GARFIELD TODD

Garfield Todd

The End of the Liberal Dream in Rhodesia

Authorised biography

Susan Woodhouse

Published by
Weaver Press
Box A1922, Avondale, Harare, Zimbabwe
<www.weaverpresszimbabwe.com>
First published in 2018
© Susan Woodhouse, 2018

Cover design: Danes Design, Harare
Maps on pp. xv and xvii: Street Savvy, Harare
Typeset by Weaver Press
Printed in Great Britain by Clays Ltd, St Ives plc

All rights reserved. No part of this publication may be reproduced, stored in a retrieval system, or transmitted in any form or by any means, electronic, mechanical, photocopying, recording or otherwise, without the written permission of the publisher, Weaver Press.

ISBN: 978-1-77922-323-4 (p/b)
ISBN: 978-1-77922-324-1 (epub)

To
Garfield and Grace Todd,
who lived this life

Contents

List of Illustrations — xi
Map of Federation of Rhodesia and Nyasaland 1953–1963 — xv
Map of Southern Rhodesia 1890–1980 — xvii
Foreword by Lawrence Vambe — xix
Author's Note — xxi
Acknowledgements — xxiii
Introduction by Trevor Grundy — xxix
List of Abbreviations — xxxv
Chronology — xxxvii

PART I – SCOTTISH BACKGROUND

1. The Todd Family — 1
2. New Zealand, 1865 — 5
3. Grace Wilson's Family — 11

PART II – DADAYA MISSION

4. Southern Rhodesia, 1934 — 18
5. 13 July 1934 — 21
6. Babes in the Bush — 24
7. That they may become Leaders — 28
8. Girls at Dadaya — 32
9. The Village Churches and Schools — 34
10. Matters Medical — 37
11. 1937: The Dadaya Family — 42
12. The Dadaya Schemes — 46
13. War comes to Dadaya — 51
14. Furlough, 1941–2 — 55
15. Judith — 57
16. A Wider Horizon — 60

17.	The Post-War World, 1945–7	63
18.	A Double Life	67
19.	Hokonui Ranch	70
20.	The Dadaya Strike	73
21.	A Bigger Picture, 1948–51	78
22.	Politics, 1949–53	83
23.	Last Days at Dadaya Mission	91
24.	Grace Todd	96

PART III – PRIME MINISTER OF SOUTHERN RHODESIA

25.	The Succession; Prime Minister of Southern Rhodesia	100
26.	December 1953 to February 1954	107
27.	The Eighth Parliament	114
28.	The Land Apportionment Act (1930)	117
29.	The Economy: Working with the Federal Government	120
30.	The Dam Controversy: Kariba vs Kafue	126
31.	Pause for Thought: Visit to the UK, 1954	131
32.	African Affairs (I)	136
33.	Visit to the USA and Canada, 1955	144
34.	1956: A Year of Crucial Importance	147
35.	African Affairs (II)	153
36.	The Political Scene, 1956	159
37.	Unrest in Southern Rhodesia: Harari Bus Boycott and Railway Strike	166
38.	A Break from Politics	173
39.	Year of Impending Crisis: 1957	177
40.	The Industrial Conciliation Bill	182
41.	African Education, 1957	186
42.	The Immorality Motion	189
43.	The Southern Rhodesia Franchise	193
44.	The Federation, 1957	201
45.	The Rise of the African National Congress	206
46.	Party Fusion and the Growing Crisis	214
47.	'Is this the Beginning of the End for Todd?'	220
48.	The Crisis Breaks	226
49.	Caucus Meeting and Second Cabinet	231

50.	'An Uneasy Month'	236
51.	'Fateful Congress'	242
52.	'Let the Dust Settle'	251
53.	Two Prime Ministers: 9 February to 23 April 1958	258
54.	8,000 Miles to the Wilderness	267
55.	'It was already too Late'	272

PART IV – 'INSPIRING AND PROPHETIC UNGUIDED MISSILE', JULY 1958 TO DECEMBER 1960

56.	A Heaviness of Heart	280
57.	The Shooting Starts (January to June 1959)	285
58.	Too Late for Gradualism	291
59.	The Wind of Change (January to June 1960)	294
60.	Exit the Colonial Office	298
61.	Exit Garfield Todd, Politician	302
62.	The Monckton Commission: Exit Federation?	313
63.	Southern Rhodesia: No Exit	317

PART V – CO-OPERATING WITH THE INEVITABLE, 1961 TO APRIL 1980

64.	The Rancher – 1961	324
65.	Southern Rhodesia and the United Nations – 1962	329
66.	'Victory over Hypocrisy' – 1963	334
67.	Enter Ian Douglas Smith – 1964	340
68.	UDI and Restriction – 1965	347
69.	Nameless at Hokonui – 1966	356
70.	Between the Talks – 1967	360
71.	Talking Again – 1968	364
72.	Cutting the British Strings – 1969	367
73.	The Republic of Rhodesia – 1970	371
74.	An Anglo–Rhodesian Settlement? – 1971	376
75.	Prison – 1972	381
76.	The Pearce Report – 1972	392
77.	Normal Restriction Order – 1972–4	397
78.	'A Zimbabwe Man' – 1975–6	402
79.	A Free Man – 1976	406
80.	The War comes to Hokonui Ranch – 1977	414

81. Smith's Rhodesian Solution – 1978	421
82. Facing Realities at Last – 1979	429
83. Death Throes of an Illegal Regime – 1979–80	439
84. 'This Peculiar, Rogue Colony' – 1980	445

PART VI – ZIMBABWE, 1980–92

85. 'Free, Legal and at Peace' – 1980	454
86. The New Era – 1981–3	458
87. 'Life is a Mixture' – 1983–5	462
88. 'Fifty Marvellous Years' – 1983–6	467
89. Sir Garfield and Lady Todd – 1986–7	473
90. Tributes and Tribulations – 1988–90	477
91. Last Years at Hokonui Ranch – 1990–2	483

PART VII – RETIREMENT, 1992–2002

92. Bulawayo – 1992–5	491
93. 'This Haven of Peace and Security' – 1996–9	498
94. Sadness and Serenity – 1999–2000	504
95. 'Her Name is Grace' – 2001	511
96. 'A Mighty Tree has fallen in the Forest' – 2002	520
Epilogue	527
Sources	529
Select Bibliography	533
Index	541

List of Illustrations

(Todd family archives unless otherwise stated)

1. Thomas Todd (I) (1823–1908), Garfield's grandfather (photo: NZ Early Settlers' Museum).
2. Thomas Todd (II) (1862–1936), Garfield's father, with his grandmother Elizabeth (née Wright) (1832–1929).
3. Mrs Edith Todd (née Scott) (1883–1957), wife of Thomas Todd (II), and Garfield's mother.
4. Belgravia, Waikiwi, Invercargill, New Zealand. Grandparents' home, built by Thomas Todd (I) (photo: courtesy of Harcourts Holmwood, Invercargill).
5. Students at Dunedin Bible College, Glen Leith, Dunedin, 1930. Garfield in middle of back row.
6. Garfield and his sister Stella (Mrs Salisbury) on his motorcycle.
7. Garfield and his wife, Grace (Wilson) (1911–2001), selected by the Church of Christ to go to Dadaya Mission, Shabani, Southern Rhodesia (photo: ACCNZ).
8. Grace at her desk as headmistress of Dadaya School.
9. Garfield grinding corn with the help of his car, watched by adopted daughter Alycen (1932–2003) and Mr Milton Vickery of the NZ Church of Christ.
10. Large classroom block built by Garfield, staff and boys of Dadaya School, with bricks made by them.
11. Garfield at the brick kiln, 1938.
12. Garfield with schoolteachers David Mkwananzi and Joram Sibanda, and the Rev. Ndabambi Hlambelo.
13. Garfield with the first daughter he delivered, Judith, 1943.
14. Garfield campaigns in the 1946 general election in Insiza constituency.
15. Grace and Judith in Cecil Square, Salisbury, after the Opening of Parliament in 1946.
16. Todds visit New Zealand in 1949: Alycen, Grace with Cynthia (born

17. 1948, also delivered by Garfield), Rua McCulloch (Alycen's nurse and companion and then her sisters') and Judith.
17. Commonwealth Parliamentary Association visit by Southern Rhodesian MPs to Kenya, 1954: Garfield and A. D. H. ('Paddy') Lloyd in sombre mood after visiting Mau Mau prison camps.
18. USA *Voice of America* interview, 1955.
19. The Todds with Grace's sister, Elsie Barham from New Zealand, at the Opening of Parliament, July 1955.
20. Camping at Mana Pools on the Zambezi River, 1957: Rupert Fothergill (Government Game Warden), Sir Robert Tredgold (acting Governor of Southern Rhodesia and Federal Chief Justice), Garfield, Archie Fraser (Chief Game Warden) and Mr Nysshens, elephant-hunter.
21. Sir Robert Tredgold, Garfield Todd and the Queen Mother, Southern Rhodesia, 1957.
22. Hardwicke Holderness with *Lost Chance*, his brilliant account of the eighth Parliament of Southern Rhodesia, of which he was a Member.
23. The famous view from Hokonui Ranch homestead, Dadaya, looking west to Mount Wedza along the Ngezi River (photo: S. Paul).
24. Joshua Nkomo, nationalist leader – 'the Father of Zimbabwe'.
25. Garfield visits Joshua Nkomo, nationalist leader, at Gonakudzingwa Restriction Area, 1965 (photo: S. Paul).
26. Grace with Dadaya teachers (left to right): David Mukonoweshuro, M. M. Nyoni, M. D. Nyoni, M. B. Nyoni, Zephaniah Phiri ('the Water-Harvester of Zvishavane'); and Dadaya missionaries Val and Bryan Kirby.
27. Cynthia and Derrick Edge with their wedding present from Alan Ritson, a neighbouring rancher.
28. Grace with the Rev. J. N. Hlambelo and Stella Salisbury, Garfield's sister.
29. Grace with Judith and Cynthia, 1965, taken as Judith was about to leave to study at Columbia University, USA.
30. Garfield is allowed out of restriction at Hokonui Ranch to visit British Prime Minister Harold Wilson at his request in Salisbury on the eve of Ian Smith's Unilateral Declaration of Independence, 1965.
31. Garfield, once again briefly allowed out of restriction, and Grace in London, 1976.

List of Illustrations

32. Three cousins meet in London, 1976: Peggy Stallworthy of Oxford, Louisa ('Louie') Todd of Moscow, and Garfield of Southern Rhodesia.
33. Part of 3,000 acres of Hokonui Ranch given to Vukuzenzele, a farming co-operative formed by a group of disabled ex-combatants.
34. Garfield builds 40 cottages for Vukuzenzele families.
35. Garfield at Great Zimbabwe (photo: Clare Chiminello).
36. Todds retire in 1992 to 47A Heyman Road, Bulawayo, where Grace creates another beautiful garden.
37. Todds celebrate their diamond wedding anniversary, 3 April 1992.
38. Garfield and his nephew Allan Todd, from Wellington, help rebuild Dadaya High School after a disastrous arson attack.
39. Foundation stone of Dadaya High School administration block, 1993, erected by the Associated Churches of Christ in New Zealand commemorating all the missionaries sent by NZ to Dadaya Mission between 1906 and 1974.
40. Garfield at the grave of the nineteenth-century Zulu Chief Mzilikazi in the Matopos area outside Bulawayo.
41. Garfield's last public meeting, 2001 (photo: editor of *The Farmer*).
42. Grace's grave at Dadaya Cemetery, January 2002 (photo: Tom Barratt).
43. Garfield's grave at Dadaya Cemetery, October 2002 (photo: Tom Barratt).

Note. The cover image of Garfield Todd and that on page xli from the Todd family archive are from an unattributed press photograph. The author and publisher will be glad to acknowledge the source should anyone be able to assist them with this information.

Map of the Federation 1953–1963

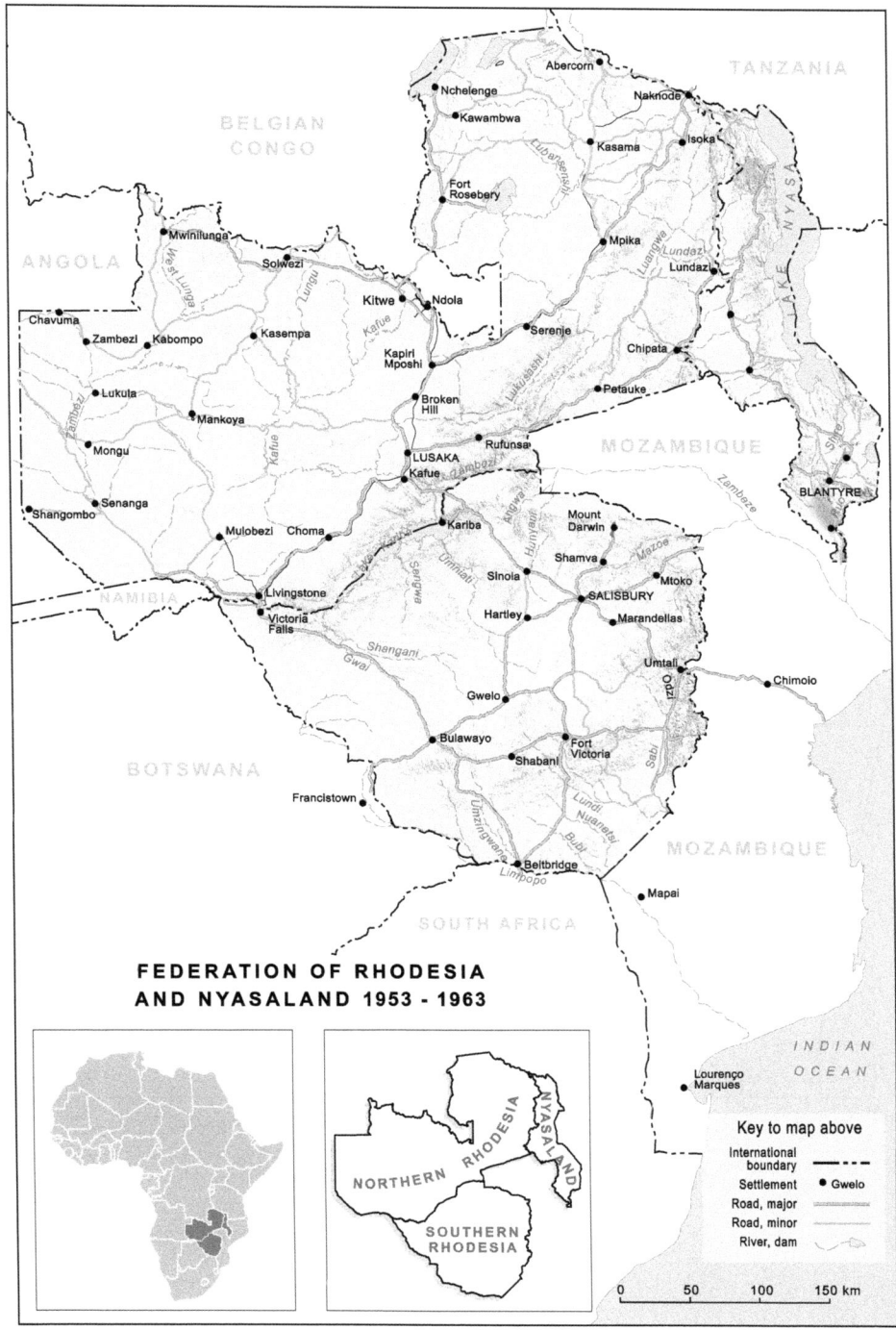

Names pre-1980	Names post-1980
Belingwe	Mberengwa
Enkledoorn	Chivhu
Essexvale	Esigodini
Fort Victoria	Masvingo
Gatooma	Kadoma
Gonakudzingwa	Gonarezhou
Gwelo	Gweru
Harari	Mbare
Lundi	Rundi
Marandellas	Marondera
Que Que	Kwekwe
Salisbury	Harare
Selukwe	Shurungwi
Shabani	Zvishavane
Sinoia	Chinhoyi
Umtali	Mutare
Umvukwes	Mvurwi
Wankie	Hwange

Map of Southern Rhodesia 1890–1980

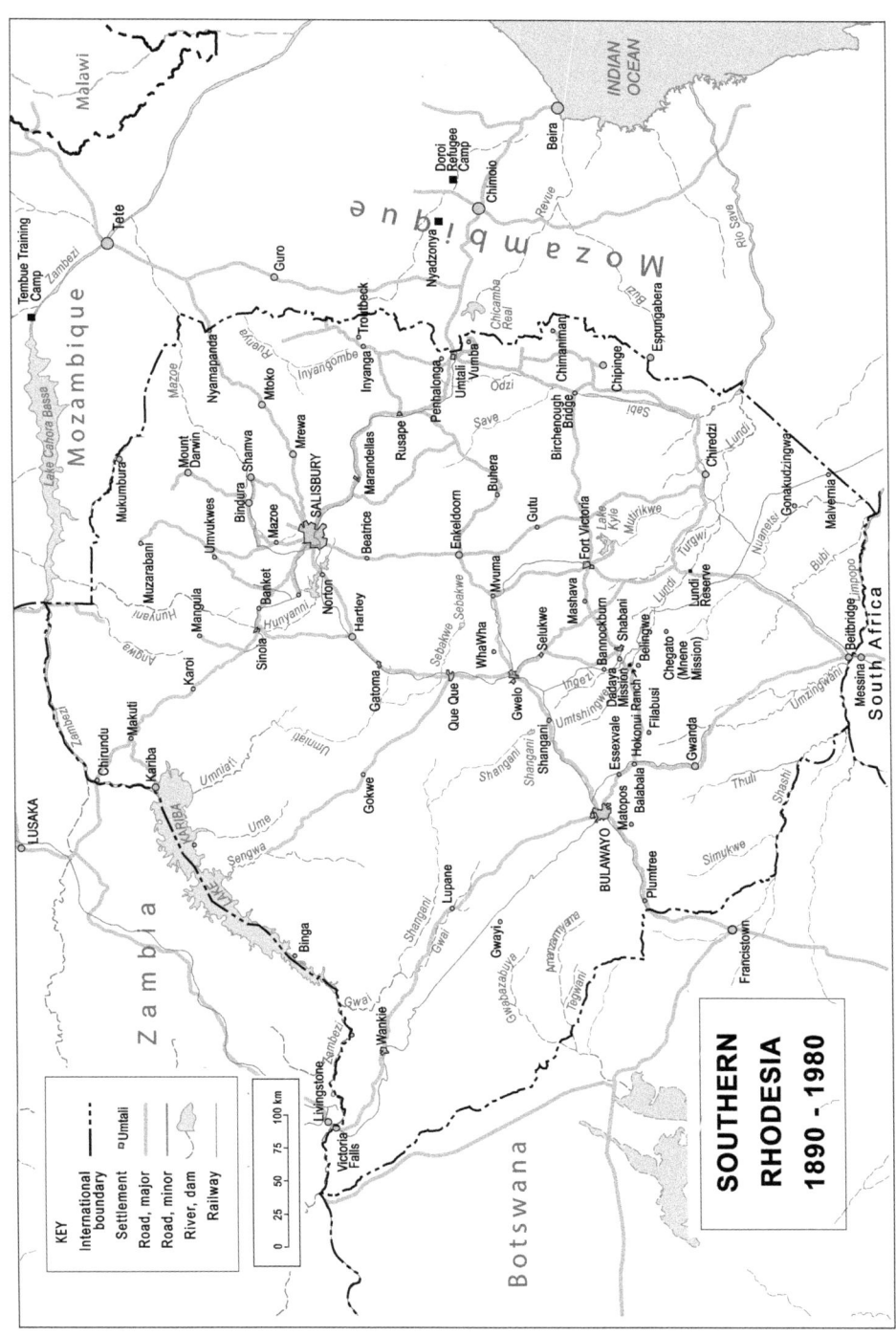

Lawrence Vambe, 1985
Photograph by Trevor Grundy

Foreword

by

Lawrence Vambe, MBE

I have every reason to count myself among the long-standing admirers of the multi-talented and exceptionally morally brave man, Garfield Todd. For my first book, published in 1972, I chose the title *An Ill-fated People: Zimbabwe Before and After Rhodes*. I wrote that book in a mood of great anger and something close to personal despair. Ian Smith was in total control of Rhodesia and so full of confidence that he could afford to taunt the seemingly impotent British Government, the Organisation of African Unity (OAU), the United Nations (UN) and anyone else who dared to question his position.

However, at long last and after all that bloodshed and tears, when black majority rule and independence came in 1980, all of Zimbabwe's people believed, to put it simplistically, that they deserved to be happy ever after.

As we all know, that was not to be the case.

Rarely has there been such a need to have a structured narrative of the past in order to cope with the present and to plan for the future. Hence the importance of this book. It could not have come at a more appropriate moment as our great country stumbles from crisis to crisis without apparent purpose or aim.

I felt honoured when asked to write this Foreword. It was the least I could do in memory of the only Prime Minister of my country whose heart I believed to have been in the right place and who, had he not been toppled by the forces of racism, might have saved Zimbabwe some, if not all, of the colossal misfortunes which have befallen its people since the demise of his administration in 1958.

I first met Susan Woodhouse when she worked for Garfield Todd while he was Prime Minister of Southern Rhodesia (1953–8) and president of the United Rhodesia Party. As I was at that time editor-in-chief of African Newspapers, then widely known and influential throughout the Central African Federation, I met Susan, who gave me personally and my fellow black journalists easy access to the country's Prime Minister, this amazing new leader in whom we Africans had both faith and high expectations.

That experience of working so closely with Garfield Todd gave her a special insight into his life and work. What distinguishes this biography is the fact that Todd himself authorised her to carry out this undoubtedly onerous task. And why? Because he stressed that Susan knew him and his wife, Grace, better than anyone else did. Todd entrusted Susan Woodhouse with what any serious biographer and scholar must rate as priceless: a collection of materials, including diaries and private letters, from which she has been able to draw freely.

Whichever way one looks at him – as a Christian missionary, educationalist, back-bench member of parliament, Prime Minister of Southern Rhodesia, twice a prisoner in Rhodesia's jails, senator in Zimbabwe, rancher, writer or private citizen – he stands out as an unembittered man with deep-rooted Christian convictions and courage. What terrible irony that during his long, fruitful life he suffered persecution not only under Ian Smith but also, and perhaps more painfully, after independence when he endured the humiliation of being denied the right to vote by Robert Mugabe, whose cause he had championed during those long years of the struggle for African freedom.

I urge young Zimbabweans to read this book. It will help them to learn more about who they are and where they come from, and how courage and greatness are not the monopoly of those who boast the loudest about how they alone possess those universally respected qualities. This is not the full story of Todd or the time in which he lived, but it is an important contribution to our country's tangled and complicated history. It is the story of a man with great courage who stood up to tyrants, whatever their political persuasion or skin colour.

Author's Note

I began work as confidential shorthand typist to the Prime Minister of Southern Rhodesia, the Hon. R. S. Garfield Todd, on 1 July 1956. The Prime Minister's private office consisted of his Private Secretary, the late Mr W. H. R. ('Wally') Allen, and myself. Part of my job was to help Mrs Todd on the social side, and to accompany her sometimes on her official duties.

On 17 February 1958, Garfield Todd ceased to be Prime Minister and became Minister of Labour and Social Welfare in the first (and short-lived) cabinet of his successor as Prime Minister, Sir Edgar Whitehead. Garfield's tenure of his new office lasted but two months. His hastily re-formed United Rhodesia Party won no seats in the subsequent general election, and he left government, to become a cattle rancher.

A year later, I accepted an invitation from Garfield to work on Hokonui Ranch. In 1965, I returned to Salisbury to keep house for my father, and became secretary to the Anglican Bishop of Mashonaland.

In 1969, I married Archdeacon John Paul of Messumba Mission in Mozambique and author of *Mozambique: Memoirs of a Revolution*.[1] For the next 40 years, we lived and worked in Scotland. Grace Todd and I corresponded regularly. We exchanged visits over the years. In 1992, Garfield asked me to undertake his biography: 'My life is but the thread which connects so many interesting people and events.' There were plenty of reasons to decline his request, but only one to accept: as he said, I knew them better than anyone else.

It has been a long haul: I visited Zimbabwe ten times, spending many weeks on Garfield's papers in the National Archives of Zimbabwe, and interviewing surviving friends and colleagues. I spent a month in New Zealand, and also visited the places in Scotland connected with the families of Garfield and Grace.

In time, an expanded version of this biography (together with Garfield's few remaining papers) will be available to researchers at the Bodleian Library African and Commonwealth Collections, University of Oxford.

---

1 Penguin African Library, Harmondsworth, 1975.

Susan Woodhouse
Photograph by Ilo the Pirate

Acknowledgements

My late husband John's immense generosity of spirit alone has made it possible for me to write Garfield's biography.

Garfield and Grace Todd were unstinting in their help of every kind, and in their hospitality at Hokonui Ranch and in Bulawayo. Judith gave me access to all her parents' letters from 1972 to 1980. Cynthia in Australia gave me permission to quote from her parents' letters to her. To them all, my thanks.

In the 25 years since I began work on this book, most of the people I mention have died. It would be tedious to write 'the late' before each name. And, anyway, they live on in my memory.

The assistance of Professor Terence Ranger (former Rhodes Professor of Race Relations, University of Oxford) has been crucial, and almost magical in the opening of doors in both Oxford and in Zimbabwe. At the University of Zimbabwe, the then Pro-Vice Chancellor, Professor Ngwabi Bhebe, introduced me to the Chairman of the History Department, Dr Pwiti, whose staff saw me through the bureaucratic hoops. I am unable sufficiently to express my gratitude for all the kindness and help I received. The other vital Harare door that Professor Ranger opened was that of the National Archives of Zimbabwe, where Dr Ian Johnstone, then Acting Director, and Mrs Sibanda and all the staff made my work over seven years not just easy but also a pleasure.

In Bulawayo, Mr Peter Genge, then Curator of the Historic Reference Collection of the Bulawayo Public Library, gave me a spare set of the Southern Rhodesia *Hansard* for the relevant years, and, on his return to the UK, has continued to offer welcome help and advice. The Senate Proceedings were harder to come by, but with help from Peter Genge and the Librarian of Parliament in Harare I managed to find some record of a few debates.

I interviewed Dr Hugh Ashton, one-time Director of the Bulawayo Municipal African Affairs Department, and Mr M. M. ('Mike') Hove, former Federal MP, both of whom had helpful and interesting views to pass on. I was grateful to Mrs Cecil Goddard for coming to see me; also Mr Douglas Hadfield and his wife, Ruth. I cannot leave Bulawayo without mentioning Mrs Paddy Fehrsen and the late Mrs Alison Rudd for wonderful hospitality and for driving me to Dadaya for the funerals of Grace and Garfield Todd in 2002.

In Bulawayo and at Dadaya, I renewed my acquaintance with former pupils and colleagues of Grace and Garfield, including two of their oldest friends, Mr David Mkwananzi, teacher for 40 years (25 at Dadaya), and Mr K. D. Dube, MBE, former United Nations civil servant. From them I got insights and stories I could not have got from anyone else. Former Principal of Dadaya High School, Mr Samuel Mutomba, had frightening memories of the 1970s and, particularly, prison in 1980. Other Dadaya Governing Board members who kindly received me were the chairman, Mr Cephas Msipa, Mr M. D. Nyoni and Mr B. J. Mpofu, who opened to me ancient files. Similarly, the late Mr Bethuel Hlambelo, retired teacher and son of the late Reverend Ndabambi Hlambelo, opened my eyes to sombre pictures of the 1959 Emergency. My grateful thanks to them all for hours of fascinating and instructive conversation. Mrs Rua Marsh (née McCulloch) had known Grace, Garfield and Alycen from 1936 and passed on many family stories.

On the way to Harare, I stopped off several times at the Norton farm of the late Sir Cyril and Lady Hatty, and spent a weekend there. They and their great friend, the late Mrs Muriel Rosin, MP 1953–62, had much to tell me. In Harare were other friends with whom to renew a happy acquaintance – the late Mrs Eileen Haddon, one-time editor of the *Central African Examiner*, who also was generous in her hospitality and left me for a long evening with the bound copies of the magazine, essential reading for the years 1957–65; and Mr Lawrence Vambe, MBE, historian of Rhodesia/Zimbabwe, and one-time Federal Public Relations Officer at Rhodesia House in London. Advocate Antony Eastwood was extremely helpful about Federal political views and attitudes in the years 1953–63.

Two other journalists I interviewed in the mid-1990s were Geoff Nyarota, who could tell me much about the Mass Media Trust, and the late minister Nathan Shamuyarira. The late Mr Ian D. Smith, only PM of the Republic of Rhodesia, very civilly allowed me to interview him, for which I was grateful. Mr M. A. ('Tony') Pedder, Hon. Sec. of the United Rhodesia Party in the 1950s, and Mr A. E. ('Abe') Abrahamson, SR MP 1953–62, wrote most helpfully from Winchester and Johannesburg respectively. Professor J. R. T. Wood generously sent me a copy of his book *The Welensky Papers*.

Another who added to my knowledge and understanding by letter was the late Peter Nathan, Dadaya Missionary and later senior official of the Education Department after Independence, and for twenty years the valued colleague of Garfield and Grace on the Dadaya Governing Board. The late Bishop Jim Thompson, who presided at the London Service of Thanksgiving for the lives

Acknowledgements

of Garfield and Grace, sent a long and thoughtful account of his acquaintance with them, for which I was deeply grateful.

In New Zealand, I met many members of the families of Grace and Garfield as well as school friends, church and college friends, and colleagues from the Associated Churches of Christ. I saw Garfield's eldest nephew Allan not in New Zealand but in Zimbabwe on several occasions. He made arrangements for me to see relatives and also obtained for me copies of correspondence with the ACCNZ. His brother, Jeff, arranged for me to interview the former New Zealand Prime Minister, the late Mr David Lange. Garfield's niece, Mrs Clare Chiminello, introduced me to the Hocken Archives and the Early Settlers' Museum, in Dunedin, where I found fascinating material about the Todd and McKenzie families. I also have to thank Clare for a photograph she took of Garfield at Great Zimbabwe. Grace's old school friends, Miss Addy Gunn and Miss Beth Morrison, were delighted to talk of her, as also were Mrs Joyce Murray and her husband, Ross, in Tauranga. Garfield's cousin, Rob Wood, drove me around Grace's home town, Winton, and took me to Belgravia, the beloved home of Garfield's grandparents. Others who kindly gave me their time included Mrs Jessie Hamilton (another cousin of Garfield's), Mrs Kathleen Caroe and Mr John Curwood (whose parents were the first couple Garfield married). Grace's niece, Elizabeth Collins, and her husband Dr Roger Collins, kindly entertained me and gave me the few letters that had survived from Grace and Garfield to her parents Elsie and Clarence Barham. I spent some time with Mr and Mrs Bill Walsh, who had been members of Garfield's congregation in Oamaru. Their memories were very fresh, and they had kept Garfield's and Grace's letters from the time they left New Zealand in 1934. I saw Grace's cousins Russell and Esmae Styles in Arrowtown, and learned much about the family as we drove around that glorious countryside. Mr Gavin Munro, former Principal of Glen Leith Bible College, Dunedin, took me to visit the beautiful building which had housed the college in Garfield's day (the owners most generously allowing me to look around the house). An old school and church friend of Garfield's, and a one-time Overseas Mission Board Secretary, Mr Ray Blampied, had lots of family and Church history to tell me. The only former Dadaya Missionary I was able to see was Mrs Isobel Knapp – the last to leave Dadaya, in 1974. My last visit in the South Island was to Oamaru, to be shown by Beryl Jacobs the little church where Garfield had ministered from 1932 to 1934. In Auckland I enjoyed the generous hospitality of Jeff Todd and his wife, Glenys, who arranged for me to meet more connections. Roger and Jennifer Gonin were wonderful hosts in Dunedin. I also met the producer of the

NZTV film *Hokonui Todd*, Richard Driver, who very kindly gave me a copy of the transcript of all the material he had recorded.

Thanks to Professor Ranger and Dr John Pinfold, the then librarian at Rhodes House, I was able to spend some weeks in the Bodleian Library African and Commonwealth Collections at the University of Oxford, and thanks to Dr James Hargrave, archivist and cataloguer of the papers of Sir Roy Welensky, I had early access to those papers. I was grateful to Lady Tredgold for permission to go through her late husband Sir Robert Tredgold's papers, and to Dr Piers Mackesey for early access to Sir John Kennedy's papers. The Bodleian Library's senior archivist, Miss Lucy McCann, has been unfailingly helpful. Garfield had hoped that the long version of his biography and his few remaining papers which I hold would ultimately be available to researchers at the Bodleian Library. Miss McCann's agreement to this is a matter of profound relief and gratitude to me.

Professor Ian Phimister kindly sent me his book *Wangi Kolia* and checked my original chapter on the Wankie Colliery strike in Southern Rhodesia in 1954; and Dr Allan Hood of Edinburgh checked my classical quotations. Derek Ingram, Vice-President of the Royal Commonwealth Society, has been generous with his time and answers to my questions; and Miss Terry Barringer of the Royal Commonwealth Society kindly sent me useful cuttings.

Until his death, the late Professor Richard Gray of the School of Oriental and African Studies was my principal adviser. I have felt keenly the loss of his advice and wise counsel. Lady Soames, widow of the last Governor of Southern Rhodesia, kindly put me in touch with Mr James Buckley, Lord Soames's private secretary at Government House, Salisbury, during the dramatic weeks in 1979–80. He in turn put me in touch with Lord Renwick. To all these I owe my thanks – and extra thanks to the last-named for sending me his book, *Unconventional Diplomacy in Southern Africa*.

I am grateful to Lady (Judy) Colman for lending me all the Southern Rhodesia papers of her father, Sir Peveril William-Powlett, Governor of the Colony from 1954 to 1959. I am similarly grateful to the Earl of Home for kindly allowing me to spend time in the Hirsel Archives at Coldstream, and to Lady Home for hospitality; to Sir Peter Tapsell, MP, for an interview at the House of Commons and hospitality; to Mr J. Peart-Binns for copies of correspondence between Garfield and the late Bishop Kenneth Skelton, one-time Bishop of Matabeleland; and to Mr Richard Lindley, formerly of ITV, for details of his foray into 'the bush' during the Rhodesian guerrilla war. My thanks are due to Dr Alex May, former editor of *The Round Table: The Commonwealth Journal of International Affairs*, for permission to quote from Garfield Todd's articles in various issues

Acknowledgements

of the *Journal* when he was the official correspondent for Central Africa, and to quote from the then editor's correspondence with Garfield. I enjoyed a delightful conversation with Mr Ewen Greenfield, son of the late Mr Julian Greenfield (one-time Federal Minister of Law), though he was far too discreet to tell me what I wanted to know! And I enjoyed several frank conversations with the late Hardwicke and Elspeth Holderness in Cheltenham.

I must record my gratitude to Forward Maisokwadzo for researching UK newspapers for me, and to the helpful staff at the Rhodesia House Library in London, the National Library of Scotland, the Edinburgh University Library and the Haddington Public Library; and to the staff at the New Cumnock Library, in Ayrshire, and at the Rothesay Archives, Isle of Bute, for their help on my visits.

I am very grateful to the following authors, who, over the years, have given me verbal permission to quote from their books: Professor Richard Gray, Norman Harris, Hardwicke Holderness, Patrick Keatley, Professor Terence Ranger, Lord Renwick, Clyde Sanger, Nathan Shamuyarira, Bishop Kenneth Skelton, Judith Todd, Lawrence Vambe and Michela Wrong.

More recently, my thanks go to the Rev. Dr Pamela Welch of Dunedin, New Zealand; to Judy Moir; to Alan Macpherson, who patiently converted me from word-processor to computer; and to Ivor Normand, copy-editor and Edinburgh collaborator. My heartfelt thanks go to Irene Staunton and Murray McCartney of Weaver Press for turning hope into reality.

Almost more than anyone else, Trevor Grundy, author, writer and journalist, deserves my gratitude for years of companionable collaboration, and for sharing with me his knowledge both of Africa – East, South and Central – and of politicians, as well as his professional expertise. Even more than all this, if possible, I have valued his continuing friendship, assistance and encouragement.

Introduction

by

Trevor Grundy

I *first met Susan Woodhouse in Bulawayo in 1993; she was interviewing Zimbabweans about the life and times of the man she was to spend the next quarter of a century writing about. We met through my great friend and mentor, Lawrence Vambe. Later, the three of us attended a lunch at the Bulawayo Club to mark Garfield Todd's 85th birthday. Lawrence said to me: 'You are having lunch with one of our truly great men. This is a day you will never forget.'*

From 1966, I spent 30 years working as a reporter in Central, Eastern and Southern Africa. In 1996, my wife and I returned to the UK to live in Edinburgh. Ten years later, the doyen of Commonwealth journalists, Derek Ingram, rang to tell me about Susan Woodhouse, who had once worked for Todd and who now needed editorial assistance. For the next three-and-a-half years, I worked alongside Susan. My concern was that the author might – because of her closeness to the Todds – be aiming for some sort of hagiographic literary monument. That fear was soon dispelled.

This is not the first book about Todd, but I like to think it is the best so far. A new generation of Zimbabwean historians will be able to draw on Todd's vast archive held by the National Archives in Harare, and on the author's Paul Collection of Todd Papers which, on her death, will be deposited at the Bodleian Library in Oxford.

Reginald Stephen Garfield Todd (1908–2002)
Prime Minister of Southern Rhodesia (1953–8)
Senator of Zimbabwe (1980–5)

Garfield Todd personified the failed liberal dream in Africa after the Second World War when Britain was dismantling her empire and attempting to create a multicultural showpiece in Central Africa – the Federation of Rhodesia and Nyasaland – to form an economic and political buffer between encroaching Marxist-influenced black nationalism in the north and an equally militant form of white Afrikaner nationalism emanating from South Africa.

This book traces the development, triumph and failure of the man who unexpectedly found himself at the very centre of political life in Southern Rhodesia during the explosive years of 1953 to 1958. The failure of Todd and the European liberals who supported him cleared the decks for what they most feared: a head-on racial collision.

As the distinguished Oxford historian, Professor Terence Ranger, said about the man often seen as the architect of a political liberal dream in Central Africa: 'The story of Sir Garfield Todd has proved very hard to tell. He was undeniably a great man – but never had the chance of doing anything great. His political career was a failure and any account of it is inevitably about the many disconcerting concessions he made, in vain, to Rhodesian opinion. His moral career was ultimately a great success, during the long period when he did not need to make such concessions. But historians are unconvincing about and unhappy with virtue.'[1]

Todd had been sent to the British self-governing colony of Southern Rhodesia in 1934 by the Associated Churches of Christ in New Zealand to take charge of their small mission station in a native reserve near Shabani. Over the next nineteen years, he and his wife, Grace, a schoolteacher, built Dadaya Mission into a network of thriving village churches and schools centred on the large co-educational boarding school. Todd's missionary years were the foundation of his premiership, and the basis of his close relationship with blacks (many of whom would become leaders of their people) and his understanding of their difficulties, frustrations and aspirations.

In 1946, Todd entered Parliament, supporting the United Party of Sir Godfrey Huggins, Prime Minister of Southern Rhodesia for twenty years. Politics in Southern Rhodesia hinged on 'the native question', namely, how two very different races can live together peacefully in one land – a small group of sophisticated white conquerors, and overwhelming numbers of unsophisticated black subject people with their own traditions and beliefs. There was little political theorising as understood in, for example, Britain. Political labels did not necessarily mean the same thing. If 'Right' meant conservatism, it manifested itself in a reluctance to do more for the Africans than was absolutely necessary. 'Left' meant a more sympathetic – 'liberal' – attitude and a determination to

---

1   Ranger, 2008, p. 225.

advance the African people towards equality of opportunity with the whites.

In her 1957 book *Going Home*, Doris Lessing[2] wrote that, for Europeans, Rhodesia was 'a country where, unlike Britain, which is ruled by the Establishment of which one is not a member, one is close to the centres of administration simply because one is white. Here, journalists get their information straight from the CID, with whom they have sundowners, and everyone has a friend who is a Member of Parliament or a cabinet minister.'

In Parliament, Todd had hoped to increase awareness and understanding by the MPs (all European) of the African people's needs and hopes. How much he succeeded in this objective is debatable, but after seven years he had established himself as an able Member and an exceptionally talented speaker. When in 1953 Southern Rhodesia was incorporated into the Central African Federation with the British protectorates of Northern Rhodesia and Nyasaland, and Huggins became Prime Minister of the Federation, the United Party elected Todd as its new president and therefore Prime Minister of Southern Rhodesia. After four-and-a-half years of painfully slow and limited liberalisation, a frightened, largely white electorate threw Todd out.

Thereafter, Todd continued his increasingly desperate attempt to persuade the whites that their only hope for the future lay in co-operating with black nationalism. Terence Ranger said that Todd's progressive views on race created 'a trajectory through the rhetorical and ideological choices that inexorably led him out of gradualism into radicalism'.[3] By writing and speaking, and lobbying influential people in Britain, the USA and various parts of the Commonwealth, Todd did what he could to avert an eventual quick march to disaster after Ian Smith's successful Unilateral Declaration of Independence in November 1965.

I first visited Southern Rhodesia in 1966, eight years after Todd had been ousted. The Federation had been consigned to history, and the whites were triumphantly all-powerful. A drunken white man in a Salisbury bar told me that Todd was a communist and miscegenist. He told a tale of Todd spanking black girls. This was a reference to a 'strike' at Dadaya School, when Todd had disciplined several girls who refused to eat the food provided. This 1947 incident brings onto the stage a teacher called Ndabaningi Sithole, once Dadaya's most promising student – and later a prominent nationalist leader. He had encouraged the girls to report Todd to the police for assault. The subsequent case caused a sensation, but Todd was found not guilty – by a white magistrate.

My bar acquaintance was still rambling on about this 'kaffir-loving Garfield

---

2   Panther Books, 1968, p. 61.
3   Ranger, 2008, p. 225.

Todd' when I left to attend a meeting of the Salisbury Economic Society. There, I heard well-educated men and women say that Todd had been removed as Prime Minister not because he was a liberal but because he was aloof, opinionated and authoritarian. They said Todd's liberalism was well neutralised by his ownership of a 25,000-acre cattle ranch.

Even Ian Smith, they said, had praised Todd for sending in the troops to prevent disorder at Wankie Colliery in 1954 after strike action by black miners threatened to bring industry to a halt. African writers are critical of Todd's handling of the Wankie strike. There is a continuing debate about whether miners were killed by the army. Maurice Nyagumbo said in his book, *With the People*, that Todd condoned the shooting dead of black miners – something Todd and his followers always strenuously denied. But Nyagumbo went to his tragic death still believing that Todd had ordered white soldiers to shoot and kill black protesters.

The Economic Society claimed Todd had embraced the liberal cause not because he believed in it but because he was in tune with his age and peers in the Commonwealth and knew the blacks would take over now that Britain had distanced itself from its former colonies. The few whites and blacks who stayed loyal to Todd after the 1958 cabinet coup said – usually privately – that yes, he could be authoritarian. For years, he had been the only European male at a remote mission station in charge of hundreds of teenagers. Under such conditions, authoritarian tendencies are hard to avoid.

Most whites in Rhodesia hated Todd, and in their pitiful ignorance and prejudice condemned him as 'a bloody foreigner, a Christian, a non-sporty type who didn't smoke or booze'. But, worse than all those, he was 'a trouble-making missionary who wanted black people to learn to read, write and argue, debate and think for themselves and question the boss'.

In 1957, Todd upset both blacks and whites: the former for a strong attack on the nationalists, then led by Joshua Nkomo, James Chikerema and George Nyandoro. During a speech in Bulawayo, Todd said they were moving too fast and putting too much pressure on him; they must slow down and drop some of their demands. He later admitted it was the only speech he really regretted making.

The whites were aghast when Todd accepted an invitation from Kwame Nkrumah to attend the celebrations marking the Gold Coast's transition from British colony to independent Ghana. Three years later, even his own supporters deserted him when he and Nkomo called for the suspension of Southern Rhodesia's constitution and for direct action by Britain to stop a now rapid decline towards racial anarchy in Rhodesia.

Introduction

One sympathetic white politician told me that Todd, like Caesar, had been done to death by men who had once seen him as a national saviour. He said that, when Todd was premier, he was like a fireman fighting a raging fire and yelling at his subordinates who were pointing their hoses in the wrong direction while fierce flames consumed the building.

Liberals at the time, and liberals since, recognise that Todd's limited widening of the franchise for blacks led to his downfall. Even Joshua Nkomo, the ZAPU leader so linked to Todd's name, said in his memoir that Todd claimed to be all for African progress 'although he did little enough about it'. But that little was enough to get him thrown out by the whites.

Todd was a big man, both politically and physically – and an editorial usually devoted to attacking, and not praising, this outspoken liberal leader described him as 'his country's lively and troublesome conscience'.[4] That conscience did not go to sleep when the day of the Europeans ended. To his eternal credit, Todd was unable to remain silent between 1983 and 1987 when a North Korean-trained unit of the Zimbabwean army, the Fifth Brigade, wiped out many thousands[5] of men, women and children during a national 'dissident-cleansing' operation known as Gukurahundi.

At the centre of everything were Todd's deeply held Christian beliefs. The man known as the great phrase-maker summed them up in a few words: 'The religion of our Lord Jesus Christ is faith, hope and love; the rest is theology'.

In 1995, aged 87, Todd told the author: 'I was a missionary. I am a missionary. I was never a politician.' But he added that he had enjoyed being an MP and a PM! Six years later, a year before he died, he wrote in a letter to her: 'Dadaya stays at the centre of things' – seven words which said where his heart lay and where it would always lie.

That letter was written three months before the death of his beloved wife, Grace, and five months before a blow landed that would have killed a lesser man – a blow that the historian Lawrence Vambe called 'one of the most disgraceful incidents in Zimbabwe's post-Independence history' – namely Mugabe's withdrawal of Todd's citizenship and of his right to vote in the 2002 presidential election. Why? Todd had committed an unforgivable crime. He had condemned corruption and despotism in Zimbabwe – as he had condemned

---

4   *The Chronicle*, Bulawayo, 29 September 1957.

5   '… the real figure for the dead could be possibly double 3,000, or even higher' (CCJP/LRF, 1997, p. 157). In an interview with Dr Sue Onslow in October 2008, Dan Stannard, former Director Internal of the CIO, said that 'Nobody knows the actual figure, but between 30–50 thousand' (Stuart Doran, *Kingdom, Power, Glory: Mugabe, ZANU and the Quest for Supremacy, 1960–1987* (Midrand, SA: Sithatha Media, 2017), pp. 534–5).

corruption and despotism in Rhodesia. After his death, Todd's daughter, Judith, frustrated Mugabe's plan to turn him into a state-approved, rubber-stamped, on-side hero by refusing to have him buried at Heroes' Acre outside Harare.

Todd's heritage is his insistence that discipline, dedication and love of one's fellow human beings, based on an overarching moral code which he called Christianity, was a person's – and a nation's – true liberator. Over the last twenty years or so, Garfield Todd has been almost completely airbrushed out of the Zimbabwe freedom story – but, as this book shows, he was greatly admired by some of Zimbabwe's most respected writers, politicians and historians.

This timely and important book comes in the 60th-anniversary year of the cabinet 'coup'. From then on, Todd was released from the clutches of European reactionaries who went on to take Rhodesia into a vile racial confrontation costing an estimated 35,000 lives. This book is a work that should give the young in Africa a wider understanding of Zimbabwe's past.

LIST OF ABBREVIATIONS

ACCNZ	Associated Churches of Christ in New Zealand
ANC	African National Congress
ANC	African National Council (1971–9)
Bodleian Library	Bodleian Library African and Commonwealth Collections, University of Oxford
BSAP	British South Africa Police
CAP	Central Africa Party
CDC	Colonial Development Corporation
CID	Criminal Investigation Department
CMED	Central Mechanical Equipment Department
CRO	Commonwealth Relations Office, London
CWA	Christian Women's Auxiliary (ACCNZ)
DM	Dadaya Mission
DP	Dominion Party
EB	Elsie Barham, Grace Todd's sister
EW	Sir Edgar Whitehead (Prime Minister of Southern Rhodesia 1958–62)
EZE	Evangelische Zentralstelle für Entwicklungshilfe
FAD	Federal Assembly Debates
FBC	Federal Broadcasting Corporation
FCO	Foreign and Commonwealth Office
FLH	Mr Francis (Frank) Leslie Hadfield
FMC	Foreign Mission Council (ACCNZ)
FMP	Federal Member of Parliament
FMU	Foreign Mission Union (ACCNZ)
FP	Federal Party
GT	Garfield Todd
GT/A	Garfield Todd's draft autobiography
HHCH	Hardwicke Holderness
HMG	Her Majesty's Government (or British Government)
IDS	Ian Douglas Smith (Prime Minister of Rhodesia 1964–79)
JGT	Jean Grace (Isabel) Todd, wife of Garfield Todd
JN	Joshua Nkomo
JT	Judith Todd (Todds' daughter – married name Acton)
LAD	Legislative Assembly Debates (Southern Rhodesia, Rhodesia)

MBE	Member of the Order of the British Empire
MDC	Movement for Democratic Change (1999–)
MLC	Member of Legislative Council
MP	Member of Parliament
NAZ	National Archives of Zimbabwe
NDP	National Democratic Party (1960–1)
NLHA	Native Land Husbandry Act
NR	Northern Rhodesia
NZ	New Zealand
OBE	Officer of the Order of the British Empire
OMB	Overseas Mission Board (ACCNZ)
PCR	Programme to Combat Racism
PM	Prime Minister
PRO	Public Records Office
RATA	Rhodesian African Teachers' Association
RCT	Robert C. Tredgold (Federal/Southern Rhodesia Chief Justice)
RF	Rhodesian Front (1962–78)
RW	Sir Roy Welensky (Federal Prime Minister 1955–63)
SP	Susan Paul (née Woodhouse)
SR	Southern Rhodesia
TPPC	Todd Papers Paul Collection
UCRN	University College of Rhodesia and Nyasaland
UFP	United Federal Party (1957–63)
UK	United Kingdom of Great Britain and Northern Ireland
UKHCSR	United Kingdom High Commissioner for Southern Rhodesia
UN	United Nations
UP	United Party (1933–54)
URP	United Rhodesia Party (1954–60)
USA	United States of America
WCC	World Council of Churches
ZANLA	Zimbabwe African National Liberation Army (military wing of ZANU)
ZANU	Zimbabwe African National Union (1963–6)
ZANU-PF	Zimbabwe African National Union (Patriotic Front): temporary union with ZAPU (1976–9), but name remains after dissolution of union with ZAPU
ZAPU	Zimbabwe African People's Union (1961–87)
ZIPRA	Zimbabwe People's Revolutionary Army (military wing of ZAPU)

Chronology

	Southern Rhodesia	Todds
1890	Pioneer column from Cape Colony occupies Mashonaland; Union flag raised at Salisbury	
1893	Defeat of Ndebele; Matabeleland occupied	
1896–7	Shona and Ndebele revolt against white rule	
1899	Legislative Council established	
1908		GT born in Invercargill, NZ
1911		Grace Wilson born in Winton, NZ
1923	Self-governing Colony of Southern Rhodesia established	
1932		GT and GW marry; adopt Alycen
1934		Todds appointed to Dadaya Mission at Shabani, Southern Rhodesia
1939	Onset of Second World War	
1941		Todds go on leave to NZ
1943		Birth of Judith Todd
1944		GT to Witwatersrand University for one year
1946	Influx of British immigrants; general election	GT elected to Parliament
1947		Dadaya School strike; Todds acquire land and move Mission; establish Hokonui Ranch
1948	General strike; general election	GT re-elected; Cynthia born
1949		Todds go on leave to NZ
1951	NLHA passed	

Garfield Todd: The End of the Liberal Dream in Rhodesia

	Southern Rhodesia	Todds
1953	**Federation** of Rhodesia and Nyasaland; URP formed	GT becomes PM of Southern Rhodesia
1954	General election	GT re-elected; Todds visit UK
1955	SR Youth League formed in Salisbury	GT visits USA
1957	Independence of Ghana; SRANC formed; URP and Federal Party fuse to form United Federal Party	Todds attend Ghana independence celebrations
1958	SR cabinet rebels against PM; Sir Edgar Whitehead elected in GT's stead; cabinet crisis continues; URP re-formed; UFP wins general election	GT in first Whitehead cabinet; URP and GT lose seats; Todds to Hokonui Ranch
1959	SRANC banned; Security Laws passed; CAP replaces URP	
1960	NDP formed; Law & Order Maintenance Act passed	GT visits UK; letter to Lord Home; resigns from CAP
1961	NDP banned; Nkomo forms ZAPU. New SR constitution	
1962	RF formed; ZAPU banned; RF wins general election	GT appears before UN
1963	ZAPU splits; Sithole forms ZANU; Nkomo forms People's Caretaker Council; End of Federation; CAP disbands	
1964	Malawi (Nyasaland) gains Independence; Northern Rhodesia becomes Zambia; Ian Smith becomes PM of SR	Judith protests against banning of the *Daily News*; convicted of illegal demo, and fined. Crisis at Dadaya Mission. GT heads new Dadaya Governing Board
1965	**Unilateral Declaration of Independence** from UK	GT restricted to ranch for a year; Judith visits USA
1966	'Tiger' talks re Rhodesia; 'Battle of Sinoia' marks the start of the Second Chimurenga	
1968	'Fearless' talks re Rhodesia	
1970		Cynthia marries Derrick Edge; Judith returns to SR

Chronology

	Southern Rhodesia	Todds
1971	Lord Home to Rhodesia for talks on settlement; African National Council formed to campaign against proposals	GT and Judith campaign against proposed settlement
1972	Pearce Commission appointed; delivers verdict – 'No'	GT restricted to Hokonui Ranch; Judith arrested; solitary confinement; Judith on hunger strike; Judith into exile
1973	Flight of whites begins; Smith/ANC (Bishop Muzorewa) talks; Vorster of South Africa talks to Kaunda of Zambia	Judith marries (in Rome)
1974	Sithole and Nkomo released from detention for Lusaka talks	Todds released briefly to visit South Africa
1975	Smith/Nkomo/Sithole/Muzorewa talks at Victoria Falls Bridge fail	Local guerrilla situation worsens
1976	Samora Machel closes Mozambique border; Rhodesian raids on Mozambique. African parties form Patriotic Front for Geneva all-party talks under UK chairmanship; no agreement is reached	GT released for 3-week visit to London; end of 4½ years restriction; GT part of Nkomo's team at Geneva Conference
1977	Abortive talks initiated by the USA	Edges leave for UK then Australia
1978	Smith agreement with Muzorewa, Chief Chirau and Sithole to form Zimbabwe-Rhodesia	Todds visit USA
1979	Muzorewa becomes PM of Z-R. Commonwealth summit in Lusaka. Lancaster House Conference signs agreement between all parties.	Todds buy house in Bulawayo; GT to Lancaster House
1980	April: **independence** as **Zimbabwe**; Robert Mugabe becomes PM	GT to NZ. On return, arrested on capital charge, later withdrawn. GT is appointed Senator; Judith returns. Grace appointed to Mass Media Trust
1982	Beginning of Gukurahundi	GT delivers last baby

	Southern Rhodesia	Todds
1984		GT's sister Edith Todd dies at Shabani; GT resigns from Dadaya Governing Board
1985	Zimbabwe general election	
1986		GT knighted by Queen
1987	Unity Accord: ZANU-PF and ZAPU	Sale of ranch agreed with Sam Mpofu
1988		GT's 80th-birthday party; GT's sister Stella dies at Hokonui
1989		GT badly burned in petrol fire
1990	Lancaster House constitution lapses; Mugabe becomes President	Dadaya School fire
1992		Todds hand over ranch to Sam Mpofu and move to Bulawayo, as does Judith. Todds' 60th wedding anniversary
2001		Grace dies in December
2002		Grace is buried at Dadaya in January; GT and Judith lose right to vote; GT has a stroke in September, dies in October, and is buried at Dadaya

Sir Garfield Todd

PART I – SCOTTISH BACKGROUND

◆•◆

1

The Todd Family

'That Scotland has still a noble peasantry, none who, like myself, have been brought up with and mingled among them will deny.'

Adam B. Todd, 1909

The story of Garfield and Grace begins in New Zealand, where both were born into families descended from Scottish immigrants of the nineteenth century. Garfield's great-grandfather, Matthew Todd, was born in 1768 in Fenwick, Ayrshire, in the west of Scotland. He was a crofter, and in 1795 he became tenant of a small farm, Craighall, near Mauchline. This was 'Robert Burns country'. Members of his family still farmed locally – and the poet was revered. Here Matthew Todd's fifteen children were born, the two youngest, by his second wife, Mary Gibb, being Adam (b. 1822) and Thomas (b. 1823), Garfield Todd's grandfather. All fifteen children lived to maturity. Adam became first a brick- and tile-maker and then a writer, ultimately editing the *Cumnock Express*, a local newspaper. In 1906, he wrote an autobiography

– and it is to this book that we owe many details of the family.[1]

Crofters' sons had to help work the farm when they were not at school, and formal education ended early. Thomas 'started in a tile works at an early age, usually working until the light failed'. Their evenings were filled with night school and study. As in so many humble Scottish homes, there was a deep respect for learning, an appreciation of literature, the habit of hard work, and above everything else a profound Christian faith and stern Presbyterianism.

In 1848 Thomas, now aged 25, was appointed manager of the Marquis of Bute's tile works at Kilchattan Bay near Kingarth on the Isle of Bute, off the Ayrshire coast. The main town on Bute is Rothesay, and here Thomas soon made the acquaintance of a local grocer. Robert Wright was a fairly well-to-do man with three small coasters as well as his business. On Thomas's first Sunday on the island, he went to the Presbyterian Church, where he met Robert's son, William, who invited him home for a meal and introduced him to his sister, Elizabeth.

Elizabeth Wright had been born in 1832; and her daughter Eliza, from whose memoir, *The House of Todd*,[2] we also learn much of the family, tells us that she was a healthy, happy child. Elizabeth attended a parish school in Rothesay until she was ten years old, when her father sent her to 'a ladies' school'. Here she learned sewing, music, dancing, French and drawing in addition to the usual subjects. She also helped in her father's shop when he was away or ill. Wright had two assistants in the shop, John Herbert and John Logan, who both later emigrated to New Zealand.

Eliza's account of her mother's childhood gives an impression of liveliness and intelligence, which soon captivated the 'tall handsome lad' from Ayrshire. On 6 November 1849, Thomas Todd and Elizabeth Wright were married at Robert Wright's home, Braeside Cottage, outside Rothesay, by the Reverend Thomas Nelson, who later went as a missionary to the New Hebrides.

The Marquis of Bute built a house for the young couple, 'The Tileries', a two-storey cottage with dormer windows on the road from Kingarth to Kilchattan Bay. The date '1849' is inscribed above the door. Thomas and Elizabeth spent several happy years in Bute, where their first child, Matthew, was born in 1850. The decline in the tile-making business saw the family move from Bute to the mining town of Sanquhar in north Dumfriesshire, but soon Thomas was urged by a friend to go to Canada. However, he did not prosper there, and after five years he had to apply to his brother, Adam, for help to return to Scotland.

---

1   A.B. Todd, 1906.
2   Todd Papers Paul Collection (TPPC).

The Todd Family

***

Things were little better there, but, after a few difficult years, Thomas was asked to manage a branch of his father-in-law's business in Glasgow. They lived at 77 Shamrock Street, where their seventh child, Thomas (II), Garfield's father, was born on 13 July 1862. Not long after, Matthew, the eldest son, fell ill and died, and the doctor advised Thomas to take his family to one of the colonies. Elizabeth had corresponded over the years with John Logan's wife in Dunedin, New Zealand, so she wrote to them to find out what might be the prospects there for Thomas.

The mail between New Zealand and Scotland took more than three months, but, when a positive reply was received from Logan, the decision to emigrate was soon made. Logan agreed to sponsor Thomas from New Zealand and, most importantly, to advance his passage money. News of his guarantee reached Shamrock Street in February 1864. This time, Thomas went ahead of the family to make sure the prospects really were as good as had been suggested.

Thomas set out aboard the *Hamilla Mitchell* from Glasgow on 8 June 1864 and reached Dunedin on 20 September. The town was doing well following the discovery in June 1861 of gold in the Arrow River, and on that spring morning Thomas saw some fine buildings. Though most of the houses were of timber, he was pleased to see some brick houses. He rented a room in George Street and within two days had found a job at the brickworks of Lambert Brothers.

***

During the long wait for news, Elizabeth gained a Diploma in Midwifery and Diseases of Women and Children at Glasgow Hospital and made shirts for sale at 2/6d a dozen. Finally, letters began to arrive from Thomas urging Elizabeth to join him: 'I will never cease to Bless God for giving me you for my wife ... If I had you and the children and the Bible God's Book I would be happy ... my dear, dear Elizabeth, my own Dear wee wife ... you and the children are all my care ... I will cease to live when I cease to love you ... Come, my love, come ...'[3]

'Only a few days ago my employer told me that he would find work for me all the year round summer and winter ... I hope you may get off in March or not later than April ... I am to get a house from Mr Lambert ...' Thomas was very concerned about the family's long journey to New Zealand and goes into great detail about what provisions Elizabeth should take: 'get as many clothes for yourself and children as you can. You must also have two pairs of shoes each ... one barrel of oatmeal and one barrel of flour ... buy at least as much coffee as will supply you twice every day for 3 months; one large smoked ham

---
3   Hocken Library, Dunedin.

… a few pounds of red herrings … some syrup for your porridge … 5 chests … put meal in one, and eggs, ham and all other eatables in a third, then have two for clothes … brass locks …' He was insistent about the brass locks.

The family left from Greenock on 2 April 1865 in the 1,160-ton mail ship *Caribou*. 'The prospect of three long months at sea with her little ones did not deter her', wrote Eliza. They arrived at Port Chalmers outside Dunedin on 13 July 1865, young Thomas Todd's third birthday – 'and there was father waiting!' Family tradition has it that he presented Elizabeth with 'a great paper bag of fresh scones and a pound of butter'.

2

NEW ZEALAND, 1865

'Industrious, persevering, patient, imbued with a deep sense of the solemnity and dignity of human life'

Professor John Collie[1]

The family stayed in the Dunedin area until 1878, when Thomas found land with good clay at Waikiwi near Invercargill; and here the family settled, first at Newfield and then, finally, in 1890 at Belgravia, where 45 acres provided land for gardens and orchards, and for each of the sons a plot on which to build a house when he married. Here began the golden age of the Todd family. The firm of Thomas Todd & Sons, brick and tile makers, was established, with John, Robert, Thomas and, in due time, Nathaniel.

Another great turning point in the Todds' lives occurred in 1878, when they joined the Church of Christ. This small church had begun in the USA (the 'Church of Christ (Disciples)') in 1802 with the breakaway of several Presbyterian congregations. The two basic principles of the Church of Christ are New Testament Christianity (including 'believer's baptism', as opposed to infant baptism) and the unity of the Church. The Church of Christ spread to Australia in the 1840s, and from there to New Zealand.

Invercargill, with its Church of Christ, would remain the centre of the family's life for decades. When Thomas Todd retired in 1893, his son Thomas (referred to now as Thomas II) became managing director, and in spite of his mild eccentricities the firm prospered. He had little time for trade unions, and had no office, often interviewing potential customers on the steps of the Post Office.

The family was very close, and all were musical. Thomas Todd I formed a family choir which practised hymns and psalms for a few minutes after

---

1   *The Story of the Otago Free Church Settlement 1848 to 1948* (Glasgow: The Presbyterian Bookroom, 1950).

dinner every day. There were four special family occasions during the year – Christmas, Thomas's and Elizabeth's birthdays and their wedding anniversary. The celebration of their golden wedding anniversary was held on 9 November 1899. Eliza wrote: 'the sun shone from a cloudless sky on wide lawns and on flowers in full bloom, on shrubs a blaze of colour. Trees that rose to a height of ninety feet sheltered the rich picturesque grounds. Bell birds and tuis filled the wood with melodious song.' Nearly 150 guests lunched in the large marquee under the walnut trees. Thomas Todd I summed up his feelings: 'Man, I never thought I would end ma days in sic a bonnie place ... I'm sure I dinna deserve a' this.'

In 1898, Thomas II married Jessie Davies of Auckland. Their son, Thomas Frederick Davis Todd, was born in 1900, but four years later Jessie died.

***

In 1907, Thomas II married Edith Scott, who had been adopted as a child by an English couple. On 13 July 1908, Thomas Todd II's 46th birthday, Reginald Stephen Garfield Todd was born. (He was named after the US President, also a member of the Church of Christ.) Shortly after his birth, Garfield was taken to receive his ailing grandfather's blessing. The death of Thomas Todd I was, Eliza wrote, 'Our greatest sorrow'.

Garfield has admitted he was 'an impossible child', but he loved all his family dearly, none more so than his parents, and his grandmother. 'My mother and father had a very good relationship. My relationship with my mother was more brother-and-sister because my father was 20 years older but we were centred on my father. My mother was a delight, beautiful, and my father was very proud of her.'[2] Thomas and Edith also had two daughters, Stella and Edith.

Garfield's memories of his grandmother, of his parents and 'the aunts', of Belgravia (which was of great importance to him) and of his 28 first cousins, remained fresh to the end of his life. In his letters over the years, there are constant happy references to the New Zealand home and family from which he came, and which he saw so seldom after he was 25. In a letter to his cousin, Dr Garfield Stewart, in 1968 he wrote: 'In our own family we have been greatly privileged ... Aunt Jane with her bicycle and her studio and art classes, frail Aunt Eliza whose health proved so uncertain that she lived for 97 years, and Aunt Mary who provided apple tarts and porridge. I can imagine myself taking the paper to Grandmother every evening at five o'clock. I used to go around and through the side door, then down the long corridor to the parlour ... I kissed

---

[2] Quotations from Garfield and Grace Todd, unless otherwise specified, are from conversations documented in TPPC.

Grandma and gave her the paper and perhaps sat on a stool at her feet for a while before going home.'[3]

The family's religious life was something Garfield accepted without question, attending church and Sunday School and later Bible class regularly. When he was twelve, he expressed a wish to become a missionary, which was in keeping with the family's missionary-minded tradition. One of Garfield's heroes was the Reverend John G. Paton, who went as a missionary to the New Hebrides; the other was Dr David Livingstone.

The Todds were early enthusiasts for the internal combustion engine. Garfield was all his life fascinated by cars. In later life, he would date events by remembering what car he was driving at the time; and, as a very old man, being driven along a busy road in Zimbabwe, he admitted that he noticed the make of every car that passed. By the age of ten, he was his grandmother's unofficial driver, and at twelve he could strip down and reassemble the engine – a talent he later had many opportunities to exercise in Africa.

During the 1918 'flu epidemic, Elizabeth helped with the nursing, and Garfield became one of the staff at the volunteer centre, filling bottles of disinfectant, answering phones and travelling with doctors so that, while the doctor was looking after the patient, he would wash dishes, sweep floors, and check on food supplies. One day, the *Southland Times*' headline was: '10-year-old boy commandeers the Mayor and his car!' The office had been offered five gallons of milk at a farm some four or five miles outside the city. 'My instructions were to get the milk in, so I went outside and stopped the first likely car ...'

In 1923, Garfield turned fifteen, and came fifth out of 439 entrants in an essay competition run by the New Zealand Churches of Christ – and left school. He was bored with his lessons. His mother had serious misgivings about this, but his father did not try to dissuade him, simply taking him into the firm. 'My father, though he loved me very greatly, had very definite ideas – if you were to manage men you started off at the bottom and each thing you did, you had to do it better than they did. It was tough. There were three of us and we were working in very soft, mucky clay. We had to cut out 50 tons a day and it was very heavy work. The shifts were twelve-hour shifts, seven days a week. So I worked from ten at night until ten in the morning. I was to get a shilling an hour, that was £4.4.0. a week. I bought a motorbike, my first, with the money. I learned a lot of practical things which served me well when I came to be a missionary. But I loathed it, the hours simply would not pass. I was a clock-watcher. I just did not like the work.' While recovering from an accident at a

---

3 GT/Garfield Stewart, 3.10.68, MS.1082/4/7, Todd Papers, National Archives of Zimbabwe (NAZ).

brick kiln, Garfield decided that he would return to high school, get his matric. and train for the ministry. 'Since that day, even the calendar has raced round.'

***

In 1927, the Church of Christ in New Zealand opened a Bible College in Dunedin. The first Principal was Dr Arthur Langan Haddon, MA, from New South Wales. A very scholarly man, Dr Haddon was considered in Church of Christ circles to be very much a liberal. Garfield counted him among the seven most important influences in his life. From him he learned the value of Christian education based on a holistic approach to life. 'True education', said Haddon, 'helps to break down prejudice and bitterness. It teaches us to open our eyes to seek that which is Christ-like in every human life.' Garfield wrote of Dr Haddon as 'a great man and a peace-loving man with a nice sense of humour. He was of course a big man in a small pond but we benefited. Where would I have been without him? He exerted a great influence on my thinking. I am greatly indebted to him for many things but especially for him leading me, during my three years at College, to a clear and unshakeable belief that life is a whole. I learned that Christ is interested in the whole breadth of life and would reconcile it all with the justice of his love.'

Garfield and Ray Vickery were the first two students to arrive at the college on 19 July 1927. As Garfield had no money, he took a correspondence course in sweet-making and paid his way through college by making and selling sweets, until he became a part-time minister and earned enough to pay his fees.

Sure of his vocation, confirmed in his beliefs and at last finding enjoyment in his studies, it came as a great disappointment to Garfield when at the end of his first year he was asked to leave college. Seventy years later, he told the story: 'In 1927 I fell in love with my first girl-friend. Betty was a member of our own Church and a delightful girl. We fell in love but I was very unpopular with her father, whom I did not respect a great deal. One day when I was with the family he took exception to something I said and made to hit me, which was very unwise because I was 19 and very strong. Even as he was picking himself up from the floor I knew I was (to use a theological expression suitable, possibly, for a theological student) in a hell of a mess. He went to a doctor and got a certificate regarding the damage I had done and brought it to the College authorities … and that was the end of my career at the theological college.'

Bitterly disappointed with himself, Garfield went back to the clay-pits, this time at Benhar, where he stayed with his brother Tom and his wife, Ivy, who were very good to him. He made friends among the tough young men he worked with. During his 'wilderness years' from the time of his suspension from theological college to his readmission in 1929, Thomas retired from Thomas Todd & Sons, and the family moved to Dunedin. The following year, the college moved to the beautiful Glen Leith house there – it and its grounds came second only to Belgravia in Garfield's memories of New Zealand. But, at Belgravia, the long life of Garfield's beloved grandmother was slowly drawing to its close. He went to see her shortly before she died: 'She lay in comfort looking through a great window which commanded the drive. The front porch of the house was dominated by a fifty-foot monkey-puzzle tree which she greatly prized … As I rose to leave, Grandmother said, "Well, Garfield, I think I should really say goodbye. You know I'm 95! Whoever would have thought it? Well, I'm ready to go whenever the Lord wills it …" The last sentient action of my grandmother's life was to put aside her offering for the following Sunday's collection for Dadaya Mission' – established by the New Zealand Churches of Christ in Southern Rhodesia.

***

Readmitted to Bible College, Garfield took courses at Otago University. A small incident during one lecture had significance for him twenty years later at another university: 'Just as Professor Edgar arrived unseen by almost all the class, two girls walked down the aisle and were "tramped" to their seats by two hundred pairs of feet in unison. Dr Edgar mistakenly thought the students were "tramping" him down the aisle and was furious … two hundred of us sat and offered neither explanation nor apology. It was really a matter of little importance but afterwards I was disgusted with myself for having done nothing at all and I determined I would not fail so miserably again.'

It was the custom for Glen Leith's students to take up part-time posts with the Churches in Dunedin when the Principal considered them sufficiently capable. Garfield went to North East Valley Church. In the winter of 1930, his sister, Stella, broke her leg in a fall on the ice. She was visited at home regularly by two friends from the teacher-training college, Alyce Crawford and Grace Wilson. During one of their visits, Garfield walked into Stella's bedroom in his shirtsleeves and braces. Much disconcerted to find the two girls there, he withdrew, reappearing in a couple of minutes with his jacket on. At 22, Garfield was over six feet tall, strong and broad-shouldered, with a mass of thick, wiry black hair, and penetrating hazel eyes. Grace, at nineteen, was a very pretty girl with sparkling blue eyes.

In 1988, Stella wrote in Garfield's 80th-birthday book that, not long after the meeting in her bedroom, 'Garfield was reading in the Dunedin Botanical Gardens, and Grace walked by. But she was not noticed. When she had gone a little further she decided to go back and say "hallo".' Soon Grace and Garfield were spending all their spare time together.

***

When Garfield's temporary post at North East Valley came to an end, he was assigned to a similar post in Oamaru, a beautiful town on the South Island coast about 70 miles north of Dunedin. He never forgot his first week's pay of two gold sovereigns. Garfield received the Church of Christ form of ordination – 'In the tradition of "where the Bible speaks, we speak", it was the simple setting aside of a person for the Ministry with prayers and "the laying on of hands".'

3

GRACE WILSON'S FAMILY

'The kind of people from whom we come were very ordinary, decent God-fearing bodies – and Scots into the bargain.'

Grace Todd

On Friday 19 August 1859, the *Sevilla* (589 tons) sailed from Glasgow with 304 Scottish emigrants aboard, among them Grace's great-grandfather, Alexander McKenzie, a farmer from Carsehead in Fowlis Wester parish, Perthshire, his wife, four sons and three daughters. On arrival in Dunedin, Alexander took up a farm at Anderson's Bay, and later opened a quarry. Alexander's son, James (Grace's grandfather), had started his working life in Scotland as an eight-year-old cowherd on the shores of Loch Katrine. All his life, James was a great reader, and he always carried a copy of *Paradise Lost* in his pocket to read while driving. It is stated in his obituary that 'he was overcome with the power of it and the tremendous use of language'. He did what he could to educate himself by reading and attending night school. Later, Alexander and James bought 400 acres of land near Pukerau in the south of the South Island.

In 1872, James, now 28, married Ann Crawford, a 25-year-old tailoress, whose parents had come out to New Zealand from Paisley in 1862 on the *Storm Cloud*. Ann and James lived in Anderson's Bay for four years, and there Annie, Grace's mother, was born. Ann bore ten children in all, but two died of TB and one from meningitis. James's passion for education and his public-spiritedness made him a leader in his small but growing local community. For 26 years, James and his brother carried the mail. An account of James and Ann's golden wedding gives some impressive facts about James: he 'held office in almost every body looking after the welfare of the district'.

Annie was one of the first children to enrol at Pukerau School. Here, Helen

Todd, Thomas II's sister and Garfield's aunt, was her first teacher – and, Grace has said, 'greatly influenced my mother, who loved her dearly'. Annie inherited her father's love of books. There was no money to buy them, so, according to Grace, she 'concentrated on the book prizes she and her siblings won at school, which is why she knew the collected works of Tennyson practically by heart. One book had to last until the next one arrived – Whittier, Browning, Scott, Wordsworth.' Annie's formal education ended when she left primary school, for although secondary education was also free, her parents could not afford the books or uniform. She went to work in an accounts office in nearby Gore, and at 25 married James Wilson, a builder and carpenter from Waitake, near Blueskin Bay in Southland. They lived in Winton, not far from Invercargill. James Wilson was an excellent builder but not a good provider, largely on account of his drinking. On Annie, therefore, fell the burden of keeping and bringing up the family. Like her mother, she made a loving home for her daughters: Winifred, born 1899; Madge 1903; Elsie 1907; and Grace, born 3 April 1911. It was a constant struggle, and later Annie took in boarders to bring some money into the house. Grace's home was the centre of her life, and that meant her mother, from whom she inherited a life-long love of books, gardening and flowers. To Grace fell the (hated) job of looking after the precious family cow.

Mrs Wilson was another devoted Presbyterian and taught in the Sunday School at Winton Church for 40 years. Grace's admiration for her mother was unbounded: 'She was a remarkable woman, well-informed and well-read. She was my standard. I could never approach her in her unselfishness or her kindness and concern for people outside the family as well as inside.'

The girls went to Winton Primary School. There was huge excitement in the family when Grace went on to the Southland Girls' High School. One of the proudest days of her life was when she first put on her school uniform. It had been accepted that Grace would be a teacher: 'I think it stemmed from my grandfather'. So, Grace went to Dunedin Teacher Training College in 1929 to take a two-year course, living in lodgings with friends. During her second year, she took English and Education at Otago University. At the end of that year, she was invited to take a specialist course in Physical Education. 'There were seven girls and seven men from Colleges all over New Zealand, and when a place was offered to me I accepted. We were a very privileged group – an elite group. It gave me another year at University and I took two more subjects for my degree, History stages 1 and 2. I remember meeting my History 2 lecturer one day and he stopped me and said, "I just want to congratulate you, Miss Wilson, you have got an 'A' for your final History paper."' Grace was persuaded to join the college's debating team, which beat Christchurch College, and she was adjudged the best speaker. She never forgot the acclamation of her fellow students as they sang: 'She's got eyes of blue, I like blue eyes now!'

Garfield was 23 on 13 July 1931, and for his birthday Grace gave him a book of daily Bible readings, *Being and Doing*, which was familiar to her. At the back, she quoted this verse from Browning's *Asolando*:

> One who never turned his back but marched breast forward,
> Never doubted clouds would break,
> Never dreamed, though right were worsted, wrong would triumph,
> Held we fall to rise, are baffled to fight better,
> Sleep to wake.

Fifty years later, she would ask: 'What made me choose that particular quotation? Was it chance, or recognition, or prophetic fore-knowledge? Who can tell? I only know that Browning might have had Garfield in mind when he wrote those lines.'

After her triumphs at college, Grace went to her first – and only – teaching post in New Zealand at Winton District High School. But the worldwide depression of the 1930s had hit New Zealand hard, and Grace's appointment ended after one term.

***

The developing friendship between Grace and Garfield did not meet with unqualified approval from Mrs Wilson, nor did their engagement. 'I think my mother did not want me to marry anybody at that time. She looked forward to my making a contribution to the community and probably doing well in my profession.' Garfield went to Winton on his motorbike for Grace's 21st birthday on 3 April 1932 and gave her a fire opal engagement ring. He has written: 'The depression was spreading its blight of misery over the world and in the uncertainty of the times Grace and I craved the security of marriage, but we could not afford to live together'. As minister of Oamaru Church, Garfield was now earning £3.10.0.

Grace became ill: all her life, she suffered from sickness at times of great strain. When Garfield found her ill, he was afraid that he would not have the right to care for her or be concerned in her welfare. Staying at Winton over her birthday, they 'talked for hours and on April 7th we rode by motorcycle to Invercargill and were married before a magistrate … The knowledge of our marriage gave us strength and much joy till we were able to add a wedding ring to the engagement one at a service at Glen Leith College by Dr Haddon – and my debt to him was increased.'

When the secret marriage came to light, the local Church community at Oamaru was scandalised, and the Church Committee had harsh words for the young bridegroom. What they were we will never know, for a subsequent Church secretary (Mrs Mavis Walsh, née Thomson) removed the page from the minute book, an exercise book kept in pencil, now in the Hocken Archives in Dunedin, and burned it.

Stella describes their secret marriage as 'the first of a lifetime's extraordinary experiences' for Grace, but for them both their marriage was also the greatest blessing. In August 1952, Garfield wrote one of his last letters to Mrs Wilson: 'I was very fortunate when I met Grace Wilson', and twenty years later he told their daughter, Judith: 'A happy marriage is the most desirable thing on earth and is a foretaste of heaven.' He adds: 'Early in our married life, I noted that Grace was at her very best in times of crisis – and I have kept the crises coming steadily.'

***

The young couple went to live for a few months at Kakanui, seven miles from Oamaru. While they were there, Garfield and Grace adopted a little girl. Born on 21 January 1932, the daughter of Grace's cousin Sheila, she had been looked after for a year by her grandparents to enable Sheila to return to work; but, as Sheila did not intend to marry the child's father, the grandparents decided to adopt her. Grace and Garfield were concerned that the little girl would be growing up with much older people, 'in a place where everyone knew her story, and it would be better if we adopted the baby and brought her up'.

'There was a great deal of opposition, even from the magistrate, through whom I had to work to get the adoption legalised.' Old Mrs McKenzie predicted that the Todds' action would be 'misconstrued' by the 'malicious'. She was right. The magistrate was right. People did assume that Garfield had fathered the child, whom they christened Alycen, and persuaded Grace to take her in as part of their family. So much was said along these lines at the time that Garfield had the adoption papers published in a local newspaper.

***

Soon after this, the little family moved into Oamaru itself, renting a small house from a member of the congregation. Every month, Garfield gave Mr Thomson a cheque for the rent, and every month, Mr Thomson failed to cash it. But not many months passed before the house burned down and almost all their few possessions were destroyed, including 300 of Garfield's books and his 'Sunday suit'. The following Sunday, he preached in a borrowed suit, several sizes too small and of rather unclerical cloth.

When the Church Committee minutes were read out to the congregation on 20 March 1934, reference was made to the fire. The minutes also reveal that, after expressing his heartfelt thanks for all the help he and Grace had received, the minister said that a vacancy had occurred in the mission field in Southern Rhodesia and that he was going to apply for the job. Garfield later wrote that in some ways his work at Oamaru was 'very fulfilling, but on the other hand I was not fully satisfied – sometimes I felt that my ministerial duties did not add up to a very useful life'.

The *New Zealand Christian* had carried an advertisement seeking a couple who would be prepared to go to Dadaya Mission in Southern Rhodesia for five years. Teaching qualifications were particularly desirable. The Southern Rhodesia Director of Native Development (later the Department of Native Education), Mr Jowitt, had told the Church of Christ Foreign Mission Board that it should be policy to send out missionaries who had some training and experience as teachers.

Garfield was shortlisted for the post and went to Nelson for an interview. This meant taking the ferry via Wellington in the North Island, with a night on board. When he embarked at Wellington, he got permission to go down to the stokehold, where he helped the stokers. 'I worked with them, firing, and then at midnight they said, "Come and have something to eat with us." By this time, the motion of the boat was beginning to make me feel a bit sick so I took two seasick pills when I should only have taken one. The stokers' mess was right up in the bow and the boat was heaving up and down, so I took another couple of pills … I didn't realise they were strong sedatives.' When he finally got to his bunk, he slept until 10 a.m., three hours after the boat docked – and three hours after the Church officials had called for him.

The youngest member of the selection committee, the Reverend Thomas Bamford, spoke of that day to the *Oamaru Mail* in January 1972: 'the 26-year-old candidate was forthright and without diffidence. A strong character but not immodest, boastful or too pushful. He spelt out his theological qualifications, then spoke of his skills as a handyman and having qualified as a brickmaker in the family brickworks.' The committee was divided between the two candidates, but Mr Bamford's support for Garfield, on the strength of Grace's qualifications, swung the vote in Garfield's favour.

Government regulations in Southern Rhodesia stipulated that because the mission was in a Native Reserve, a white male missionary must live there. As the present superintendent at Dadaya, Mr C. A. Bowen, and his wife had moved off it to a small farm nearby, leaving two women missionaries on their own, the

Foreign Mission Board wanted the Todds to leave as soon as possible. Few ships sailed between Australia, New Zealand and Africa during the Depression, but the SS *Ascanius* was due to leave Sydney shortly for Durban. It was first-class only, but the Board booked the Todds on it rather than wait months for a ship with third-class accommodation.

Preparations for the Todds' departure were rushed, but – thanks to the fire – their possessions were few and fitted into 'five small boxes', an echo of Elizabeth's journey 70 years before. After a quick round of farewell visits to some of the churches in the Dunedin and Invercargill areas, and to families, the new missionaries with their little fair-haired daughter Alycen and their boxes (one of which held Garfield's father's Sunday suit) travelled to Auckland to join their ship.

In 1983, Garfield spoke of that visit to Auckland: 'We faced the first major test of our missionary life. I had graduated from the Glen Leith College where Dr A. L. Haddon was principal. He was also a very strong exponent of what today would be called "liberation theology". Both college and principal were unpopular with a conservative minority of our brethren and this was a major reason for a last-minute attempt to stop me at the wharf ... The opposition in Auckland was a wealthy group of men who asked us to consider a proposition: if we gave up our call to Africa, generous financial backing would be given to us so that we could go to one of our wealthy churches in America where prospects would be very attractive for a young minister.'[1]

Garfield recalled in that 1983 address how 'greatly shocked' he and Grace were by this offer, but they were unaware of the church-political background and how much difficulty the Foreign Mission Board was experiencing with Mr Bowen, who had the support of the men in Auckland. Now the Chairman and Secretary of the Board, Mr Bolton and Mr Boddington, who had travelled to Auckland with the Todds, revealed to them 'the full measure of their concern ... The New Zealand brotherhood was split to some extent on the question of foreign missions. Mr Bolton and Mr Boddington said to me: "Of course, you are very young and we are not sure that you will be able to take as firm a line as we would hope." But I told them, with the confidence of youth, "Whatever instructions you give me, I will carry out."'

This was the first intimation Garfield had of a conflict that was to continue for decades – basically a conflict between conservatives (represented by Bowen and his supporters in the North Island), who saw the Church's job as to 'save souls'; and liberals, Dr Haddon and a new breed of missionary, personified to

---

1   Tübingen address, 28.5.83, TPPC.

some extent now by the Todds, who saw the work of the Church, in Christ's words, to bring the people 'life more abundantly'. The conflict would take the form of support for, or opposition to, the education of the African people.

***

The immediate families were the ones who would bear the real pain of the five-year separation. Thomas Todd was an old man, and he loved his son dearly. Mrs Wilson was glad that Grace's teaching qualifications were to be made use of, but Grace's departure was hard for her to bear. Her feelings are expressed with almost unbearable sadness in her last letter to Grace in New Zealand:

'My dear little love, This will be the last message you will receive from home while you are in New Zealand and I want it to be a message full of love and cheer. As you go away from all that you know and from much that you love, to do the work that God has called you to in a foreign land, remember that you carry our love, our warmest wishes for your welfare and true success and our prayers that God will bless you and your husband and child with his richest blessing. I am very proud and thankful that you have been called to do this special work and I pray that you will both be led and guided by our heavenly Father. He is faithful – as you try to be too. I thank God for all the joy and happiness we have had together, Grace, and may the new home in Africa reflect some of the pleasant cheer of the old home, with none of its faults. You are my dear little daughter and wherever you are my love and my prayers will follow you. All this is meant for Garfield and Alycen as well as you. Goodbye and bon voyage, from Mother.'

PART II – DADAYA MISSION

♦•♦

4

SOUTHERN RHODESIA, 1934

'It will be an ill day for the native races when their fortunes are removed from the Imperial and august administration of the Crown and abandoned to the fierce self-interest of ... white settlers.'

Winston S. Churchill, 1923

Southern Rhodesia had been colonised from South Africa at the instigation of Cecil John Rhodes, Prime Minister of the Cape Colony, in pursuit of his dream of British influence from 'the Cape to Cairo'. The British flag was raised in what was to become Salisbury on 13 September 1890. For its first 34 years, the country was administered by the British South Africa Company under a Charter granted by the British Government in 1889. The Charter gave the Company rights to undertake commercial ventures, including mining, and to set up a police force – the British South Africa Police.

In 1893, the Matabele people in the west of the country rose up against their new rulers – and again in 1896. The Mashona people in the eastern half of the country also rebelled. Both uprisings were put down by the BSAP and by locally raised volunteer forces, assisted by a relief column sent up from South Africa. Peace was finally established at an indaba (meeting) in the Matopos Hills outside Bulawayo when Rhodes with three companions met the Matabele chiefs and elders. In 1898, an Order in Council of the British Government set aside areas of the country as native reserves, under the jurisdiction of the Chief Native Commissioner and the Government Native Affairs Department. The Department, through its Native Commissioners, exercised complete control of all administrative aspects of the natives' lives.

Many settlers came from Britain, as well as from South Africa; but South African influences were predominant, with Southern Rhodesian law modelled on the Roman Dutch system. However, in 1923, when given the choice of joining the Union of South Africa or becoming a self-governing colony of Great Britain, two-thirds of the almost wholly white electorate voted for independence. When Garfield and Grace Todd arrived in Southern Rhodesia in 1934, the African population was an estimated 1,154,500. There were around 52,950 Europeans, and 4,550 people in the Coloured or mixed-race community. That year, there were 101,296 African children in village schools, almost all of which had been established by Christian missionaries who came from sixteen countries in Europe, Australasia and America. There were 1,500 African teachers, with little or no training. The Government had established two large primary schools, Domboshawa in Mashonaland and Tjolotjo in Matabeleland, where, that year, the first African children were able to enter a Standard Six class. Links between Government and missionaries were strong, though officials suspected churchmen of encouraging dangerous – even revolutionary – liberal attitudes among Africans.

The Associated Churches of Christ in New Zealand had become involved in missionary work in Southern Rhodesia through the inspiration of John Sherriff, who was born in Christchurch in 1864. A member of the Church of Christ, he felt that the Lord was drawing him towards Africa. He went briefly to Cape Town, Johannesburg and Pretoria before arriving in Bulawayo at the end of July 1897. He was sure it was to the African people that he had been sent, and this was confirmed to him by an apparently trivial incident: walking one evening in the native location, he saw, in the dim light shining through a crack in the wall of a tin shanty, a group of 'native boys' clustered round a candle trying to read English out of a book. He started a night school, screening off half of his own tiny hut, teaching English and Christianity for two hours a week. Returning to New Zealand in 1905, he met members of the Foreign Mission Council of the New Zealand Churches of Christ, who decided to sponsor a missionary to Southern Rhodesia, selecting a previous minister of the Church of Christ in Oamaru, Mr F. L. Hadfield.

Mr and Mrs Hadfield and their family went to Southern Rhodesia for a five-year term to work in Bulawayo. One of his colleagues was William Mansill, who was engaged to marry a New Zealand girl, Madge. Hadfield got permission from the Southern Rhodesian Government to open up a mission station at Ngome in the Belingwe Reserve (part of the Lundi Reserve), about 120 miles from Bulawayo and ten miles from the small mining town of Shabani. Madge had now arrived in Southern Rhodesia; and, two weeks after she and William were married, they set out, with Hadfield, for Ngome, a place so isolated that leopards lazed in the midday heat on a flat rock halfway up the nearby hill.

The journey from Bulawayo took three weeks by donkey cart. They took with them building materials for two small thatched houses, and a cow. They had six African helpers, but work was painfully slow, and both men fell ill. Hadfield had to be taken to Belingwe Hospital, 25 miles on a stretcher – a thirteen-hour journey. Later, both men got blackwater fever. Mansill died, and Hadfield, with the young widow, returned to Bulawayo, leaving a native assistant in charge. No white missionary went back to work at Ngome; but, with help from native assistants, small outstations were established at Dadaya, Fishu, Lundi and in Shabani itself. Mrs Mansill returned to New Zealand, where her daughter, Hazel, was born.

In 1917, Hadfield, now living in Bulawayo, was told by the Belingwe Native Commissioner that unless a white missionary lived in the reserve, representatives of other churches would be admitted to the area. The New Zealand Board sent Mr F. J. Phillips out for a year, and so the Church of Christ retained its tenuous hold on the reserve. Dadaya, only ten miles from Ngome but in a much healthier area, was now made the head station – and there Hadfield's son-in-law and daughter lived temporarily until the Phillips family returned, this time for five years. In 1920, Hadfield retired after fourteen years of missionary work to take up secular work, later entering the Southern Rhodesia Legislative Assembly. At the end of F. J. Phillips' term, New Zealand sent Mr C. A. Bowen and his family to Dadaya. When Hazel Mansill had completed her primary education, she and her mother returned to Southern Rhodesia and went to Dadaya, where they worked tirelessly as teachers – untrained teachers, as they had declined the NZ Board's offer of training for Hazel.

5

13 July 1934

*'Those white educators were not colonialists, nor did they bring
second-class teaching. They lighted fires in the hearts of boys
and girls.'*

Garfield Todd, 1981

In 1934, Bulawayo boasted what was held to be the longest railway platform in the world. There on 13 July to meet the New Zealand arrivals were C. A. Bowen and Hadfield's son, Philip, and his wife, Vonna (née Phillips). The Todds were dismayed to be told that they would be going straight to Dadaya – no promised three-week acclimatisation visit to the long-established Hope Fountain Mission.

Bowen piled the Todds into his Graham truck, put their luggage into the back and rushed them around Bulawayo to get things they needed: a wardrobe, two beds and mattresses, a table and chairs; canvas waterbags, a sun helmet and mosquito boots for Garfield, jodhpurs for Grace, mosquito nets for them all. After a brief call at the Native Education Department to meet the Native Education Circuit Inspector for the Dadaya area, Mr A. R. Mather, the Todds set off with Bowen for the mission.

At first, they looked about them with interest: the sparse suburbs with their bungalows and flowering trees and shrubs soon giving way to dry, brown land, empty save for scattered villages of round grass-thatched mud houses surrounded by small fields of maize, and then the low, rounded hills and beautiful mopani trees around Balla Balla, where they left the main Bulawayo–Beitbridge road to South Africa – with another 70 miles to cover. The country became flatter and rather featureless, a sameness of bare, red earth, for this was winter and the dry season, scrubby thorn bushes and a few bush-clad hills and dry water-courses, which they were told would be impassable in the rains. The cab filled with dust from the unsealed dirt road – Grace noted Alycen's fair curls were gradually turning red – and the 'corrugations' meant a long, bone-rattling drive before they finally reached the mission in the evening.

Both the Todds regretted the abandonment of the visit to Hope Fountain Mission, founded by John Moffat, son-in-law of Dr David Livingstone, little realising that this was a decision of great importance in their lives. They would go, untutored, into their work and find their own ways of doing things, ignorant of how other whites treated the natives. They would take the people as they met them, their own instincts as their guide, rather than the prevailing customs.

***

The Todds had little knowledge of the country's turbulent history but knew that here, in the previous century, the Matabele kings Mzilikazi and Lobengula had hunted the abundant wildlife and wintered the royal cattle herds. To the north lay Wedza Mountain. 'Wedza would be the axis of our lives,' Garfield wrote in his draft autobiography,[1] 'and in three homes to follow, over the next 40 years, we would move a little further round the semi-circle: but always our view would centre on the mountain. On that clear, cold morning in July 1934, Wedza was serenely set in a stillness that enveloped the whole countryside, a stillness only emphasised by the cooing of doves and the distant barking of a single dog.'

The day after the Todds arrived at Dadaya was a Sunday, and at intervals during the day the teachers called to greet them. The work of the mission would have been impossible without the African evangelists and teachers, and the most senior was the Reverend Ndabambi Hlambelo, a tall, fine-looking man, well educated and with an excellent command of Sindebele, the local language, and English. His grandfather had been one of the Impi that Mzilikazi brought with him when he left Natal. He was a forthright Ndebele, intelligent and a 'wizard' with machinery. Over the years, he became a much-trusted friend and colleague.

In a letter to Mavis Thomson back in Oamaru, Grace wrote: 'We went to Hazel's Sunday School and will never forget our introduction to real native singing: a hundred boys and girls, and they made one think of a mighty organ. I have never heard anything like it ...'[2]

The Todds soon discovered the truth of what they had been told in New Zealand about the strains between the Foreign Mission Union Executive Committee and the missionaries in the field. And what Garfield found shocked him. Within weeks of their arrival, he wrote to New Zealand: 'I'm afraid I will not be a success if I have to work under Bro. Bowen for already I am sickened

---

1 GT/A, c. 1974, TPPC.
2 I am grateful to Mavis Thomson for sight of this and other letters.

by the whole business. The position at Dadaya is intolerable ... The whole outlook and attitude to New Zealand must be changed. The missionary is made such a fuss of and set on so high a pedestal by the homefolks, that he seems to ... think he is the only one who makes sacrifices ... and if the people of the churches in New Zealand had heard all that I have heard since coming to our stations and weren't privileged to see the native people and their Christianity, I have no doubt but they would close down missions in Africa. I'm not speaking at all hastily – I just know that it is so.'[3] That letter would take six weeks to reach New Zealand.

The very day that Garfield wrote to the Secretary of the FMU Committee, Mr Jowitt paid an unexpected visit to Dadaya. As a result, Hadfield called a meeting of all missionaries at Dadaya, together with Mr Mather. Bowen made serious allegations of immorality against Garfield – 're Alycen' – which so shocked Hadfield that he turned to him and said: 'I'm sorry, Alf, but I have to withdraw my support for you.' This was one of the 'hinge moments' in Garfield's life, as it ensured that his work at Dadaya could begin – and he could be sure of Hadfield's support until the latter died in 1966 at the age of 92.

The next day, Mather and Hadfield signed a letter to Mr Jowitt: 'Arising out of a joint visit of Mr F. L. Hadfield and myself to Dadaya Mission, Mr Hadfield and I both decided to completely withdraw any support of Mr Bowen ... Mr Hadfield is notifying the NZ Board to this effect and advising that Mr Bowen be withdrawn from the field.'[4]

The monthly reports Garfield sent to New Zealand give vivid accounts of the work at Dadaya and provide insights into the reactions and attitudes of the new missionaries, but they do not always say it all. In October, Garfield wrote to Mavis rather more frankly: 'If you have read between the lines of the report which of course must appear in the *New Zealand Christian* for October, you will know that life has not been easy ... but today I am superintendent with full charge of Dadaya ... I have hardly slept in weeks.'

---

3   GT to Patrick Boddington, ACCNZ, 7.8.34.
4   TPPC: 2.9.34, referred to as 'Letter No. 6' in later correspondence. ACCNZ.

6

BABES IN THE BUSH

'From the moment he arrived at Dadaya, Todd and the Africans developed a unique relationship that translated into broad understanding of the meaning of human co-operation and friendship.'

Dr D. A. Mungazi, The Last British Liberals in Africa

In 1934, Dadaya Mission consisted of a little group of plain, whitewashed, cheaply constructed buildings: the Bruce Wright Memorial Church, two dormitories for the 22 boarders, the Beginners' School, the boys' kitchen, the electric light plant and the Mansills' house. In the twenty years since its establishment, a great increase in the number of villages, the people and their animals had largely destroyed the vegetation, and the land had become so impoverished that the stream Hadfield had swum in twenty years before was now only a dry river bed and a memory.

The Todds' house, set among syringa trees and dominated by a single great jacaranda tree, had been built in 1923 of Kimberley bricks, which were moulded from ant-hill mixed with water, and sun-dried. The ceilings were of steel sheets and the roof the usual corrugated iron. The stoep (verandah) gave protection to three sides of the house so that it kept reasonably cool in summer. It was quite substantial, a better house than they had been expecting. There was no running water, and by the end of July there was often very little left in their 80ft well at the bottom of the hill. The bathroom had hot water from a 44-gallon drum filled daily from the buckets carried on girls' heads. Pressure lamps were used when the lighting plant failed. There was a very minimum of furniture in the house – and, in the first year, if there were visitors such as Government inspectors, the Todds slept on the floor.

Dadaya Mission was the centre of work for about 30 churches, twelve with schools attached. When the Todds arrived, there were 12,000 or so people living on land held in communal tenure in the Native Reserve. By the time they left in 1953, there would be 20,000. The people were organised under headmen who, in turn, were answerable to their chiefs, of whom there were five in the Lundi Reserve. The Mission leased from the Government, at an annual rental of £100, 50 (later 100) acres of rough, dry, stony land.

'Life was good,' Grace remembered. 'We were missionaries, young, full of good intentions, admittedly arrogant in our background of belief that we had everything to give and little to receive from the people except the generous return of their friendship without which all was lost.'

***

No sooner had the Todds settled in at Dadaya than Mr Mather came for a five-day visit. Garfield describes him as a 'round, dynamic man'. He was an American citizen and had worked for the American Methodist Episcopal Church at Mount Silinda Mission in the east of the country for three years before joining the Native Development Department, where Mr Jowitt held him in high regard. Mather had a deep commitment to the cause of African education and, over many years, the Todds found in him guide, philosopher, slave-driver, colleague, supporter and friend – and, at moments of desperate financial need, interest-free moneylender to the Mission.

Mather told the young enthusiasts not to look upon blacks as being different and therefore inferior beings: 'we should not make the common mistake of looking on education here as being basically different from education in a European country', Garfield remembered him saying. 'It may be different but it shouldn't be and you must not lower your standards for the people can rise to any standard you set.' There was a conference of all the staff, and as a result Grace assumed control of all the educational work and the physical training, with Mrs Mansill teaching the primary department and Hazel the pre-primary classes, until they left in April 1935.

Soon the Todds were immersed in the excitement of this new beginning. The work of the mission depended on the preacher-teachers. Garfield describes a significant meeting with these men: 'I have just had the teachers in here with me. When they came in I told them to sit down and they sat down on the floor. I told them to sit on the chairs and they beamed. It really just breaks one's heart. I have fallen in love with the people and I think they have fallen a bit in love with me ... The people are great and some are splendid Christians. If we can only keep our health, we are going to enjoy every moment of time in Rhodesia. The hardest work just now is language study ...'[1]

---

1 GT/Mavis Thomson, 25.9.34, TPPC.

Grace was daily in the school at Dadaya – 'I found a kraal (village) school and a Central Boarding School of twenty boys ... Most of the teachers were also preachers. They lacked training but they did not lack enthusiasm or devotion. On their work our more modern edifice has been erected and it was from the thrust of their character and influence that our leaders of today have emerged. They were the heroes of their day at 30 shillings and 40 shillings a month. I visited village schools and was appalled by what I saw. The buildings were made of pole and dagga with apertures for windows and they had no doors. There were blackboards and the children sat on low benches made of Kimberley brick. The teacher had a table and chair and the children wrote on slates. There was no clock, there was no timetable. There were practically no books and there were really no aids for the teachers, all of whom were untrained. In our schools there was not one woman teacher. In our area it was difficult to get girls to come to school but in some areas girls went to school quite freely. Our teachers came in to Dadaya for a monthly meeting and we held classes to help. It was a time which was exciting and rewarding: at no time did the teachers or I myself feel that we were faced with an impossible situation.'

Grace's full-time job as headmistress of the central primary school meant that she had to find someone to look after Alycen, so a little ten-year-old girl of mixed race called Rua McCulloch became Alycen's nurse/companion.

While Grace was in the classroom, Garfield was attempting to get an overall picture of the life and work at the Mission. 'We came to speak about God, a God who in Christ is deeply concerned with the poor, the sick, the disadvantaged. The gospel of Christ which we preached was concerned with the saving of souls. But it was also constructively sympathetic with the children who had no schooling and with teachers who did their splendid best but who had no professional training and perhaps only five or six years of primary school teaching themselves.' Garfield was appalled by the need of the people: 'On every side was poverty and filth, disease and drunkenness and, worse than these physical things, were the witchcraft, the fear and degradation of the souls.'[2] 'It was not possible, we found, to look the need of the people straight in the eye and then preach vacuous generalities. So, from the love of God, came the establishment of vegetable gardens, the teaching of improved methods in agriculture ... Five hundred years ago, St Thomas Aquinas said: "A minimum of material comfort is necessary to have a spiritual life ...". I accept that statement and we have worked hard to improve both homes and churches.'

---

2 GT/A, TPPC.

Visiting the village schools, encouraging the teachers, checking up on standards and the state of the buildings was a constant part of Garfield's work. At one village, Garfield found the teacher giving the boys an English lesson, while three little girls sat drawing pictures on their slates. When he inquired why they were apart from the class, the teacher replied: didn't he know that girls could never learn English? Visiting another school, where there were few girls, he was told: 'The headmen of the kraal have forbidden them to attend for, they say, if they go to school they will learn to do as they like – in other words, they won't marry the old men who are prepared to give cattle for them.'

7

THAT THEY MAY BECOME LEADERS

'The quality of a teacher as a human being is fundamental to the quality of his work as an educator. He educates not just from what he knows and can do, but from what he is.'

W. McD. Partridge, 1985

'Garfield and I are up to our eyes preparing for the new term and deep in Sindebele', Grace wrote[1] in January 1935. But, despite strenuous efforts, the Todds never mastered either Sindebele, the language of the minority Ndebele, or Shona, the language of the majority. It is interesting to note that, when some of the local leaders were interviewed for this book, it was the Todds' failure to learn the local languages that they saw as their principal shortcoming. For Garfield, it was his 'biggest sadness. There is the language of the heart with which we tried to make up for our lack, and of course I learned enough words and phrases to be able to do the medical work and find out where the pain was.'

However, in the 1930s, the students were eager to learn English, which they saw as vital to their education and future. Many of them did not wish to be spoken to in their own language, and at Dadaya there was a self-imposed 'rule' that students would speak only in English from Monday morning to Saturday midday.

During 1935, the devoted Mansills were due to go back to New Zealand on furlough after seven years in the Lundi reserve, but their last weeks at the Mission were not easy. The new emphasis on teaching, and the building up of the school, was so contrary to Hazel's own ideas that she found it difficult to maintain good relations with Garfield. Although they hoped to return to Rhodesia, the Board did not have the money to send them back, and as they were without the teaching qualifications now required by the Government, they

---

1 JGT/Mavis Thomson.

were ineligible to be missionaries. In the event, the two women took matters into their own hands, and, supported by friends in New Zealand, returned to work with the Church of Christ in Bulawayo, Hazel earning her living in secular employment. Sixty years later, she was still teaching in the Sunday School there.

'We have everything to ourselves now, and it is bliss, not usually known on earth', Garfield told Mavis. He and Grace were now the only whites at Dadaya, and that was how it was for the next twelve years, largely due to the recession in New Zealand. The Todds were never conscious of being 'on their own', and their African assistants became increasingly capable as they took on greater responsibility. 'We were fortunate to realise so early in our time in Africa not only that the future lay within the African people themselves but that in the sleepy villages, basking in the sun, there were people who would take the future into their own hands. At Dadaya we were to be concerned with thousands of young people already being caught up in a revolution which was to exert its increasing and irresistible pressure on the whole continent of Africa. These were the men and women of tomorrow and the responsibility of the church was great ... evangelism was not the whole story. What we were trying to do was meet the need of the people in all life, medical crises, teaching, better use of the land, teaching them how to build. All these were just as important as the teaching and the preaching of the Gospel – which anyway was done better by the blacks. We began to realise this very early.'

***

All her life, Grace's principal recreations were reading and gardening. Every evening, if she was not too tired, she would read at least a few pages of one of the books sent out fortnightly by the Bulawayo Public Library. She had lovingly established a little flower garden, and a tiny square of lawn, watered by buckets of bath water when there was no rain. 'The garden is the joy of my heart', Grace wrote in 1935 to the Christian Women's Auxiliary (CWA) in New Zealand. 'I've been starved for the sight and smell of flowers these many months and on the table as I write is a lovely bowl of zinnias – at least they seem lovely to me. They are the first fruits of my garden ...' The Todds also planted hundreds of trees around the mission: gum trees, jacarandas, frangipani – and fruit trees, mango, guava and pawpaw. Sunday by Sunday, Grace played the little Todd organ which had come to rest in Africa. And, Sunday by Sunday, there would be Garfield's simple address in church, which was the high point of Grace's week. On Sunday evenings, there was a second service, and it was here that the students made their 'decisions for Christ' – a precious statistic for the Church at home in New Zealand. Baptisms took place in a local river during the rainy season.

With Mather's encouragement, it had been decided that the most important part of the school's work was the central boarding school, and its enlargement would be their priority. They set out a long-term building programme for the village schools and churches, for in many cases existing buildings were both inadequate and dilapidated. The rapid increase in the enrolment at the central school, however, largely determined priorities. Lack of money was always inhibiting and frustrating, even for simple buildings of Kimberley bricks and thatch. Food was mealie-meal (cornmeal) with vegetables or meat for 'relish'. Garfield's years in his school cadet force had given him another useful skill: marksmanship – but he only shot 'for the pot'. The conditions at the central school were primitive, especially the latrines. One of the building instructors at the mission, Joram Sibanda, remembered seeing Garfield in the mornings emptying the buckets into the pit and covering the contents with soil. 'That surprised us all, as we had never seen a white man doing such things.' A distinguished old boy of Dadaya, Sam Mpofu, would later say of Garfield: 'he set an example to the students by doing the work himself'.

Each child enrolling at the school was given an enamel plate and mug. Garfield remembered 'how proud they were for very few of them had ever had a mug and plate before … each boy made his own spoon'. Not only the children, but also the teachers, including the Todds, lived in poor conditions. Garfield's monthly reports record rapid building at the Mission – the provision of homes for permanent staff members and the improvement of a small dam. 'It is worth remembering', he wrote, 'that all the work was done with picks, shovels, spades, wheelbarrows and the odd stick of dynamite, and mostly by schoolboys, but many of the schoolboys during those first years were over age for their classes and some at the beginning were married men, older than their headmistress.'

At the beginning of 1935, the staffing of the school was adequate, as Mather had found a well-qualified couple to replace the Mansills. Grace was delighted with the arrival of a woman teacher. The Government gave grants to the Missions in respect of trained African teachers, so they were doubly welcome. The year began with 61 boys (a considerable increase over the twenty in 1934), and Garfield told Mavis: 'My family of boys has won my heart … They are here to be trained that they may become leaders of their people … We have the confidence and whole-hearted support and help of the Government and that counts for a great deal. They have given us a splendid report, mostly due to Grace's efforts, for she knows her job and has licked this school into shape …'

'We were not looking for miracles', Garfield wrote in his draft autobiography, 'but we should have been, for without a miracle Africa was unlikely to change much during our lifetime. The villages had slept in the sun for countless generations. The Moffats had worked and prayed for thirty years before they had won a convert, and as our own Mission completed thirty-six years' service in Rhodesia it had little enough to show for it. That would be our lot, too, we believed, but we were glad we had come.' From the vantage-point of 1974, Garfield added: 'Now that we can look back forty years it seems to us that Africa has walked knee-deep in miracles day by day.'

Years later, Grace wrote to a fellow retired missionary that she soon had to face 'doubt as to the wisdom, or ethics, of educating (civilising?) [sic] a primitive people ... I answered my doubts and questions in my own way, by accepting that we, and they, were already well into the twentieth century with wars, technology and ideologies to which we, and they, must learn to adjust. And that anyway it could only ever be beneficial for a child's mind and understanding to be extended, and for him to learn the skills which he would need in this bewildering and changing world.'[2]

Sometimes there was homesickness, and for Grace the longing for the cooler, greener land that had nurtured her, the beloved garden and home in Winton and, particularly, for her mother. Even Garfield was not immune from longing thoughts of home, writing to Mavis as winter approached: 'The mission is quiet as I write. Grace is sitting beside me writing, too. It is now 4.45 and a blue haze is spreading over the hills and already one can feel the air growing chillier. It is dark at 6 pm now and is not light until 6 am. How I long at times for the twilights of New Zealand of the south ...' And the next day: 'Now it is morning, crisp and sunshiney. From where I sit at my office desk I can see Grace getting around. She is wearing a khaki shirt and a particularly nice pair of grey worsted flannel longs and she looks rather nippy ... I may be far from being the most effective missionary they have out here but Grace is certainly the most efficient woman ...'

Grace's uniform of grey or khaki trousers, khaki shirt and tie was the practical dress for a physical education teacher – but, when photographs got back to New Zealand, some church members were very shocked and chalked it up as another black mark for the already controversial missionaries. The Todds were visited one day by an unexpected trio of Brethren in Christ missionaries, the two ladies wearing long skirts and bonnets. They were all very civil and the visit passed off well, but they never came back, and the Todds were inclined to blame Grace's trousers.

---

2   GT/Queenie Ladbrook, 6.12.84, MS.1082/3/6, Todd Papers, NAZ.

8

GIRLS AT DADAYA

'There can be no doubt that the women are a vital factor to moulding the character of the African community ... The social status of the African people will be seriously retarded until the women are educated.'

Kerr Report, 1952

In New Zealand, the equal status of women was established as early as 1893, when they were given the vote. We have already seen the importance of the women in the Todds' own families, so the inferior place of women in African culture had come as a shock to them. They very soon recognised that one of the greatest weaknesses of their work at Dadaya was a lack of provision in the whole area for any girl to obtain more than three years of education, barely sufficient for literacy in the vernacular. Many barriers in the African culture had to be overcome, and the most stubborn of these was often prejudice in the minds of some of the people about education – and about women.

Garfield asked the New Zealand Board for permission to establish a boarding department for girls at the Mission. 'This was the only occasion on which permission for a new venture was not immediately forthcoming. The Board felt that we were unwise to consider housing boys and girls on the same fifty acres of ground. However, we were not forbidden to go ahead. In 1935 we enrolled the first five girls.' Fifty years later, four of them were still active in the local churches.

Grace found the work with the girls one of the most important and rewarding aspects of her work: 'a great deal of the satisfaction came from the more practical subjects – the vegetable gardening, sewing, knitting, and dress-making, basketwork, laundry, the home-nursing and baby-care classes, Red Cross, the drill and sports, the choirs and all the activities associated with the church'. The girls made all their own clothes, including their uniforms as Wayfarer Guides, as the African Girl Guides were known at the time.

***

The married teachers who had arrived at the start of the year were 'treasures, for they know their work so well that it takes a real load from my shoulders', Grace told the CWA. 'Emily works beautifully with the girls … It has been amusing to see the reaction of the people of this Reserve to a Standard VII woman … From the point of view of the girls who are boarders, the coming of Emily has really been a gift from God.'

Almost every morning brought another courageous girl to the school. Some stayed, but some were forced to return to backward homes and unhappy futures. As Grace wrote to the CWA: 'The native woman has no chance of any kind. We endeavoured to gain a hearing for one girl. The reply was, "The girls are getting out of hand and the [Native Affairs] Department urges parents to report unauthorised departures from their kraals of their daughters and wards."'

The first period after morning prayers was half an hour's drill for the whole school. With the arrival of the girls, a woodworking class produced Indian clubs for them. Each evening, the girls learned to swing clubs in a myriad of rhythms, and soon they were demonstrating their great natural grace of movement and posture. As the numbers increased, Grace formed a small choir, and the Indian clubs were soon swinging to their music. Garfield wrote: 'The first performance was an overwhelming success. The boys recognised that in this drill the girls were cleverer and more graceful than they could ever hope to be, and what was equally important was that the girls were fully convinced also. They were on their way …'

In July 1935, Garfield wrote in his report: 'Dadaya School must be regarded as the key to our work in the Lundi Reserve, for it affords boys and girls the opportunity of living in healthy surroundings under Christian influence. Here for a nominal fee, payable in cash or in grain, and in some cases in work, Education, not secular, but Christ-centred, may be theirs … We trust that those who complete their training at Dadaya will be a leaven when they return to their homes on the reserve.'

9

THE VILLAGE CHURCHES AND SCHOOLS

'As far as Christianity is concerned, I wasn't too long in this country before I saw African friends whose faith was more admirable than mine.'

Garfield Todd, 1991

The supervision of the kraal churches and schools took up a significant amount of Garfield's time. One of his guiding scriptural texts was: 'I am come that they may have life, and have it more abundantly' (St John 10:10). His faith was simple, and simply stated: 'The religion of our Lord Jesus Christ is basically faith, hope and love; the rest is theology'.[1] But 'the preaching of Christ's love and the teaching of His Work and His kingdom' was the root of all the mission's work: 'the work of the churches is being carried out faithfully by the African preachers ... Our Sabbath bells may not sound as beautiful as some, but ... they call the sons and daughters of Africa to worship God ... The people among whom we are privileged to work have not worshipped material gods; but while they worshipped the Great Spirit, "Mlimo" as they called him, they could never have known God as he is revealed to us in Christ, but worshipped the "unknown god" who to them was not a God of love, the giver of every good and perfect gift, but one who must be approached with awe, one who must be appeased.'

***

In the winter of 1935, Mather went with both the Todds on a week's visit to the Dadaya outstations. At the end of his visit, he presented Garfield with a choice: either he must raise the standard of the village schools at a fairly high cost, or lose the Government grant. Garfield did not find it difficult to decide to improve the schools.

---

1   GT, Peter Ainslie Memorial Lecture, University of Natal, 1.6.1955, TPPC.

Mather directed that agricultural 'demonstration plots' be introduced. The plots were part of a small 'revolution' that was going on through the kraal schools, a revolution initiated by another former missionary of the American Board of Missions, Henry Alvord, a contemporary of Mather's. Alvord's agricultural principles were few, simple and basic: kraal manure, crop rotation and vegetable gardens. He saw that the old, wasteful practice of the burning of trees and shifting of plots every two or three years had to stop. The biggest single potential contribution towards successful agriculture in established fields was neither recognised nor used: the manure from the cattle kraals. The one-acre demonstration plot was divided into four: one plot was heavily manured and planted with maize; number two plot was planted with maize, unmanured; number three plot had a leguminous crop, usually a type of bean; and number four plot was planted with a reliable and sturdy sorghum. In the first year of planting, the results were little short of miraculous, and the lesson quickly learned.

In the first years of their life at Dadaya, many of the boys and girls were around the same age as the missionaries. 'This freedom of fellowship resulted from our lack of inhibitions in relationships between black and white. After all, we did come from New Zealand where relationships between Maori and Pakeha and Jew and Gentile were hardly noticed,' Garfield wrote. The mission ran Christian Endeavour Societies along the lines of those in New Zealand to strengthen the faith of the young people. The societies met weekly, and at full moon there was a games night when everyone marched out into the veld and supper was eaten round a campfire.

Garfield wrote of one games night when they learned something of white attitudes. An old man called Alf Holland, a former Native Commissioner, had started to mine for gold-bearing quartz not far from the Mission, and he visited the Todds on a games night. 'He stayed over and had supper with us. The Societies met, as usual, had their hymn and prayer, read the minutes of the last meeting and then adjourned for games on the drill ground below our house. Soon the air was filled with singing as the games and dancing began.'

As they watched the dancing, it broke and new partners were taken. 'A tall young man detached himself from the group, ran across the drill ground and up to where we were standing, bowed before Grace and put out his hand. Grace joined hands, excused herself and they ran together to the dance. The moon gave all the light needed to show me the look of incredulity mixed with almost horror on Alf's face. 'My god,' said Alf, 'I never saw such a thing. Do you allow this?' The rest of the evening was spent in endeavouring to explain what we thought of life in Africa. I am afraid that Alf was more than ever convinced that missions were a danger to the safety of white men.'

There was also the Improvement Society, 'where they expected to learn European ways. We had dressing competitions, for instance, for boys and girls. You looked at their hair, their nails, their shoes – everything had to be absolutely right ... There were speaking competitions. It was in the Improvement Society that people learned to speak, and run meetings.'

***

The three inhibiting factors in the development of Dadaya Mission were insufficient land, inadequate water supply and very little money. Dadaya School was known as the poor man's school with low fees and, in the beginning, primitive conditions. The situation when the Todds arrived in Southern Rhodesia was even more precarious because of the world economic recession. In order to survive, Government assistance was needed which, to the minds of some missionaries, raised a moral issue that was articulated by the Reverend Arthur Shearly Cripps, the Anglican priest and poet. Cripps warned that if the churches received Government grants, missionaries might one day find that the Church was little more than a branch of the Civil Service – and, as things turned out, the Church came perilously near this position. But in the 1920s and the 1930s such arguments carried little weight in New Zealand – or at Dadaya. In 1934, Government grants to the Church of Christ missions amounted to £329; New Zealand contributed £1,235; and school fees brought in £27.5.0 (10/6d a head per annum, but some children didn't pay, working their way through school). A total of £1,591 had to meet the wages of the missionary and seventeen other people (mainly untrained teachers), the upkeep of a car, the running costs of a clinic, the purchase of food for 80 pupils, and provision for building expansion. Some of the evangelists earned only 10/6d to £2 a month. The Government gave Dadaya an extra £70 as a result of the reorganisation that had followed Mather's August 1934 visit. Grace told the CWA: 'It would be quite impossible to run a school of nearly 70 boarding boys and girls on the money available unless it was possible for the boys and girls themselves to help substantially.'[2]

---

2 JGT/CWA, April 1935, TPPC.

10

Matters Medical

'Through this service we have come very near to the life of the people and have grown to know and understand them more fully.'

Garfield Todd, 1941

Garfield's sister, Stella, trained as a teacher with Grace, but her teaching career, like Grace's, had been abruptly terminated before it ever really began, and she had then trained as a nurse. Recently qualified in 1935, she had become ill, and it was feared she might develop tuberculosis. The climate of Southern Africa was well known to be a healthy one, so Garfield suggested she come to Dadaya. He was quite frank about a secondary, selfish motive: a qualified nurse at Dadaya would be a wonderful thing.

The three most frequent medical emergencies that Garfield was called upon to deal with were childbirth, burns – particularly to small children – and malaria. But he could also be faced with snake-bites, wounds from fights, even insanity. He had only very limited medical knowledge – five years of weekly First Aid classes with St John Ambulance in New Zealand – but he did what he could, armed with the Mission's inadequate medical supplies – a black tin box containing little square bottles of medicine including Epsom salts, a laudanum mixture and brandy. He was aided by a 'Wellcome' book on drugs, a 1900 gynaecology textbook given to him in New Zealand and, most importantly, by the help, advice and support of a remarkable man, Dr Alfred J. ('Sonnie') Ireland, Medical Superintendent of the Shabanie Mine Hospital and the only medical practitioner within 40 miles of Dadaya. Garfield soon got to know Dr Ireland and learned what he could from him. Over twenty years, Dr Ireland was unstinting in his care of the Todds, saving both their lives in serious illness – and he never sent a bill.

Garfield records that his 'introduction to the physical needs of my parishioners was harsh ... In the middle of the night, soon after we had settled in, there was a knock at the door ... There was a woman, very ill, at the Railway Compound and would I come? I took my black box, and the messenger and I set out. I found that the sickness I had been summoned to cure was childbirth ...

'That night, as well as recognising my ignorance, I learned a great many things. The first was that nature has had a great deal of experience with childbirth and can manage most cases with a minimum of help ... With some shame I have to admit that that night I had laced my prayers with brandy. I had never tasted spirits before and have luckily had no longing for them since, but that night my physical needs were great. The combination of dirt, the smell of dried sticks of meat close to my head, the filthy piece of jute sacking spread on the floor as a delivery mat, the shortage of water, and no soap in my black box. It was almost more than I could bear. Two hours crawled by and the babe was born ... I tied the cord with a piece of twisted bark, the cord parted before my scissors with a spurt of blood and another babe announced its arrival with a plaintive cry. The baby was born, the mess cleared up, the small brandy bottle was empty and I went home determined to become a more knowledgeable man.'[1]

***

Later, when Garfield was Prime Minister, the then President of the British Medical Association visited Southern Rhodesia. A gynaecologist, he listened with some astonishment to a few of Garfield's medical experiences. One story he found of particular interest: on a Sunday morning in 1944, Garfield took a service at a distant church, and afterwards two old women and an old man approached him to tell of a woman in their village who was very ill. All he had with him were the Bible and a hymn book. He took the old people with him, and after nearly an hour's drive on rough tracks they stopped at a little village of four round huts. 'The old woman led me to the smallest of the huts and I stooped down under the thatch and entered ... sunshine entered the little doorway sufficiently to let me see the patient lying on the floor. On a sleeping mat, a young woman was propped up with her back against the wall. In the centre of the hut, almost between her feet, a small fire burned ...

'I removed the covering blanket and to my consternation found that obviously some hours earlier the woman had given birth, but when the old women had seen what the spirits had done they had been so horrified that they had given "first aid" – covered everything with a blanket – and

---

1 GT/A.

decided to go to the church and ask if I would come ... The mother had delivered a live child but the throes of birth had continued until there had been a complete prolapse, not just of the vagina but of the uterus itself. The spectacle of a mixture of water, blood, the placenta with babe attached and the inverted uterus had been more than the midwife could bear. The old women had gone to the cattle kraal with a blanket and gathered a quantity of powdered cattle dung. This they had used to cover the uterine lining and had spread it around to absorb the fluids. The blanket had then been used to hide everything from sight.

'My urge was to replace the blanket and go, accepting without protest what the spirits had done ... My basic needs could be met by a piece of string, a knife, water and soap. A piece of bark was stripped from a tree and twisted into string with which to tie off the cord. A pocket knife was given me and I cut the cord. A tin of grayish water and a small piece of soap came in their turn. I took the little baby which had lain silent for several hours, dried up by its proximity to the fire. I moistened its face and mouth and almost immediately there was a little cry. The young mother with her first babe was in a state of shock ... but the little cry from her baby was probably the most potent remedy ... One of the old women accepted the child from me and wrapped it in a cloth which was unwound from her head.

'With the baby clear of the mess, I could then take stock. The placenta was probably already separated from the uterine wall and I gently cleared it away, taking with it as much of the cow dung as I could gather in my hands ... Fortunately there had not been much haemorrhaging and I now set myself with soap and water and fingers to cleaning the delicate membranes. It was a long job but eventually it was as clean as I could make it ... If it were possible I must now return the uterus to its place. On the basis that what had emerged last should be returned first I firmly began the replacement. Eventually it was all back in place ...

'The baby seemed to be all right but I expected for the mother that massive infection would take over in a few hours and there was nothing I could do. I would hope and pray that the uncomplaining mother and her child might recover. Some weeks later I heard that they had both done so, and this seemed to me to be little short of miraculous.' In 1990, when the NZTV unit was filming the Todds at Hokonui Ranch, they all visited the weir Garfield had built on the river below the homestead. While they were there, a middle-aged man came up and introduced himself as Todd Mangena, the baby who had survived that remarkable birth all those years before.

But it was not all success: Garfield never forgot another tiny baby that, no matter what he did, he could not get to breathe.

***

Before Stella left, they all visited the Wankie Game Reserve and the Victoria Falls. Wildlife photography became a hobby of Garfield's.

Stella's visit did a lot to make the medical work easier: not only did she teach Garfield a great deal, but also she trained one of the girls, Lida Malunga, and two of the older boys to assist her – and him. One of the boys was Ndabaningi Sithole, Grace's brightest student and the future nationalist leader. All the girls helped with Garfield's patients as part of their home-nursing course – and with abandoned babies as part of their homecraft course. Before Garfield built the little hospital and maternity clinic, patients were treated and nursed in a small room off the stoep of the Todds' house, often overflowing onto the stoep itself.

Motor oil was a 'recognised' if fairly basic treatment for burns. Jimmy Savory, pioneer surveyor of the Kariba gorge, records its use in the 1920s. Garfield had first used it on a man called Jonah Mantjojo who had been very badly burned in a chemical fire in Bulawayo. Hadfield brought him to Garfield because the man was pining for his own home hearby. 'He lay here for three months and at first it seemed a hopeless task to get the skin to grow healthily on his legs', Garfield wrote in his draft autobiography. 'Jonah lay there without being able to move or do anything. I put this terrible oil on and next morning he was furious with me because of the pain, but instead of the pus there were little rivulets of blood all through the burned flesh.'[2]

Garfield told the end of the story in his May 1935 report: 'We took him to his kraal this week, half his body clean pink flesh. He was greeted by the assembled village as one who had returned from the dead, and it is good to see him, atrociously fat and all smiles. It will be sometime before he is able to walk but he appears to be going to make a fine recovery and his skin is at least completely healed.'[3] We will come across Jonah Mantjojo again in 1959.

Another case was of a very badly burned child – 'so badly burned', Garfield wrote, 'that I did not dare try putting bandages on. We put him on a mattress under a mosquito net and then we just put motor oil all over his body, and kept on putting on the oil. This takes a lot of work, and as the girls in their home-nursing class learned this sort of thing, they took over.'

Two further cases were significant in their own way: 'The little son of the local Chief Mafala Matshazi, Jobe by name, fell ill when he was still only five

---

2 GT/A.
3 GT, 5/1935 Report, TPPC.

or six and his father came up to me and asked me to go down and see him. I drove down with Ndabaningi Sithole and found, I think, three witchdoctors sitting on little stools around Jobe, who was in a bad way with dysentery. I left Ndabaningi there and told him to look after Jobe and make sure that he was not given any rough food … I went back to the Mission where I would have got soup for him but I had hardly arrived there when Ndabaningi ran up saying that they were now cooking stamp mealies, which was not even as kind as grain mealie-meal. So I went down again and with the protests of the people ringing in my ears, I picked this little wraith up, put him in the car and took him up to the house. I was very rough and determined with the people in a case like that when I could see the little boy would die. We put him in a room and Grace made soup for him and before long he was fine again.'

Ngedhleni was an old village headman, and one day he walked eight miles of rough track to ask Garfield's help for his very sick daughter. They drove to the village and entered the sick woman's hut. 'Sitting around a little fire in front of it were three men, one of them I knew to be the local n'anga, or traditional doctor. I was a bit perturbed when I learned that Ngedhleni's daughter was the doctor's wife and that she had given birth only a few days previously. It was quite obvious that I was not to receive any warmth of greeting from the husband but his wishes were subservient to those of the headman. On a long mat was a form completely wrapped in a blanket, and beside it a large necklace made from all sorts of bones, from monkeys and snakes and other creatures. I presumed that the husband had been doing his best to tackle the spirit problems, and when I announced my presence and carefully pulled the blankets down from the woman's head I prayed that I might be more successful …

'Ngedhleni's daughter had a raging fever. I gave what help I could and, as the village was not far from home, I came back daily to help her recovery. Besides the particular fever there was deeper venereal infection and I suggested that when she was strong enough I should take her to Mnene Mission Hospital for more sophisticated treatment than I was able to give.' When Garfield took Ngedhleni's daughter to Mnene Hospital, her husband elected to accompany her, which was just what the situation called for.

11

1937: The Dadaya Family

'Building, gardening, cobbling, doctoring, tinkering, carpentery [sic], gun-mending, farriering, wagon-mending, preaching, schools...'

David Livingstone's Diary

If you cut out 'gun-mending' and 'farriering', and substitute 'car' for 'wagon', Garfield's days were not unlike those of his hero, Livingstone.

For the Todds, contact with anything and anyone outside the Lundi reserve was restricted except for infrequent visits to the dusty little town of Shabani, dominated by the head-gear and growing dumps of the big asbestos mine, and even fewer visits to Bulawayo. Shabani was the centre of a small European ranching and mining community, notorious for its hard-drinking residents. By this time, Dadaya was becoming quite well known among its Europeans. Dr Ireland and the Assistant Native Commissioner (the Native Commissioner's office was in the small town of Belingwe) were early acquaintances and soon firm friends; so were the local magistrate, Mr Merrington, and a most important person in Shabani, the mine manager, Mr 'Bossman' McAdam. Garfield wrote: 'Quite early we recognised the importance of trying to bridge the gulf between white and black. We invited white people from Shabani to Mission concerts and later on to shows of sewing, knitting, vegetable gardening, etc., which we started.' Garfield got on very well with the Government inspectors and also had a high opinion of some of the whites who worked for the Native Affairs Department and who lived in the town. 'There have always been specialists who knew about the people but fortunately there were a great number of white men and women in the Department who knew the people and who were known to them. No-one can attempt to estimate the contribution of individual officials and their wives whose concern led to the provision of clinics, the organising of clubs and the improving of human relationships.'

***

Recession was biting ever deeper into the life and pockets of people in New Zealand, and for five months no money was sent to Southern Rhodesia. There came the day when, in order to pay the teachers, Garfield took to the Shabani auctioneer 'our old motor-car, a filing cabinet and our beautiful kaross (of leopard skins). For the lot we received just over £10 which, together with a loan from our friend Mather kept us all alive until times improved.'[1]

'Dadaya School is still expanding almost daily and our church has outgrown its building and we must build again as soon as possible ... The Inspector has recommended an increase in grants for Dadaya School ... from £60 to £200 ... brick-making is being commenced immediately.' Not long after, Garfield wrote of 'over 160 potential leaders in training'. This was what the Todds were working for, why they had taken as a motto for Dadaya School the motto of the Southland Boys' and Girls' High Schools: *non scholae sed vitae discimus*: 'Not for school but for life we are learning'. This would later be shortened to 'Education for life'. Not all Dadaya's 'graduates' would be absorbed back into the school and churches as teachers and preachers, but many of them would be going back to their villages ready to take on worthy work.

School fees were still vital. They came in many forms: holiday labour; one boy brought a cow; others arrived with donkeys carrying sacks of maize on their backs. A boy's father counted out carefully collected threepenny pieces – 'tickies' in Southern Rhodesia. The children came from many parts of the country: one walked 200 miles from his home. Twenty-five other children walked over 100 miles to Dadaya. Garfield wrote in a report: 'We know that some have a hard time indeed before they are permitted to come while there are others whose fathers save to get their fees and then come in themselves to see their girls and boys safely to the Mission ... one father brought his boy over 100 miles by bicycle through tropical rain and mud. Another man brought his daughter nearly fifty miles and they had to walk all the way. "What will happen when the holidays come?" I asked. "You must tell me when that will be," said the father, "and I will come and walk back with her." Yet another man came thirty miles to see if there would be room for his boy. When he was told that there would be, he went back home and three days later arrived again with his son who is only about ten years old. He had the money for the boy's fees too and counted it all out in "tickies".'[2]

---

1 GT/A.
2 TPPC.

***

The Government was very anxious that the missions should all work together, but the different denominations were jealous of their own positions – except for that great ecumenist F. L. Hadfield, who had been one of the earliest participants in the biennial Missionary Conference. For many years, this was the voice of the Missionary Societies; most Protestant churches as well as the Roman Catholic Church were members. Garfield observed it all with a sharp eye: 'At my first Conference I was disturbed to see that the Catholics and High Church Anglicans did not enter the hall until after the devotional session was completed. It did seem in the 1930s that language, education, industrial conciliation were ties that bound all the churchmen together but the love of Christ had not broken down denominational barriers. The lack of Christian fellowship among some of the Missionary leaders was more than unfortunate – it was sinful – but worse was the fact that when Africans took part in the Conference they had to meet separately, so that there was a white conference and a black conference.'

At the 1936 meeting, the Todds met two of the region's Christian leaders, the Anglican Bishop Edward Paget, who would later be Archbishop of Central Africa, and Father O'Hea of the Roman Catholic Kutama Mission in Mashonaland. 'I was a great admirer of both these men and stood in some awe of them also. Bishop Paget was courageous, tall and a joyous extrovert.'

Apart from the Missionary Conference, the Todds did not have much to do with other missions except Mnene, the Swedish Mission with its fine hospital, some 40 miles away; but relations between the churches on the mission field were generally better at that time than they were between many of the 'home churches'. For Dr Haddon's student, denominationalism counted for little: 'I believe Dadaya has never been denominational, but it has always been religious.' It would be many years before some, at least, of the churches recognised that in Africa it was time to throw the history books out of the church windows.

***

By the beginning of 1937, Dadaya presented a very different appearance from 1934. New dormitories, classrooms and teachers' houses had been built; terraces laid out with 25 vegetable gardens; 600 jacaranda trees had been planted, with another 1,000 ready to be planted at Dadaya and the kraal schools. The syringa trees which had been planted the year before were now six feet high. Crops, too, were doing well – maize, peanuts and experimental cotton plants. There were 310 pupils, 220 of whom were boarders. Garfield and Grace constantly refer to the wonderful achievements of local girls. 'I wonder if you can realise what it means to the life of the Reserve to have even 57 of its girls educated in a Christian environment in such things as mother-craft, house-wifery, laundry, sewing, vegetable-gardening, besides the ordinary academic subjects.'

In 1937, Garfield made a momentous decision, telling his father he could no longer waste hours of his time 'on his back under a car with a spanner' trying to repair the broken-down vehicles that had been all that the mission could afford, and had bought a 'new' car. He describes it in loving detail and concludes: 'Even Alycen is satisfied with it … we went to Bulawayo and got over 22 mpg so that is very satisfactory for a big car. I am very happy.'

***

In the tradition of Christian Missions, Dadaya was a refuge for all sorts and conditions of people. There were many miners – 'smallworkers' – in the heavily mineralised area of Belingwe, where, for example, gold, antimony, platinum and chrome could be found. Some took an African girl as a 'wife' and established families of Coloured children. Some of them were responsible, sending their children to be educated at missions or coloured schools; others were less so, and 'wives' and children would return to the mother's village. Magistrates or the Social Welfare Department would often send such children, and others 'in need of care', to Dadaya where, Garfield wrote, 'we were glad to receive them and they became known as the "Dadaya Family". There were twenty-five to thirty in the Family and although some arrived with "criminal" records they were happily received. As each new member of the Family arrived he found that the pressures of the daily life of the community kept him in line, and the children settled in well. Most were a good average and a few were outstanding.'

12

THE DADAYA SCHEMES

'All the Africans here who did primary education before 1980 are children or grandchildren of the Grace Todd Education System.'

Dr Aeneas Chigwedere, Minister of Education,
Culture and Sport, 2002

In his draft autobiography, Garfield asked the question: 'What do you teach?' He answered it partly by writing: 'the work of a mission had a much wider significance than the teaching of what men might do – it must reveal what men and women might be ... We held that at this period in the life of Rhodesia the English language could make a very important contribution. It was given high priority at Dadaya and it began with "Good morning" on the very first day of school. We recognised that there would come a day when there would be a reaction and an increasing demand for a greater use of the vernacular, and a greater concern, too, for African culture ...

'We were humbly treading in the path which had been so clearly marked in Macaulay's famous "Minute". In 1833, when Macaulay arrived in India he found that the "Committee of Public Instruction" was "divided five against five on either side of a controversy, vital, inevitable, admitting of neither postponement or compromise ..." One group wanted the education of the people developed through the medium of Sanskrit, Persian and Arabic while the other wanted to use the vernacular and then proceed in the medium of the English language. Lord Macaulay's Minute recommended English and it proved to be so persuasive that there was no further argument.

'We were concerned only with a few villages in Africa! Schools in Rhodesia taught in the vernacular until the end of Standard Three, the fifth year of schooling. Grace immediately changed this and used English as the medium of instruction from the beginning of Standard One. When the Dadaya Schemes were produced this change made them especially useful, for the time had come to make a much greater use of English.'[1] Dadaya became noted for the standard of its English ... spoken with a New Zealand accent.

By 1938, there was a full academic course from Standard One to Standard Six. To a great extent, the curriculum, including the industrial work that the boys and girls were taught, was regulated by the Native Education Inspectors. In 1934, hardly any African woman in the Lundi Reserve had ever held a needle in her hand. A Standard Six class opened at Dadaya in 1938, and by the time a girl left Standard Six she could adapt patterns, cut out and sew every article that she and her children would require; she could make a man's shirt and knit a pair of socks. Girls also learned to care for the sick, helping to attend to patients who went to Dadaya for treatment. They knew First Aid (many of them gaining Red Cross Certificates) and had learned babycraft. Every girl could wash, iron, make baskets from grasses growing on the veld, cook appetising meals and plan a wholesome diet for a family.

The boys learned agriculture, vegetable-gardening, animal husbandry, forestry, woodwork, ironwork and building. They learned how to farm – the basis of African life. They knew how to choose a farm, how to set it out; how to improve its value and the quality of the soil; how to choose suitable stock for the various purposes they might require, and how to improve their stock; how to kill and flay, how to provide for the long months of drought. They could make bricks for their house, set out a foundation and knew how to protect the walls from the ravages of white ants; how to build and thatch. They learned when trees should be cut and how to season the timber. With a big pit saw, they learned to cut planks by hand and from those planks to make simple furniture.[2]

***

The Mission superintendent and the headmistress had routine work enough, especially with the opening of Standard Five in 1937 and Standard Six in 1938, but during that time both were engaged in even larger projects, Garfield with his ambitious building programme, including a classroom block large enough for the whole school to worship in on Sundays, and Grace preparing notes of lessons for the teachers.

One day, Mr Mather, that dedicated and energetic educationalist, had asked Grace to show him her teachers' schemes of work. She did not know what he

---

1   GT/A.
2   *Dadaya Mission 1934–41*, Garfield's account, for New Zealand, of his first seven years' stewardship at Dadaya.

was talking about, and told him so. He professed surprise because, he said, other Missions had these aids for their untrained teachers. So, Grace set about the enormous task of producing 'Schemes of Work' for every lesson on every subject for every day of every class in primary schools from Sub-A to Standard Four. It was only when other Missions began to ask for copies of her Schemes that Grace realised that nobody else had produced anything like this before. Mather had recognised not only that Grace's talent was admirably suited to the task but also that she had the dedication to complete it.

When the Todds had arrived in 1934, Grace recalled, 'there was not one trained teacher in our whole system. I was the first. It was to help these teachers and their pupils that I started the whole exercise. I started by using a Croxley Triplicate book in which I wrote by hand. It was the days before the biro pen, so I used those old indelible pencils. The first two copies went to two teachers at the Head Station where I could monitor their work. Week by week I then typed as many copies as possible and each was given to a village school teacher. At monthly meetings of the teachers we discussed the school plans and work and made adjustments to the Schemes as necessary. The Notes of Lessons were of use during the period when there were few trained teachers and few textbooks and for this reason the material had to be specific, detailed and basic ...

'In 1940, the Shabanie Mine, prodded by the Reverend Reg Burman, Methodist Minister in Shabani, opened an Undenominational School for the children of its employees. Mr Burman came to me for help with lesson material for his staff, and he persuaded the Mine Management to make a donation to provide stencils. I then set about cutting the stencils. These were Gestetner and of a marvellous quality, for we used them over and over again ... by this time others had heard of the Notes of Lessons and requests for help poured in from schools all over the country. I cut the stencils but Garfield did the duplicating and now swears he turned the handle of the Rotary Gestetner more than a million times!'

Judith remembers her mother saying she could never have created the Dadaya Schemes without Rua, who looked after Alycen.

Mr Jimmy Stewart, Circuit Inspector for Matabeleland, told Garfield: 'Native Education owes Mrs Todd and yourself its undying gratitude for the work you have put into the preparation of these Schemes.' In the midst of glowing approval came a dissenting voice from Steve Davies of the Matabeleland School Circuit Inspectorate. A Rhodesian graduate fresh out of Yale University, he told Grace: 'This is absolutely wrong from the point of view of education. What you are doing is limiting the teachers and their imagination.' Grace replied: 'But you will find they don't have the imagination, they don't have the training, and they certainly don't have the books to enable them to prepare lessons properly, nor do they know what should be the speed of advance in education, whereas it is all there for them in these Schemes for the six years.'

The day came, however, when Steve went to war and was put in charge of training non-commissioned officers. 'Next thing we knew,' Grace recalled, 'there is a letter from Steve asking for a set of the Dadaya Schemes.'

***

In spite of attacks of typhoid, 1937 had been a good year for the Todds. The world was coming out of recession, and New Zealand had been able to resume its regular remittances; Government grants had risen to £625; the first Standard Five class had done well; Red Cross lectures had started and Literary and Debating societies formed. Stella's health had benefited so greatly from the months she spent in Southern Rhodesia that when her younger sister, Edith, was also threatened with TB she, too, was despatched to Dadaya – and lived in the country for the rest of her life. Edith had trained as a secretary, and it was not long before she was well enough to get a job in Gwelo with the Todds' lawyer friend, Mr Max Danziger (who later became an MP and a minister). Afterwards, for many years, Edith was a *Hansard*-writer in Salisbury. Garfield's mother was next to visit – but she, like Stella, returned to New Zealand.

***

The introduction of Dadaya's first Standard Six class in 1938 was a very proud day in the school's history, and this year also saw the completion of the large church/classroom block, the Routledge Memorial Building. The Inspectors' reports on Dadaya continued to please both the workers 'in the field' and the donors in New Zealand: 'The Principal is to be complimented on his ingenuity in providing desks which are suited to the pupils' requirements and yet cheap and simple ... the school has reached new levels in numbers and in the efficiency of the teachers ... a more highly qualified staff is gradually being acquired ... definite cheerfulness pervades all activities. Boys are polite, courteous and always ready to obey.'

The Director of Native Education spent a weekend at the Mission and expressed satisfaction with the Routledge Memorial Building. A few days after the visit, Grace was undergoing an emergency operation in Shabani Hospital. The drive from Dadaya had been 'a nightmare journey even though it was by car and not by hand-cart,' Garfield wrote, remembering Hadfield's thirteen-hour ordeal in 1910. Grace made a quick recovery, and was very philosophical, even light-hearted, about her brush with death. 'This has been vacation time and it has been wonderful that this was so for there is still a fortnight of holiday,' she wrote to the CWA from hospital. 'I have been writing this a little at a time. My room is fragrant with flowers ...'

Grace's illness had prevented Garfield's attendance at the monthly meeting of church workers, but he was delighted that the elders had carried on in the usual way without him, reporting to New Zealand: 'The most gratifying part of the work is not what I see being done in my presence, but how capably the work is carried on in my absence. We are trying to impress upon the people that it is time they were growing up and as leaders emerge we find plenty of work for them to do ... much of what at one time Europeans had to do for the African people at Dadaya Mission, the African people are now doing for themselves. The Routledge Memorial Building is being built by Africans, almost the whole of the teaching work at Dadaya is being carried out by Africans and the school has 300 children on its roll. Far the biggest part of the actual medical work is performed by young people here. At three different parts of the Reserve bricks are being made under the supervision of our teachers – trees are being planted, school furniture made, schools and churches in the Reserves capably governed, even proper school committees functioning, and at the Mission itself so many routine tasks are taken from my sphere of duty by capable and willing hands. For all these things we thank God, but it is well for us to keep in mind that the "growing up" period has perils as well as wonderful opportunities. We ask, for the sake of the work and the people, that you will be unceasing in your prayers during these years of transition.'[3]

13 July 1938 was Garfield's 30th birthday. Writing to their daughter Judith on her 30th birthday in 1973, Garfield thought back to that day: 'at 30, we were unknown, ill-dressed, poverty-stricken missionaries in the Lundi Reserve, the only good thing being our excitement and deep happiness in the work that had come to our hands'. 13 July 1938 was also Garfield's father's 76th birthday. He, too, had been very ill in previous weeks, but on the 25th he wrote what would be his last letter to the little family at Dadaya: 'Just a few lines with the first direct Air Service mail at the cheap rate ... We all trust that you, Grace, are making a good recovery from your illness.' By the end of 1938, airmail letters from New Zealand were taking only three weeks to reach Dadaya – and Thomas Todd II had died.

---

3   GT, 5/1935 Report, TPPC.

13

WAR COMES TO DADAYA

'I rather think the secret of success in life is ... to endeavour to work miracles with what lies at one's hand.'

Garfield Todd, 1953

Two of Dadaya's most outstanding students left at the end of 1938 to go the new Teacher Training College at Matopo Mission near Bulawayo: David Mkwananzi and P. J. Mkoka Ndebele. At the end of their training, both returned to teach at Dadaya. 'What I am, whatever I shall be', wrote Mkoka to the Todds, 'I owe all to Dadaya Mission. Mr and Mrs Todd have been my parents and I have been their child – a child well cared for, a child loved and protected from all harm and danger.'[1] He was a fine man and was ordained a priest in the Anglican Church. He was also a committed nationalist, so it was a great loss to both the Church and the nationalist movement, as well as a great sadness for the Todds, when he was killed in a car crash in the early 1960s. David was a teacher for over 40 years, 25 of them at Dadaya. Jimmy Stewart once said that 'when trained teachers came to Dadaya, Grace taught them to be teachers'.

Grace told the CWA: 'The work of the school had been most satisfactory and at Dadaya the first Standard VI closed its work with all scholars satisfying the Inspector. In the past two weeks we have had two and a half inches of rain. The yearly miracle of the granting of new life to a dead landscape is taking place before our eyes. Animals that were moving frantically from place to place, desperate with hunger a week ago are moving quietly on the veldt finding new grass at every step. The greatest blessings ...'

It was a year of considerable progress, and Garfield often mentions in his

---

1 PJMN/Todds, n.d. (1937?), TPPC.

reports to New Zealand his gratitude for moral and financial support. The membership of the Foreign Mission Union – and its name – might change from time to time, but over all the years of Garfield's connection with it (and its successor bodies) this support was constant and often imaginative. Messrs Bolton and Boddington, then Ray Blampied and Lew Hunter, in particular, never visited Dadaya, but these men so many thousands of miles from Africa caught, and never lost, the vision of what missionary work should be, and what it could achieve.

The year 1939 opened in Southern Rhodesia, as everywhere else in the Empire, with people swinging between hope that war would be averted and a fearful certainty that it would not. Life went on as normal, even though all planning was hedged about with 'ifs'. The Todds were due to take their longed-for furlough in July 1939. This meant preparing every department of the Mission for their six-month absence, the establishment of a Committee to run the Mission, the allocation of new duties, and the amassing of all needed stores. Dadaya School would be closed while the Todds were in New Zealand, but the village schools would stay open and the work of the churches continue. As the year progressed and the war clouds gathered, the Todds' hopes of furlough faded. When war was declared, the Government brought in conscription for both men and women of serving age. Garfield duly registered under the National Service Regulations – but, he remembered, 'all that was required of me was to carry on with my work. I was thankful beyond words that I was able to spend my time in constructive labour when so many others were called upon to leave home and family and work for war.' For most of the war, as clergy were conscripted, all Europeans in the Shabani area were ministered to, baptised, married and buried by either Garfield or Father Bohé of the Roman Catholic Church. In years to come, the fact that Garfield did not serve in the forces would be used by his political enemies as a weapon against him, and Dadaya Mission would be referred to as his 'funk-hole'.

As the Todds had planned to be away for much of 1940, it was a quieter year than usual, but this enabled Garfield to do a considerable amount of building, both at Dadaya and at the village schools and churches. Dadaya's annual figure for medical treatments given was over 4,000, so Garfield was delighted to have an African nurse take over from him. She would also take over from Grace the weekly women's meetings. 'This appointment is one of the most important that have been made at Dadaya', Garfield told New Zealand. But of course the nurse's arrival made the need for an appropriate medical building even more urgent: 'We need huts in which to put sick people, a clinic. If you came here today you would find babies with burns living in the meal room, critical cases billeted in our house, babies delivered in our bathroom, teeth being extracted on our back verandah.'

Government grants had risen and, with the school fees, nearly equalled the total salaries of the teachers. At the end of 1940, fifteen pupils completed Standard Six. Eight would go to teacher-training colleges, three to medical-orderly training, one to agricultural school, and one to a commercial school. But one of Grace's best teachers left: 'His younger brother had recently been killed in action further north in Kenya', Garfield told the OMB, 'and Matecheta said that he must go "to take his brother's place".'

Children continued to flock to Dadaya. Turning hopeful young people away because they had no fees was one of Garfield's most painful tasks. In 1941, Grace found a little boy weeping bitterly on the office steps. On hearing what the matter was, she appealed to the principal who, in his own distress, told her angrily there was no place for a boy with no fees. But he went back to the boy and asked what he could do to earn his fees. 'I could work, sir,' he replied. 'I could herd cattle, if the missionary has cattle.' So, Manikidza M. Nyoni came to Dadaya – and twenty years later became the first African principal. Did Grace remember that her grandfather as a little boy had herded cattle on the shores of Loch Katrine in Scotland? Did part of the Todds' understanding of the people stem from their similar background, just two generations in the past?

There had been successes, and there was optimism, but Mrs Mary Phillips, widow of John Phillips, knew what was not told. In December, she wrote to Grace: 'One thing I notice about you two is that you never give a hint of the disappointments and heartaches you must continually meet with.' She knew the anxieties that daily attended the work. Garfield, too, acknowledged this when he wrote to the CWA in March 1941: 'There are times of disappointment, times of sadness ...'

***

On 3 April 1941, Grace turned 30. Her mother wrote: '"Oh, those wonderful years from thirty to sixty", someone wrote. We make mistakes all our lives, I suppose, but not so many foolish ones as we make before we are thirty ... though none of us can see youth receding without regret, if we believe that the best is yet to come, we can go on in confidence.' By now, it seemed clear that the war would be limited to Europe, so it was decided that the Todds should go to New Zealand for their furlough after all.

Garfield told the CWA that a committee had been set up of six leaders 'to advise the superintendent. Their help has been considerable and now they are to take over the responsibility of looking after the work during furlough.' The committee was never disbanded, evolving over the years with increasing responsibility into the Conference Council. Garfield wrote in his draft autobiography that when the committee was composed of five Africans and two whites, it never divided along racial lines: 'Its most usual division was of everyone else against the treasurer who hated spending money'.

14

FURLOUGH, 1941–2

'... every expectation was eclipsed by the reality.'

Garfield Todd, 1974

The Todds left Dadaya in October 1941 and travelled by train from Bulawayo to Durban to await the arrival of their Blue Funnel Line ship, as no fixed schedules of sailings operated during the war. There they saw the battleship *Renown* on her way to the Far East, where she was sunk by the Japanese. The journey to Perth was uneventful. Not so for others: the *Sydney* – due to arrive in Perth on the same day – never arrived, and, unbeknown to the Todds, they crossed the Australian Bight as the Japanese launched their attack on the American Fleet at Pearl Harbor.

Grace had a week at Winton, and they saw Garfield's mother and sister before they started a very rushed tour of the churches. Garfield addressed more than 80 gatherings, as well as having long meetings with Church of Christ officials. For nine days, they were based at the beloved family homestead of Belgravia, where Garfield took Alycen through all the old paths in the fruit and nut orchards, and showed her the initials of about 30 young members of the Todd tribe carved on many trees.

It was a gruelling two-month tour with a few brief, snatched chances of rest. They were still worn out when they began the long journey back to Africa – a journey in which nothing was certain. They went by flying boat to Sydney, where every plate-glass window had been boarded up for fear of the bombs which would have fallen but for the American Navy. Eventually they sailed for Melbourne, which had become a turbulent American base for General MacArthur. 'We had cargo to discharge and some to load, but there was a lengthy dockers' strike and there were not enough waterside workers to cope with the demand.' Garfield was one of the passengers who offered to work on the waterfront. He was drafted to a night-shift gang of eight men. The experience on the waterfront opened Garfield's eyes to some less-than-honest practices of the dockers, and to the end of her life Grace treasured a little marcasite brooch that was Garfield's 'share' of a looted crate. Garfield never made so much money in his life as he did stevedoring in Melbourne – £5 an hour. (His annual stipend had just been raised from £250 to £400.) Eventually, the strike ended, and their ship was able to leave Sydney.

Garfield was very anxious to reach Dadaya before the new term opened on 22 June, so when they docked at Durban he took a seat on a Belgian Airways plane flying to the Congo via Bulawayo, Grace and Alycen following by train. The Bulawayo airport had been commandeered by the air force, and when the plane landed at a little makeshift civilian airfield there was no transport into the city. Garfield got a lift in a mail van – a free ride was important, as he had landed with only six shillings in his pocket.

During his flight to Bulawayo, Garfield drafted his June 1942 Report for New Zealand: 'Even after all the travelling of the past eight months and all the experiences we have had, I must admit that I am so excited at being so nearly home that I cannot wait for the plane to land.' He continued his report some days later after collecting Grace and Alycen from Beit Bridge: 'News of our arrival spread and letters came with each mail from the Director of Education, from Inspectors, from the new Minister of Finance [Max Danziger], from missionaries of various other churches ...'

Restrictions on petrol and tyres had come into force. But of more importance was the excellent report Jimmy Stewart gave of the stewardship of David Mkwananzi and Mkoka Ndebele at Dadaya Mission. 'It was grand to be back again', Garfield wrote, 'but after our time in New Zealand, we found Dadaya not only quiet but shockingly drab ... the rainy season had again failed so that there was famine in the land. At Dadaya, there was no water and the gardens had completely died. Grace was deeply disturbed and it took her more than six months to find her joy again.'

15

JUDITH

*'I believe that leadership is not confined to the very great ...
but to the multitude who lead in industry, in commerce, in
education, in medicine, who show initiative, who keep the faith,
who have discernment to recognise another's need and the goodwill to meet it.'*

Garfield Todd, 1957

Dadaya Boarding School opened as planned on 22 June 1942 with over 200 boarders. Fortunately, there were a few vacant places, so there was room for Alycen. Her school in Gwelo didn't expect her back until after the war, so she had lost her place. Fewer children in school meant Grace's duties were lightened, and she was happy to be able to devote more time to their new house, for which funds had been sent from New Zealand. Grace told the CWA: 'It seems selfish to be thinking of building a house in the middle of a war but my heart has been singing within me ...'

The first difficult years were behind them, and, with a new house planned – and the joyous knowledge that Grace was carrying her first child – the future once again seemed bright. In August 1942 there was a Missionary Conference, attended by the Acting Governor and various ministers, at which Garfield was elected to the new Executive Council. The aim of everyone was, quite simply, to improve Native Education. 'All of these things were good for the morale of two isolated young missionaries at Dadaya,' Garfield wrote.

Soon reports and letters from Dadaya were once more full of bricks, baptisms and 'decisions'. Garfield had been assured of money for a new church and dormitories. Happily, he set about building a large kiln for the many thousands of bricks that would be needed. A dream of Garfield's – a maternity hospital – was about to be fulfilled with the arrival of, first, £140 from the Matthews Trust of St Andrew Street Church, Dunedin, and, second, an efficient African midwife. 'Her coming', Grace told the hospital's sponsors in New Zealand, 'will ease the work which is growing all the time.' A £60 cheque towards the clinic costs came from the retiring Native Commissioner, Mr Marshall Campbell. Friends had collected this sum for him 'to use as he wished'; without opening the envelope containing their cheque, Mr Campbell handed it to Garfield.

***

When 1943 opened, Garfield was forced to turn away 500 hopeful pupils. Even so, the intake was, at 330, 30 more than he had intended to enrol. Garfield and Grace had early recognised the extraordinary abilities of Ndabaningi Sithole. He received all his primary education at Dadaya and later became a member of the staff. He gained his matriculation through private study and, at the start of 1943, took over the teaching of Standard Six classes from Grace, leaving her free to supervise and assist in all classes. Garfield wrote with pride to New Zealand about his star student: 'Ndabaningi Sithole is in the vanguard of progress in this country and now commences his study for an Arts Degree.'

***

Judith's birth was the great event of 1943 for Grace and Garfield. With Dr Ireland away on holiday, the question was: who would deliver the baby? Grace knew exactly what she wanted, asking Garfield: 'You deliver hundreds of African babies so why can't you deliver ours?' Garfield wrote: 'I set aside a room in our house and made it as aseptic as possible while Grace made every possible preparation.' By the evening of 18 March, the Todd household was prepared for the great event, and Alycen and Rua heard the baby cry at 7 p.m. (the time was recorded by Alycen). Garfield later wrote: 'I was transported beyond time as I announced to a new mother, drowsy from a little chloroform, that Judith Garfield Todd had safely arrived. I held my lovely daughter in my hands and for the moment the whole world was three people.'

On 13 July, Garfield celebrated his 35th birthday. Writing to his mother, he expresses his delight with his new daughter: 'Judith has blue eyes and is bald, or was, but I think she is going to have black hair. We hardly know she is about and every time you go to see her you are met with smiles and laughs. Altogether she is far too good.' Grace also wrote happily to the CWA at this time: 'we have moved to the new house. It is beautiful. It is even lovelier than I thought it was going to be … The living room is very big but we want it that way as we like to have room to entertain staff and preachers on occasions … Judith is the happiest baby imaginable and both she and I have never had a moment's sickness …'

Judith

***

As Garfield wrote his annual report, he allowed himself a look at the future: 'Africans are beginning to see visions and dream dreams and at Dadaya we have some who may become leaders of their people. Their life will not be easy for their people are in the chains of ignorance and heathendom and as ignorance passes they find themselves in a world where so much is against them because they are black. The colour-bar is the curse of Africa and one of our sacred duties is to endeavour to instil into the hearts of our people a greater and wider love than is shown them. If that cannot be done then Africa might become an even darker continent ... Education will bring power but that might result in tragedy and so in mission work we strive to show that the fear of the Lord is the beginning of wisdom ... mighty forces are stirring in this continent ... Dadaya may have a very small part to play but it is nevertheless an important part and that it may do it properly depends upon you and us.'

16

A Wider Horizon

'I felt stale and unfulfilled.'

Garfield Todd, 1974

One of the new village teachers in 1944 was nineteen-year-old Robert Mugabe, who had been educated at the Roman Catholic Kutama Mission. He was a brilliant student and, like Sithole, was studying in his spare time for his Junior Certificate. Village schoolteachers were expected to collect the school fees from their pupils. One month, Garfield deducted from Mugabe's monthly salary of £3 the sum of 7/6 for unpaid fees. 'I raised quite a hell of a row,' Mugabe said years later; 'I wanted to box him.' In 1981, Senator Todd reminded the Prime Minister of Zimbabwe of this occasion back in 1944: 'two future prime ministers speaking together'.

***

The first ten years at Dadaya had been full of activity, of planning and building, and setting the Mission firmly on the road to greater development. Now the machinery was in place and running smoothly. Garfield was 35 in 1943, and, after his months in New Zealand, his mind sought a more stimulating environment. He writes in his draft autobiography: 'I felt unfulfilled and Grace was aware of this. Dadaya was a daily challenge but also a daily draining of our resources. We were well physically but when you live in a community in which you are the teacher and you are working with enthusiasm for seven days a week you are in danger intellectually, culturally and spiritually.

'I began to toy with the idea of a year at university. At first this seemed impossible. We didn't have enough money and the Mission needed all of my time. However, we talked and planned how I would meet the minimum requirements for the inspection of schools and yet fit in three years of university.

Grace gave me her full support. She had always carried the Dadaya School programme and we now had a Committee to care for the churches … I applied to the University of the Witwatersrand for first year medicine … At the back of my mind was the thought that there might be a miracle which would allow me to proceed with medicine but the main thing was that I would have a period at university.'

The decision was made, and the approval of the Church in New Zealand was received. Garfield's application to 'Wits' was successful, and permission to go was granted by the Native Education Department. He was delighted and relieved that his plans could go forward, but he was also very aware of the extra burden he was laying on Grace.

***

In his draft autobiography, Garfield paints a vivid picture of Wits University in Johannesburg as he arrived: 'In 1944 men were returning from military service and some were going to university so I found some of my own age in the first-year medical class which I entered in March. The months that I was able to spend at Wits were some of the most exciting and important of my life but they did not add much to my academic knowledge … I was just too busy.

'I had little money so I was limited in my choice of accommodation. I was able to rent a very dirty little room on the first floor of an old building in Smith Street in a very disreputable area but quite close to the Public Library in the centre of Johannesburg. I set to work and scrubbed out my room, bought a strip of coconut matting, a bed and mattress, a chair and small table. There was an electric point and I bought a hot-plate. The communal bathing facilities were terrible but except for that I was comfortable …

'At university on the first morning a meeting was held in the Great Hall. There were twelve or fifteen hundred students present and I found myself sitting beside a big Afrikaner man. We were settling down when he whispered, "Look behind you". I looked and saw an African student and I turned back questioningly. "My god", he said, "I was told that they had them here but I never expected to see one." The meeting began and to my consternation I found that its object was to call a strike of students against increased tuition fees. I felt desolate … What was to happen to my plans and my few resources? I was so deeply distressed that I stood in the Great Hall and, surrounded by a sea of unknown people, I spoke as eloquently as I could against the proposed strike. Fortunately, there were enough others who thought similarly and the strike was ruled out.'

Garfield's class was allocated an African laboratory assistant, but some students lobbied for his removal. Garfield was horrified and consulted their chemistry professor, Dr Halliday. He called the students together. 'Before the 150 assembled students I stood very nervously and suggested that the matter before us was much too important to be dealt with so surreptitiously. I suggested that if anyone wished to proceed with the protest against the provision of an African assistant he should call a meeting of the whole class and have it discussed. This suggestion was met with applause, the students returned to their benches and the matter was not raised again.'

Anger had made Garfield raise his voice and take a stand against such blatant racial discrimination. Otherwise, Garfield said, 'I would have kept quiet, because I hadn't had much to do with Europeans'; but, when the class met the following week to elect their representative, it was hardly surprising that Garfield was nominated and elected.

***

There was no miracle. Garfield's year at Wits did not lead to a medical degree; instead it led to a career in politics, for, without his experience of student life, Garfield 'would not have had the courage to stand for Parliament in Rhodesia just twenty months later'.

***

On 7 June, the day after the D-Day Landings in France, Garfield led the prayers at an ecumenical service in Shabani. At Dadaya, the Matthews Memorial Clinic was opened by Mr George Stark, Director of the Native Education Department. Garfield's 1944 Annual Report gave the churches in New Zealand all the statistics about the medical work and the Matthews Memorial Clinic – two new African nurses, 5,000 out-patient treatments, 62 babies born, 232 women attended for antenatal care, 147 people had teeth extracted. Others received medical care in their homes. 'We find heart-breaking things. The continued power of witchcraft, the burden of beer-drinking, the hardened hearts of many', Garfield wrote sadly.

As Garfield told friends: 'Africa is just as great a question mark as ever, though, and I do not think we will extricate ourselves from the tragedies of the colour-bar unless America and the Dominions take an interest in us and lend us their strength. The colour-bar is as evil here as the race-conscious theory of Hitler is in Europe. Africans are not in concentration camps, they are not being flogged and murdered, but they are just trodden down. People mistake the tragedies of under-nourishment, disease and the colour-bar in general for the mark of a race which is sub-human, instead of realising things for what they are. Those of us who are nearest to the African people are aware of the great problems ahead – many of them concerned with the rising of down-trodden people, and the way will not be easy.'

17

THE POST-WAR WORLD, 1945–7

'It has been my ideal in politics all my life to seek that no one should be handicapped by the colour of his skin and that advancement should be possible on merit to any person irrespective of race.'

Garfield Todd

The Second World War had a major influence on the pace of change in Southern Rhodesia and upon the minds and aspirations of the African people. They had been exposed to European turmoil and racism. They had heard talk about universal democracy and had absorbed most of the Allied propaganda against Hitler and Mussolini, Nazi racism and injustice. Thousands of African servicemen returned home with a much wider knowledge of the world outside the Colony. For the first time in their lives, they had met white people on equal terms – and found themselves no less brave, no less competent and no less able to cope with the demands of modern life then their white counterparts.

According to the historian Lawrence Vambe, at the outbreak of war 'The Prime Minister asked for, and was given, total African loyalty and active support, not only in terms of young men who joined the Rhodesian African Rifles and fought in the Far East, but also in gifts … Yet, sadly, when this international conflict was over, Huggins extended the Land Apportionment Act in both rural and urban areas. In order to make more land available, firstly for white Rhodesians returning from war service and secondly for new immigrants, hundreds of African families were forcibly removed from areas they had always considered their ancestral homes – "nyika dzedu" – such as Nyanga, Rusape, Vumba, and Matopos. True, alternative land was allocated to these unfortunate people but hundreds of miles away, to which they and their pathetic belongings were transported in army trucks, and left to start from scratch. As far as we black journalists, who recorded some of these stories, were made aware, no other form of compensation or assistance was given – apart from six acres of land, free transport and some seed maize. This wholesale uprooting of a whole people, families and their goods and chattels to make way for "varungu" (white people), many of whom did not come from Rhodesia, was most upsetting to them, and became political dynamite in the not too distant future.'[1]

Garfield had his own experience of this forcible removal of Africans from ancestral land when his help was sought by 2,800 tribesmen of the Ghoko Block in the Midlands. 'Never had I felt so ashamed at the conditions which my own countrymen can enforce on the African people. I was unable to help.'

Dadaya was beginning to produce the promised leaders: Garfield had become Vice-President of the Southern Rhodesia Missionary Conference, and Ndabaningi Sithole was elected chairman of the Shabani and Dadaya African Teachers' Association. On 13 July, Garfield's 37th birthday, he put his plan for the future before the New Zealand Board: a Teacher Training department to be opened at the beginning of 1949, when the first pupils would be emerging from the secondary school. This would require several well-qualified New Zealand teachers.

For the next 50 years, Africa would be caught up in what Lord David Cecil, in his classic study of Lord Melbourne, called the 'irresistible pressure of the time-spirit',[2] and after 1945 more and more Africans came to see education as the key that would unlock the door of their own, and their children's, future. In 1945, Grace put this in the context of Dadaya when she wrote to the CWA: 'There is no limit at Dadaya to what men may do and become. You in New Zealand can scarcely comprehend what this can mean to people who are everywhere underprivileged, everywhere cramped and retarded in their longing for development. Dadaya promises hope and progress.'

But, writing to her mother, Grace expressed concern about their own children's future. 'Garfield loves Rhodesia altogether. But I don't. This land has serious difficulties and problems to face and some see no peaceful solution ahead. It worries me greatly to think that our children must grow up here. For us, we have made the choice with open eyes.'

***

There were 2,500 children in Dadaya's central and village schools, where all the teaching was now done by trained African teachers. The important milestone for 1945 was the opening of the secondary department, but the more significant

---

1   Lawrence Vambe/SP, 2007, TPPC.
2   Cecil, 2017, p. 160.

event for the Todds was a visit to Shabani by the Prime Minister, Sir Godfrey Huggins. There was to be a general election in 1946, and Southern Rhodesia's political parties were rousing themselves from their habitual between-elections torpor.

Huggins addressed a public meeting at the little Nilton Hotel, Shabani, the centre of the Insiza constituency, which was held at that time by Mr Leslie Smith of the opposition Labour Party. Their programme included a promise to introduce into Southern Rhodesia all the things that the Labour Party had introduced in New Zealand – a 'welfare state'. That night, Huggins, not content with denouncing the Labour Party's policy, also roundly condemned New Zealand. What he said angered Garfield, who had been there so recently and seen how Labour policies had benefited the ordinary people. Standing at the back of the hall, he included in his ten-minute question a defence of the New Zealand Labour Party. The chairman of the meeting, the local magistrate, Mr V. W. Goddard, and the speaker consulted briefly – and the chairman closed the meeting. That evening, Huggins questioned Goddard about the heckler.

***

Garfield was invited to become a parliamentary candidate by three political parties, the last being the United Party, the party of Huggins, who wrote: 'I do hope that after considering all the Parties, you will be able to join our party.' Garfield told the Secretary of the Foreign Mission Union in New Zealand that he had accepted the PM's offer. He and Grace 'considered the matter most carefully from all angles. The natives have no direct representatives in the House and there is a strong demand that I will be an unofficial advocate on their behalf. The people of this district are making what I think is an amazing gesture in backing a missionary. I do not think that any missionary has ever been in the House, except Bro. Hadfield, and when he was elected he was a land-agent in Bulawayo. As far as our work at Dadaya is concerned, I would be ... able to spend every weekend at home and the total length of the Parliament sittings is from four to five months, in two periods, one March to May/June, and the second in November for about a month. The House usually sits from Tuesday to Friday afternoon only and all country members return for the weekend ... whether I am returned or not in 1946 (April) Sithole will be taking over the secondary subjects from me.'

Garfield knew that the Education Department and the Missionary Conference were pleased that he was going to stand. 'I know that there are many people who are very much against the progress of the Native, who are not interested in much except money and who will not be ready to vote for a missionary. But

I feel that when a considerable section of the community has real yearnings for a better and more Christian policy in our country's affairs, I must do what I can ...'

No one was left in any doubt about his attitude on racial issues. On 23 March, he gave his first speech on Native affairs in Shabani. He said that there were two main problems: 'first, the fear that a rising primitive race may swamp us economically. The fear is not so much that the black man may rise but that in the process of his doing so he will undermine all the economic standards of the white man'; and second: 'it is fear that the Native may soon exercise a growing political power and that eventually his power will be greater than our own. Intelligent, thinking Africans do not wish to see the European standard of living lowered. Their wish is to see the African standards raised ...'[3]

Throughout his campaign, Garfield was realistic about his chances, and nobody was more surprised than he when he won the seat with 330 votes to 195 and 190. 'They put me in. So then I believed they were much more liberal than I had taken them for – a belief I had to change later on.'

The UP now had fourteen MPs, as against the combined sixteen of the other three parties; in spite of this, Huggins' party would remain in office for another two years.

---

3 TPPC.

18

A DOUBLE LIFE

'The key to the future was to try to persuade the whites that the blacks were the most important potential in this country.'

Garfield Todd, 1991

In Salisbury, Garfield had a room at Meikles Hotel, a modest, whitewashed, two-storey Colonial-style building of great charm, like the Legislative Assembly. In his spare time, he did Dadaya Mission office work, spreading out his papers and account books on the long table in the Caucus Room, which was only used when the members of the governing party met with the PM and cabinet. Beyond the Caucus Room was the Prime Minister's parliamentary office, again rarely used – so, when Sir Godfrey Huggins offered Garfield the use of it he gladly accepted. He admired Sir Godfrey: 'My experience of Huggins did not give me any thought that there was "dirt" in politics. He was a good man. Sometimes he tried to be clever; sometimes he dropped a "clanger"; but I always found him a very pleasant man, very English. He was a splendid man, a bit of a dictator and he didn't take blacks at all seriously.' Garfield thought Huggins listened to him on matters concerning Africans.

In Parliament, Garfield concentrated on those issues which he could speak about with authority, and lost little time bringing African concerns before the House. In his first intervention in the Budget Debate, he told the House it must 'show a more intense interest in the native people themselves, in their conditions, in their opportunities or lack of opportunities for development, in the potential which exists in the native population of this land ... The interests of all the people of this country interlock ... We cannot instil progress until we give the whole native race a basis of education.'[1] He told the House that

---

1 LAD, vol. 26, 4.6.46, cc. 151–3.

while £10 was spent on the education of every white child, 4/- was spent on a black child.

The *Sunday Mail* of 4 June observed: 'In Mr R. S. G. Todd a new champion of the natives took the floor. He is evidently an accustomed speaker and puts points with fluency. He can be expected to make interesting and well-expressed contributions to future debates.' Garfield had passed his first parliamentary test.

***

In 1946, Mkoka Ndebele became the new Chairman of the Churches' Committee, and both J. N. Hlambelo and David Mkwananzi (who had recently married Leah, a nurse from South Africa who took the medical work off Garfield) were still on the Committee. The growing strength of African leaders was also apparent in the village churches and schools.

Grace told the CWA: 'We have grown more knowledgeable, we have grown to understand the people with the passing of the years. We have lived very intimately with a people so different from our own, and yet our growing knowledge of them has taught us that "humanity" is one. Our particular needs are different, the environment of one race may be very different indeed from that of another, but the fundamental needs of our hearts are one ...'[2]

***

A terrible drought held the land in its grip as 1947 opened. Two graduate teachers, Mr and Mrs A. W. Bell of Dunedin, now arrived from New Zealand and assumed responsibility for the planned secondary school. Dadaya could at last fulfil some of the Todds' ambitions, but they realised that a little of their own joy in their close collaboration would be lost. Garfield now had a huge building programme to fulfil – new classrooms and dormitories, and a house for the new missionaries.

***

The year 1947 also saw the arrival of many white immigrants into Southern Rhodesia – British (including some of the airmen who had been trained in the country during the war), English-speaking South Africans, anxious about the rise of Afrikaner nationalism in their own country, and refugees from war-torn Europe. Such rapid immigration brought its own problems for planners and parliamentarians – particularly in the provision of housing and schools and roads, and the acceleration of development of the smaller towns. In Parliament, Garfield became known as a 'phrase-maker', producing, during one exasperating

---

2 JGT/CWA, 2/1946.

debate, his memorable utterance: 'when reasons fail, prejudice readily comes to the rescue'.³

Not many days later, on a motion before the House to increase its members, Garfield made a speech about franchise qualifications which has been quoted against him, as an indication that his 'liberalism' was superficial and cynical: 'I believe that the African people have very great power and that there is much more difference between individuals in any race than there is between one race and another. I believe that in time many Africans of high ability will come forth from the African people and some of them are with us today. I had hoped that we might raise the conditions of the franchise to a fully civilized level, and provided people could get to that level we would take no note of race or colour ... At the present time the conditions for the franchise are so low and the economic situation of the country is changing so quickly that ... in a matter of a few years the African vote could dominate the European vote.

'There is a great surge at the present moment among the African people, with their African Voters' League and so on, to make the fullest use of the available time to get as many people as possible on the Voters' Roll. If all these Africans coming on to the Voters' Roll were fully civilized human beings with a reasonable political background then I would not worry about the matter but this is not the case ... There are some Africans I know who have the right because of their own worth to be on the Voters' Roll today. Even though their background has been poor, they have made amazing progress and their speeches would do honour to this House.

'I do not know whether this House realizes just how quickly conditions are changing in the African areas. I would say that it is only within the last five years that the more tremendous changes have been noticeable in the African areas ... it will be necessary to wait for some time before we can think of opening the Voters' Roll to all the people of this country ...

'I believe that if the African people in the next 10 to 15 years were able to control the Government of this country, it would be to their own undoing. I would fight this because I have their interests at heart.'⁴ Such was the quickening pace of post-war African advancement and aspirations that, only ten years later, Garfield would be pleading with reluctant Hon. Members to widen the franchise to allow 10,000 well-qualified Africans onto the Voters' Roll.

---

3 c. 1607.
4 LAD, vol. 27, 28.5.47, cc. 1183–6.

19

Hokonui Ranch

'In 1947 we decided to buy a piece of land for our future security.'

Garfield Todd, 1998

Garfield had long been casting envious eyes over the tens of thousands of empty acres of 'European' land beyond the boundary fence of the Reserve, where the Mission was confined to its parched 100 acres. He had approached the owners, the Rhodesia Corporation, and been sympathetically received by the managing director, Mr F. L. ('Freddie') Wigley; but minimum acreages varied from 15,000 to 70,000, vastly more than the 500 Garfield was wanting to buy for the Mission. But the whole situation was about to change.

On becoming a Member of Parliament, with a £600 annual salary, Garfield gave up his missionary stipend – but, politics being a notoriously insecure career, he now had to consider how to provide for the family in the future. He decided to buy some land and to start ranching cattle. Back he went to Freddie Wigley, who offered him 24,000 acres at 7/- an acre on easy terms. A deposit of £1,000 was required. The Todds had £400 saved, but Freddie Wigley gave them a year's option and the right to use 30 acres on which they grew a crop of potatoes, hoping to make up the shortfall. That year, the rains came on an almost Biblical scale, and not one potato was harvested. That was the end of the Todds' savings.

However, a few months later Garfield saw in the *Government Gazette* that the Ministry of Agriculture was inviting tenders for derelict game fencing in the Bikita-Ndanga and Victoria-Chibi districts. He knew some of the fencing could be salvaged and that, as fencing was in short supply, it would fetch a good price. On 13 July, Garfield's 38th birthday, he and Grace drove down to inspect the fence. The map provided by the Veterinary Department was out of date, and they found that long stretches were simply not there, so Garfield set out to follow it on foot as best he could. Due to the inaccuracies of the map, he was soon lost, and night overtook him. It was very cold, so that, although the moon had gone down, he could not stop; he stumbled on, hoping to rejoin the road. Garfield tells the story in his draft autobiography: 'It was lion country and at a soft leap I sprang up a tree feeling the thorns as miserably as I had seen them. Now I had such a nausea that I knew it was a choice between falling down or climbing down. Probably it was not a lion. I stumbled on and eventually came out on a gravel road. Which way was the car? I chose wrongly but at daybreak the car came up behind me and soon Grace had a fire going … She was as cold as I was, having decided with intense sympathy but little logic that she could not wrap herself in rugs when I was lying helpless, freezing and probably half-eaten on the lonely veld.'

To test the market, and to judge how much to offer for the fence, Garfield put an advertisement in the paper for a quarter of a mile of four-wire, steel standards and droppers, fencing for sale for £20. Garfield subsequently found that these proceedings were not strictly legal …

'We were overwhelmed with enquiries. We replied to every would-be buyer that we might be able to help in a month's time and we would advise in due course. The price? We could get £80 per mile but the cost of getting the wire out, heating and straightening strainers, beating out twisted standards, would be considerable and then it would all have to be carted up to 100 miles on the average to the nearest rail. We decided to offer £1,400 for the lot.'

Even then there were bureaucratic hitches, but finally he learned that the fence was his – and would he send his cheque for £1,400? The Department of Agriculture was quite happy to accept a cheque post-dated to the end of the month. The respondents to the Todds' advertisement were offered three miles of fencing each – 'cheque with order' – and there was money in the bank to cover the cheque. 'Then came work. Heat, lions, impossible terrain which only a tractor could cover, but out came the fencing until eventually about £4,500 was sold, and with the first £1,000 down, Hokonui Ranch was on the way to being ours, with only another £12,000 to go.'[1]

The Todds now quartered their land, searching for 500 suitable acres to hand over to Dadaya Mission: land that would have a large area for growing crops, proximity to main road and rail, power, telephone and the all-important year-round water supply. They found the ideal site, but it was just outside their 25,000 acres. Back they went to Freddie Wigley and asked for more land.

---

1   GT/SP.

'Certainly', said the obliging Freddie – but only if they took another 25,000 acres! The Todds took a deep breath, became the very embarrassed owners of 49,050 acres of ranching land – and Dadaya Mission got its 560 acres.

The name Hokonui was chosen because Garfield had been brought up on one side of the Hokonui Hills in Southland, New Zealand, and Grace on the other, and the Belingwe Hills behind the ranch closely resembled the Hokonui Hills. They had forgotten that 'Hokonui' was also the name of an illicit whisky distilled in those New Zealand hills – so they earned another black mark with the church folks back home.

***

Until 1957, Garfield did little beyond participating in the Cold Storage Commission grazier scheme for ranchers and dipping the cattle weekly, but he did invest in pedigree Afrikander bulls. He employed a foreman, Richard Dewa, a former Dadaya pupil, and half-a-dozen cattlemen.

20

The Dadaya Strike

'1947 strikes the only discordant note in this now happy condition of affairs.'

Murray J. Savage, *Achievement*

When the Todds returned to the Mission after inspecting the fence, they found themselves embroiled in a crisis. The immediate cause was a mistake by one of the teachers who was responsible for the distribution of food for the Sunday evening meal, but the trouble had its roots elsewhere. The general awakening of educated Africans to a sense of their potential, allied to a dissatisfaction with their limited opportunities, led to a ferment of ideas and desires – and this was true at Dadaya, where teachers like Ndabaningi Sithole, David Mkwananzi and Mkoka Ndebele were flexing their intellectual muscles. By July 1947, there had been strikes and disturbances at two colleges in South Africa and also at schools in Southern Rhodesia. Added to this general unrest was a recent rise in Government salary rates – which had been announced several months before the increased salary grants were sent to Missions. Dadaya Mission, for one, could not afford to pay the increased rate before receiving the increased grant. Here the teachers had a genuine grievance.

When there was no meat for the Dadaya boarders' Sunday supper, there were grumbles, but the boys ate their meal. The girls, however, fed theirs to the goats. At Assembly on the Monday morning, Garfield apologised for the mistake and as usual dismissed the school to the drill ground. The girls refused to go. This sort of disobedience was so serious that Garfield told them they would be expelled. Those who didn't want to be expelled would be punished and should go to their dormitories. They all went to their dormitories and in due course were beaten by Garfield: two cuts on the hand for girls who had only been in school for six months; four cuts on the seat for those who had been there eighteen months; and six for the girls who had been at Dadaya for two years or more.

'Corporal punishment is not often used at Dadaya,' Garfield wrote. 'It is given only in cases where there is deliberate disobedience to command or regulation, but in a case of mass disobedience we would use it. There was no severe or brutal punishment. No girl demurred or protested, and none needed to have taken the punishment if she had chosen otherwise. No girl cried out, though a number shed tears. I then told all girls to go to their dormitories with their prefects, and I went to every room and spoke for three or four minutes with each group. The girls fully realised that they had committed the most serious offence which they, as a group, could commit and they knew that they had deserved the punishment they had received.' One of the girls who had been beaten was Ndabaningi Sithole's sister.

All but about 100 boys now joined the strike. Garfield found that Sithole and Mkwananzi had encouraged the boys to go on strike to show solidarity with the girls, who in their turn had been encouraged by Mrs Canaan Sithole, Ndabaningi's wife. Eventually, striking boys and girls went to the police in Shabani with a list of grievances written by one of the teachers. They arrived at the police camp at about 7 p.m. after walking eleven or twelve miles through the bush, and the girls laid charges of assault against Garfield.

The girls were examined by the Government Medical Officer, Dr Millerick. As a result, Garfield was charged with 58 counts of assault. 'I knew that while I had given stern punishment for a most serious offence I had given no brutal punishment.' At Garfield's request, Dr Ireland also examined the girls and later gave evidence that all the injuries were of a 'very light nature'.

The case against Garfield was heard in the Magistrate's Court at Shabani on 26 and 27 August. The magistrate was Mr Farewell Roberts, from Bulawayo (as the local magistrate was a friend of the Todds). During the hearing, Garfield told the court that government methods of dealing with strikes were corporal punishment or expulsion, and black-listing of teachers by the department. He did not approve of expulsion as a means of settling strikes. 'If you take a child and correct him and keep him in your school he is still within the influence of the school. Expulsion is a very easy way for a principal. He merely tells the child to get out and his responsibility ends. But if you have any affection for the child it is not an easy way. It is well worth the difficulty of holding on to the child if in the end you can produce a good citizen. No parent has come to me objecting to the treatment but some have come pleading that their

The Dadaya Strike

children should be readmitted. I had no thought of using anything more than moderation. I carefully thought the matter out and graded punishments.'

The *Rhodesia Herald* reported Mr J. N. Hlambelo's evidence: 'he had a daughter who was punished by Todd and he had no objection to this. He had not thought it wrong that Todd had beaten his daughter on the buttocks with a sjambok. Another native said he had two daughters at the mission. He had no objection to Mr Todd's action. Advocate J. M. Greenfield … said there were a number of natives who were there who could give similar evidence. He did not propose to call them and closed his case.'[1]

Inspector Jarville said that Garfield had been very straightforward and honest in evidence. Advocate Greenfield, who represented Garfield, told the Court that the punishment of females was perfectly legal. He added: 'there has been no suggestion of indecency in court … The prosecution had not suggested the punishment was not called for. Only a prima facie case had been established and that was not sufficient for prosecution.'[2]

When the prosecution case ended, and Garfield's advocate rose to make his concluding speech, the magistrate said: 'We don't need you, Mr Greenfield … I have made up my mind and your client is innocent. Judgement was made totally on the evidence.[3] The finding of this Court is that the punishment was not immoderate and that the caning was not unduly severe. I feel that this Court should not lightly interfere in this instance. A verdict of Not Guilty will be entered on each of the counts, and the accused will be discharged.'[4]

Corroboration of Sithole's part comes from one of his colleagues, Mr A. L. Ndhlovu: 'Mr N. Sithole came to my [classroom] on the morning of 14 July. I was teaching. He spoke loudly from the door so that all the pupils could hear, and said: "See how your sisters are being thrashed" … Later at the Teachers' House Sithole was strongly advising boys to strike, advising them to go to the Police, telling them what complaints they should make, telling us teachers to use this opportunity to report Mr Todd because of "back pay" … The rest of us teachers refused to go, and they were very angry with us and called us a lot of women …'[5]

The late Bethuel Hlambelo, son of the Rev. Ndabambi Hlambelo, commented in 1995: 'Canaan incited the girls, then Ndabaningi the boys'.[6]

---

1 *Rhodesia Herald*, 27.8.47.
2 *Rhodesia Herald*, 28.8.47.
3 JGT/SP, TPPC.
4 Magistrate's Judgement, MS.390/1/2, NAZ.
5 S.482/169/6/481, NAZ.
6 Bethuel Hlambelo/SP, 1995.

Garfield dismissed Sithole and his wife, Mkwananzi, David Ndoda and J. Nyemba and was 'deeply shocked' when he heard the Department had not only declined to suspend them but had also re-employed Sithole and Ndoda at other missions.[7]

The African Teachers' Association requested a Government committee of inquiry into the Dadaya disturbances, but the President of the Southern Rhodesia African National Congress, the Reverend Thompson Samkange, took the line that it would be a mistake to criticise Todd too heavily when African teachers themselves beat both boy and girl students so frequently. Certainly Ndabaningi did; he 'warmly supported corporal punishment', according to an autobiographical note.[8]

The American historian Michael West, writing in 1992, accused Garfield of carrying out 'what was clearly a personal vendetta against the fired teachers'.[9] Garfield's anger at the teachers' involvement and at the Department's reluctance to suspend them can be better understood after reading his 1947 Annual Report to New Zealand, where he reveals that over the years he and Grace had personally helped the Sitholes and Ndoda with their college fees.

Two or three years after the strike, Garfield invited Sithole to return to Dadaya, but he declined. In the mid-1950s, Sithole went to the USA on a scholarship, and Garfield helped Canaan with her airfare to visit him. Garfield was no longer Prime Minister when Sithole asked him to write the foreword to his book, *African Nationalism*. In that book, Sithole does not even mention the strike at Dadaya. West writes: 'The reason for this silence, which amounts to a cover-up, is no mystery.'[10] By then, Garfield 'had become something of a martyr in elite African circles'.[11]

David Mkwananzi returned to Dadaya. Warm relations continued until David's death on 29 August 1995, when Garfield preached at his funeral at Dadaya. David was buried in the cemetery there. When, a few years earlier, I had asked him about the Dadaya Strike, he replied: 'Aah, that is the part of Dadaya I don't like to think about.'

Garfield did not lose touch with David Ndoda either. He became a Salvationist and in the 1990s was running a project for street children, 'Emthunzeni Wethemba' in Bulawayo, to which Garfield contributed (and the collection at

---

7   GT/Director of Native Education, 3.10.47, S.482/189/6/481, NAZ.
8   n.d., MS.390/1/9, Todd Papers, NAZ.
9   West, 1992, p. 304.
10 Ibid., p. 307.
11 Ibid.

the Todds' London Thanksgiving Service was sent to the Home).

West maintains that the Dadaya Strike (among others) 'was an important background episode in the rise of African nationalism in Southern Rhodesia'.[12] Garfield disagreed: 'the strikes had their message, but it was a message of growing intolerance of authority, white authority, I suppose, but African nationalism surely was the result of education, Christian education. Food and personal relationships were the basis of strikes. The development of African nationalism was the result of enlightenment and the hunger of the people for greater knowledge and civilisation ... its beginnings were not strikes but the work of the missionaries of the sixteen Missionary societies.'

What the strike made very clear was Garfield's attitude towards indiscipline and his ideas about punishment, justice and forgiveness. Fifty years after the Dadaya strike, Grace observed: 'it is difficult to look back from the stage at which we are at present, with schools as they are at present, and compare it with the fairly primitive conditions we were dealing with at that time. Garfield had a very special place in the community. He came at a time when it was unthinkable that a man should be present at the delivery of a baby and yet the very first thing that happened, the very first call that was made on him, was to help at the delivery of a child. That was a great break-through. He really was looked upon as a parent ... Not one of those girls chose to leave rather than be caned – and not one parent came in to protest about the treatment of their children.'

---

12   Ibid., p. 297.

21

A Bigger Picture, 1948–51

'Although you are white in skin your heart is African with ours because you know so well our African feelings'

Farewell letter to Garfield Todd from 'the African people of Dadaya', 1949

Three events of great political significance for Southern Africa occurred in 1948: in Southern Rhodesia a general strike, followed by a general election; and in South Africa, a general election brought the National Party to power, where it stayed for the next 40 years. Garfield told New Zealand the strike had given the European population 'rather a severe shock'.

The Rhodesian writer, Lawrence Vambe, wrote: 'Huggins took up a position which forced even us, who generally regarded him as our arch enemy, to accord him a good measure of respect. Far from being the work of communists, he maintained, the strike was an economic protest. The Africans also wanted a place in the sun ... we are witnessing in this country the emergence of the proletariat ... This happened in Europe ... The only difference is that in Rhodesia the proletariat happens to be black. This was a courageous thing to say ...'[1]

Huggins had survived a vote of no confidence in 1947, and somehow business in the House proceeded normally with the Budget Session in the middle of 1948, during which Garfield spoke in the debate on the Native Department vote, and coined a phrase which was soon in general currency among the Department's critics: 'We have almost a government within a government'.[2] On Native Education, he told the House: 'We have to realise that Native Education is only about to begin in this country. Only 1.3 per cent of the scholars have

---
1 Vambe, 1976, p. 246.
2 LAD, vol. 28, 31.5.48, c. 579.

reached Standard Six. There is a widespread call for efficiency. If we are going to make the native efficient we cannot start until he has a basis of education.'[3]

When a second vote of no confidence in the Government was called, Huggins lost it, and the Governor, albeit reluctantly, granted a dissolution of Parliament. During its short life, however, Garfield had been able to obtain an extension of the provisions of the Ministers' Salaries and Pensions Bill to enable a pension to be granted to Huggins' widow in due time. As Garfield said: 'in those days, you didn't make money out of your politics'.

There had been a redefinition of constituency boundaries since 1946, and the former Insiza constituency, slightly readjusted, had been renamed Shabani. Garfield had learned a great deal during his two years in Parliament and had also got to know many of his constituents. 'On the other hand, my views about Africans were a bit more generally known, but then Africans were not a threat.'[4] He defeated the right-wing Liberal Party candidate by 688 votes to 458. Two new members entered the Legislative Assembly in 1948: advocate Julian Greenfield in Bulawayo, and farmer Ian D. Smith in Selukwe.

During the campaign, Garfield attended and addressed a very significant meeting of African organisations in Gwelo, reporting to Huggins: 'Twenty or thirty present. I endeavoured to put that part of our policy which deals with franchise before the gathering but I stressed the long-term policy and told them of possible lines of action for a short-term policy. They stressed that if a twenty-year period of closed rolls were enforced, it would be twenty years of agitation against the European in this country. Criticism of the Native Department and the feeling that their main task was to keep the African "in his place"; and that against any of the injustices under this heading they had no redress. They felt that the "educated" Africans had no voice and that the Department's policy was to ignore the educated African and make a show of democracy and fair play by stepping up the Native Councils which were the voice only of the Native Commissioners concerned. They wanted some channel direct to the Minister for they felt that much information which would be of value to yourself, could not get to you. It has always seemed to me that the danger point is not the mass of Africans as such but the mass of Africans as influenced by the better off. It now is quite impossible to satisfy them – they told me very frankly yesterday that they were far from satisfied with much of what I had to say, but nevertheless they appeared to appreciate my patience and gave me a very much better hearing than I had expected from them.'[5]

***

---

3   Ibid. c. 536.
4   Oral.TO.1, NAZ.
5   GT/PM, 19.2.48, MS.1082/2/3, Todd Papers, NAZ.

In the new Parliament, Garfield again turned his attention to Native education: 'We have to raise the standard of living of the African population. Where education has been given to certain African people their standard of living has been raised quite considerably. When I speak of education I speak of it in the widest sense and not merely of an academic education. Environment has a great part to play in education. We are not going far enough in our education, we are not considering all the factors which enter into the civilisation of the native people ... We have got to go much deeper than we have ever gone before if we are to solve this problem of Native labour. What is the position of the Native people and how do they live? The great bulk live in the reserves ... In the reserves there is no ownership of land. There is uncertain individual tenure and a Native may be moved from one place to another ...

'In a colony where circumstances are changing and where there is a demand for labour, and where there is now opportunity for progress, the reserves constitute a serious handicap to the Native people. We have not been interested enough in a long-term policy to find out what are the conditions under which the native lives and in which his family is raised. These vital matters are a closed book to us. I think the time has come for a complete investigation of Native life and conditions ... Until we are willing to face facts, to concern ourselves with the lives of the Native people, we will have no satisfactory answer to the problem facing our land.'[6]

Garfield concluded his speech: 'Unless we get down to some very serious thinking and work out a new approach we will only go from bad to worse'.[7] Out of this debate emerged the appointment in 1951 of the important Kerr Commission 'to report upon the system of education for Africans in the Colony of Southern Rhodesia in relation to (a) the present and probable future needs of the African and (b) the social and economic development of the Colony'.

***

Grace had wanted to have her second baby at home, but they decided that this time she should go to Shabani Hospital. In the event, Grace left the journey too late on the night of 29 March 1948, and Cynthia Gay Garfield Todd was born at 1 a.m. on the 30th, 'at the side of the road somewhere between Dadaya Mission and Shabani', according to her birth certificate (the Registrar's clerk having written, word for word, what Garfield told him over the telephone). Not having provided for such a contingency, Garfield wrapped the baby in his sports jacket. Now that the baby had safely arrived, Grace thought they would

---

6 LAD, vol. 29, 24.11.48, cc. 255–8.
7 Ibid., c. 450.

be returning to the Mission, but Garfield insisted on continuing their journey to Shabani. However, as the urgency had gone from the situation, he was reluctant to arrive at the hospital at 2 a.m., so they waited in the car for four hours more.

***

Enrolment at Dadaya at the beginning of 1948 was 400. The Mission now had the old 100-acre site in the Lundi Reserve and the new 560-acre site on Hokonui Ranch. Many new buildings would be required at New Dadaya – classroom blocks, domestic science blocks, science laboratories, girls' and boys' dormitories, workshops for the boys' industrial work, dining room and kitchen, as well as teachers' houses.

In 1948 at Dadaya, the gradual move of the Mission to the new site continued, but the Todds' greatest excitement was the prospect of furlough towards the end of 1949. Grace told the CWA: '1934 does indeed seem a long way back and our 1941/2 visit has never felt real for that was a time of great anxiety for all'.[8]

Grace, Alycen, Judith, Cynthia and Rua arrived in Wellington just as the Knapp family – Ray and Isobel and their two small children, Brian and Beverley – left for Dadaya, where Garfield was eager to receive them. For the next couple of years, Old Dadaya would be their home, with Ray as head of the Secondary Department and Isobel as acting headmistress of the Central Primary School. The Todd family was reunited in New Zealand on 20 February, and went with Mrs Wilson to Stewart Island for a two-week holiday. Then Garfield and Grace began their work among the churches, while Rua and the children stayed with Mrs Wilson and Grace's eldest sister Win in Winton. (But Rua's mixed-race ancestry inspired another rumour among the scandalmongers of the Churches of Christ in New Zealand.) Roofing new buildings at Dadaya had always been a problem, so Garfield was particularly pleased to find, and despatch to Dadaya, a tile-making machine capable of producing 300 tiles a day, sufficient to cover 200 square feet of roofing space.

On returning to Dadaya in 1950, the Todds 'were given a wonderful welcome, "Amhlope, Mfundisi" from J. M. Sibanda – "our eyes are white" i.e. "we are well, we are no longer weeping", but the finest part of it … was to see the work going on so steadily and so well.'[9]

Dadaya Mission was split between the two sites until 1952, which made administration difficult. The arrival in January 1951 of Albert and Queenie Ladbrook eased the staffing position; and, when the new school year opened, old Dadaya was home to the Christian Leadership and Teacher Training

---

8   JGT/CWA, 1/1949.
9   JGT/CWA, 8/1950.

Department, with twelve students; the Secondary School (which would later become Dadaya High School) with 101 students; and the 'practising school' from Sub-A to Standard Six, with 247 pupils. When the Bells left shortly afterwards, Garfield again became superintendent of the 29 village schools – 100 African teachers, 3,000 pupils.

At the New Dadaya site, there was the Central Primary School of 314 pupils, with Grace as headmistress. It was here, on a hill overlooking the Ngezi River, that several staff houses were built, including the Todds'. And it was here that the Mission lands were established to provide food for the boarders.

22

POLITICS, 1949-53

'The central purpose of British Colonial policy is simple. It is to guide the colonial territories to responsible self-government within the Commonwealth, in conditions that ensure to the people both a fair standard of living and freedom from aggression from any quarter'

Arthur Creech-Jones, quoted by Sir Oliver Lyttelton, 1953

In the second half of the 1940s, a new political development was being debated between the British Government and the two Rhodesias which would greatly affect Garfield's life and career. Sir Godfrey Huggins and Mr Roy Welensky, leader of the Unofficial Members (i.e. not Colonial Office officials) of the Legislative Council, had long wished to bring the countries closer together, but Her Majesty's Government had made it clear that it would only consider such an association if the small colony of Nyasaland were included.

Early in 1949, representatives of the three African countries met at the Victoria Falls to discuss their future. The Chairman of the Conference, Sir Miles Thomas, former Chairman of the British Overseas Airways Corporation, told delegates that the success of the conference depended on its reception in Britain, and 'the measure of its success will depend on how it appeals to the Natives'.[1]

'The natives' had little opportunity to judge anything that took place at Victoria Falls that year, as the minutes were not published, but such press reports that were released aroused the deep suspicions of the politically aware Africans. The (Labour) Colonial Secretary, Mr Arthur Creech Jones, was alarmed at the spread of the 'federal cause' and visited all three territories, making himself singularly unpopular with whites everywhere he went.

In 1951, a conference of officials from all four countries concluded that on

---
1   Verbatim Report, S.26, NAZ.

every ground – 'strategic, administrative, moral and social' – some closer form of co-operation between the territories was needed. The three territories were at different stages of development: Southern Rhodesia was a 'self-governing Colony' (and came under the British Commonwealth Relations Office); the other two were British Protectorates, administered by the British Colonial Office. More importantly, the Africans of Northern Rhodesia and Nyasaland were firmly opposed to any kind of union with Southern Rhodesia. To them, it was better to stay under Colonial Office control in London than to be under the domination of the whites of Southern Rhodesia. The white farmers and miners, artisans and clerks of Northern Rhodesia, on the other hand, needed Southern Rhodesia as an ally in their fight against what they saw as the pro-black policies of the Colonial Office.

African politicians were also aware of events beyond their borders: that same year, the Governor of the Gold Coast (Ghana) dramatically released from prison the leader of the nationalists, Kwame Nkrumah, and initiated a process which led eventually to self-government for the Colony. Officials in London now had two principal concerns for Central Africa: the Africans could easily fall under the Marxist rhetoric emanating from Accra, as well as from Cairo; and the whites could be seduced by the policy of apartheid in South Africa following the National Party's victory there in 1948. A Central African federation could act as a multiracial 'buffer zone' between the two nationalisms.

***

In 1950, Hugh Beadle, Minister of Internal Affairs and Justice, had resigned from the Southern Rhodesian cabinet to become a judge. He was succeeded as minister by Julian Greenfield, who plays an important (if sometimes equivocal) part in Garfield's story. In the consequent by-election in Bulawayo North, the UP's candidate, Cyril Hatty, an industrial accountant who had emigrated from England in 1947, was elected. Of the political parties, Hatty found 'the Liberal Party were not liberal; the Labour Party didn't represent most of the workers; and the United Party were anything but united'.

During the main Parliamentary session in 1951, there were long debates on electoral law and land. Garfield saw clearly that the African masses were leaderless: it was the job of government to cultivate and co-operate with the educated or 'civilised' elite from the black community. 'I disagreed with the [United Party] dictum that the government of the people should be by the white people for the people. I believed that the government of the people should be by the civilised people for the people. I believe that it is fundamentally unsound to demand as a qualification for the vote a state which cannot be attained but must be born into. To say that most black people are uncivilised and, therefore, unworthy of the vote is, I am afraid, quite correct. But it is not true to say that all are unworthy of the vote. However, if we agree that there are some who are worthy of the vote, then the greatest measure of frustration to which we can subject them is to deny them, because of their colour, the right to vote and to have a say in the government of this country.

'The great mass of the African people are not dangerous at the present time because they are not led. But they could only be dangerous if they had really capable leaders and the capable leaders are the educated people. The educated people can be invited to share with us in the Government of this country, or they can be repressed and pushed back in among the masses. There they will find plenty to do and they will become capable – most capable, some of them – leaders of the African masses against the European order of the day, and that is a very great danger of which we should take cognisance.'[2]

The common voters' roll was retained and the monetary qualification raised from £10 per month to £20, combined with simple literacy. Garfield later explained: 'I was not very keen when Greenfield put up the qualifications but it was not too bad still. Africans of quality and calibre could get it and I never cared at any time for a universal franchise, although I would hope it would come eventually when people had reached the quite reasonable qualifications.'[3]

In April 1951, the Native Land Bill was presented to Parliament. Later to be known as the Native Land Husbandry Bill, this was described by Garfield as 'one of the most important measures that has come before the House for many years'.[4] This measure, enacted later in the year (though its implementation would not seriously begin until 1955), became one of the most contentious pieces of legislation in Southern Rhodesia's history. The 'experts', almost to a man, were enthusiastic, both as to the principle of individual ownership of land and of good farming practice; not one black nationalist had a good word to say for it, George Nyandoro going so far as to assert that it was the best recruiting agent the African National Congress (ANC) ever had. It was not only nationalists who objected strongly to the proposed legislation: as some of the Bill's provisions dealt with the allocation of land, this was seen by the chiefs as an infringement of their own long-held rights – and as giving too much power to Native Commissioners.

The Bill had its origins in 1944 when the Native Trade and Production Commission recommended the enforcement of conservation measures. It also recommended that only registered title-holders should hold land. The Chief

---

2   LAD, vol. 31, 8.2.51, cc. 3280–5.
3   Oral TO.1, NAZ.
4   LAD, vol. 32, 11.4.51, c. 51.

Native Commissioner's Report for 1947 contained this passage: 'The aim will be the elimination over a period of years of the inefficient native farmer, and those who are left will adopt farming as a full-time job with prospects of an economic living.'[5]

The Bill was also, according to Professor Richard Gray, 'an extraordinary effort to carry an entire African population through an agricultural revolution in the space of a very few years. It was unique in Africa ... The Bill, however, deprived the African of his rights to the land as enshrined in the Constitution and as envisaged by the Land Apportionment Act ... much of the status and influence of the chiefs in whom the land was previously vested would be lost.'[6]

When the Bill came before Parliament in April 1951, Garfield uttered several warnings:[7] 'The native people are frightened by this Bill and I believe they have good reason for their fear ... I think the cost of the bill to us in Southern Rhodesia in personal relations and, more than that, in economic welfare will be greater than we can bear ... All the younger applicants who want a farm are coming to the opinion ... that the way they want to farm is on their own land ... If we want co-operation from the Africans and assistance in building up this country we will have to see that they get security of tenure ... We want the conservation of our reserves and native areas but we do not want it from an unwilling and increasingly resentful native population ... We do not want native peasants. We want the bulk of them working in the mines and farms and in the European areas and we could absorb them and their families ... We should have focussed more of our attention on the urban areas ... This Bill should have come later, after we had been able to remove from the reserve 100,000 families ...'[8]

The Government set up a Select Committee (of which Garfield was a member) to investigate the question further. It took a great deal of evidence from African organisations and individuals, Native Commissioners and churchmen. 'I think it was the first time in our history that we were able to really consult with the African people as to what they wanted', he told a Forum on 'Federation, Colonialism and Race in Central Africa' at Georgetown University, Washington in 1955.[9]

The Committee also received 'radical criticisms'. To a plea from Guy Clutton-Brock, of St Faith's Anglican Mission, for more land, Garfield had replied

---

5   Vol. CNC Ann. Rep. SRG 3 over INT 4, NAZ.
6   Gray, 1960, pp. 289–90.
7   LAD, vol. 32, 11.4.51, cc. 424–9.
8   LAD, vol. 32, 23.4.51, cc. 375–6.
9   14.8.55, file MS.390/1/9, Todd Papers, NAZ.

tellingly: 'If we opened up the whole country, we would put off this day for twenty years perhaps.'[10]

Hardwicke Holderness, a Salisbury lawyer and moving spirit of the influential National Affairs Association there, had been deeply involved in the preparation of evidence for the Select Committee, on behalf of a number of concerned Africans. His understanding of, and sympathy with, the African people – especially of the urban Africans – was unrivalled among whites, but he, too, had come to believe 'that there should be a change in the system of tenure at this stage to prevent a progressive fragmentation of land holdings, provided that other reforms went ahead, for example, provision of security of land tenure for Africans in the towns'.[11]

The Bill became law – but, as Professor Gray points out, 'The three major problems, of enlisting the co-operation of Native Councils and of providing wider rural opportunities and adequate urban security, which had to be solved if there was to be any decisive advance towards a permanent racial co-operation, were ignored.'[12] Garfield saw all of the Act's failings but maintained that on balance it had been sensible and necessary.

Garfield was above all concerned with good race relations and the education of the Africans which would foster these. He told Parliament in the Budget debate in May 1952 that over 4,000 new teachers had been trained but, denied proper wages by government, two-thirds had dropped out.[13] In 1952, only 7,000 children out of 250,000 were in Government schools, he said – the rest were in Mission-aided schools, where they paid for all their equipment and books as well as school fees. While the Government gave about £600,000 to Mission education, the people themselves spent at least £175,000: 'there are many people today who are crying out for better-educated Natives ... as tractor drivers, machinery operators, medical orderlies, teachers. This country is dependent on its Native labour ... our future depends on the raising of these people ... [but] we are paying people who are educating the great masses of the people of this country £2 or £3.'[14]

***

When the Kerr Commission reported, its main recommendations – 'with equal urgency' – were: teachers' salary increases and parity between Government and Mission teaching services; increased teacher-training facilities; improved

---

10 Gray, 1960, pp. 299–300.
11 Holderness, 1985, pp. 91–92.
12 Gray, 1960, pp. 300–1.
13 LAD, vol. 33, 23.5.52, cc. 1292–3.
14 LAD, vol. 33, 26.5.52, cc. 1352, 1358–9.

facilities for industrial education; increase in the inspectorate and maintenance of a head-office staff adequate for the expanding administrative and supervisory duties, and provision of more schools in the urban areas. The Commission's Report reinforced many of Garfield's ideas on the development of the country, and its recommendations formed the basis of his own later legislation on urban housing, industrial training, labour and the industrial colour-bar as well as education.

For Garfield, the single most important paragraph of the Kerr Report was: 'the Commission has been left without the shadow of a doubt that the stability of character, the education, the professional training and the conditions of service (including emoluments, housing and pensions) of the teacher whether academic, agricultural, industrial or commercial, lie at the root of most of the problems which beset African education in Southern Rhodesia'.[15]

'An education programme can be neither framed nor carried out in a vacuum ... Two sets of circumstances have ... seriously disrupted, and ... will continue to disrupt, the character training of Africans. They are the want of adequate provision for African urban areas attached to European towns, and the occupational colour-bar ... The town-dwelling African has no need that is graver and more urgent than real home and family life ... Good character and the required skill are the only fair tests that should be applied for admission to any skilled trade or profession ... But, however slowly African education may have to go, we must see that it goes in the right direction. It must lead ... to happy home life and prosperity.'[16]

***

Garfield, as a humble backbencher, was not involved in any formal discussions of federation, nor privy to any of the planning or of the decisions made, but took part in the pro-federation campaign and in debates in the SR Parliament in November 1951 and in February 1952. For him, the South African dimension was not a primary consideration. It was in the closer alliance with the northern territories that he saw the benefit for Southern Rhodesia. He would have preferred a unitary government – simpler, more economical and more efficient – but, failing that, federation was acceptable. There was no significant African opposition in Southern Rhodesia, and he was quite ignorant of the tremendous resentment against federation in the northern territories. (That would apply to most of the whites in Southern Rhodesia.) For him, the all-important thing was the 'arithmetic': 'If the Europeans were prepared to ... change their ratio from

---

15 LAD, vol. 33, 9.7.52, c. 3632.
16 Ibid., cc. 2621–3.

1:16 in Southern Rhodesia to about 1:60 they were going to face realities ... That is how guileless I was.'[17]

In June 1952, the Southern Rhodesia Legislative Assembly debated the White Paper setting out plans for a federation. Garfield asked: 'Have we in ourselves what it takes to make this Federation a success? If we federate these three countries, we are committing Central Africa to a liberal policy. We are committing it to a policy of racial co-operation which I believe we are not so fully committed to under our present State Government.'[18]

The final conference on federation was held in London in April 1953. Two leading Southern Rhodesian Africans, Jasper Z. Savanhu and Joshua Nkomo, were sufficiently in favour of the plan to attend as members of Huggins' delegation.

The Federal Referendum was held on 10 April 1953. In Southern Rhodesia, the almost exclusively European electorate voted in favour by 25,570 to 14,729, with similar proportions in the northern territories.

The Order in Council setting up the Federation of Rhodesia and Nyasaland became effective on 3 September 1953. The following day, Lord Llewellin arrived from Britain and was sworn in as Governor-General, the British monarch's representative in the Federation. Her representative in Southern Rhodesia, a self-governing Colony, was the Governor, who acted on the advice of his ministers. Northern Rhodesia and Nyasaland, as Colonies and Protectorates, were administered by governors who were directly responsible to the Secretary of State for the Colonies in Britain.

The Africans in Northern Rhodesia and Nyasaland remained deeply hostile to Federation, but the Conservative Government in Britain either was ignorant of African feeling or chose to ignore it.

Almost as an afterthought, a Preamble was written into the Federal Constitution: 'And whereas the association of the Colony and territories aforesaid in a Federation under Her Majesty's sovereignty, enjoying a responsible government in accordance with this Constitution, would conduce to the security, advancement and welfare of all inhabitants, and in particular would foster partnership and co-operation between their inhabitants ...'.[19] Sir Robert Tredgold, one-time Federal Chief Justice, wrote that: 'The key word ... was partnership. It was to become a word of ill-omen. In this context it was ambiguous, yet most impartial people would have accepted that it implied a

---

17 Oral TO.1, NAZ.
18 LAD, vol. 33, 23.6.52, cc. 2675–8.
19 UK Command Paper no. 8753.

substantial participation in the management of the firm by each partner.'[20]

By 1958, 'partnership' had come to mean (in the words of Sir John Moffat of Northern Rhodesia in another context) 'all things to all men by meaning nothing to anybody'. And an editorial in the *Central African Examiner* stated bluntly: 'Partnership – a single-word indictment of European hypocrisy.'[21]

***

On 7 September 1953, the interim Federal cabinet was also sworn in: Sir Godfrey Huggins (Prime Minister), the recently knighted Sir Roy Welensky of Northern Rhodesia and Sir Malcolm Barrow of Nyasaland.

The end of 1951 had been enlivened for Garfield by an alarming incident. The main Shabani–Bulawayo road crossed the Ngezi River by a low-level bridge near Dadaya Mission. Particularly heavy early rains had brought the Ngezi down in spate, and though the bridge railings were still visible, the bridge itself was under water and not safe to cross. The driver of a large lorry had taken a chance and was stuck in the middle, the water rising all the time. Lines of cars had built up on the very steep approach roads on both sides of the river. There was little time to be lost in drawing the lorry off the bridge. Garfield sent for his massive, antiquated tractor, but when it came he was horrified to see not the usual trained and competent driver, but a younger man totally unused to handling it. The young driver was also horrified at what he saw and froze to the wheel as the vehicle started downhill, quickly gathering speed. Garfield realised the tractor was out of control and raced across the side of the hill towards it. He threw the driver off, grabbed the steering wheel and was able to bring the tractor to a halt just short of the cars.

Archdeacon Aldington-Hunt, who was sitting in one of the cars, described the incident to the *Rhodesia Herald* when Garfield became Prime Minister in 1953, and added: 'I thought if a man can tackle a job like that he has great presence of mind, great agility and great courage. I was delighted when I heard he had become our Prime Minister.'[22]

---

20 Tredgold, 1968, p. 202.
21 *Central African Examiner*, vol. 1, no. 17, 18.1.58.
22 *Rhodesia Herald*, 9.11.53.

23

Last Days at Dadaya Mission

'I buried Ireland and McAdam: a nice thing to do for one's friends.'

Garfield Todd, 1952

In 1952, Grace began a trial two-year Domestic Science training course for teachers in village schools. She was in her element and found the work exciting and rewarding. Nine new missionaries arrived from New Zealand – some indication of the hectic building programme Garfield had been undertaking, in addition to the building of a small weir on the Ngezi River to enable the water to be pumped up to the Mission. The coming of the new missionaries – Mr and Mrs Paul Sharfe; Mr and Mrs Hugh Carden; Mr and Mrs Peter Nathan; and three young women teachers, Shirley Beadle, Jean Scott and Jean Kermode – meant a radical reorganisation of the work. Peter Nathan would become a good friend to Garfield and to Dadaya, as well as having a distinguished career in Native Education in Southern Rhodesia. Many years later, he wrote of Garfield: 'My first impression was that he was a human dynamo cloaked in an aura of charm and grace (no pun intended). That was also my second impression and every other impression as well. We at the Mission ... did our best to match his pace but not always successfully.'[1] Garfield impressed Peter also 'with the facility he had for grasping issues and with the vision he had in seeing not only outcomes, but also possibilities'.[2] Shirley Beadle also became a close family friend and the very capable manager of Hokonui Ranch when Garfield became Prime Minister and went to live in Salisbury.

The weir on the Ngezi had made life much easier at the new site, where there was also electricity and waterborne sewerage; and soon would come the

---

1   80th-birthday-book, 1988.
2   Peter Nathan/SP, 1993, TPPC.

telephone. In the middle of all the activity of the new Mission, and of the arrival of the new missionaries, Grace fell ill and underwent an operation. For some weeks she was confined to bed, in considerable pain, but in the unrivalled care of Dr Ireland. On one visit, he went across to her bed and took her hand, saying: 'anyway, you know where to come and you mustn't delay'. Three days later, Dr Ireland had a stroke and died. Thousands of people came from all over the country, and from South Africa, to attend his funeral – the largest ever seen in Shabani. Garfield conducted the service at the interment. 'Such a man', he wrote in his draft autobiography, 'leaves behind him the only worthwhile memorial that there is – people who remember him with deep affection and gratitude. Life can be enriched by the people we live with more than by the things we achieve, and no book concerned with my family would be in balance if it did not pay tribute to the man upon whom our very lives have depended.'

***

Garfield's deepening involvement in the political life of the country and the federation campaign, and the increasing number of European staff members at Dadaya, led to the setting up of a Field Council to direct the work. Ray Knapp was appointed Principal in Garfield's place. Jimmy Stewart, now Divisional Inspector, wrote to Garfield: 'It is indeed a shock to learn that you are resigning from the Principalship of Dadaya … Much has happened since February 1938 when I first visited Dadaya. The development in both the village and Central schools has been extraordinary. A great deal of initiative, hard work and courage was required to plan the development of your educational work which is now so firmly established as to be able to carry on with the force of its own momentum. It is a lively and lasting memorial to Mrs Todd and yourself.'[3]

***

In 1953, Dadaya Mission went through the worst upheaval of Garfield's time as superintendent – 'the happiest and easiest times were the first thirteen years', as Garfield told his cousin Jim Wood (Conference Chairman, ACCNZ).[4] 'It did not seem to worry us that in those days there was not water laid on, or that there weren't any other Europeans around, or that transport was difficult (or all the other little things which seem to have grown out of their right size recently).'

The trouble began right at the beginning of the year, but the first intimation we have of it is a letter of 10 June from Garfield to the Secretary of the FMC: 'I sincerely regret to have to inform you that the relationships between Mr Carden

---

3   Jimmy Stewart/GT, CC/2/721, 27.4.53, Associated Churches of Christ in New Zealand (ACCNZ) files.
4   GT/Jim Wood, 16.9.53, MS.1082/2/6, Todd Papers, NAZ.

and members of the staff here have been so strained over the past four months that a break has had to be made. I have not written for some time as I could not bring myself to do so until I knew how things were going to go. We have kept hoping and praying that this letter would be unnecessary. I could write at very great length but I think if I keep to the main matter of personal relationships I will cover the root cause of most of our trouble ...'5

Since his arrival, Carden had succeeded in upsetting several of the female missionaries, including Mrs Knapp and Grace. He then upset the men by not bearing his part in visiting the village churches on Sundays. His reason was his fear of catching disease from the unboiled water used to dilute 'communion wine' (raspberry juice). Carden then complained about his salary and of Garfield not trusting him to sign cheques. Garfield explained that the Mission's financial situation was always so finely balanced that it required tight control by one person. Finally, Carden said that either Garfield must leave, or he should. Garfield accepted that the only solution was for Carden to return to New Zealand.

The crisis at Dadaya so alarmed the FMC in New Zealand that, without consulting Garfield, they took the extreme step of sending the chairman of the Council to Rhodesia to assess the situation. He stayed at Dadaya for over a month, and upon his return to New Zealand in August he recommended to the Council that the Mission should be closed and all the missionaries brought home. This suggestion proved completely unacceptable to the FMC, which had confidence in the strength and future of Dadaya. There, an immediate consequence of the chairman's visit was the resignation of the Cardens, the Sharfes and Miss Kermode.

Exasperation breathes through every line of what Garfield wrote at this time about Carden and the chairman's visit. In a subsequent letter to Jim Wood, Garfield wrote that the strength of the work in the previous twenty years had been the fact that 'on no occasion has [the Board] interfered or set to over-rule any action that I have taken. If it had been guided by me in its recent action, it would not have fallen into the error for which we are now all paying ...'6

Garfield did, however, understand some of the difficulties which the new missionaries encountered and which some found unacceptable: 'Dadaya has never had anything like the money that was required to run it satisfactorily', Garfield told the CWA Middle Advisory Board. 'You must realise, however, that we built the place up from very small beginnings and we grew with the place.

---

5   GT/FMU, 10.6.53, MS.390/5/3, Todd Papers, NAZ.
6   GT/Jim Wood, 28.10.53, MS.1082/2/6, Todd Papers, NAZ.

Now that we are handing it over to other people, they do not find it as easy as we did, because they are taken from good surroundings, especially those who have come lately, and are dumped into a work which is inadequately financed and in which everybody has to live in conditions which are difficult.'[7]

The Churches of Christ in New Zealand then set up a Commission of Enquiry to take submissions from those concerned and to make a report on its findings. At the end of its deliberations, Garfield wrote to Dr Haddon: 'Both the Field Council and ourselves have received cables from the Board which show that confidence has been re-established between Nelson and Southern Rhodesia.'[8] He wrote to the FMU: 'It has been a great joy to my wife and myself to know that the position has now been clarified and that the work will receive the full support of the people in New Zealand ... you will find that we will be glad to help in any way that we can ...'[9]

Garfield was aware at the time he left Dadaya that 'in the last years life has become more and more complicated and busy and many of the things that I wished to do, I failed in', as he told his brother in October 1953.[10] But it may well be that, during the early months of the Carden affair, Garfield 'took his eye off the ball' and paid insufficient attention to helping the new missionaries to settle in. Parliament and the referendum campaign took him away from Dadaya, but the most serious distraction was Grace's illness. She has said that Garfield looked to her for sensitivity. It is significant that the Carden crisis coincided with her illness, when Garfield was desperately worried – and deprived of her wisdom and counsel.

***

In a letter to Reg Burman of 3 September 1953, Garfield reviewed his and Grace's Mission years: 'You know that we have been at Dadaya for almost twenty years and as far as I could see, we probably would have stayed there for the next twenty. The break has been made ... I think it is all to the good because I had got too much bound up with it and I am quite sure other people who have come recently must have found it rather difficult to work in with a dictatorship which has been established for so long. Mind you, as I have told the new staff, I haven't minded serving under Grace at all!!'[11] Ten years later, Garfield told Ray Blampied, Chairman of the NZ Board: 'Older people like ourselves have had

---

7   GT/CWA, 22.10.53, MS.390/1/14, Todd Papers, NAZ.
8   GT/Dr Haddon, 12.3.54, MS.390/1/8, Todd Papers, NAZ.
9   GT/FMU, 12.3.54, MS.390/1/8, Todd Papers, NAZ.
10 GT/Thomas F. D. Todd, October 1953, MS.1082/2/5, Todd Papers, NAZ.
11 GT/Reg Burman, 3.9.53, MS.390/1/14, Todd Papers, NAZ.

our day of almost apostolic rule – it probably was not at all good for us.'[12]

During the course of 'their day', Garfield and Grace had seen the mission grow out of all recognition. They would be the first to say that their contribution was but part of the greater whole: the excellent (and dreadfully ill-paid) African teachers and preachers; the New Zealanders who supported them at home and the New Zealanders who came to join them; and the Native Education Department officials: George Stark, A. R. Mather, Jimmy Stewart and many others. As F. L. Hadfield wrote in the *Dadaya Mission Jubilee Commemoration Issue 1906–1956*: 'all have carved their niche in the history of Dadaya by their deep understanding of the problems that beset the missionary and of their earnest desire to work in as close harmony as possible'.[13] All could take pride in the Mission's development, most clearly reflected in the last statistics that will be quoted: the number of village schools had increased from 12 to 33, the village churches from 12 to 37; the staff in the whole circuit had grown from 12 to 150; the boarders at Dadaya School had increased from 20 boys to nearly 600 boys and girls; the total enrolment in all schools from 700 to 4,000. In addition, a secondary school and a teacher-training college had been established.

'What we have done over the last twenty years cannot be undone, because it has been working in the lives of the people and these hundreds and thousands of people are now scattered around Rhodesia getting on with their life work', Garfield told Stella. 'The last twenty years has been a period of almost complete happiness and tremendous progress.'[14]

---

12 GT/Ray A. Blampied, 14.7.64, MS.390/6/4, Todd Papers, NAZ.
13 FMU, ACCNZ, TPPC.
14 GT/Stella Salisbury (née Todd), 27.10.53, MS.390/1/5, Todd Papers, NAZ.

24

Grace Todd

'I have come to believe that a great teacher is a great artist and that there are as few as there are any other great artists. Teaching might even be the greatest of the arts since the medium is the human mind and spirit.'

John Steinbeck

In Southern Rhodesia, in the mouths of whites, 'missionary' was often a pejorative term, but Garfield had 'never been ashamed of being a missionary. I never shall be. Not once have I regretted the years I have devoted to the work.'[1] 'My missionary career I am grateful for, and am proud of it', Garfield said in interviews for this book. 'If I had to choose the missionary period or the political one there just isn't any choice at all. I was a missionary. I am a missionary. I don't hold that I was ever a politician but I was a Member of Parliament and I was a Prime Minister and I enjoyed both roles.' So far from regretting his missionary career, Garfield held that it was an important preparation for being Prime Minister: 'If I am of any real use to Southern Rhodesia over the next few years it will be largely because for the last twenty years my wife and I have been living in native reserves and working with the African people.'[2]

Garfield told the World Convention of the Churches of Christ in Edinburgh in 1960 that at Dadaya Mission, 'although we did not fully realise what was happening, we had brought a message which not only saved souls and brought people to a knowledge of the transforming love of God, but which also brought a new dignity and a thousand new and disturbing questions'.[3]

***

---

1   *The Chronicle*, 14.9.53.
2   *Rhodesia Herald*, 1.7.54.
3   World Convention, Edinburgh, 5.8.60, TPPC.

Garfield's cousin, Nell Wood, wrote to Grace from Invercargill in August 1953: 'I know Gar would agree with me in feeling that he could never have done so much without your companionship, your encouragement and at times even your suggestions'.[4] This was a message of great comfort to Grace, as her last three months at Dadaya, after Garfield had gone to Salisbury, were difficult: with the Knapps and the Ladbrooks she was trying to rebuild harmony among the New Zealanders; she was preparing her Domestic Science students for their final exams; and, although Judith and Cynthia remained at Dadaya with her, she felt the divided family acutely. The Carden debacle had deeply distressed her both on her own account and on Garfield's, and impaired her serenity to the point where she told her sister Elsie: 'my feeling at the moment is that I shall thankfully shake the dust of Dadaya from my feet. I never expected to feel that way … I have had twenty years of very hard work here, and while it has been richly rewarding and I have on the whole been very happy, it is certainly time I moved on.'[5]

Years would pass before gradually the African people became aware of what Grace had achieved. First came a Certificate of Outstanding Service from the Rhodesia African Teachers' Association in 1968. Twenty years later, Dr Eddison Zvobgo, Minister of State in the Department of Political Affairs, heard about Grace's Schemes and got their story from her. He was so impressed that he had a copy handsomely bound, with 'Dadaya Schemes' and 'J. Grace Todd DLH' in gold lettering on the cover, and went to Bulawayo to present it to her. (The honorary doctorate was conferred upon Grace in 1978 by Eureka College in the USA.)

Shortly before Grace died in 2001, the Rotary Club of Bulawayo presented her with a Services Rendered Award 'for dedicated and lifelong service to education at Dadaya Mission and Zimbabwe'. The Citation stated that the teaching of aspects of domestic science 'contributed towards the all-important task of modernising the African society and to the emancipation of the African woman. "Education for Life" – Full pursuance of the School's motto at Dadaya facilitated the production of men and women of trained intellect, who loved the dignity of labour. Many of them have made and are making significant contributions towards the quality of life throughout Zimbabwe. Lady Grace has been a great achiever and nation-builder in our country in her own right. The people greatly respect and love her also as a pillar of the

---

4   Nell Wood/JGT, 15.8.53, MS.1082/2/6, Todd Papers, NAZ.
5   JGT/EB, 4.10.53, Mrs Collins' Papers. I am grateful to Mrs Collins for sight of this letter and others.

Todd family of Zimbabwe and New Zealand.'[6]

Dr Aeneas Chigwidere, the Zimbabwean Minister of Education, Culture and Sport, gave the address at Grace's funeral in January 2002. In the course of it, he said: 'I am an historian and educationist. In 1997 ... I discovered that the African education system [Garfield] expanded and developed was in fact the Grace Todd system that was then known as the Dadaya Scheme ... Grace Todd's African Primary Education System remained intact with very minor cosmetic changes right up to 1980. I am a product of the Grace Todd Scheme; all the Africans here who did primary education before 1980 are children or grandchildren of the Grace Todd Education System ... education schemes throughout the world are products of Education Commissions and Education Task Forces. The Southern Rhodesian African Education System was the product of one person ...'[7]

***

George Stark, Director of African Education, wrote to Garfield shortly before the latter left Dadaya: 'How delighted I am that you have been elected leader of the UP and will therefore be Prime Minister ... My warmest congratulations. We shall miss you very much indeed from the Joint Conference and its Standing Committee. You were a tower of strength to me there. But what good fortune it is to have a man of your calibre and liberal views in the Government controlling the destinies of the Colony. We wish you all success as you embark on your very arduous duties. And what I have said goes also for Mrs Todd. Together you have built up the Dadaya Mission to its present outstanding position as an educational institution – together you have given the very best to the education of the African – together in the political field you have earned the respect and goodwill of the people of the Colony.'[8]

In 1956, Dadaya Mission celebrated its Golden Jubilee with a Jubilee Commemoration Issue. Under the title 'Our Heritage', F. L. Hadfield wrote – and he well knew what he was writing of – 'It is a simple matter to classify highlights in a Mission's history ... But the history of a Mission is more than these things. It is the story of personal hardships, of physical suffering, of discomforts, of voluntary exile from friends and loved ones, of disappointments, of great ideals, and always of a constant giving of oneself and travelling that second mile. But even this does not represent the history of a Mission. What of the indigenous Church and the loyalty and faithfulness of those who worship each Lord's Day?

---

6   Resolution of the Board of Directors of the Bulawayo Rotary Club meeting, 2.10.2001, J. Todd Papers, c/TPPC.

7   Dr Aeneas Chigwedere, funeral address for Grace Todd, TPPC.

8   George Stark/GT, 15.8.53, MS.390/1/5, Todd Papers, NAZ.

Think of Tom Ngole, who preached at Dadaya when it was an outstation before there was a resident missionary ... Think of J. N. Hlambelo, Jackson Mvubu, Wesley Sibanda, with a total of more than a century of Christian witness for Christ in the Lundi Reserve. "And their name is legion" ...'[9]

'Dadaya stays at the centre of things. I can hardly believe that Grace and I had twenty years there – twenty years of unbelievable privilege.'[10]

'From the beginning, God was in Africa ... We were neither architects nor builders of the New Africa but were just two of the countless workers who were making bricks; concerned with individuals one by one.'[11]

---

9 Dadaya Mission: Foreign Mission Union of the Associated Churches of Christ in New Zealand. Jubilee Commemoration Issue 1906–56, printed by Rhoprint, Bulawayo, 5530 – 1/5/56. TPPC.
10 GT/SP, 26.9.2001, TPPC.
11 GT/A.

PART III – PRIME MINISTER OF SOUTHERN RHODESIA

'This little sea of hope'

Nathan Shamuyarira, *Crisis in Rhodesia* (1965)

♦•♦

25

THE SUCCESSION; PRIME MINISTER OF SOUTHERN RHODESIA

'The most important office of a prime minister: that he provide enlightened, just and fearless leadership.'

Senator Garfield Todd, 1983

At no time did Huggins make any move as regards 'the succession' – who would become Prime Minister of Southern Rhodesia in his place. Garfield himself had no thought that he was in any way a chosen successor – on the contrary, he felt Huggins did not want him on account of his missionary background. However, the Governor of Southern Rhodesia, Sir John Kennedy, a man of known liberal views, was definitely interested in the succession. He liked and respected Garfield as a man, a missionary and an MP, so when Lord Swinton, the new Conservative Secretary of State for Commonwealth Relations, visited Salisbury in July 1953, Kennedy invited Garfield to Government House to meet him.

Swinton also talked with Huggins, and upon his return to London, wrote to the Governor: '[Huggins] is as clear as we are that Southern Rhodesia is the key ... Huggins would like to have Todd as Prime Minister but thinks that too much for the Party to swallow in one gulp ... Huggins thinks Todd much the best man but can't rush him into Prime Minister.'[1]

***

The 'succession' would be decided at the United Party's Annual Congress, when a new president had to be elected in Huggins' place; whoever was chosen would automatically become Southern Rhodesia's new Prime Minister. There was an air of excited anticipation when delegates, elected from Party branches, together with SR MPs, converged upon the Jewish Guildhall in Bulawayo on 14 August 1953. Garfield and Grace were just about to enter the hall when, to Garfield's surprise, a member of the cabinet, Patrick ('Ben') Fletcher, tried to persuade him not to stand.

Julian Greenfield, Huggins' Minister of Justice, Sir George Davenport and Todd were nominated. Davenport withdrew; Fletcher refused to stand. When voting took place, Congress divided 50:50. The Chairman (Humphrey Gibbs) gave his casting vote for Greenfield because of his experience. There was 'pandemonium in the hall' – and the meeting broke for lunch. The Todds and Greenfield lunched together; and, on their return to the hall, Greenfield told Congress that he really wanted to 'go Federal', and so he withdrew. Garfield was duly elected President of the United Party.

Sir John Kennedy told Lord Swinton: 'The reception of Todd as leader has been distinctly tepid. Huggins thinks he has the qualities and that it may be all right in the end. He is of course a very unknown quantity except as a backbencher.' Swinton replied: 'Todd is the best bet we could have ... Greenfield would have been hopeless as he is as full of doubt as an egg is of meat. Todd will take hold as Prime Minister and you can help him: of course, Huggins will ... [he] will realise that if Southern Rhodesia went wrong it could dish the whole future of Federation.'[2]

On 17 August, Garfield issued a statement: the office of Prime Minister was not something he had really contemplated, 'but having had it handed to me I do not lack enthusiasm. I am not frightened. I have had plenty of problems in my life – these are merely of a different kind. I have experienced people around me. I am certain of their co-operation.'[3]

---

1   Lord Swinton/Sir John Kennedy, 3.8.53, Kennedy Papers, Bodleian Library.
2   Kennedy's unpublished memoirs, Bodleian Library.
3   *Rhodesia Herald*, 17.8.53.

Press reaction within the Colony was also 'tepid'. The *Sunday News* (Bulawayo) said in a leading article that the UP 'rightly rejected the course of vacillation, but in so doing had to choose a leader about whom there must of necessity be rather more of faith and expectation than conclusive knowledge and proof of his suitability and adaptability'.[4] *The Chronicle* observed that Garfield was 'comparatively young in years and political experience but he has proved himself to be a clear thinker and a level-headed debater'.[5]

Cyril Dunn, then the *Observer* correspondent in Salisbury, writes: 'When Lord Malvern was given the Federal throne there was nobody left in Southern Rhodesia to compare with Mr Todd in experience and intellectual stature.'[6]

Hardwicke Holderness expresses the views of himself and fellow-liberals in Salisbury: 'It seemed to us an astonishing decision when we heard about it, and greatly encouraging ... [It] must signify a readiness for change in a liberal direction on the part of at least a substantial proportion of the white electorate.'[7] Todd seemed to have 'a sufficiently common touch and must have made a very strong impression to overcome the contrary factors so prejudicial to his chances – no common experience at 'club' level, either the Salisbury Club or the Salisbury Sports Club, and being a "God" man and perceived to be a good man'.[8] 'There was something fundamentally to be trusted about Garfield Todd.'[9]

In New Zealand, the first newspaper to pick up the story of Garfield's election was the *Dunedin Sports Special*! Under the headline 'Former city man PM of Southern Rhodesia', it carried a picture of the local boy. Garfield's mother wrote: 'If you two were as excited as I was, then you would not have been fit for much ... you know just how proud dear old Dad would have been of you. I know that you will always fill your very high position with dignity and honour.'[10]

Sir John Kennedy's term as Governor of Southern Rhodesia ended in November 1953, but he has left this picture of his brief association with Garfield: 'I ... found him delightful and easy to work with in his new role of Prime Minister ... One could not but hope that Todd's acceptance by the electorate, so predominantly white, might prove to be an indication of a more liberal approach to racial policy.'[11]

---

4 *The Sunday News*, 16.8.53.
5 *The Chronicle*, 17.8.53.
6 Dunn, 1959, p. 154.
7 Holderness, 1985, pp. 123–4.
8 HHCH/SP, interview, 1993.
9 Holderness, 1985, p. 167.
10 Edith Todd/GT, 17.7.53, MS.1082/2/5, Todd Papers, NAZ.
11 Kennedy's unpublished memoirs, Bodleian Library.

Garfield knew that with a general election not many months away, he might lose his position as suddenly as he had achieved it. He had always felt privileged in his political life in being associated with men of high principle, and in the knowledge that politics in Southern Rhodesia were decently conducted, but he was well aware that he lacked several qualities that make a good politician. He would be the first to acknowledge that he was, as Kennedy had pointed out, 'a political innocent' – or, in Grace's words, 'the most naive person who has ever been in politics'.

Garfield told his friend and former pupil, K. D. Dube, 'I hope that I may have the opportunity to carry on the work here according to my lights for some time … I will do what I consider right and do it to the best of my ability during the time that I may be allowed to be Prime Minister.'[12]

Garfield 'immediately set a pace, volume and range of work, which was astonishing. He habitually worked a sixteen-hour day, and was tireless in his efforts to promote a better understanding between the European settlers and the Africans.'[13] Garfield rose early to clear his in-tray in order to spend more time with people, including his cabinet ministers. The main responsibility of the SR Government was Native Affairs, but in addition there were the Treasury, the Irrigation Department (although major works would be a federal responsibility, the Department was to become heavily involved in preparations for the Kariba dam), the Public Works Department and the Department of Roads and Road Traffic.

***

In a moment of despair, Grace once told Garfield: 'If you had told me that you were going to become Prime Minister, I would never have married you.' But she was not 'tremendously excited or moved or scared by any of the things that happened all the way through … it seemed a natural progression from what he was doing, working on a wider scale for the benefit of the community, for the benefit of the country'. Until November, however, she remained at Dadaya, to see her Domestic Science students through to their final exams, going up to Salisbury as occasion demanded – and one of the demands was turning a lovely but run-down old Government-owned house, Northward, into the official residence of the Prime Minister. There were great changes forND the three girls. Alycen had hankered to return to New Zealand ever since their last visit. With her parents' move, the time seemed opportune and she left Rhodesia – to return only on rare, brief visits. Judith and Cynthia went

---

12 GT/K. D. Dube, n.d., MS.1082/2/6, Todd Papers, NAZ.
13 Biography of GT, *Current Affairs Bulletin of the University of Sydney*, vol. 24, no. 2, 26.5.59, 'African Nationalism', TPPC.

daily to David Livingstone School in one of the nearby avenues.

Grace went to Salisbury for the opening of the new sitting of Parliament and 'saw Gar take his place as Prime Minister on the cabinet benches, and also saw Sir Godfrey Huggins sitting in Gar's old seat on the back benches – a unique occasion! Gar is loving it all, and I do hope that he gets the chance of another full term as PM to see what he can do.'[14]

When Grace was permanently settled at Northward, she set about creating a beautiful and tranquil garden, and continued with her Native Education committee work and with the Girl Guide Association (which soon absorbed the Wayfarer Guides into the mainstream movement). She would later spend many hours on committees for the Association of African Women's Clubs and the St Giles Rehabilitation Centre. One thing Grace was dreading about her new life was the inevitable public speaking. Garfield, himself one of the outstanding speakers of the day, was full of praise: 'She did not like addressing meetings … but if she had to speak, she spoke excellently, and she made friendships. She did remarkably well as Prime Minister's wife. From the point of view of a man in the public eye, I could not have asked for a more capable wife … The finest thing from my point of view about my wife is that in emergencies she never falters, no matter what may be said or what may happen.'[15]

Garfield told Elsie Barham's husband, Clarence: 'Grace is complaining that, after twenty years of doing things together, we have now reached the point where she stays at home and looks after the house, while I go out and earn the living. She complains that I do not give her enough news, and I have apologised for not being able to take her to the cabinet meetings.'[16] But Garfield 'discussed everything with Grace, including secret material'. Hardwicke Holderness writes that the more he got to know the Todds, 'the more I learned to appreciate their complementary qualities: he basically the decisive, and in some ways boyish, man of action, and she the sage lady with intuitive foresight'.[17]

The country was peaceful and there were few security concerns. There were no bodyguards for ministers – and this held true to the end of Garfield's premiership. There were no gates between the whitewashed pillars at the entrances to Northward, the front door was not locked – and, although the doors of the Legislative Assembly might be locked at night, at least one window had a defective catch which enabled Garfield to climb in if he forgot his keys.

Every week, Garfield took a day off to go down to the ranch; and, while

---

14   JGT/EB, 5.10.53, Mrs Collins' Papers.
15   Oral TO.1, NAZ.
16   GT/Clarence Barham, 25.2.54, MS.390/1/14, Todd Papers, NAZ.
17   Holderness, 1985, p. 167.

he was always careful to keep a proper distance from the Mission, these visits gave him news of what was going on. The six-hour car journeys enabled him to catch up on his papers and reading.

Some white Rhodesians found it embarrassing that their Prime Minister was a missionary, but they misunderstood Garfield's belief that politics and religion, and all life, were one. He told the Asian Adult Education Institute in Gwelo on 30 May 1956 that it was 'the rankest nonsense to say that [politics and religion] do not mix. The only politics that do not mix with religion are the kind that do not serve truth, justice and right, and the fundamental value of the individual.'[18]

***

Southern Rhodesia was in many ways very British, and nowhere more so than in regard to Parliament and the Civil Service. The Speaker of Parliament ranked immediately after the Prime Minister. The Civil Service was largely locally recruited, with technical advisers brought in as occasion demanded. The integrity of civil servants was never questioned.

The creation of Federation upset all previous political arrangements in the constituent territories. Urgent questions now arose about the formation of parties to fight the Federal general election in December 1953 and the Southern Rhodesian general election the following year. Huggins chose the name 'Federal Party' for his now Federation-wide former United Party. The Confederate Party, who had opposed Federation, formed the opposition in the Federal sphere.

The Southern Rhodesian general election was scheduled for March 1954. The United Party, of which Garfield was now President, was opposed by the anti-Federation Rhodesia Party, whose members largely came from the old Labour Party. Soon, however, leaders of the Rhodesia Party suggested a merger with the United Party; but, when this fell through, certain prominent members of the party joined the United Party individually, including a leading Salisbury accountant, Geoffrey Ellman-Brown, and a Salisbury solicitor, A. R. W. ('Rube') Stumbles. On 5 November, the United Rhodesia Party (URP) was formed under Garfield's leadership. The clarification of the political situation enabled the SR general election to be brought forward from March to January 1954.

***

There was one legislative matter that had to be dealt with before Parliament was prorogued – an amendment to the Peace Preservation Act. Accusations of undemocratic behaviour have been levelled at Garfield on account of the security legislation enacted by his Government. The proposals for Federation in 1953 had led to disturbances in Northern Rhodesia and Nyasaland. A

---

18 *Rhodesia Herald*, 31.1.56.

contingent of the BSAP, under Superintendent Ken Flower, had been sent to restore order in Nyasaland. He later wrote a report on the security situation which warned that the same kind of violence could quickly spread to Southern Rhodesia. In the 1950s, fear of the spread of Communism was very powerful in the Western world, with a particular anxiety for the vulnerability to its influence of the African population. The 1948 strike by African workers in Salisbury and Bulawayo had come as an enormous shock to whites, and the impact of the Mau Mau movement in Kenya was also not to be underestimated. This was seen as another reason to strengthen existing security legislation. As a result of Flower's report, an amendment to the Peace Preservation Act of 1901 was prepared and passed by Parliament.

***

Between his assumption of office in September 1953 and the general election at the end of January 1954, Garfield was engaged in the normal business of government – congestion on the Rhodesia Railways as they tried to juggle the requirements of chrome, copper and tobacco exports with petrol and oil imports, and the vital coal supplies from Wankie on which the power stations depended; continued discussion on the rival merits of two proposed hydro-electric schemes on the Zambezi River at Kariba and Kafue; and the controversial Inter-Territorial Movement of Persons Bill, to control the entry of Asians into Southern Rhodesia. Garfield was concerned that there should be no influx into the Colony of Asians who would take jobs for which increasingly capable Africans were becoming eligible.

Once Parliament had risen, Garfield made a comprehensive tour of all the departments of government to find out how they worked – an activity which earned him praise from *The Chronicle*: 'His researches into the working of departments already are equal to that of many commissions of inquiry of the past.'[19] Garfield was also engaged in a programme of speaking around the country: 'the idea of appointing a special body to go thoroughly into the franchise ... is one to be welcomed';[20] 'If you are going to take natives out of the reserves, you must be prepared to give them satisfactory tenure of land in our industrial areas ... tenure of land is of paramount importance to the country and industry.'[21] 'We recognise the uselessness of spending millions of pounds to develop the country if that country were to be subjected to the tragedy of racial hatred and strife ...'[22]

---

19 *The Chronicle*, 14.1.54.
20 *Rhodesia Herald*, 13.11.53.
21 *The Chronicle*, 21.11.53.
22 St Andrew's Night Banquet, Gwelo, 27.11.53, MS.1082/5/3, Todd Papers, NAZ.

26

DECEMBER 1953 TO FEBRUARY 1954

'Nearly all men can stand adversity, but if you want to test a man's character, give him power.'

Abraham Lincoln

In the Federal general election of December 1953, Huggins' Federal Party won 24 of the 26 elected seats, although the Confederate Party, led by Dendy Young, QC, polled nearly half as many votes. The pro-Federationists in Northern Rhodesia and Nyasaland were similarly successful, but African opposition remained solid, and their directly elected representatives, Mr Dauti Yamba of Northern Rhodesia, and Mr Wellington Chirwa of Nyasaland, were effective members of the Federal Assembly – particularly the latter, who became a formidable opponent of Sir Roy Welensky.

The URP's election manifesto stated that the keynote of its policy was to maintain the standards of Europeans, to improve the standards of Africans and to preserve racial harmony. Over 50 people, mostly men, offered themselves for selection for the 30 seats. All were 'professionals' from the 'real world' rather than experienced politicians. The average age was younger than in the previous Parliament. Garfield told a Bulawayo audience that the URP had chosen 'a band of men and one woman [Mrs Muriel Rosin] who are not people who will easily toe the line marked by the leader'.[1] One of the five lawyer candidates, Hardwicke Holderness, was selected for Salisbury North. Garfield wrote to him: 'I expect you will be a frightful nuisance in the House but by the list of people we have got we are going to have a number of strong men and Sir Godfrey always reckoned that strong men are a nuisance.'[2]

---

1   *The Chronicle*, 13.1.54.
2   Holderness, 1985, p. 126.

Garfield was a tireless campaigner. Holderness describes his performance as a speaker: 'He had a commanding platform presence – tall, clean-cut, powerful build: shock of dark hair – and a command of the English language and delivery which no doubt owed a lot to his training as a preacher but, adapted to dealing with the whole range of national affairs (and, incidentally, still spoken with a discernible New Zealand accent), seemed to be sufficiently down to earth and appropriate for politics; and heckling and hostile questions usually provided fuel for the best part of the performance – highly intelligent, instantaneous and humorous.'[3] A few years later, a newly arrived university lecturer, Dr T. O. Ranger, felt that he 'knew for the first time the meaning of the word "charismatic"' when he saw Garfield speak. 'Energy and charm flowed from him almost without his willing it ... All this force seemed wasted on the Prime Minister of little Southern Rhodesia.'[4]

At all his meetings, Garfield sought to reassure European voters of his intentions. At Braeside, Salisbury: 'The Europeans in the colony will only be safe and secure if they work in harmony with black people.'[5] At Bulawayo, he said that the URP insisted the standard of living for Europeans had to be maintained.[6] On 19 January, Garfield addressed a meeting of the National Affairs Association in Bulawayo on the subject of racial harmony, telling his audience that 'by equality the URP did not mean social equality but the equality of all races before the law of the land'.[7]

The Southern Rhodesian electors – in number roughly equal to the ratepayers of Aberdeen, Scotland – went to the polls on Wednesday 27 January. Garfield toured polling stations in his Shabani constituency and cast his own vote; then he flew to Salisbury to await results. Shabani's result was always the last to be declared, but at 2.15 on Thursday 28th he learned with some relief that G. Todd had polled 759 votes as against 273 for the Confederate candidate, L. Leary. The URP had won an overwhelming victory in the country, with 26 seats out of 30. Of the 30 MPs, 20 were newcomers, including William Addison, who became Speaker of the House. What Garfield's new men lacked in political and parliamentary experience they made up for in their knowledge of the worlds of commerce, industry, mining, agriculture, the law – and the

---

3   Ibid., p. 134.
4   Ranger, review of Weiss and Parpart, 1999, in *The Bulletin of the School of Oriental and African Studies*, 63/1 (2000), pp. 154–5. I am grateful to Professor Ranger for making this available to me.
5   *Rhodesia Herald*, 5.1.54.
6   *The Chronicle*, 13.1.54.
7   *The Chronicle*, 20.1.54.

country. Although the Confederate Party had polled 22.6 per cent of the vote, they had won not a single seat. The four elected Independents formed the official opposition.

Later that day, Garfield announced his new, five-man cabinet, with himself as Minister of Justice and Internal Affairs; Ben Fletcher retained Native Affairs; George Davenport, Minister of Mines, Land and Surveys; Cyril Hatty, Minister of the Treasury; and one of the newcomers to Parliament, Geoffrey Ellman-Brown, Minister of Roads and Road Traffic. On Friday 29 January, Grace watched as Garfield and his cabinet were sworn in by the Acting Governor, Sir William Murphy, a former Governor of the Bahamas and now a farmer in Southern Rhodesia.

When Garfield was contemplating the selection of ministers, the people he would 'naturally have gone for were Hardwicke, Paddy [Lloyd] and the Palmer brothers. But ... I would not have lasted a week so I was a bit pragmatic. Hardwicke is the one I should have had as Minister of Justice and Internal Affairs. It would have been a fearful risk to take him and it would probably have wrecked us ... I was prepared to take the risk on that but he would not come in because he thought that being a cabinet minister would spoil his relationship with his African friends.'

Garfield said he 'found strength in every expression of confidence and goodwill that came his way' in telegrams, telephone calls and letters – not least the letter of congratulations from Lord Swinton: 'I do congratulate you ... It is a great personal triumph and I feel I know you well enough to be very sure (if I may say so) that it will give you confidence without any swelling of the head.'[8]

***

The first meeting of the new cabinet took place on Tuesday 2 February – but neither the Prime Minister nor his Minister of Native Affairs was there. Garfield had encountered the first test of his ministry, of his strength and standing as a national leader and his credibility as a liberal.

In 1953, the Anglo-American Corporation took over the vital Wankie Colliery from Powell-Duffryn Ltd. Six months prior to the change of ownership, the management had received warnings from Government officials about the appalling conditions underground.[9] Both Powell-Duffryn and Anglo-American had ignored this warning. Towards the end of 1953, the cabinet

---

8 Lord Swinton/GT, File P7, Box 167635, Records Office, NAZ.
9 Phimister, 1994, p. 130. I am indebted to Professor Phimister for permission to quote extensively from this book.

was made aware of more rumblings of trouble at Wankie, but these had been on a very small scale and were largely concerned with the introduction by the Company, without proper consultation with the workforce, of new equipment and working practices.

On 25 January, notices appeared outside Wankie No. 1 Colliery telling black miners to come out on strike on 1 February. Meetings on Wednesday 27th (polling day) were attended by hundreds of underground workers who were told by their leaders that if Europeans did not resort to violence, then Africans wouldn't either. A Government Industrial Relations Officer, Mr R. N. Ketteringham, in his February 1954 report, pinpointed many of the African grievances, which included low wages, unhygienic conditions, 'harsh treatment by European supervisors and miners and no effective system of communication' between workers and management.[10] There was a system of tribal representation, with 'elders' from 38 different tribes forming a loose body to negotiate with the company. Under the Masters and Servants Act, which regulated African labour affairs (the responsibility of the Native Affairs Department), strikes were illegal. This strike was organised not by the 'elders' but by 'boss boys' (or foremen). Few of the strikers spoke English, Shona or Sindebele. 'It proved impossible to obtain any concrete demands from the strikers', wrote Ketteringham, 'or to persuade a delegation to interview the chief compound manager. The strikers demanded that [he] should interview them en masse on the football field. This was refused by the management' – but the mass meeting did not disperse. Sub-inspector A. Weston of Wankie BSAP realised that trouble was brewing on a larger scale, so Colonel A. S. Hickman, Acting Commissioner of the BSAP, ordered additional police detachments to go to Wankie. Later a contingent of Northern Rhodesian police was drafted in because a majority of the striking workers came from there. At this point, the colliery management issued a statement denying any knowledge of the men's grievances or the causes of the strike.

On 1 February, over 9,000 African underground workers at the colliery came out on strike. As coal was not only the sole source of power in the Federation but also fuelled the all-important Rhodesia Railways, the strike threatened the economic life of the Federation. The company's priority was to keep mechanical production going at No. 2 Colliery. Appeals were broadcast for European miners from other parts of the country to travel to Wankie – and every European man in the place, whether employed by the mine or not (except the BSAP), went underground. Above ground, 9,000 angry and idle Africans

---

10   Department of Labour Files, Box 147883, Records Office, NAZ.

waited for someone to listen to their grievances.

Garfield writes: 'Instead of presiding over my first cabinet meeting of the new Parliament, I sent an apology and flew [with Ben Fletcher] to the Wankie Colliery ... I recognised two facts: the men had grievances and no adequate machinery to let them be known. Also there was a second problem, because every white man seemed to have gone below surface to keep the machines operating. I could not risk an outbreak of violence and so called out the army, not to break the strike but to keep the peace.'[11]

Garfield met the men on the playing field, but communication was well nigh impossible. He toured their living quarters – and was horrified. After hours underground, men had to stand in line sometimes for an hour before they received their staple diet, dry mealie-meal (cornmeal). Then they had to cook it. Between ten and twelve men crowded into rooms made for three or four. One of the Europeans who went underground to fill in during the strike was similarly appalled: 'The No. 1 hostel was a terrible place and conditions there were very bad. It was the first time the Blacks realised how badly they were treated.'[12]

When representatives of the strikers failed to negotiate with company officials, the strikers disowned their representatives. An African clerk tried to put management's views but was assaulted. For some time, his recovery was in doubt, but after that there was no further violence. In fact, the men were well behaved almost throughout the strike. Under the provisions of the recently passed Peace Preservation Amendment Act, a curfew was imposed, together with a ban on gatherings of three or more persons, and permission was given for the police to arrest and search without warrant. On 2 February, Salisbury Radio Station broadcast instructions to members of the 1st Bn Royal Rhodesia Regiment to report to the Salisbury Drill Hall immediately.

Garfield had had no thought of sending troops to Wankie until he had seen the situation, he told Parliament in May. 'I am quite convinced, now that the events have passed, that we did take the right decision. Yes, we had the police. At first there was not a great number of those and, after all, even when the security forces were at their full strength, we then had 700 ratings of one kind or another and in Wankie we had 15,000 to 17,000 [strikers] ... most of them are of a fairly primitive order.'[13]

On his return to Salisbury, Garfield told reporters that the Government was 'determined to go on producing coal at Wankie with whatever labour was

---

11   GT, Foreword to Holderness, 1985, p. 3.
12   A. G. Koen, Oral Archives 264, NAZ.
13   LAD, vol. 35, 5.5.54, cc. 811–12.

available and was not prepared to have Wankie close down because of an illegal strike'.[14] At Wankie, the Native Commissioner announced to mass meetings of strikers that if they returned to work, a Labour Board would be appointed to investigate their grievances. But 'if they did not return to work, they would be signed off'.[15] By the evening of Thursday 4th, 920 strikers had gone back to work, local stores had reopened, and two or three strike leaders had come forward to discuss matters with the Native Commissioner, who had given them permission to address a mass meeting of striking miners. Garfield said that 'the date of the labour board's first meeting would be announced as soon as all the strikers had gone back to work … The strikers had greeted the security forces with goodwill rather than resentment.'[16]

In the end, only 300 strikers asked to return home to Northern Rhodesia; the rest went back to work. Six men were arrested and appeared in court on 1 March. They were found guilty of making 'diverse statements and acts urging employees of the Wankie Colliery Company to stay away from work'. They received suspended sentences of three months' hard labour and, as natives of Northern Rhodesia, were deported.

The Wankie Native Labour Board was established on 11 February. Its remit was to 'consider the terms and conditions of employment of the African employees of the Wankie Colliery Company Limited and to make recommendations thereon'.[17] The board reported to cabinet on 20 March. Its findings included inadequate pay scales; insufficient consultation with tribal leaders; grossly insufficient accommodation for the men; inadequate sanitary accommodation; candlelight only in the older collieries; abuse of the bonus system; and unacceptable rationing arrangements. A fundamental weakness was the absence of negotiating machinery between employer and employees.

On the matter of 'calling out the army', Garfield told Parliament on 5 May: 'We felt that while we might get a certain amount of criticism through taking precautionary action … it would be nothing to the trouble which we would lay up for ourselves in our own consciences and in our own hearts if, because we had not taken this precautionary measure, there had been any lives lost at Wankie.'[18] *Time* magazine observed: 'Garfield Todd kept his head and by so doing, saved many others … The results of such rare good sense were little

---

14 *Rhodesia Herald*, 4.2.54.
15 *Rhodesia Herald*, 5.2.54.
16 Ibid.
17 File MS.1086/2/1, Todd Papers, NAZ.
18 LAD, vol. 35, 5.5.54, cc. 1811–12.

short of electrifying.'[19] It has been asserted that an inexperienced Prime Minister over-reacted; and some African reaction to the calling out of the army was very critical – and has continued to be over the years – but Garfield has never wavered in his view that what he did was right. Two opposition MPs, Mr 'Robbie' Williamson and Mr 'Jack' Keller, had a field day in Parliament but could not shake Garfield: 'I maintain the Government had a serious responsibility to make sure that everybody, both black and white, was safe ... law and order shall be maintained and ... everyone, black or white, shall have a healthy respect for law and order ... the security forces who were in Wankie were not there to interfere with the strike.'[20]

The Wankie strike is part of Southern Rhodesia's history; it has also become part of Southern Rhodesia's folk-history. Garfield had always hoped to write an account of the Wankie Colliery strike of 1954 and to 'set the record straight as far as my own actions were concerned'. Grace, perhaps, does this for him: 'Garfield's whole life is evidence of his single-minded determination to see Africans develop and advance until power sharing, at least at legislative level, has been achieved. Any action by groups which thwarted or annulled his aims he dealt with firmly. Strikes, which affected the economy of the nation on which depended the financial power to implement his aims, he regretted and opposed. That does not mean that he was unaware of the disabilities under which such groups laboured. This was demonstrated by the events of the Wankie strike ... within days of his taking office. It was crucial that a new and untried Prime Minister should be seen to act quickly and firmly. Because there was a very real security problem he called out the Army, not as was later claimed, to break the strike, but to contain a possibly violent situation. In the event it did all pass off peacefully.'[21]

In 1959, Garfield said: 'I do not suggest that while I was Prime Minister of Southern Rhodesia I did not make mistakes – but I do not think I made a mistake at Wankie.' It is still alleged that Africans were killed at Wankie in 1954, but it is generally accepted that the first Africans killed in a riot since 1890 were the eleven men shot in Bulawayo on 24–25 July 1960.

***

One thing the Wankie strike did was to emphasise the urgent need to put in place conciliation machinery in disputes between employers and their African employees.

---

19 *Time* magazine, 22.2.1954.
20 LAD, vol. 35, 28.7.54, cc. 957–8.
21 JGT/SP, June 1995, TPPC.

27

THE EIGHTH PARLIAMENT

'The quality of the House was higher than for some years.'

British High Commissioner to the Federation of Rhodesia and Nyasaland

On 13 April 1954, the Acting Governor of Southern Rhodesia opened the Eighth Parliament of Southern Rhodesia – 'surely the most agreeable parliament in all history to be a member of', writes Hardwicke Holderness.[1]

The coming of Federation opened a new world for the whites of Salisbury and Bulawayo who wanted more out of life than *braais* (barbecues), rugby, cricket and beer-drinking. There was an increased tempo to life, and almost overnight there was a sizeable diplomatic community in Salisbury which brought a welcome degree of sophistication to the social life of the city. The arrival of academic staff at the university stimulated its intellectual life, and economic life also took off. Federation was going to be worth paying for, the Europeans began to think – and they seemed ready to pay the price: 'partnership'.

To give Africans 'the opportunity to learn, to develop character and leadership' had been Garfield's reason for entering politics, he had said in a radio talk in New Zealand in 1949, 'and the rest lies with the people'.[2] African Affairs was the largest single responsibility of the SR Government, and the conduct of African Affairs was in the hands – the grip – of the Native Affairs Department. Since 1945, Garfield had viewed with concern the increasing power of the department over the lives of Africans. By 1954, he recognised that it was more of an obstacle to change than an instrument of change. As he wrote in his draft autobiography in the early 1970s, 'The importance of the Department …

---

1 Holderness, 1985, pp. 136–7.
2 TPPC.

cannot be overestimated ... At least some members of the Native Department did not believe that it was possible for Africans to break away from savagery. It was impossible, they held, for missionaries or anyone else to eradicate the fear of spirits or a belief in witchcraft. What missionaries believe is that Africans belong as intimately to the family of man as any other ethnic group.'[3]

The department should have been run by people with sound degrees as a basic requirement – 'instead, it was staffed largely by people with a secondary school education to which, over the years, were grafted examinations in subjects such as anthropology, Native Customary Law and languages ... When despite the system people began to move forward in educational and political awareness, signs of great and increasing stress appeared.'[4]

***

Garfield had early on recognised that he would have to steer a careful course in his negotiations with the Federal Government, with its very experienced ministers and senior civil servants. For some time, his task was made more difficult by the inevitable confusion arising from this period of changeover. Certain responsibilities, such as education and agriculture, were divided between governments on racial lines, with European interests being the responsibility of the Federal Government. The transfer of whole departments was comparatively simple; more difficult was the transfer of key individuals. There were fears that the depletion of the Southern Rhodesia Civil Service would leave the Territorial Government with a very 'limited number of administrative and clerical civil servants from which to draw for their own requirements'.[5] The transfer of the most senior men meant a loss to the Southern Rhodesia Government of a valuable body of knowledge and experience, thus compounding the lack of experience of the new cabinet elected in January 1954. The whole operation was a stiff test of the new Prime Minister's competence but, as the Secretary for Labour, Jack Armstrong, would later describe him, Garfield was a 'first-class administrator'.[6]

In June 1954, Garfield and his government were faced with another strike, this time by some of the white firemen on the Rhodesia Railways. The position of fireman was an essential step on the way to becoming a very highly paid engine-driver – a jealously guarded 'European' occupation. The Rhodesia Railways Workers' Union had a wide and active membership on both sides of the Zambezi River. Welensky had been an engine-driver for most of his

---

3 GT/A, 1973–4.
4 Ibid.
5 Cabinet Memorandum, SRC(54)190, 30.8.54, File S.3242/10, NAZ.
6 Jack Armstrong/SP, April 1958.

working life, and a Union official, and was now Life President of the Union. As the Rhodesia Railways operated in Northern as well as Southern Rhodesia, the Northern Rhodesia Government was peripherally involved. Furthermore, the ringleader of the strike was a recent immigrant into Southern Rhodesia from Britain – and immigration was a Federal responsibility, so that Government also became involved. European labour matters were handled in Southern Rhodesia by the Department of Internal Affairs. Garfield, as minister, therefore became personally involved in all the intricate negotiations.

The experience of both the Wankie strike and this short, but complex, dispute served to confirm his view that all labour matters should be the responsibility of a single, dedicated department.

28

THE LAND APPORTIONMENT ACT (1930)

'What probably made the Land Apportionment Act acceptable to many of us was the fact that it was fading out.'

Garfield Todd, 1970

Land. Land. Land. The first thing that needs to be said in the context of the Land Apportionment Act is that most of the white settlers of 1890 and their successors had no understanding of the spiritual importance of the land to the African people of the country. Land and what lay under its surface had brought the Europeans to Southern Rhodesia. Land and its importance to both races lay at the root of most of the problems that faced everyone in Southern Rhodesia. The African Reserves had been set aside for exclusive African use before Southern Rhodesia attained self-government in 1923, and were enshrined in the country's Constitution. In 1930, there were Native Reserves – areas of lighter, sandy soil, easily worked – for the half a million Africans; land set aside for the 50,000 or so Europeans (the more fertile areas, with a heavier soil, more suitable for tractors than ox ploughs); and two smaller areas: National Parks and Native Purchase Areas.

Garfield recognised that the Land Apportionment Act had been useful, saying as late as 1957: 'It had seemed a completely sensible and natural provision when it was introduced and it continues to have a most important part to play in the life of the country.'[1] 'If there had not been a Land Apportionment Act there is no doubt that Europeans, with their capital resources, would long ago have bought up most of Southern Rhodesia.'

When in 1954 Garfield attempted to amend the Land Apportionment Act

---

1 GT, article for *Optima*, magazine of the Anglo-American Corporation, vol. 7, no. 4, 1957.

in four very minor, very specific areas, he realised that white acceptance of 'partnership' and what it meant was but skin-deep. The proposals caused great strain in the party – and also within the cabinet. The amendments were necessitated by developments that followed Federation: African diplomats had to be free to live in 'white' areas; provision must be made for multiracial hotels and clubs; and the first black advocate, Herbert Chitepo, required chambers alongside his white colleagues in Harvest House in the centre of Salisbury. Most important of all, however, was the establishment of a multiracial university in Salisbury, which had been under discussion even before Federation. Sir Godfrey Huggins was in favour of the establishment of a university with British entrance standards, which meant that the institution had to be multiracial. But such a university in a white area meant that amendments to the Land Apportionment Act must be made before a single black student or black lecturer could take up residence there.

When the draft bill was published, reaction was immediate: the *Umtali Post*, for example, said that 'it is an attack on the safeguards the European enjoys at present'.[2] Hardwicke Holderness went to the heart of the matter when he said in Parliament that among whites the conservatives' point of view arose out of their ignorance of educated Africans: 'there is no other way for these people to go than the European way ... what they want to do is be accepted on their merits. There is in Southern Rhodesia a whole section of African people who are knocking on the door of Western civilisation.' Then he turned to a spectre haunting whites in Africa – the rise to power of African nationalists with Marxist leanings. 'There are demagogues. Let us face it, and there are great temptations for the demagogues to become black nationalists. But one thing I am convinced of. At this moment, and I do not know how long it will last, but I do not think it will last more than another few years if things do not go the right way – at this moment the leadership of these people is firmly in the hands of people who do not want black nationalism, people who want western civilisation, people who want racial co-operation, and people who will come in 100 per cent, as liberals, co-operating in our Western way if the door is not closed on them.'[3] (Less than three years after that statement, the reformed Southern Rhodesia African National Congress was launched by James Chikerema and George Nyandoro, among others, who decided to turn their backs on white liberals and conservatives alike.)

At the end of a long debate, Garfield reminded MPs that his views on race relations had been totally consistent: 'I believe that only if we move reasonably

---

2 *Umtali Post*, 29.10.54.
3 LAD, vol. 36, 9.11.54, cc. 2388–90.

with the times and only if we are prepared to let common sense and decency have its way and meet our problems one by one without leaving too big a time-lag will we be able to carry on and build up the good feeling which today exists between the races here.' His recent Commonwealth Parliamentary Association visit to Kenya at the height of the Mau Mau rebellion had left a brutal and lasting impression on him and made him more than ever determined that he 'would leave nothing undone which I could do in my own responsibility to make sure that race relations in Southern Rhodesia and Central Africa were not only maintained but improved'.[4]

Inevitably, the amendments were considerably watered down, but the university opened in 1956, and the vexed question of multiracial hostels was settled within three years by the wishes of the students themselves and the ratio of their numbers. Garfield maintained the principle of the 'free vote' for his MPs throughout his administration; on this occasion, six of them joined the opposition to vote against the Third Reading of the Bill.

---

4 LAD, vol. 36, 11.11.54, cc. 2594–6.

29

THE ECONOMY:
WORKING WITH THE FEDERAL GOVERNMENT

'The state finances were not based on the number of people living in each area but on the amount of money spent in the past on those particular services.'

Garfield Todd

Garfield considered that his only hope of 'introducing necessary but unpopular change was to make an outstanding success of the economy'.[1] But there were almost insurmountable difficulties with the economy. Becoming a part of a federation of states seriously circumscribed Southern Rhodesia's freedom of financial action. Its proportion of federal revenues was set by the Fiscal Commission at 13 per cent in 1952 – before the extent of its responsibilities had even been determined – and the Commission, Cyril Hatty told the cabinet in 1955,'appeared to proceed on the basis of inadequate logic and inaccurate arithmetic'.[2] The Government's ability to raise money locally was also severely limited. Furthermore, any proposal to raise money overseas had to go through the Federal Loans Council. To compound the Government's difficulties, again in Hatty's crisp tones, 'the Federal Government did not co-operate'.[3]

The balancing act was to counter the present difficult situation and at the same time provide for the economic development which alone would make possible the advancement of the African people. Garfield, Hatty and Ellman-Brown worked closely together on the economy – in some ways they 'really ran the country from the point of view of practical affairs'.

---

1 GT, Foreword to Holderness, 1985, p. 3.
2 Memo, SRC(55)144, 21.7.55, File S.3242/4 f. 6, NAZ.
3 Interview, C. J. Hatty, 6.7.97.

The Economy: Working with the Federal Government

Holderness writes: 'The first problem was a shortage of capital ... A lot of capital was locked up in government-owned enterprises like the Iron and Steel Commission [RISCOM] and Triangle Sugar Estates and the Central Mechanical Equipment Department.'[4] If these organisations could be put into order and taken over by private enterprise, some vital capital would be freed.

A short strike at the RISCOM steelworks near Gwelo in January 1954 had highlighted some of the problems there – and brought a blistering report from the Assistant Native Commissioner at Que Que: 'Bad organisation ... the appointment of a resident General Manager ... imperative and urgent necessity ... I do not think the management ... fully realise the seriousness of last Saturday's trouble – anything could have happened and the police would have been powerless to control such a large mob had it got out of hand.'[5]

Ellman-Brown set up a Commission of Inquiry to examine the whole future of the steel industry in Southern Rhodesia. Its report concluded that private enterprise might be interested in acquiring the works if they were put on a proper basis, but it would probably take four to five years to achieve this.[6] 'These were terrific days', Hatty said in an interview in 1994, 'because we were having to battle to get things going. In 1955 Geoff and I went overseas and we saw various people, heads of concerns that were already in the country ... we tried to turn RISCOM to RISCO ... Government had to take the initiative in industrial development at this stage.'[7]

By the end of 1954, the Southern Rhodesia cabinet was getting impatient at the Federal Government's attitude and lack of energy and action. The Federal Constitution provided for the establishment of an Economic Planning Council, but, in spite of constant pressure from the Southern Rhodesia Government, the Federal cabinet was so determined not to implement this provision that the Council only came into being after Garfield left office.

***

Immigration, a Federal responsibility, soon became an area of disagreement with the Federal Government. Garfield wanted to see more immigrants coming into Southern Rhodesia, as only by this means could the country's vital industrial growth be assured. In his end-of-session statement in October 1953, he referred to the importance of immigration, primarily from Britain. He was opposed to assisted passages and the 'new Australians' mass immigration. 'My own feeling

---

4   Holderness, 1985, p. 140.
5   INV.4.1.53 (no. 548/54) dated 23.1.54, Labour Dept files, Box 100486, Record Office, NAZ.
6   Cabinet Memorandum, SRC(54)159, 28.6.54, File S.3242/10, NAZ.
7   C. J. Hatty/SP, interviews for this book.

is not that we should spend large sums of money to get people here, but rather to find money for the development of Kariba and Kafue ... and the expansion of the Electricity Supply Commission ... If we can get the money here we have got to get the people here to spend the money. The crux of the matter was to raise capital, both for the government and private enterprise.'[8]

'The Federal Government's performance was depressing from the start,' wrote Hardwicke Holderness in August 1963.[9] 'The key to the situation, for both the Federation and Southern Rhodesia, lay in Southern Rhodesia. The new Southern Rhodesia Parliament seemed more vigorous than the last. And the progressives seemed to be making headway.'

***

One of the first decisions the Federal Government had to make was where to establish the Federal capital. During the early months of Federation, when government departments were being set up, it made sense for it to be in Salisbury alongside the Southern Rhodesian Government. There were many who thought that for political reasons the Federal capital should be located in Northern Rhodesia – Livingstone and Lusaka were mentioned – but senior civil servants quietly but firmly vetoed the idea, no doubt with the tacit encouragement of everybody else concerned with the Federal Government and the Federal Assembly. The Federal cabinet decided that a purpose-built capital should be established at Warren Hills, a pleasant wooded area outside Salisbury, and that the Government would meantime remain in Salisbury. Inevitably, the Warren Hills site was found to be far too costly to develop – and the Federal Government made its politically disastrous decision to remain in Salisbury.

***

By the end of 1954, the Southern Rhodesia cabinet was getting impatient at the Federal Government's lack of energy and action. At the beginning of 1955, Southern Rhodesia was forced to cut back on expenditure, mainly because of shortfalls in funds coming into the Federal purse. One piece of good news, however, was the appointment of an immigration attaché in London. By October, the Federal Government had made a complete volte-face, intending to 'obtain the maximum number' of 'desirable new Rhodesians that can beneficially be absorbed in the Federal economy'.[10]

Garfield was well aware of the sensitivities of the Federal Government; but, as

---

8   GT, Inauguration of the Methodist Men's Fellowship in Bulawayo, *Rhodesia Herald*, 5.3.54.
9   *Central African Examiner*, vol. 7, no. 3, August 1963.
10 Memo, SRC(55)203, 24.10.55, ff. 27–9, 32, File S.3242/15, NAZ.

he wrote in an article in September 1955, 'we are all citizens of the Federation and what I say "federally" in this article is said because of my rights as a Federal citizen'.[11] Evidence of the mounting frustration of Garfield, Hatty and Ellman-Brown with 'the slow way in which the Federal Government people were moving on certain economic issues'[12] came in a speech Garfield made to a URP audience in Umtali on 4 November. He knew he would cause controversy but took comfort from the knowledge that Hatty and Ellman-Brown were fully in agreement that things were seriously wrong, and that he must speak out.

Garfield said the Federal Government had 'achieved much in its two years in office ... We recognise our enormous debt to Lord Malvern ... Since the work of the territorial administrations was conditioned by the success or lack of success of the Federal Government ... a responsible territorial leader could not keep silent if he felt that the development of his own country was being threatened by the action or inaction of the Federal Government.' Three main things threatened the future: the first was 'our inability to raise the funds reasonably required to develop our greatest potential – the African population'.[13] The second was the danger of extremists of both races working to subvert the constitution. The third was 'the difficult period the Federal Government is experiencing. This is a matter of the very greatest importance to us all ... there are a number of most vital matters which are not being tackled with the imagination, efficiency and determination which we must demand of our Federal Government. I must point out that liberal forces in this Federation are being divided in their loyalties – not on the grounds of their liberal beliefs but because of a lack of cohesion and efficiency within the Federal Government ... there is talk of another party with the same ideas as ourselves. The only difference between this party and the Federal Party would be that they would be dynamic and energetic, but I believe that changes can be made in the Federal Party.'[14] Three days later, the *Rhodesia Herald* reported: 'a group of business and professional people in Salisbury is interested in trying to form a new political party ... to be run on progressive lines ...' to challenge the Federal Party.[15]

Garfield's speech created a storm of discussion and criticism. He responded to the criticism by saying that his speech was not motivated by political expediency; strong action must be taken, and taken now; and, as far as 'another party' was

---

11 GT, 'What we do now will determine our path later', in *Rhodesian Graphic*, September 1955.
12 A. D. H. Lloyd, Oral LL.2, NAZ.
13 *Rhodesia Herald*, 5.11.55.
14 Ibid.
15 *Rhodesia Herald*, 8.11.55.

concerned, 'it is impossible to divide up the people in the Federation into two groups of that kind ... That is why I wanted the Federal Government to put its house in order – so as to make it possible to keep all these people behind the Federal Party.'[16]

Garfield's speech was important in more ways than one: it not unnaturally aroused the anger of the Federal Government; it fostered an immovable suspicion in Welensky that Garfield had Federal ambitions; it alienated the Federal Party; and it upset a section of his own party whose esteem for Lord Malvern made them resent any criticism of him, particularly when the Federal Prime Minister was out of the country (a point that had not occurred to Garfield). But it was gratifying – and surprising – for Garfield to receive approval in the *Rhodesia Herald* editorial the next day: 'It was one of the most outspoken political statements of recent years and required courage to make it, which is a measure of the importance which Southern Rhodesia's Prime Minister attaches to the subject with which he dealt. It can be put in a sentence as the need for a more dynamic or energetic approach to affairs by the Federal Government and the Federal Party.'[17]

David M. Cole, a friend of Welensky's, writing in the 'Politics and People' column of the *Sunday Mail*, commented: 'In bringing these points out into the open [Todd] did the country a service'.[18]

***

The Federal Government's decision to site its capital in Salisbury meant that Southern Rhodesia now had to decide where its own capital should be established. Garfield's preference was for Bulawayo, failing which Gwelo. A Select Committee was set up to examine all the facts and report, but an unsatisfactory Committee produced an unsatisfactory report, so the Government appointed a Commission of Inquiry. The terms of reference were to ascertain 'whether it will be in the interests of the colony of Southern Rhodesia and of the Federation ... and its constituent territories that the capital of Southern Rhodesia should be in some place other than Salisbury and if so, which place'.[19]

The Commission's Report concluded that 'The advantages of keeping the capital in Salisbury outweigh the advantages to be gained by a move regardless of the consideration of cost'.[20] MPs from Matabeleland and the Midlands were furious – and, during a bad-tempered debate, allegations and accusations of

---

16   *Rhodesia Herald*, 10.11.55.
17   *Rhodesia Herald*, 8.11.55.
18   *Sunday Mail*, 13.11.55.
19   21.6.55, Department of Labour Files, Box 69829, Records Centre, NAZ.
20   Report, 28.9.55, para. 45(b), ibid.

less-than-honourable conduct were bandied across the floor of the House. When Garfield summed up the debate, he concluded by saying: 'we have the advice and judgment of three men who ... have the quality of being disinterested, which is one that none of us can have'.[21] Fletcher, Hatty and five URP MPs from Matabeleland voted with the opposition against the recommendation.

---

21 LAD, vol. 37, 2.12.55, cc. 2086–91.

30

THE DAM CONTROVERSY: KARIBA VS KAFUE

'So, Kariba is not a dream after all.'

Monsieur André Coyne, consulting engineer

Jimmy Savory of the Irrigation Department was one of the first civil servants whom the Todds had met after their arrival in Southern Rhodesia. Garfield says in his Oral Archive: 'He had done a survey of the Zambezi Escarpment and recognized the fantastic possibility of Kariba without knowing more than that it could take an ocean of water.'[1] A dam at Kariba had been Savory's dream for years, but engineers and mining experts attached to the copper industry in Northern Rhodesia favoured a dam on the Kafue River, a major tributary of the Zambezi, which, smaller and less costly than Kariba, could be completed more quickly.

'Nothing much happened with the Kariba dam scheme until about 1953–4', Jimmy Savory writes, 'when the matter of the supply of further electrical power not only to Southern Rhodesia but to Northern Rhodesia as well became urgent. At that time there was a considerable body of opinion in the northern territory in favour of a scheme on the Kafue river ... We of course were in favour of the Kariba scheme, and fortunately we were in a very strong position because our Department ... had for many years taken all available recordings both on the Zambezi river and the Kafue river.'[2]

In August 1953, Sir Godfrey Huggins, at this time Prime Minister-designate of the Federation, agreed to support the Northern Rhodesia Government in building Kafue, but on certain conditions regarding the sourcing of finance, and with assurances that the Kafue scheme 'could be constructed within the amount

---

1 Oral TO.1, NAZ.
2 Savory, 1984, p. 105.

of £31 million proposed'.³ Southern Rhodesia, however, did not consider that that scheme alone would provide adequately for all its requirements. When the Federal Government took over responsibility for hydroelectric schemes, it confirmed the decision to go ahead with Kafue. But this decision did not stifle debate. The difficulty for the Southern Rhodesia Government lay in the fact that hydroelectric schemes were a Federal responsibility and, technically, the subject of Kariba should not even be discussed in the Territorial Parliament. Garfield would change that. In Parliament on 6 May 1954, he was asked by several MPs to clarify the situation. He replied that an adequate supply of cheap power was more important than the question of which scheme should be built first. 'The availability of money is perhaps the most important factor and we do know that Kariba will take a great deal more money to build than Kafue ... I am given to understand that when the matter goes before the financial experts it will go before them not as the Kafue scheme only but the two schemes will be placed before them and the recommendations of experts on the electrical side will also be taken into consideration.

'If it is possible at all to find the money, it is in the best interests of the Federation to go ahead with the larger scheme. The first stage of Kariba is expensive but after that the succeeding stages are less expensive. That is because in the first stage you have to build the dam ... We feel, if it is at all possible, that the Kariba project should go forward and we shall continue to make representation along those lines.'⁴

This impromptu statement 'unleashed a torrent of trouble for all of us', Welensky told a friend.⁵ He promptly refuted what Garfield had said. The *Rhodesia Herald* the same day took Garfield to task for speaking on a Federal matter. But Garfield's outspokenness found favour with the editor of *The Chronicle*: 'Mr Todd spoke of new facts and figures of which the Federal Government was, according to Sir Roy Welensky, unaware – is still unaware – when the decision to back Kafue was taken.'⁶

Garfield and Jimmy Savory, now Acting Director of the Irrigation Department, remained convinced that Kariba was the right project to start on – all that had to be done now was to find the exact spot for the dam wall. 'One day,' Garfield recalled, 'Jimmy Savory came in and said "We have found the rock!" This was "sound rock at river bed level ... the sub-stratum being almost as sound as

---

3   Malvern's Statement on Hydro-Electric projects, 1.3.55, File F/164/728, NAZ.
4   LAD, vol. 35, 6.5.54, cc. 867–9.
5   RW/J. Wallace, 1954, File 679/6, Welensky Papers, Bodleian Library.
6   *The Chronicle*, 11.5.54.

good granite. Under the river bed itself the rock is excellent to a great depth."[7] "So what are we going to do?" asked Jimmy. "Are we going to try to go ahead with it?" And I said, "I am not going to have a cabinet meeting until Tuesday ..." "You mean you could let us know by next Tuesday? I thought it would be months."'

On Tuesday 14 May, the cabinet duly met and had before it a memorandum[8] referring to a report of 8 May from Savory which advised that the analysis of the construction requirements of the Kariba project had been completed.[9] These included 'aerial, ground and soil surveys; drilling, hydrological installation, international agreement, road access, rail construction, housing, consultants, telephone, quarry, sand tunnels, site excavation, coffer dams, concreting of dam, water storage basin, removal of natives, excavation of power house foundations, power houses, water transport equipment, steel assembly plant, barometer demarcation, fish ladder ...'

The Territorial Prime Minister's intervention in the great dam debate was 'either a courageous attempt to prevent a major blunder being effected or it is parochialism of the worst sort', observed one politician.[10]

On 28 June, Huggins announced that, since the debate in the Federal Parliament early in March, 'the information with regard to both Kafue and Kariba has altered very materially'.[11] Later, the French firm of Duffaut, Tisne and Misson was appointed. André Coyne was invited to 'associate himself with them ... as one of the world's greatest experts on this subject'.[12] A mission from the International Bank (to whom the Federation would look for finance) was invited to investigate the general economic and financial position of the Federation.

During the Southern Rhodesian Parliament's Budget session, Savory comes back into the story: 'I happened to be in the House when the Department of Irrigation estimates were due to come up. We did not have provision for any work at Kariba, but there was provision on a miscellaneous vote for certain expenditure there. Shortly before this was to come up ... the then Prime Minister, Mr Garfield Todd, came over to me where I was sitting in the Civil Servants' seats behind the Speaker and asked: "what really is the position regarding

---

7   *The Kariba Project*, Federal Government Publication, 1956, Ref. FG-P over POW, NAZ.
8   SRC(54)114.
9   Ref. 293/43/6 of 11.5.54.
10 A. E. P. Robinson/Welensky, 21.6.54, File 633/1, Welensky Papers, Bodleian Library.
11 *Rhodesia Herald*, 29.6.54.
12 Huggins' Statement, 1.3.55.

Kariba?" I was able to tell him that only the previous night we had completed our calculations and that in our opinion a scheme could be built at Kariba very much larger than anything at Kafue, and that it would take at most only a year longer to do. Mr Todd said, "Thank you very much, that's exactly what I was hoping to hear.""[13]

Garfield subsequently saw Huggins, and later remembered that Huggins 'was very quiet. Then he said, "well, Kariba is the biggest thing that I will be doing of that nature during my time and I would be determined not to make a mistake".' By Christmas the suspense was over: 'the Kariba project should be started first'.[14] No final decision could be made by the Federal Government until a clear picture of the financing of the scheme was available. And Welensky still backed Kafue.

On 1 March 1955, Sir Godfrey Huggins became Viscount Malvern, and on that day he announced the Federal Government's decision in favour of Kariba. He made an exhaustive statement to the Federal Assembly on the long-drawn-out history of the investigations that had preceded that decision. The Federal Government's decision was subject to only two conditions: André Coyne must give his final approval, and the International Bank's Economic Mission must also approve. How Coyne gave his final approval is told by Jimmy Savory: 'We took M: Coyne and company down our track along the foot of the gorge next to the water, and showed them the proposed site from there first. Then we drove them up the face of the hills at a point where a Land Rover could get up, and from there walked back to a point immediately over the site. We had marked this on both banks with whitewash at various points to show heights and so on. Coyne spent a long time up there asking many questions, and then we started walking back to the Land Rover … he turned to me and said: "So, Kariba is not a dream after all" … After further inspection the following day, M: Coyne became extremely enthusiastic about the Kariba site and left us in no doubt as to his opinion.'[15]

Even before the financial arrangements had been completed, the Federal Prime Minister authorised preliminary works to be started at Kariba. The site access roads gave the Roads Department many difficulties. A road 'had to be created to go right down the escarpment' capable of taking huge loads on very large vehicles. 'They got really stuck at one area and cast around for help. This came from Jimmy Savory. He found a way through the difficult part, simply

---

13   Savory, 1984, p. 105.
14   Hydro-Electric Working Party Conclusions and Recommendations, File F/170/3, 13.12.54, Federal Government files, NAZ.
15   Savory, 1984, p. 107.

by observing the route taken through there by the elephants – so he designed a route on the elephant trail.'[16]

A banner headline in the *Rhodesia Herald* on 24 April 1956 read: 'WORLD BANK BACKS KARIBA: All funds now assured.' On 17 May 1960, the Queen Mother opened the Kariba dam, and among the proudest of the spectators were Garfield Todd and Jimmy Savory (who was awarded the OBE in the 1960 New Year's Honours List).

One of the most serious consequences of the Kariba decision was the future of the Africans living in the vast areas of Southern and Northern Rhodesia which would be flooded. There was controversy about displacing more than 50,000 Batonka people from their homes and religious sites. On 9 August 1956, Garfield said in Parliament: 'It is a very great sadness to the Government to have to move them from that area, although in actual fact in many ways they will now be brought into contact with facilities and assistance which they have not enjoyed in past days ... there have been no schools, no stores, no clinics, but now that roads are being opened, water points established, land development officers appointed, these people will live in areas, more or less of their own choosing, where they will be able to enjoy a better life than they have been accustomed to in the Zambezi Valley. Nevertheless, it is not a pleasant thing to move tribes from their hereditary area.'[17]

---

16 Sir Cyril Hatty, interviews for this book, TPPC.
17 LAD, vol. 39, 9.8.56, c. 811.

31

PAUSE FOR THOUGHT:
VISIT TO THE UK, 1954

'The outlook was promising.'

Sir Robert Tredgold, *The Rhodesia that was My Life* (1968)

In his autobiography, Sir Robert Tredgold has this to say about Garfield's impact on the country in the early years of his administration: his 'ability and manifest sincerity and the frank manner in which he handled even the most controversial issues had allayed the doubts'.[1]

For his part, Garfield had learned a lot – from the strikes, from working with the Federal Government, and from a Commonwealth Parliamentary Association visit to Kenya. In November 1954, the new Southern Rhodesia Governor, Admiral Sir Peveril William-Powlett, arrived to take up his duties. In spite of having little political experience, Sir Peveril proved himself to be understanding of Garfield's hopes for the country – and very supportive in times of difficulty. The new Governor and Lady William-Powlett received early evidence of the divided society into which they had come: European scouts were drawn up on the long Bulawayo railway platform; African scouts were outside the station. The picture presented by Southern Rhodesia at the end of 1954 and in the early part of 1955 was observed and commented on by many people. The journalist and historian Lawrence Vambe wrote about the way many white newcomers to the Colony attempted to break down the colour barrier: 'Americans did the most to make partnership a practical reality'.[2] John Parker captures perfectly the years immediately after Garfield became Prime Minister: 'an exciting time. Rhodesia, tucked away behind its barriers of time and distance for so long, was

---

1 Tredgold, 1968, pp. 225–6.
2 Vambe, 1976, p. 257.

brimming over with activity. The mood was expansion. Capital and people were flooding in, bringing with them new outlooks and novel ideas. For ten years, Salisbury ... became the cosmopolitan capital of Africa south of the Sahara. It is strange now to recall how real it all was, when so much of it has turned out to be illusion.'[3]

Garfield reviewed the year at the Gatooma St Andrew's Night Banquet. After speaking about the great opportunities opening up in Central Africa, he returned to his central belief – the need for racial partnership and a better life for the African people: 'We are faced with a wakening African population ... [who] are now making demands for schooling which are too great to be met by the colony's available funds ... I believe that ... the African has it in him to progress in the field of industry and commerce to a far greater degree than is sometimes admitted.'[4]

The Federal Supreme Court was opened in 1955 by Lord Kilmuir, Great Britain's Lord Chancellor. Garfield writes in his draft autobiography of a disturbing conversation they had. Kilmuir 'had not been greatly impressed by some of our judges and he spoke to me at length about the desirability of making our conditions of service good enough to encourage outstanding men to join our bench. "The day could come", he warned, "when the future of your country may depend upon the quality of your judiciary." As I sat and listened to Lord Kilmuir, his warning seemed as unreal and outrageous as to suggest that a Prime Minister of Rhodesia might break his oath of allegiance and rebel against the Queen.'[5] Neither Kilmuir nor Garfield would have foreseen that day – or the day when a Southern Rhodesian judge would head a 'tribunal' to determine, in dubious circumstances, whether a former Prime Minister should continue to be held in solitary confinement without trial.

Despite complaints that nothing really significant had changed in Southern Rhodesia, there were small signs of improvement on the racial front: the formation of the Capricorn Africa Society, which boasted members such as Herbert Chitepo, Leopold Takawira, Nathan Shamuyarira, Lawrence Vambe and Enoch Dumbutshena, as well as liberal whites; and a multiracial club for men and women, the United Club, opened in Salisbury. The Cathedral Club at the Anglican cathedral was quietly welcoming young working people of all races to its Sunday evening social gatherings. But, apart from these and some private homes, there were few places, and few social occasions, where the races could mingle on equal terms.

---

3   Parker, 1972, p. 11.
4   27.11.54, MS.1083/1, Todd Papers, NAZ.
5   GT/A, 1973–4, Todd Papers, NAZ and TPPC.

Pause for Thought: Visit to the UK, 1954

As Garfield went into 1955, he recognised more and more clearly his basic dilemma: to make vitally necessary changes in the lives of the African people, with the acquiescence of his European electorate. In 1991, he told the producer of the New Zealand Television team making a documentary about the Todds: 'this was terribly frustrating. And also to suggest things that were just half what you wanted and so on. But you know, one thinks one's being wise ... I was not only going as carefully as I thought I could, but I was going far quicker than I could maintain.'[6]

Garfield was not and never would be wedded to any particular political principle, except democracy. He recognised that things were moving very fast in Central Africa – that 'native policy was a living and growing thing'. He repeatedly told large European audiences about the need to make the vision of a non-racial society work. In April 1955, he told a Conference of Rotarians of Southern Rhodesia in Salisbury: 'Governments can do very little about some of the most important things concerning race relations and especially ... the attitude of the peoples one to another. It is one thing to speak of the importance of mutual respect ... I believe the first step towards solving our problems in race relationship is a searching of our own hearts. It may be objected that I place too much responsibility ... on our own European peoples. That is where the responsibility must be placed. We came here to live among primitive peoples. We have changed their ways of living ... We have demanded something which is for their own good – that they should accept civilisation. We have brought them another religion. We have taught them new ways, we have brought them into industry and we must set the example in race relations ... Relations between the races are bedevilled by prejudice and fear and it is time that a little more ordinary human kindness was introduced.'[7]

An occasion of 'bedevilment' came during a visit to Salisbury by Sir Edmund Hillary and George Lowe, who had climbed Mount Everest in May 1953. They addressed a packed Salisbury cinema, and afterwards there was a reception for them at Northward. During the earlier part of the evening, the Indian High Commissioner telephoned Grace to ask when the party would be. 'Come with all the people from the lecture,' she replied. The High Commissioner said quietly: 'I will not be there: no Asians are allowed in the Palace Theatre.' 'Hillary telling the story of Everest and the Indian High Commissioner could not be there! I could not answer him because I felt so shocked.'

***

---

6   NZTV, Typescript l/V, 11.4.91.
7   *Rotarian*, 20.4.55, MS.1083/1, Todd Papers, NAZ.

Commonwealth Relations officials were surprised to find that a Commonwealth Prime Minister had never visited Britain, and in 1954 they arranged for the Todds to have a few weeks getting to know their motherland. It was also very important for Garfield to meet British officials, politicians and men of influence. He had serious matters to discuss with the Commonwealth Relations Office, finance companies and other bodies, principally the need to raise money for African housing.

George Addecott, of the Zambezi News Service in Salisbury, having observed Garfield from the press gallery for eight years, did his best for him, with this despatch to the *Daily Mail* in London: 'A zeal to turn Africans into good citizens dominates all Garfield Todd's thinking about race relations and guides his government's Native Policy: "we want to see that any millions we can get for Southern Rhodesia are spent in such a way that our Africans will not suffer a sense of frustration. I am genuinely interested in the policy of partnership between white and black ... There is a great urge for more education, better housing and health services. There will be some difficult periods to live through. But you cannot always run satisfactorily on the side of safety – you have got to take risks." London will like the look of this tall, suntanned man from the empire's wide-open spaces. ... There is a great deal of true modesty in his make-up; but no hint of doubt. He has the incisive manner of one who recognises what ought to be done and intends to see it through. This quality of concentrated moral purpose marks him as one of Africa's coming men.'[8]

The Todds enjoyed a good press in Britain. The *Manchester Guardian* wrote that Garfield Todd 'is immediately impressive ... and has a useful flow of language. The subject on which he is most eloquent is the need for native housing schemes to replace the slums and shanties that grow up so quickly in African towns. He is quite an expert on the practical side of building.'[9] The *Scotsman* wrote: 'an amazing and interesting person to meet ... he made it clear that he is both practical and idealistic regarding the future of his country. Great changes are taking place in Southern Rhodesia ... and Mr Todd views the future with optimism and enthusiasm.'[10]

An interesting comment was made in a New Zealand paper of 6 July: 'Mr Todd revealed himself at a Press Conference in London as a powerful personality imbued with the idealism – tempered with realism – which is so necessary in the present transitional state of African political development.'[11] That journalist,

---

8   19.6.54, File P.7, Box 167635, Record Office, NAZ.
9   *Manchester Guardian*, 1.7.54.
10 *The Scotsman*, 1.7.54.
11 File P.7, Box 167635, Record Office, NAZ.

and – later – the historian Robert Blake, captured Garfield's consistent approach to the politics of his country: 'idealism – tempered with realism'.

A visit to Edinburgh was almost a 'homecoming' for Garfield and Grace. The highlight of their visit north of the Border was a state dinner given for them in the Lower Banqueting Hall in Edinburgh Castle. On their return to London, Garfield had further talks with Lord Swinton, R. A. Butler, the Chancellor of the Exchequer, and officials from their departments. But little concrete assistance was forthcoming.

From beginning to end, the visit was a great success (except in the raising of money for Southern Rhodesia), leading both the Todds to a lifelong love for the United Kingdom, and particularly London and Edinburgh. To people of the Todds' intelligence, knowledge and wide interests who, well-read though Grace might be, had lived for over 40 years in very restricted societies, this sudden broadening of their horizons was intoxicating. The contact with older cultures and societies, with people of outstanding experience and ability, was a revelation. Garfield in particular would never thereafter lose the appetite for such encounters.

32

AFRICAN AFFAIRS (I)

'There was not the land for everyone.'

R. M. Davies, Director of African Agriculture

The Native Land Husbandry Act (1951)

As a subject for study, historical research and academic theses, the Native Land Husbandry Act of 1951 presents a well-tilled – even an exhausted – field; and this is not the place for yet another lengthy consideration of its intentions, merits and failures. The Act had been designed to improve African agricultural practices and gradually to substitute individual, freehold tenure for communal ownership of land in the reserves.

In 1951, Garfield had said: 'If we opened up the whole country we would put off this day for twenty years perhaps'. He saw all too clearly the defects of the controversial Act and deplored instances of its maladministration, but he had seen enough of soil erosion, over-grazing and the impoverishment of the land by over-population in the Lundi Reserve to recognise the necessity of pressing ahead with the implementation of the Act. As he told the Gatooma St Andrew's Night Banquet in November 1954: 'peasant farming is certainly not our answer and it is up to us to think in terms which have some relation to the vast needs of our population'.[1]

The Act was implemented in a few areas 'to test out techniques and find the best way of setting about applying the Act', wrote the Assistant Director of the Native Agriculture Department. 'The reaction of the people was so encouraging that it was then decided to speed up the implementation.'[2] The official attitude

---
1   27.11.54, MS.1083/1, Todd Papers, NAZ.
2   D. Robinson, *Concord*, July 1956, vol. 1, no. 8.

to the Act continued to be enthusiastic. The head of the Department of African Agriculture, Mr R. M. Davies, described it as 'The finest Act that had ever been put on the Statute Book in Rhodesia.'[3]

Implementation, however, was proceeding at a pace which would take many years to complete, so in 1955 it was decided to speed it up. One of the factors that influenced Garfield in favour of the Land Husbandry Act was that possession of individual title deeds would enable farmers to obtain loans to help them develop their land. In Parliament in July 1955, he told MPs that 'if the government does not do something, and if it does not do it quickly, the position in the rural areas will be past remedy'.[4]

In August 1955, the *Bantu Mirror* had sounded a negative note when it described the spiritual importance of the reserve: to the African it was 'a sanctuary. This idea of common ownership of land cemented tribal bonds and loyalty.'[5] But, the following year, the paper gave the Government its support: 'The African of Southern Rhodesia has time and again shown that he is alive to changing conditions: for that reason he has accepted progressive reforms readily. The Land Husbandry Act which, among other things, had the effect of passing the power over land from the chief to the individual, was a revolutionary piece of legislation but the opposition against it was not as strong as one would have expected in the circumstances.'[6] But the groundswell of African antagonism gathered pace; George Nyandoro, a founder of the Southern Rhodesia ANC, in 1957 famously said: 'The Land Husbandry Act is the best recruiter Congress ever had.'[7]

February 1958 saw Garfield abruptly removed from office, but his views on the real usefulness of the Land Husbandry Act remained unchanged. Surprisingly, he found support in an editorial in the *African Daily News* of 9 September that year: 'The Land Husbandry Act is intended to give permanent holdings to rural Africans, for which they can draw title deeds. When a man has a title for his land he is much more firmly rooted to that piece of ground than in a communal system ... But the principle of individual land holding which underlies the Act is unassailable and is accepted throughout the world.'[8] Nathan Shamuyarira has written: 'Africans detested the harsh authoritarian manner'

---

3   R. M. Davies/SP, interview for this book.
4   LAD, vol. 37, 21.7.55, c. 1047.
5   *Bantu Mirror*, 15.8.55.
6   *Bantu Mirror*, 16.6.56.
7   Quoted in Sanger, 1960, p. 28.
8   *African Daily News*, 13.9.58.

in which officials threw their weight about in executing the Act.[9] Michael M. Hove, former FMP and Parliamentary Secretary, agreed. He said in 1993: 'the legislation was not too bad but the administration was bad'.[10] The anecdotal evidence of harsh decisions, of people being moved not just once but twice or even three times, of unsympathetic and bureaucratic officialdom, is too great to discount.

Lawrence Vambe, one-time editor-in-chief of African Newspapers Ltd, recalled that the opposition to the NLHA was 'bitter and sustained'.[11] Forty years later, he said: 'It was a good thing because it was intended to encourage good husbandry and ensure the proper utilisation of the soil. But it was introduced at the wrong time (1951) and by the wrong government ... We were deeply suspicious and in no mind to look at the positive side. Unfortunately, Todd inherited that kind of thing as PM.'[12]

Garfield decided that on balance the Act was 'sensible and necessary' – and trusted that, with time on his side and the provision of security of tenure in the towns, the gamble would come off. He made a start in the urban areas – but time was not on his side. Later, he realised 'how little I had understood the situation: the truth about the depth of the relationship of the African and his land ... I suppose I am ignorant regarding the Rhodesian background. It was there when we came, the population was less than a million and there was so much land that it seemed of little consequence ... only visionaries like White and Cripps[13] recognised the truth.'[14] There was not the land for everyone.

'The government', write Birmingham and Ranger, intended 'to create a contented and prosperous peasantry.'[15] Instead, it 'created a landless class harbouring a great deal of ill-will towards the agents of government'.[16]

African urban housing

After the Second World War, Southern Rhodesia's industrialisation meant that tens of thousands of Africans moved from their traditional homes in the rural areas into urban settlements around cities and towns where they had no freehold rights and rarely any decent rented accommodation, and where their

9   Shamuyarira, 1965, p. 91.
10 Interview, 26.7.93.
11 Oral 233, NAZ.
12 Interview, 13.7.93.
13 Reverend John White, Methodist missionary; Reverend Arthur Shearly Cripps, Anglican missionary.
14 GT/SP, 25.6.2002.
15 Birmingham and Ranger, 1983, p. 366.
16 Ibid., p. 372.

living conditions were atrocious. By 1953, it was estimated that there were 100,000 Africans living in townships outside Salisbury and a similar number in Bulawayo. The 1952 Report of the Kerr Commission into African Education in Southern Rhodesia commented on the situation: 'These conditions if they persist will make the essential task of character formation of African children in urban areas well-nigh impossible.'[17]

Shortly after taking office, Garfield told the Bulawayo Chamber of Industries: 'If you are going to take natives out of the reserves you must be prepared to give them satisfactory tenure of land in our industrial areas.'[18]

Funds to build African housing was one of Garfield's most important objectives when he went to Britain in 1954. The immediate housing needs – a backlog of many years' neglect – were 19,000 single and 7,500 married quarters, which would cost £6m over the next three years. After that, the annual increase would be for 15,000 units at an annual cost of £2.5m, which the Government would need to fund locally. The Colony's share of the Federal Loan Funds would not be sufficient to enable the Southern Rhodesia Government to give extra money to the Municipalities to build the houses. Garfield explained to officials at the CRO that his Government 'had to make proper provision for urban African communities on a considerable scale. It was the aim of his Government to give freehold tenure in certain urban areas … Experience elsewhere, particularly in Johannesburg and Nairobi, had shown that if this problem were neglected it brought as a consequence political and social unrest on such a scale that enormous sums had to be spent by Government first on quelling the unrest and then on providing a remedy.'[19]

Garfield's conversations in London with Lord Reith, chairman of the Colonial Development Corporation, went well. He reported to cabinet on his return to Salisbury: 'It had then been clearly stated by Lord Reith at the conclusion of the meeting that the prime minister could count on the unanimous decision of the Board to give a loan of six million pounds payable over a period of, say, three years. Lord Reith, moreover, had expressed no objection whatsoever to news of this intention being made public which in fact had been done in London. There was, however, some technical difficulty regarding the ability of the Board to make a loan to a self-governing colony but … the legal officers of the Corporation were satisfied that it would be in order for the CDC to make a loan direct to the Southern Rhodesia Government.'[20]

---

17   Quoted by Todd, LAD, vol. 33, 9.7.52, c. 3621.
18   *The Chronicle*, 19.11.53.
19   CRO meeting, 29.6.54, MS.390/1/6, Todd Papers, NAZ.
20   Cabinet meeting 42, 22.7.54, MS.1086/2/2, Todd Papers, NAZ.

Garfield had seen Swinton, who 'expressed himself as satisfied with their [the CDC's] decision. Further, he had been assured by the CDC that any loan made by them did not come within the purview of the Capital Issues Committee of the [HM] Treasury' and, on that basis, he assumed 'that the loan would not need to be raised with the sanction of the Federal Loan Council'.[21]

On 5 October, Garfield had to tell his colleagues that 'he had now been informed ... [by] the Secretary of State for Commonwealth Relations that there was now only a prospect of the CDC being able to grant a loan of £1m only almost as a token'.[22] Lord Reith had been misled about the Corporation's ability to make £6m available to Southern Rhodesia – a self-governing Colony which was not part of the Colonial Office's jurisdiction. Garfield was shocked by the British Government's attitude to what he had assumed was a firm commitment by Reith and the CDC – he was still 'something of a political innocent' – and disappointed that all he could hope for was a fraction of what was needed and what, he thought, had been promised.

This was an occasion when Garfield's acknowledged lack of government experience at cabinet level put him at a considerable disadvantage when dealing with the British Government. His seven years on the backbenches had given him no knowledge of inter-governmental processes. The departure of so many senior civil servants to the Federal field had also left the Southern Rhodesian service short of the necessary expertise. A new Prime Minister, a new Cabinet Secretary, a new High Commissioner in London, were learning the hard way. Even the £1m was initially withheld but eventually found its way to Southern Rhodesia, giving the Federal Minister of Finance an opportunity to say that he managed to procure it in order to save Garfield Todd's face. Two small home-ownership schemes totalling 6,000 houses were launched in Salisbury and Bulawayo with that £1m, together with funds raised from other, local sources.

As increased land tenure for Africans in the urban areas was vital to the SR Government's hopes of reform of African land settlement, the inadequacy of HMG's response was a double blow. Garfield's failure to raise the money he knew was so desperately needed – and the manner of it – was a bruising and disillusioning experience for him. He had confidently expected HMG to understand that it would have been cheaper for them to help him build houses in 1954 than to wait a few years and put out the fires of inevitable discontent.

---

21   Ibid.
22   Cabinet meeting, 5.10.54, MS.1086/2/2, Todd Papers, NAZ.

African Affairs (I)

African education

One of Garfield's main aims in 1954 was an extension of the primary school system, which in turn meant the training of more teachers. Parliament grudged increased spending on African education, but on 1 July 1954 the Treasury Minister, Cyril Hatty, had announced a doubling of the Native Education budget and also the Government's intention to charge tuition fees in Government urban schools, in line with those already charged by missions in the rural areas. It was in an attempt to attract foreign capital for African Education as well as housing that Garfield's 1955 visit to the USA was planned. During his absence, the new Director of Native Education, Mr H. C. Finkle, with his deputy Mr C. S. 'Steve' Davies and their officials, worked on an ambitious scheme for a five-year expansion to be launched in March 1956.

In February 1956, Garfield appointed himself the first Minister of Native Education. He enjoyed working with his old friends, Finkle and Davies. Finkle's rather irreverent attitude is best illustrated by a telegram he sent to one of his inspectors: 'When commonsense conflicts with regulations, choose commonsense'.[23] On the day of his appointment, Garfield wrote to his old friend and mentor, A. R. Mather (now retired to the USA): 'This morning I took over the portfolio of Native Education, taking the department out of the arena of Native Affairs and the Secretary for Native Affairs ... I so clearly remember those first few months when you had a great deal to do with getting us going at Dadaya.'[24]

An editorial in the *Bantu Mirror* exclaimed at 'this great piece of news: the separation of African education and Native Affairs. Every African believes that Education is the only weapon he can use effectively in his desperate bid for advancement and to be of any use, that education should not be confined to a few who will almost invariably tend to use their influence for the cultivation of extreme nationalistic views but it should be so spread that the whole nation is composed of people with an average education.'[25]

Shortly after the establishment of the new Department, Garfield was invited to address the Harari African Cultural Association on the subject of his 1955 visit to the USA, and in 1991 described the occasion:[26] 'How free and easy things were! ... there was no security problem for a start, you never went round with policemen ... I went down with my wife ... and of course she was

---

23 P. Nathan/SP, n.d. but 1993, TPPC.
24 GT/A. R. Mather, 1.2.56, MS.1082/2/7, Todd Papers, NAZ.
25 *Bantu Mirror*, quoted in *The Chronicle*, 18.2.56.
26 Unpublished NZTV interview, 1991.

better known than me because she was known in education circles, and all the educated people became teachers ... There was a packed meeting, we had a very nice time. African votes of thanks were usually delightful speeches. Samkange[27] gave the vote of thanks, and when he had done so, added thanks for making African education a division of its own, with the PM as Minister of African Education, finishing: "With all his experience in African education, no doubt there'll be problems which he may not himself be able to solve, and we would like to ask him if on an occasion like that, he would not turn to his cabinet, but he would ask Mrs Todd."' This remained one of the proudest and happiest moments of the Todd 'partnership'.

To form the Department of African Education was one thing; to do what had to be done was another; but to find the money to do it was something else again – so Garfield doubled the Native Tax (all African men over sixteen paid an annual 'head' tax of £1). The ministers were horrified, foreseeing a riot or a revolution. Garfield said: 'There won't be a riot or a revolution. All the money that is collected in this £1 a head is going to be spent on forward moves in the education of the people. They will accept it. My ministers, who did not know the people as well as I did, not having been missionaries, did not really believe it, but it did not stop me doing it and I don't know of any outcry from the people ... It was an outrageous thing to do, and quite unjust in one way, but it was the only way I could get the money.'

Garfield prepared the public by writing three articles for the *Rhodesia Herald*. In the first one, on 13 March, he used a phrase which gained some notoriety: 'What is demanded of us together is to co-operate courageously and generously with the inevitable, so that the changes that are rapidly occurring will take place in an atmosphere of growing confidence and goodwill ... The danger is not met by the preaching of equality, or integration, or pleading for a universal franchise, but in the provision of education, in the establishment of new values ... This is the challenge which faces us, which confronts Government itself, but it cannot be successfully met without the full co-operation of our African people themselves.'[28]

In his second article, on 14 March, Garfield stated that education was 'the key to the future of African progress', and set out the financial difficulties. The headline to his third article, on 15 March, was: 'The choice before us today is orderly progress or stagnation'. He warned that if schools were not provided 'then extra police and prisons will certainly have to be', and that the entire

---

27 Stanlake Samkange, who went on to become Professor of African American Studies at North-Eastern University, Boston.
28 *Rhodesia Herald*, 13.3.56.

education system was in danger of being 'bogged down' with 300,000 children in lower primary classes, and only 5,000 or 6,000 emerging from Standard VI each year.[29]

***

Lawrence Vambe told the Asian Adult Education Institute: 'the decision of the Southern Rhodesia government to give security of tenure in the towns ... has had a tremendous impact on urban African public opinion ... The change in Government policy, coupled with other schemes such as the five-year education plan, have had a tonic effect on Africans.'[30] And, years later, he wrote: 'It was largely through mission education that we became aware of ourselves as part of the family of man and acquired the political sophistication necessary for our struggle.'[31]

---

29 *Rhodesia Herald*, 15.3.56.
30 *Rhodesia Herald*, 9.8.56.
31 Vambe, 1972, p. 234.

33

VISIT TO THE USA AND CANADA, 1955

*'It is amazing to witness the interest and understanding which
Mr Todd aroused.'*

Unnamed US Information Agency official in charge of policy
and program in Africa

In its need to obtain funds for development, the Southern Rhodesia Government arranged a visit to the USA for Garfield in July and August 1955. The American Consul-General in Salisbury, Mr Loyd V. Steere, was also anxious that Garfield should go there, and readily opened doors for him in Washington.

Garfield's visit to the USA was a joy to him and a success in almost every way. Without any previous connections to the country, he discovered an affinity with the people; the range of technological achievements (and the cars) excited him; and the widening of his horizons was almost stunning. Garfield would always be at home with 'American hustle and bustle', not very different from his own. His letters shimmer with the excitement and novelty of so much he is seeing and experiencing, and wonder at the kindness and friendliness of the people he meets. Garfield could indulge his love of films and theatre – and he never failed to bring home a long-playing record of the latest musical.

He also found great interest in the Federation and Southern Rhodesia and a degree of knowledge of their affairs which astonished him. But in spite of the interest and concern for the Federation and its problems in government, commerce, industry, philanthropic institutions – in spite of numerous well-received media interviews – not one cent in funding was forthcoming.

Garfield was a speaker at a Georgetown University Forum in Washington on 'Federation, Colonialism and Race in Central Africa'. At the end, he was asked: would the ultimate result of his policies be 'that finally the white man will lose political control in Africa? Would he be prepared to face that?' Garfield's reply was unequivocal: 'I am. I believe that we are laying now the foundations of co-operation and I am not concerned so much whether it is a black man or a white man who is in control as that it is civilised. Christian people who have got the right motives and who will run the country well. There are at least I think 30% of our people in Southern Rhodesia, Europeans, who would violently disagree with me on that statement.'[1]

In the USA, Garfield made private visits to some of the American Church of Christ (Disciples) churches and universities – notably Butler University in Indianapolis, where he received an honorary degree.

***

Canada was the next stop. Garfield attracted a great deal of media attention there. After he visited Ottawa, the influential *Toronto Globe and Mail* carried a report of his address to the Canadian Institute of International Affairs: 'The missionary and the politician are harmoniously blended in the vigorous personality of Garfield Todd. His idealism stems from the conviction that the native population is capable of development if given a chance. He is realist enough to know that unless the enormous gap between the blacks and whites is narrowed the future will be empty for both blacks and whites. "Time is not on our side", he said.'[2]

On his way home, Garfield had a few days in London, where he saw politicians, bankers and officials – and met the new Secretary of State for Commonwealth Relations, Lord Home. He also addressed members of the *Round Table* editorial board: 'If we cannot discover how to live together in justice, money will not save Central Africa.'[3] He told the *British Weekly*: 'Unless a genuine multi-racial society is created, it is all of no use. We cannot diminish or remove certain social tensions by law – it must come by itself.' When asked how far his experience in the mission field contributed to his work now, Garfield replied: 'If I am of any use now it is because of my being on intimate terms with the Africans in my mission work.'[4]

Garfield had been invited to visit the Gold Coast by the Governor, Sir Charles Arden-Clarke, and he relished the opportunity to witness a country shrugging off colonialism and moving towards independence. Thirty years later, he told a Bulawayo audience: 'I was looking for ideas that might help my own government as I considered that the time had come to make vast

1   Georgetown University Forum, 14.8.55, MS.390/1/9, Todd Papers, NAZ.
2   *Toronto Globe and Mail*, 22.8.55, MS.396/1/4, Todd Papers, NAZ.
3   *East Africa and Rhodesia*, 15.9.55.
4   *British Weekly*, 22.9.55.

changes in our electoral laws in Southern Rhodesia.'⁵

In seven weeks, Garfield had travelled 23,600 miles; held 50 conferences with Government officials, industrialists, representatives of foundations and of commerce and industry; given 28 addresses and eleven radio talks; and made seven TV appearances. Opposition MP, Jack Keller, questioned the Prime Minister about his expenses; Garfield replied: '£1,402.17.1, of which £1,082.3.9 was chargeable to public funds'.⁶

---

5   25.7.85, 75th Anniversary of Milton High School, Bulawayo, MS.1083/4, Todd Papers, NAZ.
6   LAD, vol. 38, 20.11.55, cc. 1858–9.

34

1956: A Year of Crucial Importance

'The year 1956 must go down in the history of Zimbabwe as one of crucial importance.'

Lawrence Vambe

The year 1956 is the 'year of Suez' – of Colonel Nasser of Egypt and the nationalisation of the Suez Canal; of the ensuing war between Egypt and Britain, France and Israel; of the Hungarian uprising and its brutal suppression by the Soviet Union; and of a crackdown by the South African authorities on what it perceived as Communist sympathisers. The nationalism of Colonel Nasser gave strong impetus to nationalist movements throughout Africa – and in Britain, in Whitehall and Westminster, something akin to a revolution took place in her whole relationship with her colonies as she tried to readjust her world role, withdrawing from Empire into Europe.

***

By the end of 1955, Europeans in Southern Rhodesia had found their lives enhanced by Federation – without, apparently, having to pay the price they had steeled themselves to expect. The change in attitude from April 1953 was palpable. This was matched by 'the alarm and despondency which is already too apparent among the African people in the Federation', as Dr Andrew Doig of Nyasaland told the Federal Assembly.[1] That was not a happy place. Hardwicke Holderness found it 'a depressing debating chamber' except when Mr M. I. Wellington Chirwa (Nyasaland African Representative), Sir Roy Welensky or Sir John Moffat was addressing the House. And Mr Chirwa emerged as the ablest parliamentarian of them all. 'It was he who carried on the fight against

---

1 FAD, vol. 3, 16.3.55, cc. 3935–9.

Federation before the force of African nationalism had gathered strength.'²

A general review of the Federal Constitution was planned to take place between 1960 and 1963, but the desire for 'enhanced status' for the Federation soon began to take centre stage with the Federal Government, supported by the knowledge that the Gold Coast would become independent in 1957. By May 1956, Malvern was becoming very impatient with the British Government, writing to the Secretary for Commonwealth Relations, Lord Home, that 'the time has come when independent status should be given to the Federation'.³

Greenfield shared Welensky's deeply rooted dislike and mistrust of the British Government – and he would become increasingly bitter as the years went on. In a speech to the Ndola and District Caledonian Society Banquet on 30 November, he 'predicted a "long and bitter struggle" before the Federation advanced to recognised nationhood. But that advance ... "our kith and kin in the United Kingdom will never be able to stop"'.⁴

Garfield was 'not concerned so much with the metaphysical concept of a free and independent Federation' as he was 'with the security and welfare and advancement of the inhabitants of the Federation'.⁵ In 1985, when he was interviewed for the television series *End of Empire*, he spoke of the early agitation for constitutional reform: 'as soon as we started Federation came the call for Dominion Status in 1960, and the Africans felt the handcuffs were being put on them'.⁶

The October 1956 visit to the Federation by Lord Home and a Commonwealth Parliamentary Association delegation from the House of Commons did nothing to help inter-governmental relations. It came as a shock to Welensky and Huggins to find there was almost no difference between the views of the Conservative and Labour MPs on the question of African advancement. Europeans had always regarded the Conservative Party as their allies at Westminster.

Lord Malvern retired on 31 October 1956 amid outpourings of genuine affection and praise. The following day, the newspapers carried tributes to his long service to Southern Rhodesia and the Federation. The *Rhodesia Herald* quoted Garfield: '"Courage, straight-forwardness and plain speaking marked the man. But with this has gone deep human sympathy and understanding"... and after warm references to the various achievements of Lord Malvern, Mr Todd says, "We, the people of Southern Rhodesia, salute the man to whom we

---

2 'The Locust Years', *Central African Examiner*, August 1963, vol. 7, no. 3.
3 Malvern/Home, 10.5.56, File 196/3, Welensky Papers, Bodleian Library.
4 *Rhodesia Herald*, 1.12.56.
5 LAD, vol. 39, 9.8.56, c. 809.
6 Mss.Brit.Emp.1985, S.572/2, Bodleian Library.

owe our greatest debt.'"[7] 'There is no tribute adequate to the occasion ... for of all people, Southern Rhodesians are the most grateful and have for you and Lady Malvern the deepest affection.'[8]

Garfield saw the flaw in Malvern: his lack of any 'estimation of either the value of Africans or even their potential leadership'.[9] Unfortunately for both Southern Rhodesia and the Federation, his successor as Federal Prime Minister shared that flaw. The English Edwardian doctor, who had come to Southern Rhodesia for his own health in 1913, was succeeded by a burly engine-driver of Swedish-Dutch stock, who had been born in the Colony in 1907. Welensky was Prime Minister of the Federation from 1 November 1956 to 31 December 1963 – the end of Federation. During those years, for good or ill, he towered over the Central African political scene – as he had towered over the Northern Rhodesian political scene since 1938, and as he had dominated the industrial scene on the Copperbelt before that.

In 1955, Don Taylor's biography of Welensky was published.[10] Colin Legum reviewed it for the *Observer*: 'The tragedy of Sir Roy's career is that neither before Federation nor since has he succeeded in winning the confidence of the African political leaders – or even really seriously tried ... But without the support of Africans Sir Roy can never hope to become the leader of a really multi-racial Rhodesia.'[11]

***

In February 1956, Garfield announced that '1956 will be franchise year'.[12] The SR Government set up a Commission 'to decide what qualifications mark a civilised responsible citizen, regardless of race. We in Southern Rhodesia are committed ... to the common voters' roll for all races.' 'The franchise', writes Hardwicke Holderness, 'was really the common focal point of African aspirations and white fear of change ... Garfield was not sufficiently aware of the significance of the franchise and how important it was to get cracking on it.'[13] Support for Holderness's view comes from Dr Hugh Ashton, Bulawayo's one-time distinguished and liberal Director of African Affairs. Writing to Holderness after the publication of *Lost Chance*, he comments: 'you regret the delay in tackling electoral reform and the Industrial Relations act. If Todd had

---

7   *Rhodesia Herald*, 1.11.56.
8   GT/Malvern, 1.11.56, PRO file, Box 16733, Records Office, NAZ.
9   Oral TO.1, NAZ.
10 Taylor, 1955.
11 *Observer*, 3.7.55.
12 *Rhodesia Herald*, 10.2.56.
13 Holderness, 1985, p. 176.

acted while the iron was hot both would have been law before the next elections came along to stir things up and there would have been time for Africans to have got on the roll in sufficient numbers to counteract the inevitable swing.'[14]

Garfield remained firmly of the opinion that it simply could not have been attempted earlier: 'We had to fix the financial side first'. There was another reason for the delay, revealed in a top-secret memo written to the Commonwealth Relations Secretary by Sir Arthur Benson, Governor of Northern Rhodesia, and sent to Garfield under cover of a letter of 26 January 1957: 'Two years ago and more both Mr Garfield Todd and I were very anxious to get ahead with consideration of what franchise arrangements should be made in our respective territories in time for the next General Elections. Mr Garfield Todd refrained from pushing the matter then ... because he was urged by the Minister concerned in the Federal Government [Greenfield] not to get ahead of the Federal Government in its consideration of what should be the basis for the Federal franchise ... Todd refrained also from appointing a Commission on the franchise (in spite of his election-time undertaking to do so); and flew to Lusaka to have discussions with me before, feeling he could wait no longer, he eventually established it.'[15] That meeting took place in February 1956.

The extension of the franchise to the point where real choice and power devolved on the African majority was basic to Garfield's hopes and intentions for African advancement, and towards total integration. He saw clearly the danger of not sharing power. Known as a 'liberal' long before he came to power, he soon made it clear that the franchise was an important issue: 'it would be wrong permanently to prohibit Africans, however responsible and civilized they become, from taking a reasonable part in the government of the country just because they were black'.[16]

When Garfield was in Britain in July 1954, he was questioned on the anomaly that 'Africans sat in the Federal Assembly but not in the parliament of Southern Rhodesia'. In reply, he said that 'he preferred the Southern Rhodesian system, which sought to keep colour out of politics'. It was 'much better that men, irrespective of their colour, should become voters because they qualified in the normal fashion, not because they were white or black'.[17]

Back home, Garfield was keeping up the pressure on the white electorate, writing in 'The Next Step – Federation's Future' for the *Rhodesian Graphic*

---

14 Hugh Ashton/HHCH, 6.10.88, *Lost Chance* follow-up project, Holderness Papers, Bodleian Library.
15 MS.1080/5/3, ff. 323–4, Todd Papers, NAZ.
16 *Rhodesia Herald*, 13.11.53.
17 *East Africa and Rhodesia*, London, 8.7.54.

1956: A Year of Crucial Importance

of September 1955: 'What we do now will determine our fate later ... there is no doubt that one of the major problems before us is to determine what is a reasonable standard for the franchise in Central Africa ... and then honestly to welcome every African who can make the grade.'

The task of steering a franchise bill through the House would fall to the Minister of Justice and Internal Affairs. In interviews for this book, Garfield explained that Greenfield and Sir Robert Tredgold 'brought great pressure' on him to give A. R. W. Stumbles the portfolio – which he had himself held until then because he 'didn't want Stumbles'. His two legal advisers were strongly of the opinion that the minister should be a lawyer, of whom there were five in the House. Hardwicke Holderness had already turned the job down; neither Paddy Lloyd nor Ben Baron could take it on because of their professional commitments; and Reginald Knight, QC was Deputy Speaker and Chairman of Committees. Stumbles, it will be remembered, had voted against the Land Apportionment Amendment Act earlier in the year, so it was not surprising that his appointment at the end of November 1955 'was something of a shock' to Holderness. He correctly saw it as 'ominous'.[18]

On 19 April 1956, Stumbles announced the names of the Commissioners: Sir Robert Tredgold (Chairman); South African-born Sir John Murray, Southern Rhodesia's Chief Justice; and Rhodesian-born Sir Charles Cumings, Resident Director of the British South Africa Company and a retired Chief Justice of the Sudan.

The Commission's Terms of Reference were few, short, simple and broad: '(1) to consider and report on a system for the just representation of the people of the Colony in its Legislative Assembly under which the government is placed and remains in the hands of civilised and responsible persons and in particular to consider (a) the qualifications and disqualifications of persons who are entitled to vote in an election for a member of the Legislative Assembly; (b) the qualifications and disqualifications of persons entitled to nomination as candidates for election ... under the existing law of the Colony and make recommendations as to any changes that should be made in the law to achieve the first-named objective; (2) to consider any other matters which, in the opinion of the Commissioners are relevant to the foregoing matters.'

Philip Mason, author of *The Birth of a Dilemma* (1958) and *Year of Decision* (1960), visited Southern Rhodesia in May 1956 and told the Rhodesian National Affairs Association: 'Any franchise system for Southern Rhodesia must take three things into consideration: the surging uprush of Africans for a

---
18 Holderness, 1985, p. 165.

bigger share of power; the question of capital; and the fact that political power was at present in European hands.'[19] There were, Mason said, three courses open: 'domination might work but nobody wanted it; territorial apartheid was an economic impossibility; so the only remaining course was increasing integration'. Though universal franchise was the ideal system, it could not be introduced into Southern Rhodesia – 'it was a dangerous system to introduce too quickly'. He rejected communal rolls, proportional representation and a second house.

---

19 *Rhodesia Herald*, 12.5.56.

35

AFRICAN AFFAIRS (II)

'There is nothing positive which legislation can do to ensure good industrial relations. It can only provide a legal framework which may or may not be constructively used by employers and employees ...'

Hardwicke Holderness (1985), p. 150

Industrial relations

The Wankie Colliery strike of 1954 had highlighted the need for proper negotiating machinery between African employees and their employers, and the need for proper regulation of African working conditions and wages. The existing labour legislation – the Industrial Conciliation Act of 1934, as amended in 1945 – had provided for the establishment and recognition of trade unions, but the fundamental principle of the Act lay in the definition of an 'employee' as 'any person employed by or working for an employer, and receiving or being entitled to receive, any remuneration *but does not include a native*' (my italics).

African labour affairs were regulated separately and were the responsibility of the Native Affairs Department. In April 1946, a division of Native Labour was formed within the Department, with white labour officers responsible for enforcing all legislation dealing with African employees. The following year, the Native Labour Boards Act was brought in with regulations providing for the prevention and settlement of disputes in industry between employers and native employees. It was also charged with recommending to the Government minimum conditions under which natives in specialised industries and areas could be employed. But the Act operated in a generally piecemeal way.

In 1952, the cabinet set up an inter-departmental committee 'to examine in detail the whole question of development of African trade unions with a view to producing a scheme which might in due course be referred to a select committee'.[1] The wide-ranging Kerr Report on African Education had this to say about African employment: 'Good character and the required skill are the only fair tests that should be applied for admission to any skilled trade or profession.'[2] By 1954, there were, in fact, several lively, unofficial African trade associations – e.g. the Railway African Workers' Union – wielding unofficial power and receiving unofficial recognition, brought loosely together under the umbrella of the Federation of African Trade Unions (later known as the Trade Union Congress).

A Native Industrial Workers' Unions Bill was drafted by the Native Labour Department and came before the Legislative Assembly in the second half of 1954, and a Select Committee was appointed to study it and make recommendations. The MPs appointed to the Select Committee included Garfield (Chairman) and Holderness, who had been involved in the preparation of the Bill. The Select Committee took over a year to prepare its report. During its deliberations, members of the Committee visited Northern Rhodesia, South Africa – where there were many meetings, as almost all Southern Rhodesia's white trade unions were branches of much larger South African unions – and the Belgian Congo, where they met executives from the traditionally secretive Belgian mining conglomerate, Union Minière. Evidence from within the Colony was taken from 'people representing the whole spectrum of relevant opinion in the country', including, 'impressively, ... Charles Mzingeli, Joshua Nkomo, James Bassoppo-Moyo and three other Africans jointly representing the African Unions'.[3]

At the end of November 1955, Garfield established the Ministry of Labour, with himself as its first Minister. African labour matters were removed from the jurisdiction of the Native Affairs Department, and European labour affairs from the Ministry of Justice and Internal Affairs.

The following March, the Committee reported. One of its key recommendations was to reject the Native Industrial Workers' Unions Bill because its provisions for native unions would perpetuate 'the racial basis of the existing machinery and this ... would be detrimental to the interests of European labour, African labour and the interests of the country as a whole'.[4]

---

1   Report of the Native Labour Board on African Industrial Conciliation, 17.9.53, A.B. 50/1954, MS.1083/4/1, Todd Papers, NAZ.
2   Quoted by GT, LAD, vol. 33, 9.7.52, c. 3621.
3   Holderness, 1985, p. 155.
4   Report of Select Committee on NIWUB, para. 45, in Holderness, 1985, p. 161. The full Report can be found under SRC/56/62 of 6.4.56, File S.3242/17, NAZ.

The Committee's main conclusion was that there was a 'real basis for co-operation' and that what needed to be done could be achieved by 'extending the machinery under the Industrial Conciliation Act ... to include Natives by extending the definition of "employee"'.[5]

There were two other important points in the Report. One was the attitude of present union leaders in Southern Rhodesia: 'Almost without exception, European Trade Union leaders were confident that the existing European trade unions would open their doors to Africans.' The other was an emphasis on skill and training, and apprenticeships. When Garfield presented the Report on 27 March 1956, he said: 'there are some Africans who are skilled – not very many but there are many Africans who are semi-skilled ... but I think it was the American Consul-General who said, "that is true; they are just like the workers in Detroit"'.[6] For Garfield, 'the crux of the report' was the 'recommendation that the definition of "employee" in the Industrial Conciliation Act should be extended to include natives'.

More important than the conflicts of interests, he said, was 'the very definite common interest which exists between labour of both sections ... Unless we have men of character, and men who can give capable leadership, the trade union movement will not be able to make its full contribution to satisfactory industrial relations'.[7] The following day, the *Rhodesia Herald* told its readers that when Garfield 'had completed his introduction every member of the house on both Government and Opposition benches joined in loud applause which lasted for nearly two minutes'.[8]

The *Bantu Mirror* referred to 'heartening' reading, an 'indisputable' indication 'of the rapid spread of racial tolerance that has for some time been noticeable in the Federation ... We trust with the additional educational facilities being made available to Africans the time will soon come when workers of different races but with similar training and ambitions will have no cause of disputes occasioned by rivalry between white and black.'[9]

Reaction everywhere was positive. The *Rhodesia Herald* commented: 'Throughout the debate, it was impossible to escape the feeling that here was industrial history in the making. The introduction of the "partnership" concept into the Colony's industrial conciliation machinery ... was generally welcomed ... There was an undertone of surprise, too, almost of astonishment, that most

---

5   Ibid., para. 50a.
6   LAD, vol. 38, 27.3.56, cc. 2237–8.
7   Ibid., cc. 2364–5.
8   *Rhodesia Herald*, 28.3.56.
9   *Bantu Mirror*, 28.3.56.

of the industrialists and European and African Trade Union leaders interviewed by the Committee had accepted the principle of multi-racial unions.'[10]

Prosperity and advancement

During the Budget Debate in Parliament on the Native Education Vote in July 1955, Garfield had been almost in despair as he listened to his Minister of Native Affairs, Patrick Fletcher: 'I have always maintained that there must for a very long time to come be differential arrangements in the field of native affairs. The social and economic structure of a multi-racial state with races on different standards must be riddled with differentials and we must accept these practical propositions and not be side-tracked by parrot-cries such as "partnership". Those people who rush round the country ramming partnership down our throats are a perfect nuisance.'

Having made this oblique attack on Garfield, Fletcher turned his fire openly on Hardwicke Holderness: 'The only people who can afford the luxury of speed in this regard are people like the hon. member for Salisbury North ... I am becoming hardened and quite immune to this poking finger of partnership. The people who poke those fingers seem to think that ... Federation has brought something new in that regard. How wrong they are.'[11]

Shortly before his death in 2002, Garfield wrote: 'Of course, on the evidence of Ben's speech I should have had the courage to fire him straight away!'[12] Fletcher's 'something new' in native affairs was the fact of Federation – of the 'arithmetic', to Garfield, the essential part of Federation. Acutely aware of African impatience, and that 'time is not on our side', he recognised that European opposition to partnership between the races was growing at the same time as nationalism was gaining momentum not only in Northern Rhodesia and Nyasaland but throughout Africa.

While Africans increasingly hinted that force might be needed to end European paternalism, Dr Ralph Bunche, Under-Secretary for Special Political Affairs at the UN, was saying: 'African colonialism may threaten the peace of the world in the next decade ... In the process of "liquidating African colonialism ... the job of the UN is to show these people that their aspirations can be realised in a reasonable time without resort to violence".'[13] The Europeans in Southern Rhodesia took little notice of such reports – and warnings – or, indeed, of the UN. Federation was booming, and they saw no reason to expect anything

---

10 *Rhodesia Herald*, 4.4.56.
11 LAD, vol. 37, 20.7.55, cc. 954–5.
12 GT/SP, 30.8.2002, TPPC.
13 Dr Bunche in Michigan, USA, reported in *Rhodesia Herald*, 30.1.56.

different. *The Economist*'s special correspondent in Rhodesia commented: 'There is, in short, no gainsaying the sunshine of prosperity which at the moment gilds this Central African semi-dominion.'[14]

***

Plans for handing over to private enterprise the troubled and expensive Rhodesia Iron and Steel Commission, with effect from 1 January 1957, were finalised in 1956. *The Chronicle* gave credit where credit was due: 'the Government took over more than one difficult legacy from its predecessors. The CMED was "in the red", so was RISCOM ... today it can claim with justifiable pride that it has put both RISCOM and CMED on their feet ... There is in fact more concrete evidence of successful management by the Territorial Government than by the Federal Government ... despite ideological similarities the URP is something much better than a pale reflection of the Federal Party.'[15]

Cyril Hatty continued to complain, with justification, that Southern Rhodesia found it hard to borrow – and Africans at grassroots level to complain that they had seen fewer benefits from Federation than had been expected; but enough was happening in the field of African advancement to encourage several of the leading Africans 'to work from within Garfield Todd's party'. Nathan Shamuyarira wrote that: 'By 1956 a stage had been reached when Africans had begun to regard the government as their own ... African activity in the URP was not extensive but it was effective; the few URP Africans enjoyed a degree of confidence from their community which the Africans in today's white-led parties could never claim. But in those days the URP Africans were looked up to for advice and the redress of grievances.'[16]

Holderness observed that African membership of the ANC was 'part of the urgent desire on the part of the people of Africa to participate fully in the management of their national affairs ... It is not a new phenomenon ... the most relevant example is the labour movement in England during the nineteenth century ... it was pretty obvious that having achieved federation in the face of the feeling of the people in the north ... we would be in trouble unless we could convince these people of the good faith of Southern Rhodesia.'[17]

Garfield's contribution to the debate on 20 July 1956 took the form of a wide-ranging address. Mrs Todd and I watched proceedings from the Distinguished Strangers' Gallery – rather anxiously, as we knew the PM had 'flu. The *Rhodesia Herald*'s gallery correspondent wrote next day: 'For eighty minutes yesterday

---

14 *The Economist*, 11.2.56.
15 *The Chronicle*, 4.6.56.
16 Shamuyarira, 1965, p. 21.
17 LAD, vol. 39, 17.7.56, cc. 239–40.

afternoon, the Prime Minister rose from the ranks of politicians into the select band of statesmen, when he made what Members of the Southern Rhodesia Parliament, and observers, rank as probably the best speech of his political career ... Effortlessly he toured through the present and future plans of the Government for running the Colony, and he outlined what he regarded as the country's position in the Federation. He spoke on a very high policy level, and the quality of his speech is best illustrated by saying that its length was not noticeable, as he held the House almost spellbound.'[18]

Garfield had no prepared speech, no typed notes – just a few headings jotted down on an envelope. Throughout those 80 minutes, he stood in his customary relaxed attitude, hands loosely clasped in front of him. 'The hon. Leader of the Opposition has asked me to make a clear statement regarding the position of Southern Rhodesia in its relationship to the Federation ... on both sides of the House the over-riding desire and determination of the people is to see that Southern Rhodesia plays its part as fully as it can for the development of the people of the Federation ...'

Garfield spoke of lack of co-operation by the Federal Government; of difficulties with the Loans Council; of the anti-white attitude of the Northern Nationalists; of the Commonwealth Relations Office reluctance to include Southern Rhodesia in the Federal constitutional talks – and of the generosity of Southern Rhodesian Africans in accepting the doubling of their tax.

Garfield concluded: 'Southern Rhodesia, we hold, is a self-governing colony and we believe that gives us a status which has importance ... We cannot do our work fully without knowing everything of importance that is going on in other parts of the Federation. I believe that we are endeavouring, as a responsible government, actively to carry out progressive policies for the benefit of all our people in this country. We maintain that it is of vital necessity to have the closest co-operation at all levels between the peoples and also the Governments of the Federation, and to this end we are ready in every way to co-operate.'[19]

---

18 *Rhodesia Herald*, 21.7.56.
19 GT, LAD, vol. 39, 20.7.56, cc. 318–41.

36

THE POLITICAL SCENE, 1956

'If we are going to become closer to the Federal Party, it must be on the basis that we are being strong together in a more forthright policy.'

Garfield Todd, 1956

Opposition to both the Federal Party in Federal affairs and the URP in Southern Rhodesia was growing. Right-wing Europeans were feeling that the advancement of 'the African' was proceeding at a pace which threatened their own position. In February 1956, this opposition coalesced into the Federation-wide Dominion Party. Its principal policy was that 'political control must remain within the hands of the European for the foreseeable future'.[1] The Party's policy received endorsement at the Federal by-election at Sebakwe in Southern Rhodesia in April 1956 when Robbie Williamson, who had been the DP MP for Gwelo in the Southern Rhodesian Legislative Assembly, defeated by nineteen votes the Federal Party's Dr I. M. Hirsch.

The *Rhodesia Herald* of 13 April warned that the URP was likely to face 'criticism of its policy for advancing the African and for the sums of money it is spending on this work'.[2] Local Dominion Party activists were vocal in their condemnation of the Prime Minister, and were blamed for a 'smear campaign' against him. The right-wing whites perceived Garfield as the principal architect of liberal policies and so used whatever means they could to damage him. Garfield, in this at least a true politician, took it in his stride, but it was the cause of great anger and unhappiness to Grace.

At the subsequent by-election in Gwelo, the DP candidate, Mr C. F. S.

---

1 The Dominion Party's 'Policies and Statements of Principles, Salisbury 1957'.
2 *Rhodesia Herald*, 13.4.56.

Clarke, won by a majority greater than the URP vote. The recent decision on the territorial capital might have had something to do with this, but there was no doubt the URP had suffered a major defeat. Garfield himself was neither surprised nor too worried by the result, which maintained the party status quo in the Legislative Assembly.

***

In February 1956, Garfield said 'the particular weakness of the Federation was the lack of co-ordination between the Federal and Territorial Governments on joint issues'.[3] Subjects of major concern were the growth and development of industry, power and transport. 'These matters were federal responsibilities. Nevertheless ... they were matters in which Southern Rhodesia had a great interest.'[4] Even the *Rhodesia Herald* became critical of the Federal Government, commenting that Garfield's remarks made 'it clear that the attitude of the Federal Government toward them and its refusal to act in a situation in which they feel a strong sense of urgency, has aroused what amounts almost to a spirit of rebellion ... the desirability' of the four governments acting as a team 'is self-evident'.[5]

Malvern replied: 'We have always recognised the principle of consultation and will continue to do so, but the Federal Government is responsible only to the Federal Parliament and to the electorate all over the Federation – not to the Territorial Governments.'[6] Malvern's remarks received surprisingly harsh treatment in press editorials: 'Mr Todd's plaints might never have been voiced had the Federal Government itself shown more energy and drive in this business of attracting new industries.'[7]

***

Hard on the heels of the Gwelo by-election came the URP's Annual Congress – in Gwelo. When the papers were sent out, the press was not slow to pick up a resolution from the Marlborough Branch in Salisbury: 'That in view of the apparent decrease of confidence in the Federal Government, the United Rhodesia Party take whatever steps may be necessary to prevent the Government of the Federation falling into the hands of reactionary groups at the next Federal Election.'[8] The *Rhodesia Herald*'s editorial, on the day before the Congress

---

3   *Rhodesia Herald*, 9.2.56.
4   Ibid.
5   *Rhodesia Herald*, 10.2.56.
6   *Rhodesia Herald*, 11.2.56.
7   *The Chronicle*, 13.2.56.
8   Congress Minutes, File MS.1086/1, Todd Papers, NAZ.

opened, said that 'the more enthusiastic members of the URP are irritated by the seeming inaction and caution of the Federal Government and Mr Todd and some of his ministers make no secret of the fact that they do not see eye to eye with the Federal Party leaders on such important subjects as immigration and industrial development ... the sensible thing for the URP to do would be to amalgamate with the Federal Party ...'[9]

The highlight of Congress was always the President's Address. Garfield's address in 1956 was one of the most significant speeches of his political life. It caused an immediate furore in political circles and had far-reaching consequences not only for his own career but also for Southern Rhodesia. *The Chronicle* noted that it was 'a carefully prepared policy statement drawn up with the full approval of his cabinet'.[10]

Garfield spoke of the differences in outlook that had become 'increasingly apparent' between the URP and the Federal Government – 'A main disagreement ... stems from Kariba itself ... The Federal Government holds that Kariba is so big that it must dominate the entire economic scene until power is flowing from it. The Southern Rhodesia Government believe that the decision to build Kariba has as its corollary the necessity to press forward widespread development, with such immigration as is required to make possible this development.'

Garfield then returned to the subject of loan funds. His Government, Garfield said, considered that 'no adequate programme has been formulated and that the outlook of the Federal Government on this matter precludes any hope of obtaining the necessary funds ... if new sources for loan funds are to be tapped, the Federal Government must do it ... This is so fundamental that we could not join their camp unless the attitude of the Federal Government were to change radically.'[11]

Garfield referred to the activities of the African National Congresses in Nyasaland and Northern Rhodesia, and again warned: 'the URP Government is so exclusively a territorial organisation that we are unable to assist our friends in the north, both European and African ... we have no jealousy of the present Federal Party Government – we have no jealousy of their present or future leadership. What we require is a more dynamic policy, a wider vision, a greater determination to press forward with maximum development.'

There was, Garfield stated, 'no future for a political party which concerns itself in isolation with territorial matters only ... There are two possible

---

9   *Rhodesia Herald*, 21.6.56.
10 *The Chronicle*, 25.6.56.
11 Presidential Address, URP Congress 22.6.56, Minutes Annexure 'A', MS.1086/1, Todd Papers, NAZ.

alternatives ... If in Congress the Federal Party feels that there is merit in what we say and if it is ready to improve its own policy and make it acceptable to a greater proportion of the people of the electorate in Nyasaland, Northern Rhodesia and Southern Rhodesia, then we should link up with them for the benefit of the Federation ...

'But if new policies regarding immigration, general economic planning, and constitutional development are not advanced by the Federal Party – policies which are acceptable to ourselves and to the great number of people in the three territories, who are critical of the present government, what does the United Rhodesia Party do? I believe that we must have a part in these wider issues. If this view is accepted by Congress and if the Federal Party does not make it possible for us to join them, then we must seek a liaison with people of like mind to ourselves in Northern Rhodesia and Nyasaland and ... challenge the Federal Government ... This I would bitterly regret but our whole future is at stake – the success of the Federation – our high hopes for the development of a progressive and happy society – all of those things depend upon courage – upon vision – upon action – now!'

Garfield at his most eloquent and forceful always received a storm of applause from his audience, the criticism coming later. 'Congress agreed completely with all the points of criticism of the Federals raised by Mr Todd', reported the *Sunday Mail* correspondent, present in the hall.[12] But his challenge to the Federal Party was disturbing to a number of the delegates, many of whom were active members of both parties.

As a matter of courtesy, Welensky had been sent a copy of Garfield's speech; and he issued an immediate statement, which Garfield read to the delegates in the afternoon – where it came 'as a bombshell'. 'It was difficult to imagine a more unfortunate address by the leader of a territorial government to his Party Congress', said Welensky.[13]

Garfield commented that Sir Roy had not replied to some of the main points of his speech. 'I knew that I was going to embarrass this Congress. I did it most deliberately ... We have no wish in any way to be separated from our friends in Northern Rhodesia and Nyasaland. On the contrary, it is our aim to co-operate with them.'[14]

The amended Marlborough resolution that was agreed included an instruction to the Party Executive 'to enter into immediate negotiations with the Federal Party in order to ascertain what measure of co-operation or fusion can

---

12 *Sunday Mail*, 24.6.56.
13 Ibid.
14 Minutes of URP Congress 22–23.6.56, p. 36, MS.1086/1, Todd Papers, NAZ.

be brought about forthwith in the Federal and Territorial sphere'. The results of such negotiations, and recommendations of the President and Executive, were to be brought to a special party congress, following the Federal Party Congress. Failing a satisfactory agreement on the lines of the President's address to Congress as a result of the negotiations, 'the URP will be compelled to give serious consideration to whether it must not take an active part in Federal politics'.[15]

The editor of the *Rhodesia Herald* commented on Garfield's 'fighting speech': 'As a speech by its leader to the Congress of a political party it was a masterpiece. But as the opening gambit in what Mr Todd makes clear is a bid for closer association ... with the Federal Party, the tactics, to say the least, are unusual ... There is little doubt ... that the sympathy of the majority of the public is on Mr Todd's side. Indeed, even in the Federal cabinet there is substantial agreement (though unexpressed) with such statements of Mr Todd's that spending on a federal scale has been inadequate and that it is necessary to get new industries "on the drawing boards" now.' However, the editor thought that 'by couching his invitation ... in terms that are virtually an ultimatum, [Mr Todd] is making it extraordinarily difficult for the Federal Party to come to terms with him and so bring about this highly desirable situation'.[16]

Julian Greenfield, Federal Minister of Law, and Welensky's able political lieutenant, had also been thinking along the lines of party fusion. The Federal Party already operated in territorial politics in Northern Rhodesia and Nyasaland, so formal entry into the politics of Southern Rhodesia could be a logical step. The metamorphosis of the URP into the Southern Rhodesia division of the Federal Party would also give the senior members of that Party a position of authority. This aspect of fusion had not been lost on Garfield, but he felt that ideals common to both parties, the acceptance by both of the principle of genuine partnership and the strength of the liberal element in the United Rhodesia Party, would not lead to any slackening of the pace of African advancement in Southern Rhodesia.

In a Federal Party paper, Greenfield wrote that the FP and the URP 'should stand together' and called for a 'merger of the URP within the Federal Party or failing this at least an alliance and a better understanding between the two parties'.[17] Greenfield's phrase 'within the Federal Party' is very significant: in his view, 'fusion' meant absorption of the URP, rather than a merger with the Party.

15　Ibid., p. 37.
16　*Rhodesia Herald*, 23.6.56.
17　'Intervention in Territorial Politics', 15.6.56, File 516/4, Welensky Papers, Bodleian Library.

Greenfield and Garfield met informally to discuss the fusion proposal, and afterwards Greenfield told Welensky that Garfield had 'no desire to oust you from the succession'. Greenfield reported that Garfield had agreed that 'I should chair the talks ... He is willing either for a fusion or a less close tie up'.[18] Welensky's own view was that there 'cannot be a link-up of the two parties but there is no reason why we should not get to the point of a working arrangement'.[19]

Nowhere was Garfield's political inexperience so evident as in his whole approach to, and negotiations for, fusion. After initial meetings with Greenfield and others, he left discussions to other URP members who also proved themselves no match for the very much more professional FP team.

***

On 9 August, in the Legislative Assembly, Garfield clarified his views on the necessity for collaboration, maintaining that a phase in the affairs of the Federation had been reached 'where determination to succeed in our venture should bind us into one company. We are not here to question the authority of any Government in its own sphere of action.' He referred to the right of the territories to consultation between governments. In Paragraph 42 of the Federal Constitution, it was 'laid down that the governments of the Federation and the territories shall consult together on all matters which are of common interest and concern ... the crux of the matter lies in how much we want to co-operate together and to consult together'.[20]

He went on to speak of Africans in Southern Rhodesia taking resolutions to Party congresses – as happened at Gwelo when, for example, a resolution allowing Africans to drink European beers and light wines was passed – and if a change was desirable they could have it made into law 'because they have the power of the vote behind them. But when Africans look to the African National Congress for political change, is the strength which is behind it, the vote? ... or ... the boycott, the strike, intimidation and witchcraft? ... What we are asking for is simply the implementation of the Federal Constitution, not just in the letter, but also, and particularly, in the spirit.'[21]

On 5 September, the Joint Negotiating Committee of the URP and the Federal Party met and formulated a recommendation on the fusion of the parties to be put to Congresses of both parties: 'that the two Parties should be combined

---

18 File 516/4, Welensky Papers, Bodleian Library.
19 Ibid., 14.8.56.
20 LAD, vol. 39, 9.8.56, cc. 807–8.
21 Ibid., cc. 818–24.

into one Party to operate in the Federal and all Territorial spheres'. If accepted, there would then be special congresses of both parties on the same day and at the same place early in 1957 at which the constitution and policy of a joint party would be considered. Then there would be a joint session to adopt a constitution, agree a policy and choose a name for the Party.[22]

At the Federal Party Congress later that month (at which Welensky was elected President), Malvern, who remained as Prime Minister, opposed the merger, as he saw the URP's '"main motive for wanting to merge is to try to increase the influence Southern Rhodesia has on federal policies …" [a merger] would only intensify northern suspicion of the influence of Southern Rhodesia … If there were just one political party operating in both Federal and Territorial fields, then the Federal Government would automatically be blamed for anything in the native policy of the Southern Rhodesia Government.' However, he added: 'Any political stability, maturity and advancement which would be forthcoming for the Africans in the future would come from the Africans of Southern Rhodesia.'[23]

The merger was proposed by Sir Edgar Whitehead, former Southern Rhodesia Minister of Finance, seconded by Greenfield and carried. As the principal beneficiary of the fusion of the parties would, in 1958, turn out to be Whitehead, it was a neat little coincidence that he should have proposed it. Garfield, not a member of the Federal Party, was not at the Congress. One reason for his less than whole-hearted desire for fusion was his fear, later to be amply justified, that instead of the URP sharpening up the Federal Party approach, the Federal Party might blunt the edge of his party's liberalism. Aware as he was of the changing attitude of some Europeans, even within the URP, on African advancement, a clear alliance of genuinely liberal forces would have been preferable.

---

22 Federal Party Congress, 15.9.56, File 482/9, Welensky Papers, Bodleian Library.
23 *Rhodesia Herald*, 17.9.56.

37

Unrest in Southern Rhodesia: Harari Bus Boycott and Railway Strike

'Politics of confrontation entered the scene.'

Enoch Dumbutshena

Harari was anything but a model township: 'That people could lead decent, self-respecting lives there, cultivating qualities of goodness and cheerfulness, was a miracle in itself', wrote the *Rhodesia Herald*.[1] Under the authority of the bureaucratic and unsympathetic officials of the Salisbury Municipal Native Affairs Department, and the stringent Pass Laws, the people's liberty was severely circumscribed. Into this unwholesome desert blew the strong wind of the City Youth League.

The City Youth League had been formed in Salisbury in 1955 under the leadership of James Chikerema and George Nyandoro. Lawrence Vambe describes the League's dramatic arrival: 'They acted like a gale-force wind in the township'.[2] Chikerema had been educated at the Roman Catholic Kutama Mission (where his nephew Robert Mugabe and Lawrence Vambe were also educated) and had then studied law in Cape Town. Nyandoro was the great-grandson of one of the Shona Chiefs who took up arms against Cecil Rhodes' white settlers in the 1890s. Other talented leaders of African nationalism in Southern Rhodesia were Edson Sithole, Paul Mushonga, Henry Hamadziripi and Joshua Nkomo. What these younger, energetic new arrivals on the scene wanted was real change *now*, not in some distant future. African nationalism's Southern Rhodesia cast was beginning to assemble.

An issue ready-made for their purposes was the raising of bus fares into

---

1 *Rhodesia Herald*, 21.9.56.
2 Vambe, 1976, p. 277.

town. Two years earlier, the United Transport Company had been given a monopoly of African and European bus services within a radius of sixteen miles from the Salisbury General Post Office. When the company wanted to employ African drivers and conductors on their buses, which would have reduced their costs considerably, the Salisbury City Council turned down the proposal. The company raised the return bus fare to Salisbury to 1/6d – pointing out that African fares were still 50 per cent lower than European fares. As African wages on average were only 10 per cent of European wages, African passengers were unimpressed.

Several meetings were held in the African townships, a boycott of the buses proposed, and an action committee formed. By Sunday 16 September, plans for a boycott were well advanced. Late that evening, Garfield and Government officials met representatives of the bus company and the Municipal Native Affairs Department. The Action Committee was invited to attend, but only 'observers' from Mabvuku Township turned up. A statement was issued shortly before midnight: 'The Government is aware of the proposed boycott of buses in Salisbury by African users and has taken steps to ensure that the action committee ... will be guided towards the correct channel for negotiations'; and, to 'ensure that there is no interference with the liberty of those who wish to travel, suitable measures have been taken by the police'.[3]

The following day, thousands of Africans walked, cycled or took taxis to work. The intention of the Africans had been simply to boycott the buses, but trouble started at Market Square in Harari at 5:30 p.m. when a bus carrying African passengers home from work was stoned. Soon a large crowd had to be dispersed with tear gas, but about 300 roamed through the township in gangs, causing damage to African and European property and raping several girls in the Carter Hostel, which they wrecked. Cars travelling along the main Beatrice Road were stoned. After two ambulances had been stoned, they were withdrawn; casualties were taken to Harari police station and stretchered to the ambulances. By midnight, the situation was said to be 'fairly quiet'.[4] Garfield went to Harari that night.

At Garfield's Thanksgiving Service in London in 2003, Lawrence Vambe spoke movingly about meeting him amid the wreckage of Market Square: 'Early that morning I rushed to the main bus station where it all began. What a scene of destruction I saw! Yet my attention was drawn to the very sad-looking, lonely figure of the Prime Minister, come to see for himself. I was speechless, till he

---

3   Statement, 16.9.56, PRO file, Box 167633, Records Office, NAZ.
4   *Rhodesia Herald*, 18 and 19.9.56.

greeted me first: "How very sad", he said to me, to which I could only agree.'5 Vambe expanded on this memory later: 'What he and I saw was most heartbreaking. As I was about to go away, disgusted by what I had seen, I recognised one of the organisers. He ... [was] clearly gloating over the evidence of what he and his colleagues had achieved by brute force, beating up savagely men and women who wanted to go to their jobs, and smashing buses – the buses which had transformed the city's transport system for black workers. This young man was Henry Hamadziripi and I heard him say, "We have fixed Todd ... he cannot tell lies now and say Africans are happy."'6

Garfield told the Press: 'The African people of Southern Rhodesia are stunned and almost unbelieving at what has taken place. Evidence of the fact that the number of active rioters was not large is that in Salisbury today almost every employee is quietly at work. The evidence available has convinced me that the riot was not planned, but that the hooliganism was sparked by buses arriving at Harari in the dusk carrying passengers.'7 Thirty-three arrests were made: sixteen for rape or indecent assault and seventeen for various forms of public violence.

Urgent meetings were held with representatives of the bus company, at which Garfield and Ellman-Brown were shocked and angered to learn that the heavily used African bus services were subsidising the thinly patronised European services. The URP Congress had asked the Government to set up a wide-ranging Urban African Affairs Commission of Inquiry, whose terms of reference would include transport facilities; but Garfield realised this issue could not wait, and immediately appointed a commission specifically to inquire into transport for Africans in Salisbury. Its personnel included Joshua Nkomo, and its remit was later extended to Bulawayo. When the Commission reported towards the end of November, it recommended that the basic minimum wage – for all Africans whose conditions of service were governed by the Native Labour Boards Act – should be increased from £4.15.6 a month to £5.10.0. It had not needed a Commission to tell Garfield that low wages were at the heart of many problems facing the Government – and the Africans! – but any attempts to raise them, thereby hitting the European pocket, were met with fierce resistance.

***

There is a chilling postscript to the bus boycott in Nathan Shamuyarira's book *Crisis in Rhodesia*: 'It was in a true sense a landmark in the history of African organisations in Southern Rhodesia ... Girls in Carter House ... were raped

---

5   L. Vambe, Thanksgiving Service for the Todds, London, 13.2.2003, TPPC.
6   Lawrence Vambe/SP, 2007, TPPC.
7   Statement, 18.9.56, PRO file, Box 167633, Records Office, NAZ.

– and immediately there was an outcry from Europeans that this was utter barbarism ... It was in fact calculated revenge by the strikers for the way in which the girls had defied the strike orders and boarded buses.'[8]

Fifty years later, Lawrence Vambe said: 'That sickening manifestation of violence against their own people back-fired and antagonised countless potential members. As long as Todd was in power, so long did the mood of hope and trust in the Missionary-cum-Prime Minister last.' But the occasion had given Vambe 'the first evidence of what became in the future ZANU(PF)'s [9] ready weapon: use of force against their own people'.[10]

***

It will be remembered that the Wankie Colliery and the Rhodesia railways were key to the economic life of Southern Rhodesia. In September 1956, thousands of African railway workers threatened to go on strike because of the huge discrepancy between white and black pay rates. We have also seen that labour matters within the organisation were complicated by the fact that the railways operated within both Rhodesias. In May, the Federal Government took up the question of grading and pay structures on the railways. The Railway Industrial Council, with representatives of both the Railway African Workers' Union (RAWU) and the Rhodesia Railways, met to discuss the whole question of African pay, but without agreement. Following established procedures, the Labour Department then set up an official arbitration body – a Special Industrial Council, again with representatives of both sides. It was agreed in advance that the findings of that body would be binding, once the Government had approved the award. Two months later, however, the RAWU formulated excessive demands, backed by a strike threat. Large meetings were held at which strong opposition was expressed to the arbitration negotiations.

By September, the process of arbitration had been concluded, and the wage award, to come into effect on 1 October, was announced on 20 September. It was greater than the railway administration had offered, but fell short of what the Africans were asking for. The Governments of Northern and Southern Rhodesia accepted it, but the Africans considered the new wage structures to be unsatisfactory and called a strike, principally in Bulawayo, the railways' headquarters.

On Sunday 23rd, at 11 p.m., the Governor of Southern Rhodesia declared a State of Emergency. (When the strike ended, there was a debate in Parliament.

---

8   Shamuyarira, 1965, p. 43.
9   Zimbabwe African National Union (Patriotic Front).
10 Lawrence Vambe/SP, 2007, TPPC.

Most of Garfield's comments on the strike come from his statement of 4 October during that debate.) 'In Salisbury the Monday morning turnout of African railway workers was higher than is normal for Mondays. Six hundred police reservists had been on duty from the early hours and no union leaders had been detained. In general throughout the whole of the railway system the Africans were very law abiding.'[11] The *African Daily News* reported that 'leaders from all centres condemn Bulawayo stoppage' – and confirmed that all other centres were at work.[12] On Tuesday, word reached Salisbury of a very large meeting in Bulawayo ('not in as good a state of mind as ... earlier meetings') which had started at 7 a.m., so the Government stopped all further meetings there. That day – Tuesday 25th – the general manager of Rhodesia Railways gave the strikers an ultimatum: return to work on the 27th or be dismissed.

Nine leaders, including Knight Maripe, RAWU Secretary, were detained. On Wednesday 26th, Maripe was released and had talks with Government officials. He 'offered to do anything he can to get the Africans back to work. He is no longer detained ... All was quiet in Bulawayo and there were no incidents during the night.'[13] Labour Officers and police contacted older strikers, who showed evidence of wanting to return to work, 'but they were still afraid of that very intimidation which big mobs have on African people. It is a very important factor, and a very worrying one at the present time.'[14]

The strike ended; no train had to be cancelled, and no time was lost in loading or offloading goods trucks during the strike, according to the Railway Administration.[15] By 10 a.m. on the Thursday, 1,000 men were back at their jobs. The Rhodesia Railways clerks worked all day signing off 1,775 workers – and signing 1,680 on again – at bottom rates for their grades. From the end of January 1957, they would be reinstated.[16] At noon on Friday 28 September, the State of Emergency was lifted.

Criticism came from overseas newspapers about the way Garfield handled the strike, and he was condemned for using tear gas; but again he told Parliament that he would 'sooner face the criticism for being too quick off the mark in a case which concerns law and order than perhaps to be more dilatory ... the fact that the strike went off at half-cock was because of the things we did, the

---

11 LAD, vol. 39, 4.10.56, c. 89.
12 *African Daily News*, 24.9.56.
13 Press Release (5), 26.9.56, PRO 38/56, Box 167633, Records Office, NAZ.
14 GT, LAD, vol. 39, 4.10.56, c. 899.
15 *Rhodesia Herald*, 27.9.56.
16 General Manager's circular no. 16, 16.11.56, Labour Department Files, Box 53158, Records Office, NAZ.

action we were able to take under the law of the land'.[17]

It was not to be expected that Garfield's liberal critics Paddy Lloyd and Hardwicke Holderness would support the Prime Minister on this occasion. The former deplored the calling-up of police reservists, the use of 'tear gas on peaceful strikers' and the declaration of a state of emergency when 'with mature judgment it should have been realised that in the situation which existed it was unnecessary'.[18] Garfield replied the following day: it was true 'that if we had arrested, and had been able to arrest several people quite a while earlier we might have averted a strike, but ... we did not have sufficient evidence ... to take any action until the strike actually occurred'.[19]

Holderness said: 'There is a very serious danger in a country like this of creating two nations ... We must realise that of the new people who are being embroiled in the industrial revolution, who are manifesting these signs of political consciousness and energy, that with these new leaders, we must realise that we really get nowhere unless we command their allegiance, unless our leadership is up to commanding their allegiance; and not by force. There are common interests and there is plenty of reason to co-operate and, thank God, still at this stage there is the greatest willingness to co-operate rather than be forced into any racialist way of tackling the matter.'[20]

The State of Emergency also brought fierce condemnation from J. Z. Moyo of the Southern Rhodesia ANC: 'Public peace and order was not at stake as the strikers were not in any way violent. We very strongly feel that unless all democratic forces are marshalled against some of these irregularities which threaten the freedom of the people, we shall sooner than we are aware find ourselves deep in a police state.'[21]

Concord, the journal of the Interracial Association, in its review of the year, also attacked the use of tear gas: 'It was a totally unnecessary order ... Is this the way in which the Prime Minister expects to achieve racial Harmony in Southern Rhodesia? ... His action has left a legacy of bitterness and anger ...'[22] 'Rumblings and outbreaks are symptoms ... remedies for the roots of the trouble are required – now. What are those remedies? An inquiry into African urban living conditions will provide some answers. But inquiries take time. For the

---

17 GT, LAD, vol. 39, 4.10.56, c. 903.
18 A. D. H. Lloyd, LAD, vol. 39, 4.10.56, cc. 908–10.
19 LAD, vol. 39, 5.10.56, c. 968.
20 LAD, vol. 39, 4.10.56, c. 929.
21 J. Z. Moyo/Minister of Internal Affairs, 24.10.56, Labour Department Files, Box 5158, Records Office, NAZ.
22 *Concord*, December 1956, vol. 1, no. 10.

man who pays exorbitant bus fares and suffers pathetically inadequate wages, even six months is too long. Time, in Central Africa, is on no one's side ...'

***

The situation Garfield found himself in is best summarised by the London *Observer's* correspondent, Cyril Dunn: 'Mr Todd was entitled to a formal verdict of "not guilty" on his handling of the threatened railway strike ... the most interesting, if somewhat saddening, thing about the debate was the spectacle of Mr Todd, who only two or three years ago was himself a backbencher chiding the government for illiberal behaviour towards Africans now enduring the same sort of talk from his own liberal wing without evident signs of discomposure ... One never had a better opportunity of contemplating the dilemma of the white liberal leader in Africa who can proceed along the road of good intentions only with white support.'[23]

---

23   Quoted in *Rhodesia Herald*, 9.10.56.

38

A Break from Politics

*'The fulfilment of such plans would give us the greatest pleasure
and satisfaction.'*

Garfield Todd, 1956

Garfield and Grace learned from their friends, Dr Emory and Myrta Ross, that Mr Lansdell K. Christie, a New York millionaire with extensive mining interests in Africa, principally Liberia, was interested in acquiring a block of land for experimental ranching. Garfield wrote to Mr Christie saying that though he had hoped to develop Hokonui Ranch and eventually to break it up into 30 to 40 self-contained mixed farms, he had reluctantly come to the conclusion that he should sell at least 40,000 acres because he simply did not have the money or the time to do this. He finished his letter: 'If you are at all interested you will let me know. I cannot ask you to fulfil dreams for me and only if by great good fortune your ideas and mine synchronised, would it be right to go ahead.'[1]

Christie replied promptly, proposing a partnership in Hokonui, which 'delighted' Garfield, who wrote back: 'With the land and capital available, I would suggest that the first step is to get the ranch fenced and fully stocked and I believe that will take four years.' He finished his letter with the assurance 'the fulfilment of such plans would give us the greatest pleasure and satisfaction. We would, of course, maintain our financial interest in the Company and I would continue my personal interest as at present.'[2]

A partnership between Hokonui Ranching Company and Lansdell K. Christie was duly arranged. Christie injected £70,000 capital into the business, and, over a couple of years, Garfield oversaw the erection of miles of fencing, the

---

1   GT/Lansdell K. Christie, 26.7.56, MS.390/1/10, Todd Papers, NAZ.
2   GT/Lansdell K. Christie, 14.8.56, ibid.

establishment of water points in the new paddocks thus created and the gradual purchase of cattle, including pedigree Brahman bulls. A cattle manager, Mr John Kirby, was engaged.

***

The year 1956 had been over-full of drama: not only the routine of government but also many visitors, including two successive Secretaries of State for Commonwealth Relations, and Lord Reith, who brought not so much a breath of fresh air to Salisbury as an invigorating blast of it. Then there had been the launching of the new Department of African Education, and its ambitious five-year plan; contentious issues like the siting of the territorial capital; and manifestations of unrest in the country. Politically, too, there had been extra activity with the Gwelo by-election and the party congress, with the repercussions of the proposed party fusion. In the Federal field, there had been worrying developments in Northern Rhodesia and Nyasaland (which carried serious implications for Southern Rhodesia), the arrival of a Federal Prime Minister very different from Lord Malvern, and everywhere the hardening of European attitudes – which would continue unabated in 1957.

The Todds spent the Christmas and New Year 1956–57 holiday at the house they had bought during the year from Paddy and Alan Henderson at Noetsie near Knysna in the Cape, where the Atlantic rolls in magnificently – a paradise for swimmers and surfers. The house was one of about a dozen round a quiet bay, and for many years their annual holidays were spent there. When later it became impossible for Garfield to obtain a visa to visit South Africa, the Todds sold the house back to the Hendersons.

Grace continued her activities with the African Women's Clubs and the Girl Guides – the incorporation of the Wayfarer Guides into the mainstream movement was a great joy to her. She often questioned the usefulness of her life in Salisbury. In his draft autobiography, Garfield recalls that 'one evening, when Grace came home exhausted from the social day, she said, "I've often been as tired as this at Dadaya but the difference is that at the Mission I never had to ask myself if it was worth the effort."'[3] The social engagements of one kind or another seemed trivial and unending but all demanded – and received from her – the best she could give, all of her interest and charm, whether as guest or host.

Dadaya Mission celebrated its Golden Jubilee in 1956 with the laying of the foundation stone of Dadaya Church. Another milestone came on 7 September when Garfield signed the Notarial Deed of Donation to Dadaya Mission of the 560 acres of Hokonui Ranch land, valued at £18,574.10.0.

---

3   GT/A, TPPC.

A Break from Politics

***

The year 1957 opened badly for the Central African Federation, with the death of the Governor-General, Lord Llewellin. The loss of his long experience in politics and government, so early in Welensky's premiership, meant the removal of a wise and helpful influence. He was succeeded in October by the Earl of Dalhousie. With him came a very shy young ADC, Lord James Crichton-Stuart, whom Garfield first encountered in the Government House swimming-pool. He introduced himself with the words: 'The last time our families met was when my grandfather was tile-maker to your great-grandfather.'

Garfield enjoyed unexpected meetings, and kept them coming with his habit of offering lifts to hitch-hikers on his long journeys from Salisbury to Dadaya. On one occasion, Garfield said his name was Todd and then asked what his passenger did. 'I'm a reporter. What do you do, Mr Todd?' came the answer. Greatly to his credit, the newly arrived reporter did not keep the story to himself: 'How was I to know that the Prime Minister of Southern Rhodesia was fond of giving people lifts and talking to them?'[4]

***

In March 1957, the Gold Coast became independent Ghana, with Kwame Nkrumah its first Prime Minister. Sir Michael Blundell records that when Mr James Griffiths, a one-time Labour Colonial Secretary, was asked why he had given Ghana independence, he replied: 'And what was the alternative? Bloody revolution, man, bloody revolution.'[5] And that is still the answer to all such questions.

Sir Malcolm Barrow represented the Federation officially at the independence celebrations, but Garfield and Grace were invited as Nkrumah's personal guests. Independence Day was 6 March – the anniversary of the Fantee Bond made by the British with the people of the Gold Coast in 1844. That night, Garfield was in the stadium early to watch proceedings. He later wrote: 'I got to about the sixth row, near where Nkrumah was to speak ... I had never seen such a vast concourse of people ... The people were particularly pleasant to me' – warning him of pickpockets at one stage. 'A great ovation was given to the Prime Minister and the Ministers who were with him. I must say I felt that the Prime Minister did not measure up to the occasion ... [but he] received a tremendous hearing ... It was all over in 15 minutes and the great crowd turned quietly and in a most orderly way homewards.'

Garfield asked one man what he considered 'freedom' would mean. 'I don't

---

4   Harris, 1971, p. 176.
5   Blundell, 1994, p. 94.

know', came the reply, 'but I expect that it will mean more hard work.' Forty years later, Garfield added another little detail: 'That night, when the Union Jack was to be lowered and the Ghana flag went up, there were Bedemah, Nkrumah and Busia all dancing in their prison uniforms. I thought, how incredible, they had been to prison! I little thought I, too, would go to prison.' Standing out in all his memories, however, was 'a little girl of ten or eleven who met me on a footpath. She gave me a great smile and raised her arm, "Freedom, White Man", she shouted.'[6]

On their return to Southern Rhodesia, Garfield showed his cine-film of Ghana's independence to large African audiences when he attended political or religious meetings in the townships. But Ben Fletcher, Minister of Native Affairs, is reported to have said, in a rare flash of humour, that being required to watch Garfield's Ghana film was what finally drove him to resign from the cabinet.

---

6   JGT and GT, 1993; and JGT at Combined Women's Institute of Balla Balla, 1957, File MS.1082/5/5, Todd Papers, NAZ.

39

YEAR OF IMPENDING CRISIS: 1957

'One of the frightening things about today is the speed of change.'

Garfield Todd, 1957

In April, the Todds celebrated their silver wedding. To commemorate the anniversary, Garfield bought a fifteen-acre plot of land at Inyanga in the high, beautiful eastern districts of the country. A rough road to the plot was made by the Achilles Construction Company of Umtali, and a shelf created on the hillside on which to build; Garfield took brickmakers up from the ranch, buying sand from nearby Rhodes Inyanga Estates to make bricks for a gardener's house; Grace spent happy hours planning a little cottage and its garden, and their friend Mike Pearce planted trees for a windbreak.

Mention is made of the Achilles Construction Company and buying sand because, as Welensky told Malvern in November 1957: 'I need hardly tell you that there is the usual crop of rumours about [Todd] building a house at Inyanga'.[1] One of those rumours was that Garfield used Government vehicles to make the road. Inventing 'rumours' – innuendos, scandal, lies – became something of a cottage industry among Garfield's opponents, but during 1957 the campaign accelerated. Ralph Palmer, in his Oral Archive, refers to a 'terrific smear campaign ... going about the country. I believe old Matabele Mac was one of the instigators.' He refers to the 'government road-builder at Inyanga' and 'sex with a coloured woman. There were all sorts of horrid things like that – all completely unfounded.'[2] Stumbles says, 'there was nothing really concrete you could put into words to make up a smear campaign, although some of the

---

1 RW/Malvern, 7.11.57, File 643/5, Welensky Papers, Bodleian Library.
2 Oral PA.4, NAZ.

others may have done so'.³ There were those who considered that Stumbles himself had a hand in the 'campaign', but the late Dr Ashton of Bulawayo believed Greenfield 'thought up the smears'.⁴ Opposition MP Stewart Aitken-Cade thought the campaign was started by 'disgruntled members of the Federal Party. They recognise Mr Todd's noted force of character and his ability to influence people as a threat to themselves.'⁵ Garfield says in his Oral Archive: 'Until my own attempted character assassination, I never saw anything that I really thought was horrible'.⁶ In fairness to 'Matabele Mac' (John Macdonald, MP) it must be recorded that, before he died some years later, he apologised to Garfield.

***

1957 was the year when Garfield hoped to bring to fruition the first part of his plans for the steady advancement of the African people and the establishment of a true partnership state in Southern Rhodesia. But it was a year that saw the forces of reaction begin to gather. Garfield recognised that, with an election due in 1958, the more reactionary members of his party – and of his cabinet – were beginning to worry about the 'danger of going too quickly for the electorate', just as he recognised the increasing frustration of the African people because he was not keeping pace with their constantly rising aspirations – and his own hopes.

In May, Garfield was able to announce the setting-up of the Urban African Affairs Commission under Mr R. P. Plewman, who had been a member of the Commission of Inquiry into the Siting of the Territorial Capital. The terms of reference were wide-ranging and comprehensive. Garfield had high hopes that the Plewman Commission would give him a sound basis for a coherent programme to deal with the growing and urgent problem of making a permanent and wholesome urban environment for Africans, but by the time the Commission reported to cabinet in March 1958, Garfield was out of office. His successor, Sir Edgar Whitehead, ignored the Report, preferring his own policies.

***

August 1957 brought Garfield sharp personal anxiety: the years of unbroken work and stress finally undermined Grace's strength, and she had a physical breakdown. It was two months before she was able to write to her sister Elsie: 'At long last I am beginning to experience a renewal of strength and interest ...

---

3   Oral ST.6, NAZ.
4   Interview, 23.7.94.
5   *Rhodesia Herald*, 4.12.57.
6   Oral TO.1, NAZ.

I am sure that there is nothing wrong with me that rest and patience will not mend ... For a long time now everything had become increasingly an ordeal ... Eventually I had a bad go of eczema on my hands and face and then started my old nightmare of not being able to keep down any food ... It has all been physical, and it is my physical strength that seems threatened ... The stupidity of it is that it is Gar who carries the heavy burdens, not I. This year has really been frightful ...'[7]

During Grace's illness, I moved my typewriter to Northward to be there whenever Garfield had to be elsewhere. Morning and afternoon, I had tea with her in her bedroom, and during these quiet hours together she told me stories of her beloved home and her youth in New Zealand, and of their early days at Dadaya Mission.

When Grace was well enough, she went for a month to Inyanga's Troutbeck Inn, where she planned their hoped-for house and garden. But dreams were destined to be just that – dreams. No cottage was built, no garden was made, the little trees were destroyed in a bush fire, and the plot was sold a few years later when bankruptcy threatened the Todds. After her month at Inyanga, Grace returned to Salisbury and shortly afterwards went to Britain with Paddy Henderson for three weeks. The constant anxiety over Grace, her absence from his side, and – most important of all at the time – the loss of her wisdom and counsel all took its toll on Garfield and played its part in the events of the last months of 1957.

***

The URP Congress took place in September 1957. In his Presidential address, Garfield dealt particularly with industrial conciliation (and the increasing work in the Labour Department which meant he would soon divest himself of that portfolio); with the Plewman Commission on Urban Affairs, and the economic position and development plans; and with African education and the franchise: 'This has been the most difficult year that your representatives have had. On the one hand we have had to consider some very controversial measures and on the other there has been a reaction to the work the Government has done concerned with Africans ... What the country needs is strong and purposeful leadership ... The second point I wish to stress is that while I am sure this Party, and I believe the country, has confidence that this Government will never flinch from its determination to maintain law and order and guarantee security to all our citizens, the maintenance of good relations between peoples

---

7   JGT/EB, 28.10.57, Mrs Collins' Papers. I am grateful to Elizabeth for sight of this and other letters to her mother.

and races must be based on known and trusted policies of fair dealing for all our people.'[8]

Garfield's consciousness that members of his cabinet and caucus were becoming increasingly unsettled inspired the final passage of his address: 'When we come to the election of officers I will ask you to recognise that if you vote for me to continue as your leader, I will take it that that vote is also for the honouring of our policy.'[9] When the election took place, there were two nominations: Garfield and Fletcher. Fletcher immediately stood up and said that the cabinet was a united and happy team and that no change of leadership could improve it.[10]

What Garfield did not know at the time was that H. D. Wightwick (pronounced 'Wittick'), MP for the Eastern Districts, and Norman Straw, MP for Rusape, were behind a move to replace him with Fletcher, and that the latter, together with Ellman-Brown, persuaded them not to proceed but to wait until the Party Fusion Congress (due in March 1958) before raising the question of the leadership. Two months later, Fletcher told Garfield that, 'the reason they had not pushed it then was that they considered that the fusion negotiations … were delicately poised and as I was leading them it was considered inadvisable to disturb the situation at that point. This means that Mr Fletcher made his statement on the unity of the cabinet when he, and perhaps others of my ministers, was biding his time having already decided to turn me out.'[11]

***

In October, a Commonwealth Parliamentary Association delegation from Westminster visited the Federation: four Conservatives, led by the Hon. Richard Wood, and three Labour MPs, including James Callaghan. The latter proceeded quickly to upset the delicate sensibilities of the Europeans in Central Africa by asserting that Dominion Status should not be given in 1960. Garfield wrote in his December *Round Table* article: 'At first an attempt was made to condemn Mr Callaghan … but it was soon quite evident to those who wished to know the truth that all members [of the delegation] were unanimously of this opinion.'[12] During a joint meeting of Federal and Southern Rhodesian MPs, Wood spoke of the difficulties of assessing African opinion; but, though they had been able to hear representatives of only a tiny minority, 'Nevertheless, that opinion was deeply opposed to Dominion Status in the very near future and the removal

---

8   Presidential Address, URP Congress, 20.9.57, MS.390/2/3, Todd Papers, NAZ.
9   Ibid.
10 GT's 'Notes on Recent Events', Caucus Meeting, 14.1.58, TPPC.
11 Ibid.
12 GT, *Round Table* article, December [1957?].

of the protective status in Northern Rhodesia and Nyasaland and our opinion is that until we get an expression of views in favour I believe we would be acting irresponsibly if we advised the Government of Her Majesty to ignore her solemn pledge.' Wood also spoke of 'a general absence of contact, between Africans and Europeans except on the basis of employer and employee. We feel that partnership is unlikely to work unless there is more contact.' Of the franchise, Wood said: 'In very few of the conversations which we have had with politicians all over the Federation has the question of the franchise been long absent.'[13] When the recently established fortnightly magazine, the *Central African Examiner*, commented on the Delegation's report, it noted that 'a five-week visit, well spent, is long enough to get beyond superficialities and prejudices; written by the four Conservative and three Labour Party members ... the report is unanimous and commands extra respect on that account'.[14]

---

13   UK CPA Delegation meeting, 25.9.57, File 195/12, Welensky Papers, Bodleian Library.
14   *Central African Examiner*, vol. 1, no. 17, 18.1.58.

40

THE INDUSTRIAL CONCILIATION BILL

'I believe that this government ... has endeavoured to face the facts ... It has endeavoured to do what is needed and what is best for the Colony.'

Garfield Todd, 1957

Peter Gibbs, Industrial Adviser, commented in the *Central African Examiner* in January 1957: 'All that the Industrial Conciliation Bill seeks to do is this: to legislate realistically for a state of affairs that has come about by evolution, and which has certainly not developed from any sense of liberal idealism imposed arbitrarily by Mr Todd or anyone else.'[1]

Garfield's aim with this Bill was to open 'the door of advancement to Africans but at the same time ... to maintain sound standards of skill and conditions of employment'.[2] Parliamentary draughtsmen set to work to produce a Bill for an amended Industrial Act, and a redrafted Apprenticeship Bill. In the weeks between publication and debate in May, Garfield met delegations and addressed organisations whose membership was worried about some of its provisions. Back in August 1956, he told the Chamber of Mines that the proposed Bill would 'see that any trade unions formed would be "democratic bodies, capably and sensibly led". Mr Todd said it was obvious that where industries were going ahead, Southern Rhodesia would not be able to get all its skilled men from Europe. Africans would go right to the top in trades, and even more so with cheap power from Kariba.'[3]

On 9 August, Garfield addressed the Salisbury Chamber of Industries, and here, too, hoped to allay some of the employers' fears – and apparently

1   *Central African Examiner*, vol. 1, no. 17, 15.1.58.
2   GT, *Round Table*, no. 193, December 1958.
3   *Rhodesia Herald*, 9.8.56.

The Industrial Conciliation Bill

succeeded, the President, Mr J. de Haas, writing afterwards: 'I feel that you have given us all the confidence that the government is moving in the right direction.'[4]

In March 1957, Garfield told the Mineworkers' Congress in Gwelo: 'Africans will be subject to the provisions of the Industrial Conciliation legislation in exactly the same way as Europeans. They will be entitled to form and apply for the registration of trade unions although it is hoped that where trade unions are already in existence provision will be made for them to include Africans in their existing organisations. Multi-racial or non-racial unions ... would be entitled to have branches according to categories or degrees of skill.' Addressing European fears, he said: 'I am deeply concerned that the fear of workers today that they will be replaced by Africans at lower wages will be removed. The Bill should remove this fear ... We are determined to safeguard the European standard of living ... [with] proper grading of jobs at just rates of pay, dependent on the economic worth of the job itself.'[5]

At the Chamber of Mines AGM, the President wanted to know 'the implications of this Bill because it looks as if the Africans could swamp the Europeans in industry'. This was the underlying fear of all Europeans – that they would be 'swamped' by the greater numbers of the Africans as they advanced. Garfield replied: 'There is no attempt at the moment to force the issue ... [but] unless the Colony continued along "progressive" lines it might find itself "prodded" along unsatisfactory lines.'[6]

A major difficulty with the European trade unions was that most were branches of long-established South African unions whose ideology reflected that country's history and current political situation, and by the end of April 1957 their influence was becoming stronger. The *Rhodesia Herald* editorial on the morning of the Second Reading debate highlighted this: 'The first organised white Trade Union Opposition ... has come almost direct from South Africa with little pretence that it is even a partly Rhodesian rejection.'[7]

In introducing the Second Reading, Garfield said: 'The crux of the new Bill is the omission of six words from the present ... Act: "but does not include a native" ... I have received many letters and memoranda from various organisations ... but this new principle is apparently accepted by everyone and it is because of this that I have felt fully justified in proceeding with the Second Reading.' Any South African connection would be severed: 'No trade

---

4 J. de Haas/GT, August 1956, MS.390/3/2, Todd Papers, NAZ.
5 GT, Mineworkers' Congress, Gwelo, 30.3.57, File P.4a, Box 167636, PM's files, Records Office, NAZ.
6 *Rhodesia Herald*, 16.4.57.
7 *Rhodesia Herald*, 2.5.57.

union or employers' organisation shall be registered under this Act unless it has a governing body situated in the Colony and its officials are resident in the Colony,' Garfield quoted from the Bill. And the question of political influence was briskly dealt with by 'a prohibition on the use of trade union funds for political purposes'.[8]

The House listened to Garfield with close attention – and applauded as he finished. That was just the beginning of a protracted battle. On 8 May, Keller went on the attack. Well briefed by his friends in the South Africa-based unions, he quoted their memoranda to support his opinions: 'everyone in the country of all sections objects' to the Bill, which amounted to 'unnecessary and unwarrantable government interference'. After a tirade against 'big business', he gave a 'warning' to 'the white worker ... to beware of the hon. the Minister who through this Bill is going to repress him, to curtail his freedom, to restrict his liberty, to push him out of the country'. The Bill, Keller maintained, was one of the 'most pernicious pieces of legislation yet brought before this parliament ... The white man's organisations are to be taken from him and the black man is to take his place.'[9]

Garfield tried to dismiss Keller's fears that the provisions of the Bill would lead to the employment of fewer Europeans: 'This Bill aims to ensure the full employment of all races ... we are not suggesting powers which would hurt trade unionism in general in its legitimate aspirations.'[10]

Holderness writes: 'One of the benefits that could be expected ... would be in the field of ... the relationship between the less well-endowed whites and talented and up-and-coming blacks.'[11] He tried to explain why 'the reception of the Bill was quite different from the enthusiastic one' accorded the Report of the Select Committee of the Native Industrial Workers' Unions Bill, 'whose recommendations were supposed to be incorporated in it'. The officials drafting the Bill, 'instead of simply taking the existing Industrial Conciliation Act and putting into an amending Bill the changes which we had been at pains to specify in the Report, had decided ... to try to kill a number of other birds with the same stone ... In short, it was a bit of a mess.'[12]

The fundamental principle of bringing Africans within the scope of the Industrial Conciliation Act had been condemned by none. After a further couple of days' debate, Garfield proposed that it be adjourned and a second Select

---

8   LAD, vol. 39, 2.5.57, c. 1356.
9   LAD, vol. 39, 8.5.57, cc. 1654–67.
10 LAD, vol. 39, 17.5.57, cc. 1916–24.
11 Holderness, 1985, p. 213.
12 Holderness, 1985, pp. 188–9.

The Industrial Conciliation Bill

Committee set up. His action was seen by the press as 'another setback' for him.

Cyril Dunn, Salisbury correspondent of the *Observer*, describes these events only two years later: 'The Report on which the Bill was based was, by Southern Rhodesian standards, a remarkably liberal document. It was plainly not the intention of those who signed its recommendations to do anything but forward the interests of the African worker within the limits imposed by the partnership idea. Yet when the Bill went to the House, Members ... made speeches which were substantially extracts from memoranda supplied to them by white pressure groups.' Some made it 'almost scornfully clear' that 'the Minister's ideas did not at all reflect the mature and responsible opinions of the Colony's most important citizens – the white employers and the white trade unionists'.[13]

A revised Bill was published in December, but with Parliament in recess there would be no debate before February 1958 – and by that time Garfield had been succeeded as Prime Minister by Sir Edgar Whitehead.

---

13 Dunn, 1959, pp. 165–6.

41

African Education, 1957

'It was only when I became Prime Minister and gave the first decent grants to Missions that they realised that I really meant what I had been saying.'

Garfield Todd

The late Nathan Shamuyarira, journalist, nationalist and long-serving Zimbabwean minister, considered that Garfield's acceleration of African education was his great contribution to society and to Zimbabwe: 'with his attempt to bring the Africans into the system by trying to bring in African headmasters and make them inspectors. He wanted the capable Africans to be brought along. The teaching profession formed very much a background for his political action. He knew how able they were. What he was offering was very small but the principle he was fighting for was the correct one. He increased African participation in Government.'[1]

The implementation of Garfield's five-year plan, introduced in 1956, gathered momentum during 1957. After fifteen months, it had already resulted in the double streaming of classes in four secondary schools, additional classes for teacher training, doubling the number of Domestic Science courses, and increased grants to mission schools. Then came the Native Education Bill of 1957, which provided for the establishment of the Native Education Advisory Board, the introduction of the Unified Teaching Service – bringing together teachers in Government and Mission schools – and a teachers' pension scheme.

During the Budget Debate in July 1957, members expressed their anxieties that the African Education budget had topped the £2m mark. Garfield reminded them that the people themselves had contributed a quarter of that amount: 'As

---

1 Interview, 29.6.94.

we move from picks and shovels to an increasing degree of mechanization, both on the farms and in industry, so the quality and capability of our labour force has also to increase ... the African people themselves clamour in thousands to enter vocational courses ... and we simply have not provided the courses for them ... we have not got one technical school in the African education system.'[2]

Opposition members – remembering the beginnings of Mau Mau in Kenya – spoke of politically minded teachers, imbuing pupils with political ideas and encouraging political activity, all of which Garfield refuted with some heat.[3] He then replied to Stockil's 'usual annual charge ... I was responsible for a headlong plunge into bringing forward the African people at an untoward rate ... this Government ... has endeavoured to face the facts ... to do what is needed and what is best for the Colony ... [people say] "the development of the native people is too fast". Of course it is too fast. It is unavoidably too fast ... I regret that such enormous strains are being placed upon them and upon their social life and so on. It is almost more than a people can bear ... But the marvellous thing ... is that the native people are proving themselves adaptable in a most remarkable way to the changes with which they are being faced ... It is we who have decided that the native will be pushed forward at this rate and it is up to us to see that the stage of transition is carried through as carefully and as confidently as we can ... so that everyone may benefit from the development which is taking place.'[4]

One of the most radical provisions of the five-year plan was for post-Cambridge Certificate technical training. A technical college was established at Luveve, near Bulawayo, under the inspired direction of Dr James McHarg, a Salvationist and musician. But McHarg experienced difficulty in 'placing' his graduates in white-owned – and largely white-manned – firms. When the college was closed by the Rhodesian Front Government after 1962, McHarg arranged with overseas schools and firms – some as far distant as New Zealand and Australia – to take some of his pupils.

In September 1957, Garfield handed over the portfolio of African Education to 'that good old right-winger', Stumbles: 'I thought I could do that safely', Garfield said in 1993, 'because the whole thing was now set and we were on our way ... Stumbles was given the portfolio for unworthy reasons. My ministers were wanting the electorate to see a change in my image and as African Education had been receiving a good deal of my time and attention it

---

2   LAD, vol. 40, 25.7.57, cc. 363–71.
3   Ibid., cc. 372–3.
4   Ibid., cc. 374–6.

was considered to be a popular move to hand it over to a right-winger.'[5]

The plan ran into difficulties through an even greater demand than expected. Stumbles, without reference to cabinet, instructed Missions not to engage more untrained teachers or to open more forms in the lowest standards. While Garfield was on holiday in December 1957, Stumbles followed this up with a cut of £66,000 on the 1958/9 Estimates. In February 1958, Garfield formed his second cabinet; Stumbles' successor, Ralph Palmer, restored all the cuts and announced that the Government had 'agreed to make available the full amounts envisaged under the plan'.[6] A week later, Garfield resigned as Prime Minister.

---

5   GT/SP, 1993, TPPC.
6   Press statement, PRO/20/58, File MS.1085/1/2, Todd Papers, NAZ; PRO file Educ.1-5, Box 167634, NAZ; reported in *Rhodesia Herald*, 10.2.58.

42

THE IMMORALITY MOTION

'A cloud no bigger than a man's hand. A Rhodesian African had arrived home from Europe with a white wife ...'

J. A. Gray, *South Africa*

The Southern Rhodesia Immorality Suppression Ordinance of 1903 made it a criminal offence for a white woman to have sexual intercourse with a native male. In 1916, the Act was superseded by the Immorality and Indecency Suppression Act, with a similar provision. A proposal at the time that the law should also apply to white men and black women was rejected, as was a resolution to the same effect passed by the Rhodesian Women's League in 1921.

In 1956, interest in the Immorality Suppression Act was reawakened when it was learned that a schoolteacher, Patrick Matimba, from the Rusape area, who had gone overseas for his secondary education, was hoping to return to his homeland with his white Dutch wife. The arrival of the Matimbas raised the problem of where the mixed-race couple could live, but it also 'aroused among a lot of white voters steeped in the Southern African tradition a sense of outrage which defied any attempt to resolve it by appeal to reason', writes Hardwicke Holderness.[1] The Rusape branches of the Federal and United Rhodesia Parties held a meeting to discuss the question of interracial marriages in the country, and about 350 people 'called for legislation against mixed marriages' – and a general election 'if the request was not carried out', reported the *Rhodesia Herald*.[2]

The Minister of Native Affairs, Fletcher, sharing these opinions, circulated to cabinet a memo proposing an amendment to the Land Apportionment Act

---

1 Holderness, 1985, p.184.
2 *Rhodesia Herald*, 13.2.57.

to define the race of a woman by her husband's race. The two quite distinct subjects – amendment to the Immorality Suppression Act and the Matimbas' return – became inextricably mixed up. According to Holderness, again, 'what members of the caucus had been coming across were accusations that this – Patrick Matimba and his white wife breeding Coloured children – was the kind of thing the URP approved of, and the inevitable result of "partnership". And some of them thought it was absolutely vital to do something to clear their own and the party's name.'³

The Press kept up the pressure – egged on by one of the URP backbenchers, who, in violation of caucus privacy rules, reported on discussions there. Cabinet minutes do not give any idea of personal views expressed by ministers individually, but debate later clearly showed Garfield's determination not to be a party to the hysteria of the day. He found the matter both depressing and distasteful and resisted Fletcher's efforts to make the cabinet act to amend the Immorality Suppression Act. The minutes of cabinet meeting 9 of 26 February 1957 merely state: 'Immorality Suppression Act. Cabinet agreed that the Act should remain as it now was without amendment.'⁴ Fletcher therefore approached a backbench MP with the suggestion of a private motion that the Government amend the immorality law. Max Buchan, who though reactionary in his views had an immense liking and admiration for Garfield, thought Fletcher's approach had the PM's backing, and agreed.

Garfield cleared the matter up once and for all when he spoke at the Leadership Congress in February 1958: 'I am not really dictatorial, but in this particular matter I did state that I was not prepared to stay as a member of the cabinet if the cabinet brought up this particular measure from the government'.⁵

All the briefing papers that came to Garfield from the police and the Justice Department suggested that miscegenation between white men and black women was on a relatively small scale. The concluding paragraph of a confidential memorandum from the Officer Commanding CID gave Garfield powerful ammunition: 'From the police point of view it must be said that any such legislation, although it might serve as a nominal deterrent, could only be enforced by continued clandestine observation and intrusion of a type which would probably not be tolerated by our public.'⁶

The debate on the motion 'That the Immorality and Indecency Suppression act be amended to prohibit illicit sexual intercourse between a European male

---

3   Holderness, 1985, p. 184.
4   Cabinet meeting 9, 26.2.57, MS.1086/2/5, Todd Papers, NAZ.
5   GT's Notes, Congress 8.2.58, MS.1085/1/1, Todd Papers, NAZ.
6   Memo, 27.4.57, Reference 883/57, BSAP Headquarters, TPPC.

and an African female' took place on 1 May. Holderness comments that 'it all seemed slightly crazy'.⁷ 'But for Garfield Todd the motion, crazy though it might be, had critical implications. If he were to come out against it, whatever his reasons and however well expressed, it could count as an indelible black mark against him as a politician looking for white votes and as Prime Minister depended upon by his colleagues to command them. All of them, Fletcher, Ellman-Brown, Stumbles and even Hatty, had made it clear before Garfield spoke that they would support the motion. Garfield's speech was well researched and as conciliatory as possible but uncompromising.'⁸

Garfield began by saying that the motion was 'frankly a racial measure and not a measure that is concerned with morality'.⁹ He questioned Buchan's assertion of support from the Churches, and wondered if Buchan had put before the Churches what was involved. 'This is not a moral question: it is a racial question ... I have spoken about this matter to Africans including a number of leading Africans ... so far I have not met one of them who demanded that we pass the amendment under discussion this afternoon, but they want the law that is on the Statute Book repealed, and I think there are many reasons why it should be.'

Garfield, seconded by Ben Baron, moved an amendment to omit all the words after the introductory 'That miscegenation be deplored'. Lloyd, seconded by Eric Palmer, wanted the act repealed. Both amendments were lost. As usual, Garfield had given the House a 'free vote' – and the final voting was fifteen for, including all four of Garfield's ministers, and nine against: Garfield, Holderness, the Palmer brothers, Lloyd, Baron, Davenport, Abrahamson and J. M. Macdonald. After the vote, in some distress, Buchan sought out Garfield to assure him that he would not have put the motion at all if he had not been led to believe that the PM supported it.

Garfield had support from the Press: 'The debate ... has given the world the unfortunate impression, on the basis of no facts that we can discover – indeed the census statistics rather suggest the opposite – that we need such a law ... Worse, there has been controversy on racial lines ... when it is more than ever necessary, for the sake of quiet progress, to adopt a non-racial approach to public business and allow questions of race to be governed by the enduring arbiter of social convention ...'¹⁰

The *Gwelo Times* and the *Nyasaland Times* printed an article by Eric Robins,

---

7   Holderness, 1985, p. 186.
8   Ibid., pp. 185–6.
9   LAD, vol. 39, 1.5.57, cc. 1327–8.
10 *Rhodesia Herald*, 6.5.57.

which congratulated Garfield on his 'gallant stand' and awarded him the 'badge of Courage' in the debate. 'Mr Todd, the ex-missionary, stood firm … He voted against it – at grave risk to his prestige. At that moment he rose in stature above the experiences of the politician and the blinkered viewpoint of the bigot. Those who have little opportunity of assessing the sincerity and resolution of their Prime Minister can be left in no doubt now of his outstanding calibre as a man and a leader.'[11] The National President of the National Council of Women of Southern Rhodesia told Garfield that Buchan 'did not have the "written and verbal approval of the NCW and of the National President of the NCW, SR" …'.[12]

The message from the lobbies of the House at the end of the debate had not been lost on Garfield. It was a clear shot across his bows, warning him that party unity was disintegrating under the strains of racially controversial issues. He wrote to all his MPs on 3 June 1957: 'In the criticism of my lack of leadership there is enough truth to make us all think. We have two important matters before us – Industrial Conciliation Bill and the franchise. Of broader concern is the appearance of lack of unity – a matter to which I have given little attention for there is also strength in our freely expressed differences …'[13]

Garfield saw the miscegenation debate as a crucial event in his political career. Cyril Dunn did too, but for different reasons. He writes: 'This, according to some white liberals in Rhodesia, was the hour of Mr Todd's enlightenment and self-discovery. He spoke against the Bill with a depth of feeling rarely shown by one who habitually hid his emotions behind that wide and brotherly smile.'[14]

In 1957, Paddy Lloyd's amendment to the Buchan motion calling for the repeal of the Immorality Act had been lost. Among those voting against it were Hatty, Stumbles, Quinton, Knight and Cleveland; all would be members of Whitehead's cabinet, and all would vote for the repeal of the Act when Whitehead proposed this the following year.

***

On 6 June 1957, the Federal Party lost a by-election at Mrewa to the Dominion Party, its large 1954 majority overturned by the popular local farmer, Winston Field. This defeat, and the swing to the right by the electorate which it represented, had a profoundly unsettling effect on the Federal Party – and, to a slightly lesser extent, on the URP.

---

11 *Gwelo Times* and *Nyasaland Times*, 10.5.57.
12 National Council of Women, National President/GT, 15.5.57, TPPC.
13 GT/URP MPs, 3.6.57, File P.3, Box 167632, Records Office, NAZ.
14 Dunn, 1959, p. 166.

43

THE SOUTHERN RHODESIA FRANCHISE

'The dilemma of the white liberal leader in Africa who can proceed along the road of good intentions only with white support.'

Colin Legum, 1956

The Tredgold Commission hearings began on 17 January 1957. Evidence was taken from the whole range of opinion, including, on the right, the Dominion Party and bodies like the Segregation Society and the League of Empire Loyalists (whose leader, A. K. Chesterton, was a former propagandist for Sir Oswald Mosley's British Union of Fascists in the 1930s).

From the left, evidence came from African trade unions and the Southern Rhodesia African National Youth League and the SR ANC, which proposed universal adult suffrage based solely on the ability to complete the voter's enrolment form unaided. Evidence was given by African bodies – a majority prepared to co-operate with the European and a more extreme minority. 'Both were profoundly mistrustful of the European attitude to them. The Commission felt that it would have a deep psychological effect if larger numbers of the responsible type of African could be admitted ... on reasonably low qualifications. This could be done if a device were found to ensure that the voters with the high qualifications were not swamped by the Africans so admitted.'[1]

On 12 March, the Southern Rhodesia cabinet debated the Commission's Report and concluded that although the proposals 'seemed to be eminently practical and acceptable ... some possible changes might have to be considered'.[2] When it came to the voters' roll, the Commission did not fail Garfield: it recommended 'that the country should at all costs stick to the common voters'

---

1 Minutes, Inter-Governmental Franchise Committee meeting, 7.3.57, SRC(57)49 of 16.3.57, S.3242/20, NAZ.
2 Cabinet meeting 11, 12.3.57, MS.1086/2/5, Todd Papers, NAZ.

roll and avoid adopting a system of "group" or racial representation'.[3] Garfield had long ago decided 'to maintain the common roll' despite repeated attempts by Lord Home to persuade him to 'take more Africans into his government and administration'.[4] 'What Home had tried to do was to persuade me that a pseudo B-vote would allow as many Africans as whites to go to the booths, whites to cast a vote which had power and blacks to go through the motions so that the British Government could show the world how just she was.'[5] By 1976, when Home wrote his book, Garfield's minor attempt to increase the number of Africans on the voters' roll had caused his downfall; Whitehead, whose electoral act had brought a few thousand Africans onto a B-roll, had also been repudiated by the largely white electorate; and the powerlessness and tokenism of African representatives elected on a racial roll had been amply demonstrated in Smith's Parliament.

In his autobiography, Sir Robert Tredgold gives an account of the Commission's reasoning and philosophy: 'the key to the political future rested in the franchise ... to this day, large numbers of the European inhabitants ... consistently ignore it ... They seem unable to grasp that, however good a government may be, the consent of the governed, upon which it must ultimately rest, will not continue unless these can see for themselves that it is good ... If we were to achieve any practical result, we had to find something that not only seemed equitable to ourselves, but that had a chance of acceptance by the electorate, which was overwhelmingly European.'[6] For Tredgold, to consider 'the just representation of the people' was more 'fundamental and important' than to keep the Government 'in the hands of civilised and responsible persons'.

In its Conclusion, the Report states: 'Unless the mass of the people can make its voice heard, it will never be satisfied that it is receiving justice in the ordinary affairs of its daily life.'[7]

The Report recommended that the existing means test should be abandoned in favour of 'a combined means and education test which would provide, in effect, four doorways to the franchise, three of them 'ordinary' and one of them "special"'. The first required income of £50 a month with literacy (ability to complete the form unaided); the second £40 a month and Standard Six (primary education); the third £25 a month and Form 4 (four years' post-primary education); and the fourth (Special) £15 a month with literacy. 'Door

---

3   Holderness, 1985, p. 178.
4   Douglas-Home, 1976, pp. 124–5.
5   GT, MS.1091/2, Todd Papers, NAZ.
6   Tredgold, 1968, pp. 211–12.
7   Tredgold Commission Report, lines 825–34, Misc. Reports 1955–7, RG-4, NAZ.

4 would be special in that the votes of voters qualified by that route would be subject to devaluation, if necessary, so as to count for not more than one half of the total votes cast in a constituency by 'ordinary' voters.'[8] The Commissioners did not think that this limitation on the 'special' votes would ever come into operation. 'It was, as it were, a safety device in the electoral machine, which one hoped and believed would never be required.'[9]

This would have given Africans a real say in the Government. It was hardly surprising that subsequent discussion would concentrate on the 'special' vote – and its possible devaluation. The Report was favourably received by the URP caucus (Parliament was in recess). Tredgold writes that the Report was 'generally acclaimed by the press and the public'.[10] The *Rhodesia Herald* considered that if the plan were 'accepted by the country it will change radically the complexion of elections and the attitudes of candidates to their constituents'[11] – an important point.

In June 1957, the editorial in the first issue of the *Central African Examiner* commented on the Tredgold recommendations: 'essentially make-shift in character, but they are a step forward in that thousands more Africans will get the vote'.[12]

***

On 30 April, the Tredgold Report was debated in Parliament. Holderness writes that a 'reactionary mood ... seemed to infect' the House. Garfield 'spoke in conservative terms but indicated pretty clearly that, so far as he was concerned, whatever formula did emerge should be such as to make eligible for the vote at least the kind of people the Tredgold Commissioners had in mind in proposing the Special qualification'.[13] Garfield reminded the House that the URP had promised 'to take whatever steps we could to preserve racial harmony, to avoid the undesirable principle of separate representation on racial lines, to build up security and confidence within the Colony ... We are indebted to the Commission ... for its recommendations ... also for its statement of the case for the just representation of the people ... and for argument so compelling that we dare not ignore it ...

'It is not enough in a democracy to have power in the hands of those best qualified. It is dangerous to be governed by an oligarchy ... even more dangerous where the top group to whom you are going to give the franchise ... is mostly

---

8   Holderness, 1985, p. 178.
9   Tredgold, 1968, p. 218.
10   Ibid.
11   *Rhodesia Herald*, 15.3.57.
12   *Central African Examiner*, vol. 1, no. 1, 7.6.57.
13   Holderness, 1985, p. 188.

from the race which is a minority and, in this country, a small minority ... no security can be achieved unless the franchise is given to the greatest number possible ...'[14]

Garfield spoke about 'door 4': 'Is £15 and literacy a fair test? ... the number of people who get only £15 a month include people who hold quite responsible posts ... If in Canada we asked if trained teachers, transport drivers, experienced policemen, should be given the vote, no one would doubt that they should be given the vote ... our economic set-up means that people who in other countries are considered because of the work they do and the responsible part that they play in industry and in the life of the community, capable of having the vote, in Southern Rhodesia they might not get a vote, simply because our national income is as yet very low.'[15]

Garfield told Sir Arthur Benson that he believed the number involved would be no more than 5–6,000,[16] 'but ... my big difficulty is to get my people to be liberal enough in their outlook'.[17]

Caucus discussion of the franchise increased H. D. Wightwick's disillusionment with Garfield and his policies, and on 5 June he called on Garfield to resign: 'There ... comes a time when opinions on some major issue become so divided as to be irreconcilable. I believe that not only you but all of us have reached this point.' He wrote of divisions in the party, of 'liberal measures which are, in this country at least, regarded as being almost revolutionary in character'; of 'a widening of the gap because you are now increasingly introducing measures which force a clearer definition of the divisions ... It is my belief that you, as Prime Minister, do not command the support of the country as a whole.'[18]

Garfield was not surprised by Wightwick's well-publicised attack. He was aware of the widening split within the party – but he was determined to stand firm when it came to the franchise and the need as he saw it to enfranchise responsible (and very underpaid) African teachers, nurses, policemen and agricultural demonstrators. Opposition also came from within the cabinet, with Ellman-Brown going so far as to threaten to resign. Garfield, who had a liking for the man as well as a high opinion of his ability, managed to dissuade him, but it was another straw in the wind.

Garfield addressed the annual general meeting of the Interracial Association in Salisbury on 15 June. Once again, we owe our knowledge of events to

---

14 LAD, vol. 39, 30.4.57, cc. 1241–7.
15 Ibid., cc. 1248–9.
16 GT/A. Benson, 23.5.57, MS.1082/2/8, Todd Papers, NAZ.
17 Ibid.
18 H. D. Wightwick/GT, 5.6.57, Holderness Papers, Bodleian Library.

Holderness, then President of the Association, who quotes the Association's Minutes: 'Mr Todd said he agreed completely with the Tredgold Report where it says that we must make it possible for every individual to have a place in the sun. This did not mean that what we call European standards would be lowered, but that opportunity to work for and attain those standards must be given to all Rhodesians. Tolerance, understanding and more of the vision of Rhodes, who abhorred race antagonisms, was needed now ... We were in danger of becoming a race of fear-ridden neurotics ... if legislation further to implement that policy ... was so changed as to continue to keep off the rolls our 6,000 Africans who have had 10 years of education and who work as teachers, medical orderlies, and so on, we would be so betraying the spirit of Rhodes that, said Mr Todd, he would not continue to lead his party. However, he was confident that our legislators would meet the spirit of the challenge of the Tredgold Report.'[19]

'That set the cat among the pigeons', wrote Stanlake Samkange 30 years later.[20] 'Good stuff', wrote F. L. Hadfield on 17 June, 'stick to your guns ... the franchise issue is demanding the very stand you are taking ... The only people to be afraid of are ourselves if we lack the courage to take the right course.'[21] C. D. Smith wrote from Ndola: 'Is it too much to hope that your splendid example will encourage some of our Federal Ministers to remember that they, too, were elected on a policy of partnership?'[22] The *Rhodesia Herald* said the speech was 'a courageous statement ... Mr Todd has taken his stand and we congratulate him ... It may well be that in doing so he is committing political suicide, but ... what alternative is there but apartheid and baaskap ...'[23]

'To anyone knowing what was going on behind the scenes', Holderness would write in January 1958, 'it was absolutely essential if a franchise on the Tredgold lines was to be passed, that Todd should give a sort of "ultimatum"' ... but the former ministers never liked being compelled to go that far, and they were absolutely furious that Todd should give a public ultimatum, and even more furious that the meeting which provided the timely occasion for him to do so was one which happened to be organised by the Interracial Association.'[24] J. A. Gray wrote in *South Africa*: 'Some people never forgave him'.[25]

---

19 Holderness, 1985, pp. 196–7.
20 S. Samkange, contribution to Garfield's 80th-birthday book, 1988, J. Todd Papers.
21 FLH/GT, 17.6.57, MS.1082/5/3, Todd Papers, NAZ.
22 C. D. Smith/GT, 18.6.57. Ibid.
23 *Rhodesia Herald*, 17.6.57.
24 Holderness's notes on Caucus Meeting, 14.1.58, TPPC.
25 J. A. Gray, in *South Africa*, 14.6.58.

***

When the URP caucus met on 19 June, in spite of hints that it would be bitterly divided, 'it was apparent that the blockage had been cleared', writes Holderness.[26] The proposals agreed to were substantially along the lines of the Tredgold recommendations, but with two 'doors' to the Special qualification, not one: door '4' with £20 a month and literacy; and now door '5': simply Standard Eight. Proportional limitation would apply to Doors '4' and '5'. Press comment was largely favourable, but disappointed Africans did not agree, James Chikerema saying the proposals were 'a political fraud'.[27]

After the caucus meeting, Garfield embarked on an exhaustive campaign to 'sell' the new franchise to the electorate, addressing audiences large and small throughout the country. Other MPs were also addressing meetings, but not all with Garfield's message, as the franchise was causing more political interest – and anxiety – than any other issue during Garfield's administration. By the time Parliament opened, they had been so unsettled by their constituents that an emergency caucus meeting was called on 12 July. Once again, Garfield managed to calm the over-excited and win over the waverers.

The Electoral Amendment Bill came before Parliament on 1 August. Though illness had reduced the official opposition to two – both Keller, by now a very sick man, and Stockil were in hospital – the unofficial opposition on the Government benches meant there was no easy ride for the Bill, which Stumbles, as Minister of Justice and Internal Affairs, introduced. 'The Proposals enshrined in this Bill are ones for which all of us on this side of the House must and do take our full share of responsibility …'[28]

The debate continued on 6 August, when Keller rather heroically was back in his seat – and back on form. (That evening, a meeting in Straw's Rusape constituency passed a vote of no confidence in the Prime Minister.) An expectant House did not interrupt when Garfield spoke on 8 August: 'I know that some people are wondering why, all of a sudden, we are having so much talk about industrial conciliation, and other subjects. They have not fully realised how widespread are the changes that have been taking place in Southern Rhodesia and throughout the Federation during the last ten years.' He referred to his address to the Interracial Association AGM: 'some people have said that this was a threat and verged on blackmail, but surely that was not so. There simply came a point in my own thinking where I believed it was in the interests of

---

26 Holderness, 1985, p. 197.
27 *Rhodesia Herald*, 25.6.57.
28 LAD, vol. 40, 1.8.57, cc. 548–50.

the country that I should state my position.' On the question of the special qualifications, Garfield told the House that it was these 'which challenge our good faith ... We have a section of our people who, through no fault of their own, are allied to the native wage ... a very low figure and we have no choice but to keep those wage scales low ... the hope is that the special qualifications will ... cover this interim period of fifteen or twenty years before they will automatically fall away ... We all recognise that the proposals ... are not perfect. They could not be perfect ... because they are catering for a situation which is not perfect.'[29]

Every time it seemed that agreement had been reached within the URP caucus, it dissipated as uncertain MPs were lobbied by anxious constituents. When caucus met on 14 August, it agreed to a means qualification for 'door 5' of £12.10.0 a month: 'a figure which in debate most members stated they accepted as being a fair one to admit Africans who could measure up to a standard 8 education, but earn very low wages'.[30] During the debate in Parliament, the figure of £12.10.0 a month was reduced to £10, which brought closer alignment with the B-roll proposals of the Federal Electoral Bill.

When it came to the Second Reading vote, Wightwick was joined in the 'No' lobby by the two opposition MPs and Straw and Wingfield. Wightwick protested again at the Third Reading and was supported by Keller, who made the most of what turned out to be his last opportunity to attack Garfield in Parliament: 'This Bill represents nothing more and nothing less than a base betrayal of the white people of this country ... We are breeding, Sir, and nursing thousands of lazy, good-for-nothing loafers in this country ... The country is run by a negrophile Government ... I oppose every word, every comma printed in the Bill.'[31] Stumbles' summing-up was brief. The last of some 50 divisions was called, and five URP members joined three opposition members in the 'No' lobby; but that was their last throw, and the Bill was successfully read the third time. Stumbles' regulations governing the Bill were very discouraging of new voters, and, although the President of the Southern Rhodesia ANC did his best for Garfield, urging 'Africans to enrol as voters soon',[32] by March 1958 only 158 had registered as 'special' voters.

A subsidiary provision in the Act turned out to have great significance at the General Election the following year: the introduction of preferential voting. Although the Electoral Amendment Act applied for only one general election,

---

29 LAD, vol. 40, 8.8.57, cc. 708–15.
30 *Rhodesia Herald*, 15.8.57.
31 LAD, vol. 40, 31.8.57, cc. 1071–7.
32 *African Daily News*, 21.12.57.

the passing of the Act was a defining moment for Southern Rhodesia, as well as for certain individuals. Among the Europeans, it divided the 'liberal' from the 'reactionary'; among the Africans, it raised political awareness as nothing else had done. The passing of the Act was a matter of great satisfaction to Garfield. It was 'the first irrevocable step which I believe we have taken in Southern Rhodesia under the heading of partnership'.[33] He also recognised that the right wing of the party had now declared its determined opposition to any future liberal steps the Government might wish to take.

Garfield writes in his draft autobiography that in 1957 'I had been quite sure that there was no future for whites in Rhodesia unless we were prepared to share political power with Africans.'[34] He told the New Zealand TV unit in 1991: 'I don't regret that I did what I did, because if I had not done that I would have betrayed myself and everything I stood for.'[35]

---

33 GT/Mrs F. Bolton 28.8.57, MS.1082/5/3, Todd Papers, NAZ.
34 GT/A.
35 *Hokonui Todd*, 1992.

44

THE FEDERATION, 1957

'The Federal Franchise today is the biggest road block to a happy future.'

Garfield Todd, June 1959

The Southern Rhodesia Government watched with some concern as the Federal Government pursued its Dominion Status ambitions. In April 1957, Welensky went to London to continue Malvern's discussions on 'enhanced status' for the Federation, as well as amendment of the Federal Constitution to allow the enlargement of the Federal Assembly, and the proposed new Federal franchise. At the end of the talks, the United Kingdom Government issued this declaration: 'Her Majesty's Government ... are opposed to any proposal ... for the secession of any of those Territories from the Federation'.[1] Announcing that the statutory conference to review the Federal Constitution should be convened in 1960, the declaration went on: 'The purpose of this conference is to review the Constitution ... and in addition to agree on the constitutional advances which may be made. In this context the conference will consider a programme for the attainment of such a status as would enable the Federation to become eligible for full membership of the Commonwealth.'

The agreement Welensky brought back from London – sometimes referred to as the 'April 1957 convention with HMG' – has been seen as one of the most significant developments for the Federation, and one of the factors in its demise. Immediately, alarm bells began ringing. It was April 1957 – and 1960 was only three years away. Africans in the northern territories realised that they had less than three years in which to convince both the British and

---

1 Welensky, 1964, pp. 76–7.

Federal Governments of their opposition to the Federation, and particularly one with 'enhanced status'.

Stanlake Samkange, who always favoured co-operation, wrote in the *Central African Examiner*: 'It must be recognised that Nyasaland Africans have now set their feet on the narrow road of nationalism which they hope will lead them to self-government on the Ghana model. What does Dominion Status mean to an ordinary African? It means the white man has full and unfettered power to do as he pleases.'[2]

After attending his first meeting of the Commonwealth Prime Ministers' Conference, Welensky addressed the first Northern Rhodesia Industrial and Commercial Show: 'He believed ... that when 1960 came London would be found reasonable and he knew that in return London would find the people of the Federation ready and willing to accept their duty to continue to protect the interests of the backward elements of the country's population.'[3] British MP James Johnson wrote in the *Manchester Guardian*: 'enormous harm is being done in Northern Rhodesia and Nyasaland by the unequivocal statement by Sir Roy Welensky that he expects independence by 1960'.[4]

Only a month later, Wellington Chirwa told the Federal Assembly that Africans in Nyasaland 'want to secede ... It is wrong to pre-judge the case and say in 1960 you cannot secede.'[5] In September, the Federal Prime Minister paid the first of his three visits to Nyasaland. (The others were a pre-general election rally in December 1958, and an airport conference with the Governor during the 1959 Emergency.) He met Angoni chiefs, who told him 'that their fears of Federation were justified'. Nyasaland – before federation talks – was quiet and maintained only law and order. 'But during Federation very strong misunderstandings between the government and the governed arose because the rights of the latter were not considered ... Federation was imposed and this means that Nyasaland belongs to the settler and not to the Africans.' Federation was still opposed for fear of Southern Rhodesia's African policies, copied from South Africa.[6] The Nkata Bay chiefs boycotted Welensky's visit, and at Blantyre 'no more than a dozen' went to hear him. When Sir Roy was asked if he was not disappointed at the absence of Africans, he replied: 'I do not think they are really interested in politics. Those who are interested are represented here.'[7]

---

2   *Central African Examiner*, vol. 1, no. 1, 7.6.57.
3   *Rhodesia Herald*, 9.7.57.
4   Quoted in *Rhodesia Herald*, 2.8.57.
5   FAD, vol. 8, 13.8.57, c. 1277.
6   *Rhodesia Herald*, 27.9.57.
7   *Central African Examiner*, vol. 1, no. 9, 28.9.57.

The Federation, 1957

***

In Southern Rhodesia, consideration of the Federal Franchise had run parallel with its own franchise discussions. The Southern Rhodesia Government was not required to approve any federal legislation, but Garfield was concerned about the divergent views on the franchise between the two governments. The Southern Rhodesia cabinet discussed Federal citizenship and the franchise on several occasions but 'considered that the Federal Government was ill-advised at this juncture to attempt to legislate ... the essential consideration for the governments was to devise a minimum standard on civilisation which could be applied throughout the Federation'.[8]

In July 1956, Malvern and Greenfield had met the Secretaries of State for Commonwealth Relations and the Colonies in London to discuss the Federal Franchise. Benson was there, but not Garfield: the Prime Minister of the most significant of the three federated territories was not invited. A report of the meeting was sent to the territorial governments in September 1956, but the Southern Rhodesia Cabinet Secretary, Gerald Clarke, politely replied that the Government did not feel it could usefully put forward any views until its commission had reported.[9] Later, it recorded that 'a dual roll for the election of members of the Federal House on a racial basis would be likely to be completely unacceptable'.[10] The Federal Government maintained its determination to legislate for a two-roll system against all the representations of Tredgold and Garfield. It is interesting to note from Greenfield's Oral Archive[11] that he was himself against the dual-roll proposals but went along with the rest of the Federal cabinet.

On 5 July 1957, the Special Correspondent of the *Rhodesia Herald* wrote: 'The franchise itself will largely decide the fate of partnership. Sir Roy's franchise policy, as foreshadowed so far, threatens to plunge the Rhodesias in the long run into exactly the same racial brew as the Union. Todd's policy, which he wants the Federation to follow at least in principle, seeks to diminish racial extremism all round.'[12]

The Federal Electoral Bill was presented to the Federal Assembly on 18 July. Of the two rolls, the 'A' roll was overwhelmingly European, and the 'B' roll overwhelmingly African. The 'A' roll alone would elect the 44 ordinary members. Of the fifteen members to represent African interests, two Europeans

---

8 Cabinet meeting 18, 3.5.56, MS.1086/2/4, Todd Papers, NAZ.
9 G. B. Clarke, 13.10.56, Federal File F.236/CX 28/1/1, NAZ.
10 Cabinet meeting 46, 22.11.56, MS.1086/2/4, Todd Papers, NAZ.
11 Oral GR.2, NAZ.
12 *Rhodesia Herald*, 5.7.57.

would be nominated by the Northern Governors (as before); four Africans in the Northern Territories would be elected indirectly by Africans (as before); and the remaining nine (including the Southern Rhodesian European and two Africans, as provided in the Constitution) would be elected by both 'A' and 'B' rolls. In other words, 44 members would be elected by Europeans; nine by a European majority; two would be appointed – and there would still be only four (indirectly) elected Africans.

Africans JGT were quick to see that four out of 59 was a considerably reduced ratio from four out of 36. An inevitable result of the two rolls was that those on the lower roll would see themselves as 'second-class citizens', which was not the case in the Southern Rhodesia common roll entry by 'doors 4 and 5'.

The *Manchester Guardian* editorial on 18 July drew a parallel between the situation in Central Africa and that in South Africa before the Union had self-government: 'Britain conceded self-government trustingly to the relatively liberal Union of Botha and Smuts. Fifty years after, we confront the Union of Strijdom and Verwoerd. The liberal impetus was not enough to carry South Africa up to, and over, the brow of the hill. In the same way, Britain cannot finally relinquish her remaining responsibilities in Central Africa until the hump of the hill is past.'[13]

The Constitution Amendment Bill was passed by the Federal Assembly on 31 July. The African Affairs Board of the Federal Assembly, the constitutional 'watchdog' of African interests, considered it to be a 'differentiating' measure. It had therefore to be referred to the British House of Commons. The Conservative Government disagreed with the Board, and in November its majority in the House of Commons saw the African Affairs Board's objection brushed aside.

When the Commonwealth Secretary visited the Federation in October, Garfield unsuccessfully 'pled with Home to disallow' the Federal Electoral Bill, due for its second reading in December.[14] He still considered the proposals grossly unfair to the African people – and he was profoundly uneasy about their effect. Sir John Moffat made a devastating attack on the Bill in a hushed and tense Federal Assembly: 'The balance of influence in this House has been most materially shifted in the European favour.'[15]

Cyril Dunn writes of the debate in *Central Africa Witness*: 'Sir John, who attended the conference at which the Federation's constitution was agreed upon, declared "categorically" ... that if it had been disclosed there that the compromise reached with such effort and concession would in due course be

---

13 *Manchester Guardian*, 18.7.57.
14 GT/JGT, 13.3.60, MS.1082/4/1, Todd Papers, NAZ.
15 FAD, vol. 8, 16.12.57, c. 1983.

altered unilaterally by the Federal Government, agreement would never have been reached and the Federation might never have been created. Describing the Bill as "unholy" and capable of bringing "lasting disgrace to us as Europeans", the unemotional voice went on: "One of our duties as a minority and as a people holding absolute power is that we cannot abuse our own power for our own benefit. This is absolute and admits of no exception. Its practical application to politics is that we can leave the balance of power between ourselves and Africans as it is, but if we choose to alter it we can alter it in only one direction, and that is to give the Africans a larger share …"[16]

The Bill passed its second reading in December, and its third on 9 January 1958. It was accepted by a two-thirds-plus-one majority. Again, the African Affairs Board objected to it as 'a differentiating measure' and made its report. To Greenfield's annoyance, it was reserved for Her Majesty's assent and was duly debated in the House of Commons. The Conservative Government persuaded the House to disregard the Board's opinion, and the Bill became law.[17]

The watchdog had barked; the watchdog went unheeded. Sir John Moffat resigned as Chairman of the African Affairs Board, and in Nyasaland Dr Andrew Doig retired as a member of that Board and as one of the nominated European representatives of African interests in the new Federal Assembly of the Central African Federation. Doig wrote to the Speaker of the Federal Assembly (who, in defiance of precedent, did not read his letter to the House): 'The setting aside of the reservations of the African Affairs Board in regard to the Constitutional Amendment and the Franchise Bills has so weakened the position of the Board as to render it quite ineffective as a safeguard of African interests.'[18]

In Northern Rhodesia, Sir Arthur Benson received the news by telegram: 'my reaction was one of absolute profound shock. I was shattered by it. It seemed to me that that was probably the end of the Federation.'[19]

---

16 Dunn, 1959, pp. 125–6.
17 FAD, vol. 8, 16.12.57, c. 1981.
18 Doig, 1997, p. 46.
19 Lapping, 1985, p. 470.

45

THE RISE OF THE AFRICAN NATIONAL CONGRESS

'What lies before us – co-operation or unrelenting racialism? The happiness and general well-being of the European cannot be maintained if there is discontent and misery among the great African population.'

Garfield Todd, 1953

Quotation has frequently been made from the Kerr Commission Report of 1951. Among its insights into the Colony's problems was this, quoted by Garfield in the Legislative Assembly the following year: 'Nothing can prevent a formation and steady growth of a group of well-educated Africans which, although for a long time to come relatively small, will have an influence among the mass of less privileged Africans wholly disproportionate to its size.'[1]

In the Federation, hotels were whites-only. In 1955, the Roman Catholic Diocese of Salisbury was raised to the status of Archdiocese, Bishop Aston Chichester was made archbishop, and the Papal Legate came to Southern Rhodesia for the formal inauguration of the 'Ecclesiastical Province of Southern Rhodesia'. The Government wished to give a dinner in his honour at Meikles Hotel; and, as the occasion was of some importance – and some delicacy, with a guest list that included Bishop Dhlamini of Natal, the first African bishop in Southern Africa – Garfield himself went to see the general manager, Mr Bull. When the situation was explained to him, Mr Bull famously replied: 'If his Holiness the Pope was coming, and he was black, he would not be allowed into Meikles Hotel!'

***

The African National Congresses in Northern Rhodesia and Nyasaland had

---

1   LAD, vol. 32, 9.7.52, c. 3623.

become increasingly active and vocal since the imposition of Federation. Hardwicke Holderness told Parliament in July 1956: 'if things had not changed as they have over the last three years, we would have had a National Congress movement here, and I am confident in saying that if we had had a National Congress here, it would have found a leadership here just as determined and just as confident, and in my view more effective, than the leadership of the Congress movement in the North ...'[2]

At its third meeting in 1957, the cabinet formally agreed to the abandonment of the term 'native' in favour of 'African'.[3] This was announced in March, and henceforth, for example, the Native Affairs Department would be known as the African Affairs Department. Whether that meant a change of attitude in the department would remain to be seen. The gesture amused men like James Chikerema and George Nyandoro, who read the writing on the white man's wall, but upset right-wingers in the growing Dominion Party. Other small forward moves followed, with Africans being permitted to participate in the National Lottery, and the 'expediting' of the proposed new and less irksome system of registration of Africans.

All these little forward moves were watched by the ANC in Nyasaland and Northern Rhodesia, where fears grew that Britain might be persuaded by them to grant Dominion Status to the Federation in 1960. Meanwhile, in Southern Rhodesia, where the largest Nyasaland ANC branch was established in Salisbury, Garfield was still trying to remove white fears. He told the annual dinner of the Salisbury Chamber of Commerce that 'there were people who fear that the advancement of some sections of the population would cut down what was available for ... "the privileged group ... there will be enough for everybody. There should be opportunity for all here in the country ..."'[4]

On 5 June, it was announced that the ANC was to be re-formed in Southern Rhodesia, which profoundly upset the whites. Pressure came also from the police to 'act tough', but it was Garfield's own dislike of racialism of any kind in politics that persuaded him to 'talk tough' on nationalism. In an interview with the *Rhodesia Herald*, he said: 'The new African National Congress movement in Southern Rhodesia will be closely watched by the Government. "Much as we deplore the emergence of a racialist organisation, the Government will not take any action so long as there is no subversive activity or any kind of threatening behaviour towards those who may not

---

2 LAD, vol. 39, 19.7.56, c. 284.
3 Meeting 3, 15.1.57, ibid.
4 *Rhodesia Herald*, 7.2.57.

agree with the promoters of this organisation."'⁵

Stanlake Samkange wrote in the *Central African Examiner*: 'Perhaps interest in this congress has arisen from the assumption that it will be militant, nationalistic and anti-white. Although it is correct to suppose that the Congress will be nationalistic in character, it is important to remember that no nationalist movement begins by being extreme or anti-white. They are generally moderate to start with ... in Southern Rhodesia the opportunity for co-operation between black and white still exists, although it may well be out of the question within a few years.'⁶

That same month, in an article for *Optima*, the magazine of the Anglo-American Corporation, Garfield wrote of the change in black–white relationships that had come with partnership: 'There is no doubt that Africans throughout the continent are becoming more fully aware of the responsibilities which must accompany the granting of such rights ... there is a rising tide of black nationalism to meet the white nationalism ... The movement does call for domination in government by the African people as such, a demand which is quite as unacceptable and dangerous as are the demands made by white nationalists. These are the two extremes and the truth is not with either of them. The future of the country does depend upon government remaining in the hands of enlightened and responsible people and it depends also upon the maintenance of what we term European standards. At the same time opportunity must be provided for Africans to advance to those standards ...

'There are still a good many Europeans who do not recognise that the welfare of the country depends upon our making the very best and fullest use of the potential of every citizen ... The fear expressed is that, as the African becomes skilled, he will be prepared, because of his background of a low standard of living, to do work for lower wages and under worse conditions ... All our endeavours to build a happy and secure nation rest ultimately on our ability to make possible for all the people a wholesome and secure family life ...'

Garfield wrote of the evolution of behaviour patterns between the races, and went on: 'It is difficult to change the old behaviour patterns. Africans, even though they may be doctors or teachers, are not admitted to hotels or theatres or restaurants, and when they go to post offices they enter by special African entrances ... [which] disturbs most deeply the emergent group who are the most significant people; significant, not only from the point of view of themselves, but also from the influence they may have on the mass of their own race ... These are the people who will determine how the great mass of Africans will

---

5   *Rhodesia Herald*, 5.6.57.
6   *Central African Examiner*, vol. 1, no. 2, 22.6.57.

act, and it is this group which demands the honest and generous implementing of partnership. It is this same group of educated Africans who demand a larger say in government.'[7]

The Government was obviously apprehensive about the advent of the reinvigorated ANC, 'which put life and spirit into the black fight for parliamentary representation'.[8] Occupation Day 1957 – 12 September – came; and, while Europeans in Salisbury were paying tribute to the Pioneers at the memorial and flagstaff in Cecil Square, a couple of miles away in Harari hundreds of Africans were marching with placards reading 'down with white domination', 'down with police rule', 'Congress will oppose racial discrimination', 'we have no intention of giving our land to someone else'. Joshua Nkomo, President of the new ANC, was reported as calling for peaceful behaviour during 'our stroll through Harari. This is a peaceful procession.'[9] The Youth League leaders, Chikerema and Nyandoro, became Vice-President and Secretary-General respectively. They backed Nkomo's call for peaceful protests, but they had already, privately, decided that the only way to remove whites from power was by violence.

In 1959, Garfield wrote an article about the birth of the ANC, in which he said: 'Africans in Southern Rhodesia, pressed by land shortages, unable to get freehold land in town, excited by the new thoughts which experience and education have brought, and confronted with the accomplishments of black men throughout all the rest of Africa, have decided that there must be changes.'[10]

The first statement of principles of the ANC begins: 'Its aim is the national unity of all the inhabitants of the country in true partnership, regardless of race, colour or creed. It stands for a completely integrated society, equality of opportunity in every sphere, and in the social, political and economic advancement of all. It regards these objectives as the essential foundation of that partnership between people of all races, without which there can be no peaceful progress in this country …'[11]

The 'Fortnightly notes and Comment' column in the *Central African Examiner* of 28 September made a very important point: 'What would have strengthened the congress case and made its aims more acceptable to Europeans would have been their public recognition in the policy statement,

---

7 *Optima*, vol. 7, no. 4, December 1957.
8 Obituary of James Chikerema by Trevor Grundy, 26.3.2006, Institute for War and Peace Reporting.
9 *Rhodesia Herald*, 13.9.57.
10 GT for *Africa South in Exile*, 1959, TPPC.
11 Quoted in Parker, 1972, p. 64.

that all of this will take years, if not a generation.'[12]

The day after Occupation Day, Guy Clutton-Brock, founder-member of the ANC and widely credited with formulating its 'aims', addressed the Rhodesia National Affairs Association meeting in Salisbury. Holderness reckoned that Clutton-Brock 'had his ear closer to the ground than the Native Department or Special Branch'.[13] A large audience came to listen to the quiet-voiced, gentle-mannered lay missionary from St Faith's who would one day be the only white man whose ashes were buried alongside notable nationalists at post-Independence Heroes' Acre. 'The African National Congress is not produced by a handful of machinating agitators subverting an otherwise docile people', he said. '"It is the result of a spiritual movement deep down in what Mr J. B. Priestley has called the common man, which this highly materialistic civilisation has released. It is manifest on the continent from the Cape to the Mediterranean, from Ghana to Uganda ... In Central Africa it is crystallising into the form of the ANC. We can thank God that it has not yet taken – and I hope it never will take – any international totalitarian form." It was a grave mistake, he said, for the government or anyone else to under-estimate the strength of feeling. "We have a prime minister who is a fine man but he is subject to considerable pressures ... I hope the pressures to discredit and suppress the congress before 1960 will not prove too great for him."'[14]

Lawrence Vambe describes the results of the ANC actions as having a 'crucial psychological effect: that of removing from the minds of the common folk the paralysing fear of white authority ... It was almost like removing the fear of death in a people.'[15]

Only Europeans like Hardwicke Holderness and his friends, and overseas journalists, troubled to get acquainted with the leading ANC personalities. The Minister of Native Affairs, even in his new guise as Minister of African Affairs, sought no meeting with this new political force. Indeed, one of his complaints about his PM was that the latter saw African leaders on his own – without the Chief Native Commissioner in attendance! Garfield 'had meetings with Africans that he never told me about ...'[16]

An early white recruit to the ranks of ANC sympathisers was Dr Terence Ranger, recently arrived from England to teach at the University College of Rhodesia and Nyasaland. In his Valedictory Lecture on retiring as Rhodes

---

12 *Central African Examiner*, vol. 1, no. 9, 28.9.57.
13 *Lost Chance* follow-up project, Holderness Papers, Bodleian Library.
14 *Rhodesia Herald*, 14.9.57.
15 Vambe, 1976, p. 279.
16 Oral FL.1, NAZ.

Professor of Race Relations at Oxford University in June 1997, he spoke of the early days of the ANC: 'I had found an earnest, emancipatory atmosphere in mass nationalist rallies, where the crowd was educated in the history of Greek democracy and of past African achievements, and where over two or three years the timid huddles of people which came to the first nationalist meetings were transformed into self-confident gatherings of twenty or thirty thousand people. It seemed obvious at the time that an oppressed people was finding its mind and voice ... three years' actual experience of African nationalism had convinced me that it was about human rights rather than about their denial ...'[17]

***

At the URP September 1957 Congress, Garfield made no specific reference to the week-old ANC, but it was clearly in his mind when he spoke of 'a combined effort to make our country the best on earth – not the finest for the privileged only, but a country of hope and opportunity for all our people'.[18]

The growing popularity of the white, right-wing Dominion Party, the increasing fears of URP members about Garfield's – and the party's – African advancement agenda, and the formation of the ANC, all caused grave disquiet to the other members of his cabinet. On Sunday 24 November, Fletcher visited Garfield at Northward to express their concern about the party's chances in the 1958 general election if he continued to give the impression that he was only concerned with the African, and to demand that he take a stronger line with the SR ANC. Against his better judgement, but in an attempt to preserve the unity of the cabinet, Garfield agreed. At the end of his life, he said: 'There is only one speech of which I felt ashamed and that was the St Andrew's speech I gave in Bulawayo. Things were getting tense (my excuse) and Ministers were quite open that my support of African development would lose them the coming election. I took the opportunity ... to warn Joshua Nkomo and his men that they were going too far in their opposition to us ...'[19]

Garfield said: 'One of the most difficult tasks of Government is to balance responsibility on the one hand with the desire to make further concessions towards the growing liberty of the individual citizen – particularly the African ... we have been ... concerning ourselves with the preparation of further security legislation which is of course of a restrictive nature ... What follows is said in the hope that public opinion, both European and African, will be so roused

---

17 T. O. Ranger, Valedictory Lecture, St Anthony's College, Oxford, 19 June 1997, 'Living Africa: Making and Writing History in Zimbabwe'. I am grateful to Professor Ranger for permission to quote this extract.
18 Presidential Address, URP Congress, September 1957, TPPC.
19 GT/SP, 29.7.2002, TPPC.

in the support of freedom for the individual and the maintenance of good relationships between the races and between the forces of law and order and the people themselves, that we may yet be able to refrain from bringing our new security measure before Parliament in February next. In Southern Rhodesia there is no cause for alarm and in general the relationships between our peoples are good ...'

Garfield said that Joshua Nkomo was well educated, capable and responsible, but the name '"Congress" was not reassuring, for its popular appeal was likely to be on the lines of the northern Congresses ... The constitution which was accepted was a reasonably responsible document but we did not know whether Mr Guy Clutton-Brock and the others who helped frame it meant it to be a rule of conduct for Congress members in Southern Rhodesia, or propaganda ... Africans who join the present political parties are termed "sell-outs", "Judas Iscariots", "foolish people" and they are warned that they will be dealt with in due course ...

'In a totalitarian country resistance and violence may be the only means which are available to the people, but in Southern Rhodesia there are democratic ways of approach to authority ... It is the first duty of the Government to provide protection for all our people, and this we will continue to do, even if it means introducing further legal restrictions. If, on the other hand, leaders in Congress and particularly Mr Clutton-Brock and Mr Nyandoro would throw in their weight with the forces of law and order, if they would give their support to the cause of racial harmony, we could in the next three months halt the erosion which has started and make further restrictions unnecessary.'[20]

Garfield saw Nkomo in the Prime Minister's office in Bulawayo on his way to the family holiday in South Africa two weeks later. At their meeting, Garfield 'received an assurance from [Nkomo] that his organisation would not break the law but would be faithful to the terms of the sound Constitution'.[21] Garfield wished to keep on friendly terms with Nkomo and the other African leaders. Paddy Lloyd approved of Garfield's meeting with Nkomo, at that time 'a very mild nationalist ... It was the effort of a Prime Minister to reach a modus vivendi with a man whom he knew had considerable support among his people and it was a statesmanlike thing to do rather than a foolish thing to do.'[22]

Nkomo, meanwhile, had done what he could to help Garfield. The *Central African Examiner* of 21 December referred to a speech by Nkomo: 'Mr

---

20 GT/St Andrew's Night Banquet, Bulawayo, 30.11.57, Ref. PRO 88/57, TPPC.
21 *Sunday Mail*, 14.9.66.
22 Oral LL.2, NAZ.

Nkomo ... rightly calls the Prime Minister 'a man in whom Africans have confidence' ...'.[23]

'Of course, Guy and I were working for the same end, the bringing in of the African majority to a democratic system', Garfield wrote in 1995.[24] 'However, I was on the side of legality and working from the existing structures to a new order. Guy saw that that was a hopeless endeavour and worked entirely with the people ... a position which eventually and in desperation I had to accept for myself.'

---

23   *Central African Examiner*, 21.12.57, vol. 1, no. 15.
24   GT/SP, 14.2.95, TPPC.

46

Party Fusion and the Growing Crisis

'I sincerely believe that the influence of the United Rhodesia Party liberals will be submerged by the reactionary forces in the United Federal Party.'

Leopold Takawira

In July, the *Central African Examiner* published an article by Enoch Dumbutshena in which he expressed the fears of Africans at the 'intended fusion'. It 'had been hoped that the URP was going to split, the liberal wing following Mr Todd and the reactionary wing finding a home in the Dominion Party or joining the unprogressive wing of the Federal Party under Sir Roy Welensky'.[1]

Party fusion was debated at the URP's Congress in September. Garfield correctly but rather tactlessly pointed out that, 'the URP had no influence in Federal Party discussions as they did not have a vote at their Congress. Once fused they could influence the joint policy.'[2] Congress having voted for fusion, the URP appointments to be made would be for the interim period only. Nathan Shamuyarira and Chad Chipunza expressed reservations about fusion, because the Federal Party had no African branches. *The Chronicle* correspondent observed that 'the [United Rhodesia] Party is keen on merging but it has no intention of submerging'.[3]

At the Federal Party Congress on 22 and 23 November, URP members who were also Federal Party members were not sufficiently watchful of URP interests and let pass the opportunity to question some of the Federal Party's statements, for example regarding the membership of the Southern Rhodesia

---

1 *Central African Examiner*, 20.7.57.
2 URP Congress Minutes, 20.9.57, MS.1082/1/6, Todd Papers, NAZ.
3 *The Chronicle*, 23.9.57.

Executive of the fused party, the United Federal Party.

The editorial in the *African Weekly* of 27 November commented that the failure of the Federation to earn the 'loyalty and respect' of the African people 'could be laid at the door of the Federal Party as a whole and its leadership in particular'. The paper questioned whether 'the URP is going to maintain the niche that it had carved or was beginning to carve in the hearts of the African people' following party fusion.[4]

Dr Claire Palley points out that, 'If the Federal Government wished to take action in any field it would override Territorial views'.[5] This was a fear that liberal URP members had harboured – and with reason. Welensky now had control over the affairs of the Southern Rhodesian party, even though the URP had neither accepted fusion nor dissolved itself.

After the Federal Party debate, Greenfield announced: 'The adoption of the new constitution [of the UFP] would form a framework *into which the URP could merge*' (my italics). At the time, the URP, again manifesting inattention and poor judgement, did not appear to notice this hint of their new, inferior status. Greenfield's statement went on to speak of the joint congress of the two parties which would follow: when 'the branch position has been adjusted it will be necessary to hold a territorial congress of the UFP for Southern Rhodesia. This congress will include the present URP MPs and Federal MPs who represent constituencies in the colony, besides members of the *central executive of the UFP and URP* and delegates from the UFP branches' (my italics).[6]

The chairmen of the United Rhodesia Party branches at Harari and Highfield resigned in protest against fusion. In the end, the powerful Federal Party machine took over; the URP, instead of becoming the Southern Rhodesia wing of the United Federal Party, found itself unable even to persuade Greenfield to abide by earlier – announced – decisions as to, for example, the position of the URP Central Committee. Ultimately, Greenfield, Welensky and senior Federal Party (now UFP) officials collaborated with Garfield's rebellious ministers to force his resignation as Southern Rhodesia Prime Minister.

***

The cabinet crisis occurred because the Government had to face racial matters at the same time as the country entered the pre-general election period. Hardwicke Holderness noted in February 1958 that by mid-1957 the

---

4   *African Weekly*, 27.11.57.
5   Palley, 1966, p. 359.
6   *Rhodesia Herald*, 25.11.57.

'conservatives' in the party had decided they must get rid of Todd if the party was to win the next election. 'They thought this would come about naturally in conjunction with fusion.'[7] He also wrote, in his own election manifesto for the 1958 general election: 'Having worked happily for three-and-a-half years with a perfectly straightforward man – inexperienced as a Prime Minister, capable of making mistakes, but with integrity and a streak of brilliant ability and leadership in public affairs – they now built him up, in their own minds and by grumbling to their friends, as a sort of monster consumed with ambition and bent on undermining the security of the European population.'[8]

There had been a number of signs of dissatisfaction in the party: the change of mood on the Industrial Conciliation Bill; Fletcher's behaviour over the Immorality Motion, and the vote at the end of the debate; Wightwick's well-publicised letter demanding Garfield's resignation; and party disquiet over the franchise. In August, Ellman-Brown had threatened resignation over increased spending on African education.

Holderness's account of the growing crisis continues: 'After the September Congress several private meetings had taken place between Stumbles and Ellman-Brown and then Hatty had been brought in, and when the three of them had found themselves in agreement about their complaints against Todd, they had brought in the old hand, Fletcher.'[9] In his own Oral Archive, Fletcher says: 'Hatty and Ellman-Brown and the other ministers came to me and said that Todd had done things and made statements that infuriated them, and they were not going to serve under him any longer … So then I said, "you know, I have been against Todd all along … the only honourable thing to do in this case is to tell him".'[10] Fletcher had been 'against Todd all along' but had served in his cabinet for four years!

The Oral Archivist probed interviewees on the subject of the 'underlying reason' for the cabinet rebellion over the following years but discovered nothing. There are several mysterious references, for example in Fletcher's Oral Archive: 'these are not to be published yet'. The interviewer has a note here: 'Hatty and Ellman-Brown assembled a large number of specific charges against Todd … They never used them, for some reason unknown' (to Fletcher). '"At the last minute" they did not bring them forward. They related to the misuse of government money.'[11] There is no evidence here – on

---

7 'Notes, General Meeting, Salisbury North URP Branch, 3.2.58', TPPC.
8 'The real issue in the Election', June 1958, File 531/1, Welensky Papers, Bodleian Library.
9 Holderness, 1985, p. 219. Fletcher refers to this in his Oral archive: Oral FL.1, NAZ.
10 Oral FL.1, NAZ.
11 Ibid.

the contrary, the size of Garfield's bank overdraft in 1958 would indicate that he was subsidising Southern Rhodesia's Prime Minister to a considerable extent. When Cyril Hatty was asked about the 'deeper and more subtle reasons', he was emphatic in denying the existence of any such grounds of complaint against Garfield.[12]

***

So, Fletcher went to Northward to challenge Garfield on the afternoon of Sunday 24 November – 'immediately after the projected United Federal Party – to which Mr Todd had previously committed himself in good faith – was formally brought into being by the one-sided action of the Federal Party'.[13] Garfield was totally unprepared for Fletcher's message. For many weeks, anxiety about Grace had been his principal preoccupation. His account of the Fletcher interview notes that: '[Mr Fletcher] told me that Ministers had held private meetings and had decided to resign the following morning. I cannot tell adequately of my feeling of shock. At last Congress, Mr Fletcher had said that the cabinet was a team, a happy one, and one in which no change in leadership could bring improvement, and I fully believed that this was a truthful and correct statement ... Mr Fletcher said that he had really nothing to do with the situation for it was only recently that he had been brought into the confidence of the others. He said the Ministers believed that in the country there was dissatisfaction with my leadership and had therefore decided to withdraw their support of me.'[14]

Garfield was anxious to hear direct from the other ministers what their views were. He expected them next morning, but, owing to some muddle, none of them appeared; alone came Hatty in the afternoon, and added to the confusion by saying that Fletcher acted without his authority and 'I myself have never thought that the political situation was irretrievable'.

On Monday, Garfield saw Welensky, and on the morning of Tuesday 26th he met the full cabinet. 'There was no difference between us on general policy. The Ministers were generous in their praise of my leadership and work up to six months earlier. They complained that I had not given so much care and thought to cabinet recently as I usually did; but themselves acknowledged that I had been under a heavy strain because of my wife's serious illness. Their real complaint was not on policy or practice; but on political reaction to me throughout the country ... they believed that so many people were of the

---

12 Interview, C. J. Hatty/SP, 6.7.97.
13 *The Chronicle*, 1.2.58.
14 GT's 'Notes on Recent Happenings 23.1.58', File PM.50/80, Box 167639, Records Office, NAZ.

opinion that I was too pro-African that the Party would not be able to win the next election. A long discussion took place and at the end of it we agreed that there would be full unity ...'[15]

The story broke on 27 November with a report in the *Rand Daily Mail*, but with no mention of the ministers' resignation threat: 'Policy differences among members of the Southern Rhodesia cabinet may result in the resignation within the next few days of Mr R. S. Garfield Todd ... secret meetings of both cabinet ministers and backbenchers have taken place in the Federal capital every day since last Thursday ...'[16]

In reply to this, Garfield issued a statement which included the sentence: 'My ministers and I are not only fully united in our policy but also in our confidence in one another, and I believe we have good reason for such confidence in the light of achievement and development over the past four years'.[17] Garfield believed that his denial was 'the truth'.[18]

The United Kingdom High Commissioner, Mr Rupert Metcalf, in a long despatch to the CRO in London in January 1958, observed rather sharply that the ministers 'appear to be more pre-occupied with pursuing their own short-term plans and ambitions than pulling together as a team'.[19] The *Rhodesia Herald* editorial on 29 November commented that, 'a very vicious whispering campaign is under way in the Federation ... the possibility of the Prime Minister's resignation discussed ... Were the acknowledged leader of liberal thought to be pushed out at the first opportunity after fusion ... it would be a serious shock to a substantial section of opinion within the Federation and a powerful weapon in the hands of the Federal Government's opponents overseas.'[20]

Fletcher says in his Oral Archive that 'Todd admitted that he was doing wrong and promised to mend his ways, and he promised to make statements and contradict impressions.' When Fletcher was asked by the Oral Archivist 'what concessions to the right' Todd made, he replied: 'He did not make any really.'

Metcalf, in his despatch referred to above, writes: 'The cabinet is said to have threatened to oust Mr Todd if he did not take a strong line, but finally

---

15 Ibid.
16 *Rand Daily Mail*, 27.11.57.
17 PM's statement, 27.11.57, MS.390/2/2, Todd Papers, NAZ.
18 GT's 'Notes on Recent Happenings 23.1.58', File PM.50/80, Box 167639, Records Office, NAZ.
19 UKHCSR/G. E. B. Shannon, CRO, 10.1.58, Ref. CA 433/310/1 (DO35/7643), CRO, PRO, UK.
20 *Rhodesia Herald*, 29.11.57.

ministers grudgingly agreed to postpone the decision ... to give him time to try to warn Congress off further mischief-making.'[21]

---

21 UKHCSR/G. E. B. Shannon, CRO, 10.1.58, Ref. CA 433/310/1 (DO35/7643), CRO, PRO, UK.

47

'Is this the Beginning of the End for Todd?'

'The events of the Todd/Whitehead period had very wide-spread repercussions and in no small way are responsible for what has happened.'

Sir Roy Welensky, 1975

During the hot, difficult weeks of November and December 1957, the Southern Rhodesia Government had another major concern: a review of the appalling wages paid to African employees, which had prompted unrest in 1956. In January 1957, Garfield, as Minister of Labour, had set up the Urban Industries Native Labour Board 'to investigate conditions of employment of natives in those industries for which no other Labour Board has been established'.[1]

The board reported on 19 June 1957, with recommended amendments to the 1953 regulations. The most important of these was for a minimum monthly wage for adult male Africans employed in Salisbury and Bulawayo of £6.10.6; in other municipal areas, £6.0.3; and in Town Management Board areas £5.10.6.[2] (A white shorthand-typist in a Civil Service typing pool earned around £60 a month.)

Cabinet discussed the report at six consecutive meetings and also with all the other labour boards. The report was submitted to the Federal Prime Minister's department, because Rhodesia Railways, one of the largest employers of African labour, would be affected, and satisfactory discussions were held with the Federal Government. Before new regulations were published, they were also sent for comment to the Federated Chambers of Commerce and the Association of Rhodesian and Nyasaland Industries (ARNI, whose President

---

1   SRC(57)117 of 21.6.57, File S.3242/21 NAZ.
2   Ibid.

was A. E. Abrahamson, MP). Garfield and his labour officials had unofficial and confidential discussions with a number of industrialists. On 30 August, the cabinet 'agreed that it was likely that industry would be prepared to accept the necessity for higher starting wages'.[3]

The new labour award would be announced on 16 December 1957, effective from 1 January following.[4] Garfield was due to go on holiday on 16 December, but offered to delay his departure to be present when the new regulations came into force. However, the cabinet 'pressed' him to go off as planned. 'I was leaving the matter of the wage regulations in the hands of Fletcher, Minister of Native Affairs, who for years had dealt with native labour boards and should have been able to have dealt satisfactorily with any position that might arise.'[5] (Fletcher would, as usual whenever Garfield was away, be acting Prime Minister.) Garfield later wrote: 'The cabinet, and especially Ben [Fletcher], were adamant that they would cope. We were unanimous in our final decisions. I was worried but I went on my way.'[6] Garfield genuinely believed what he had said in his statement about cabinet unity, and had no suspicion that there might be continuing resentment and dissatisfaction among his ministers.

The new minimum wage rates were announced in the press on 18 December and, the *Rhodesia Herald* reported, 'brought strong protests from the textile industry ... [which] claims the increase ... has been thrust upon it without warning ... To the building industry, the new regulations were not a complete surprise ... [employers] have been aware for some time of possible changes and within limits have planned accordingly ... In some sections of industry, the new rates will have little effect as existing payments are based on similar or even better schedules.'[7]

The jute industry was a part of the textile industry, and sent two representatives to that Board. H. D. Wightwick, MP, managing director of Rhodesia Jute Industries, who was a powerful voice in that industry, had declined an invitation to serve on the Board. He complained to the Department of Labour that his Umtali Jute Company had not been fairly treated. At his request, the Textile Industry Board, which had been consulted before the award was made, was recalled. Labour officials, ARNI and Garfield's ministers all became embroiled – and, by the time everyone concerned was convinced that there was no case to answer, Wightwick had launched a more outspoken personal attack on Garfield.

---

3   Cabinet Minutes meeting 29, 2.9.57, File MS.1086/2/5, Todd Papers, NAZ.
4   Meeting 33, 16.10.57, ibid.
5   Ibid.
6   GT/SP, 20.9.2000, TPPC.
7   *Rhodesia Herald*, 18.12.57.

On 26 December, Wightwick issued a press statement announcing his resignation from the United Federal Party. It was published in the *Umtali Post* on the 27th: 'I no longer have confidence in either the judgment or the leadership of the Prime Minister ... and I cannot continue as a Member of Parliament to associate myself with the increasing tendency for major political and economic decisions to be imposed on the country without the fullest discussion in the party caucus or Parliament ...

'Mr Todd has been hasty, tactless and inept in his handling of political matters'; the wage rise had been 'imposed in a manner which the Press has rightly dubbed "ham-fisted" ... It seems certain that in this matter Mr Todd has not consulted with either the Members of his own party or with the Federal Government.'

Wightwick concluded: 'Apart from his failure as a Minister of Labour Mr Todd has, in many political utterances, made it clear that his personal beliefs are apt to affect his judgment as a Prime Minister. I can no longer continue to be branded as one of his supporters.'[8]

The Cabinet Secretary cabled Garfield a long précis of Wightwick's statement and went on: 'Umtali Executive [i.e. UFP] have decided not repeat not to ask for Wightwick's resignation from Parliament and they appear to support him stop Herald Leader says resignation no surprise and half-expected before this but has unusual significance present time and now gives concrete form to rumours of party dissension and dissatisfaction among section and good thing matter has come into open stop situation thus precipitated calls for clarification.'[9]

Garfield replied the next day, the 28th: 'Thanks telegram stop if ministers think it desirable could return by January 5th'. This was not received by the Cabinet Office until the 30th, and received the immediate response: 'No need to return earlier than you have arranged.'[10] Garfield was 'delighted' to receive this reply, and issued a press statement which pointed out that Wightwick had neither criticised nor opposed his election as party leader at the party's congress, and his attempt now to remove him was undemocratic: 'consultations with the Party Caucus have been regularly and fully maintained'.[11]

An editorial in the *Umtali Post* pointed out that Wightwick was 'not elected to parliament to represent industry. He was put there by the voters ... Mr Todd has served the Colony well ... he is the best man for the job of Territorial Prime Minister ... and under his guidance Southern Rhodesia has gone far towards

---

8   *Umtali Post*, 27.12.57.
9   Telegram, Gerald B. Clarke/GT, 27.12.57, File MS.390/2/2, Todd Papers, NAZ.
10 Gerald B. Clarke/GT, 30.12.57, File 50/90, Box 167639, Records Office, NAZ.
11 *Rhodesia Herald*, 28.12.57.

solving some of the racial problems which, more than anything else, could call a halt to progress if neglected.'[12]

The Chronicle warned its readers that, 'The issues at stake are far wider than those enumerated by Mr Wightwick. He is conducting what virtually amounts to a personal vendetta against the Southern Rhodesia Prime Minister, but Mr Todd would be the first to admit that it is not his own political future that matters, so much as what he stands for ... [Todd is] a leader who in ability and drive certainly has no equal in the Southern Rhodesia Parliament ... It is no secret that his liberal approach has earned him many political enemies and caused uneasiness even within the ranks of his own party ... [but] he has a large following – many believe his mixture of firmness and liberalism is the only realistic approach to the African problem ... We firmly believe that a vote of no confidence in Mr Todd at this moment in our political history would do irreparable damage, not only to Southern Rhodesia's reputation, but to that of the whole Federation. It would be interpreted, not without justification, as a hardening of European attitudes against African political and economic advancement.'[13]

The *African Daily News* editorial commented: 'If [Todd] is removed because of his desire to build a modern industrial society in which both Africans and Europeans have an equal stake, white Rhodesians have no leg to stand on with their claim that they believe in the policy of partnership ... The wage increases ... are necessary and timely.'[14] Abe Abrahamson, as ARNI president, issued a New Year message in which he said 'organised industry has accepted the latest wage award in a responsible manner'.[15]

In mid-1960, Wightwick wrote a revealing letter to Welensky: 'I had precipitated the Todd crisis with the avowed intention of eliminating him from continuing to play any part in the Government of Southern Rhodesia ... You were generous enough to remark to me that you thought the country owed me a debt for what I did and that it should not be forgotten.'[16]

***

The exceptionally hot, dry weather that had tried tempers so sorely in November and December gave way to more than usually heavy rains, with overflowing rivers, bridges either submerged or washed away, and general disruption of road traffic north and south of the border with South Africa. New Year 1958

---

12   *Umtali Post*, 27.12.57.
13   *The Chronicle*, 28.12.57.
14   *African Daily News*, 28.12.57.
15   PRO File 3/58, Fletcher Statement, 4.2.58.
16   H. D. Wightwick/RW, 7.6.60, File 683/4, Welensky Papers, Bodleian Library.

brought a knighthood for Fletcher on Garfield's recommendation.

At the end of cabinet meetings in early January, when the Cabinet Secretary had withdrawn, there were lengthy discussions among the ministers, clearly flustered by the noises coming from Umtali. Gerald Clarke was a loyal civil servant, giving his loyalty to the Government of the day, and he was extremely worried about what was going on. After one cabinet meeting, as he walked past my desk, he muttered out of the corner of his mouth: 'Get him back!' A couple of days later, Garfield telephoned to say he would return on the 9th.

Cabinet met on 7, 8 and 9 January and discussed the labour award at each meeting, with the Secretary for Labour, Mr Jack Armstrong, and the Adviser to the Department present at the first two. On the 9th, after a meeting with Abrahamson and a senior ARNI official, 'it was now clear that no purpose would be served by receiving representatives of the Jute industry'.[17] Abrahamson said 'that there had been unanimous acceptance in the industry for the minimum wage' and made it clear that there would be difficulties if 'the industry, which had made the most trouble and had shouted the loudest, seemed to get away with their representations'.[18]

On 9 January, Garfield and Grace flew to Salisbury, where they were met by Fletcher, who, heedless alike of hovering reporters and interested observers crowding the windows of the terminal building, immediately engaged the Prime Minister in obviously serious discussion. Garfield writes of his airport conversation with Fletcher: 'You may imagine my shocked surprise when I stepped off the 'plane at 8:25am and was told by Sir Patrick Fletcher that things were in a bad way and that Ministers wished to meet me the next morning to tender their resignations. I asked if anything had happened to account for such action. Sir Patrick said that it had resulted from the complete fiasco in the labour situation ... [they] had become so frustrated and angry over the way I had mishandled the whole thing that, after several cabinet meetings, they had all decided that I had shown complete incompetence and that they would therefore put in their resignations ...

'I was so shocked to be treated in this fashion on my return that I felt like fighting them and not going out as they wished me to do. Sir Patrick warned me against such a course of action and said that I had a great responsibility upon my shoulders and that I should not make any trouble. He warned me particularly of the reaction overseas ...'[19]

---

17 Notes of meeting, ARNI representatives and Cabinet, 9.1.58, File MS.1085/4/4, Todd Papers, NAZ.
18 Cabinet meeting 4, 9.1.58, ibid.
19 File PM.50/80, Box 167639, Records Office, NAZ.

'Is this the Beginning of the End for Todd?'

On arrival at Northward, Garfield studied all the cabinet minutes and papers and was fully briefed by Jack Armstrong about the whole labour-award situation – an almost routine affair which Fletcher and Wightwick between them had blown up into a crisis. It was clear that the ministers had laboured under a great many misapprehensions. When he met the cabinet next morning, Garfield went through it all very carefully with them. Ellman-Brown wanted to discuss the general political situation and Garfield's leadership, and the latter said he was prepared to do so 'as long as we discussed leadership in relation to the political situation and did not link it with any supposed maladministration of Labour for I refuted any allegation that my Department or I had shown incompetence ... nothing further was said regarding the labour situation'.[20] Garfield felt completely vindicated when he read in the *Rhodesia Herald* of 16 January: 'Higher wages have not led to African dismissals'.

Cyril Dunn writes that the ministers 'believed they had discovered mistakes which would allow them to attack Mr Todd, not for any excess of zeal for partnership, but for his incompetence. As it happens, the Ministers seem to have erred ... But a cabinet which had wanted a change of leadership for some time was evidently not to be diverted and went ahead with general allegations of "lost confidence".'[21] Clyde Sanger sums up: 'The grounds for resignation were flimsy but they were the best that Fletcher and Ellman-Brown could find.'[22]

---

20   Ibid.
21   Dunn, 1959, pp. 170–1.
22   Sanger, 1960, p. 145.

48

THE CRISIS BREAKS

'You cannot always run satisfactorily on the side of safety – you have got to take risks.'

Garfield Todd

Geoff Ellman-Brown, one of Garfield's rebellious ministers, told the Oral Archivist at NAZ: 'I think Hardwicke Holderness's book dealing with the build-up to the Todd crisis ... is a fair account of all that.'[1] Holderness has also left many notes on the significant political events of 1958, one of which explains the actions of the ministers: when it became clear that their allegations of incompetence and maladministration did not stand up, 'they resigned on the question of what they referred to as his "Leadership". In order to substantiate the allegation of bad leadership they talk about "dictatorship". But this is really quite silly, because they fully agree that right up until the middle of [1957] ... there could not have been a happier team or better leadership ...'[2]

In his own 'Notes on recent happenings in the political situation in Southern Rhodesia, 23.1.58', Garfield writes that 'At first, I found little courage to stand against their expressed will. They had told me quite definitely that they would not continue to support me ... Ministers were not concerned ... with either Caucus or Congress, but with effecting an immediate change in the leadership of the Party ...'[3]

When Garfield met his ministers on 10 January 1958 and they had concluded their discussion of the Labour Award, the matter of Garfield's ability, or otherwise, to lead the party to victory in the next election was brought up.

---

1   G. Ellman-Brown, Oral 235, NAZ.
2   TPPC.
3   23.1.58, File PM/50/80, Box 167639, Records Office, NAZ.

'Each man stated that he would withdraw his support and someone suggested that I might like time to think the matter over. They all agreed to wait 24 hours. I then asked if they were putting in their resignations and they said they would if I wanted them to do so. I then asked each one if he was quite decided in his action and when I was assured that all were, I said that as they had no further decisions to make they might as well give me their resignations ... I would then be in a position to take such action as I considered best ... we rose and spent a little time making our farewells for our four years' work together was finished and we all had regrets.'[4]

But there was obviously some misunderstanding on the ministers' part, for according to Ian Hancock, who interviewed many of the 'principal players' in the drama, they 'expected that the Prime Minister would take note of a unanimous vote of no confidence and promptly submit his own resignation to the Governor'.[5] This is borne out by the fact that, later in the day, the ministers met with certain departmental advisers to consider 'a very important matter ... which they had only the moral right to consider if they were, in fact, the government (and not a group of men who were putting in their resignations)'.[6]

Garfield consulted Tredgold throughout the crisis, and now he sought to establish what would be the legal position of any action he might take. He was advised, 'that if he resigned the Governor would have to ask him to form another government and that he should not bring the Governor into a political quarrel. Similarly, if he asked the Governor to dissolve Parliament and hold a General Election at once, the Governor would have to refuse since this was constitutionally a party matter and not something which concerned national interests.'[7]

As a result of his talks with the Governor and Sir Robert and constant discussion with Grace, now fully restored to health, Garfield decided he would accept the ministers' resignations and carry on with a new cabinet. Cyril Dunn admirably captures this moment – and a fundamental part of Garfield's character: 'When things came ... to their inevitable point, Mr Todd's genial exterior was shown to cover an internal framework of pure steel.'[8] Garfield was ready to resign if this were the right thing to do. 'I saw clearly that my duty was to continue with government if I could do so. This I had to test ... Ill-health is a fair reason for resignation. Inadequacy as a leader should ... be determined

---

4   GT's 'Notes on Recent Happenings 23.1.58'.
5   Hancock, 1984, p. 69.
6   GT's 'Notes for Congress', 8.2.58.
7   Sanger, 1960, p. 156.
8   Dunn, 1959, p. 171.

by the Party. The Party Congress, under our constitution, has complete control over the appointment or dismissal of its leader.'⁹

On 11 January, the *Rhodesia Herald* speculated: 'Todd may seek a vote of confidence. Liberalism under fire.' Garfield read this before driving to the airport to meet Lansdell Christie and his lawyer. He had hoped to take them to the ranch and the Victoria Falls, but now it was Grace who would introduce them to Hokonui. Having driven them to Northward, Garfield prepared for his press conference at noon – rather impatiently waiting for the resignation letters of his ministers. 'When 10.15 came I realised that Ministers were probably so sure that I was myself resigning that they were not going to send in their resignations. I therefore rang Mr Hatty ... his reply was a question: "Do you require them?" I said I did and that I had a Press Conference at noon.' They arrived fifteen minutes later – and, as Fletcher baldly states in his Oral Archive, 'Todd had no cabinet'.¹⁰

At noon, the press arrived in force at the PM's office. The *Gwelo Times* reported that Mr Todd spoke with 'an impressive display of dignity and flashes of humour'.¹¹ Garfield read his statement about the events of the immediate past, Fletcher's airport bombshell, the meeting with the ministers and their resignations. They 'had regretfully come to the conclusion that the measure of criticism levelled at me at present would make it impossible for the Party to win the next election ... they had decided to withdraw their support of me. At the recent Party Congress no indication was given by any Minister that there was dissatisfaction within the cabinet.

'I am determined to go back to the Party and give them an opportunity to express their will. I know that there are people who want me removed from the Premiership but there are also many people who have supported me and encouraged me and I have no intention of meekly stepping aside to permit four men who may be quite wrong, even in their summing up of the political situation, to have their way. A change of leadership might be in the best interests of the country ... I have no wish to cause a split in the United Federal Party. I am a moderate, as a fair appraisal of my administration over the past four years will prove. Within the ranks of the United Federal Party there are a great many moderates, but there are also extremists, both liberal and reactionary. The danger at the present moment is ... from moderates who allow fear to sway them to such an extent that the reactionary element may take control of the United Federal Party ...

---

9   GT, *Central African Examiner* questions, 28.1.58, File MS.390/2/2, Todd Papers, NAZ.
10 Oral FL.2, NAZ.
11 *Gwelo Times*, 17.1.58.

'Whoever is to lead Southern Rhodesia at this time must recognise the vital importance of calling upon the support, co-operation and loyalty of both Europeans and Africans. This is no time for wavering; this is no time to embrace policies of fear; for we have come to our year of decision, our election year ...'[12]

The FBC lunchtime bulletin that day gave the general public its first news of the ministers' resignation. The crisis was under discussion in the Federal Cabinet, where Greenfield advised that Todd would have to resign when his cabinet rebelled. Sir Athol Evans, Secretary for Home Affairs, was 'firmly of the opinion that [the ministers'] action was wrong for themselves and principally for Southern Rhodesia'.[13]

The ex-ministers had their say in the Sunday papers of 12 January, maintaining that Garfield had 'confused our personal regard for him, his ability and his capacity for work with our opinion as a Prime Minister'. They had lost confidence in him as a leader, a view 'shared by many in the party ... we were only concerned with the true interests of stable government'.[14]

Garfield decided to go to a Party Congress as 'the right and proper place to decide questions of leadership'. He writes in his 'Notes on recent happenings ...': 'This reason alone fully justifies my stand ... I speak with humility, but with conviction and some knowledge, when I say that my removal from office at this moment would be widely interpreted abroad to indicate a rejection of Southern Rhodesia's moderately liberal stand ... I know also that to the great African section of our population this is how the position would appear.'

Garfield's first duty was to appoint a cabinet. At another press conference on Sunday evening, he said he would announce on Tuesday the names of the new ministers. 'This will actually mean that Southern Rhodesia will have been without Ministers for two days only, a shorter space of time than normally might follow a general election.'[15]

Monday's newspapers were full of comment on the political situation and Garfield's statement, together with speculation on his position, which the *The Chronicle* described as 'precarious for the simple reason that, unlike some Rhodesian politicians, he refused to compromise on principles or to camouflage liberal legislation to make it more palatable to European opinion'.[16] Garfield's new 'team', from among his loyal backbenchers, consisted of Sir George

---

12 SRG Press Statement, PRO/6/58, 11.1.58, File MS.390/2/2, Todd Papers, NAZ.
13 Sir Athol Evans/HHCH, 6.9.88, *Lost Chance* follow-up project, Holderness Papers, Bodleian Library.
14 *Sunday Mail*, 12.1.58.
15 PM's Press Statement, PRO/9/58, 12.1.58, File MS.390/2/2, Todd Papers, NAZ.
16 *The Chronicle*, 13.1.58.

Davenport, Ralph and Eric Palmer, Abe Abrahamson and Paddy Lloyd. Sir George was an obvious first choice for Garfield, and he readily agreed to serve. His ability, unassailable integrity and public spirit gave the new cabinet a firm foundation. The Palmer brothers were long-established, wealthy farmers from the Norton area near Salisbury, described by Lawrence Vambe as 'distinctly different in outlook from most' farmers.[17] Once again, Garfield had not chosen Holderness as Minister of Justice – 'I thought he would be the last straw'[18] – but his legal training, his total honesty, his unique understanding of the attitudes of educated Africans, and his unwavering, humorous and candid friendship made him a most important adviser and ally.

Garfield's new cabinet gave him great personal support and encouragement. Sir William Murphy considered it 'a fine team ... a distinct improvement on its predecessors'.[19] The *Rhodesia Herald* described the new ministers as 'men who, in private life and as backbenchers in Parliament, have proved themselves capable and successful'.[20]

---

17 Vambe, 1976, p. 228.
18 GT/SP, TPPC.
19 Sir William Murphy/GT, 15.1.58, MS.390/1/4, Todd Papers, NAZ.
20 *Rhodesia Herald*, 15.1.58.

49

Caucus Meeting and Second Cabinet

'It is not pleasant to be betrayed by people whose loyalty one should be able to trust.'

Garfield Todd

By the end of Tuesday 14 January 1958, Southern Rhodesia had a new cabinet, and the final battle lines had been drawn for a leadership Congress on 8 February. However much the rebel ministers proclaimed that Garfield's liberalism was not the *casus belli*, however much they spoke of Garfield's failures of leadership and so on, the impartial observer was quite clear. As the *Rand Daily Mail* put it: 'The main criticism of Mr Todd has been his so-called "ultra liberal" outlook, and his cabinet felt that this ultra-liberalism would lose them the next election.'[1]

Garfield told Caucus it was being held 'simply to bring members more fully into the picture'.[2] The planned Congress would 'give all members the opportunity to express their views and also to have their democratic share in making decisions regarding leadership'. Garfield also gave his reasons for not recalling Parliament: 'If this were a tussle between two different parties for support ... then such a course of action will be correct.' The present dispute was not between two parties, but within a party; and not a dispute about policies but about personalities – 'it is an issue to be referred to Congress ... for decision. The question before the Party is primarily that of deciding on their leader ... then the question of who is to be Prime Minister will also have been settled ...'

Garfield was followed by the ex-ministers. Hardwicke Holderness took detailed notes of the meeting; quotations from those notes follow, as what

---

1   *Rand Daily Mail*, 14.1.58.
2   'PM's Notes for Caucus', 14.1.58, MS.390/2/2, Todd Papers, NAZ.

the ex-ministers said at Caucus formed the substance of their speeches – and accusations – at the Leadership Congress on 8 February when the press was not present and of which no record has been found, though they gave individual statements to the press.

Fletcher had been 'worried over the PM talking at every street corner on racial matters ... disturbing effect on the African ... building up racial pressure ... Fletcher had insisted on fusion.' Regarding 24 November: 'An undertaking was given to do the utmost to make the Government work ... The next morning when the Ministers told the PM they intended to resign there were two alternatives open to the PM: he could resign or carry on. "We told him we were prepared to carry on as a Caretaker Government." The PM interjected to deny this. Fletcher said anyway the PM must have been very naive not to understand the position. ... They had said "when you are ready for them we will hand in our resignations".'

Stumbles had opposed the Land Apportionment Bill. 'He explained to the PM that to achieve the liberal goal we are all after we must be certain to retain the votes of all Europeans.' He had objected to the PM making statements about the franchise proposals which had come to be known as the 'Todd proposals'. All the ex-ministers were shocked at the PM making a statement to the Interracial Association.

On immorality suppression, Stumbles thought there was an agreement in cabinet to act as proposed in Buchan's motion, and was astonished when the Prime Minister took a different line. When it came to the ANC, Stumbles 'proposed to legislate, being worried about security ... and understood that the PM was in favour of legislating ... After the URP Congress Stumbles took over Native Education ... problems began cropping up.' Stumbles and Ellman-Brown felt that the PM's conduct had been such as 'to give rise to a feeling in the country that he was "a sort of Saviour"'. Todd was wrong to see Nkomo ...

Ellman-Brown came next: 'For the first three years the cabinet had been a "wonderful team" ... he soon found that [Hatty and he] had exactly the same ideas on development.' (Hatty interjected here that Todd was with them.) The franchise worried Ellman-Brown ... the PM was 'determined to dictate the policy'.

Ellman-Brown was worried about Garfield's attitude to the miscegenation issue. 'Since then Todd had "ignored me completely in every sphere". Co-ordination had gone. The system of cabinet had not worked properly for the last four or five months. The PM had "pushed matters aside in cabinet – the same attitude as he adopted in Caucus".'

Garfield also took notes during the Caucus meeting, and here writes: 'There was dissent from members present and Mr Eric Palmer, the Whip, spoke up and said that he had not received one complaint from members of the Caucus regarding the running of the Caucus'.[3]

Ellman-Brown 'had advised the PM not to keep talking about the African, and to give up Native Education ... He should show the country he was concerned with "general development" ... Their attitude was that it was 'not what the PM has done, but what he is making people believe, and particularly the African, that he has done'. 'They had lost confidence in the PM's ability to lead the people.'

'Another cause of concern to Ellman-Brown was the "infiltration into the Party of the extreme left". He thought this was doing tremendous harm ... He had told the PM also that there was not room in the same party for Ellman-Brown and Holderness. Holderness should be removed from the caucus. The PM should not have seen Clutton-Brock or Nkomo ... The support which the PM was getting in the African papers was evidence that he was not taking the tough line agreed upon.'

Hatty's 'evidence was given with the air of a man who was in a bad state of nerves and not at all happy ... In the middle of 1957 he felt a change had been taking place. The cabinet had begun differing between themselves ... discussions (on franchise) had indicated that a split in the "basic co-ordination" was beginning to take place. In the discussions of the security question, he felt that the situation was deteriorating. There was a smear campaign against Todd.

'Hatty felt that it was essential to do something to get Todd out of the limelight ... Hatty was concerned about the Party's chances at the next election. After that meeting it was perfectly right to say that there was "complete accord", and Hatty as well as the PM had said this to reporters ... Hatty understood that action would be taken at this stage which would lead to Holderness leaving the caucus ... The ministers had never done any lobbying ...'

Finally came Quinton, who had joined the Government in September 1957: 'It was apparent to him that the Ministers were worried and they were not a "complete team" ... pressures were rising throughout the country, created by the PM's interviews with all and sundry. The PM's interview with Nkomo in Bulawayo had "put a halo round Nkomo's head". Quinton warned the Prime Minister about "over-liberalism" and the pressure of Holderness in Caucus. Quinton told the Prime Minister that Holderness would have to review his position ... the atmosphere in cabinet "strained" ...'

---

3   GT, 'Caucus Notes', MS.390/1/10, Todd Papers, NAZ.

Garfield's Notes record that 'The only important thing that he said was that he, in going round the native reserves, had been concerned with the rise of such groups as the ANC. He said that a senior official of the Native Department had told him that they would continue to have difficulties with Africans just so long as I was prepared to grant interviews to any African at the drop of a hat. He attacked the over-liberalism of the Party and of my leadership.'

In Garfield's 'fairly short' reply, he cleared up the position on the Labour Regulations – 'The concern of the Ministers had been based on a misunderstanding of the position. The PM denied ignoring Ellman-Brown ... and being "dictatorial" at cabinet or Caucus meetings. The situation during the last six months had been a difficult one, personally, for him, and he thought that all the Ministers had been in a rather bad state due to overwork.'[4]

When the meeting adjourned for lunch, four of the five members of the new cabinet (whose names had not yet been announced) were sworn in by the Governor. (Davenport would be sworn in on his return to the Colony the following day.) The 'rebels' also met – and were joined by six MPs. Later, two others joined the ex-ministers. As J. A. Gray wrote on 14 June 1958 in 'The eclipse of Garfield Todd' in the magazine *South Africa*: 'The majority of the party caucus was against the Prime Minister, as the rebels well knew, having taken the precaution of testing how the wind was blowing before they acted.'

Before Caucus resumed that afternoon, the Fletcher group issued a statement in which they announced 'that they had lost confidence in the Prime Minister ... [who] had been irresponsible in calling for the resignations of the retiring ministers before he had formed the new cabinet ...'[5]

When Caucus resumed for an hour at 3.30 p.m., Garfield announced the names of his new cabinet. 'Although this is a caretaker government, I am proud of the capability of the men who are serving in it.'[6] Caucus finally broke up at 4.30 p.m., and only then was Garfield able to have time with his American visitors to discuss the development of Hokonui Ranch. Before dinner, however, he had another press conference. Garfield was always keen that the public should know what its Government was doing – at a time of crisis, this was doubly important.

Garfield told the assembled press: 'I could not submit to the strong temptation to lay down a burden which has been a heavy one, but which, now that I have been deserted by these friends, is almost intolerable. I am fully aware that

---

4   Holderness's 'Memo for Private File of HHCH on Caucus meeting on Cabinet Crisis held on 14 January 1958', TPPC.

5   Undated note [14.1.58], PRO File 1-4, Box 167634, Records Office, NAZ.

6   GT's Statement, PRO/12/58, 14.1.58, File MS.390/2/2, Todd Papers, NAZ.

enormous pressures are being built up to have me removed from office, but I also have been made aware of the wide measure of support which is being given me.'[7]

'The crux of the [ministers'] complaint was that they believed that so many people were of the opinion that I was too pro-African, that the party would not be able to win the next election.'[8]

---

7   PRO/11/58, PRO File 1-4, Box 167634, Records Office, NAZ.
8   GT's notes, 23.1.58, File PM 50/80, Box 167639, Records Office, NAZ.

50

'An Uneasy Month'

'The dispute, which from this distance has always seemed rather foolish and petty ...'

The Times

The day after the Caucus meeting, *The Chronicle* stated the constitutional position: 'The Prime Minister can carry on until he fails to win a no-confidence motion on the leadership in the House – unless the Governor chooses to dismiss him.'[1]

Notwithstanding the ministers' protestations, Africans in Southern Rhodesia clearly saw the issue as one of African advancement. A resolution passed by African voters at a meeting in Harari stated: 'We are very perturbed by the action of the four ministers ... If this spirit were to continue and be the guide in the politics of this land, the African people will be left with no alternative but to break faith completely with the Europeans.' They pledged their 'support for Mr Todd on his broad-mindedness and progressive outlook and the brave stand he has taken on this cabinet crisis, in the interests of the country as a whole'.[2]

The *Manchester Guardian* rather agreed with the Africans of Harari and staunchly supported Garfield, who, 'though far from radical in outlook, is a major figure on the more liberal side' of the UFP.[3] The paper quoted the president of the Southern Rhodesia ANC: Todd '"is a man in whom Africans have confidence". The right-wingers would like to get rid of Mr Todd before the next election, and evidently hoped that he would go quietly. But the Premier is a man of courage and resolution ... He may still fail and this would be a serious set-back. But it would have been much more serious if he had meekly

---
1   *The Chronicle*, 16.1.58.
2   *African Daily News*, 15.1.58.
3   *Manchester Guardian*, 15.1.58.

stood down before the dissidents, or if he had trimmed his sails to suit them.'

The *Scotsman* was quoted in the *Rhodesia Herald* of 15 January: "'It has been said of Mr Todd that he does not represent any large body of white Rhodesians but only the 'better self' of most of them" – that he thinks and tries to act in the way the majority of them would like to do if they were not driven to act otherwise by what they consider to be the necessities of their own survival. On that precarious basis of moral force, plus, it must be stated, a very astute exploitation of political manoeuvre, Mr Todd has preserved a delicate balance between the extremists ... Far too many whites see in Mr Todd's liberalism a betrayal of their interests and a threat to their very survival ... And far too many Africans among whom are some of the leaders who must shape African minds for the future, even while they admit his sincerity, regard Mr Todd's achievements as merely imposing a false front of liberalism which stifles opposition without implying any real change of heart in the white camp, and so frustrates the straight fight which they would like to make for African domination and full self-government ... can Mr Todd survive to hold the middle way of controlled and reasonable progress? And, if not, then, can the Federation hold to that road?"[4]

***

We have seen that the Federal cabinet and officials were closely involved in what was happening in Southern Rhodesia, and particularly with the ex-ministers. The day after the Caucus meeting, Stumbles saw Greenfield, who reported to Welensky that Stumbles 'was convinced that Fletcher will carry the day ... [Fletcher] is guiltless of any intrigue ... I am myself inclined to think that Ben may be the best of a bad job'.[5] As for Fletcher's virtuous abstention from intrigue, we have it from the man himself that he 'led the movement to throw Todd out'.[6] Quinton says the cabinet met in Fletcher's house; 'it was from there that all plans were made'.[7] Abrahamson, however, says that while 'Ben wanted to be prime minister I don't think [he] was the arch plotter ... because I don't think he was capable of being the arch plotter ... I think he saw ... an opportunity to realise a life's ambition'.[8] Quinton told the Oral Archivist: 'We dealt with Welensky on the whole thing and he agreed with us.' When a somewhat startled interviewer asked him 'Welensky was privy to all this?',

---

4   *Scotsman*, 14.1.58, quoted in *Rhodesia Herald*, 15.1.58.
5   J. M. Greenfield/RW, 15.1.58, File 501/1, Welensky Papers, Bodleian Library.
6   Oral FL.1, NAZ.
7   Oral QU.1, NAZ.
8   Oral AB.2, NAZ.

Quinton replied: 'He knew all about it.'⁹ Garfield, who had known Fletcher since at least 1946, considered Fletcher to be the ringleader. 'He was in close contact with Roy Welensky, who, he believed, was supporting him as the new leader of Southern Rhodesia.'¹⁰

Welensky was working hard to change the argument, telling his biographer, Don Taylor, now the editor of *New Commonwealth*: 'Don't swallow the story that this is an issue based on liberalism ... that is bunk and it is a state of affairs that has been deliberately created.'¹¹ Taylor responded with a warning: 'Tough, unafraid to speak his mind, transparently honest, Southern Rhodesia's Premier commands the respect of moderate African opinion. Extremists, both black and white, may dislike him, may use every device to get rid of him, but to most friends of the Federation in Britain anxiously watching its great experiment in race relations, their efforts look suspiciously like those of men hell-bent on digging their own graves.'¹²

The editorial in the *Central African Examiner* of 18 January considered: 'What is really at stake ... is nothing less than the ideal to which the Federation was dedicated. If Mr Garfield Todd has ultimately to resign, partnership will be a phrase greeted only with a bitter laugh, a single-word indictment of European hypocrisy.' The writer goes on to list Garfield's 'several large political mistakes' but considers that the ex-ministers had 'offended worse ... While Fletcher was Acting Prime Minister he called no caucus meeting to learn his parliamentary colleagues' views, but merely planned with his group ... an election would force Sir Roy Welensky to declare his hand ... His inaction, so far, may seem splendidly Olympian to some; to many others, it looks like fence-sitting ... Only he can now save Todd.'¹³

Another writer in the same issue considered that the result of Garfield's stand would result in his disappearance 'from any role of any importance in political life. Mr Todd is a man of integrity and ability. The past week has shown that he is a man of great courage also – what he lacks is political intelligence in the sense of strategy. There is now but one hope for Mr Todd and that is to force the Federal Prime Minister ... to declare his attitude to the present Southern Rhodesian fracas.'¹⁴ Welensky had his opportunity to do just that at a United Federal Party meeting in Harari on Sunday 19 January. He commented on

---

9   Oral QU.1, NAZ.
10 GT/SP, 1993, TPPC.
11 RW/Don Taylor, 17.1.58, File 674/7, Welensky Papers, Bodleian Library.
12 *New Commonwealth*, 4.2.58, quoted in *Rhodesia Herald*, 5.2.58.
13 *Central African Examiner*, 18.1.58, vol. 1, no. 17.
14 Ibid.

the crisis gripping Southern Rhodesia: 'I have no power and no authority to intervene in a territorial matter'; he hoped the crisis would be 'settled as quickly as possible'; 'Mr Todd is a man of high standing and integrity'. It was not enough, and the first comment was not even true: as head of the UFP he had all the power he needed, if he wished to use it. (And very shortly, he would use it – against Garfield.) The *Central African Examiner* was very critical: 'This important Sunday morning meeting did less than no good ... Todd supporters ... concluded therefore that Welensky was unwilling to give Todd even the mildest backing ...'

Cyril Dunn, the *Observer*'s Salisbury correspondent, made an important point: '[the ministers] bungled things. Instead of dropping him swiftly and silently through the trapdoor as planned, they fell through it themselves and with world-rousing clamour ... White Rhodesians are, in fact, startled and dismayed by the violence of overseas reaction to their idea of discarding Mr Todd; they are clearly surprised to find him internationally respected. But it seems his former ministers were induced to strike when they did because they believed the majority opinion in the United Kingdom was already with them. By ratifying Sir Roy's plans for giving Africans no more than a trifling say in Federal affairs, the House of Commons led the anti-Todd faction here to suppose there was no longer any need for Southern Rhodesia to go as fast or as far with African advancement as Mr Todd desired.'[15] In an *Observer* 'Profile', Dunn writes: 'If Todd is too liberal for the settlers to accept, Southern Rhodesia should abandon its partnership pretensions altogether. African faith in racial partnership, always slight, would surely vanish if Todd were to go.'[16]

Both Todd and Fletcher being unacceptable to the UFP hierarchy, the behind-the-scenes manipulators were now concerned with a 'compromise candidate'. Welensky had in mind Sir Edgar Whitehead, Federal representative in Washington. An exchange of telegrams secured his agreement in principle.[17]

***

On 17 January, Alf Adams, the UFP Secretary, issued a statement about the forthcoming Congress: 'Three hundred delegates will attend the congress. Included will be two delegates from each Party branch in Southern Rhodesia and the Executive Committee of the United Federal Party ... the executive of Mr Todd's former United Rhodesia Party will not attend unless they do so as branch delegates or MPs.'[18] This last statement caused great indignation

---

15 *Observer*, 19.1.58.
16 Ibid.
17 File 501/1, Welensky Papers, Bodleian Library.
18 *Rhodesia Herald*, 17.1.58.

among the former URP members: the Party had not been dissolved, nor had it yet ratified fusion on the basis of the two documents on which the Federal Party had ratified it. Further, Greenfield had earlier announced that the URP would form the Southern Rhodesia section of the UFP, and the URP's Executive Committee would form the territorial Executive. Garfield had agreed to a congress of the territorial UFP, rather than the URP, because he felt fusion had gone so far that he must do so – despite protests from some supporters who felt he was loading the dice against himself. The exclusion by UFP diktat of the URP Executive in favour of the UFP Executive which included members from Northern Rhodesia and Nyasaland, was, as the *Central African Examiner* pointed out, 'palpably unfair'.[19] Garfield objected strongly that members of the UFP Executive Committee, who did not even come from Southern Rhodesia, should be involved in any way, let alone vote on the leadership of the Southern Rhodesia party, but Greenfield was adamant.

Garfield got some valuable support from *The Chronicle*: 'By their rigid adherence to a constitution which they (Greenfield and co.) believe to be ratified but which has not been seen – let alone accepted – by the United Rhodesia Party, they are damaging the party far more than they realise.'[20] Clyde Sanger writes of Greenfield's part in 'the removal of Todd ... the congress was loaded before it assembled ... it is clear that Greenfield's constitutional rulings played a considerable part in Todd's defeat'.[21]

Garfield was not afraid of what might be said at the Congress. He did not fear being ambushed by unexpected allegations which he would not be able to refute or challenge; but, as the ex-ministers' accusations had already been made public, he was anxious that the press should be present (except as was customary during the actual Election of Office-Bearers) to record and publish his defence. In this he was opposed by Welensky, Greenfield and T. P. Cochrane, Chairman of the Federal, not Territorial, UFP. Garfield sent an angry statement to the press – which was promptly handed over to Welensky, who demanded that sections be deleted before publication. Even press standards were subverted in the UFP's determination to be rid of Todd.

The day before Congress, *The Chronicle* called once again for the press to be admitted: 'Because the public has been kept guessing too long ... congress should also insist that the proceedings be thrown open to the press.'[22] In the event, the decision was made by the Congress. It was a curious feature of the

---

19 *Central African Examiner*, 1.2.58, vol. 1, no. 18.
20 *The Chronicle*, 23.1.58.
21 Sanger, 1960, p. 137.
22 *The Chronicle*, 7.2.58.

debate that it was 'the accusers' who did not want the press to be present, and 'the accused' who did.

Right up to the eve of Congress, Garfield was endeavouring to ensure he had a fair hearing. He wrote to Welensky that morning: 'I am deeply shocked to find that I have been put down as speaking after Fletcher and before the other four ex-ministers ... I certainly cannot be asked to speak before I know the accusations against me ...'[23]

---

23 GT/RW, 7.2.58, File 501/1, Welensky Papers, Bodleian Library.

51

'Fateful Congress'

'The United Federal Party survived because it jettisoned Todd.'

Colin Leys

Saturday 8 February 1958 was a heavy, overcast day, hot and sultry, with dark clouds perpetually threatening, but never delivering, more rain. Hardwicke Holderness told Stanlake Samkange: 'Todd laid on the finest piece of adult education, in the place where it was most needed, that could have been designed. And the Congress evaded the issue …'[1]

Holderness was in the Presbyterian Church's Kennedy-Grant Hall that day, as was Nathan Shamuyarira, but other locally based observers – Cyril Dunn, Clyde Sanger and Frank Clements – have also left us vivid accounts of the 'Todd crisis' which convey very clearly the prevailing mood, the confusion, the frenetic political activity, the excitement, the sense of shock, the disappointment – and the jubilation – and the sheer electrifying drama of the Congress. The principal participants in the action have left their memories in their Oral Archives; and Greenfield, Stumbles, Smith and Welensky – all of whom were at Congress – in due course wrote about the events in published accounts. Welensky observes briefly that its 'principal and very dramatic decision was firmly to reject Mr Todd';[2] and Smith, equally briefly, writes: 'Todd was defeated and Sir Edgar Whitehead elected to replace him.'[3]

There was one other observer in the Hall – Grace; she, too, wrote an account of the Congress, for Lansdell Christie. While she can hardly be regarded as neutral, her political awareness and her unparalleled knowledge of the events

---

1   HHCH/Stanlake Samkange, 21.2.58, TPPC.
2   Welensky, 1964, p. 90.
3   Smith, 1997, p. 35.

'Fateful Congress'

leading up to the Congress and of the personalities involved, together with her perceptive intelligence, lend weight to her comments and conclusions. The following day, the *Sunday Mail*'s picture of the Todds arriving at the Hall shows her elegant, smiling and serene beside a cheerful Garfield.

Shamuyarira saw that 'the Congress was packed with federal delegates who had never been [Todd's] supporters'.[4] At the 'top table' were Garfield's two cabinets, separated by Welensky, who sat silently all day in the middle of the long table behind a Union Jack. As earlier agreed, Garfield, seconded by Fletcher, proposed Greenfield as Chairman. The first thing the Chairman did was to request anyone who was neither an authorised delegate nor an *ex officio* member to leave the hall. Grace sat quietly on.

'Early in the conference', reported the *Central African Examiner*, 'the newly elected, independent chairman, Mr Julian Greenfield, demonstrated his impartiality by prefacing the motion on the admission of the Press with his personal view that it would be undesirable, because of distorted reporting. The Press was excluded by a vote of two to one … [Greenfield] thus followed the party line of trying to inhibit public discussion … of the vital issues on which the whole crisis hangs.'[5] Grace writes: 'This became significant later, since we learned that the speeches of the rebel ministers were in the hands of the Press the day before. Garfield had refused to give his speech to the Press, since he knew a vote was to be taken at the Congress on this point.'

Representatives of press and journals from Britain, America and many other parts of the world, as well as Southern Rhodesia, had assembled and now stood watching outside the Hall, seeing but unable to hear a word. Once the curtains were drawn, Dunn writes, 'the occasion was both tedious and funny. The congress sat for fourteen hours and through most of this time the reporters eavesdropped with energy and initiative … But modern design does not lend itself to secrecy; by applying an ear to airbricks set in the outer walls it was possible to hear a fair amount of what went on within, while the Party struggled for its soul or its survival. But did this long and voluble day in February, 1958, see the first blow struck in the planned murder of Central Africa's white liberalism? It certainly seemed so to some.'[6]

***

At around eleven o'clock, that small inner circle of the United Federal Party – Welensky, Greenfield, Cochrane, Adams – received confirmation from

---

4 Shamuyarira, 1965, p. 23.
5 *Central African Examiner*, 15.2.58, vol. 1, no. 19.
6 Dunn, 1959, pp. 151–2.

Washington that their *deus ex machina* was prepared to fly in as a possible 'uniting' leader. Their knowledge of the general membership of the Congress, with its strong 'federal' bias, was sufficient to assure them that the Whitehead plan could be sold by using high-minded appeals to party unity. One almost begins to feel sorry for Fletcher, who had no idea that the rug was about to be pulled from under him.

But now is not the time to be sorry for Fletcher; it is time for him to fire the opening salvo in the ex-ministers' attack on the Prime Minister. It lasted for one hour and 25 minutes. Shamuyarira gives us this account: 'Fletcher, a tired and cantankerous man whose thinking had been set since the old days ... tried to centre his attack on the charge that Todd had been dictatorial in cabinet, but the truth came through his mass of accusations. He talked of Todd's promises to Africans over land and schools, he objected to Todd meeting Nkomo ... Todd had opposed an "immorality" law amendment ... He attacked Todd for making a major speech about the franchise "to the Inter-Racial Association – of all places!" While he complained that Todd had taken all the credit for progressive legislation, he swung his arguments round to add: "He has stirred up the natives to want more than they can be given."'[7]

The *Sunday Mail* account included 'charges of "dictatorship", "acting in an unparliamentary manner" ... it had become accepted overseas that he was a liberal. Mr Todd had attempted to perpetuate that idea, and it was false ... Europeans were being driven away, and Mr Todd had embarrassed the Government by his advanced legislation ... [He] had attacked and made an enemy of [Lord Malvern] in front of the Africans. Then he had turned against Sir Roy Welensky.' Todd had made 'impetuous statements' and 'shown himself to be against the Federal Government and to side with the Colonial Office if he could ...

'Mr Todd had been against cabinet and caucus, and had aroused false expectations and racial dissatisfaction. The Rhodesian was a liberal but he did not want this sort of thing rammed down his throat. Mr Todd had no qualities of leadership. He did not follow Parliament, but was guided by political expediency and personal ambition. The majority of his party in Parliament had no confidence in him ...'[8]

Ellman-Brown made 'one of the hardest-hitting' speeches.[9] The *Sunday Mail* reported: 'Mr Todd had lost all sense of judgment and balance in his anxiety to keep himself in the public eye ... He had blatantly ignored his backbenchers

---

7 Shamuyarira, 1965, pp. 23–4.
8 *Sunday Mail*, 9.2.58.
9 *Rhodesia Herald*, 10.2.58.

and cabinet meetings had become a farce. He had ignored the advice of his ministers and run down the Federal government, particularly in overseas eyes ... Mr Todd was quite unsuitable to lead a stable government. The action by the former members of the cabinet had been taken to preserve liberalism and not to destroy it.'[10]

The only reference to Cyril Hatty's part in the attack on Garfield comes from the *Sunday Mail*: 'Mr Hatty won applause when he remarked that probably there had been faults on both sides. He was near to breaking down when he said that he had placed Mr Todd on a pedestal and then seen him crash.'[11]

Stumbles' accusations included the complaint that 'Mr Todd had not kept him informed on security reports. To this Mr Todd is reported to have replied that security liaison was the Prime Minister's job, and that Mr Stumbles' security responsibility was in the realms of internal affairs with the police. Top security was always on a Prime Minister to Prime Minister level ... [Todd] had, entirely on his own initiative and without consultation with his Cabinet Ministers, largely discarded the five-year African education plan.'[12] 'When the Prime Minister opposed the Immorality Motion ... he was not in fact keeping in line with security reports that had come from Bulawayo ...'[13]

Finally it was Quinton's turn: his complaint was that Todd 'had visited the offices of the African National Congress in Bulawayo regularly'. He also said, 'Mr Todd had told him when he was appointed four months ago that he would break up the Native Affairs Department ... this removal of a department that had done so much to develop the African people and build good race relations could not be countenanced by Congress.'[14]

At this point the Congress broke for lunch, and afterwards the accusers still held the floor. There were no new allegations or hideous revelations which the rebels had hinted at to justify their action. Grace was scornful: the rebels' attack was 'weak in the extreme ... what was as plain as a pikestaff was their rejection of Garfield's endeavours honestly to implement the policy of partnership ...'[15]

When Garfield rose at about 3.00 p.m. to answer his accusers, the level of excitement and expectation in the Hall was almost tangible. The *Central African Examiner* correspondent wrote: it was 'a speech of an hour and forty-five minutes of which I was lucky enough to "overhear" thirty minutes. He was

---

10   *Sunday Mail*, 9.2.58.
11   *Sunday Mail*, 9.2.58.
12   *Rhodesia Herald*, 10.2.58.
13   *African Daily News*, 10.2.58.
14   *African Daily News*, 10.2.58.
15   JGT/Lansdell K. Christie, March 1958, MS.1082/3/1, Todd Papers, NAZ.

answering each and every accusation in the minutest detail, citing exact chapter and verse for every action. The complete master of his material, he employed it with astonishing fluency, compelling conviction, and an unerring sense both of timing and humour. Brick by brick, the incriminating edifice of his opponents' case was demolished. Explosions of applause mounted in volume and frequency, and he closed to something like a demonstration.'[16]

The Chronicle reported that, 'Although feelings were strongly divided over the leadership issue ... those on both sides agreed that Mr Todd was the dominant figure ... Many say that he completely cleared himself of the accusations ... "The rebels' arguments were mainly trivial and were easily demolished"'.[17] Even Peter Reay of the *Rhodesia Herald*, never noticeably sympathetic to Garfield, had to report that 'Unquestionably the most brilliant speaker at the Congress was the Prime Minister ... who after his ninety-minute speech won a thunderous ovation from supporters and opponents alike. As one delegate was heard to remark afterwards, "I don't care on whose side anyone is, that was a magnificent speech." ... On Saturday [Mr Todd] was calm and factual in answering his accusers and his replies were detailed. But interlarded into his very serious subject he slipped jokes, which won laughter every time. He had to deal with the attack of five accusers ... and he did so with unfaltering lucidity. He moved from point to point with superb skill ... Mr Todd denied emphatically that he had ever exhibited tendencies to be a dictator and he told congress of the number of cabinet meetings and parliamentary caucuses held, select committees appointed and the number of times he had addressed meetings in his constituency to prove that he had always been open in his dealings with his fellow Ministers, the party MPs and the electorate.'[18]

Holderness wrote: 'It was a courageous and memorable performance.'[19] He told Stanlake Samkange: 'Todd made an absolutely brilliant speech, and his whole attitude throughout the Congress was so obviously that of a man of integrity and principle who had also mastered to a rare degree the art of political oratory. It made a tremendous impression, and had the red herring of Whitehead not been drawn across the proceedings, I think it is pretty certain that Todd would have won the day, notwithstanding all the factors against him.'[20]

At the moment when the atmosphere still crackled with the echoes and excitement of Garfield's speech, the independent chairman adjourned Congress

---

16 *Central African Examiner*, 15.2.58, vol. 1, no. 19.
17 *The Chronicle*, 10.2.58.
18 *Rhodesia Herald*, 10.2.58.
19 Holderness, 1985, p. 222.
20 HHCH/Stanlake Samkange, 21.2.58, TPPC.

for an hour and a half. Grace told Christie that 'Our side pressed for an immediate vote on the leadership directly following Garfield's speech, but were overruled from the Chair, who insisted that we break at that point for dinner.'[21] The afterglow of Garfield's triumph was still upon the Todds and the Hendersons when they returned to Northward for dinner; and it was a joyous meal. But Greenfield's 'performance' had also been masterly, allowing the impressions of Garfield's speech to be dissipated over the sundowners and dinner tables of the Salisbury Club, Meikles Hotel and scores of private houses across the city.

***

'At 8.30 pm, batteries recharged and judgment doubtless sharpened, [the delegates] reassembled to cast the vital vote', reported the *Central African Examiner*.[22] First Fletcher and then Garfield replied to the afternoon's debate.

Replying – and now he could be heard by the *Sunday Mail* reporter outside – Garfield 'referred to the vital need to push through the planned parliamentary programme – particularly in view of the possibility of trouble with Africans in the North. He was confident that there were sufficient MPs in the House who would back the programme. Unfortunately there had been differences among members of the Government, and the country had been dealt a bad blow. Perhaps he had been to blame as well as Sir Patrick, but he felt that whatever happened the electorate should have a say as soon as possible.' Aware of Whitehead's projected nomination, 'he appealed to delegates not to put into office someone who was in some other sphere of business, and not even in the country. Congress had to think of another alternative – whether it was Sir Patrick or himself. Despite all that had been said and all the accusations that had been made it was not going to break his heart, or that of his wife, if they walked from the Hall free people that night.'[23]

Members of Garfield's second cabinet spoke in his support, but that was only a curtain-raiser to the third act: the vote. 'After the two inevitable nominations to the party leadership, came the bombshell that had already exploded, the too-much expected *deus ex machina* ... to redress the balance of the Federation. Sir Edgar Whitehead's nomination was greeted with delighted applause – the way of escape from an intolerable dilemma.'[24]

Fletcher opposed the nomination of Sir Edgar Whitehead, protesting that the crisis involved himself and Mr Todd, and he felt that Congress should

---

21   JGT/Lansdell K. Christie, March 1958, MS.1082/3/1, Todd Papers, NAZ.
22   *Central African Examiner*, 15.2.58, vol. 1, no. 19.
23   *Sunday Mail*, 9.2.58.
24   *Central African Examiner*, 15.2.58, vol. 1, no. 19.

decide between himself and Mr Todd. In the first ballot, Fletcher received 73 votes, Whitehead 122, and Garfield 129. Garfield would have agreed with Fletcher that the vote should be between the two of them. He wrote later to W. F. Rendell, Member of the Legislative Council (Northern Rhodesia): 'On the second ballot it was left for Sir Patrick's followers to decide who was going to be Prime Minister of Southern Rhodesia. There was no doubt who it would be after that.'[25]

Mr Leonard Tracey, who had seconded Whitehead's nomination, wrote to Garfield the following day expressing his 'personal admiration' for him and his 'great regret that you should have been placed in this predicament. A man of sound judgement said to me "Whitehead has won, but the moral victory lies with Todd".'[26] For many delegates, the appeal to 'party unity' had been genuine and decisive. Todd 'had gloriously won the day and routed his enemies', wrote the correspondent of the *Central African Examiner*. 'Yet it was still they who were to pull him down.'[27]

Garfield addressed Congress a second time: 'It is a pity that Sir Edgar is not here to get the congratulations of Congress himself, but as I have come second in the poll and as Prime Minister at the moment, we will carry on the Government until Sir Edgar comes ... I would hope that all the members of the Party who are in the House will work loyally if we have to go through a session of Parliament, so that we may be able to hand over to Sir Edgar Whitehead still a united team. When he arrives my cabinet and I will hand him our resignations but we will endeavour to assist him in any way so that he may come in under the most auspicious circumstances. Now I would just like to say how much I have enjoyed serving you and the country for the last four years. It has been a very great privilege and although in some ways I may have disappointed you, I still have done my best and I go without regrets and without bitterness.'[28]

***

'Todd's last hope was the intervention of Roy Welensky on his behalf,' writes Ian Hancock. 'Instead the Federal Prime Minister affected a neutrality which neither convinced the Todd supporters at the Congress nor carried conviction when repeated down the years. Very simply, the federals wanted Todd out of the way; he was a source of party dissension ... It was important, however, that the Southern Rhodesians administer the act and be seen to have done so.'[29]

25 GT/W. F. Rendell, 14.2.58, MS.390/1/3, Todd Papers, NAZ.
26 Leonard Tracey/GT, 9.2.58, MS.390/1/1/3, Todd Papers, NAZ.
27 *Central African Examiner*, 15.2.58, vol. 1, no. 19.
28 *Sunday Mail*, 9.2.58.
29 Hancock, 1984, p. 69.

'Fateful Congress'

The *Sunday Mail* reported what Welensky said: 'I feel that the final remarks made by Mr Todd just now should set the tone for the future relationship within the Party ... a decision has been taken and as leader of the Party I should expect both factions to give Sir Edgar Whitehead every opportunity of making a success of the task that faces him ... I think the attitude of Mr Garfield Todd has been magnanimous, I think that is perhaps an understatement, and I sincerely hope that the clear lead given by the Congress this evening will be followed by the Party ... We want unity and stability.' Welensky continued: 'Let the dust settle now before you make up your minds in regard to your individual actions – other than to keep the Party together.'[30]

Grace concluded her account for Lansdell Christie: 'And so it ended, with Garfield going out with head high and with integrity and honour. The letters we have had, hundreds of them since then, have been amusing in that they are all letters of congratulation, which appear to overlook the one important fact that he is no longer PM, but which one and all speak with admiration and gratitude of the stand he made, the fight he fought and the victory he won.'[31] It was in this spirit that the Todds and Hendersons returned to Northward for the last time that long day, stopping on the way for Garfield to ask a *Sunday Mail* newspaper-seller for his poster 'TODD AND FLETCHER BOTH OUT'.[32] At midnight, once home, where I had been waiting all that day, Grace and the Hendersons sank gratefully into easy chairs. Garfield and I went into the kitchen to make Ovaltine for us all. A late telephone call came from Steve Davies, telling Garfield, 'You may think it is a defeat, but I can assure you that things will never be the same again'.[33] Garfield had 'made a graceful exit, free from petulance or rancour'.[34]

For the African people, Todd's defeat was 'a catastrophe', writes Shamuyarira.[35] '"Let the dust settle down", [Welensky] said several times. The few African delegates in the hall could only see dust settling on their hopes ... A sad but perhaps a treasured, compliment was paid to Todd at that time when an African composed a song which became a best-selling record:

> "Todd wasichiya,
> Hamba kahle mudala" ...
> (Todd has left us,
> Go well, old man) ...'

---

30 *Sunday Mail*, 9.2.58.
31 JGT/Lansdell K. Christie, March 1958, MS.1082/3/1, Todd Papers, NAZ.
32 TPPC.
33 GT/SP, 2002, TPPC.
34 *The Chronicle*, 10.2.58.
35 Shamuyarira, 1965, p. 25.

***

Thirty years later, Julian Greenfield, the 'independent' chairman of that 'fateful congress', wrote an astonishing postscript to it: 'Had Todd been able to win the day on 8 February, things for the Federation and Southern Rhodesia might have gone right.'[36]

---

36 J. M. Greenfield/HHCH, 15.8.88, *Lost Chance* follow-up project, Holderness Papers, Bodleian Library.

52

'LET THE DUST SETTLE'

'For a man to have high office in Rhodesia he must prove that he is tough on the African.'

Maurice Nyagumbo

On the morning of Sunday 9 February, Garfield held an informal press conference in his office. The *Rhodesia Herald* reported: 'Mr Todd was very cheerful, but looked tired ... Asked if he thought the election of Sir Edgar would satisfy the London critics, Mr Todd thought for a moment and said he was almost sure it would ... He thought that the present political situation would only really be solved by an early general election ...'[1]

Sir Patrick Fletcher issued a press statement on Sunday calling for Garfield's immediate resignation, but Hatty, Ellman-Brown and Stumbles immediately dissociated themselves from it. The observant reader will have noticed that Cyril Hatty features but slightly in the account of the crisis and the congress. There was no Oral Archive to consult about Hatty's memories of that time, but in the late 1980s he wrote: 'After the decision of the Party Congress to invite Sir Edgar Whitehead over, I ... pondered with dismay the political mess we had precipitated; and its aftermath which, in my view, was hardly a solution.'[2] When in 1997 I asked Sir Cyril about the cabinet crisis, he simply put his head in his hands and said: 'I can't bear to think about it.'[3]

***

During the brief but most welcome lull in political activity before Whitehead's arrival on Wednesday 12 February, Garfield was able to reply to some of the

---
1   *Rhodesia Herald*, 10.2.58.
2   C. J. Hatty, *Lost Chance* follow-up project, Holderness Papers, Bodleian Library.
3   Interview, SP, 2.7.97.

messages he had received. He told Elsie Barham, Grace's sister: 'We are actually looking forward very much to a time of quietness ... We have had a wonderful time in Salisbury and now leave without any regrets.' He described the congress as 'a wonderful day' which 'completely vindicated the stand that my side had taken. I have been very happy to have had the opportunity, if I had to go out, of retiring on as sound a note as we were able to do at Congress ...'[4]

Kingsley Dinga Dube, Old Dadayan, now working for African Newspapers Ltd in Salisbury, told Garfield: 'The African people are very disappointed and feel let down by the Europeans of this country, but they feel consoled a bit that Sir Patrick found himself without a significant following at the Congress. He has ended a long political career rather ignobly, and so will Welensky if he will not be bigger in his heart.'[5] Garfield replied: 'The important thing is that if possible Sir Edgar should get a team of liberal men who would be able to reinstate and strengthen even further the ties between African and European in this country. If he cannot do that, then he has failed. I have been tremendously impressed with the quiet dignity of the African people and their readiness to wait to see how things turn out before committing themselves ...'[6]

Frank Rendell, MLC of Northern Rhodesia, saw Garfield's defeat as 'a seeming victory for the illiberal element of Southern Rhodesia ... I am convinced more than ever that our survival in Africa, if it can be secured despite rampant nationalism ... can only depend on a practical expression of partnership, as far as can be safely given, being exercised. Again unfortunately, many of the Federal Party higher-ups pay only lip service to this principle ... and are as blind to the likely future events as the people they represent.'[7] With Rendell, Garfield shared some of his disquiet about the future: 'Our great trouble is that one of two things must happen: either somehow we must clear up the UFP and see that it stands for honest partnership ... or else at some point we will have to inaugurate a party that will do this thing ... There is no doubt that our time is short, and it seems to me that the Federal Party itself has been captured by illiberal elements ... Sir Roy obviously favoured the other side and gave us no support whatever. He could have brought Congress together ... but the Congress handed over to Sir Edgar the decision which was theirs to make ...'[8]

In another letter from Northern Rhodesia, Sir Arthur Benson wrote with his customary frankness and passion: 'If you could only know the hearts of so

---

4   GT/EB, 14.2.58, MS.390/1/2, Todd Papers, NAZ.
5   K. D. Dube/GT, 10.2.58, File MS.390/1/2, Todd Papers, NAZ.
6   GT/K. D. Dube, 13.2.58, MS.390/1/2, Todd Papers, NAZ.
7   W. F. Rendell/GT, 'Sunday' [9.2.58], MS.390/1/3, Todd Papers, NAZ.
8   GT/W. F. Rendell, 14.2.58, MS.390/1/3, ibid.

many thousands of us and how they have been torn by the things they have done to you and how they have been uplifted in joy at the wonderful fight you are making and have made ... Whatever happens ... you have won. Because the hearts of all good and true men (and they are in the majority) are with you and your cause. This to you just as I go off to the UK to fight my end of the battle over franchise etc. There are faint hearts and cowards there, too, I am afraid. If there had not been, you would not have had to go through with that burden you have had. Sit-on-the-fencers, and cower when someone with a big belly says 'Boo' to them! ... Bless you ... I wish you could both know how much so very many of us admire you both, if that is not too weak a word.'[9]

The *African Daily News* editorial expressed 'deep disappointment that Mr R. S. Garfield Todd, the man whom [our people] trusted more than any other white politician, is on his way out of office'. This was 'a severe blow to the forces of co-operation in this country'.[10] The news had 'distressed the Africans of Southern Rhodesia – politicians, trade unionists, and commoners. Reports we have received all point at general disappointment.' The paper goes on to quote K. T. T. Maripe, president of the SR African Trades Union Congress; Charles Mzingeli; Grey Bango, Bulawayo trade unionist; and J. M. N. Nkomo, president of the SR ANC. Nkomo 'thought Mr Todd was going slower than the circumstances demanded. The African people are now horrified and distressed that Mr Todd has been crucified by his colleagues, caucus and the UFP Congress which assumes to represent moderate opinion. His sin is that of trying to implement the policy enshrined in the constitution ... the Rhodesian electorate was not ready for partnership. The congress ignored a candidate solidly backed by the African people ... Mr Garfield Todd was described as "a great man who will go down in the annals of the colony's history as a man who was sacrificed on the altar of liberalism".'[11]

Sir William Murphy wrote: 'You alone emerge from this sorry business not only with undiminished but with enhanced reputation'.[12] Stanlake Samkange, at Indiana University in the USA, told Garfield: 'You have personally lost nothing; if anything you have proved that it is possible for human beings to attain high office and still stick to principles which they hold dear'.[13]

Professor S. Herbert Frankel, who had been consultant to the Plewman Commission (its report lay in the Cabinet Secretary's safe), wrote from Nuffield

---

9   Sir Arthur Benson/GT, 16.2.58, MS.390/1/10, ibid.
10   *African Daily News*, 9.2.58.
11   *African Daily News*, 10.2.58.
12   Sir William Murphy/GT, 11.2.58, MS.390/1/3, Todd Papers, NAZ.
13   Stanlake Samkange/GT, 18.2.58, MS.390/1/3, ibid.

College, Oxford: 'I am glad that ... you continued to struggle up to the last moment ... it is all that liberals can do, since they are not strong enough to form a large party of their own ...'[14]

'The finest' letter Garfield received at this time came from Mr A. G. Haldane, the international consultant he had first met in the USA in 1955, telling of his feelings of 'surprise, shock and almost unbelief' at the 'disastrous political developments in Salisbury': 'Your racial policy has created prestige for Southern Rhodesia internationally, has created a future for African and European alike, and hope for them in that future ... Rhodesia needs inspired politicians ... You have inherent qualities of leadership ... which, unfortunately, are all too scarce in the Federation ... You have much reason to be proud of in what has been accomplished through your leadership in a comparatively short space of time ... You know truth and you have much courage – use them – at every propitious opportunity.'[15]

***

Mr Sydney Swadel, editor of *The Chronicle*, had supported Garfield's cause throughout the crisis – which, as he wrote to him later, 'should never have arisen'.[16] On Monday 10 February, he headed his editorial 'All but the laurels': 'Mr Todd, who would still be the leader had the decision rested on a straight vote, felt strongly that this was a clear-cut issue between himself and his former Ministers and that no outside influence should be brought to bear ... In many ways he was entitled to this straight verdict from the party on his leadership, because it would then have been a simple vindication or rejection of his policy and administration ...'[17]

The *Umtali Post* was unusually generous to Garfield: 'His sincerity cannot be questioned'; he was 'a man who has shown as much integrity, courage and dignity in his going as he did in fulfilling the responsibilities of his office'.[18] *The Times* said Garfield 'stands out among the European political leaders of Southern Africa in that he has been prepared to risk office because of his championship of African advancement'.[19]

An article on the Congress in the *Central African Examiner* of 15 February started uncompromisingly with the statement that 'The circumstances attending the overthrow of Mr Garfield Todd ... reflect little credit on the standards

---

14 Prof. S. H. Frankel/GT, 17.2.58, MS.390/1/2, ibid.
15 A. G. Haldane/GT, 27.2.58, MS.390/1/17, ibid.
16 Sydney R. Swadel/GT, 18.2.58, MS.390/1/10, ibid.
17 *The Chronicle*, 10.2.58.
18 *Umtali Post*, 10.2.58.
19 *The Times*, 11.2.58.

of public life in the colony or, indeed, in the Federation as a whole ... For some years now a consistent campaign against Todd has been waged by certain elements in this country, and not least by the press. The tragedy is that the one politician who has the courage to speak out for the underprivileged African majority has incurred suspicion and even active dislike for that very reason.' The fear of the Federal Party's leadership was that, 'Todd's outlook, if carried into practice, would lead ultimately to the eclipse of white civilisation and all it stands for ... It is this fear ... which has led to a consistent and not over-scrupulous campaign throughout the country for the discrediting of Todd and for the elimination of him and his supporters from public life.'[20]

***

Over succeeding years, there was much debate about the involvement of Welensky, Greenfield and the Federal Party generally in Garfield's removal from office. The general consensus seems to be that Greenfield was clearly guilty, Welensky less so. When, in the following March, I asked Sydney Sawyer, Federal MP, about this, he hesitated briefly before replying that he didn't think Welensky had been involved.[21] Sawyer was close to the leadership of the UFP, and this reply seems pretty conclusive of Greenfield's complicity, if not of Welensky's innocence.

Frank Clements writes: 'At any time during the leadership crisis a few words from Sir Roy would have preserved Garfield Todd's position, but Sir Roy never spoke them and at no time has there ever been any pretence that what happened was disagreeable to Sir Roy.'[22]

Patrick Keatley's *The Politics of Partnership* was published in 1963, and in it he is typically forthright: 'Mr Todd was cast away ... in a palace assassination conducted under the benign imperial gaze of Sir Roy Welensky.'[23] Sir Robert Tredgold writes of the fact, 'which is incontrovertible, that a large part in engineering [Todd's] downfall was played by people in the Federal sphere of politics, including some Federal ministers'.[24] Alan Gray, in his Quarterly Chronicle for *African Affairs* (July 1958), would seem to sum up contemporary opinion: 'As guilty as those who spun the tissue which was to be Mr Todd's shroud were those who were suddenly struck by paralysis.'[25]

There is evidence in Welensky's papers that supports the view that it suited

---

20   *Central African Examiner*, 15.2.58, vol. 1, no. 19.
21   March 1958, interview, S. Woodhouse.
22   Clements, 1969, footnote, pp. 129–30.
23   Keatley, 1963, p. 326.
24   Tredgold, 1968, p. 226.
25   *African Affairs*, vol. 57, no. 228, July 1958, p. 170.

Welensky very well to get rid of Garfield. For instance, in a letter to Don Taylor, Welensky writes: 'I can tell you this much: had we not got rid of [Todd,] the UFP would have suffered defeat in the Territorial election.'[26] (Note the 'we'.) It is interesting to read in many letters which Garfield received after the Congress that Welensky's guilt in this matter is virtually taken for granted. It can also be said that, if Welensky had not desired the removal of Garfield, he could have stopped Fletcher as early as November 1957. Welensky's eyes were firmly fixed on the Federal general election due within the year – and, as *Time* magazine commented in May, he was 'worried about his party's electoral chances if the opposition tars it with the label of "liberal"'.[27]

Enoch Dumbutshena wrote much later, in Garfield's 80th-birthday book: 'Without being told, Africans believed that Sir Roy Welensky and Julian Greenfield were "through and through" against Garfield.'[28]

Garfield is quite clear about Greenfield's part in his downfall. When the New Zealand writer, Norman Harris, visited Hokonui Ranch in 1970, Garfield spoke of a politician who was 'my friend. I knew he was a schemer, but I thought our friendship would be above that. I trusted him to be fair and just. He was the person I was closest to and really he organised my undoing.'[29]

Robert Blake states: 'Todd himself has never believed that the Federal Prime Minister was involved at all closely in the affair'[30] – but there is evidence that this does not accurately reflect Garfield's opinion. The *Central African Examiner* of 17 January 1959 reported: 'More than any other single person … Todd feels he owes his defeat to Sir Roy Welensky. For he feels, probably rightly, that a word from the Federal Prime Minister during the Southern Rhodesia cabinet crisis might have saved him.'[31] Claire Palley wrote that 'Mr Todd maintains that his subsequent downfall was engineered by Sir Roy Welensky, the Federal Prime Minister.'[32]

In interviews for this book, Garfield was quite clear: 'Welensky's influence could have helped me very greatly if he had wanted to step in. I don't think he wanted me to stay in – rather the opposite.'[33] And very shortly before his death, in one of his last letters, Garfield wrote: 'Welensky was neither astute enough nor

---

26 23.7.58, File 674/7, Welensky Papers, Bodleian Library.
27 *Time* magazine, 24.5.58.
28 E. Dumbutshena, GT's 80th-birthday book, J. Todd papers.
29 Harris, 1971, p. 172.
30 Blake, 1977, p. 31.
31 *Central African Examiner*, 17.1.59, vol. 2, no. 17.
32 Palley, 1966, footnote on pp. 357–8.
33 GT/SP, TPPC.

liberal enough to give the leadership which just might have saved the situation.'³⁴

***

Tredgold writes: 'Those who brought about [Todd's] downfall should have foreseen the disastrous effects it would have upon African opinion. Had they done so they might have gone to almost any lengths to avoid it.'³⁵ In Garfield's Oral Archive, he quotes the late Ndabaningi Sithole, a leading nationalist for decades in Rhodesia/Zimbabwe: 'The noise of my falling, as I was thrown out, awakened the nationalist cause.'³⁶

---

34   GT/SP, 30.8.2002, TPPC.
35   Tredgold, 1968, p. 227.
36   Oral TO.1, NAZ.

53

Two Prime Ministers:
9 February to 23 April 1958

'The Congress evaded the issue and left it to Whitehead to decide.'

Hardwicke Holderness

On his arrival in Salisbury on Wednesday 12 February, Whitehead's immediate objective was the formation of a cabinet, and once that was completed (and Garfield had resigned as Prime Minister) he would be sworn in as the new Prime Minister. Then it would be necessary for him to find a seat in the Legislative Assembly, as Article 37 of the Colony's Constitution laid down that a minister of the crown, not an MP, could hold office for no longer than four months before being elected to Parliament. Quickly established in a suite at Meikles Hotel, Whitehead lost no time in acquainting himself with the situation into which he had been parachuted, seeing Greenfield, Garfield, Sawyer and Fletcher before 10 o'clock that night. Interviews continued on Thursday and Friday as Whitehead explored all possible combinations of pro- and anti-Todd factions.

Holderness described events in his letter to Stanlake Samkange: the '"liberals" … were all set to form a new party if the Congress were to decide in favour of Fletcher and Co. During Whitehead's negotiations this question of the new Party was a basic consideration in assessing each of the proposals that came forward.'[1]

Late on Friday, Whitehead was obliged to announce that he had failed to form a cabinet. On Saturday 15th, Garfield called a meeting of the former ministers in that Meikles Hotel suite and asked: '"What is going to happen now? Who is going to be leader?" They looked at each other and eventually I saw all eyes turn to Ben … I said, "Fine. The Governor is down in Bulawayo but he will be back tomorrow. I presume we advise him when he comes back."

---

1 HHCH/Stanlake Samkange, 21.2.58, Holderness Papers, Bodleian Library.

Ben was absolutely adamant that I should get on the telephone although it was late ... "All right," I said, "I will go and ring the Governor." I went out, and sitting in the anteroom were Adams and Sawyer. They both stood up and asked what had happened. When I told them that Ben would take over from me and that I was now going to ring the Governor to get him back that night to swear Fletcher in – I think it was Sawyer who said, "Oh no, Roy will never accept that".' So, Whitehead tried again.

When Whitehead asked Garfield if he would serve in a cabinet with Hatty and Ellman-Brown, he readily agreed – he admired both men's abilities. So, with Todd, Ellman-Brown, Hatty and Davenport (who was acceptable to everyone), Whitehead only needed a lawyer. Holderness, Lloyd, Baron and Stumbles were all ruled out for various reasons. Advocate Reginald Knight remained – and he accepted.

At Whitehead's request, Garfield called a caucus meeting for 11.00 a.m. on Sunday 16th. After five hours, Garfield issued a statement announcing the composition of the new cabinet, and saying that, Straw apart, Caucus had agreed to give 'their unanimous support to the new Government'.[2] Garfield would serve as Minister of Labour and Social Welfare. The *Manchester Guardian* reported that 'Southern Rhodesia is coming out of its crisis rather better than seemed likely a fortnight ago ... and Mr Todd is in [the cabinet] ... It is to [Whitehead's] credit that he has insisted on having Mr Todd in though not, as was hoped, as Minister for Native Affairs, where he could have done more than anyone to allay the African suspicions aroused by the whole manoeuvre ...'[3]

On the afternoon of Monday 17 February, the Governor returned to Salisbury, and within a few minutes, the Prime Minister's official car drew up outside Chaplin Building (now Mashingaidze House), picked up Garfield for the last time and took him to Governor's Lodge to resign his office. The following day, Whitehead was sworn in as Prime Minister.

***

Grace and Garfield had already moved out of Northward and into a Government flat in the suburb of Avondale, which would be a pied-à-terre for them while Garfield remained in cabinet. From now on, Hokonui Ranch would be home, and they drove down the day after the swearing-in – taking twelve gallons of paint for their new house, which was the one John Kirby had built when he became ranch manager the previous year. Grace and her gardeners set about applying some of those twelve gallons of paint, and 'her heart sang' at the

---

2 Press Statement, 16.2.58, PRO File 1-4, Box 167634, Records Office, NAZ.
3 *Manchester Guardian*, 17.2.58.

thought of living there permanently. She remembered gratefully the letters friends had written over the past weeks – and also an article in the *Rhodesia Herald* 'Cabbages and Kings' feature (although it showed complete ignorance of her Mission life): 'Mrs Todd has done a magnificent job during the four years her husband has been Premier. Although she has never loved overmuch being in the limelight – for years she lived a secluded and very quiet life on the Shabani Ranch – she has never avoided her public duties and has performed them with distinction ...'[4]

The article prompted her Salisbury neighbour, Lady Fletcher, to write: 'Many hard and bitter words have been said during the past few weeks, and, so, it made me happy to read the tribute paid to you ... I want you to know that I am only one of many who endorse that tribute and hope that you will always be happy in whatever you do and wherever your steps take you. May God bless you, with love, Dollie.'[5]

***

In spite of natural disappointment at his untimely departure from office with the job half-done, and his sadness at the defection of friends and colleagues – as well as his anxiety for the country's future – Garfield's cheerful demeanour never deserted him. There was much, in fact, to encourage him in the letters that came expressing satisfaction at his inclusion in Whitehead's cabinet. Sydney Swadel, editor of *The Chronicle*, wrote immediately: 'My own hope is that the new cabinet will be able to work together. The middle of the road policy has held power for so long in Southern Rhodesia that any able politician who joins the opposition ranks is liable to stay there for the deuce of a long time.'[6]

A more surprising, and possibly even more encouraging, letter came from John Roberts, leader of the UFP in Northern Rhodesia's Legislative Council: 'It was with great relief that I heard that Whitehead had managed to form a government supported by the Caucus and, reading between the lines, I cannot help but feel that it was to a large extent through your own goodwill, effort and co-operation that he was able to do so.' Roberts expressed his 'personal admiration for the manner in which you have conducted your thoughts and efforts during this very sad chapter ... it is extremely noble of you to have accepted a portfolio ...'[7]

The new Minister of Labour and Social Welfare had a small suite of offices in a recently constructed, anonymous Government building. With his senior civil

---

4   'Cabbages and Kings', *Rhodesia Herald*, 12.2.58.
5   Dollie Fletcher/JGT, 12.2.58, MS.1082/3/1, Todd Papers, NAZ.
6   Sydney R. Swadel/GT, 18.2.58, MS.390/1/10, ibid.
7   John Roberts/GT, 18.2.58, MS.390/1/3, ibid.

servants, Garfield was among friends: Jack Armstrong, Secretary for Labour, and Major Peter Kenworthy, Under Secretary, had been with him from the formation of the department; while Mr F. S. Caley, the Director of Social Welfare, was a very old colleague who had introduced many members of the 'Dadaya family' to the Todds. With his knowledge of his portfolios, Garfield found them a light load, but there was much that he missed in the backwaters of Central House, and in Twickenham Court in Avondale: meeting the interesting people who visited the country – though many still sought him out – and having his destiny in his own hands and the stimulus, interest and excitement of being at the centre of events, with the opportunity to initiate policies and direct affairs and get things done. If this is power, then, yes, he had enjoyed it – and he missed it.

The Todds returned to Salisbury for the opening of the new session of Parliament – and a no-confidence motion in the Government by the Opposition, now, with the addition of newly independent Wightwick, numbering five. Fletcher sat on the back benches. As Garfield took his seat beside Davenport, the Leader of the House, he knew the tradition of parliamentary privilege would mean that he could expect some very plain speaking. The Leader of the Opposition, Stewart Aitken-Cade, spoke quite mildly, even complimenting Garfield for not deviating from his principles. Aitken-Cade then went on to review the work of the Government during its four-year existence, and wound up his speech with a comprehensive condemnation: 'This Government has done the country such harm that it will take us years to recover.'[8]

Aitken-Cade had only provided the prologue; the real action began with Keller, who may have been a very sick man but there was nothing of the invalid about his attack on Garfield and the rebel ministers: 'Our troubles started when the now deposed Prime Minister was appointed leader of the party ... it is due to his fanatical outlook and the unbridled egotism of the former Prime Minister ... that we must apportion the blame for the unhappy events of the past few weeks', though his ex-ministers must take their share of the blame: 'They have brought the country into disrepute and seriously damaged its reputation ... By political manipulation Parliament is to be muzzled and the people kept ignorant of the true state of affairs – a story yet to come to light because we have not yet heard the true state of affairs, but we will hear it one of these days if I have anything to do with it.'[9]

Keller then launched into a more personal attack on Garfield, repeating the old allegations of improper use of transport and of 'covering up'. Reverting to the Ministers' 'rebellion', Keller repeated allegations he understood to have been

8   LAD, vol. 40, 26.2.58, cc. 1131, 1138–9.
9   Ibid., cc. 1140–1.

made by them, quoting from newspaper reports of Ellman-Brown's speech. 'And finally he said that he was disgusted with his leader's actions. But unfortunately he did not detail the actions and I want to know what are the actions that were not detailed ... personally I am as disgusted with the whole affair as are most thinking people. He has not only embarrassed people in this House, he has destroyed confidence overseas, and he has done everything possible to jeopardize the future of the white men of this country ...'[10]

Wightwick and Stockil took their turn but added nothing new. It was then Davenport's unhappy lot to have to answer the attack; and he rose to the occasion with a speech variously described by the Leader of the Opposition as 'grandfatherly' and by the *Rhodesia Herald* as 'colourless'. Government backbenchers kept quiet. Davenport came out in support of Garfield: 'I am very sorry indeed that [Keller] saw fit to criticize our previous Prime Minister. I do not know where he gets his information from as to the wrongful use of Government transport and so on ... I deprecate it very much ... I have no hesitation whatsoever in contradicting it.'[11]

Garfield was the only other Government member to speak, admitting that there had been 'difficulties within our own ranks, and what one might say might not always be wise. It is perhaps just as well that time should be given for wounds to heal ... I believe that people have acted honestly according to their own lights.'[12] But when replying to Keller's allegations of personal impropriety, Garfield's anger came through clearly: 'The privilege of the House is given so that people may speak freely, but not that they may speak dishonourably of one another. I may say that over the past few weeks both my family and myself have had to put up with a great deal of whispered comment throughout this country, covering all sorts of things, by people who apparently, in one way or another, are determined to oust me from politics ... I have endeavoured over the years that I have been in this House to maintain the honour and rightness of the position of a member of Parliament and a Minister of the Crown; and the reason that the slander that has gone around in past weeks has not made more impression upon my family or myself is because it is completely untrue. But if [Keller] would like to make the statement that he has made this afternoon in public, and publish it in full in one of the newspapers of the Colony, then the hon. member will hear from me.'[13] The no-confidence motion was duly defeated by 21 votes to five.

---

10   Ibid., cc. 1143–4.
11   Ibid., cc. 1153–4.
12   Ibid., c. 1157.
13   Ibid., cc. 1157–8.

The *Rhodesia Herald* was very critical of Keller – and had 'every sympathy' for Garfield. 'Public life will become completely intolerable if men in high places are required to answer every splenetic attack on them without a tittle of evidence being forthcoming ... Mr Keller said too much that left a nasty taste and ... too little to enable Mr Todd to answer him.'[14]

***

Early in March, the Southern Rhodesia ANC held its conference: the African people, who had left the squabbling to the Europeans, now had their opportunity to express their feelings. Joshua Nkomo told delegates that 'The time has now come that unqualified partnership be practised or nothing at all ... What we want is treatment and regard of Africans as human beings in the land of their birth ... and it is the Africans themselves who must decide this now.'[15] An appeal was made for all Africans in European-run parties to withdraw their support forthwith. Garfield's removal from office 'was a clear indication that Europeans were not prepared to co-operate with the Africans'. Vice-President James Chikerema said that Africans in the European parties were being used to strengthen Welensky's claim that African opinion supports his 'moves to consolidate settler control here'.

***

The time had come for Whitehead to choose a parliamentary seat and fight his by-election. He could have chosen any one of a dozen safe seats but chose Hillside, in Bulawayo, 500 miles from his own home, and traditionally anti-government.

'The by-election campaign was a disaster,' Abrahamson wrote, 'and Edgar's defeat was blamed not on over-confident non-activity but on Garfield.'[16] Whitehead lost by 691 votes to 604. Clyde Sanger writes: 'The sight of a Premier defeated at a by-election added an unexpected twist to the whole depressing drama. Whitehead did not increase his stature by putting the blame on Todd, but he was tactically wise to do so.'[17]

On 18 April, the Governor granted a dissolution of parliament. A general election would be held on Thursday 5 June, with nomination day 15 May. But first came another crucial Caucus meeting, on Wednesday 23 April. Whitehead could no longer avoid the choice that, as Garfield had pointed out, Congress had side-stepped. His dilemma lay in the fact that his own instincts were on the

---

14   *Rhodesia Herald*, 28.2.58.
15   *African Daily News*, 3.3.58.
16   A. E. Abrahamson/SP, 3.6.97, TPPC.
17   Sanger, 1960, p. 157.

liberal side but he had been back in Southern Rhodesia long enough to realise that the European electorate was in retreat from more liberal policies.

Holderness's 'fall-back position' of the revival of the URP was now under serious discussion among the Todd group. On the day before the next Caucus meeting, Welensky called Whitehead and Garfield to a meeting. They discussed the situation, and the two prime ministers asked if Garfield would consider leaving the political scene before the meeting. Garfield described his response later: 'I believed that my withdrawal from politics would be a betrayal of a large section of the people, both European and African, and that such an action would be completely negative and would solve nothing.' He believed that it was 'in the country's best interests that we face our problems and not sidestep them'.[18]

At 10.00 a.m. on Wednesday 23 April, Caucus met. Debate centred on 'the dropping of Todd ... the effects of fusion ... and the influence of left-wingers in the Party'. Some of Garfield's supporters thought dropping him would be either no answer or positively disastrous; Paddy Lloyd maintained that it would be a 'submission to having our progress dictated by the "pace of the white miner on the Copperbelt"'. Six others – including Fletcher, Stumbles and Ellman-Brown – thought 'Todd must be dropped'; they and Wingfield 'were emphatic about the evils of left-wing "infiltration" into the Party'. Abrahamson, who had by this time left the Todd group, proposed a vote of confidence in Whitehead, which was carried by fourteen votes to eight.

Garfield said: 'It was obvious that the Prime Minister had made his decision to retain the Fletcher–Straw group. I pledged my loyalty to his leadership but he had made up his mind ... I went further and stressed that this group should go to the Dominion Party, who had invited them to come ... This would have left the country with a choice between the Dominion Party policy and a clear-cut UFP policy. We had no wish to leave; but we saw the Prime Minister surrender to the reactionary element ... we had no option but to leave the caucus and the party.'[19] Thirty years later, Garfield remembered 'one of the worst moments in my life – the occasion when Edgar, with head bent, said he could not go to the next election with Todd in the party'.[20]

Garfield, the Palmers, Ben Baron, Max Buchan, Hardwicke Holderness and Paddy Lloyd stood up and left the caucus room. Garfield remembers the elation that was in the room as they walked out. Whitehead apart, these were the men (for there would have been only sadness in Muriel Rosin, who

---

18 GT's Address, Inaugural Congress of the revived URP, 3.5.58, TPPC.
19 Inaugural Congress of the revived URP, 5.5.58, TPPC.
20 GT/SP, interview, 1993.

was 'going federal') who had been his colleagues for four years, men whom he had trusted and with whom he had worked and who, until a couple of months before, he had considered supporters and even friends. His group went to a committee room, rather shaken by what had happened. After a few minutes, Garfield left them to compose a statement while he returned to his office to write his letter of resignation to the Prime Minister: 'My dear Prime Minister, Following upon today's events, I now send my resignation as a member of your cabinet. It has for some time been apparent to us all that there is a divergence of opinion between members of the Caucus as to whether my continuing service has been in the best interests of the Party. It has been made clear to me in talks with leaders of the UFP that it is my withdrawal, together with those who are of like mind, which is desired. I should have been happy, if circumstances had so allowed, to have served under you, Sir, either as a member of your Government or as a backbencher ... I take this step now, not of my own wish, but with reluctance and regret.'[21]

The Prime Minister's reply was not long in coming: 'My dear Todd, I have received your resignation with regret but agree with you that in view of today's events I have had no option but to accept it. I wish to thank you for your services in my cabinet and the loyalty you have given to me while serving under my leadership. I regret that political differences within the party have made it impossible for us to continue to collaborate.'[22]

Paddy Lloyd issued a statement on behalf of the 'Todd group', saying they had resigned from the UFP because 'We believe that it no longer represents the principles for which we stand and upon which we were elected to Parliament ... the split was due to fundamental differences in the interpretation and execution of policy ... We are now satisfied that the spirit of compromise within [the UFP] is destructive of the best interests of Southern Rhodesia. It is our intention to revive the United Rhodesia Party in order to implement the policy which has given the country a unique record in progressive administration ...'[23]

'The choice before us after we had withdrawn from the Caucus', Garfield explained in May, 'was whether or not we should stay in politics, and if we decided to do so, how we would go about it. Within our group the majority wished, for personal reasons, to leave politics; but we had to face our responsibility to the people who had elected us, and our responsibility to that section of the party which had supported my leadership at Congress

---

21   GT/EW, 23.4.58, File PRO 1-4, Box 167634, Records Office, NAZ.
22   EW/GT, 23.4.58, ibid.
23   *Rhodesia Herald*, 24.4.58.

… In April the Prime Minister himself sanctioned and participated in the dismemberment of his parliamentary group. Sir Edgar was not empowered by Congress to disregard the one hundred and twenty-nine votes which supported my group.'[24]

---

[24] URP Inaugural Congress, 5.5.58, TPPC.

54

8,000 Miles to the Wilderness

'Your representative owes you, not his industry only, but his judgement; and he betrays instead of serving you if he sacrifices it to your opinion.'

Edmund Burke (1729–97)

After the Caucus meeting on 23 April 1958, Garfield drove to Belingwe to address a pre-arranged meeting. He told his audience how impossible it had been for him and his supporters to remain longer in the UFP – but at the same time he did not wish to leave. 'There are some things which stand out and they cannot be gainsaid. The patched-up state of the party was not acceptable to the electorate, vide Hillside.'[1] A decision had to be made, which should have been made at Congress: 'whether Rhodesia will fearlessly pursue the policy of partnership – on the one hand maintaining standards Europeans have set, and on the other opening fully the door of opportunity to the African people. You cannot publish that you will, and lie back in the traces – that is political expediency – that is what the UFP has chosen ... I would sooner be in the political wilderness with my principles intact.'

The decision to revive the United Rhodesia Party and to contest the general election on 5 June gave Garfield and his friends six weeks in which to prepare, but during that time they also had to recreate a party structure, formulate and print a party policy statement and – probably most difficult of all – get financial backing. But an even closer deadline was nomination day – 15 May – leaving 21 days in which to find 30 good candidates. Difficulties were compounded by the unfinished business of 'fusion', for example, the differing status of branches.

---

1   GT Notes, April 1958, MS.1084/1/2, Todd Papers, NAZ.

The Todds were now living at Hokonui Ranch, where communications would always be difficult – 265 miles from Salisbury, 110 from Bulawayo, largely on untarred roads – and, fifteen miles away in Shabani, the oldest manual telephone exchange in the country. With twelve subscribers on the party line, confidentiality was impossible. Most of the arrangements were made and decisions taken in Salisbury or Bulawayo without Garfield. The enthusiasm and dedication of URP supporters all over the country saw to it that a policy document was prepared, approved and printed in time for an inaugural party congress on 3 May. A programme was drawn up for Garfield to speak in as many constituencies as possible, as well as in the main centres in his own vast constituency. He now began a marathon electioneering programme. In Shabani, Garfield knew that he would have a tough fight: the voters there included a high proportion of European miners and a considerable number of people of Afrikaner extraction. Many of the local ranchers were also right-leaning in their views on the all-important subject of African advancement. It had always been surprising that Garfield should represent such a constituency, but now he rejected a 'safe seat' in Salisbury to stay with it.

Three days after the Caucus meeting, the *Central African Examiner* brought encouragement to the URP: Garfield, 'with six Parliamentary followers, has thrown down the gauntlet. He was right to do so. And he was right even if his action results in so severe a split among moderate elements in Southern Rhodesia that both the UFP and Mr Todd's new party go down in defeat. He was right even if the outcome of his decision is to leave the country to five years of rule by Mr Winston Field's DP, a party which ... is reactionary, segregationist, and travelling, even if it has not yet awakened to the fact, towards a South African solution to a Rhodesia problem. Mr Todd and his friends are right because they will give the voters of Southern Rhodesia the opportunity they should in honesty have been given in January of this year ...'[2]

Holderness writes: 'The chances of winning a majority of seats in the House must have seemed non-existent from the start, but there were others besides us who felt that even if we only got one seat it would be significant ... It was no good trying to contest all thirty seats, but important to contest enough to make possible an overall victory in theory at least.'[3] There was great enthusiasm, excitement, friendship and unbelievable hard work.

When it came to money, the former URP treasurer, John Allen, CA, although now a member of the UFP, decided that, 'because fusion had not

2   *Central African Examiner*, 26.4.58, vol. 1, no. 24.
3   Holderness, 1985, p. 226.

been ratified by a special URP congress, the merger had not been official and therefore the URP funds should be handed back'.[4] Garfield approached Sir Ronald Prain, but he had already agreed to support the UFP. An approach to Mr Harold Hochschild was also unsuccessful, but Sir Stephen Courtauld came to the support of the URP. Sir William Murphy agreed to act as chairman of the party.

Saturday 3 May was the day of the URP Inaugural Congress in Salisbury. Garfield began his address: 'The United Rhodesia Party is alive and in action and I believe this is good news for Rhodesia. I am determined to do everything in my power to set Rhodesia firmly once again on her sound and liberal cause.'[5]

Nomination day was 15 May, and the URP held a rally in Salisbury to present its twenty candidates, who, Professor Kenneth Kirkwood maintained, represented 'undoubtedly "the cream of Southern Rhodesia" – a phrase used even by political opponents'.[6]

Ian Hancock considered that they 'constituted the ablest and most accomplished group ever to stand as one party in White Rhodesia history. Not one could be described (except in white Rhodesia) as a crank or a radical; only one was under thirty and a third were over fifty; most could point to a war record or long service in public affairs, including membership of the United Party or of the Federal Party or of the old URP; all were successful and respectable figures in the professions, business, mining and farming ... But the quality of the candidates and the deliberate attempt to offer an image of responsibility and common-sense, could not undo the reputation, sedulously fostered by the UFP and the DP, of wide-eyed innocence and a willingness to sabotage White rule and the existing standard of living.'[7] Educated Africans watched the campaign closely and with considerable background knowledge of individuals.

The UFP and DP contested all 30 seats. Garfield's opponents in Shabani were Mr V. J. ('Tom') Goddard, a local farmer and former magistrate, for the UFP, and Mr I. B. Dillon, a miner, DP, who told Parliament in 1959 that his 'entry into politics was to get Mr Garfield Todd out of the political system'.[8] Holderness, at Salisbury North, which he had represented during the Eighth Parliament, found himself pitted against Whitehead. Lord Malvern lent his

---

4   *Rhodesia Herald*, 28.4.58.
5   URP Inaugural Congress, 3.5.58, TPPC.
6   Kenneth Kirkwood, 'Points for Collin', Kirkwood Papers, Bodleian Library.
7   Hancock, 1984, pp. 73–4.
8   LAD, vol. 43, 15.7.59, c. 298.

considerable prestige to Whitehead's campaign, which distressed the URP, who felt he should have remained aloof from the contest; but Whitehead was taking no chances. *South Africa* commented that Malvern's 'intervention must have contributed considerably, if not decisively, to the discrediting of Mr Todd and his United Rhodesia Party'.[9]

***

Garfield was the first to cast his vote at Shabani before the start of a tour of his constituency, visiting as many polling stations as he could. His feat of addressing 48 meetings in 43 days could only have been performed by a man of exceptional physical and mental stamina and vigour. He covered nearly 8,000 miles, for most of which he was behind the wheel, though Grace drove him whenever practicable. She went early to vote at Dadaya, but otherwise remained at Hokonui Ranch all that day. Shabani results were always 24 hours later than other places, and it was not until Friday 6 June that the count there was completed. By that time, Garfield knew that the URP had lost every other seat it had contested and that the UFP was set to win the election – albeit only with the help of the second votes of URP supporters. At Shabani, the first count gave Dillon (DP) 477, Todd 365 and Goddard 230 – so Garfield still stood a chance, if at least 113 UFP voters had cast their second vote for him. But only 61 UFP supporters did so – 52 gave Dillon their vote, and 117 UFP voters simply did not use their second vote. Garfield was so shocked, as well as disappointed, by the result that he was unable to mask his reaction. He had been right when he said a couple of days earlier in Bulawayo: 'The UFP would rather accept the possibility of a DP government than advise its supporters to give their second vote to the United Rhodesia Party.'[10]

Exhausted as much by the emotions of the last two days as by the events of the preceding six months, Garfield returned to the ranch. Grace was sitting on the homestead verandah watching for him, and knew he had lost when she saw him, head bent, come round the corner of the house. 'That was the moment when I was more angry and more hopeless about the future for this country than any other.'[11]

***

In a 74% poll, the Dominion Party received 45.7% of votes cast (18,314) and won thirteen seats; the United Federal Party 42.4% (17,064), seventeen seats; and the United Rhodesia Party 11.7% (4,663), no seats. The URP

---

9   *South Africa*, 14.6.58.
10 GT, Bulawayo, 3.6.58, MS.1093/1/2, Todd Papers, NAZ.
11 JGT/SP, interview, 1998.

percentage rose to 14.9% in the seats the party contested.

'When Todd's candidates were all defeated,' Clyde Sanger wrote, 'Africans went about greeting each other with that special embrace which denotes sympathy at the death of a friend.'[12]

---

[12] Sanger, 1960, p. 158.

55

'It was already too late'

'The golden years when [Grace] and you led the way in dignity and honour to new understandings of changing times.'

Peter Mackay to Garfield Todd, 2002

The result of the general election was not just a great disappointment to the URP, its candidates and its supporters; it was a complete disillusionment. Their firm belief in the 'essential liberalism' of Rhodesians, on which they had been building for five years, had proved disastrously wrong; and it was this more than anything else which overwhelmed them. We have seen how much faith Garfield had placed in this – and its conclusive demolition was a blow from which it would take him months to recover. A letter he wrote four years later to Sir John Moffat of Northern Rhodesia, whose Liberal Party suffered similar annihilation, shows how he was feeling that weekend in June 1958: 'One is tempted to let the whole thing rip.'[1]

On Saturday 7 June, Garfield was interviewed by a *Sunday Mail* reporter: 'Mr Todd said the strength of the illiberal faction had been under-estimated. Clearly it was at least fifty percent. "That is a sinister thing ... there are quite a lot of people who are just not prepared to have the African coming on to the voters' rolls".'[2]

The *Rhodesia Herald* of 11 June referred to the 'gallantry' of the URP's candidates[3] – and the same word cropped up repeatedly in the letters Garfield received. These men had given Rhodesians a choice – and a last chance – but they now felt shocked, bruised and isolated – at least until they read the comments from overseas papers. The recognition there – and in that remarkable

---

1 GT/Sir John Moffat, 6.11.62, MS.390/1/25, Todd Papers, NAZ.
2 *Sunday Mail*, 8.6.58.
3 *Rhodesia Herald*, 11.6.58.

Midlands newspaper, the *Gwelo Times* – helped Garfield and Grace to maintain their cheerful equilibrium, untouched by bitterness or resentment.

'The rejection of Mr Todd and his party has set the seal of public approval on political expediency and compromise', ran the editorial in the *Gwelo Times* on 14 June. 'Thus closes one of the most fateful chapters in this country's history – and one which, in our view, is a blot upon that history. The circumstances which led up to the ultimate defeat of Southern Rhodesia's last Prime Minister are discreditable in more ways than one; and that a man of his outstanding and widely recognised abilities and qualities should have been subjected to so infamous a campaign of personal defamation is something of which this country should be thoroughly ashamed ...

'The fact that those who lent him their practical and moral support all through were by all standards reputable and well-known Rhodesians is enough to give the lie to his detractors, but there is no doubt that incalculable harm was done among unthinking and easily influenced people by the methods used to turn public opinion against him. Strange as it may seem, Mr Todd's greatest handicap in the battle he fought so courageously was the fact that he was ... a missionary. For it is sad but true that people like to keep their religion and their politics in water-tight compartments, and are unwilling to see Christian principles (particularly in human relations) too overtly applied to the affairs of state. Sad but true, again, – and proved over and over again in history – is the fact that men of mediocre abilities have an instinctive desire to persecute and discredit those who display qualities which are too conspicuously superior to their own ...

'We believe it is true to say that his detractors have deliberately attempted to blind themselves and others to the ethical rightness of his approach to our major problem – race relations – by casting doubt upon his personal integrity; and this is a piece of indefensible political strategy which will leave a permanent stain on our national character.'[4]

In the meantime, the letters flooded into Hokonui. Many correspondents echoed what the Anglican Archbishop of Central Africa said, that they were concerned not so much about the people who had been returned as about those who had *not* been returned.[5] The quality of URP candidates was commented on time and again by the people who wrote to Garfield, among whom were civil servants. Mr Erskine Grant-Dalton, Clerk Assistant of the Federal Assembly, wrote: 'The electorate could not find it possible to return even one just man

---

4   *Gwelo Times*, 14.6.58.
5   *Rhodesia Herald*, 5.7.58.

... do not cease to struggle for the principles you advocate. They will prevail.'[6] The Todds' old friend and encourager, Jimmy Stewart, wrote in indignation: 'The treatment accorded to yourself in particular and to your gallant band of enlightened failures was a tremendous shock ... We were all very proud of the standard you have raised ... We believe that the candle you have lit will never be put out in Rhodesia.' 'Your ideals will remain', wrote Dr E. C. Malherbe, Principal and Vice-Chancellor of Natal University.[7] Professor S. H. Frankel wrote from Oxford: 'You coped with characteristic courage and it is not your fault that Southern Rhodesia is not yet advanced sufficiently to understand your message ...'[8]

Disappointed letters came from many Africans, clearly seeing the end of white protestations of partnership. D. G. Mhambi wrote from Livingstone: 'you put the whole country to a test and they were found wanting ... the white electorate totally rejected the development of an African on human basis'.[9] J. A. C. Mutambirwa from Waddilove Mission: 'I am so deeply shocked by the results ... I feel I must write to you ... You are the man who has a greater insight into the future of this great country ...'[10]

University people, Capricorn Africa Society members, a former mayor of Salisbury, Maurice Went of the Rhodesia Railway Workers' Union, the Federal Eurafrican Society, all wrote. Mrs Jessie Lovemore (who had arrived in Matabeleland before 1880) told Garfield that 'in the end right will overcome'.[11] She went 300 miles to vote for him.[12]

Sir George Davenport wrote on his last day at the Ministry of Mines: 'I had hoped and fully expected that both you and Paddy Lloyd would be returned to Parliament. You are much too valuable a man to be lost to the country if only for five years.'[13] The Librarian of Parliament, Philip Laundy (author of *The Office of Speaker*), wrote: 'With the opening of the Southern Rhodesia Parliament tomorrow I think with regret of the Parliament that is no more and those whose valuable services have been lost to the country as a result of the election. Although I am required to have no political sympathies I feel compelled to let you know how deeply I regret the fact that you will not be heading the procession of Members tomorrow. I was deeply shocked by the

---

6 Erskine Grant-Dalton/GT, 6.6.58, Todd Papers, NAZ.
7 E. C. Malherbe/GT, 14.6.58, MS.390/1/3, ibid.
8 Prof. S. H. Frankel/GT, 7.6.58, MS.390/1/3, ibid.
9 D. G. Mhambi/GT, 8.6.58, ibid.
10 J. A. C. Mutambirwa/GT, n.d., MS.390/1/3, ibid.
11 Jessie Lovemore/GT, 10.6.58, MS.390/1/3, ibid.
12 *Rhodesia Herald*, 5.6.58.
13 Sir George Davenport/GT, 10.6.58, MS.390/3/3, Todd Papers, NAZ.

eclipse of the URP. I did not think that courage and integrity would count for so little with the electorate ...'[14]

***

While the overseas press was relieved that the Dominion Party had been defeated in spite of winning a majority of the votes, it mourned the departure of Garfield from the Southern Rhodesia scene, which the *Scotsman* feared 'was likely to confirm Africans in their opposition to any change in the direction of freedom from Westminster'.[15] Colin Legum in the *Observer* also looked at the wider Federal scene and commented that Garfield's defeat had dealt a 'shattering blow' to 'the image of the Federation as a cradle of Liberalism'. The URP's 'total annihilation ... will serve as a warning to other would-be liberals that Rhodesian settler opinion is unwilling to support even the diluted Liberalism offered by Mr Todd'.[16]

The *African Daily News* commented: 'In the eyes of some Africans the result of the Southern Rhodesia General Election is seen as a rejection of the policy of partnership by Europeans ... the forces of liberalism, they say, are waning, giving way to reaction.'[17]

The *Central African Examiner* reported that 'Scarcely any African imagined that the [United Rhodesia] Party, with so many high-calibre candidates, would be completely wiped out, and that Mr Todd and Mr Lloyd would lose their seats ... They believe that Todd was rejected because he "espoused the African cause" ... Many politically conscious Africans now believe that in the struggle for their advancement, they will have to "go it alone" ...'[18]

Robert Blake, writing towards the end of the 1970s, is also quite clear in his summing up: 'In retrospect the year 1957 and the first few months of 1958 can be seen as a turning point in the history of the Federation and the colony. When it began there was a chance – a slender one no doubt – that the educated African would try to realise his aspirations with[in] the framework of the Constitution. By the end that chance had slipped away for ever.'[19]

In 2003, at a service of thanksgiving for the lives of Garfield and Grace Todd in London, Lawrence Vambe, historian, journalist, and witness over 80 years of the troubled scene in Central Africa, told his audience: 'We Africans were bitterly shocked ... [we believed] that Todd was being ditched because of

---

14 Philip Laundy/GT, 30.6.58, MS.390/1/10, ibid.
15 *Scotsman*, 7.6.58. quoted in *Sunday Mail*, 8.6.58.
16 *Observer*, 8.6.58.
17 *African Daily News*, 7.6.58.
18 *Central African Examiner*, 14.6.58, vol. 2, no. 1.
19 Blake, 1977, p. 296.

his pro-black agenda. From then on, we flocked to the banner of the African National Congress.' However, he added, this enforced departure from power 'was perhaps a blessing in disguise for Garfield Todd. African nationalism was on the march and unstoppable ...'[20]

***

'What was Todd's so-called programme of reform?' Greenfield scornfully asked the National Archives Oral Archivist. 'I never saw it.'[21] But it had been there for all to see. The URP 'Native Policy' at the 1954 general election stated: 'The keynote of the URP's policy is to maintain the standards of Europeans, to improve the standards of Africans, and to preserve racial harmony. To achieve these ends it is essential to ... create the atmosphere of contentment in which Communism cannot breed. This calls for adequate housing, security of land tenure, education and some measure of political development.'[22] No one could say Garfield sprang any surprises on the electorate.

At the end of the one term of office vouchsafed to him, Garfield had to his credit undoubted achievements. He had forced the Europeans to look at the facts of life in Central Africa in the mid-twentieth century. He had shown them what partnership really meant. He had clearly drawn the alternatives before them. That they didn't like what they saw was not his fault, nor did it alter his own beliefs. Nathan Shamuyarira said in 1994 that Garfield made 'a great contribution to society and to Zimbabwe. His greatest contribution was his attempt to bring the Africans into the system ... He wanted the capable Africans to be brought along ... What he was offering was very small but the principle he was fighting for was the correct one. He increased African participation in government ...'[23]

Garfield's 'great achievement (and it is an important one)', wrote the UK High Commissioner in Southern Rhodesia to Lord Home in January 1958, 'is that he in Southern Rhodesia has won and retained the confidence of moderate Africans to a far greater extent than any other politician in the Federation'.[24] For the *African Weekly*, Garfield's 'greatest achievement' was African 'participation in European-initiated parties'.[25] An editorial in a later issue commented: 'In the African community [the Todd Government] has a good record of progressive legislation ... Better housing, a wider franchise, improved education facilities,

---

20 L. Vambe, Address, St Martin's-in-the-Fields Church, London, 13.2.2003, TPPC.
21 Oral GR.2, NAZ.
22 MS.390/2/1, Todd Papers, NAZ.
23 Interview, 29.6.94.
24 UKHCSR, January 1958, PRO CRO 7531.
25 *African Weekly*, 5.2.58.

plot-ownership in the rural areas, a less vexatious pass system, and a non-racial approach to the vexed question of industrial conciliation, are among the many progressive measures that are linked with the name of the URP. It could also rightly claim to have maintained and even increased the spirit of goodwill between the races ...'[26]

Garfield's steady erosion of the power of the Native Affairs Department, bringing the African people into the mainstream of government activity, comes high on the list of his achievements. The message this sent out elicited unprecedented co-operation by the Africans, notably in the doubling of the Native Tax. The provision of security of tenure in urban areas was only a small step, but it was the establishment of a principle. The industrial-conciliation legislation not only brought African trade unionism into the mainstream of industrial activity, but it also removed the South African influence on white trade unions. A few significant breaches of the monolithic Land Apportionment Act proved that it was not impregnable – and, finally, there was the franchise legislation. Though but a part of what Garfield had hoped for, it did at least open the door to a wider participation by Africans.

Blake writes: 'Todd tried to tackle some of the major obstacles to African advancement. It is often said that more progress was made by Whitehead who succeeded him. This is true, but only in the sense that a ship moves more rapidly in an arctic sea than the ice-breaker that goes ahead of her. Whitehead's achievement was to build on Todd's foundations, but he would have accomplished little had they not been laid.'[27]

***

Garfield's hopes for the country when he became Prime Minister were formed many years earlier as a missionary and could be said to apply also to the calling of a politician – 'to serve people'. In 1943, he told the New Zealand Overseas Mission Board that 'One of our sacred duties is to endeavour to instil into the hearts of our people a greater and wider love than is shown them. If that cannot be done, then Africa may become an even darker continent.'[28] 'There is power in a readiness to serve people because of a love for what is right and just', Garfield told the Capricorn Africa Society.[29]

When a Central African federation was being discussed in the Southern Rhodesian Legislative Assembly in 1952, Garfield saw clearly that 'If we federate these three countries we are committing Central Africa to a liberal

---

26 *African Weekly*, 24.4.58.
27 Blake, 1977, p. 292.
28 GT, Report, July 1943, TPPC.
29 *Rhodesia Herald*, 26.2.54.

policy, to a policy of racial co-operation, which we are not so fully committed to under our present state government.'[30] Garfield committed himself, wholly without cynicism, to that 'liberal policy'. He was 'genuinely interested in the policy of partnership between white and black', as he told George Addecott in June 1954.[31] He considered politics to be God's work as much as the Church, and saw the need for a 'recognition by our people of the humanity of Africans', as he told the Salisbury Rotarians in 1955.[32] Garfield's well-known phrase – 'co-operating courageously and generously with the inevitable' – could be said to sum up his intentions for Southern Rhodesia. He hoped to come to an understanding with the Africans and to share government with them – but in the end, 'I was unable to persuade the white electorate which had given me power that we had no option but to come quickly to an understanding with our fellow citizens and to share government with them.'[33]

'There was only one thing to be achieved and that was to lay a political foundation on which you could build a non-racial community sharing in Government', Garfield told the New Zealand Film Unit at Hokonui in 1991. A peaceful transition could have been made: 'In my estimation there's no doubt about that, because the whole African population was ready to negotiate ... would have been prepared to take what I would offer ... That was the time, because blacks were ready ... Whites never were ready to negotiate and that was the key time and they missed their opportunity ...'[34]

Richard Gray 'vividly' remembered a discussion between Nkomo and M. M. Hove, MP, in Bulawayo in January 1956. 'It was quite clear that Nkomo desperately wanted peaceful evolution but already was reluctantly convinced it was impossible.'[35] Nkomo was asked by the NZ TV team: if Garfield Todd had stayed in power, would there have been a peaceful transition to democracy? He replied: 'No. It wouldn't have been possible ... like us he was devoted to peaceful change ... He was trying to further the oneness of the people of his country ... but all of us failed ... we had come to realise that the concessions could not really bring about what some of us wanted to bring about – one man, one vote.'[36] But Nathan Shamuyarira disagreed: if the whites had agreed 'to share power and permit participation in government, and if they had taken that

---

30 LAD, vol. 33, 23.6.52, c. 2678.
31 GT, File P.7, Box 167635, Records Centre, NAZ.
32 19.4.55, MS.1083/1, Todd Papers, NAZ.
33 GT, National Union of South African Students, Johannesburg, 2.7.63, MS.390/1/28, Todd Papers, NAZ.
34 TPPC.
35 Interview, Prof. Richard Gray/SP, 24.4.2001, TPPC.
36 NZTV, *Hokonui Todd* recording, 22.4.1990.

road, then UDI and violence would have been prevented'.³⁷

Cyril Dunn delightfully described the Eighth Parliament as an 'almost laughably urbane and rational world'. The passage, however, goes on: 'It was, as things have turned out, a fading picture. Its gentle colouring was of the sunset. The Government and all its liberal claims are gone, and with them most of those white Members who, in an all-white House, defended the ideal of a common roll ... But for five years they sustained an illusion in Southern Rhodesia – that on a basis of rigid racial segregation they could build a multiracial sanctuary. It may be claimed that they made significant changes, that they altered the whole trend.'³⁸

When the University of Otago conferred their LL.D. on Garfield in 1979, the citation included this comment: 'If men of ideals abandon [politics,] they leave it to men who have none. One of Garfield Todd's great achievements has been to demonstrate that politics and principles are not incompatible, that men of integrity and faith can be effective political leaders though, or rather because, there is always a point beyond which they will not compromise for the sake of retaining power ... Historians agree that [1958] was a turning point in Rhodesian history. With the fall of Garfield Todd the country lost its one chance of a peaceful transition to majority rule and legal independence.'³⁹

Professor Dickson Mungazi writes that Todd, 'never knew what race was as he saw Africans as precious human beings ... in turn, the Africans saw Todd as a man whose Christian principles and values extended far beyond the ordinary ... Given the conditions of the times, such a relationship ... was rare in the quality of the message it carried for the country ... a man whose contribution has left an important imprint on the history of Zimbabwe.'⁴⁰

---

37 Interview, 29.6.94.
38 Dunn, 1959, p. 87.
39 University of Otago, December 1979, TPPC.
40 Mungazi, 1999, pp. 175–6.

PART IV – 'INSPIRING AND PROPHETIC UNGUIDED MISSILE',[1]
July 1958 to December 1960

♦•♦

56

A HEAVINESS OF HEART

'Todd: "The White who gave the black man hope".'

John Parker, *Rhodesia: Little White Island* (1972)

The brief period from July 1958 to December 1960 was a pivotal moment in the history of Central Africa. At the end of it, the fate of the Federation and its constituent territories would be sealed; and everything that would happen to Southern Rhodesia had been clearly spelled out.

In April 1957, the Federal Prime Minister, Sir Roy Welensky, demanded Dominion status for the Federation in 1960. This lit a fuse which burned slowly

---
1 T. O. Ranger, 1995, p. 171.

until the return to Nyasaland in 1959 of Dr Hastings Kamuzu Banda (the self-exiled African nationalist leader) ignited the smouldering resentment of Federation among Africans in the north. In early 1959, states of emergency, of varying duration and violence, were proclaimed in all three territories. In Nyasaland, 57 Africans were killed. This brought Central Africa to the reluctant attention of the British Government. The Conservative Party's increased majority after the UK general election of October that year strengthened the hand of Prime Minister Harold Macmillan against his vociferous and obstructive right wing – and, while Lord Home remained as Secretary of State for Commonwealth Relations, Macmillan was able to appoint the liberal Iain Macleod as Colonial Secretary.

The new Colonial Secretary wrote an article in the *Weekend Telegraph* of 12 March 1965 about the granting of independence in Africa, in which he said that 'The tempo accelerated as a result of a score of different and deliberate decisions. For myself, some months before the election ... I had convinced myself that for all the manifest dangers of moving quickly in Africa, the dangers of being too slow were greater.'

***

In November 1957, *The Chronicle* had commented that Garfield 'has largely become the embodiment of something that should never be stilled – the national conscience'.[2] The same paper had earlier described Garfield as the country's 'lively and troublesome conscience'.[3] It was in a desperate attempt to awaken his fellow Europeans to reality before it was too late, and to help them achieve some sort of sound future in Zimbabwe, that Garfield bent his energies – not just during this crucial period, but for the next twenty years.

***

On 13 July 1958, Garfield celebrated his 50th birthday. He experienced a mixture of relief that the responsibilities of government were over, and great anxiety for the future of himself, his family and Southern Rhodesia. But there was also a feeling of hurt. Twelve years later, he told Norman Harris of 'the shame of being thrown out, which is not a nice thing, and the annihilation of character'.[4] Garfield chose not to ask for a pension. 'In those days you didn't make money from your politics.'[5]

Hokonui Ranch, fifteen miles from Shabani, had been registered in 1955 with a total capital of £56,000; 49,050 acres in the middleveld, 3,000 feet above

---

2   *The Chronicle*, 23.11.57.
3   *The Chronicle*, 29.9.57.
4   Harris, 1971, p. 167.
5   GT/SP, TPPC.

sea level, with 40 miles of river frontage. There were a butchery, petrol station and four stores on the ranch (but the profits from Dadaya Store were used for missionary work). While Garfield was living in Salisbury, Shirley Beadle had managed all the ranch work until the Christie partnership, when John Kirby had taken over management of the cattle, leaving her with the oversight of the commercial undertakings. But, when Garfield was unexpectedly freed to live and work at Hokonui, Kirby's employment was ended on terms which enabled him to begin ranching on his own account earlier than he had expected.

Bannockburn was the commercial centre of the ranch. Here the Rhodesia Railways siding had grown into a station on the main line to Lourenço Marques (later Maputo), and here was a European 'township' of sixteen families. Ten times that number of African families lived in a compound a little way away. The store and butchery benefited from the communities, but otherwise the railway was a nuisance: broken fences enabled cattle to get onto the line, with a weekly death toll; and sparks from the steam engines brought frequent grass fires which could destroy thousands of acres of grazing. The coming of diesel engines was very welcome – and should have meant the release of more water from the Railways dam on the Ngezi River in drought years. The political attitude of the railway authorities and local officials was so unsympathetic to Garfield that it was always difficult to persuade them to fulfil their statutory obligations – still less provide emergency assistance. The stores also benefited from proximity to the Lundi Reserve – the constant traffic of people and donkeys laden with maize for the grinding-mill made for a lively scene which Garfield enjoyed through the open door of his office.

On taking over the ranch in June 1958, Garfield spent a month going through all the ranch operations, checking organisation and systems, and trying to get to grips with the financial situation. Christie had visited Rhodesia in January 1958 at the height of the cabinet crisis, but Garfield had spent only a few hours with him. Six months later, Christie threw everything into disarray, telling Garfield he wished to break the partnership and get his money back as quickly as possible – all £70,000 of it. This was a considerable shock to Garfield, who found it difficult to understand Christie's complete change of mind over Hokonui. The increased anxiety of the ranch situation, on top of his physical exhaustion and the aftermath of the first half of the year, culminated in Garfield's collapse during a church address in Bulawayo in September. Fears of a heart attack proved unfounded, but Dr Paul Fehrsen ordered a month's complete rest.

In an attempt to clarify matters with Christie, Garfield flew to New York. 'Emory Ross took me to see him and went in first on his own. When he came

1. Thomas Todd (I) (1823–1908), Garfield's grandfather.
NZ Early Settlers' Museum

2. Thomas Todd (II) (1862–1936), Garfield's father, with his grandmother Elizabeth (née Wright) (1832–1929).

3. Mrs Edith Todd (née Scott) (1883–1957),
wife of Thomas Todd (II), and Garfield's mother.

4. Belgravia, Waikiwi, Invercargill, New Zealand.
Grandparents' home, built by Thomas Todd (I).
First published in the Southland Times, 2/12/95. Reproduced with the kind permission of Ian McCallum of Harcourts.

5. Students at Dunedin Bible College, Glen Leith, Dunedin, 1930.
Garfield in middle of back row.

6. Garfield and his sister Stella (Mrs Salisbury) on his motorcycle.

7. Garfield and his wife, Grace (Wilson) (1911–2001), selected by the Church of Christ to go to Dadaya Mission, Shabani, Southern Rhodesia.

8. Grace at her desk as headmistress of Dadaya School.

9. Garfield grinding corn with the help of his car, watched by adopted daughter Alycen (1932–2003) and Mr Milton Vickery (NZ Church of Christ).

10. Large classroom block built by Garfield, staff and boys of Dadaya School, with bricks made by them.

11. Garfield at the brick kiln, 1938

12. Garfield with schoolteachers David Mkwananzi, Joram Sibanda, and the Rev. Ndabambi Hlambelo.

13. Garfield with the first daughter he delivered, Judith, 1943.

14. Garfield campaigns in the 1946 general election in Insiza constituency.

15. Grace and Judith in Cecil Square, Salisbury, after the Opening of Parliament in 1946.

16. Todds visit New Zealand in 1949: Alycen, Grace with Cynthia (born 1948, also delivered by Garfield), Rua McCulloch (Alycen's nurse and companion and then her sisters') and Judith.

17. Commonwealth Parliamentary Association visit by Southern Rhodesian MPs to Kenya, 1954: Garfield and A. D. H. ('Paddy') Lloyd in sombre mood after visiting Mau Mau prison camps.

18. USA *Voice of America* interview, 1955.

19. The Todds with Grace's sister, Elsie Barham from New Zealand, at the Opening of Parliament July 1955. Southern Rhodesia Government Press photograph.

20. Camping at Mana Pools on the Zambezi River, 1957: Rupert Fothergill (Government Game Warden), Sir Robert Tredgold (acting Governor of SR and Federal Chief Justice), Garfield, Archie Fraser (Chief Game Warden) and Mr Nysshens, elephant-hunter.

21. Sir Robert Tredgold, Garfield Todd and the Queen Mother, Southern Rhodesia, 1957.

22. Hardwicke Holderness with *Lost Chance*, his brilliant account of the eighth Parliament of
Southern Rhodesia, of which he was a amember.
Holderness family archive

23. The famous view from Hokonui Ranch homestead, Dadaya,
looking west to Mount Wedza along the Ngezi River (photo: S. Paul).

24. Joshua Nkomo, nationalist leader – 'the Father of Zimbabwe'.

25. Garfield visits Joshua Nkomo, Nationalist leader at
Gonakudzingwa Restriction Area, 1965
Photo Susan Paul

26. Grace with Dadaya teachers (left to right): David Mukonoweshura, M. M. Nyoni, M. D. Nyoni, M. B. Nyoni, Zephaniah Phiri ('the Water-Harvester of Shabani'); and Dadaya missionaries Val and Bryan Kirby.

27. Cynthia and Derrick Edge with their wedding present from Allan Ritson, a neighbouring rancher.

28. Grace with the Rev. J. N. Hlambelo and Stella Salisbury, Garfield's sister.

29. Grace with Judith and Cynthia, 1965, taken as Judith was about to leave to study at Columbia University, USA.

30. Garfield is allowed out of restriction at Hokonui Ranch to visit British prime minister Harold Wilson at his request in Salisbury on the eve of Ian Smith's Unilateral Declaration of Independence, 1965.

31. Garfield, once again briefly allowed out of restriction, and Grace in London, 1976.

32. Three cousins meet in London, 1976: Peggy Stallworthy of Oxford, Louisa ("Louie") Todd of Moscow, and Garfield of SR.

33. Part of 3,000 acres of Hokonui Ranch given to Vukuzenzele, a farming co-operative formed by a group of disabled ex-combatants.

34. Garfield builds forty cottages for Vukuzenzele families.

35. Garfield at Great Zimbabwe
Photo: Clare Chiminello

36. Todds retire in 1992 to 47A Heyman Road, Bulawayo, where Grace creates another beautiful garden and relaxes.

37. Todds celebrate their diamond wedding anniversary, 3 April 1992.

38. Garfield and his nephew Allan Todd, from Wellington, help rebuild Dadaya High School after a disastrous arson attack.

39. Foundation stone of Dadaya High School administration block, 1993, erected by the New Zealand Churches of Christ commemorating all the missionaries sent by NZ to Dadaya Mission between 1906 and 1974.

40. Garfield at the grave of the nineteenth-century Zulu Chief Mzilikazi in the Matopos area outside Bulawayo.
Photo Susan Paul

41. Garfield's last public meeting, 2001
Photo: editor of The Farmer.

42. Grace's grave at Dadaya Cemetery, January 2002.

43. Garfield's grave at Dadaya Cemetery, October 2002.

out he said, "Garfield, I do not know what has happened but Lansdell is not the same man."[6] The result of discussions with Christie was a repayment programme which became increasingly burdensome. The most difficult years of Hokonui's life came to an end in 1965 when Christie died. Only then was it found that he had had a brain tumour, which had changed his whole nature and personality. On Christie's death, his accountant eased the repayments; the debt was finally repaid in 1968 when Garfield sold 19,000 of Hokonui's acres at £2 an acre to Mr Percy Hall, the successful owner of Shushine Buses of Shabani, who went on to become an equally successful farmer.

***

Garfield attended a conference of the defeated United Rhodesia Party in Gwelo on 29 June 1958 at which it was agreed 'that the need for the party's continuance was greater than ever'.[7] 'Mr Todd has a point of view. He begins with the assumption that the Africans are, like it or not, as important a part of the human community in Rhodesia as any part, and goes on from there to plan positively for their integration into the economic and political life in ways which (he hopes) will develop and not strain the fabric ... he does not believe that in Southern Rhodesia this can be safely left' to the United Federal Party.[8]

Garfield addressed meetings where he could, but found it impossible to attend all the URP committee meetings arranged in Salisbury – a round trip of 530 miles and ten hours' driving – and it was not long before there were rumblings of discontent within the party. Garfield's elusiveness would always present a problem for the URP and its successor, the Central Africa Party. At the end of October, Garfield met Sir John Moffat, Federal MP, Unofficial Member of the Northern Rhodesia Legislative Council, to discuss proposals for the formation of a liberal front to fight the next Northern Rhodesia territorial election.

***

Garfield began 1959 in New Zealand, where he had been invited to attend the Sixth Commonwealth Conference of the Royal Institute of International Affairs at Palmerston North. Meeting many high-calibre Commonwealth representatives was intensely stimulating to him, and, coming at a time of crisis in the affairs of Central Africa and in his own political thinking, had a profound influence on him. He told Grace: 'My thinking will be changed for all time from

---

6   GT/SP, TPPC.
7   *The Chronicle*, 30.6.58.
8   *The Chronicle*, 1.7.58.

this visit'.⁹ But, by now, news of the declaration of a State of Emergency in Southern Rhodesia had decided Garfield to return earlier than planned.

***

On his return to Hokonui, Garfield found to his amazement and delight that Grace had taken over the management of the cattle. For the next 25 years she found endless interest and pleasure in the work, but it was no sinecure – the weekly dipping programme meant she spent long hot hours every day checking every beast as it went through the dip, supervising the branding, the de-horning and injections, choosing cattle for the butchery, and recording everything – to the admiration of the Animal Health Inspectors.

---

9   GT/JGT, 18.2.59, MS.1082/3/1, Todd Papers, NAZ.

57

THE SHOOTING STARTS (JANUARY TO JUNE 1959)

'The power of the executive to cast a man into prison without formulating any charge known to the law is in the highest degree odious and is the foundation of all totalitarian government.'

Winston S. Churchill, 1943

In 1959, disturbing events in Central Africa tumbled over each other, with the Belgian Congo leading the action. Riots in Leopoldville with 'at least 500 dead'[1] prompted the Belgian Government to speed up self-government. Events in the Belgian Congo would have a significant influence on the neighbouring Federation, where Sir Roy Welensky was concentrating on gaining Dominion status in 1960. His second concern was the growing strength of the African National Congress in Nyasaland, which, in its fear of the Federation being handed over to the settlers in 1960, was fomenting trouble. Ministers' fears mounted with several large Congress meetings in all three countries, but particularly in Nyasaland on 24 and 25 January. It was alleged at the latter that 'a murder plot' was hatched. This became the subject of an investigation by the Nyasaland Government, and then by Her Majesty's Government-appointed Devlin Commission.

On 26 January, there was renewed rioting in the Congo, with more refugees fleeing through the Federation on their way to South Africa. On 15 and 19 February, there were further riots at Karonga in Nyasaland, and King's African Rifles and Royal Rhodesia Regiment reinforcements were sent from Southern Rhodesia. On 24 February, police killed five Africans. Further disturbances inevitably followed, and on 3 March the Governor of Nyasaland declared a state of emergency. Fifty-two Africans were killed and 1,322 detained without

---
1   *Rhodesia Herald*, 12.1.59.

trial – including Dr Banda and other Congress leaders, who were flown to Federal prisons in Southern Rhodesia.

***

Meanwhile in Southern Rhodesia, during January, there had been anxiety but no outbreaks of violence. Whitehead told Parliament that certain territorial units had been called up 'in case the Nyasaland trouble spread to the colony'.[2] The next day, six days before the Nyasaland emergency, the Government issued a proclamation of a state of emergency. It was rumoured at the time, and confirmed later, that the Southern Rhodesia state of emergency had been declared at the wish of the Federal Government so that the Southern Rhodesia African Congress should not follow the northern congresses' action and so prevent the despatch of necessary forces to Nyasaland.

One European, Mr Guy Clutton-Brock, was arrested along with 435 Africans. More arrests followed, bringing the number to nearly 500. 'Most of the African congress officials arrested in Bulawayo ... were responsible people who did not fall into the government category of "rabble-rousers"', the Director of the Municipal African Affairs Department, Dr Hugh Ashton, wrote in his annual report for 1959.[3] Many teachers from the Shabani area were arrested, including Bethuel Hlambelo, son of the ageing Pastor Ndabambi Hlambelo, Garfield's right-hand man at Dadaya Mission. When arrested, he was 'shackled and handcuffed' to ex-Dadayan Jonah Mantjojo, whose burns Garfield had treated with motor oil many years before. They were taken to Khami Prison near Bulawayo, where, Bethuel said, they 'mixed with Nyasaland detainees and learned a lot'.[4] Many became 'bitter men', they said on their release; 'we all feel a deep sense of injustice over the arrests'.[5]

'Towns are tense, but there is no violence', reported the *Rhodesia Herald* on 26 February.[6] In truth, the whole country was not just 'tense', it was stunned. Clyde Sanger writes: 'As one of the released detainees described it months later, "there had not been even a glass broken".'[7]

***

On 8 February, the Central Africa Party was launched. Press reaction was surprisingly favourable: 'A genuine liberal party led by men of conviction and

---

2   *Rhodesia Herald*, 25.2.59.
3   *The Chronicle*, 29.1.60.
4   Bethuel Hlambelo/SP, interview, 22.6.95.
5   *East Africa and Rhodesia*, 2.4.59.
6   *Rhodesia Herald*, 26.2.59.
7   Sanger, 1960, p. 255.

standing is a real need in the Federation. Sir John Moffat and Mr Garfield Todd can provide that party ...'[8]

The declaration of the state of emergency so soon after the CAP was launched meant that it was quickly in business. Stanlake Samkange told a CAP meeting in Highlands, an affluent Salisbury suburb, that the party 'might be the last chance the Europeans would have to form a liberal party which would be accepted by Africans', but he warned 'that the Africans would not join any political party unless they were sure that many Europeans supported it'.[9] Samkange was right. The CAP won four seats (one African) in the Northern Rhodesia general election: the UFP thirteen (two Africans); the DP one; the ANC (Nkumbula) one; and four African Independents.

***

Garfield was 'enthusiastically welcomed ... by a large number of Europeans and Africans'[10] on his arrival at Salisbury airport on 4 March 1959. He later issued a statement: 'All that we have worked for over the years is in jeopardy and time has run out ... There is only one policy which can guarantee the safety of all our citizens and that is the policy of partnership, but the policy cannot flourish in a country where there is a rigid colour bar. These two concepts are irreconcilable. Under our present circumstances the colour bar is the responsibility of Europeans and not Africans. However, unless it is broken massively and immediately, it will not pass from this land.'[11]

Garfield told F. S. Joelson, owner and editor of *East Africa and Rhodesia*: 'Events have moved more quickly than I believed possible – and that in itself is warning enough to me of the future. What we cannot succeed in doing is to awaken the European population to their danger and their opportunity ... to co-operate with the inevitable.' His meetings with the State Department in Washington, and with Her Majesty's Government in London, Commonwealth leaders and UK High Commissioners, had convinced him even more firmly that 'our policies ... are the only ones which will make it possible for [the European] to stay in this part of the continent under conditions which would be tolerable ... I do not know yet what I can do except tell the truth as I see it.'[12]

***

Garfield called on the Prime Minister, and later told the former Governor, Sir

---

8   *Evening Standard*, 9.2.59.
9   *Rhodesia Herald*, 7.3.59.
10 *African Daily News*, 5.3.59.
11 *Rhodesia Herald*, 10.3.59.
12 GT/F. S. Joelson, 13.3.59, MS.390/1/7, Todd Papers, NAZ.

Peveril William-Powlett, that he was 'shocked beyond measure to find that he had taken these wrong and illiberal actions in the belief that if he did so he would get the backing of the mass of the African people'.[13] Garfield followed up his visit to Whitehead with a letter exhorting him to bring suspects to trial rather than detaining them.[14]

On Saturday 14 March, Whitehead went to the African suburb of Highfield to address a meeting. When it 'broke in disorder', writes Superintendent Ken Flower, 'we saved Sir Edgar from being lynched by arranging his undignified exit through a kitchen window'.[15] The Southern Rhodesia government promptly banned meetings in African townships until further notice.

Garfield, who had planned a meeting for 16 March in Highfield, transferred it to the Athenaeum Hall in Salisbury – 'one of the most remarkable political gatherings held in the Federation'.[16] Excited anticipation was widespread, and the atmosphere, even in 'white' Salisbury, tense. In the corridors of Parliament, members were anxious and indignant.

The *Rhodesia Herald* reported that 'All available police were called out ... to control a tidal wave of Africans who converged on the Athenaeum Hall to listen to Mr Garfield Todd.'[17] The *African Daily News* headlined its story: '7,000 Africans travel by car, cycle and on foot to hear Todd'. 'From far and wide they flocked, white and black, to meet the man whom many believe holds the key to racial peace in Central Africa', reported the South African magazine *Drum* next day.[18]

Garfield arrived an hour early and found a crowd of Africans outside an already packed hall. The *African Daily News* takes up the story again: Mr Todd 'was greeted with a great shout of admiration and welcome but when he raised his right arm for silence, there was utter silence'.[19] He told the crowd that he would hold a second meeting and the people responded with a murmur of approval and stayed quietly outside the hall, their number being added to constantly during the hour following. 'Europeans, including fashionably dressed women, stood among the Africans ... Africans stood on top of buses parked in the street ... content with the sight of Mr Todd speaking ...'[20]

At the end of the first meeting, Garfield removed his coat, the audience

13 GT/Peveril William-Powlett, 15.9.60, MS.390/1/15, Todd Papers, NAZ.
14 GT/EW, 11.3.59, MS.396/1/10, Todd Papers, NAZ.
15 Flower, 1987, p. 10.
16 *The Chronicle*, 17.3.59.
17 *Rhodesia Herald*, 17.3.59.
18 Reprint of 'The Gathering Storm' (1958) in *Drum*, 1990.
19 *African Daily News*, 17.3.59.
20 *The Chronicle*, 17.3.59.

streamed out and the hall rapidly refilled. At this second meeting, roughly a third of the audience was European, and Garfield was 'heckled and interrupted frequently. The most violent heckler was a European woman ... a member of the League of Empire Loyalists. Another heckler stood up to say, "you are a sell-out, Mr Todd, you are selling our country to the munts!²¹"'²² At the end of the second meeting we left, and the hall filled for the third time. By then Garfield had shed his tie, his shirt stuck to his back and his voice was hoarse. At the end of the third meeting, there were 1,000 people waiting to fill the hall a fourth time, but at 10.30 p.m. Garfield said that he was just too tired to continue, his voice confirmed this and the people went quietly away.

Clyde Sanger was present on that 'amazing and heartening evening'. Garfield's 'was the first positive and hopeful voice raised in a month of negative malice and fear ... After the meeting I ferried back some Africans to the townships and I asked one car-load why they had walked so many miles to hear a politician who had lost all political power. "Because we wanted to be made happy" one answered for the rest.'²³

***

Garfield told William-Powlett that Whitehead 'was so terribly wrong about the attitude of the African people, for in the actions that he took he finally lost any chance of winning the confidence of the African people of the country'.²⁴ One of Whitehead's actions was to present to Parliament three Bills designed to halt the advance of African nationalism within the colony, and specifically to ban the Southern Rhodesia ANC.

The Bills were greeted with a storm of protest from the press and from legal and church organisations. Sir Robert Tredgold, Federal Chief Justice at the time, denounced the Bills. He writes that there had been 'nothing to justify these drastic curtailments of ordinary liberties'.²⁵ The Protected Places and Areas Act was described by the only Independent MP, Dr Ahrn Palley, as being 'to a large extent' the South African Suppression of Communism Act.²⁶ Dr Palley, of Jewish South African extraction, would become a stern critic of Whitehead and of Ian D. Smith, and was for many years the only voice of real opposition in Parliament.

---

21   *Munt:* since 1948, an offensive South African term for a black African (from Bantu *umuntu*, 'a man').
22   *African Daily News*, 17.3.59.
23   Sanger, 1960, p. 271.
24   GT/Peveril William-Powlett, 15.9.59, MS.390/1/15, Todd Papers, NAZ.
25   Tredgold, 1968, p. 228.
26   LAD, vol. 42, 12.3.59, c. 2390.

On 24 March, 50 ANC leaders and Guy Clutton-Brock were released. The following day, the four members of the Devlin Commission arrived to look into the causes of the Nyasaland disturbances. It reported in July 1959, rejecting 'the evidence, such as it is, for the murder plot'.[27] But it found that 'Nyasaland is – no doubt, only temporarily – a police state'.[28] The Report was a grave embarrassment to the British Government, and many believe it was the Devlin Commission that signalled the effective end of the Central African Federation. Thirty years later, Enoch Dumbutshena, one-time Chief Justice of Zimbabwe, said that from that time onwards 'African nationalism never looked back'.[29]

---

27 Cmnd 814, para. 174.
28 Cmnd 814, para. 2.
29 E. Dumbutshena, contribution to GT's 80th-birthday book.

58

Too Late for Gradualism

'In Africa, there is never enough time. The hands have come off the clock, and it is later than we think.'

Garfield Todd, 1959

Garfield undertook a hectic programme of visits and addresses for the Central Africa Party. His speeches were as much about helping the party to keep up with his thinking as they were about warning the electorate and encouraging new members to join. The CAP's Inaugural Congress took place on the anniversary of the URP's defeat in the Southern Rhodesia general election. Hopes were high; the press table was well attended (with generous 'column inches' the next day); and the speeches by Garfield and Sir John Moffat were warmly received. Garfield was elected president, with Sir John and Stanlake Samkange vice-presidents. One of the happy aspects of the CAP for Garfield was association with these two men. Samkange's humour and light-heartedness matched his own. The party went energetically through all the motions expected of a political party, with a lot of people giving a lot of time and effort and money, but within a year it had virtually collapsed. It made little impact on the political scene. A fundamental problem was the future of Federation: Sir John opposed it, but Garfield felt it still had a chance of success. The departure in March 1960 of some highly respected ex-URP stalwarts, the sudden death of Dr Colin Campbell (vice-chairman of the SR division) and Garfield's own resignation in August 1960 discouraged the whites; and the party's failure to attract Europeans in any numbers disheartened African members, who gradually drifted away, many into nationalist parties. A remnant of the party survived long enough to make a useful contribution to the Southern Rhodesia constitutional conference at the end of 1960.

Garfield 'was in an impossible position', according to the Zimbabwean historian, Lawrence Vambe; 'very idealistic, unrealistic, in his aim for a moderate black/white political party. In a way, perhaps, Todd was being naive in thinking he could arrest this radical black movement.'[1] Garfield's connection with the CAP was his last formal political activity. Terence Ranger, himself briefly an executive member of the party, has written of Garfield's CAP days as 'an exciting time. One never knew what the leader was going to do or say. One only knew that it was never going to be politically wise but that it was almost always going to be morally right.'[2] Always, Garfield was in trouble with the CAP. He told William-Powlett that 'not everybody agrees either with the CAP or its president, particularly the latter'.[3] Ranger, however, says that in 1959 Garfield 'did not run too far ahead of the Party majority and was clearly the CAP's greatest asset'.[4]

***

Opposition MPs were watching Garfield, and reading his speeches in the press. Mr William Harper, who would come to prominence in the Rhodesia Front after 1965, promised: 'If the country gives us the power, we on this side will alter the franchise or make any laws that may be necessary to see that political power remains in the hands of the European.'[5] I. B. Dillon, MP for Shabani, found that his victory over Garfield was 'a hollow victory, because the damage that this man is doing now is much greater than if he had been sitting in this house'.[6]

The Prime Minister tried to calm the House: 'If there is one part of Africa where things are really under control it is this part of the world ... There is no defect that cannot be overcome, not even the attitude of the British Labour Party. We can continue this success story we have achieved for sixty years ... it not only can be done but will be done. As good Rhodesians we are pulling together.'[7]

***

After the British general election, which gave the Conservatives a majority of 100 in the House of Commons, Garfield spoke to the Conservative Associations of Oxford and Cambridge universities. He travelled home via Paris and Accra (where he had three days as the guest of the Prime Minister of Ghana). In Paris,

---

1 Interview, Lawrence Vambe/SP, July 1993, TPPC.
2 Ranger, review of Weiss and Parpart, *Sir Garfield Todd and the Making of Zimbabwe* (1999), in *BSOAS*, vol. 63, no. 1 (2000), pp. 154–5.
3 GT/Peveril William-Powlett, 13.7.59.
4 Ranger, 1995, p. 171.
5 LAD, 9.7.59, vol. 43, cc. 252–3.
6 Ibid., 15.7.59, c. 298.
7 Ibid., 9.7.59, cc. 252–3.

he had talks with senior officials over the sweeping changes which General de Gaulle's government had introduced in the French colonies. The situation there, he later told *The Chronicle*, 'had a tremendous bearing on other African countries. By walking alongside the African, the French had opened up a new way of solving what were hitherto insoluble problems.'[8]

---

8   *The Chronicle*, 29.10.59.

59

THE WIND OF CHANGE (JANUARY TO JUNE 1960)

'We have probably lost the future.'

Garfield Todd, 1959

On 1 January 1960, the National Democratic Party was formed in Salisbury and 'quickly established itself as the true successor to Congress'.[1] Many leading Africans joined, including Dr Pswarayi and Leopold Takawira from the CAP – an early indication that the party's days were numbered now that there was a legal African party for such able men to join. The NDP was an immediate success, with its emphasis not on equality but on majority rule. Vambe writes that the NDP, 'because of the greatly improved quality of the men drawn to it, seemed to send a chill of greater apprehension down the spine of the administration and the white settlers …'[2]

***

When Garfield returned from holiday in South Africa early in 1960, he spent two days in Salisbury on his way to the ranch. From there, he wrote to a friend in the USA, Robert C. Keith of *Special Report*: 'I may say that things are moving so quickly now that I notice a deterioration in a month. 1960 I am afraid is going to be a very difficult year.'[3] Garfield told the *Sunday Mail*: 'If it can be shown that Her Majesty's Government in Britain will accept her responsibilities and use her powers under the Constitution to see that justice is done to all sections of our community, then there is still hope that people of all races will be able to co-operate in Central Africa to build a democracy. If we are to have

---

1 Ranger, 1995, p. 176.
2 Vambe, 1976, p. 283.
3 GT/Robert C. Keith, 23.1.60, MS.390/1/17, Todd Papers, NAZ.

the nationalism of a group then it will be black nationalism.'⁴

***

Also in January 1960, Harold Macmillan, the British Prime Minister, visited Ghana and then Central Africa. In Salisbury, he spent time with a group of 'young black political activists', and then saw Garfield – a meeting arranged at the Prime Minister's request. Macmillan told Garfield he had been 'enormously impressed' by the 'young blacks', according to Graham Boynton. Macmillan's last words to Garfield were: 'Keep up the good work. You're right, you know.'⁵

On 19 January, Macmillan gave his major speech in Salisbury, his audience spread between two cinemas – and for this occasion Africans were allowed into the whites-only cinemas. Welensky's introduction was typically blunt: 'People in the Federation and the United Kingdom had got to face up to [the fact] that our problems were not going to be solved by anyone other than the people of this country, white and black.'⁶

On 3 February, Macmillan addressed the South African Parliament in Cape Town, repeating unreported remarks he had made in Accra: 'The wind of change is blowing through this continent and, whether we like it or not, this growth of national consciousness is a political fact. We must all accept it as a fact, and our national policies must take account of it.'⁷

***

Garfield spent some weeks from January to March in the USA, speaking at various Midwest universities. He received an LL.D. from Milligan College. The citation 'did him proud', he said – 'World-wide recognition for consecrated Christian service and for eminent statesmanship' – but no part of it pleased him more than the comment that, 'in education, largely thru [sic] his wife's professional skill, the mission acquired a unique reputation for wisdom in preparing lesson materials'.⁸

On these extended tours, letters from Grace were particularly important. She now wrote, in great anxiety, of the ranch in yet another drought year: 'I am truly anxious about the cattle and the grazing here ... I think that already we should be making plans to sell some stock'; and of the situation in the country. She had heard that, 'if the Government took action against you or if you were molested on your return, that would be the signal for an outbreak by other

---

4   *Sunday Mail*, 17.1.60.
5   Boynton, 1998, p. 55.
6   *Rhodesia Herald*, 20.1.60.
7   H. Macmillan, SA Parliament, 3.2.60, TPPC.
8   Milligan College, LL.D. Citation, 26.2.60, MS.390/4/3, Todd Papers, NAZ.

people. We must take absolutely no risk of that.'⁹

When Garfield reached London on his way home, he heard again from Grace: 'Here there is certainly a feeling of unity among the Europeans in the face of an awareness (at last) of what is happening in Africa. They are determined not to give way a further inch. There is a hardening of opinion against Macleod since the Kenya agreement ... Whitehead ... has all white Rhodesia, the Press, the lot behind him in his insistence on the removal of the reservations from the (SR) Constitution ... I fear too much, of course, I fear your further participation in the political drama here. I fear so greatly for our financial future this terrible year ... We had 0.9" of rain last night.'[10]

Garfield saw Lord Home in London and addressed a meeting of the Back Benchers' Commonwealth Committee at the House of Commons, which included several of the new, younger MPs, like Peter Tapsell, Humphrey Berkeley and Chris Chataway. The Committee's secretary later wrote: 'You were a great inspiration and a source of much-needed information ... One of my own particular worries is that so much of the news that we get is coloured by the political views of the right-wing politicians in Africa' – which was exactly what the powerful Salisbury–Robins, Welensky–Whitehead group intended, and which alone could be said to justify Garfield's visits to London. Garfield had an evening with the Macleods and two hours' talk with Joshua Nkomo. He saw Enoch Dumbutshena, who was hoping to read for the Bar and, crucially, was able to obtain the SR Chief Justice's recommendation for him.

In London, Garfield received news of the CAP's territorial congress in Gwelo – and also a cable from the party secretary, John Lovegrove: 'Regret Wigley, Jousse, Lloyd, Gibbs, Sacks, Lewis, Henderson resigned ground territorial policy'.[11] While it was no doubt good for the CAP that it should not be seen as a 'one-man band', Garfield's inspiration, energy and personality were necessary for its coherence. Nowhere was this better illustrated than at that Congress in Gwelo. The principal disappointment was a change of attitude on the part of leading African members: neither Stanlake Samkange nor Mbirimi, though continuing for the time being at any rate their membership and support of the party, was prepared to stand as vice-president. Garfield's unrivalled knowledge and experience was missed in debates, but so was his personal prestige, clarity of thought and power of persuasion. Although it was over the franchise that the seven men had resigned, there was also a general feeling that the party was pandering too much to African aspirations and that, in doing so, it was

---

9   JGT/GT, date 'ant-eaten' but Feb/Mar 1960, MS.1082/4/1, Todd Papers, NAZ.
10 JGT/GT, 12.3.60, MS.1082/4/1, Todd Papers, NAZ.
11 HJL/GT, Cable 22.3.60, MS.390/4/3, Todd Papers, NAZ.

The Wind of Change (January to June 1960)

losing contact with the whites – its inevitable dilemma. By the end of March, the CAP had also lost Ndabaningi Sithole, to the NDP, and Max Buchan, who had followed Garfield so loyally all through the cabinet crisis, finally broke with his party.

Garfield told journalists on his return home that he had recognised that 'We white people now have our final chance to make adjustments possible and with the assistance, protection and friendship of HMG in Britain. The change in the attitude of the conservatives in England is ... that the British Government will no longer acquiesce in our present belief that privilege is our right because we are white ... The challenge comes to a privileged group of 80,000 white electors. It demands of us that we relinquish our privilege but not our rights.'[12]

The CAP had given up any pretence of operating in Nyasaland, and at the end of June Sir John Moffat told Garfield that he thought the Federal Division of the CAP should be dissolved. The verdict of the *Central African Examiner* was: 'The tragedy of the Central Africa Party is that, with right and logic on its side, with all the ultimate answers on the tips of its leaders' tongues, it is caught between the two worlds of the present and the future, with no apparent notion of how to get from the one to the other. In this predicament it is unique among local political parties, who essentially live in only one world.'[13]

***

Meanwhile, in London, a deputation of Africans from Southern Rhodesia – Michael Mawema, Moton Malianga, Dr Bernard Chidzero, Enoch Dumbutshena and Paul Mushonga – was received by the Commonwealth Relations Secretary: 'Mr Michael Mawema of the National Democratic Party, who led the group, said that the talk took place "in a very cordial atmosphere" and they were well pleased with the result ... They handed Lord Home a twelve-page memo which calls on the British Government not to cede its reserved powers over Southern Rhodesia legislation ... The deputation had been relieved to find Lord Home giving the impression that the British Government had no intention of handing over its powers of veto ...' (on the SR Reserved Clauses).[14]

---

12 *Rhodesia Herald*, 28.3.60.
13 *Central African Examiner*, 16.7.60, vol. 4, no. 5.
14 *Guardian*, 29.4.60.

60

EXIT THE COLONIAL OFFICE

'We could have postponed independence, but only by the rule of the gun and at the risk of bloodshed. As it was, we devolved power too quickly but with goodwill.'

Nigel Fisher, *Iain Macleod*

In 1965, Iain Macleod wrote: 'It has been said that after I became Colonial Secretary there was a deliberate speeding up of the movement towards independence. I agree. There was. And in my view any other policy would have led to terrible bloodshed in Africa. This is the heart of the argument.'[1]

Sir John Moffat of Northern Rhodesia had received permission from the Nyasaland Governor to visit Dr Banda in prison in Southern Rhodesia, but Greenfield, as Minister of Law responsible for Federal prisons, refused to allow the visit. The *Guardian* interpreted this as 'further evidence of the complete subordination of the Colonial Office's interest in the two northern Federal territories to that of the Commonwealth Relations Office ... and the Federation'.[2] Banda was, however, allowed a visit from his legal adviser from London, Mr Dingle Foot, QC, MP, and within hours a transcript was in Welensky's hands. When Patrick Keatley reviewed Welensky's book in 1964 in the *Central African Examiner*, he wrote of 'the blunt revelation that Sir Roy ... had means of eavesdropping on the private conversation between a lawyer and his client ... this appears in the eyes of even his most devoted Tory supporters to run counter to one of the basic principles of British justice ...'[3]

Rhodesians were aware of what had been going on in the Kenya Constitutional Conference and became even more hostile to Macleod at its

---

1 Quoted in Fisher, 1973, p. 142.
2 *Guardian*, 7.1.60.
3 *Central African Examiner*, June 1964, vol. 7, no. 12.

conclusion, which would result in the transfer of power from settlers to black Kenyans. When Macmillan and Macleod decided that Dr Banda should be released both as a gesture of goodwill to Nyasalanders and so that he could talk with Macleod as a free man, Home and Welensky were horrified, and the Governor, Sir Robert Armitage, tried hard to prevent it. But, in spite of warnings of violent repercussions in Southern and Northern Rhodesia, Banda was released. Macleod thought that 'in jail Banda was a myth, out of jail he would be a man, and I thought that I could deal with men'.[4] Banda was flown to Zomba, where discussions between the three men went well: rapid advance to majority rule was conceded for a promise of peace in the country.

The Nyasaland state of emergency ended on 15 June; at the end of the month the Nyasaland detainees were released; in July the Constitution Conference opened in London; and agreement was reached in early August.

***

Constitutional progress in Nyasaland meant that some promise of similar progress in Northern Rhodesia must be given. Macleod paid his first visit to the colony at the end of March 1960 and found it 'puzzling and worrying ... almost everybody I met drew entirely different conclusions from the same set of facts'.[5] The coming independence of the Congo hung over all discussion of Northern Rhodesia's affairs, as nobody held very sanguine views of the Belgian colony's future.

Welensky had probably seen that Nyasaland was a lost cause, but Northern Rhodesia was different: he dug in his heels to save it. There lay the greater part of the Federation's mineral wealth – and there lived and worked 70,000 truculent Europeans, largely employees of the big mining companies. In 1959, Sir Arthur Benson had been succeeded by Sir Evelyn Hone, formerly Chief Secretary. Northern Rhodesia had its state of emergency 'in some ways similar to that in Nyasaland but on a smaller scale', noted the *Guardian*. 'The Government dealt with it in an exemplary way. Charges were brought against those thought to be the ring-leaders and these were sentenced. The rest were not sent to detention camps but restricted. Little by little they have been allowed to return home without publicity and its attendant status of martyrdom until there are only five left.'[6]

In the middle of all this came tragedy: Mrs Lilian Burton of Ndola and her two children were injured when their car was stoned and set on fire. Mrs

---

4   Shepherd, 1994, p. 201.
5   Macleod/Macmillan, PRO.PREM.11/3076, 31.3.60 and 3.4.60; see also Shepherd, 1994, p. 204.
6   *Guardian*, 8.1.60.

Burton died a week later, 'with no revenge in her heart, according to her husband. "She died with no malice, she would want no revenge on the African people as a whole. She would not want her death to embitter feeling between the races."'[7] The four men responsible were caught, tried and imprisoned. But the incident would not quickly be erased from the European memory, and, together with tales of attacks on Catholic missions in the Congo, strengthened feelings against the Colonial Secretary's efforts for African constitutional advance in Northern Rhodesia.

At midnight on 1 July 1960, the Congo became independent. The Federal Government declined an invitation to be present at the celebrations. Almost immediately 'all hell broke loose', writes Michela Wrong in her brilliant account. 'Told there were to be no immediate moves to "Africanise" an army exclusively commanded by Belgian officers, Congo's troops mutinied, whites were beaten and raped and the Belgian technicians who ran the country's administration headed en masse for the airport.'[8] Refugees, with hair-raising accounts of their experiences, also headed in considerable numbers in their cars for the Northern Rhodesian border. Customs and immigration formalities were waived; in every town Government mechanics worked over a two-day public holiday to deal with car repairs; food and accommodation were organised by the voluntary societies. Within a month, the river of refugees had swept through the Federation and across the South African border, but it left a detritus of fear, anger and hate behind it. The stories of real horror and atrocities convinced the whites of Southern Rhodesia that they must resist African advancement at all costs.

***

A constitutional conference on Northern Rhodesia would be held later in the year. Informal talks began in September, triggering immediate anxiety among whites, but Macleod went ahead. John Roberts, leader of the UFP in Northern Rhodesia, boycotted the conference, but Sir John Moffat and other independent Europeans attended. Welensky made negotiations as difficult and protracted as he could and obtained enough concessions to upset the Africans. But Kaunda agreed to try to sell the proposals to his people with the help of the Governor, Sir Evelyn Hone, and succeeded pretty well. After an all-too-brief incumbency, Macleod was succeeded at the Colonial Office in 1961 by Reginald Maudling. In February 1962, agreement was reached along Macleod's lines, and in 1964 full ministerial government was introduced

---

7   *The Chronicle*, 17.5.60.
8   Wrong, 2000, p. 65.

to Northern Rhodesia, with Kenneth Kaunda as Prime Minister. In October of that year, Zambia became an independent republic within the British Commonwealth.

61

Exit Garfield Todd, Politician

'It is just possible that the European population will learn the lesson in time.'

Harold Macmillan, 1960

On 19 July 1960, Sketchley Samkange, Michael Mawema and Leopold Takawira of the National Democratic Party were arrested. A protest meeting was held following the arrests, and next morning the crowd started marching from Highfield and Harari, and sent representatives to seek a meeting with Whitehead. 'The Prime Minister refused to meet them, so the people decided to march to his office ... On the outskirts of Harari township they were stopped by lines of police, with armed soldiers standing by.'[1] Stanlake Samkange had been watching events, and later wrote: 'What began as a peaceful demonstration, by people who have no votes, had ended in a riot.'[2] Stanlake himself was arrested on a charge that he had been helping to build barricades, and spent the night in the cells. His wife announced that, as such physical effort was entirely foreign to his nature, he must be innocent. The CAP put up bail and, when he was subsequently found not guilty, paid his £600 legal costs. On 20 July, 'police fired several volleys of tear-gas bombs to disperse large crowds of Africans demonstrating against the arrest of the three leaders'.[3] Whitehead promptly banned all processions in Salisbury and called up police reservists.

Joshua Nkomo, in London, told the *Guardian* that the arrests in Salisbury 'were wholly unjustified and represent a dangerous pressure against the very Africans who believe in a moderate, non-racial solution to Rhodesia's problems ...'[4]

---

1 Ranger, 1995, p. 183.
2 Samkange, Newsletter, 27.7.60.
3 *Guardian*, 21.7.60.
4 *Guardian*, 22.7.60.

Exit Garfield Todd, Politician

Garfield, on his way to London and the USA, was staying in Cyprus with the Governor, Sir Hugh Foot, when he heard of the trouble in Southern Rhodesia. Grace wrote to him: 'Could you believe that the authorities would be fools enough to arrest ... the three moderates! ... When will they learn that sooner or later they must come to terms with the African leaders, and that every moderate leader imprisoned will be replaced by one less moderate, so that the final reckoning will come with violently nationalistic leaders ...'[5]

There were riots in Highfield that night which, Dr Ahrn Palley told the House the next day, did not support the Prime Minister's contention that the situation was under control: 'politically speaking', the events of the last few days 'have driven the last nail into the coffin of partnership'.[6] As public meetings had been banned, the CAP invited diplomats, businessmen, journalists and members of the NDP to a private gathering. Sketchley and Stanlake were both present. Stanlake 'argued that government was solely to blame for the damage that had been done to property, to person and to race relations. The CAP Executive then wrote to Whitehead telling him of the meeting and urging him to proclaim his belief in 'full multi-racial democracy and to announce a programme of planned advance towards majority rule'.'[7] Ranger observes: 'In many ways this was the CAP's finest hour.' He quotes Stanlake that, at this time, 'the CAP was very close to the NDP'.[8]

Stanlake told the meeting that 'In Harari and Highfield ... there is widespread hatred of Europeans. And unless African grievances are met, Southern Rhodesia will have far worse troubles than last week's disturbances.'[9] Nathan Shamuyarira said 'that as other territories got their independence Africans would demand more and more rights and in stronger terms'. Moton Malianga said: 'Africans are one day going to rule this country, but if they are given treatment like this they are going to take revenge.'[10]

The CAP statement of 22 July was fully reported in the *Rhodesia Herald*: the Government was using 'the powers given them under legislation which has converted this country into what is, for nine-tenths of the people, a police state, for their own ends'.[11]

***

---

5 JGT/GT, 21.7.60, MS.1082/4/1, Todd Papers, NAZ.
6 LAD, vol. 45, 22.7.60, cc. 562–5.
7 Ranger, 1995, p. 185, quoting *Evening Standard*, 25.7.60.
8 Ibid., p. 185, quoting Samkange, Newsletter, August 1960.
9 *Sunday Mail*, 24.7.60.
10 Ibid.
11 *Rhodesia Herald*, 23.7.60.

Over 24–25 July in Bulawayo, riots led to excessive police action and to the deaths of eleven Africans. In London, Garfield heard the reports of the deaths 'with horror', writes Ranger,[12] who goes on to quote remarks by Garfield at a meeting of the CAP territorial executive on 26 August.[13] 'When he heard of the Bulawayo shootings, he was at once convinced that a chapter had been closed. European overt leadership was gone. He had heard while in London of joint meetings between the CAP and NDP and of CAP leaders standing bail. So he thought CAP might be moving in his own direction towards cooperation with the NDP.'

Garfield was working on a CAP memo for Home when he contacted the African leaders, Joshua Nkomo, Enoch Dumbutshena and Paul Mushonga. (Dumbutshena and Mushonga had been in the group of NDP leaders who had been received by Home in April.) Garfield told Grace: 'they came to the hotel. We had a long talk and then decided to put out a joint statement ... they had a Press Conference laid on for the evening ... We then delivered it to CRO. Home was at the House of Lords and his secretary ran along and gave it to him.'[14]

This is the complete text of the letter, which no newspaper in Southern Rhodesia ever published in full:

'The Secretary of State for Commonwealth Relations:

My Lord,

For some years we have pleaded with our governments to extend the franchise so that we might enjoy political stability in Central Africa. The United Federal Party governments, however, have chosen to play politics with the even more reactionary Dominion Party and have paid scant attention to the voice of eight millions of voteless people. When protests have been made our Governments have used the pretext of maintaining law and order to stamp out criticism and dissent, and have not hesitated even to use their military might to do this. Government policies are now maintained by force of arms and are directly responsible for the present unrest.

'Ranged against the great mass of our people are 200,000 whites with police, an army and an air force: four percent of our population, in the name of civilisation, have ranged themselves against the great body of people of our country, refusing liberty, denying justice and flouting the lessons of history.

'It is imperative that Her Majesty's Government accept the responsibility for taking immediate action to establish a new and democratic regime in

---

12 Ranger, 1995, p. 189.
13 T. Ranger's notes of the meeting. I am indebted to Prof. Ranger for sight of these.
14 GT/JGT and JT, 27.7.60, MS.390/6/7, Todd Papers, NAZ.

Central Africa. At present Britain is supporting an undemocratic and unjust form of government which, if left to itself, must soon disintegrate, causing widespread suffering to all sections of our people.

'If Britain finds herself unwilling to intervene decisively in this situation within her colonial sphere, a situation in which 80,000 voters are permitted to govern 8,000,000 by military might, then Her Majesty's Government must state this clearly and now. Those people who are now protesting against their Governments in Central Africa will then know that they must depend upon their own strength to gain liberty. We recognise that eventually this would lead to intervention by the United Nations Organisation but that there would be much regrettable and unnecessary suffering before this happened.

'We pray that Her Majesty's Government, justly proud of having, in recent years, brought some five hundred million people to freedom, will not flinch from the task of upsetting the present regime and of guiding and assisting the establishment of democratic rule by the people of our land.

'Because of our deep concern to see harmony between the races and justice and opportunity for all citizens, we ask –

1. That an immediate statement be made to the effect that Her Majesty's Government will intervene in the affairs of Central Africa to establish democratic governments so that the will of the people is implemented.

2. That the Constitution of Southern Rhodesia be set aside and a democratic order substituted for it.

3. That Her Majesty's Government come to immediate agreement with the Federal Government that no troops from the Union of South Africa will be called upon, or permitted to intervene in Central Africa. If South African troops were to be used in Central Africa, it is doubtful if there would be a healing of wounds in the next twenty years.

4. That, following an immediate statement of intent to set aside the Constitution of Southern Rhodesia, adequate armed forces should be made available from the United Kingdom to ensure that changes in Government are made peacefully. It must be recognised that should British troops be sent to Southern Rhodesia to support the present Government against the people of the country, the prestige of Her Majesty's Government would be so damaged that it would be extremely difficult for Britain to assist in any later attempts to establish a democratic system.

5. That all necessary measures be taken to bring each of the territories to self-government within the next five years and that elections at the point of self-government should be based upon a universal adult franchise.

6. That immediate moves should be made to transfer powers from the Federal Government to the States. Concurrently with these changes the

three territories should be given equal control over what remains of the Federal machine, which should then become the servant of the territories and no longer their master.

Signed by   ENOCH DUMBUTSHENA
              PAUL MUSHONGA
              JOSHUA NKOMO
              GARFIELD TODD

London
July 25th, 1960'[15]

In his draft autobiography, Garfield goes into more detail about that day: 'I thought that Lord Home would be greatly interested to hear the African reaction to what was happening in Rhodesia. Joshua Nkomo was in London and was willing to talk. I suggested that he come with me and, if Lord Home wished to see him, he would be immediately available. When we arrived and I had explained matters to the secretary he left us and was away for some time. When he returned it was to announce that as I had brought Joshua Nkomo with me, my appointment had been cancelled by Lord Home. I was deeply shocked.' Half an hour later, CRO officials were scouring London to find Garfield because he had given the letter to the press.

At the press conference,[16] Nkomo spoke first: 'all the African people wanted was a say in the running of the country and what we got was bullets'. Garfield told the press that, for the past two years, it was obvious that the Africans had been growing increasingly bitter and it was only a matter of time before things blew up. 'But the whites did not learn the lessons of the Congo. The only lesson they could see was that they should not give anything further … There is nothing the whites in the federation can do to remedy the situation and so we look to the only power that is available – Her Majesty's Government … Unless something is done and done quickly, there will be years and years of serious trouble. The European population is very frightened.'

Garfield wrote in his letter to Grace of 27 July: 'Then to BBC for Home Programme and had ten minutes of hard questioning … along to the House at 10:30 for a debate. Met a dozen young Conservatives and had a long discussion with them on the Press statement which everyone was now reading. Then to the House and an all-night debate. At 3:45 the subject of Rhodesia was raised and had a very fine presentation and reception from the young Conservatives – but then a shocking and blistering reply from Alport' (Minister of State at

15 File MS.390/6/7, Todd Papers, NAZ.
16 TPPC.

the Commonwealth Relations Office). Peter Tapsell wanted to see 'the British Government summoning a conference for Southern Rhodesia similar to that held for Kenya ... It is essential that HMG should now take a political initiative in Southern Rhodesia. For too long the Southern Rhodesia Government have been preaching partnership and practising apartheid.' Mr H. A. Marquand said 'the very men now in prison were having tea with me in the House of Commons only a few weeks ago ... men who had ideas of the rate of progress that could be achieved which were not hasty or intemperate but reasonable ...'

Alport's 'blistering reply' dealt first with the statement which appeared 'to be a request by the four signatories for intervention by force by the United Kingdom with the object of abrogating the Southern Rhodesia Constitution and overthrowing the present Southern Rhodesia Government. It further appears to invite HMG to abrogate the Federation Constitution as well.' He found it difficult to believe that the four signatories 'could have fully understood the implications' of their request. 'Nothing could have done a greater disservice to Southern Rhodesia in particular and the Federation in general at this juncture than the publication of a document which cannot in any way assist the restoration of stability and tranquillity in this territory and which represents a negation of long-established constitutional practice in the United Kingdom.' He spoke of the Monckton Commission, recently appointed by HMG, which 'will provide us with calm and wise advice on the future pattern of the Federation'. He did not consider the document 'as representing wise and calm advice' for Southern Rhodesia's future.[17] As will be seen, Mr Cuthbert (later Lord) Alport would change his views markedly and become a friend and supporter of Garfield.

Next morning, Garfield went to the Colonial Office, where, he told Grace, he 'had a delightful reception from Macleod ... "God bless you" was the parting from Macleod. I expect things are grim at home as far as I am concerned but I have much to tell you and, Gracie, your letters have been wonderful. I think that what I have said is right – I have spent hours and hours and hours working on the thoughts, praying about them. The whites are in a vicious circle. How can it be broken? Can any local politician do it?'

The CAP reacted furiously. At midnight on 26 July, Garfield had a telephone call from Salisbury to say he was no longer Federal leader of the party; in Northern Rhodesia, Sir John Moffat dissociated the Northern Rhodesian CAP from Garfield's letter, but told the *Evening Standard*: 'Mr Todd's action is nothing like as serious in its implications as the Federal Prime Minister's action

---

17 House of Commons debates, vol. 627, 26.7.60, cc. 1541–62.

in threatening "to go it alone".'[18] Garfield spoke to the *Rhodesia Herald*'s London correspondent about 'his personal political future in the federation', saying that it was 'grim, very grim … but I have done what I set out to do if I can convince some people at least that it is later than they think. My political future? I have none except to speak up on what I believe to be true.'[19]

At Hokonui Ranch, Grace was writing in despair: 'I hardly know what to say … you no doubt have good reasons for all you do but how I long for it NOT to be you.'[20] Garfield realised with great concern that Grace was having a bad time as she tried to come to terms with what he had done, as she read the local papers and received unending telephone calls – from Ralph Palmer and John Lovegrove of CAP, baffled by Garfield's action; some from equally bewildered friends and supporters. Calls from angry strangers could at least be intercepted. In an attempt to convince Grace that he had acted not impulsively but after deep thought, he told her:[21] 'I would have cabled you yesterday morning but there really was no way of getting news to you before you would be embroiled in it all – and that I regretted that with all my heart. I knew that there would be trouble … and no doubt much more to come … but I am sure that I am right … The suggestion is extreme but I know of no other means for getting us from 'here' to 'there', as John Moffat puts it – and we must get to 'there' … and there is little enough time. Britain cannot help us under our present political set-up. She can do it for Nyasaland, for Northern Rhodesia, she can break up the Federation – but if she is to do it for Southern Rhodesia she can only help a willing electorate, or she, as a last resort, can substitute another machine … I know that I, personally, have reached the ultimate – or so it seems – and that the future, as it should be, lies clearly before me for the first time. What of course will happen, what attempts will be made to trip up the inevitable is quite another matter.'[22]

A few days later, Garfield cabled Grace, 'surer than ever'.[23] Grace did not think sending the letter to Home had been wise. She told Garfield on 28 July: 'I can tell that people here are deeply offended, and I expect your enemies are gloating. But I know this to be entirely consistent with all your thinking and although I do not know why you did it in just this way, you may well be absolutely right. Anyway, darling, this is another step along your way – our

---

18 *Evening Standard*, 9.8.60.
19 Ibid.
20 JGT/GT, 27.7.60, MS.1082/4/1, Todd Papers, NAZ.
21 GT/JGT, 28.7.60, MS.1082/1/11, ibid.
22 GT/JGT, 28.7.60, MS.1082/1/11, ibid.
23 GT/JGT, telegram 2.8.60, MS.1082/1/11, ibid.

way – to whatever destiny lies in store.'[24] But, 30 years later, Grace would say: 'you know how I have disliked, even hated and feared, the publicity which my family attracts'.[25]

Garfield's conviction that he had been right in his action received reassurance from three unexpected and significant sources. He wrote a second letter to Grace to tell her of a visit he had had from Mr Guy Hunter, author of *The New Societies of Tropical Africa*, and his wife: 'they had read and listened and he had come to congratulate me. You have put into the circle a thought, and a solution which people will try to reject – which people will decry, but which they will not be able to evade for it is the only way.'[26]

A letter from Philip Mason, distinguished historian and observer of Africa, brought him 'the best of good wishes and encouragement. You will be meeting a storm of obloquy I know, and I hope you will feel it is a help to know that one observer at least admires your courage and believes that your stand has probably helped.'[27] Sir Hugh Foot wrote: 'We do hope that your voice will be increasingly heard – and that people will listen to you in time … we felt when we listened to you that there is hope yet – though time is no doubt dreadfully short …'[28]

On 28 July, Macmillan made Lord Home Foreign Secretary, replacing him at the Commonwealth Relations Office with Mr Duncan Sandys. There were questions in the House of Commons about Southern Rhodesia – and one answer from Alport, with its oblique reference to South Africa, is worthy of note: 'we should not forget the lessons of history, and one of those lessons is that if one devolves power on an overseas community it is not subsequently easy – or possible – to take it back again'.[29]

By assuming that the CAP and the NDP were very much closer than was the case, Garfield had placed the CAP, confused and anxious, in a very difficult position. On the evening of 27 July, the CAP held an Extraordinary Meeting in Salisbury. Among those attending were Stanlake Samkange, Ralph Palmer, S. M. Mbirimi, Hardwicke Holderness, Tony Pedder, John Lovegrove and T. O. Ranger, himself the target of personal attacks by MPs of both Assemblies in Salisbury. The following day, the Federal Central Executive of the CAP also met – with Garfield's resignation in their hands. 'It became clear that members did not necessarily disagree with Mr Todd's statement, although many did,

---

24 JGT/GT, 28.7.60, MS.1082/4/1, ibid.
25 JGT/SP, 22.4.90, TPPC.
26 GT/JGT, 28.7.60, MS.1082/1/11, Todd Papers, NAZ.
27 Philip Mason/GT, 28.7.60, MS.390/1/19, ibid.
28 Sir Hugh Foot/GT, 28.7.60, MS.290/1/25, ibid.
29 House of Commons *Hansard*, vol. 627, 28.7.60, c. 1942.

but that they considered that it was the manner in which it was made that had caused the trouble. It was felt that Mr Todd had no right to make a statement of this nature without consulting other Party leaders … It was decided to accept Mr Todd's resignation in such a way that the least damage should be done to African support and opinion.'[30] The party issued a careful statement: 'Mr Todd, having come to the conclusion that the situation in Southern Rhodesia has become so desperate that only some outside intervention can save us, has resigned from the leadership of the CAP so as to leave the Party unhindered in its policy of working for reform within the country itself. The Party does not disagree with Mr Todd that the situation has reached a desperately critical stage and that unprecedented measures are necessary …'[31]

The *Rhodesia Herald* printed comments made by Garfield in a telephone interview: 'The new situation in Rhodesia has made me realise that we will not be able to make decisions which must be made with the political machinery that is available to us … The British Government … cannot give us the assistance we need unless it sets aside the obstacle in its way which is the present Constitution … I realise time is short and the situation in Southern Rhodesia, if allowed to develop without a wide change in the franchise, will follow the South African pattern with increasing tension and outbursts of violence from time to time …'[32]

The *Guardian* wrote Garfield's political obituary: he had 'ended to all practical purposes his political career … To the end he was more a missionary than a politician. The letter he wrote to Lord Home … was penned from the best of motives. But it has inevitably led to his resignation and this will just as inevitably lead to the breaking up in Southern Rhodesia of the Central Africa Party, the only truly multi-racial party in the Colony. It was, without doubt, a disastrous letter. Mr Todd has always believed in shock tactics … The immediate reaction to his warnings has always been general antagonism and a lack of heeding. Later may come the desired effect …'[33]

The next day, Garfield wrote to Grace, quoting Philip Mason's letter. He went on: 'I know that you will have been much upset and I hope that I won't have to make you worry – at least away from me – so much again … I knew that I was dropping a block-buster but everything was ready and open for the doing of it … While a year ago we could perhaps still have made our own decisions we are now past that and must get Britain's help or wander on till we strike real trouble.'[34]

---

30 CAP, MS.390/2/4/2, Todd Papers, NAZ.
31 Ibid.
32 *Rhodesia Herald*, 29.7.60.
33 *Guardian*, 30.7.60.
34 GT/JGT, 31.7.60, MS.1082/1/11, Todd Papers, NAZ.

Garfield's letter to Lord Home produced a great deal of anger and bluster, and a great deal of unpleasantness for himself, but could have saved British governments, both Conservative and Labour, a colossal amount of time, energy, effort, money and loss of reputation – as well as tens of thousands of Southern Rhodesian lives – had the Conservative British Government of 1960 not left it to a Conservative British Government of 1979 to act – on the blueprint he had largely drawn.

***

The question now arose of how Garfield was to return home without precipitating demonstrations. He flew to Paris, where he booked on the next UAT flight to Livingstone – six days later. During Garfield's enforced stay in Paris, he got acquainted with a jeweller. He opened the conversation by asking if Monsieur spoke any English. 'Well,' came the reply, 'my twenty years in Adelaide help.' From that point it was but two steps to his private office, and two minutes to the pouring of two glasses of Napoleon brandy. It will be remembered that Garfield had drunk brandy once in his life – after the difficult birth of the railway ganger's baby shortly after the Todds' arrival at Dadaya in 1934. This time, the brandy was undoubtedly far superior in quality but the quantity far greater, and much conversation was required to give him time to 'appreciate' the honour. There would be one more brandy in Garfield's life – in 1979 – in very different, and frightening, circumstances.

Garfield bought a hat in Paris, and when he arrived at Livingstone Airport not even Grace recognised him.

***

There was a lengthy CAP meeting in Salisbury at which Garfield explained fully what had led him to collaborate with the NDP people on the letter to Home. Terence Ranger was present and wrote a detailed account. (I am greatly indebted to him for his unpublished transcript of those notes.) Garfield said that 'he did not know 'how far CAP had progressed' in its thinking locally and so gave an offer of resignation as leader. He hoped this would not be accepted because he hoped that he would be able to lead the two parties into alliance with each other … He had been very proud of the CAP and most of his best friendships had been within it. But he must be frank and say that 'I really think the CAP should be wound up'. … He had come to serve the African people as a missionary and was now ready to join them 'in a humbler way' … Ralph Palmer disagreed entirely with Todd …'

Ranger said: 'The attitude of the NDP to Europeans was much in the making and one could contribute to shaping it by showing that Europeans were prepared to follow African leadership now as well as in the future ... Mr Holderness said that he had reached Mr Todd's conclusions two years ago ... Todd postponed his decision until the next day but said that he 'had no hope now' of the CAP being effective ...'[35]

That evening, Terry Ranger resigned from the CAP, joining the NDP the following day. Stanlake Samkange, Samuel Mbirimi and seven other leading Africans resigned. The CAP announced Garfield's resignation on 2 September. The *Rhodesia Herald* led with the story: 'Todd quits politics – I have failed after 14 years, he says'. "I cannot see the future clearly, but what I can see alarms me. When I see something I can do which will offer a peaceful solution, I will take action ... I have no plans, no affiliations.' ... Open leadership by the European must now be succeeded by open leadership by the African, he said, and Europeans must be prepared to serve wherever they could.'[36]

***

Sir John Moffat told Garfield he intended to maintain personal contact with the SR party. 'I hope you have not been unduly affected by the SR reaction to your London Statement. The Bulawayo riots turned the whole SR world upside down and they were incapable of reasoning ... I think you must make a point of commenting on current events as usual. Your African backing is more solid than ever ... Your time will come – and may not be far distant.'[37] In 2007, Professor Ranger wrote in a review[38] of Professor M. Casey's *The Rhetoric of Sir Garfield Todd: Christian Imagination and the Dream of an African Democracy* (WACO Baylor University Press, 2007) and Judith Garfield Todd's *Through the Darkness – A Life in Zimbabwe* (C. T. Zebra, 2007): Garfield Todd's 'followers never understood where he was going or why he was going there'. And, in an interview that year with Trevor Grundy, he said: 'In a way you can say that nothing became Garfield's life so much as the leaving of it, his political life, because most of the remarkable positions he took came after he'd ceased to be Prime Minister.'[39]

---

35 T. O. Ranger, unpublished manuscript, TPPC.
36 *Rhodesia Herald*, 3.9.60.
37 Sir John Moffat/GT, 20.8.60, MS.390/2/4/2, Todd Papers, NAZ.
38 *Britain–Zimbabwe Society News*, November 2007.
39 T. O. Ranger/Trevor Grundy, 2007, TPPC.

62

THE MONCKTON COMMISSION: EXIT FEDERATION?

'Long experience, quite apart from instinct, tells the settlers that whenever they allow a disinterested body to examine their affairs the verdict is generally unfavourable.'

Patrick Keatley

On 11 October 1960, the Report of the Monckton Commission – 'The Advisory Commission on the Review of the Constitution of Rhodesia and Nyasaland' – was published. Since 1957, almost everyone in the Federation, from its Prime Minister downwards, had had their sights fixed – in hope or apprehension – on 1960 and the Federal Review Conference. The appointment of the Monckton Commission in 1959 arose from anxiety in Whitehall and the Federation about the Conference.

Sir Arthur Benson, Governor of Northern Rhodesia, had always been in favour of Federation and thought that the Federal Government 'was throwing away the most wonderful opportunity that had happened in Africa'.[1] Sir Robert Tredgold states that 'It was apparent to all, except those who did not wish to see, that the Federation was breaking up and that it could only be saved by desperate measures.'[2] Garfield put it more bluntly: 'the Monckton Commission was formed only to save the face of the Federal Government'.[3]

The Commission's terms of reference were 'to advise the five governments in preparation for the 1960 Review on the Constitutional programme and framework best suited to achieve the objects contained in the Constitution of 1953, including the Preamble'.[4] It consisted of 26 members: thirteen nominated

---

1 Tredgold, 1968, p. 208.
2 Ibid., p. 207.
3 GT speaking at Livingstone, *Rhodesia Herald*, 30.11.59.
4 LAD, vol. 43, 21.7.59, cc. 459–60.

by the British Government (including members from the Commonwealth); and thirteen from the Federation, nominated by Welensky, under the distinguished Judge, Lord Monckton.

The Labour and Liberal Parties refused to participate because the possibility of secession by a member state was, at Welensky's insistence, outside the Commission's terms of reference. These refusals set the African leaders in the Northern Territories against the Commission. But although there was no official Labour Party representation, the British Government very shrewdly appointed Lord Shawcross, an eminent judge and former Labour cabinet minister, to the Commission. He promptly upset the Federal Government by saying that the Commission's terms of reference did not preclude discussion of secession or, if it felt it right, the acceptance of secession of one part of the Federation.

The Commissioners, including five Africans, had arrived at the Victoria Falls on 15 February 1960. From there they travelled to Lusaka (Northern Rhodesia) and Blantyre (Nyasaland) before their last stop, Salisbury. They were 'a strangely mixed gathering', according to Lord Crathorne: 'they contained many sources of potential discord ... However, Monckton found that they achieved if not unanimity at least an extraordinary measure of agreement.'[5] Birkenhead places the credit for this on Monckton's 'brilliant chairmanship'. He was able to bring along with him the white Rhodesian Commissioners, one of whom, Geoff Ellman-Brown, said: 'Monckton himself was very able and we had very good secretaries'.[6] Ellman-Brown told Garfield that '"anything which was decided upon must have the backing of the African people or it would get us nowhere ..." He had changed his whole attitude to the African situation', Garfield told Sir Peveril William-Powlett, the former Governor.[7]

The Report[8] had been in the hands of the five Governments since 5 September 1960. (There was a minority report from Manoah Wellington Chirwa and H. C. Habanyama, who could not accept federation in any form.) In the Introduction, the Report commented on the boycott of the Commission's hearings by Africans in the Northern Territories, and on 'the intimidation with which these boycotts were enforced'; but, 'despite the effect of intimidation on the free expression of opinion, we were left in no doubt that genuine opposition to Federation ... has grown more intense during the last seven years ... The dislike of Federation among Africans in the two Northern Territories is widespread, sincere and of long standing ... It is associated almost everywhere with a picture of Southern

---

5   Birkenhead, 1969, pp. 344–6.
6   Oral 235, NAZ.
7   GT/Peveril William-Powlett, 1.12.60, MS.390/1/15, Todd Papers, NAZ.
8   Cmnd 1148.

Rhodesia as a white man's country' (p. 16, para. 27); 'racial feeling ... has grown sharper and stronger. It now appears to many Africans that only the presence of the European community politically entrenched behind the Federal Constitution stands between them and the form of freedom already granted to their fellow Africans in most other parts of the continent' (pp. 18–19, para. 32); 'Federation was imposed against the will of Africans in the Northern Territories' (p. 19, para. 33); and the failure to take any steps 'to demonstrate the reality of racial partnership ... Sincere efforts have been made, especially in the last few years, to remove the colour bar, but it still operates and...exists in Southern Rhodesia to a degree that causes such offence as to make association with Southern Rhodesia appear insupportable to Africans in the Northern Territories' (p. 19, para. 34).

Africans were critical of the franchise and of British Government treatment of the African Affairs Board over the Electoral Act, interpreting it as a demonstration of 'the British Government's unwillingness to resist pressure from the Federal Government' (pp. 19–20, para. 36). The siting of the Federal capital in Salisbury, alongside the Southern Rhodesia Government, 'enhanced African fears that the laws and practices of Southern Rhodesia will be imported into Federal policy' (p. 20, para. 39); 'rule from Salisbury is distrusted as too much influenced by European interests and by the native policies of Southern Rhodesia' (pp. 20–1, para. 41).

There was a 'large volume of European opinion hostile to Federation ... too-rapid increase in the political power of Africans' (p. 21, para. 44); 'White Southern Rhodesia nationalists believe that Federation has been an obstacle to their constitutional advance' (p. 22, para. 45). Paragraph 49 (p. 22) was particularly important: 'Although the weight of opinion among Europeans in all three territories, and among Africans in Southern Rhodesia, is for Federation to continue, the strength of African opposition in the Northern Territories is such that Federation cannot, in our view, be maintained in its present form.'

The Report concluded: 'we are convinced that no form of federal association, however reformed, can succeed so long as many of its peoples feel that they are being kept in it against their will and can break out only by force. We therefore recommend that under certain conditions there should be an opportunity to withdraw from the association.'

***

In a statement to the press, Garfield said the recommendations 'provide the last pattern for white participation in the life and government of Central Africa ... The report makes recommendations which could result in a wide sharing of political power, a new government with new leaders and a new hope. This is bitter medicine for those who have openly proclaimed white supremacy, and also for our Government which has preached partnership but has failed to practise it. But it gives hope to all who are alive to the danger of race hatred and who wish to serve their country and its people.'[9]

---

9   *The Chronicle*, 13.10.60.

63

Southern Rhodesia: No Exit

'1960 could be the year of adjustment or the year when we fail ourselves and our children.'

Garfield Todd

There was evidence of Garfield's unpopularity among Europeans: driving home from Bannockburn, a carload of whites chased his car through the ranch. He did not dare stop and challenge them, as his young daughter Cynthia was with him. A threatening telephone call from the Rhodesian Republican Army (later banned) was intercepted. And he never forgot the day he was quietly sitting in an airport lounge and 'a fellow passing threw some silver coins at me: thirty pieces of silver'.[1] Ten years later would come assassination attempts, but for now he was more troubled by his decision to 'quit politics' than he was by his unpopularity.

In September, Whitehead's car was stoned in Highfield, and he was unable to address a meeting of Africans which he had arranged. There were 1,200 in the hall – and 2,000 police and troops outside. Tear gas was used.[2] A few days earlier, the NDP had held an 'orderly' meeting in 'white' Salisbury, attended by 500 Africans and 150 Europeans – when the 'police were not needed'.[3]

The July killing by security forces of eleven Africans in Bulawayo was a watershed for Southern Rhodesia. Not just lives were lost, but a cherished record – that no African had been killed in a race riot in the country since 1896.

On 8 October, six Africans were killed in Gwelo, which highlighted grievances there. On the same day, another six were killed by police in Salisbury. Clyde

---

1 GT/SP, 1993, TPPC.
2 *Rhodesia Herald*, 13.9.60.
3 *Rhodesia Herald*, 9.9.60.

Sanger wrote: 'Southern Rhodesia has suddenly become the area in Central Africa of most danger ... Changes can only come through a white electorate which is still remote and stubborn ... it is the saddest fact that the Southern Rhodesia Government persists in looking to its electorate for guidance rather than stepping out ahead.'[4]

Whitehead's response to the riots and killings was to prepare 'drastic new legislation' with a minimum mandatory sentence of five years' imprisonment for 'throwing stones at a moving vehicle' – which he described as 'tantamount to attempted murder'.[5]

***

Tuesday 25 October saw the publication of the detail of the new security measure, the Law and Order (Maintenance) Bill. It was greeted with a barrage of criticism from all sides – except Parliament. *The Chronicle* editorial commented: 'in its raw form' it 'puts the totalitarian lid on, and clamps it firmly down. Liberty of speech, of movement, of assembly public or private, the liberty of the press, liberty to advise people to stop work, even the liberty to use bad language ('opprobrious epithets') on the job, all these liberties will be, although not destroyed, entirely at the mercy of the police and the executive.' The editorial went on: 'There is plenty of legitimate discontent ... Are we going to fight to remove its causes? If we are not, we deserve never to get out of this impasse.'[6] The *Rhodesia Herald* had serious objections: the bill fettered the discretion of the courts and gave 'virtually unlimited powers to the police ... This hastily drafted, panic-stricken legislation must be withdrawn and suitably amended.'[7]

Churchmen, Jewish religious leaders, the press, the legal profession, the University, all protested vigorously against the bill. But 'Sir Edgar Whitehead seems unperturbed', commented the *Guardian*; 'he said he believed the alarm in the country was "grossly exaggerated"'.[8]

In protest at the Law and Order (Maintenance) Bill, the Chief Justice of the Federation, Sir Robert Tredgold, PC, KCMG, QC, resigned. (As the Federal Supreme Court was also the Court of Appeal from Southern Rhodesia, he would be compelled to adjudicate upon cases under the new laws.) Sir Robert described the Bill as an 'anthology of horrors ... It almost appeared as though someone had sat down with the Declaration of Human Rights and deliberately

---

4 *Guardian*, 11.10.60.
5 *Rhodesia Herald*, 14.10.60.
6 *The Chronicle*, 26.10.60.
7 *Rhodesia Herald*, 27.10.60.
8 *Guardian*, 31.10.60.

scrubbed out each in turn ... The cumulative effect of the security laws was to turn Rhodesia into a police state ... a state in which the police and the executive are given or assume complete control over all political activity ... I foresaw that it would compel the Courts to become party to widespread injustice and I let it be known that, if the government persisted with the main features of the Bill, I would resign my position as Federal Chief Justice ... but the Government ignored my warning and proceeded inflexibly with the Bills.'[9]

To the *Rhodesia Herald*, Sir Robert's resignation 'is news of top importance for all races living here ... In the past he has said he would not consider entering party politics again but might support a movement to create a "united front" ... He is bound to attract a broad cross-section cutting across present political boundaries.'[10] But the *Rhodesia Herald* was wrong – the *Chronicle* was wrong – Sir Robert himself was wrong. They had fallen into the same trap that had caught Garfield and the URP – they over-estimated the liberality, understanding and intelligence of the European electorate. Although more than 1,000 people attended a meeting in white Salisbury to hear Sir Robert speak, the country did not respond – and another opportunity to leave the dreary path of oppression and revolt was lost.

When the Law and Order (Maintenance) Bill, slightly amended, came before the House on 22, 23 and 24 November, debate lasted for over 50 hours. Dr Ahrn Palley, Independent MP, called 165 divisions on amendments he had proposed to its 58 clauses, for the most part standing alone in the 'No' lobby. 'Dr Palley compared the provisions [of the Bill] with the legislation used by the Nazis to destroy democracy in Germany after they had come to power by constitutional means.'[11]

***

Garfield's letter and Tredgold's resignation had failed to shake Rhodesians from their complacency. There remained only the hope that the Constitutional Conference planned for 1961 might in some way stop the Colony's descent into the bloodshed which Garfield and Sir Robert feared. Lord Home had 'assured' Garfield 'that it was not possible, under the powers which the United Kingdom Government retained, for them to bring pressure to bear on Southern Rhodesia to have a conference similar to those held for other colonial territories'.[12] But, with Home out of the Commonwealth Relations Office, the British Government was preparing to hold preliminary talks with Sir Edgar

---

9 Tredgold, 1968, p. 229.
10 *Rhodesia Herald*, 2.11.60.
11 *The Chronicle*, 26.11.60.
12 GT's article in *Central African Examiner*, May 1962, vol. 5, no. 12.

Whitehead at the same time as the Federal Review Conference. It was hoped that Whitehead would take a delegation from all parties to the Conference. Whitehead sought the removal of the reserved powers in the Constitution – but the NDP wanted a conference at which the 'Colony's whole constitution would be reviewed, and at which the discussion would centre around the franchise, which they rightly regard as the only real safeguard' of their interests.[13]

In the end, Whitehead agreed to include the NDP and CAP in his delegation to the Federal Conference, which began on 28 November. The Southern Rhodesia talks (as well as the Northern Rhodesia Constitutional Conference) would begin in London on 14 December. The *Sunday Times* of 28 November printed an article by Garfield which dealt with both the Federal Review Conference and the Southern Rhodesia talks: 'The acid test of racial co-operation is a readiness to share political power. A majority of the white electorate of Southern Rhodesia and of the Federation has not been prepared to do this. Her Majesty's Government, in the best interests of all, including the white people of Central Africa, must now insist upon a very wide extension of the franchise.'[14]

The Federal Review Conference was soon in trouble: 'the three principal delegations of African nationalists walked out'.[15] The NR Conference and the SR talks were postponed by one day. This, Whitehead said, 'was designed to teach them a salutary lesson which was long overdue ... I would like to reassure the people of Southern Rhodesia that the antics of the African racialists will not affect the established aims of the Southern Rhodesia Government in any way'.[16] Whitehead announced that he had decided to exclude the NDP from the Southern Rhodesia delegation to both Territorial and Federal conferences.

As a result, the delayed Southern Rhodesia talks started badly. The *Daily News* told its readers: 'even the Dominionites and the African moderates were not happy with Sir Edgar's exclusion of the NDP delegation ... It was the two-man delegation of the CAP which put spanners in the works of the Conference and brought it to a complete standstill. As soon as the Conference began Mr Palmer stood up and protested strongly against the exclusion of the NDP pointing out that it represented a substantial section of the population and if Sir Edgar did not make satisfactory explanation of the matter, the CAP would be forced to consider its whole position at the Conference. Sir Edgar replied that he had excluded the NDP because their walk-out from the Federal

---

13 *Central African Examiner*, 24.9.60, vol. 4, no. 9.
14 GT article in *Sunday Times*, 28.11.60.
15 *Guardian*, 13.12.60.
16 *The Chronicle*, 14.12.60.

Review Conference had made it impossible for him to allow them to attend the Southern Rhodesia Conference.'[17] Mr Sandys, Commonwealth Relations Secretary, adjourned the conference.

Monday 19 December saw what Tony Pedder called 'the only really effective hour' of the Central Africa Party.[18] As adviser, he had accompanied Ralph Palmer and Advocate Walter Kamba, the CAP's official representatives, to the Federal Review Conference. Ralph and Tony brought together the NDP representatives and 'Abe' Abrahamson (now a member of Whitehead's cabinet), and tried to resolve the impasse. 'In a long meeting with Joshua Nkomo and his colleagues Abe is said to have used all his skill as a mediator to talk Mr Nkomo into burying the hatchet.'[19] Nkomo was persuaded to write a 'handsome letter of apology' to Whitehead.[20] The crisis passed.

Almost the only claim to fame of the Federal Review Conference – apart from its rapid disintegration – is the fact that this was the first time the Federal Prime Minister had met the African leaders from the Northern Territories. According to Colin Legum, 'Welensky's attitude to the nationalist leaders is that they can be safely ignored as not representing genuine African opinion'.[21] After the African leaders had walked out, 'proceedings at Lancaster House are about to become a dangerously hollow farce', the *Guardian* had commented on Friday 16th. On Saturday 17th, Welensky wound up the general debate, and Duncan Sandys summed up for HMG. It was agreed that consideration of the future of the Federation should be deferred until further progress had been made at the two territorial conferences. The Southern Rhodesia talks resumed in January 1961 in Salisbury with Whitehead in the chair.

The Federal Review Conference never reconvened.

Only a year earlier, Garfield had said: 'If the Federation breaks up, it will be the responsibility of the Federal Prime Minister and the members of the United Federal Party'.[22] Lord Home agreed (if for a different reason): 'The final opportunity of preserving the Federation was lost when Sir Roy Welensky ... refused to accept the (Monckton) Commission's findings as a basis for discussion with HMG ...'[23]

***

One of Garfield's most significant remarks – at the time largely ignored, though

---

17 *Daily News*, 24.12.60.
18 Oral PE.2, NAZ.
19 *Rhodesia Herald*, 21.12.60.
20 *Guardian*, 20.12.60.
21 *Observer*, 4.12.60.
22 *Rhodesia Herald*, 4.12.59.
23 Home, 1976, p. 133.

in later years often quoted – was made in an article on Native Education: 'What is demanded of us together is to co-operate courageously and generously with the inevitable.'²⁴ Four years later: 'Change is disturbing, revolutionary change with which we are faced in Southern Rhodesia is intolerable, but I am afraid it is irresistible. For twenty-six years I have worked for policies of opportunity for all and circumstances have now demanded of people like me that we should make a clear and unequivocal choice between true patriotism and white privilege. I know that my future lies with patriotism, with Africa and with her people of whom I wish to be one.'²⁵

'White liberals fought for ideals and recognised the inadequacy of their own strength,' he wrote in mid-1960, 'but the people who are taking over the fight will strive with much greater intensity ... because they are the people who are denied the vote ... These are the people who have now entered the lists and the outcome of the battle is beyond question for they have right on their side and their power will be irresistible ... Whites can no longer evade the great issue of our times. They must be prepared to declare themselves for the maintenance of an undemocratic order based on superior military strength ... or they must range themselves on the side of a democratic order working rapidly towards a universal franchise.'²⁶

The year 1960 saw the end of Garfield's career in formal politics, but for the following twenty years he was driven to continue his urgent warnings to the country's leaders and electorate – and, most of all, the British Government – to recognise the danger they were in, accepting every invitation to speak or write that came his way.

Garfield's visit to Kenya in November 1954 had profoundly affected him: 'I came back ... with a new determination in my mind to leave nothing undone which it lay in my power to do, to promote harmonious race relations in this country and I suggest that the promotion of harmonious race relations is not a matter of words but of deeds.'

In June 1995, Grace wrote: 'It was with [Garfield's] defeat as Prime Minister that African nationalism won its greatest momentum. At that point even moderate African support fell away, the argument being that if Todd, the known friend of African advancement, could not carry the white electorate along his road, no other white leader could, and [the African nationalists] had better get on and do it themselves. And from then on Garfield also accepted that interpretation of the situation, and more and more, though by no means

---

24 *Rhodesia Herald*, 13.3.56.
25 *Central African Examiner*, 31.7.60, vol. 4, no. 5.
26 *Central African Examiner*, 13.8.60, vol. 4, no. 6.

immediately, began to support the nationalist cause.'[27]

***

Garfield Todd, Garfield Todd,
How will it end?
In black votes, or red gutters
– You choose, my friend ...[28]

---

27 JGT/SP, June 1996, TPPC.
28 Quoted by Sanger, 1960, p. 318.

PART V – CO-OPERATING WITH THE INEVITABLE, 1961 to April 1980

♦•♦

64

THE RANCHER – 1961

'For the first time in my life I am able to go out each day to the duties of a farm which I find of the greatest blessing to one's soul.'

Garfield Todd, 1960

In July 1959, I went to live and work at Hokonui. The Todds' enjoyment of their new life was palpable, no matter how long Garfield's hours building dams or supervising a butchery and store, or how long and hot Grace's hours at the cattle dip. Prime minister, rancher, family man – Garfield was always the same. I never ceased to be amazed by his capacity for hard work. But to him it was all enjoyment, never work. I hardly recognised Grace: the abrupt change from public life to cattle-manager had transformed her. The lightness of her step was

The Rancher – 1961

matched by her relaxed and contented air. In addition to her management of the cattle, for two years Grace supervised Cynthia's studies at home through the Government's correspondence college.

The homestead at Hokonui Ranch was characterised by beauty and tranquillity. Its modest bungalow was surrounded by a garden Grace was gradually creating from a rocky hill – but she freely acknowledged she could have done little without her two gardeners. The site John Kirby had chosen was both inspired and totally impractical: 150 feet above the Ngezi River, from which came the all-important, year-round supply of water, and reached at the end of three miles of rough, bone-shattering track. A visiting New Zealander, Norman Harris, described the stoep as 'the focal point of the ranch-house, and from it one's attention is always seized by the huge vista: the disappearing river, Mount Wedza, the thin line of a distant train, far-off hills'.[1] In the house, a cook (for 30 years Jellinah Masuku) and two housemaids made their own cheerful contribution.

As soon as they had moved in, Garfield started building – and continued pretty well non-stop for the next fifteen years: first, a guesthouse, as there was an unending stream of visitors. Anyone who wanted to talk to Garfield had to stay the night. Servants' quarters followed, an office, chicken-houses, weirs to improve the ranch's vital water systems; and on the next hill, some 200 metres from the homestead, Garfield built a cottage for his sister, Edith, a *Hansard*-writer at both the Legislative and Federal Assemblies. A guesthouse for her, and another at the homestead, followed over the years – and finally a swimming-pool.

There were hippo in the river – and the occasional crocodile – and sometimes a small herd of kudu would appear on the other side and pause in a perfect tableau, their delicate ears pink in the sun, before moving silently away. At evening, a small flock of white egrets would fly below the house, following the valley to their roost downstream. There were doves, tiny, vivid sun-birds by the kitchen door, and usually a pair of pied wagtails on the lawn before the house. The sounds of the veld were all around: the crickets, the 'humph-humph-humph' of the hippo, the chattering of monkeys, the barking of baboon and the song of the birds – in particular the liquid call of the emerald-spotted dove, and the 'g'way' of the grey lurie – and the lowing of the cattle and the voices of the men collecting a herd in a nearby paddock.

A visitor told Grace that going to Hokonui was 'like stepping into another world. The setting, the view and the solitude – a wonderful haven of peace.'

---

1   Harris, 1971, p. 175.

Grace quoted this in a letter to Garfield (then in London), adding: 'to us ... it is a haven and a paradise', but in his absence 'it was an empty shell'.[2] Within a very few months, and in their different ways, all the family became deeply attached to Hokonui and the happy life they enjoyed there.

Two thousand cattle carried the Todds' hopes for the future, but Garfield's continuing struggle to keep the ranch financially viable was not helped by an unsympathetic bank manager in Shabani and an increasingly unreasonable Christie in New York. Much time was spent negotiating with creditors (largely wholesale suppliers for the stores); persuading his store and butchery customers to pay their bills; and frequent stock-taking to minimise losses caused by pilfering storemen. Later, he would employ only women, whom he found more efficient and more trustworthy! Christine Mukokokwayira would prove a most capable manager of the ranch's commercial activities, including the store and eating house in the Shabanie Mine's Maglas township.

***

Politics were never very far away. Banda's Malawi Congress Party triumphed in Nyasaland's general election; the Northern Rhodesia Constitutional Conference produced a satisfactory outcome; and, at the Southern Rhodesia Constitutional talks, agreement was finally reached between all parties – except the Dominion Party. There would be a multiracial Constitutional Council and a Bill of Rights, though, significantly, this would not affect existing legislation. The Legislative Assembly would be enlarged from 30 to 65, but the Common Roll was abandoned in favour of an 'A' roll (higher qualifications), largely European, electing 50 members in 50 constituencies, and a 'B' roll (lower qualifications), largely black, electing 15 members in 15 'electoral districts'. The 3,000-odd blacks on the Common Roll were arbitrarily transferred to the 'B' roll. The 'A' roll, largely white, had political power; the 'B' roll, political frustration.

Garfield was one of the first to condemn the 1961 proposals. He told *The Chronicle*: 'These proposals will not solve any of our problems, because they are unacceptable to the majority of the people'.[3] Astonishingly, however, Joshua Nkomo and Ndabaningi Sithole did accept the proposals. Nkomo's London colleague, Leopold Takawira, immediately repudiated the agreement and Nkomo's acceptance on behalf of the NDP. Nkomo withdrew his acceptance and later put the matter to an unofficial referendum of his supporters – only 471 out of more than 100,000 voted 'yes' – but it was too late.

Whitehead put the Constitutional proposals to a referendum on 26 July.

---

2 JGT/GT, 9.10.59, MS.1982/3/1, Todd Papers, NAZ.
3 *The Chronicle*, 22.7.61.

He promised 'to maintain law and order even if it meant ruling "with a rod of iron"'.⁴ He won the referendum by 41,949 votes to 21,846 in a 77 per cent poll, and declared: 'We have killed the NDP! Extremism is dead!' the *Rhodesia Herald* reported. 'I had complete confidence in the electorate. The electorate always solves such problems.'⁵

One of the things which angered the Europeans, and aroused their contempt for Africans, was the extent of intimidation by blacks of blacks. The few African members of the UFP were for the most part the victims. But, as Garfield wrote in *Liberal News*: 'While [intimidation] is at its crudest in the petrol bomb … many Europeans join in the witch hunt and employees, both black and white, dare not reveal their true political sympathies for fear of losing their jobs'.⁶ *The Chronicle* said of intimidation: 'It is never easy to define the line beyond which normal social pressures become forceful intimidation. The week before banning the NDP, Whitehead's troops had killed one African and wounded another fourteen with gunfire, and arrested nearly 600 women. So there was certainly intimidation on the government side.' Whitehead defended his action by citing 'intolerable intimidation'.⁷

Increasing lawlessness in the rural areas under new, young political leaders was rapidly undermining the traditional authority of the chiefs. The Government now sought not only to uphold their authority but also to involve them more closely in its own strategy. To Garfield this was 'wicked. What we are doing is using these men as a buffer between the Government and the mass of the people and both the chiefs and the Government are going to suffer.'⁸

***

During the early 1960s, Garfield visited the USA annually on lecture tours of Midwestern colleges. The fees he earned helped to keep the ranch afloat, and his paid travel enabled him to visit London and keep in touch with HM Government and friends, as well as politicians in the USA. He benefited greatly from these weeks away, always finding stimulus and fresh ideas from meeting interesting people. He could also keep in touch with the American churches. The 'price' for his absences from Hokonui was paid by Grace, on whom devolved responsibility for the ranch, but she was willing to have it so. Before leaving in 1961, Garfield began the construction of a weir on the Ngezi River. Grace recorded its progress.

---

4   GT, *Liberal News*, August 1961.
5   *Rhodesia Herald*, 27.7.61.
6   *Liberal News*, April 1961.
7   *The Chronicle*, 11.12.61.
8   GT, MS.390/1/13, Todd Papers, NAZ.

Garfield Todd: The End of the Liberal Dream in Rhodesia

In New York in September 1961, Garfield was the guest of the Rosses in Gramercy Park. They discussed the difficulties with Christie and the possibility of subdividing the ranch into about 40 well-watered farms of 1,000 acres each – a long-held ambition of the Todds. Grace, writing on 13 October, asked Garfield: 'Has the time half gone yet? Darling, we must NEVER do this again. My love for you and need for you is all mixed up by my longing for you to be here to look after the pump. To such depths have I come.'[9] The river had stopped flowing, and it had been necessary to pump the water into tanks to keep the irrigation system working. On the 18th, Grace continued her 'chronicle of catastrophe ... there is not a thing in the world you can do, so you must read this with detachment. Even I have reached a state of suspended animation: as each new disaster falls, I am no longer thrown into transports of rage, grief, anxiety, frustration ...'[10]

By the time Garfield returned to Hokonui, the rain had come and he saw the just-completed weir full and running over. He immediately got down to work on the plan for the subdivision of the ranch that he had put to Emory Ross. Recent legislation, providing for blocks of land to be transferred to the 'unreserved land' category, meant that the ranch could be opened up to farmers of any race. The scheme, long envisaged, was very dear to the hearts of Garfield and Grace, and over the next few years planning consumed hundreds of hours of their time in consultations with technical and financial people in Rhodesia, and in correspondence with others in the USA and the UK; but, when the Rhodesian Front came to power in 1964 and rescinded the 'unreserved land' legislation, the scheme had to be abandoned.

***

On 7 December 1961, Britain surrendered her Reserved Powers in Southern Rhodesia to Whitehead's government. The next day, the NDP – the only well-supported African political organisation – was banned, as were all public gatherings for a month. Opposition to the Land Husbandry Act in the rural areas had taken on a more violent form with the burning of school buildings, teachers' houses, dip-tanks and beer-garden shelters.

On 17 December, the Zimbabwe African People's Union was launched in Highfield.

---

9   JGT/GT, 13.10.61, MS.1082/1/11, Todd Papers, NAZ.
10 JGT/GT, 18.10.61, ibid.

65

SOUTHERN RHODESIA AND THE UNITED NATIONS – 1962

'This is the time when white liberals find it difficult to know what they can possibly do to assist.'

Garfield Todd

On 27 November 1961, in New York, the UN General Assembly reaffirmed 'the objectives and principles enshrined in the Declaration on the granting of independence to colonial countries and peoples contained in its resolution 1514 (XV) of 14 December 1960'.[1] Paragraph 5 of the Declaration provided that 'Immediate steps shall be taken, in Trust and Non-Self-Governing Territories and all other territories which have not yet attained independence, to transfer all powers to the people of those territories ... in order to enable them to enjoy complete independence and freedom.' A special committee of seventeen members was appointed to examine the application of the Declaration, and in December the Committee was requested by the General Assembly to 'consider whether the territory of Southern Rhodesia has attained a full measure of self-government'.[2]

The African nationalists now took their fight to the UN. There, the British representatives (including Sir Hugh Foot until he resigned) argued that Southern Rhodesia remained a British dependency, but Britain could not intervene in its internal affairs because it was 'a self-governing colony': 'Well, is this place a colony or isn't it?' asked the exasperated Chairman.[3] The Committee of Seventeen now set out to answer this question.

Sir Hugh Foot writes: 'From then on I became increasingly concerned that we

---

1 UN General Assembly 1066th plenary meeting, 27.11.61, Ref. A/RES/1654 (XVI) 28.11.61.
2 UN General Assembly A/C.4/L.729 19.12.61.
3 Keatley, 1963, p. 392.

would throw away all the good-will we had earned in the world by enlightened and progressive colonial policies. I feared that we should find ourselves in African affairs isolated with Portugal and South Africa in opposition to intense and unanimous African and Asian opinion.'[4]

At Nkomo's request, Garfield agreed[5] to appear before the Committee of Seventeen, and gave his evidence on 21 and 22 March 1962. Nkomo later wrote in Garfield's 80th-birthday book: 'I had heard Todd speak on several occasions and had been immensely impressed by his oratory. But on this particular day his oratory was most devastating. Facts against the 1961 constitution flowed in fast sequence ... and got a most thunderous ovation from all the delegates, except of course, that of Britain ...'[6]

The speech Garfield gave to the Committee of Seventeen he later described as 'probably the most important political speech of my career'.[7] He began: 'Frankly, I am using New York as a back-door to London; I am here to endeavour to prod Great Britain ... into accepting the responsibilities which the representative of the United States says are acknowledged to be its responsibilities, and into using the powers which the United Kingdom representative apparently admits Great Britain still retains ... I believe that my country of Southern Rhodesia is in grave danger, and ... I am concerned that Great Britain shall play her part in the future of our land ...'[8]

Of the Declaration of Rights included in the Constitution, he said it was 'quite useless and therefore is not acceptable to the African people ... The Declaration of Rights has been used to justify the decision of the United Kingdom to hand over powers which she might have used to protect the African people of our country ... to an almost exclusively white electorate. The withdrawal of British influence from the affairs of Southern Rhodesia would be a tragic happening, for it will leave us to our own travail, to bloodshed and to the eventual rout of the white people.' Garfield then went through the Rights, one by one, demonstrating how inadequate each was to protect the individual.

'This has been a horrible speech, a most distressing speech from my own point of view. For I understand the problems of the Prime Minister of Southern Rhodesia. Who should understand them better? I know that every law he is bringing to his aid, every extra policeman, every restrictive regulation, every

---

4 Foot, 1964, p. 215.
5 JN/GT, 16.3.62, MS.390/1/12, Todd Papers, NAZ.
6 Nkomo, GT's 80th-birthday book, 1988.
7 GT/Prof. Michael Casey, 23.1.2001, c/TPPC.
8 Verbatim record of meetings of UN GA Special Committee A/AC.109/PV.17 of 30.3.62 (re 21.3.62); A/AC.109/PV.18 of 30.3.62 (re 22.3.62).

tear grenade, every riot gun is needed ... I also know that unless Her Majesty's Government in the United Kingdom can now intervene, the Prime Minister will either be thrown out, as I was, or go on to the inevitable conclusion which will be one of riots, bloodshed and economic attrition ...

'Only the United Kingdom can assist the white electorate in making the changes necessary, even to save themselves ... [The whites] hold supreme political power...I am pleading for my country; for white people, as well as black people ... We, the white people, have been judges in our own cause, and no man is good enough for that ...'

On 28 June, Britain took the extreme step of walking out of the UN debate on Southern Rhodesia. On the final vote that day, the large bloc of Western votes which previously had lined up with the UK turned into 'yes' votes or abstentions. leaving the UK quite isolated except for the 'no' vote of South Africa and the non-participation of Portugal. When Sir Hugh Foot was later informed by Lord Home that Britain would take no new initiative on Southern Rhodesia, he resigned: he 'could no longer speak as an advocate of a policy which I didn't agree with'.[9]

Back in Rhodesia (once more drought-stricken), Garfield told a meeting of the Rhodesia National Affairs Association in Salisbury: 'Don't run. Don't fight. There is no cause to run. It would be stupid and outrageous to fight. Why not move forward, ready to co-operate fully and without fear with what is, after all, the inevitable?'[10]

***

The editor of *Round Table* now told Garfield, with his 'personal regret', that the editorial committee wished to end Garfield's association with the magazine on account of a 'serious rift' between Garfield's opinions and those of the majority of the committee. Mr Morrah had withstood earlier demands for his sacking but now found himself overborne and obliged to find a correspondent 'more in sympathy with official policy, both in Salisbury and in Whitehall'.[11]

But at least the long-running saga of the transfer of Hokonui land to the Mission finally ended in September. The latest delay had been occasioned by Garfield's last letter to his lawyer lying unopened in Mr Lardner-Burke's Gwelo office for five weeks.

***

On 10 August, Whitehead tabled bills to tighten up the Unlawful Organisations

---

9 *Observer*, 11.11.62.
10 *Rhodesia Herald*, 11.4.62.
11 DM/GT, 1.8.62, MS.1082/1/13, Todd Papers, NAZ.

Act and the Law and Order (Maintenance) Act. Church leaders wished to protest but were in a difficult position: they well knew that, broadly speaking, their European membership (from whom came most of their funds) would support the Government and criticise their leaders for 'mixing politics with religion'. This dilemma faced them for the next eighteen years. Sir Robert Tredgold was not so inhibited, and declared: 'These Bills are not only objectionable in themselves but could not have been validly enacted once the Declaration of Rights ... had come into effect ... [this] is a breach of faith by the Government ...'[12]

Another wave of violence and arson broke over African townships across the country, blamed by the press on ZAPU, so it was hardly surprising that on 20 August the party was banned and its leaders restricted to various parts of the country. 'The violence and horror are not only on the side of the nationalists but also on the side of the Government forces', Garfield told George Purnell in New Zealand.[13]

***

On 30 October 1962, Northern Rhodesia held its general election – and a coalition of the ANC and the United National Independence Party formed the new Independence government. The defeat of all the Liberal Party candidates, under Sir John Moffat, was a matter for regret. 'What is there to say?' asked Garfield in a letter to him; 'can we expect to get through to the next era without suffering and bloodshed?'[14] Sir John replied to Garfield's 'most welcome' letter with a question of his own: 'As one wanderer in the wilderness to another, how does your bit of desert compare with my bit of desert? ... we shall have an African government in December and as the swing in power has already occurred the need for a Liberal Party disappeared ...'[15]

When the new Prime Minister of Northern Rhodesia, Kenneth Kaunda, thanked Garfield for his letter of congratulation, he told him he realised 'that what we do here will go a long way towards helping your cause there, and that any misbehaviour on our part will make your work doubly difficult. I will keep in touch.'[16] Kaunda was as good as his word, and from time to time Garfield visited him in Lusaka, on one occasion narrowly escaping assassination.

In December 1962, Nyasaland's right to secede from the Federation was accepted by the British Government, and the following year a similar concession

---

12 *Central African Examiner*, September 1962, vol. 6, no. 4.
13 GT/George Purnell, 20.10.62, MS.390/1/25, Todd Papers, NAZ.
14 GT/Sir John Moffat, 6.11.62, MS.390/1/25, Todd Papers, NAZ.
15 Sir John Moffat/GT, 22.11.62, MS.390/1/27, Todd Papers, NAZ.
16 Kenneth Kaunda/GT, 19.12.62, MS.396/1/10, Todd Papers, NAZ.

was made in respect of Northern Rhodesia. In a mercifully short time, the moribund Federation was put out of its agony; but these were months of unexpected and uncharacteristic firmness on the part of HM Government, while Welensky continued to smoulder with anger and resentment. The recently appointed Secretary for Central Africa, Mr R. A. Butler, told the House of Commons that all the territories would proceed through the normal processes to independence.

***

Whitehead assumed that, as he had won the 1961 referendum on a 2:1 vote, so would he win the general election in 1962. Polling day was 14 December and resulted in a dramatic win for the Rhodesian Front, with 35 'A'-roll seats. Whitehead won 15 'A'-roll and 14 'B'-roll seats. Ahrn Palley, in a four-cornered fight, retained Highfield. Of the 60,000 African voters eligible to register and vote, 9,814 registered and 2,923 voted. The CAP was routed and disbanded early in 1963.

All Rhodesia was stunned by the election results – even, it was said, the Rhodesian Front. By 14 December 1962, the once all-powerful United Federal Party had lost control in all three territories of the Federation. On 15 December 1962, Whitehead handed on the baton – the 'rod of iron' – to his successors, Winston Field and Ian D. Smith.

66

'Victory over Hypocrisy' – 1963

*'Victory over Hypocrisy. The Southern Rhodesian elections are of
the past: their consequences of the future.'*

Central African Examiner

***

The Rhodesian Front was a collection of all the former anti-establishment forces in the country, led by Clifford Dupont, an immigrant lawyer from Britain; Winston Field, a wealthy farmer and leader of the Opposition in the Federal Assembly, who was well liked and respected; D. C. Lilford, an even wealthier farmer (but not so highly respected) and behind-the-scenes 'fixer' on the political right; and Ian D. Smith, MP, who had started out in the Federal Party. The Rhodesian Front would hold power virtually until independence was given to Zimbabwe in 1980. Jaspar Savanhu, Federal MP, gave the African perspective: 'a government of ignorant men with a nineteenth-century mentality – men who are leading their fellow whites to certain disaster'.[1]

***

In 1962, the Federal Government, on Whitehead's initiative, had refused to renew the residence permits of two outstanding liberals, Terence Ranger and his wife Shelagh. Early in 1963, they were declared prohibited immigrants and given two weeks to leave the country. No reason was given. No charge – no evidence – of illegal or subversive activity was brought against them. Over the next fifteen years, the list of deported university lecturers, journalists and churchmen lengthened; repressive law succeeded repressive law; nationalist leaders were in and out of restriction or detention; and soon Africans began slipping over the borders into Zambia, Botswana and Mozambique. What started as a tiny trickle became a steady flow and finally a flood as young men

---
1   FAD, vol. 20, 10.7.63, c. 499.

and women left for military training – to return, years later, with their AK47 rifles to inundate the whole country.

***

The Preservation of Constitutional Government Bill was introduced into the Southern Rhodesia Parliament early in 1963. It placed certain inhibitions on criticism of Southern Rhodesia either at the UN or elsewhere outside the country. Grace was worried about the Bill when she wrote to Garfield, in the USA, on 24 March: 'Darling, please don't make press statements in London. Things are jolly dangerous here, I feel. This Bill and the other amending Bills give the government such extraordinary power.'[2] She wrote again on 2 April: 'PLEASE don't give anybody any reason or excuse to put you in prison. It is here at Hokonui that I want you ... the abundance of richness in my life comes from my association and relationship with you ... you are the heart and sun of my life. All its meaning and delight has you for its mainspring.'[3] It was with more than his usual relief that Garfield returned to Hokonui to take some of the strain off Grace; but he had returned to an unhappy country, with the African nationalist movement in danger of a fundamental split.

***

A new recruit to the ranks of the Government's vocal critics was the recently elected Anglican Bishop of Matabeleland, the Right Reverend Kenneth Skelton. He and Garfield became close friends and colleagues during the next eight years. In his book *Bishop in Smith's Rhodesia*,[4] Skelton writes of the Law and Order Maintenance (Amendment) Bill – the 'Hanging Bill' – and wonders if Rhodesia had already become a police state. Sir Robert Tredgold answered the question in 1967: 'The cumulative effect of the security laws was to turn Rhodesia into a police state ... a state in which the police and the executive are given or assume complete control over all political activities.'[5]

The Preservation of Constitutional Government Bill was the one that particularly worried Grace. The Minister told the House 'it was highly dangerous for Southern Rhodesia that certain persons should be permitted to go overseas and into neighbouring territories and make treasonable and subversive statements with complete impunity'; the Bill set out 'mainly to punish those who sought to advocate the suspension of the existing Constitution'.[6]

In April 1963, Garfield wrote three articles for the *Sunday Mail*. 'To

---

2 JGT/GT, 24.3.63, MS.1082/1/15, Todd Papers, NAZ.
3 JGT/GT, 2.4.63, MS.1082/1/15, Todd Papers, NAZ.
4 Skelton, 1985, p. 48.
5 Tredgold, 1967, pp.230–1.
6 LAD, vol. 52, 12.3.63, cc. 1245–6.

understand the change in Britain's attitude to us we must recognise that most, if not all, the members of the Commonwealth have advised Britain that Southern Rhodesia, under a minority Government, will not be accepted into the association.'[7] In his second article, Garfield drew attention to the country's economic ills – no investment capital, rising unemployment, white emigration – which were the result of the undemocratic Constitution (including the limited franchise), Government refusal to acknowledge that Rhodesia was part of Africa, repressive legislation preventing the African people from participating in the life of the colony. Rhodesians saw the UK, the USA and the UN as enemies; South Africa and Portugal as their friends.[8]

In his third article, Garfield stressed again Britain's responsibility in Southern Rhodesia: she was 'intervening in our affairs by dismembering the federation ... a peaceful solution to our problems could be achieved only by negotiation'.[9]

***

In May, the Governor-General left: 'Old Roy looked a very broken man after he had said farewell', Sir Humphrey Gibbs told Sir Peveril William-Powlett. It marked the beginning of the end of 'all he had fought for'.[10] Welensky told Lord Salisbury: 'I feel now that we have got to look to South Africa and to the two Portuguese states for our friends. It doesn't seem as if we can look anywhere else.'[11]

In June 1963, the Federal Dissolution Conference took place, at which Mr Butler, head of the Central Africa Office, did *not* promise Mr Field independence for Southern Rhodesia.[12] On 1 October, the Order in Council which allowed Southern Rhodesia to take over Federal legislation was passed. Unfortunately, Federal Acts were not made subject to the Bill of Rights or to the supervision of the Constitutional Council.[13]

The motto given to the Federation in 1953 was 'Let us deserve to be great'. Only a decade had passed since Mr Roy Welensky, in his last speech to the Legislative Council of Northern Rhodesia, in 1952, had spoken of 'a great chance now to set an example to Africa by producing a policy that will show that people of different colour and different creeds can live side by side. There is no excuse if we fail.'[14]

---

7 'Don't let anger or fear sway us', *Sunday Mail*, 21.4.63.
8 GT, *Sunday Mail*, 28.4.63.
9 GT, *Sunday Mail*, 5.5.63.
10 Humphrey Gibbs/PW-P, 20.5.63, William-Powlett Papers, Bodleian Library.
11 RW/Lord Salisbury, 9.5.63, File 665/5, Welensky Papers, Bodleian Library.
12 Butler, 1971, p. 225.
13 *Central African Examiner*, November 1963, vol. 7, no. 6.
14 RW, *African Weekly*, 30.12.53.

In December 1959, Garfield had told a CAP meeting in Highfield: 'If the Federation breaks up it will be the responsibility of the Federal Prime Minister and the United Federal Party.'[15] In 1994, he wrote: 'Welensky utterly failed'.[16] Welensky puts all the blame on Britain. The tragedy of Welensky himself is summed up by the *Central African Examiner*: 'one who could have been great but chose merely to be powerful'.[17]

***

In August 1963, the long-simmering discontent within the nationalist movement with Nkomo's leadership finally boiled over. When ZAPU was banned in September 1962, all the leaders inside the country had been arrested and restricted for three months in the reserves. After some hesitation, Nkomo, outside the country at the time, returned and was restricted to his home area. Sithole had been in Dar-es-Salaam when ZAPU was banned, and he set up an emergency headquarters for a new party there – the Zimbabwe African National Union. He returned to Southern Rhodesia at the end of July and on 8 August launched the new party there. Nkomo responded by forming the People's Caretaker Council, in effect those members of ZAPU who remained loyal to him.

There were several elements to the split, including disagreements over policies, and personalities, but not, initially, tribalism, though this would become increasingly important. The rupture destroyed the Africans' principal and most powerful weapon – unity – and for years distracted the nationalists in internecine violence from their long-term objective. It proved costly in lives and lengthened the independence struggle.

Garfield was deeply shocked by the split. He felt that, once again, 'personality over policy' had counted for too much. He joined the committee of nine, chaired by UCRN lecturer Matthew Wakatama and including Dumbutshena and prominent African clergy, which tried by private mediation to bring the two sides together; but they failed. Garfield continued to support Nkomo to the end, though he never became a member of ZAPU. That did not prevent him from recognising Nkomo's deficiencies as a leader; but he maintained his contacts with both groups throughout the turbulent and difficult years that followed.

***

At this time, Garfield was gravely anxious about the deteriorating situation on the mission, in part reflecting the disturbance in the political situation,

---

15 *The Chronicle*, 4.12.59.
16 GT/SP, 13.1.94, TPPC.
17 *Central African Examiner*, 28.3.59, vol. 2, no. 22.

but also arising from the attitude of the Mission superintendent, Ray Knapp, to indiscipline in the school – which even manifested itself during a church service. Knapp was unable to control the situation, so Garfield got up from the congregation and went onto the platform. This action alone had an immediate effect on most of the pupils – and, by the time he had finished speaking, they were quiet. 'Dadaya has rocked this past week as probably never before,' Garfield told Lew Hunter, Chairman of the Foreign Mission Union in New Zealand, 'and I have been almost broken-hearted ... My own experience this past week has stunned and infuriated me.'[18] Ray Knapp resigned. It was a sad day for all concerned at Dadaya, not least Ray himself, who had earned from the Africans the nickname 'Rudo', meaning love. It was an additional tragedy that, unknown to anyone at the time, he was already suffering from terminal cancer.

To deal with 'the present period of disaffection and intrigue', Garfield told Lew Hunter, 'it is necessary to bring the people together, to inspire some enthusiasm in the ranks of both teachers and church workers, to establish definite standards of conduct with concern for the spiritual life of the church'.[19] A Dadaya Governing Board was set up and on 19 October held its first meeting, with Garfield in the chair. An executive committee was appointed – Garfield, Ray Knapp and Peter Nathan, now headmaster of the Shabani Primary School. That day, a vastly relieved Garfield wrote to the FMU: 'Saturday the 19th October has been a good day at Dadaya ... we agreed that there should be a committee with full authority in this country and seeking from yourselves increasing authority in place of the New Zealand Council'.[20]

Garfield knew all his time and energy were needed on the ranch and was reluctant to take on the heavy Dadaya commitment, which he recognised would be a major distraction from that work; but, as he told Lew Hunter, 'I have no choice but to find the time for Dadaya. The situation is as serious as that ... the mission has been breaking to pieces ... our selfish reaction has been to keep right away from it but when the crisis really came the other day I knew that there was no option.'[21] For the next twenty years, responsibility for the whole range of the mission's development and concerns, large and small, once more fell on Garfield.

Ray Knapp's short illness and his death on 5 March 1964 were deeply shocking to the local community, as well as to everyone at the Mission and

---

18 GT/Lew Hunter, MS.390/1/28, Todd Papers, NAZ.
19 GT/Lew Hunter, October 1963, MS.390/1/28, Todd Papers, NAZ.
20 GT/FMU, 20.10.63, TPPC. I am grateful to the Associated Churches of Christ in New Zealand (per the late Allan J. Todd) for the copy of this letter.
21 GT/Lew Hunter, 11.11.63, MS.390/1/28, Todd Papers, NAZ.

school. His wife, Isobel, continued to work at Dadaya until 1974, when she retired to New Zealand. Among Garfield's tasks now at Dadaya was keeping up the morale of the missionaries. He recognised that he and Grace had known 'the golden years of white missionary endeavour' in the country, and that the next generation, brought up on the stories of those years, were bewildered by the changes going on around them. He tried gently to adjust their idea of their role to suit the new realities – and the increased ability of the people. The situation called for 'a great deal of humility and spirituality' – but, as he told the OMB, the experience of Ray's death had 'done a great deal to break down barriers and bring people closer together'.[22]

Dadaya High School expanded greatly over the next couple of years, with Garfield supervising the construction of extra classrooms, dormitories and laboratories.

---

22 GT/OMB, 6.4.64, MS.390/6/4, Todd Papers, NAZ.

67

ENTER IAN DOUGLAS SMITH – 1964

*'[The Southern Rhodesia Government would] take the pattern
already set by the South African Nationalist Government.'*

Wellington Chirwa, FMP

The resignation in October 1963 of Harold Macmillan as British Prime Minister had brought Lord Home (as Sir Alec Douglas-Home) to 10 Downing Street. Duncan Sandys, at the now-combined Commonwealth and Colonial Office, was responsible for Central African affairs. In Southern Rhodesia, two new Government appointments had been made which were reassuring: Evan Campbell, whom Field had defeated in the Federal by-election at Mrewa in 1956, went to London as the new Rhodesian High Commissioner; and Major-General John Anderson – a man for whom unconstitutional action would be unthinkable – became General Officer Commanding the Rhodesian Army.

In January 1964, Field went to London to press the issue of independence for Southern Rhodesia, but returned unsuccessful. At the end of March he went again; but on 2 April, in his absence, a Rhodesian Front caucus meeting decided that their leader had to be replaced. At a cabinet meeting on the 9th, after his return to the country, Field agreed to stand down. The Rhodesian Front chose as their next leader Ian Douglas Smith. Hardwicke Holderness considered Smith 'tough, narrow, tortuous'.[1] Robert Blake writes that Smith was 'a master of ambiguity ... skilled in the art of double-talk ... the epitome and symbol of the white Rhodesian Ascendency caste ... echoed their thoughts and reflected their opinions'. Blake also quotes Lord Malvern on Smith:

---

1 Holderness, 1985, p. 230.

'devious, parochial, suspicious'.[2] The whites had made for themselves a god in their own image, and they now settled down to worship him.

***

In February 1964, nearly 150 members of ZANU and ZAPU had been placed in restriction, and by 3 April another 135 Africans had been 'detained' at Wha Wha camp near Gwelo. Further evidence of Government determination to keep the lid on African nationalism came with the Preventive Detention (Temporary Provisions) Act of 1959; and certain sections of the Unlawful Organisations Act, 1959, were extended, enabling the Government to ban the two parties and detain all the leaders still at large. Smith sent Nkomo, together with Josiah Chinamano and his wife, Ruth, to Gonakudzingwa Camp, in a hot, arid area in the south-east of the country near the border with Portuguese East Africa. The name meant 'where the banished ones sleep', and here Nkomo was kept for the next ten years. Garfield made public his support of the People's Caretaker Council at a press conference on 17 April – which earned him the epithet 'scum' from Welensky.[3]

Later in 1964, Garfield and Holderness were invited to London as guests of the Africa Bureau to lobby British politicians on the Rhodesian situation and to address public and private meetings. On his way to Britain, Garfield flew to America to see Christie and Goldberg. He also addressed the UN General Assembly's Committee on Colonialism, renewing his plea for pressure on a '"reluctant Britain" to take action now to "avert further bloodshed" and secure the release of nationalist leaders'. 'Mr Smith's government, he said, was well aware of the "smouldering rebellion in the hearts of four million people".'[4] *Time* magazine reported: 'Todd's fear was that Smith planned to declare Southern Rhodesia independent without British consent ... the committee urged Britain by a vote of 19 to 0 to give majority rule to Southern Rhodesia's Africans and to restrain the white extremists ...'[5]

Garfield and Iain Macleod took part in a debate at the Oxford Union on the motion 'That Southern Rhodesia should not be permitted independence until there is majority rule'. 'It was a grand debate ... Iain Macleod was marvellous', he remembered 30 years later. The voting was 570 to 56, and Macleod told Garfield: 'I have never won a debate with figures like that!'[6] *The Times*' report on the debate included this statement from Macleod: '"Sooner or later men must

---

2 Blake, 1977, pp. 360–1.
3 RW/Austin Ferraz, 9.4.64, File 745/8, Welensky Papers, Bodleian Library.
4 Reuters, RC 2330 and 2333, 27.8.64, MS.1082/1/12, Todd Papers, NAZ.
5 *Time* magazine, 11.5.64.
6 GT/SP, TPPC.

get round a table and thrash out their differences." ... Southern Rhodesia was not being denied independence because its government was white. "It is because it represents a minority. It is because this minority is so small, not because of the colour of their skins."[7]

At the end of their visit, Garfield and Holderness sent a letter to the British Prime Minister, setting out their proposals for Southern Rhodesia's future; but, as Holderness later wrote, 'nothing came of it – partly I believe because Douglas Home was either disinclined or too weak to stand up to Smith and company. Probably a bit of both ...'[8]

***

The year 1964 brought to Hokonui many visitors, including three Cambridge undergraduates. The eldest was Jim Thompson, an Anglican ordinand who was engaged to Sally, the daughter of Garfield's cousin in Oxford, Peggy Stallworthy. Jim went on to become Bishop of Stepney in the Diocese of London, and then Bishop of Bath and Wells.

Twenty years later, Jim described his stay at Hokonui as 'one of the most important times of my life'.[9] He expanded on that statement a few years later: 'On our journey south ... we stayed with white expatriate families and I had been distressed by the complete lack of trust between the families and their black servants ... It was therefore a wonderful revelation to find at Hokonui that a quite different relationship existed between the black people and Garfield and Grace ... [their] obvious respect for black people as individuals which we encountered ...

'Talking with Garfield and Grace was to see the planet through different eyes ... My time at Hokonui was one of the turning points of my life and I never saw things quite the same way again ... Garfield and Grace had the power to make you feel at least a foot taller and very special.' Jim never forgot a light-hearted mealtime discussion: had Garfield said grace? Voting was 2:3 against. 'I am a democrat', said Garfield. 'Let us bow our heads. We thank thee, O Lord, a second time for food ...'[10]

***

Early in May, cattle dip-tanks in the Lundi Reserve were damaged, and there were incidents of arson. The police established a temporary camp in the area and began investigations. On the morning of Saturday 23 May, a young man

---

7   *The Times*, 15.5.64.
8   HHCH, GT's 80th-birthday book, J. Todd papers.
9   Bishop Jim Thompson/JGT, 24.5.84 (postmark), MS.1082/3/6, Todd Papers, NAZ.
10 Bishop Jim Thompson/SP, 20.4.93, TPPC.

called Philemon Siziba, with a bandage round his head, cycled to Bannockburn Store to see Garfield and tell him of his experiences at the hands of the police. Two teachers from Wedza School were also in the store, and they translated (and witnessed) Philemon's statement. Garfield immediately took Philemon to the Government medical officer in Shabani, Dr Mavros (son-in-law of Ben Fletcher). Dr Mavros said of course he would treat Philemon, but he was not prepared to make any statement about him. The same happened when Garfield took Philemon to the Shabanie Mine Hospital. Garfield then telephoned his own doctor in Bulawayo, who said he would be prepared to treat Philemon that day and make a statement. So, Garfield drove the young man 112 miles to Bulawayo and there engaged advocate Leo Baron for the defence.

Twenty-three men had been arrested in the reserve and taken to Shabani, but later six were released. Of the seventeen remaining, ten, including Philemon, had been beaten by the police. When the case came on, as Garfield told Dr Kenneth Kaunda, 'The magistrate heard evidence on Tuesday and Wednesday. Mr Baron by this time had shown that he would be leading eleven or twelve of the suspects to claim that they had been beaten up severely by the police. It then became apparent that there were reports available from the Government clinic on the condition of several of the accused who had had to be sent for medical treatment after their beatings. Mr Baron led the evidence of the doctor from Bulawayo regarding Philemon.'[11] On the Thursday morning, the magistrate dismissed all the accused, with the statement that 'undue pressure had been exerted by the police'. The interest taken by the people from the reserve was quite spectacular, with crowds attending daily.

***

The extent to which Smith influenced the generally rather parochial, uninformed and not wildly intelligent whites of Rhodesia to rush to their destruction soon became apparent. Day after day, from April 1964 until 11 November 1965, in the press, on radio and TV (and in Parliament), Smith repeated the need for independence – illegal, if necessary – as the only solution to the country's ills, political, economic and social. He went round the country addressing large meetings of enthusiastic Europeans – for example, a 'cheering 900-strong crowd' at Bulawayo: 'I have said that in my lifetime, at any rate, we are safe in this country from this abominable thing – a nationalist government.'[12]

One place where Smith did *not* voice his opinions was at the Commonwealth Prime Ministers' Conference, as he was not invited to attend. In the event,

---

11 GT/Kenneth Kaunda, 15.7.64, MS.390/1/12, Todd Papers, NAZ.
12 *Rhodesia Herald*, 6.6.64.

Central Africa was represented by Dr Hastings Banda, Prime Minister of Malawi, which received its independence only two days before the Conference opened.

***

Early in August 1964, Garfield was invited by the Academic Freedom Committee of the National Union of South African Students at Witwatersrand University to deliver the Richard Feetham Lecture on Academic Freedom. Twenty years earlier, this was where his political journey had begun, with his plea for fair dealing for a non-European laboratory assistant. Now his address had the arresting title: 'Danger! Men thinking!'

'Academic freedom is a flower which blooms only in a suitable climate. I doubt if we shall see it flourish again in its full beauty either in your country or in mine until wide-spread changes have been made in the structure and infra-structure of our national life.' Garfield spoke of his hopes in 1953 for 'a non-racial regime ... I had hoped that our Federation would have contributed to men's understanding of each other ... We were proved not big enough – we lacked the faith to trust our fellow men ... The very hardest thing we can be called upon to do is to face facts, unpleasant facts, facts before which we stand condemned. I know, for no man can stay for years in a position of power without having some regrets when he looks back upon his record ...'[13]

***

The Minister of Law and Order, Garfield's former lawyer, Mr Desmond Lardner-Burke, announced the banning of the *Daily News* on the ground that its publication was 'contrary to the interests of public safety or security'.[14] Twenty-four hours' notice of the banning enabled Judith and like-minded students at the university to mount a protest outside Parliament while the Order was being debated; but, as the law demanded that seven days' notice of a protest be given to the authorities to enable police permission to be obtained, Judith and her friends knew that their protest would be illegal. It was a very quiet demonstration, the students simply sitting on the road outside Parliament holding placards: 'Freedom RIP', 'Cry, the Beloved Country', 'Wipe out police brutality', 'Farewell, Freedom of the Press'. As these were confiscated by the police, the students produced copies of the *Daily News* with the headline, 'Chikerema Calls for End to Violence'.

When the students were ordered to disperse, they moved to a 'No Parking' area near the House and sat down again with their newspapers. A large crowd

---

13 GT, 'Danger! Men thinking!' University of the Witwatersrand, 6.8.64, TPPC.
14 LAD, vol. 57, 25.8.64, c. 1277.

gathered, and police reinforcements arrived. All the students were placed under arrest and driven to the main police station. As one lot of students was removed, others watching spontaneously filled their places until they in turn were taken away.

The banning of the *Daily News* received a great deal of adverse publicity, with the local press arguing strenuously that the *Daily News* had repeatedly deplored violence. Most of the electorate, of course, were in favour of the Government's action against what they were told was a subversive newspaper providing a voice for Nkomo and the nationalists. The motion banning the paper was passed by 24 votes to 18.

Early in October, 81 of the accused were tried and all were acquitted. The organisers of the protest, Judith, law student Byron Hove and two other white students, were tried together. Garfield attended the trial on the first day and on the third and last day, when all were found guilty and fined £25 each. Judith was given permission by the magistrate to make a statement from the dock. She said she had been 'demonstrating against the system of Government we are under, the effects of this system on my country ... I demonstrated because the parties I support have all in turn been banned, because the people I recognise as my political leaders have been restricted or imprisoned, and because the only newspaper in this country that was courageous enough to effectively oppose the Government has been silenced. My wish was to protest peacefully and in silence; I was denied even this right ... If I cease to protest then I begin to identify myself with this system I am fighting.'[15] The statement was received in an astonished – and largely admiring – silence. Garfield paid the fines for Judith and Byron (who didn't forget: 25 years later, when Dadaya suffered a disastrous fire, he sent a substantial donation to the Reconstruction Fund). But life for the Todds would never be the same again.

***

On 15 October, the Labour Party won the British general election. Smith had announced a referendum on Independence in November. To satisfy British demands, he also planned to test African opinion at an *indaba* of chiefs – a proceeding that was quite contrary to African custom. Smith told the *Sunday Mail*: 'We need [independence] to attract investment, immigrants and to defeat the Communists ... these communists realise that when we get independence they have lost the main battle ... We are going to ensure that Africans will get a just share of the country ... we will live side by side, he in his own place, us in ours.'[16]

---

15 *Central African Examiner*, November 1964, vol. 8, no. 5.
16 *Sunday Mail*, 18.10.64.

On 21 October, Dr Palley asked Smith for a guarantee that he 'does not mean to go on to a unilateral declaration of independence'. The Prime Minister replied: 'I have given an undertaking before that we will never do this without informing the public and getting an opinion from them.'[17] Smith gave another assurance about UDI during another debate on 27 October.[18]

The *indaba* – 'that secret, stage-managed, police-guarded operation'[19] – took place from 22 to 26 October. The area was sealed off by police and soldiers, and no member of the public was allowed in. The *Central African Examiner* published an article, 'The Truth Will Out', which contained statements – 'checked, cross-checked and corroborated by eye-witnesses' – highly critical of the Rhodesian Government's tactics and assertions of a 'fair and genuine exchange of views on independence'.[20] Paddy Lloyd told Sir Peveril William-Powlett that the *indaba* was 'a fraud ... 17 chiefs and 13 headmen taken to it ... [who] refused on arrival at Domboshawa to take part are now in Gonakudzingwa'.[21]

Several things happened on 24 October, well away from the closely guarded *indaba*: Zambia became independent; Southern Rhodesia became 'Rhodesia'; and Major-General John Anderson, General Officer Commanding Rhodesia, was 'retired on grounds of age' – he was 51. There followed the removal from office of Mr Evan Campbell (replaced in London by Brigadier Andrew Skeen); of the Secretary for Defence and Foreign Affairs, Mr Barney Benoy; and of the Secretary of Central African Airways, Mr Rupert Pennant-Rea. Mr Stan E. Morris, once the Chief Native Commissioner, was succeeded by Hostes Nicolle, who was reputed to be fluent in six vernacular languages.

The referendum took place on 5 November. Rhodesian Front posters proclaimed: 'To vote 'YES' means unity – not UDI'. To the question: 'Do you want independence under the 1961 Constitution?', 58,091 answered 'YES'; only 6,096 voters distrusted Smith's assurances. It was a surprisingly low poll, 61.6 per cent; but, though in effect only 55 per cent of the electorate gave Smith a vote of confidence, it was enough for his purposes.

---

17 LAD, vol. 59, 21.10.64, c. 205.
18 LAD, vol. 59, 27.10.64, cc. 417–20.
19 *Central African Examiner*, Christmas 1964, vol. 8, no. 6.
20 *Central African Examiner*, December 1964, vol. 8, no. 6.
21 A. D. H. Lloyd/PW-P, 5.11.64, William-Powlett Papers, Bodleian Library.

68

UDI AND RESTRICTION – 1965

'If anything brought about a position where the European feared for his future, it would be the beginning of the end of responsible government in Southern Rhodesia.'

Garfield Todd, 1958

In London, 1965 opened with the funeral of Sir Winston Churchill. In Gonakudzingwa, Joshua Nkomo and hundreds of his supporters were turning detention into an opportunity for education and training. Garfield visited a few times (until prevented by law) and spoke of these visits at Nkomo's 70th birthday party in September 1989: 'the camp was a hive of industry, of political discussions and planning and of vibrant influence'.[1] 'The morale at Gona is very high and everyone is sure that the UK must act', Garfield told Judith;[2] but when, a few days later, Garfield had a long discussion in Salisbury with the Commonwealth Secretary, Arthur Bottomley, and the Lord Chancellor, Lord Gardiner, he was 'so deeply concerned because they obviously could not "do" anything that I decided to go to Gona the next day ... They are facing the fact that the battle must be won in Rhodesia ...'[3]

It was during Mr Bottomley's visit that the 'five principles' that would govern the granting of independence to Rhodesia were formally stated. These, and the fact that they had been agreed to by the Conservatives, brought considerable satisfaction to Garfield, Nkomo and millions of others:

'1. The principle and intention of unimpeded progress to majority rule, already enshrined in the 1961 constitution, would have to be maintained and guaranteed.

---

1 J. Nkomo's 70th birthday, TPPC.
2 GT/JT, 22.2.65, MS.1082/3/2, Todd Papers, NAZ.
3 GT/JT, 28.2.65, ibid.

2. There would also have to be guarantees against retrogressive amendment of the constitution.
3. There would have to be immediate improvement in the political status of the African population.
4. There would have to be progress towards ending racial discrimination.
5. The British Government would need to be satisfied that any basis proposed for independence was acceptable to the people of Rhodesia as a whole.'

(Later, a sixth 'principle' was added: 'the need to ensure that, regardless of race, there is no oppression of majority by minority or of minority by majority'.[4])

Later, the slogan 'No independence before Majority Rule' (NIBMAR) was used to cover the principles.

The *Central African Examiner* reported increasing Government control of broadcasting and television and the sacking of RBC's news director, Mr John Appleby. 'That Mr Appleby, who could never have been described as a flaming liberal, had to go was a measure of the RF Government's intentions.'[5]

In the general election of 7 May, the RF made a clean sweep of the 'A'-roll seats but did not bother to contest the 'B'-roll seats. Ten 'B'-roll African MPs formed the United People's Party and became the official Opposition. Ahrn Palley won Highfield. One of the Government's first actions was to declare a state of emergency over a large area which included Gonakudzingwa 'so that all the restrictive processes ... are in operation', Garfield told Judith.[6] At the same time, Leo Baron was restricted for twelve months to within a fifteen-mile radius of the Bulawayo Post Office. 'Everything is horrible and the river is lower than in a normal November ...'[7]

***

Brigadier Andrew Skeen wrote an account of his brief tenure at Rhodesia House.[8] Among his old friends in London was, significantly, the Chief of the Defence Staff. Skeen writes that British politicians and officials had not 'realised that the RF had ceased to be a political party and had become a national movement, of which Mr Smith was not only the leader, but its incarnation'.[9] Smith 'was in essence the incarnation of his party and Rhodesia as a whole, and ... he spoke

---

4 House of Commons Record, vol. 723, 25.1.66, c. 42.
5 *Central African Examiner*, May 1965, vol. 8, no. 1.
6 GT/JT, 8.6.65, MS.1082/3/2, Todd Papers, NAZ.
7 GT/JT, 16.6.65, ibid.
8 Skeen, 1966.
9 Ibid., p. 23.

for us all and had our absolute confidence'. This echoes the opinion of Jim Sinclair, one-time President of the RNFU (and post-Independence Commercial Farmers' Union): 'Smith brought out the worst in the white population and then personified it.'

Discussions between British ministers and Smith proceeded acrimoniously for the next few months against a background of Rhodesian Front invective against '"pseudo liberals, pseudo intellectuals, and do-gooders" ... white people who try to break down barriers ... dedicated Christians ... and others with strong moral consciences'.[10]

***

Garfield told Judith: 'Smith is ruthless and quite determined to keep whites in control for ever. About the only voice raised is Skelton's: good on him ... If Britain lets us down as most people believe she will it will be a sad day for the commonwealth and for the world. It will also be a sad day for us.'[11] Garfield's peace of mind was assailed on all sides: the political situation; the ranch, with big losses at his butchery in Shabani; doubt about the subdivision, the Mission and his health. He told Lew Hunter in New Zealand, who had written rather desperately for information that had not been forthcoming: 'I simply do not have the time to give real assistance and can only help to keep things ticking over without making a satisfactory contribution in that hard work. It has been the hardest year I have had and is not yet easing ...'[12]

***

On 3 October, Smith and Lardner-Burke went to London in a final attempt to persuade the British Government to grant independence on the 1961 Constitution. They returned to Rhodesia on the 12th. That night, the British Prime Minister made a television broadcast explaining why he had refused Smith's request. He finished the broadcast: 'Prime Minister, think again'.[13] Wilson early ruled out 'the use of force' – which some held to be a fundamental mistake – but his service chiefs would have made it clear anything else would have been out of the question.

Garfield had accepted an invitation to participate in a Teach-In on Rhodesia at Edinburgh University. He hoped to see Smith before he left to tell him of the visit, but the Prime Minister's office said he was too busy. At the end of a heavy day in Salisbury, and before going to the airport, Garfield had an early supper

---

10 *Central African Examiner*, August 1965, vol. 9, no. 1.
11 GT/JT, 6.9.65, MS.1082/3/2, Todd Papers, NAZ.
12 GT/Lew Hunter, 19.9.65, MS.1082/2/10, Todd Papers, NAZ.
13 Wilson, 1971, pp. 149–50.

with Michael and Eileen Haddon. He later told Judith about the dramatic events that followed: 'When dinner was almost finished the phone rang and Eileen came to say that I was wanted. I spoke but there was no answer. Although I did not know it, the police, as soon as they heard my voice, had slipped into two cars and were on their way to catch the elusive criminal! I put the phone down and decided I would put my bags into the car while I waited for the person to dial again ... I slipped the bags in and as I closed the door two cars flashed in. I thought it was the press and ... was about to ask them what papers they represented when, with great embarrassment, Inspector Bristow said, "We are from the CID, Mr Todd, and I am sorry but we have to serve an order on you." "What kind of an order?", I asked. "You are to be restricted to your ranch for twelve months." I laughed and said, "My wife is going to be delighted to hear this" ... So I went on my way in the Mercedes with a detective beside me, and a police car behind me!'[14]

Eileen was given permission to telephone Jim Biddulph, a former chief political correspondent of the *Rhodesia Herald*, and currently Salisbury correspondent for a London paper. She also telephoned Grace – who takes up the story in a letter to her sister, Elsie Barham: 'I was full of a quite unusual foreboding. Just after the time Gar's plane would have left, the phone rang and it was Eileen, who said: "Grace, brace yourself, my girl!" and I knew that there had been an accident and that Gar was hurt! When I finally got round to realising that Eileen was telling me that Gar was restricted – and to the Ranch – I went limp – with relief! That relief and thankfulness carried me through the next few dramatic days ...'[15]

About the time Eileen was phoning Grace, the announcement was made over the BBC, 'and from then it was a circus', Grace told Elsie. The press and TV of the world were already in Salisbury waiting for Smith's UDI. About a dozen press or TV units rang Grace that night, 'saying they were just leaving Salisbury and would be arriving soon ... Gar arrived, tired but cheerful, about 1:30am'.[16]

At about 3.30 a.m., the first newspapermen arrived at Hokonui. 'From then on,' Grace told Elsie, 'the maids made coffee, tea, sandwiches, breakfasts for numerous news men who kept arriving by car, jeep, even three charter planes. It was absolutely fantastic. The *Rand Daily Mail* reported: "The day was blazing hot and it was a super spectacular 'TODD A-O' occasion. The world's Press and television networks were having a jamboree at the old homestead ... The

---

14 GT/JT, 29.10.65, MS.1082/3/2, Todd Papers, NAZ.
15 JGT/EB, 29.10.65, TPPC. I am indebted to Mrs Barham's daughter, Mrs Elizabeth Collins, for a copy of this letter.
16 Ibid.

Olympian Todd profile, the graying good looks, the genial charm, the familiar emotive phrases, the still strong New Zealand accent were being captured for the world, pinpointing the real nature of Rhodesia's tragedy so much more effectively than any words from Mr Smith, Mr Bottomley or Mr Wilson."'

'At 8am that Tuesday morning we heard over South African BC that Judith was on her way to Edinburgh to take Garfield's place at the "Teach-In" – and so I had someone else to tremble for and agonise over! ... All the time, Tuesday and Wednesday this interviewing marathon was going on ... And then ... Judith was speaking to us – from Edinburgh, just an hour before she was due to speak ...'

Forty hours after getting up at 4 a.m. on Monday, Garfield was finally able to get to bed, and by then 'the enormity' of the action had made itself felt. 'It is hard to believe that in a British country where I have once been Prime Minister I should be deprived of my freedom', he wrote to J. M. T. Sibanda.[17] To have Garfield safe at Hokonui for a whole year was a source of secret satisfaction to Grace.

Garfield told Judith: 'Ian Smith told *The Times* that I had been making trips to Zambia where I concerned myself with activities and he mentioned sabotage and killings! Two lawyers have told me that this interview exceeded the bounds of privilege ... Anyway almost far worse things have been put to my account over the years ...'[18]

The *Daily Telegraph* reported that 'it is regarded in Whitehall as a major blunder'.[19] The *Rhodesia Herald* quoted Garfield: 'If people outside are a bit shocked at what has happened to me, let them consider that this has happened to many hundreds of good citizens who happen to disagree with the Government of today ... The problem before Britain is not a UDI. It is to bring the people here in Rhodesia to majority rule and then to get independence ... There are 4 million Africans here and no one is going to push them around for too long ...'[20]

Under the headline 'Gaffe over Garfield', *The Chronicle* editorial regarded Garfield's restriction as 'the ill-considered act of a government under strain ... By this one rash act the government has washed away all sympathy for Rhodesia's cause ... Mr Todd is a former prime minister now restricted by his own government. Such things are supposed to happen only in banana republics – or in those emergent African states which Mr Smith is so prone to criticise. That they should happen under a government that constantly boasts

---

17 GT/J. M. T. Sibanda, 5.11.65, MS.1082/5/8, Todd Papers, NAZ.
18 GT/JT, 29.10.65, MS.1082/3/2, Todd Papers, NAZ.
19 *Daily Telegraph*, 19.10.65.
20 *Rhodesia Herald*, 20.10.65.

about maintaining civilised standards (the British way of Life) is simultaneously laughable and tragic ...'[21]

By Thursday 21 October, the press had departed from Hokonui Ranch, leaving Garfield free to frame his appeal to the Minister of Law and Order against his restriction. It was turned down. At Hokonui, all the difficulties of restriction – and fears of a UDI – were briefly submerged in the Todds' delight in the reports of Judith's success at the Edinburgh University 'Teach-In'.

Smith told the *Times* that he had restricted Garfield 'because of his visits to Zambia to contact people who were aiding and abetting saboteurs'.[22] The *Sunday Mail* also quoted 'Todd's denial ... "This is absolutely untrue" ... Mr Todd denied rumours that he was planning to go overseas to help to establish a government in exile.'

***

After their brief foray into Rhodesia's drought-stricken countryside, the media men returned to the city to wait for UDI, and were soon re-energised by the arrival of the British Prime Minister with a team of 50 experts. Wilson invited Garfield to Salisbury – and the Rhodesian government made elaborate arrangements for him to go under escort. Grace told Elsie: 'I think when Gar drove off with these two security men to visit the PM of Great Britain the enormity and grotesqueness of the situation really struck me.'[23]

On his arrival at Government House, Garfield was faced by a 'battery of cameramen, some greeting me from earlier days at the Ranch. Bottomley was there to meet me and gripped me with both hands and was so cordial ... "Harold wants to come out and meet you here in front of the Press." It was very kindly done and ... soon the PM appeared and walked down the verandah and out to greet me.'[24] This contradicts Prof. J. R. T. Wood's statement that 'Wilson was not on hand at 6pm to greet the last visitor, R. S. G. Todd.'[25]

After talking for one-and-a-half hours, Wilson asked Garfield to return to Government House the following day, so a separate order was obtained from the minister to allow Garfield to stay overnight with friends outside Salisbury. At Government House, Garfield saw 'Joshua and his delegation including Leo B. and Josiah and Enoch the Advocate Dumbutshena', he told Judith.[26] 'Wilson congratulated me on the restriction. It did the UK Govt considerable good ...

---

21   *The Chronicle*, 20.10.65.
22   Quoted in *Sunday Mail*, 24.10.65.
23   JGT/EB, 29.10.65, TPPC.
24   GT/JT, 19.10.65, MS.1082/3/2, Todd Papers, NAZ.
25   Wood, 2005, p. 421.
26   GT/JT, 29.10.65, Todd Papers, NAZ.

[Wilson] will give a Press interview to everyone at 9pm but only what Smith wants will eventually be put over the air.' Wilson tried but failed to persuade the two nationalist groups to reunite.

***

On 3 November, Smith asked the Governor to sign a proclamation of a state of emergency, supported by an affidavit from the Commissioner of Police setting out his '"deep apprehension over the future security of the country" because of trained terrorists and material in Zambia and Tanzania', writes the Governor's biographer, the late Dr Alan Megahey.[27] 'Gibbs asked for, and was given by Smith, "a complete denial that this proclamation had anything to do with a UDI" ... Thus reassured ... the Governor signed.'[28]

'The emergency declaration allowed for sweeping controls covering all aspects of political, civil and economic life including full police powers of 30-day detention ... and total censorship of everything published within Rhodesia.' This last provision was in spite of an assurance from the minister: 'You are going to be perfectly all right – there is no question of censorship.'[29]

***

At the eleventh hour of the eleventh day of the eleventh month, UDI was declared. Twelve men (including the Duke of Montrose) signed the documents. Immediately afterwards, the Prime Minister and Clifford Dupont went to Government House, where Sir Humphrey Gibbs dismissed them and the rest of the ministers. The date had been carefully chosen by Smith to emphasise Rhodesia's contribution to Britain's victories in the two World Wars, but it gave great offence to many who saw it as a desecration of the memory of the hundreds of thousands of members of the British – including Rhodesian – forces who had died in those wars.

At Hokonui that momentous morning, Garfield dictated into his tape recorder a letter to the Stallworthys: 'Edie is doing my letters for me ... Cynthia is in Shabani doing the banking, and Grace is down at the bottom of the Ranch in the transporter taking herders to round up cattle.'[30]

In Bulawayo, Leo Baron had been arrested and was now in prison. Bishop Skelton listened to Smith's 1p.m. broadcast: 'It is difficult to convey the feeling of desolation which came over opponents of the Rhodesian Front's policies as

---

27 Megahey, 1998, pp. 106–7.
28 Ibid.; Megahey's first quotation is from the Governor's Note, HVG Archives, SB/3.
29 *Sunday Mail*, 7.11.65.
30 GT/J. and P. Stallworthy, 11.11.65, MS.1082/5/8, Todd Papers, NAZ.

they listened ... to Smith's "Declaration"', he writes.[31] 'But the most damaging assertion came at the end of Smith's "Address to the Nation" which immediately followed ... "We have struck a blow for the preservation of justice, civilization and Christianity."' The commemorative issue of the Declaration, garlanded in red and green flame lilies, bore on the reverse, in tiny red letters, a date – '20.10.65'. Before the echoes of Smith's broadcast had died away, into the offices of newspaper editors walked government censors.

That afternoon, the Governor summoned the press and made a statement, which would never be published or broadcast in Rhodesia – but, as many people listened to the BBC, SABC and Zambia Radio, what he said would percolate through to the public. He quoted a message from Mr Bottomley: 'I have it in command from Her Majesty to inform you that it is Her Majesty's pleasure that, in the event of an unconstitutional declaration of independence, Mr Ian Smith and other persons holding office as Ministers of the Government of Southern Rhodesia and as Deputy Ministers cease to hold office ...'[32]

On 12 November, the leading article in the *Rhodesia Herald* was censored in its entirety.

***

Grace told Elsie: 'I am full of foreboding about the immediate future ... Here at the ranch we continue, with heavy hearts, our own particular battle with our own financial and economic problems.'[33] Since Leo Baron's arrest and imprisonment, Garfield feared he also would be taken into custody – and, as Grace relates, when a couple of days later a car drove up after dark, 'Gar took one look and came to me and took my hands. He just stood looking at me, and said, "Yes! It's the police. I don't know how you will manage". Then he went out to meet them. I heard them speak, and then Gar came quickly inside and said "No" ... He was served with an order restricting him from using the telephone ...'[34]

The December 1965 edition of the *Central African Examiner* (vol. 9, no. 5) carried a notice on the front cover that 'all material in this newspaper has been subject to government censorship'. And a very thorough job the censor had made of it: no page escaped; the editorial page was blank and half the next page, and so on. After that, the *Central African Examiner* simply ceased publication. And with it died freedom of speech in Rhodesia.

31 Skelton, 1985, pp. 74–5.
32 Sir Humphrey Gibbs, 11.11.65. Misc. File, RH, Hirsel Archives. I am grateful to the present Earl of Home for access to the Hirsel Archives.
33 JGT/EB, 12.11.65, Mrs Collins' Papers, c/TPPC.
34 JGT/EB, 17.11.65, Mrs Collins' Papers, c/TPPC.

On 17 December, Wilson banned oil imports into Rhodesia, and on 28 December petrol rationing was announced (the coupons had been printed on 25 October). On Christmas Day, all but the first three words – 'Fret not thyself' – of the leading article in the *Rhodesia Herald* were censored. This is the beginning of Psalm 37 in the Authorised Version of the Bible. The verse continues: 'because of evil-doers, neither be thou envious against the workers of iniquity'.

***

In her biography of Smith, Phillippa Berlyn quotes Lord Malvern: the Government committed 'a most dishonourable and disreputable act'.[35] But in December 1977, Smith told her: 'Looking at it through hindsight, really it was the correct decision, because it worked. I often marvel at how well it has worked ...'[36]

---

35 Berlyn, 1978, p. 142.
36 Ibid., p. 183.

69

NAMELESS AT HOKONUI – 1966

'I live my life trying to be ready to do what seems required of me but recognising that if there is no practical way then I must be quiet and not fret about it.'

Garfield Todd, 1966

While Ian Smith was riding high on the success of his rebellion, Garfield Todd, restricted to Hokonui Ranch, was at an 'all-time low' in health and spirits. The difficulties caused by his restriction increased his anxiety about Hokonui; and, unable to go to Shabani, he was soon forced to close the profitable butchery there. Garfield told me in March they had 'nearly gone under'.[1] Exasperated alike by some of the Dadaya missionaries, who found it hard to work under an African principal – the excellent Manikidza M. Nyoni – and by certain actions of the Overseas Mission Board in New Zealand, Garfield resigned as Chairman of the Dadaya Governing Board. Peter Nathan took over.

Friends – and strangers – continued to visit the Todds. Bishop Kenneth Skelton found the ranch 'an island of sanity in a land which had gone mad'. 'It was clear to me also that during that period when recognised African leaders were out of circulation, Garfield's steadfastness (which was known through the "bush telegraph" even when he was incommunicado) was a great strength to the African people.'[2]

John Worrall also visited Hokonui, later writing: 'During one visit to the Todd Ranch [Garfield] gave me his binoculars and showed me the main railway line from Mozambique to Rhodesia which runs through his ranch.' Garfield told him: 'From here I can watch the trains breaking sanctions – taking asbestos

---

1 Susan Woodhouse's 1966 Journal, 23 March, TPPC.
2 Bishop Kenneth Skelton/SP, 21.4.93, TPPC.

out of Rhodesia to Lourenço Marques and see the same trains bringing back sanctions-busting petrol – through my land. They say I am subversive but why do they allow me to sit here at this strategic point counting trucks?'[3] Garfield relayed the number of those petrol tankers/asbestos trucks to his friend Bishop Kenneth for onward transmission. Worrall was shortly afterwards deported from Smith's Rhodesia – as were fellow-journalists James Biddulph and Roy Perrott (the *Observer*, London), and the British Deputy High Commissioner, Mr Stanley Fingland. The BBC was also ordered out of the country.

The imposition of sanctions caused great bitterness among Rhodesia's Europeans; but, as Bishop Skelton writes: 'I never heard an African say that sanctions ought to be removed before they had achieved the desired result. They were the one piece of evidence the Africans of Rhodesia had to assure them that the world cared. "We would rather starve than have sanctions removed."'[4]

***

Rain came at last to Hokonui, but too late for the maize. However, the grass recovered and the cattle regained condition. Grace wrote rather despairingly to Judith (who had been joined in London by Cynthia): 'All at once it became quite intolerable to me, this way of life which is serfdom for Dad, though he never complains, and which for all of us means work with very little relief.' Grace then writes of 'the comfort and the happiness of the kind of relationship which Dad and I enjoy. I know what a real joy it is, these days when he is working so hard, to come home here in the evening. And as for me, my day begins with his homecoming. It is a relationship which armours one against the "slings and arrows of outrageous fortune".'[5]

When Garfield's deteriorating health could no longer be ignored, Dr Paul Fehrsen of Bulawayo went to see him at Hokonui. Latent malaria was finally diagnosed and successfully treated with a new drug. Renewed health meant that Garfield felt able to resume the responsibilities of Chairman of the Dadaya Governing Board, and he once more took hold of mission and school matters – which was just as well, as the OMB made endless, often petty, demands for detailed reports from the Headstation. But, in Bulawayo, Mr Hadfield, 'FLH', died, aged 92. Garfield grieved that he could not attend the funeral of the man whose support in 1934 had been crucial to his career. And in New Zealand, Grace's eldest sister, Win, died following a sudden stroke. Grace felt her loss

---

3   *Rand Daily Mail*, 20.1.72.
4   Skelton, 1985, p. 83.
5   JGT/JT, 19.4.66, J. Todd Papers.

acutely, especially as she was not able to attend her funeral.

In May 1966, there was the first reference in the Todds' correspondence to what would become an increasing problem for Grace: the onset of osteoarthritis. In spite of pain-killing drugs, the only relief she could find was to rest, and though for the most part she managed to live her usual busy life, she had all the anxiety of not knowing when she might be laid low, sometimes for several days, with a sudden attack.

Garfield told Judith not to come home yet: 'It is neither easy nor will it be easy in the future, I'm afraid ... Those who care for Africa will need great patience, a sensitive understanding, a love great enough to shield one's self from being overcome by many attacks ... for there will be as much evil and self-seeking in Africa as anywhere else and in primitive conditions evil appears more frightening or repugnant than when it has the veneer of London upon it ...'6

***

Grace wrote to Judith on 17 October: 'At midnight tonight Dad's restriction is supposed to end ... I have no idea about what will happen ... if all goes well today, Dad ... intends to attend Tunmer's sale in Gwelo, where we shall be selling 30 young heifers! ... This afternoon [Dad] rang the local police. Mr McEwan said ... that he had already ascertained that there was to be no further restriction. It was almost unbelievable to have that relief and reassurance ...'7

Garfield told Judith on the 20th that 'Except for the business aspect it was not too bad. My heart goes out to all those, including Leo, who are in horrible conditions, separated from their families.'8 Great welcomes awaited Garfield from friends and strangers in the Maglas Township of the Shabanie Mine, where he had established an eating house, and from pressmen and photographers in Gwelo. He told the *Rhodesia Herald*: 'This has become a reign of censorship, secrecy and propaganda, and I must say I do not like that. But I have been here 30-odd years and came with a purpose. I intend to stay.'9

Garfield continued to be outspoken, telling Ronald Legge of the *Sunday Times*, who visited Hokonui: '"My release from restriction is completely meaningless in the context of the political scene in Rhodesia" ... To one accustomed to the current Rhodesian scene, it was like going back in time to talk to this realist-visionary who holds just as strongly today – and perhaps with even deeper conviction – the principles that caused him to be ousted

6 GT/JT, 29.5.66, J. Todd Papers.
7 JGT/JT, 17.10.66, J. Todd Papers.
8 GT/JT, 20.10.66, J. Todd Papers.
9 *Rhodesia Herald*, 19.10.66.

by a conspiracy of his cabinet colleagues who regarded his policies as "too liberal" ... "If there is to be non-racial government it will have to come from the African, not the European" ... The outstanding impression of my visit was the profound pessimism with which he regards the possibility of a peaceful settlement of the independence dispute.'[10]

***

In December, Smith agreed to talks with the British Government on board HMS *Tiger*, off Gibraltar. The sea was rough; seasickness afflicted many; and the ship did not stay at anchor but went round in circles going nowhere, which is as good a way as any of describing the talks. Smith agreed terms with Wilson, subject to the approval of his cabinet – who promptly rejected them, which was just as well, for, as Garfield told Judith: 'Wilson again went further than any of us want him to do ... With a bit of propaganda [Smith] could have picked up the package and held it high as the victory for himself that it was ...'[11]

---

10 *The Sunday Times*, 23.10.66.
11 GT/JT, 12.12.66, J. Todd Papers.

70

BETWEEN THE TALKS – 1967

'The Europeans in the Colony will only be safe and secure if they work in harmony with the black people.'

Garfield Todd, 1954

In general, all was going well at Dadaya, where Manikidza Nyoni was proving himself a good Principal, but there were still difficulties with the Overseas Mission Board in New Zealand. Garfield told them: 'The situation is now becoming so serious that a conference of heads of churches is being called ... I am sure it is not possible for members of the [OM] Board to understand how difficult it is to live under circumstances where at any time one of our brethren in the churches may be picked up by a police truck and taken away without trial of any kind, perhaps for years ...'[1]

The Church of Christ had become a member of the newly established Christian Council of Rhodesia, with Garfield one of its representatives. The Council owed its inception largely to Bishop Kenneth Skelton. It co-ordinated fund-raising for development projects initiated by the churches and scholarships, and set up training courses. But principally it provided a forum for the churches to discuss political matters, which were specifically excluded from proceedings at the Christian Conference (hitherto the only 'church' forum) under its constitution.

After his release from restriction, Garfield was elected to the Executive, where, Bishop Skelton writes, his 'wise contributions ... were also invaluable in helping the Council to maintain African morale'.[2] The Council passed a resolution on the RF Government's policy of 'separate development': 'We believe

---

1   GT/OMB, 21.3.67, MS.1082/2/10, Todd Papers, NAZ.
2   Bishop Kenneth Skelton/SP, 21.4.93, TPPC.

that the legal and physical separation of our people into racial groups would be an offence against Christian ideals of the brotherhood of all men under the fatherhood of God. We believe such separation would be against the economic and political interests of our land ...'[3]

Leo Baron was allowed to leave the country with his wife, Barbara. Garfield told Judith: 'There was a question as to how much longer he could sanely bear it all.'[4] His 'tremendous talents'[5] were put to good use in Zambia, where in 1971 he was sworn in as a Judge of the High Court.

***

Garfield and Grace went to Noetsie for three weeks over Grace's birthday in April. Grace told Judith: 'I swing between extremes of hope and pessimism. Sometimes I think that the white people here are so powerful, so sure, so determined – they will never go back. Then I am amazed – and constantly this is so – at the vast number everywhere of capable Africans holding down important jobs, and I believe these people have the future in their own hands.'[6]

Garfield had not been able to see Benjamin Greenberg in New York since Christie's death at the end of 1965. Now that he was free, and had caught up with the affairs of the ranch, and his health had improved, this meeting could be delayed no longer. He was due to give an address at the University of Toronto in October, which meant that his travel expenses to North America would be covered. He would see Judith and Cynthia in London. Furthermore, he wished to go to New Zealand for direct contact with the Overseas Mission Board. The minutes of an OMB meeting on 7 September had included this disquieting paragraph: 'It was also agreed that we should write to Mr Todd and suggest that we do not wish to be drawn into any political controversy and would appreciate his avoiding any occasion which could cause embarrassment to himself or to this Board.'[7]

To read the above in conjunction with the Dadaya Annual Report of September 1967 shows clearly how far from understanding were those Church of Christ members meeting in Nelson. They did not want any 'occasion' of 'embarrassment', while in Rhodesia 'the people face the greatest difficulties they have ever known and there is uncertainty and fear'.[8]

The possibility of Garfield's citizenship being removed was very real, and he

---

3   Christian Council of Rhodesia, 14.2.67, MS.1086/3/1, Todd Papers, NAZ.
4   GT/Judith and Cynthia Todd, 21.4.67, J. Todd Papers.
5   GT/Judith and Cynthia Todd, 21.5.67, TPPC.
6   JGT/JT, 30.4.67, J. Todd Papers.
7   OMB, Minutes, 7.9.67; Savage, *Forward into Freedom* (1980), p. 93.
8   Dadaya Annual Report, September 1967, TPPC.

felt obliged to warn Mr Greenberg of the Government's increased powers over its opponents. In Parliament, Lardner-Burke told a questioner that Garfield had been restricted in 1965 because he was 'a threat to the security' of the country – and if he again became 'a threat to the security' of the country, he would again be restricted.[9]

Garfield wrote to Grace from Sydney on 6 October: 'At Perth at 4:30am there was a full TV set up with other newsmen!' When Garfield arrived at Sydney, he was met by 'the biggest team of TV and Newsmen I have ever encountered. One TV after another for nearly an hour.'[10] On Saturday 7th, Garfield told Grace: 'The NZ interlude I almost fear. It is wrong that I should not be excitedly contemplating it but I am not. I simply do not know how it will turn out but I will go quietly and I will do my best, my love.'[11] Before Garfield met the OMB, there were several press interviews, with good coverage in the newspapers, and church addresses. Garfield did what he could to dissuade New Zealanders from supporting the pro-Smith Aid Rhodesia Movement, whose strength in both Australia and New Zealand shocked him.

Garfield met the OMB in Nelson on 13 and 14 October. First, he gave the Board a comprehensive review of the Rhodesian political scene, adding: 'We as Christians have a responsibility to the 4 million Africans. We have no option but to say that things are wrong, and these views are supported by the Africans ... If Africans can get help from anywhere, they will take it ... Thought of violence is loathed, but perhaps this may be resorted to because the Christians are not forthright and strong enough ...'[12]

The meeting reconvened on the morning of the 14th, and at '4:50pm' Garfield wrote to Grace: 'The day is over, with time to spare and ended with a warm tribute by Ron Chapman[13] to your influence at Dadaya and all that you did in many ways to help ... What a difference today from the letter I earlier received ... it has been a very good visit and everyone on the Board seems appreciative.'[14] The OMB gave approval for a considerable enlargement of Dadaya High School, which would mean more construction work for Garfield.

***

Garfield 'was exhausted when he returned, but also exhilarated', Grace

---

9 LAD, vol. 68, 15.8.67, c. 928.
10 GT/JGT, 6.10.67, MS.1082/4/1, Todd Papers, NAZ.
11 GT/JGT, 7.10.67, MS.1082/4/1, Todd Papers, NAZ.
12 GT/OMB, Notes of meeting, 14.10.67, MS.1082/2/10, Todd Papers, NAZ.
13 Principal of Dadaya School for two years earlier in the 1960s.
14 GT/JGT, 14.10.67, MS.1082/4/1, Todd Papers, NAZ.

told Elsie.[15] At Bulawayo airport 'things were a bit tense', Garfield told his daughters,[16] but at least he was free – in spite of a request by an MP that the Minister of Internal Affairs, Mr William Harper, take action about Garfield's 'false ... statements damaging to Rhodesia' made overseas. The minister replied that the Government was studying the reports 'and obviously it will have to look into the veracity of these statements before it can commit itself'.[17] No action was taken against Garfield, so presumably his statements were found to be true.

Shortly after his return to Hokonui, Garfield had a severe attack of 'flu and then cracked a couple of ribs in a fall. During his enforced inactivity following this accident, he and Grace had long discussions about the future which led to important decisions. He told Mr Greenberg: 'We believe that we should endeavour to bring our affairs under full control. We are therefore selling 28,000 acres of our land and all our cattle. We would offer the trustees of the Lansdell Christie Estate the sum of £18,000 in full settlement of all claims ... within the next ninety days.'[18] Substantial acreages were sold to neighbouring ranchers George Moorcroft and Bob Mattison. The Todds went ahead immediately with the sale of the complete herd, getting high prices. Grace told Cynthia: 'If all goes on as we expect and hope, it seems, although it is almost too incredible, that our long years of strain and anxiety are at an end. We shall be left with the house and bit of land round it, and also the land across the river, from Wedza to the Belingwe Road ...' [19]

---

15 JGT/EB, 11.12.67, Mrs Collins' Papers.
16 GT/Judith and Cynthia Todd, 6.11.67, J. Todd Papers.
17 LAD, vol. 69, 3.11.67, cc. 1031–2.
18 GT/Benjamin Greenberg, 11.11.67, Ranch File, J. Todd Papers.
19 JGT/Cynthia Todd, 9.12.67, J. Todd Papers.

71

TALKING AGAIN – 1968

*'We face the worst drought since 1924, and "God's Sanctions"
as the people term them are likely to be more devastating than
Harold's.'*

Garfield Todd, April 1968

Sir Robert Tredgold's autobiography, *The Rhodesia that was My Life*, was published in 1968. For Garfield and Grace, Sir Robert's book was the first publicly expressed and authoritative vindication of all that they had tried to do politically. Garfield told him his book was 'not only a joy to read and full of interest but I have found in it both help and comfort ... In your book you mark out clearly areas of truth ... [we] felt very deeply with you and for you as you traced your growing concern with racial attitudes. I know well the anguish of spirit caused by trying to "face political realities". I am all the more grateful that you were able to say what you did regarding my own efforts to consider people as people rather than as whites with privilege and Africans without rights.'[1]

***

In June, Wilson initiated tortuous and secret steps to ascertain if talks could be resumed with any reasonable prospect of success. Finally, arrangements were made for them to take place at Gibraltar on the British warship, HMS *Fearless*. They failed. Smith's explanation this time was that the British were obsessed with African majority rule – and he was determined there should not be majority rule in Rhodesia during his lifetime. Garfield told Judith that Smith 'must have a settlement but it must be on his terms'. 'He doesn't seem to

---

1   GT/RCT, 28.4.68, TPPC.

recognise that the terms are all too nearly his own.'²

The Flag of Rhodesia Bill, removing the Union Flag and substituting a Rhodesian one, was introduced into the Rhodesian Parliament before the *Fearless* talks started – as was the Indemnity Bill, protecting security forces against legal action for mistreatment. These were highly provocative actions by the Rhodesian Government, but the British Government turned a blind eye to both.

***

In September, the rain came at last to Hokonui, and the money to repay the Christie loan was handed over in New York. In November, Garfield went to Edinburgh to speak in a University Union debate in opposition to the motion 'That this house approves of a negotiated Rhodesian settlement'. The Scottish paper, the *Daily Record*, reported that Garfield said: 'What Rhodesia needs is a solution more than a settlement. The whites there have to learn to understand the African and live with him. They won't do it, you see. They depend on the Africans not to be people.'³ The reporter described Garfield as 'a tall, tanned, incredibly handsome 60-year-old who looks exactly the way Hollywood would imagine an elderly, wise, humane, liberal politician to look'. After telling readers of Garfield's early life, the article goes on to quote him: 'It wasn't until the 'fifties that the Africans started being really aware, and the whites to become terrified out of their minds ... Nothing corrupts quite as much as privilege, and particularly privilege based on race ... The Blacks will get their freedom eventually, of course. By blood if not by ballot box.'⁴

***

The year 1968 brought an award for Grace from the Rhodesian African Teachers' Association. Garfield proudly copied to the Overseas Mission Board extracts from '"*RATA – Views and Reviews* – A Monthly Newsletter of the Rhodesian African Teachers' Association" ... on 14 December 1968, 16 people were presented with certificates of merit in recognition of outstanding services they had rendered in promoting the interests and activities of RATA and African Education.' (Of the sixteen, five had had long association with Dadaya Mission; Grace was the only woman and the only European.)

'Dadaya is perhaps best known for the "Dadaya Schemes" which were written and produced for the whole country by Mrs Todd.

'Receiving her certificate, Mrs Todd, amid enthusiastic applause from the

---
2   GT/JT, 10.11.68, J. Todd Papers.
3   *Daily Record*, 20.11.68.
4   Ibid.

audience, said she had been moved, delighted and made very proud by the tribute RATA had paid her. She said, "Those of us receiving these awards are fortunate to be present to listen to the generous things you have said and to be able to thank you personally. Very few people have this happy experience …"

'She concluded: "In thanking you, Mr President and your Association, for this award, which I most deeply appreciate, I should like to thank also all those boys and girls, now men and women, and the teachers who passed through Dadaya during the 20 years I taught there. I know very well, and concede here today, that from them I received far more than I gave and learned far more than I taught."'

Grace wrote to the RATA President, Mr Hay I. Malaba: 'The emotion of "glad surprise" which I experienced yesterday was so overwhelming and my expression of thanks so inadequate that I feel I must write to you immediately. All my life I shall carry with me my remembrance of the heart-warming welcome I was given when I came to accept this award. When I stood before the delegates gathered at your Conference I could hardly speak. I have never sought or expected recognition for any contribution I was fortunate enough to make, and to be given the warm affection and appreciation of my African colleagues was a reward far beyond anything I could expect or hope for. I want you and the other members of the Executive to know that that was the proudest moment of my life. No honour from any government could give me such pleasure and pride as that which you conferred upon me yesterday, and I send to you my sincere and grateful thanks.'[5]

---

5 JGT/Hay I. Malaba, 15.12.69, MS.1082/4/4, Todd Papers, NAZ.

72

CUTTING THE BRITISH STRINGS – 1969

'If we fail in non-violent action, then violence will be accepted by the people as the only effective weapon left to them.'

Garfield Todd, August 1965

In March 1969, John Worrall, long-time correspondent for the *Guardian*, the *Rand Daily Mail* and the *Johannesburg Sunday Times*, wrote an article on Garfield, entitled 'The loneliest White Man in Rhodesia'. He quoted Garfield: '"I feel so remote from it all yet I feel it seething very strongly all round me because I am very much a Rhodesian." Charming and relaxed though he seems ... Mr Todd, nevertheless, gives the impression of boiling with frustration at not being able to play a part in the Rhodesian tragedy. "All one can do is keep up personal relationships and bear a personal witness to events."'[1]

***

In May 1969, the World Council of Churches, to which the Christian Council of Rhodesia was affiliated, held a Consultation on Racism in Notting Hill in London, under the chairmanship of the General Secretary of the WCC, Dr Eugene Carson Blake, and US Senator George McGovern. The Chairman of the Christian Council of Rhodesia, Dr Herbert Chikomo, and Garfield were invited to attend.

The Consultation 'proposed a detailed programme to combat racism, which was adopted, almost without any change, by the WCC Central Committee meeting at Canterbury in August of the same year. This became the Programme to Combat Racism.'[2] Garfield was on the Consultation drafting sub-committee and remembered that the PCR resolution was the only time in his life that his

---
1   J. Worrall, Gemini News Service, GG 435, 28.3.69, MS.1082/1/13, Todd Papers, NAZ.
2   Mr Boudewijn C. Sjollema (then WCC staff member)/GT, 13.1.97, TPPC.

first draft was returned with the request that he 'make it stronger'.³

The Statement issued by the Consultation included these paragraphs in Appendix C (Statement of the Consultation on Racism, London, 19–24 May 1969, pp. 97–8): 'The identification of the churches with the STATUS QUO means today, as before, that it has remained, in effect, part of the racial problem and not a means of eliminating it. If the churches are to have any relevance in these critical times, it is imperative that they no longer concentrate their attention on the individual Christians who are fighting racism ... the Church is a community, a group ... and it is therefore necessary that issues of racism be addressed by a group. Individual commitment is commendable – but not enough ... Therefore, the Church must be willing to be not only an institution of love, but also an institution of action, making inputs into societies to help effect a new balance of power that renders racism impotent. The Church must come to realize that in our institutionalized world the closest approximation to love possible, is justice.'⁴

'One of the activities of the Programme to Combat Racism was the operation of a Special Fund to Combat Racism from which the WCC Executive Committee allocated (symbolic) amounts of money to groups of the racially oppressed, including liberation movements. Grants were made in all continents, but white racism in southern Africa became the special focus of the PCR and the Fund.'⁵ The five-year Programme to Combat Racism was adopted by the WCC in August 1969. It is perhaps just as well that Garfield's close involvement in the birth of the PCR was not more widely known in Rhodesia at the time, for it caused tremendous anger and bitterness, especially in the European sections of the churches.

***

On 21 May, the Rhodesian Government published its constitutional proposals which, Smith said, represented 'a formula "which will reconcile racial differences of race, culture and society of all the people who live in Rhodesia"'.⁶ 'The Government of Rhodesia believe that the present Constitution is no longer acceptable to the people of Rhodesia because it contains a number of objectionable features, the principal one being that it provides for eventual African majority rule and, inevitably, the domination of one race by another and that it does not guarantee that government will be retained in responsible hands.'⁷

---

3   GT/SP, 1999.
4   Vincent, 1970.
5   Boudewijn Sjollema/GT, 13.1.97, TPPC.
6   *The Times*, 21.5.60.
7   1969 Constitution White Paper, *MOTO*, vol. 11, no. 6, June 1969.

The editorial in the *Guardian* on 22 May found that Smith's constitutional proposals make Rhodesia 'a permanent police state ... censorship, preventive detention and restriction, abolition of an appeal system after trials on certain charges, compulsory powers to search and seize property, the denial of bail ... Mr Smith's policy is a direct invitation to violent resistance, and must bring racial war nearer ...'[8]

Smith might consider his new constitution a 'world-beater', but, for Garfield, 'the RF's constitutional proposals were "a brutal warning" that the rights of men and human decencies were not to be allowed to stand in the way of the RF's determination to maintain white supremacy', as he told *The Chronicle*.[9]

At the referendum on 20 June, on an 85 per cent turnout, 72.5 per cent of voters accepted the constitution; 81 per cent accepted Republic status. Two days later, the Governor was able to lay down his burden. Sir Humphrey and Lady Gibbs remained in Rhodesia as private citizens for another fifteen years. Sir Humphrey was made a Privy Councillor and was awarded the Queen's personal honour of GCVO. Lady Gibbs was made a Dame Commander of the Order of the British Empire.

When Sir Humphrey died in November 1990, Garfield, who had always admired him greatly, wrote: 'Sir Humphrey Gibbs set a standard of loyalty to Her Majesty the Queen and of rectitude to the laws of Southern Rhodesia which was in stark contrast to the treasonable and humanly abysmal conduct of the rebel administration of that time. Sir Humphrey, with the strong and devoted support of his wife, Dame Mollie, endured with steadfastness the slander and the indignities to which he was subjected in the attempt to make him leave Government House and desert his post as legal Governor ... He lived a life of service to the country and the people and died an honourable man.'[10]

***

A great deal had been happening at Hokonui Ranch – now 17,500 acres in extent – where, under a revolutionary new system, the cattle paddocks, hitherto of 1,500–2,000 acres, were being broken up into 400–500-acre units. There was much new fencing required, as well as several new water points, and everyone had to get used to new routines. But this activity was exciting and positive and gave the Todds great interest and a most welcome antidote to politics. Grace told a correspondent: 'I try to comfort myself with the remembrance of all the many children and young people who have passed through our hands, and can

---

8   *Guardian*, 22.5.69.
9   *The Chronicle*, 28.5.69.
10 *GT, The Times*, November 1990, TPPC.

only hope that they benefited in some way or another from that contact and subsequent enlargement of mind.'[11]

Garfield found it difficult to be interested in what was happening in Parliament because it seemed to be quite divorced from the people and real life, he told Judith.[12] There did, however, seem something still to be done when it came to the Land Tenure Bill, which would follow from the new constitution. The Bill gave equal land to the two principal racial groups: 260,000 whites and 4,000,000 blacks. It was the 'occupation' of the two land categories that exercised the churches. The definition given 'meant that inter-racial churchmanship could be forbidden; ... an amendment designed to safeguard such worship was rejected by the Government'.[13] The Act was attacked by the Christian Council, the church leaders and the Roman Catholic hierarchy, Bishop Donal Lamont stating: 'In conscience we cannot and in practice we shall not obey.'[14] Skelton writes: 'For once, Government took notice of our objection. They did not change the law, but they gave us an assurance that any minister or missionary going about his normal duties from one area to another would not be deemed to be breaking the law.' The church leaders said plainly that the new Constitution and Land Tenure Act 'entrenched racial discrimination and could not therefore be reconciled with Christian faith ... We affirm that the Church intends to carry on its work in areas of either race and with such occupation by either race as the work requires.'[15]

---

11   JGT/Penelope Gordon, 31.10.69, MS.1082/4/4, Todd Papers, NAZ.
12   GT/JT, 28.10.69, J. Todd Papers.
13   Skelton, 1985, p. 106.
14   Grant, 1980, p. 145.
15   Skelton, 1985, p. 109.

73

THE REPUBLIC OF RHODESIA – 1970

'White Rhodesia was a civilisation in decay ... it had become a "frozen" society, a society incapable of development and change.'

Victor de Waal, *The Politics of Reconciliation*

In 1970, an Official Secrets Bill was introduced in Parliament, exchange-control measures were tightened, and the Government further strengthened its hand with a new Law and Order (Maintenance) (Amendment) Bill 'intended to create a new offence of knowingly harbouring or assisting terrorists', Lardner-Burke told Parliament.[1]

On 2 March 1970, Rhodesia was declared a Republic, and its green-and-white flag replaced the Union Flag. 'God Save the Queen' was replaced by Beethoven's 'Ode to Joy', with patriotic Rhodesian words, and an English lawyer, Clifford Dupont, took up residence as the first President in Salisbury's most beautiful colonial dwelling. But, legally, nothing had changed: the declaration was not recognised in British or international law. The British Residual Mission had been closed the previous year, and now a further nine consular offices – including the USA – were closed. South Africa and Portugal alone remained.

Garfield and Bishop Kenneth Skelton drafted a resolution for the Christian Council's Annual General Meeting in Umtali on 4 March, which set the tone of the churches' relationship with the two-day-old Republic's government: 'The Christian Council of Rhodesia is deeply concerned by the trend of recent developments in this country. It has noted particularly the acceptance by the electorate of an admittedly racialist constitution condemned by most church leaders as in many respects completely contradictory to Christian teachings; the introduction of a Land Tenure Act based upon racially separate development

---

1 LAD, vol. 76, 6.2.70, c. 1970.

which not only is incompatible with Christian commitment to non-racial free development but also permits interference with the free worship and witness of the Church ...'[2] In a sermon preached by Bishop Skelton that evening, he quoted 'a recent statement on the Land Act which had said: "The policies of Church and Government are fundamentally opposed ... the two sides are in total disagreement in principle and in practice."'[3] The sermon caused an outburst of anger among white churchpeople, but Bishop Skelton had the full support of his fellow Heads of Denominations.

The Roman Catholic Bishop in Umtali, the Rt Rev. Donal Lamont O.Carm., kept up the pressure in a letter to the editor of the *Rhodesia Herald* published on 20 March: 'The State may determine what it considers to be legal but, in a Christian country, it is for the Church to say what is right or wrong ... [The new constitution] now controls the lives and destinies of all Rhodesians ... I consider that the men who framed that document are the real terrorists in this country. Remember, physical violence or physical terrorism is not the only kind there is. Moral violence or moral terrorism is as real but it is a much more terrible thing ... the crowning insult, while paying lip-service to a Bill of Rights ... "no court of law shall inquire into or pronounce upon the validity of any law on the ground that it is inconsistent with the Declaration of Rights".'[4]

Both the World Council of Churches and the British Council of Churches passed resolutions in support of the church leaders in Rhodesia. Garfield found 'hope and joy' in 'the attitude of the churches at the moment ... we have been quite amazed at their unanimity', he told Mrs Moira Symons of Hope Fountain Mission. 'The secret is that the African people are beginning to let their voice be heard and it is significant that their voice is heard in this way through the churches ...'[5]

One voice that would not be raised in Rhodesia in future was Bishop Skelton's. His departure – due to 'pressing family responsibilities' – was a loss to the Church in Rhodesia (and particularly the Anglican Church), to the struggle against Smith, and to the Todds personally, for he had been a great friend, colleague and supporter. Garfield told the Bishop: 'We will specially miss you for you were one of the few that could be truly depended upon: no histrionics but great perception and admirable courage.'[6] To Garfield, Bishop

---

2   Item 70/30, Minutes of the CCR AGM, 4.3.70, MS.1086/3/2, Todd Papers, NAZ.
3   Skelton, 1985, pp. 107–8.
4   Rhodesian Constitution, Chap. VII, Part I, 84.
5   GT/Moira Symons, 25.5.70, MS.1082/4/1, Todd Papers, NAZ.
6   GT/Bishop Kenneth Skelton, 1.6.70, MS.1082/4/2, Todd Papers, NAZ.

The Republic of Rhodesia – 1970

Skelton wrote: 'Your friendship meant more to me than I can say.'[7]

***

On 10 June, there was a general election in Rhodesia. Again, the RF won all the white seats. The moderate Centre Party contested sixteen white and eight black seats, winning seven of the latter. New rules meant that Dr Palley could not stand at Highfield. The Government's strategy of turning African chiefs into their people's political leaders took off with the opening of the new multiracial Senate early in June. On the 11th, the state of emergency was extended for a further year. On 16 June, Lardner-Burke reported that at the beginning of 1970 there were 148 detainees – 'hard-core subversives'[8] – but the figure had been reduced the previous day to 147 by the death in detention, after three days in a coma from untreated diabetes, of Leopold Takawira, Shamuyarira's 'Lion of Zimbabwe'.[9]

On 3 September, the WCC announced the first grants to eighteen groups, including US$7,000 each to ZAPU and ZANU – and brought a renewed outcry in Britain and Rhodesia against the Programme to Combat Racism. *The Chronicle* reported a WCC spokesman as saying: 'We have assurance in writing from the groups concerned ... These groups all have social welfare programmes such as childcare and help for mothers, and that is where the money will be used.'[10]

Garfield told the *Sunday Mail*: 'No Christian wishes to see force used but a growing number of members of world churches held that the violence being done to the spirit of the black man in South Africa and Rhodesia is intolerable and that it must be resisted ... The aid is being given for social welfare programmes, not for armaments, and, in fact, if it were for arms, the total is so small it would hardly make a rifle's difference.'[11]

***

Cynthia had returned to Rhodesia in 1969 and now was to marry Derrick Edge, a former policeman with a four-year-old daughter, Kim, from a previous marriage. They would make their home at Hokonui, with Derrick becoming Garfield's assistant – ultimately to take over from him. On 21 November, Cynthia and Derrick were married by Garfield in the Dadaya Church with Kim by their side. For a few short years, Hokonui Ranch was home to three generations, giving great happiness to them all.

---

7 Bishop Kenneth Skelton/GT, 30.8.70, MS.1082/2/4, Todd Papers, NAZ.
8 *Rhodesia Herald*, 17.6.70.
9 Shamuyarira, 1965, p. 18.
10 *The Chronicle*, 5.9.70.
11 *Sunday Mail*, 10.9.70.

The historian and writer, Robert Blake, writes of a visit to Hokonui at this time: 'I was enchanted by [Todd's] intelligence, kindness and humour, and by his intriguing combination of other-worldliness and realism'. Blake quotes part of a conversation with Garfield: 'It has been my ideal in politics all my life to see that no one should be handicapped by the colour of his skin and that advancement should be possible on merit to any position irrespective of race ... But how can one expect the Europeans to give up all this when they haven't got to. Living as we do, all of us here are guilty; but I sometimes think it is asking for a generation of white saints to hope that they will voluntarily abandon what they hold ... You asked about the crisis of 1958. Well, I was very angry at the time and I do not believe in giving up ... but I can see the point of view of Ellman-Brown and Co. They were convinced that I would lose them the next election, and they were probably right, you know ...'[12]

Norman Harris was another visitor to Hokonui. He was a New Zealander gathering material for a book about fellow-countrymen who had made their name abroad. When the book was published, there was a 30-page chapter on Garfield, entitled 'A Man for Our Season'.[13] More than anyone else who has written of Garfield, Harris captured his manner and speech in everyday life and conversation; the ranch, its activities and problems, the whole 'feel' of life at Hokonui.

Harris writes: 'The doors on to the patio are left wide open; the music of the Eroica Symphony and the Emperor concerto, of Berlioz and Rachmaninov, sweeps out into the warm African night ... [Garfield] sat at ease, very much at ease, his glass of Coca Cola on his knee, his hands wrapped around the glass. Farmer's hands. Grey wavy hair parted just off centre ... A face in which one could see Scots blood – and see the New Zealander too ...

'"Ingenuous and guile-less that I was," he says rather tersely, "I went into parliament thinking that I was going to tell them all what was happening, and that they'd be glad to know. But they didn't want to know." He speaks of his great love for Rhodesia, for the country – this Africa – and the people ...

'Perhaps people are not used to seeing a man so close to those around him. He is indeed so obviously close and affectionate, to anyone, and especially to his family ... "We are very close. My wife and I, you see, for thirteen years we were the only two whites ... We've got a bit selfish and perhaps too self-satisfied, having been together for so many years, it just grows that way. All we need now is each other." He does, however, have close friends among Africans ... He will not brook the argument that there is some form of mental barrier between the

12 Blake, 1977, pp. 317–18.
13 Harris, 1971, pp. 150–80.

races. "Differences, yes, especially of background, but not barriers …"

'His own weaknesses? "Lack of diligence. Stickability … People have said I've been dictatorial – I suppose there must be something in it if that is so … From the point of view of regrets … we regret the arrogance that we had in the first years in Africa and that perhaps we haven't lost yet." He states that his passion is not simply for the African person but for Rhodesia … Was there a time when Africa suddenly took a hold? "The day we arrived, I think. For months we kept on saying, isn't this marvellous, how wonderful – so much of interest every day, the need of the people. It was all too glorious …"

'A last question: Does he consider his day-to-day life a happy one? "Oh yes. Extremely happy. I remember being told by my father of how my grandfather at Waikiwi in Invercargill, having set up a manufacturing business and having a very pleasant old house and a nice big orchard and wide lawn, on his golden wedding day, with his wife on his arm, looked around his not very affluent estate, but nevertheless said, 'I can't believe that God has blessed me so greatly.' And as a child I thought that was awfully nice, when you're old to feel that way … Well, I've felt that way for a very long time."'

***

A letter Garfield wrote to Grace for her birthday continues this theme: 'If the country were normal one could almost plan ahead and map out our days, our work, our money … We may not have built an Empire but I believe we can give God thanks that we have established a home – a lovely home in a beautiful garden … In a way we have achieved but in other ways – with both our lives and our home, perhaps we have come to the point of harvest – a point where we may be able to offer more to our three children, their children – and to the people around. If leisure is possible it must be spent in love.'[14]

---

14 GT/JGT, 1.4.70, MS.1082/3/1, Todd Papers, NAZ.

74

AN ANGLO–RHODESIAN SETTLEMENT? – 1971

'I know that my future lies with Patriotism, with Africa and with her people of whom I wish to be one.'

Garfield Todd

The year 1971 began badly for Rhodesia's remaining liberals: the multiracial Cold Comfort Farm Society was banned in January, and on 1 February Guy Clutton-Brock was deported. In March, his wife, Molly, returned to Britain. The farm was confiscated.

***

By April, Garfield reckoned Hokonui Ranch could be left to the combined care of Judith and Derrick Edge, allowing Grace and himself to take a long holiday in Britain, Paris and Greece. They had dreamed of this for years, all Grace's reading nourishing her desire year by year. They began with a Greek island cruise, and then it was 'beautiful' Delphi. Grace told Judith: 'Everywhere there are spring flowers and the song of birds and everywhere the stupendous view. ... the trip has been lovely for us ... There is snow on Mt Parnassus.'[1] Later, Grace wrote: 'We saw and did enough ... to last a lifetime. But it has only whetted my appetite, especially for Greece.'[2] From Turkey, Garfield wrote of Istanbul: 'I have never imagined what the undisturbed dirt of centuries would look like but I have seen it in Istanbul.'[3]

Lord Malvern died on 7 May while the Todds were in Athens. The *Rhodesia Herald* published a tribute from Garfield: 'He had served with Lord Malvern for twelve years and was grateful to have known so well "a man whose ideals

---

1   JGT/JT, 8.5.71, MS.1082/3/3, Todd Papers, NAZ.
2   JGT/SP, 6.12.71.
3   GT/JT, 18.5.71, J. Todd Papers.

and honour were never in question. Lord Malvern had a great respect for the law and was true to his oath (as a Privy Councillor) to 'advise for the Queen's honour and public good without partiality ... to avoid corruption ... and to observe and do all that a good and true counsellor ought to do to his Sovereign Lord' ... Lord Malvern was a surgeon, family doctor, politician and farmer. Healing was his profession and good health for the community his objective. Farming became his great love but circumstances led him into politics and he gave Rhodesia twenty-five years of honourable service.'"[4]

On 9 June, Garfield attended the memorial service at St Martin-in-the-Fields Church, London (where, 32 years later, would be held a service of thanksgiving for the lives of Grace and himself). Bishop Kenneth Skelton preached – he, too, quoted Malvern's oath as a Privy Councillor, and spoke of Malvern's 'paternalism', not 'outrageous ... a generation ago'. He said: 'What was significant was his willingness to admit readily the necessity of adjusting his views in a developing situation ... He was able, even in old age and infirmity, to see the need of change far more clearly than his fellow-citizens and was not afraid to say so. Nearly twenty years ago he warned that to try to maintain white supremacy in Southern Rhodesia could be done only by "a police state in perpetuity".'[5]

***

Garfield was still heavily involved in the affairs of the Christian Council of Rhodesia, whose fears about the consequences of the Land Tenure Act were being fulfilled with the removal not only of the Tangwena people from their ancestral lands on Gaeresi Ranch, Inyanga, but also of 5,000 people from their ancestral lands in the Stapleford Forest near Umtali. Soon thousands would be evicted from the (Methodist) Epworth Mission, near Salisbury; then it was the turn of the Roman Catholic Chishawasha Mission. 'Many people know no other home than the mission land or the "European" land on which their families have lived often for several generations. We cannot accept the description of such as "squatters".'[6] The Tangwena people finally went into Mozambique – where they were a great help to Rhodesian guerrillas who fled over the border.

Garfield had completed the building project at Dadaya, and he spoke at the opening of the new Science block. He afterwards told Jack Grant: 'When I looked at those young people I wondered really how much longer they will accept our "white" domination'.[7]

---

4   *Rhodesia Herald*, 8.6.71.
5   Bishop K. Skelton, Address at the Service of Thanksgiving for Lord Malvern, 9.6.71, TPPC.
6   *MOTO*, 2.10.71.
7   GT/Jack Grant, 19.10.71, MS.1082/4/11, Todd Papers, NAZ.

A general election in Britain had brought the Conservatives back to power. The new Prime Minister, Mr Edward Heath, was determined to get 'the Rhodesian problem' out of the way before he began negotiating Britain's entry into the European Common Market. British commercial and industrial interests were also pressing for a solution. The Foreign Secretary, Sir Alec Douglas-Home, undeterred by the failure of the *Tiger* and *Fearless* talks, was prepared to explore once more the possibility of settlement negotiations with Smith.

In November, the *Guardian* featured an article by Richard Gott, who had recently visited Hokonui. 'Garfield Todd thinks there will be a settlement between Britain and Rhodesia. "If there is, my hope is that it will mean something new, a new situation ... there must be an opening of doors, a new chance for the Africans to assert themselves." I sense that he is disappointed that the Africans have so far failed to do more. When we discussed the Zimbabwe nationalist movements he said he was disgusted with the way the people outside had behaved themselves – always quarrelling ...'[8]

Sir Alec repeated his statement that there would be no going back on the five principles. But Peter Jenkins, writing in the *Guardian* on 10 November, reckoned Sir Alec's 'chances of success' were 'exceedingly slim ... In fact, there is virtually no hope of a settlement ... the five principles simply will not stretch to accommodate Mr Smith. Majority rule means majority rule, not a never-never parity ... There is no principled or honourable settlement to be made with Rhodesia. There never was and there probably never will be.'

On the same day, *The Times* printed a letter from Lord Acton and Garfield: 'The British Government has not grasped the fundamental truths about Rhodesia. The white Rhodesians are not prepared to accept majority rule ever. The black Rhodesians do not want independence under a Rhodesian Front Government ... To avoid violence, Britain's duty is to persuade the whites to change their opinions or leave the country ... In a 1971 white Rhodesian context, no settlement, tragically, could be honourable.'[9]

A very significant remark of Sir Alec's to Garfield at this time was quoted by the latter at the Tübingen Festival, in Germany, in 1983: 'When I heard him say that each time Britain negotiated with Mr Smith they had to make further concessions to him I knew the Mission would fail, for success depended upon concessions being made to the blacks, not to the whites.'[10]

---

8   *Guardian*, 9.11.71.
9   *The Times*, Lord Acton and GT letter, 10.11.71.
10 GT, Tübingen Festival, 28.5.1983, TPPC.

An Anglo–Rhodesian Settlement? – 1971

At 11.00 a.m. on 24 November, the British Foreign Secretary and the Prime Minister of the rebellious Republic of Rhodesia signed an agreement. When Garfield heard this, he asked: 'Which has survived, the Five Principles or Smith?'[11] It would, however, have to pass a test of acceptability by the people of Rhodesia – this 'principle' alone survived amid the shattered fragments of the other four. The settlement proposals would now be put to the people of Rhodesia as a whole by a Commission under the chairmanship of Lord Pearce.

Lord Alport's significant reaction was quoted in the *Sun*: 'The only solution in the long run will be for the Africans to find their own way of achieving power in Africa. And the methods which they use are not going to be the neatly balanced constitutional procedures that are included in these present proposals.'[12]

Garfield's reaction, having studied the proposals, was: 'I would not recommend them even to myself.' And immediately he wrote to Judith: 'This is it! ... For the first time in the history of Rhodesia the future – or at least the next step – can be turned down or acquiesced to by the African people. This is simply not recognised by the whites, nor is it yet beginning to be appreciated by blacks ...

'We [must] also get people to appreciate the fact that despite the readiness of whites to accept the terms – it will be beyond them if the African people say NO ... What must be done is to clarify the issue and then bring maximum pressure to bear on government ... Of course there are problems for there is no machinery for getting such things across but we now have a chance to get some movement among the people – and we must do all that is possible.'[13]

The government issued a White Paper containing the proposals, first in English; later in Shona and Sindebele.

Judith returned home. She and her father devoted all their energies to widespread dissemination and discussion of the terms in the White Paper. They spoke at meetings whenever invited, largely in the Shabani-Belingwe area. Garfield arranged with *MOTO* for the magazine to print a page in each issue explaining the proposals simply in English, Shona and Sindebele to counter government propaganda.

Grace wrote: 'Britain has left too much to the good faith of the Government here, and who has faith in these men? ... And there we shall be, all 5 million Africans, and the white minority, outside the Commonwealth and cut off from

---

11 GT/A.
12 *Sun*, 29.11.71.
13 GT/JT, 27.11.71, J. Todd Papers.

Britain. When UDI was declared, little did we imagine that Britain would in time deal with rebels, and, as Wilson said at the time, "legalise the loot" … Judith said Lord Alport's statements had been superb. Not EVERYBODY thinks Gar a felon!'[14]

---

14 JGT/SP, 6.12.71, TPPC.

75

Prison – 1972

'The secret of happiness is liberty, and the secret of liberty is courage.'

Pericles, 495–429 BC

On 15 December 1971, Garfield attended a meeting of the Christian Council of Rhodesia Executive. They considered a British Council of Churches' report on the White Paper; a report of the delegation which interviewed the Foreign Secretary; and a paper, *Think Again*, which had been prepared by its own National Affairs Committee, of which he was a member. It was subsequently published by the Mambo Press in Gwelo as a special supplement to the magazine *MOTO* of 18 December – 'Time of Decision'.

Joshua Nkomo in Gonakudzingwa got in touch with the recently released Josiah Chinamano to set up a front organisation to co-ordinate African opposition. On 16 December, the African National Council was launched, with Bishop Abel Muzorewa, of the American Methodist Episcopal Church, to head it. From first to last, this was a David-and-Goliath affair, as the new ANC was opposed by the army and police, the Government's wide-ranging security laws, and its control over political meetings, the press, radio and TV. Already Goliath was at work, through all its channels, particularly in the rural areas, telling the people how advantageous were the proposals. Two hundred ANC applications for meetings in Tribal Trust Lands were turned down by Government authorities. 'Normal political activity' throughout the testing period had been promised – and, said the cynics, 'normal political activity' was what they got.

In Bulawayo, 'a boisterous but peaceful crowd of nearly 1,000 crammed into the 500-seat Stanley Hall, Makokoba, to hear Mr Todd … a greater number surrounded the hall'.[1] They heard him denounce the proposals as 'basically unacceptable because, while they are signed by a Douglas-Home and a Smith they are not signed by a Shumba or a Moyo or an Nkomo. The only document which we could accept is one agreed between the present administration and representatives of the African people and then ratified by Her Majesty's Government.'[2]

***

Early in January 1972, the first members of the Pearce Commission arrived at the Victoria Falls Hotel. On 11 January, Lord Pearce arrived – and there were serious riots at the Shabanie Mine as a result of inept handling by the mine authorities of a strike by 400 Africans. One man was shot dead, others were injured, and there was extensive damage to mine township buildings. When Garfield heard the news, he rushed into Maglas to check on the safety of his employees at the eating house, which he found undamaged, the employees locked inside. They let Garfield in – and, as they sat talking, he became aware of noise outside and found a dozen or so strikers surrounding his car, singing, dancing and washing it with a bucket of water and their hands.

There were outbreaks of violence in various places in the Midlands; on the 17th, police used tear gas to break up a crowd of more than 5,000. In all, fourteen Africans were killed and many wounded by police. By the end of that day, Garfield records in his draft autobiography, he thought he and Judith 'had done all that lay within our power to secure a "NO" vote', and the following day they went to their last meeting. By the end of that day, Superintendent Tomlinson of the BSAP served them with detention orders signed by D. W. Lardner-Burke, Minister of Law and Order:

> 1. You are hereby notified that it appears to me that it is expedient in the interests of public safety or public order to make an Order against you in terms of subsection (1) of section 16 of the Emergency Powers (Maintenance of Law and Order) Regulations, 1970.
> 2. The making of this Order is based on a belief that you are likely to commit, or to incite the commission of, acts in Rhodesia which would endanger the public safety, or disturb or interfere with the maintenance of public order.
> 3. NOW, THEREFORE, in terms of subsection (1) of section 16 ... I do hereby order that you shall be detained by being kept in the place described in the Schedule to this Order until the revocation or expiry of the Declaration of a Public Emergency in Rhodesia or until this Order is revoked or varied.

---

1 *The Chronicle*, 11.1.72.
2 GT, Makokoba, 10.1.72, MS.1082/4/11, Todd Papers, NAZ.

4. Under the provisions of subsection (1) of section 50 of the aforesaid Regulations, this Order shall come into force immediately it is delivered or tendered to you, but you have the right to object and to make representations in writing to me within seven days after the Order has been delivered or tendered to you stating the reason or reasons why you consider that the Order should be revoked.

5. In addition, you are advised that, in terms of subsection (1) of section 30 of the aforesaid Regulations, you may at any time within three months beginning on the date on which your detention was ordered, apply in writing to me for your case to be reviewed by the Review Tribunal established by section 25 of the aforesaid Regulations, and in any such application you should state the reasons why you consider that the detention order should be reviewed.

Given under my hand at Salisbury this 18th day of January 1972.

Schedule: Gatooma Prison.

Judith's order varied only in the 'Schedule' – 'Marandellas Prison'. The police searched the house and cars, showing no interest in Garfield's six assorted firearms. When the police learned that most of his papers were at the Bannockburn house, they took Garfield and Judith there – which gave Grace the opportunity to telephone Peter Niesewand of the *Guardian*, in Salisbury. Within minutes, the news was on the BBC – and round the world. At Bannockburn, the police found that Garfield's extensive 'archive' would take some time to search ...

Garfield, Judith and the police returned to the homestead for dinner, the family in the dining room, the police on the stoep. Afterwards, as Grace saw Garfield and Judith into one of the police cars, she said: 'I am very proud of you both.'[3] Judith writes: 'The memory I took with me was of her standing in the headlights of the police cars, strong and brave, waving us goodbye.' The police convoy left, first for Gatooma 200 miles away, and then a further 130 miles to Marandellas. Grace returned to the house – to take the first of scores of telephone calls from TV, radio and press reporters.

***

Grace told friends: 'After they had gone, the head of the Security Branch, Superintendent Tomlinson, stayed on with assistants and over the next 24 hours they searched wardrobes, cupboards, suitcases, offices, storerooms, cars and in the end took away nearly 10,000 papers and documents for examination ... When I was handed the signed list of files and documents "seized", I asked when I could expect them to be returned and the reply was, "Those papers required

---

3   Todd, 1972, p. 101.

for the case against your husband and your daughter will be retained and the others will be returned to you as soon as possible." I replied, "in that case, they will all be returned".' All were returned.[4]

***

Four hours after leaving Hokonui, the convoy reached Gatooma Prison. Judith later wrote: 'I watched my father walking over to the prison block, visible through the high fence of barbed wire. He was tired and stooping and his white hair shone under the lights …'[5]

It was 'one o'clock in the morning of January 19, 1972,' Garfield writes in his autobiography. 'Mr Seward of the Special Branch introduced me to the Superintendent. We shook hands.' Garfield was horrified to find he was to be fingerprinted: 'I have done nothing criminal. I'm not charged with any offence.'[6] 'There was a space for "signature of the accused" but before Mr Seward handed me the pen he reached forward and put a line through "of the accused". I was surprised, moved, by his action … Seward apparently did not think of me as a law-breaker and probably the jail superintendent did not shake hands with each new prisoner, so he too did not consider me a criminal …'

Garfield was allowed to take only pyjamas and toilet things from his suitcase, and was searched before he left the office. He was then taken 'through more gates and across a wide concrete courtyard. We stopped at an iron gate in the wall. Mr Edwards produced keys, released the two locks and we entered a tiny courtyard. More locks and I entered my cell. There was a prison bed with a coir pad, blankets, sheets and pillow with broad black arrows stamped on it. Mr Edwards explained that the single dim electric light high in the cell roof was controlled from the courtyard … I was in solitary confinement but, as the Government's embarrassment grew in the face of overseas criticism, it was denied that I was held in solitary confinement: I was just "segregated from other prisoners" …

'I was deeply concerned for Judith, now in her cell at Marandellas prison, but more especially was I concerned for Grace … If ever we needed strength it was now and I sought quietness and confidence for my family and friends … I found prison life rough. However, I slept soundly but when I woke in the morning and my eyes focused on the barred openings which served as windows I found it extremely difficult to believe that I was in jail in the country I have loved and served for so many years. It is not easy for a person who has a devoted respect

---

4   JGT/'Friends', 8.3.72, MS.396/1/21, Todd Papers, NAZ.
5   Todd, 1972, pp. 102–3.
6   GT/A.

for the law and who will not contemplate violence, to accommodate himself to the fact that he is in prison. Also, if one is to go to prison it is much too late to begin at 64! ... But if I was shaken, what about Judith, what about Grace? Judith was 28 ...

'I could imagine something of the frightful strain that Grace, at Hokonui, would have to endure ... in all her daily business contacts she would face unpleasantness, if not open enmity from many whites, for most would accept that Todd and his daughter Judith were traitors to their race ... Despite all that Derrick could do, Grace would be carrying an enormous load of work and responsibility ...

'I was shaken by what the Government had done to ME and to MY family, but in my reaction there was arrogance ... in Mr Smith's opinion we deserved to suffer with the African people, for, with the people, we were fighting for justice and against race privilege and authoritarian rule ... If I were black, this imprisonment might go on for years ... As I was white it would not be bad for me for even in adversity there are privileges for whites. I have benefited at every turn from being a member of the white community and I share the guilt of my fellow whites ...

'The little courtyard each morning was unlocked and added to my living space by the warder ... On two occasions I was surreptitiously visited. The first time it was just fingers slipped through the peephole in greeting. On the second occasion there was the sound of frenzied sweeping just outside the door, followed by silence. Then a whispered, "Are you all right, sir?" Next morning ... the peephole was covered by a steel plate. That put me entirely on my own.'[7]

Garfield had been allowed to take his typewriter with him, and over 20 and 21 January he wrote his first letter, from 'State Prison, Gatooma'.[8] 'Dearest Family, How often I have addressed letters with this phrase ... So, it was a cell ... and for a cell, better than many a place I have stayed in during the years I went around the schools, especially those in the low-veld. My room is 13' by 13' ... There is a bathroom across the courtyard where there is a full-size bath and a basin with cold water ... Judith, who patently knows more about prisons than I do, advised me to take plenty of cash. I thought I had a little but found that I was wrong. Actually, I need it only for a daily paper which I am allowed. As I have no money at all Superintendent Edwards lets me have his the next morning ... For me the news of the day is that I am to be visited this afternoon by Mr Smedley and Sir Glyn Jones [respectively Secretary-General of the Pearce Commission, and former Governor of Nyasaland]. I have a clean change of

7 GT/A.
8 GT/Family, 20–21.1.72, MS.1082/3/3, Todd Papers, NAZ.

clothing and my shoes are out being cleaned. My whole establishment has been swept and polished ... I have arranged my bed so that it is as good as a lounge and the happy thought of putting in my own cherished pillow was marvellous ...

'When it rains, as it may soon do again, the drops come right into my room from the open courtyard and I find this pleasant – the view of the sky is quite spoiled by the steel netting which roofs the little courtyard – but to be "outside" is still pleasant ... This cell is really a summer habitation because there is no glass in the windows ... Yesterday afternoon was good. I was so pleased to meet both of these men again ... We had a grand talk and they have promised to come again before they leave Rhodesia. The last prison visit Glyn Jones made in SR was to call on Banda in Gwelo!' Garfield borrowed ten shillings for newspapers from Sir Glyn. Mr Smedley told Judith: 'For someone who when I had last seen him had been prime minister I thought he bears incarceration with cheerfulness and fortitude'.[9] Later, Lord Pearce visited Garfield with Mr Smedley. Garfield was shocked to learn that Josiah Chinamano and his wife, Ruth, had also been arrested that day and were similarly 'detained', i.e. imprisoned. Ruth's conditions were so bad that she did not even have a bed.

'Grace came to see me and I walked across the yard where many African prisoners were at their chores ... I entered the superintendent's small office and there was Grace who came straight to my arms ... the superintendent did not exist. A precious half-hour together and then back to my cell for another week, but warmly thankful.'[10]

'Grace was full of confidence, armed with many papers to discuss and her usual happy self', Garfield told a friend.[11] The cost to Grace of appearing 'her usual happy self' can be gauged from a letter she wrote to her sister a few weeks later: 'Strange that throughout this period it was with almost a sense of relief that I drove off from Gatooma prison. Deeply as I longed to see Gar and be with him, it was always hateful. To be met at the gate of the "cage" by the Superintendent; then the great outer door of the prison unlocked at our approach, and taken to the Superintendent's office. There I would wait for Gar to be brought from some inner confine, another grille gate would be unlocked and he would be escorted in by a European warder. The superintendent remained throughout. Each time I drove away from prison in near despair, yet with relief as of an ordeal endured.'[12]

'You can live in a country where it's legal to detain people without trial,

---

9   H. Smedley/JT, 21.10.72, MS.390/6/9, Todd Papers, NAZ.
10 GT/A.
11 GT/'Mona', 22.1.72, MS.1082/1/18, Todd Papers, NAZ.
12 JGT/EB, 6.3.72, Mrs Collins' Papers.

but when it actually happens to somebody in your own family, you can hardly believe it,' Grace told the NZTV Unit in 1991.[13] 'I couldn't really believe that we, who had been law-abiding citizens all our lives, could find ourselves in the situation. I didn't at the beginning know that detention means a prison cell.'

After Grace's first visit, Garfield wrote to her and Judith: 'This has been a great day because it was the first visit from Grace. Marvellous to see you ... and wonderful to know that all is well at home.'[14] Grace had brought all the letters she had received, but later this was forbidden, so she simply listed the names of the correspondents for Garfield and Judith.

From Gatooma, Grace went on to visit Judith, who was 'in a far more pleasant place than I could have hoped', she told Garfield.[15] After this first visit, Grace's weekly 640-mile round trip would take her first to Judith, then to Garfield, staying the night in Salisbury with Jack and Ida Grant. Years later, she told Ida: 'I have much to remember with thankfulness but my thoughts always return to the haven of kindness and understanding you provided.'[16]

'I want you to try to shed all your worries and anxieties about us all', Grace told Garfield. 'I am sorry that when I come for that brief time to see you I must bring you all my troubles and the complexities of the work. But gradually I will get to know it ... take this time, which I hope will be short, as a mixture of a discipline, in the way of using your time, and a rest, enforced but nevertheless valuable ... [the letters] speak of you with such admiration and pride and love. I wish you could read them, for it would fortify you to do so as it does me ... Put all your concern and anxiety for us – and for all others – into the hands of God and commit yourself to Him also, darling. Let the burden go. Relax and even ENJOY [sic] this experience and the rest. Tell me if you can how you occupy your mind during the long night hours which must be the worst.'[17] The light bulb high in the ceiling of Garfield's cell was too weak for him to read during the early days of his incarceration, but when this was replaced with a stronger bulb he experienced again the joy of reading – Alan Paton's biography of Hofmeyr, Alport's *Sudden Assignment*, R. A. Butler's *The Art of the Possible*, Bethge's *Bonhoeffer*, and the New English Bible, where Garfield found 'special pleasure' in reading the apocryphal books. 'I found so much of interest in earth and heaven, so much wisdom, earthy and divine.'[18]

---

13 NZTV, unpublished transcript.
14 GT/JGT and JT, 21.1.72, MS.1082/3/3, Todd Papers, NAZ.
15 JGT/GT, 21.1.72, MS.1082/3/3, Todd Papers, NAZ.
16 JGT/I. Grant, 26.11.84, MS.1082/3/6, Todd Papers, NAZ.
17 JGT/GT, n.d., MS.1082/3/3, Todd Papers, NAZ.
18 GT/A.

When Garfield was allowed his radio, his 'conditions were vastly improved', he writes. 'My prison walls were breached and voices from all over the world spoke in my cell. I have always appreciated the BBC but now I was able to share with millions who have, over the past 50 years, breathed the "freedom" which comes from London. There was a great deal of news of Rhodesia ... I smiled to myself as I lay night after night hearing Grace given publicity on a world scale such as had never been afforded to Judith or me. Day by day she spoke of the mounting evil of the Smith regime and of injustice to the people at large and to her own family. I was deeply moved, knowing something of what this was costing her. Smith thought he had silenced opposition from the Todd family but, far more effectively than Judith or I could have mounted it, came a withering attack as Grace took her stand demanding justice for the people ...'[19]

Grace told Judith later: 'I was mercifully given a measure of strength and also of calmness and peace, which certainly did not come from within myself. I know one rises to challenge and a crisis, but this was beyond that. It enabled me to face those long days of driving and travelling, face officials and a hostile Bank Manager, even to undertake those TV interviews ... I was afraid and tired and troubled, but I am certain that what upheld me during those days of great strain was the fact – not the knowledge – that people were praying for me and for you both.'[20]

Garfield received the *Sunday Times* of 23 January, which contained Judith's 'diary', sent off just before she was arrested. He writes: 'The front page spread was so enormous that Mr Edwards failed to see it. I walked on air as I read Judith's faithful account of the events of the past six weeks as we had worked, not to wreck negotiations but to find a settlement which might prove to be a solution to our immense problems.'[21]

Grace wrote to Lardner-Burke protesting against the continued detention of her husband and daughter, stressing the consequences for Garfield's health of his conditions.[22] Her second letter two days later was more urgent: 'My fears for my husband have been realised. On Wednesday of this week he suffered an attack of his chest complaint. He was seen by a doctor[23] and made light of it while I was with him. But ... even if care is taken it will be some weeks before he is well again. I write therefore to offer my request

---

19   GT/A.
20   JGT/JT, 17.3.74, J. Todd Papers.
21   GT/A.
22   JGT/Minister L/O, 3.2.72, MS.1082/5/12, Todd Papers, NAZ.
23   Dr Mavros, son-in-law of Ben Fletcher.

to you that my husband should come home.'²⁴ Neither letter received any acknowledgement.

***

Before Garfield had even reached Gatooma, the British Foreign Secretary had wired the High Commission in Salisbury for the full facts of the arrests, which he would need to answer questions in the House of Commons.²⁵ Smith assured Sir Alec Douglas-Home, through the British Residual Mission in Salisbury, 'that the reasons ... were not based on their publicly stated opposition to the settlement proposals ... solely on considerations of security and the maintenance of law and order in Rhodesia. Recent events in Gwelo have clearly shown that without the maintenance of law and order it is not possible for the Peace [sic] Commission to carry out its task effectively'. It was, however, 'possible that criminal charges may be laid after current investigations had been completed'.²⁶ The Foreign Secretary sent the head of the Rhodesia Department at the FCO, Mr Philip Mansfield, to Rhodesia 'with a warning to Mr Ian Smith that any chances of a settlement are now touch-and-go'.²⁷

As in 1965, so in 1972: representatives of the overseas press were gathered in Salisbury and they gave Garfield's arrest the widest publicity. Again, Smith came in for strong criticism, Lord Pearce stating: 'If people are detained simply to silence them, then even in existing conditions, it is not allowing normal political activity.'²⁸

***

Garfield had been very concerned for Judith, and this, together with the onset of his chest complaint, stopped him writing letters for a few days; but by 2 February he was back at his typewriter. He had reason for his concern, however, for Judith had embarked on a hunger-strike in protest against her 'illegal detention'. Peter Niesewand telephoned the news to Grace.²⁹ Grace told Judith her action was 'terrible news ... I haven't any words for my concern, but also my love ... I shall come to you as soon as they will let me, darling ... think of us. I must try to see Dad, too.'³⁰ As a result of her hunger-strike, Judith was moved to Chikurubi High Security Prison near Salisbury for three weeks.

---

24 JGT/Minister L/O, 5.2.72, MS.1082/5/12, Todd Papers, NAZ.
25 Tel. no. 86 18.1.(1972), File CP.14/6, FCO 36/1266 (Part A), Public Records Office, Kew.
26 Ibid.
27 *Daily Mail*, 20.1.72.
28 *The Times*, 21.1.72.
29 *Guardian*, 7.2.72.
30 JGT/JT, n.d., J. Todd Papers.

The anguish Judith's hunger-strike caused her parents was almost overpowering. To Garfield, ill in his cell and already desperately anxious about her and Grace; and to Grace, not only also desperately anxious about Judith and Garfield but also burdened with the care of the ranch – and keeping the bank manager at bay – this news was the heaviest blow. The consequent withdrawal of all Judith's privileges meant Grace was not able to see her, which added to her and Garfield's distress. 'That was a terrible time', Grace said.[31] When Garfield heard Judith had gone on hunger-strike, he did so, too – 'in solidarity'. He made no announcement, not even telling Grace; he simply disposed of most of his meals down his cell's open WC.[32]

When Grace saw Garfield, she found him 'depressed, angry, and fearing that he would not survive the winter in gaol', Peter Niesewand wrote in the *Guardian*. 'The past three weeks have had a very bad effect on him.'[33] The Director of Prisons refused permission for Grace to visit Judith. At a press conference on 10 February, Smith, in reply to a question about the detainees from Peter Niesewand, said: 'We "are satisfied on the evidence before us at the moment that this is the most suitable way of dealing with the incredible state which existed in this country for a few weeks, when there was intimidation violence, rioting, looting, burning and in fact some people even lost their lives." He was asked if this meant he linked the four detainees with this state of affairs. Mr Smith replied: "That is correct. I don't say they are the only people responsible, but the action we took was because of the situation which existed."'[34]

When Grace visited Garfield after the press conference, his 'reaction to Mr Smith's charges was one of relief. At least he knew what they had in their minds. "Of course the charges are preposterous and now that Mr Smith has committed himself he will have to try and find proof of this. Of course no proof exists."'[35]

Grace sought the advice of Advocate Paddy Lloyd on the question of an appeal to the Review Tribunal, and Paddy visited Garfield. Superintendent Edwards at first refused to allow the customary private meeting of lawyer-and-client and only relented when Paddy agreed that a warder might 'observe' them out of earshot, to see that no messages were passed. The upshot of all the discussion was that 'ON NO ACCOUNT' (as Paddy instructed Grace) should either Garfield or Judith apply to the tribunal, which, though headed by a judge,

---

31 JGT/SP, TPPC.
32 *Hokonui Todd*, NZTV Film, 1992 transcript.
33 *Guardian*, 8.2.72.
34 *Guardian*, 11.2.72.
35 *Guardian*, 14.2.72.

did not comply with the safeguards of a normal trial and could only make recommendations to Lardner-Burke.

Lord Pearce protested to the Foreign Secretary, who in turn protested to Smith, 'that in the absence of any satisfactory explanation of the reasons for recent detentions, particularly those of Mr Todd and his daughter and of Mr and Mrs Chinamano, the inference must be that they were detained to inhibit the free expression of opinion ...'[36]

***

The cold wet weather that had contributed to Garfield's illness gave way to sun and warmth. This helped to restore his spirits and his health. On 12 February, he told Grace: 'I simply do not understand what has happened to me over the last ten days but neither in mind or body have I been anything like normal. I believe that my mind is clear and I suppose the basic trouble has been my chest and then Judith's hunger-strike which terribly concerned me.'[37]

Garfield wrote to Judith, also on the 12th: 'It has been so terribly distressing that Grace could not visit you ... The Superintendent tells me that you are ... back on ordinary diet. I am glad you have done this. I am especially glad because of the burden which Grace had to bear. She is wonderful when she is here but in the night I am sure that she has some difficult hours and I thought that it is right that we should not add to the minimum load which must be borne.'[38]

***

After six weeks in solitary confinement, Garfield and Judith were released into 'restriction' within 800 metres of the Hokonui homestead.

---

36 Alec Douglas-Home/IDS, 10.2.72, File PREM 15/1171 as amended by cable, 11.2.72, File CP.14/6, FCO 36/1266 (Part A), PRO, Kew.
37 GT/JGT, 12.2.72, MS.1082/3/3, Todd Papers, NAZ.
38 GT/JT, 12.2.72, J. Todd Papers.

76

THE PEARCE REPORT – 1972

'The excitement of the Pearce Commission was such that we have never seen before or since. For the first time in most people's lives they were allowed free political discussions.'

Grace Todd

'Health and humanitarian grounds' were the reasons given by the authorities for the change of place of detention. 'Could not the detention arrangements made now have been made at the beginning?' asked the *Rhodesia Herald*.[1] *The Times* reported: 'Lord Pearce said he was bound to infer that the detentions had been made to inhibit the free expression of opinion.' Mr Smith disagreed: the detentions 'were definitely linked with acts of intimidation and violence. Charges have still not been preferred against any of the four.'[2]

During detention at Hokonui Ranch, Garfield and Judith were not allowed to communicate 'by word of mouth, in writing or otherwise', with anyone outside the family, without the permission in writing of the protecting authority – Mr D. W. Wright of the BSAP in Gwelo.[3] Mr Wright was the soul of courtesy in his dealings with the Todds, and was sometimes more generous with his permits than Grace wished – but no permit was granted to any African visitor except the principal of Dadaya School, David Mukonoweshuro.

While the Todds had been preoccupied with the effects on their own lives of the 'test of acceptability', the Pearce Commissioners were quartering the country, interviewing hundreds and attending meetings of thousands. The Commissioners flew back to Britain on 11 March. Their report was expected at the end of April.

---

1   *Rhodesia Herald*, 23.2.72.
2   *The Times*, 23.2.72.
3   D. W. Wright/GT, 22.2.72, MS.1082/5/12, Todd Papers, NAZ.

The Pearce Report – 1972

***

Grace wrote on 24 March: 'Gar is far from well and I wished that he could have the quietness he needed … Hokonui continues to live up to its reputation for crises of some magnitude. In ourselves we are serenely happy to be together and only long for fewer interruptions and calls upon us.'[4] Garfield's sister Stella arrived from New Zealand that month. Garfield and Judith were now allowed to write non-political letters, freeing some of Grace's time. All the files and papers which were taken away by the Special Branch were returned on 6 April. On 3 April, Grace celebrated her 61st birthday, and on the 7th she and Garfield celebrated 40 years of marriage. For the first time, both Garfield's sisters were at the family dinner, along with Jack and Ida Grant. By 8 April, Grace could write: 'Garfield has good health once again and Judith is fine, but their own "happiness, despite detention without trial", is tempered by the knowledge that so many others remain in prison and some have been there without trial for more than eight years …'[5]

***

On 23 May, Sir Alec presented Lord Pearce's Report to the House of Commons. Simultaneously, the findings of the Commission were broadcast over the BBC and the Rhodesia Broadcasting Corporation. At Hokonui, the Todds listened with joy and gratitude to Lord Pearce's conclusion: 'We are satisfied on our evidence that the Proposals are acceptable to the great majority of Europeans. We are equally satisfied, after considering all our evidence including that on intimidation, that the majority of Africans rejected the Proposals. In our opinion the people of Rhodesia as a whole do not regard the Proposals as acceptable as a basis for independence.'[6]

Lord Pearce's conclusions regarding the detainees were contained in three paragraphs:

> 147. Detention of Mr and Miss Todd and Mr and Mrs Chinamano … We asked the Rhodesian authorities why they had been detained … They gave a categorical assurance that detention was not based on the Todds' publicly stated opposition to the Settlement Proposals, but solely on considerations of security and the maintenance of law and order …
>
> 148. On 7 February, in the absence of any … satisfactory explanation from the Rhodesian Government … the Commission must infer that the purpose of their detention is to inhibit the free expression of opinion …

---

4   JGT/SP, 24.3.72, TPPC.
5   JGT/'Friends', 8.4.72, TPPC.
6   Paragraph 420, Cmnd 4965, Chapter 13, p. 112.

149. ... although we are conscious that we may not have the full facts we feel compelled to infer that these detentions were an interference with normal political activities. But we do not think that they had any marked effect. Indeed, we are inclined to think that they were counter-productive.[7]

On the evening of this momentous day, Mr Smith made an angry and contemptuous statement on radio and television: 'When one reads this report, in spite of its naivety and ineptness, the only responsible conclusion that one can come to is that the answer should have been YES. Tragically ... the whole thing has landed up on the rocks, through their bungling of the test on which the British Government insisted, against our advice ... we shall govern firmly and that we shall not tolerate any attempt to disturb the peace and harmony to which, in very large measure, the country has returned since the departure of the Pearce Commission ... when you read this report you will share my disbelief that a British commission could reach a conclusion which is so unrealistic, contrary to the evidence in their own report, and so palpably against the interests of all Rhodesians and particularly of the Africans.'[8]

The *Rhodesia Herald* reported: 'Mr Smith described the Pearce Commission as a "group of foreigners, stumbling around" ... He believed 94% of the African population trusted the government. Asked how he knew 94% of Africans trusted the government, Mr Smith replied: "Well, because we understand the tribal system. We work with the tribal system, through the Chiefs Council, and we have a unanimous vote of support from the Chiefs Council. That is how we know ..."'[9]

The reasons for African rejection of the Proposals were principally 'mistrust of the intentions and motives of the Government': 'apprehension for the future'; 'resentment at what they felt to be the humiliations of the past and at the limitations of policies on land, education, and personal advancement'; 'as soon as Independence was recognised and sanctions revoked, a Government which had torn up previous constitutions would do so again'; the RF 'was committed to the perpetuation of white supremacy'; 'the guarantees against constitutional change were inadequate'; 'no African had been involved in the negotiations'; the 'time to majority rule was too indefinite and too long'. Previous speeches by Mr Ian Smith saying that there would be no African rule in his lifetime were constantly quoted. 'Most refused to accept statements by the British Government that there would be no further negotiations' (paras 311–17).

---

7   Pearce Report, Cmnd 4964, Chapter 6, pp. 39–40, paras 147–9.
8   *The Chronicle*, 24.5.72.
9   *Rhodesia Herald*, 26.5.72.

The Pearce Report – 1972

The Commission's examination of all allegations of intimidation was detailed and exhaustive – as detailed and exhaustive as had been the Rhodesian Government's 'dossier' on the subject. A further 'dossier', containing 'intimidation by Rhodesian authorities against Africans opposed to the settlement proposals', and prepared by 'a team of British lawyers', was also studied. The Report concludes: 'It was our considered view that, had there been no intimidation, there would still have been a substantial majority against the Proposals ... the Africans' rejection by a substantial majority was a genuine expression of opinion' (paras 411–18).

Whatever the shortcomings – and short-sightedness – of British politicians, on two occasions the members of British Commissions on Rhodesia gave Europeans the opportunity to change direction; but on both occasions – Lord Monckton's Commission in 1960 and Lord Pearce's in 1972 – the Rhodesians stubbornly refused to take the chance they were offered to turn away from the path of inevitable violence and bloodshed.

***

From Hokonui Ranch, Grace wrote: 'We are tremendously grateful that the answer has been unequivocal, grateful also for the paragraphs on the detainees ...'[10]

By early June, when the complete Report had reached Hokonui, Grace wrote another circular letter to friends: 'I have just read the 200-page "Pearce" Report. It marks an important milestone on the way to self-government by the people ... There seems to be just no hope when we face the "white" rejection of the findings. Yet real hope does lie in African reaction ... There is hope, too, in a paragraph from evidence given to the Commission by Mr Joshua Nkomo who has been detained without trial for eight years and still holds a position of supreme political leadership in the hearts of African people. He writes, "Finally we would like to emphasise to the Commission that we unreservedly reject these proposals because they do not satisfy universally accepted conditions of independence for all our people; they are racial and discriminatory, and we believe that if implemented they engender feelings of hostility between black and white citizens of our country and bring about bloodshed and untold human suffering. This must not be allowed to happen. We therefore appeal to you, Lord Pearce, to impress upon the British Government to abandon these proposals and summon a constitutional conference at which leaders of all sections of our population will take part ... We on our part are prepared to work resolutely for a constitutional settlement that will give peace and security to all citizens of our country irrespective of colour."'[11]

---

10   JGT/SP, n.d. [May 1972], TPPC.
11   JGT, 5.6.72, TPPC.

Early in July 1972, Lardner-Burke gave Judith permission to leave Rhodesia for London, but subject to her detention order remaining in force. Newspapers and magazines were still prohibited from mentioning her name. Judith left Hokonui on 13 July (Garfield's birthday), and was driven to Bulawayo by Cynthia and Derrick without a police escort.

While at the time Grace marvelled at Garfield's acceptance and apparent freedom from frustration, she later admitted: 'I think I was not aware during those years of how the enforced immobility fretted him'.[12] However, he could enjoy being at home with Grace; he could enjoy sitting on the stoep of an evening, admiring the beauty of the view, the sunset. He was happy to exchange the metal mesh roof of his cell courtyard for the glorious canopy of the Milky Way on Hokonui's velvet black nights. He listened to opera and Gregorian chants, to the Orpheus Choir and music from King's College Chapel, to *Joseph and the Amazing Technicolor Dreamcoat* and *Zorba the Greek*, to Mahler, Mozart, Beethoven, Rachmaninov and Vivaldi – and to the sounds of the bush around the house.

The 800 metres had been stretched on one side to take in the cattle dip (and correspondingly reduced on the other). He enjoyed being present there – the whole process, and the contact with the men and beasts. But this was the only place of work on the ranch he could go to: stores, petrol station, post office, butchery, eating house, slaughter-poll – all were out of bounds – as were the mission and the large school for which he was responsible. The office work only could be done from home.

He continued his reading, including Hans Küng, whose *On Being a Christian* contained words that would find an echo in Garfield's theology: 'He is a God who does not make empty promises for the hereafter nor trivialise the present darkness, futility and meaninglessness, but who himself in the midst of darkness, futility and meaninglessness invites us to the venture of hope.'

---

12   JGT/Pauls, 15.12.77, TPPC.

77

NORMAL RESTRICTION ORDER – 1972–4

'The last Prime Minister of Rhodesia able to state that during his term of office no person was killed by security forces, no person was detained without trial ... is detained under emergency powers taken by Mr Smith.'

Grace Todd

The Christian Council of Rhodesia re-elected Garfield to its Executive, as did the United College of Education, so the 'non-person' at Hokonui was not forgotten by his friends. This fact was gradually changing Garfield's mind about writing his memoirs, which became one of three major projects which he worked on during 1972–4; the other two were the building of a swimming pool and the raising and strengthening of the weir on the Ngezi River below the house, both ambitious construction projects being within his 800-metre restricted area. Garfield began with the pool, 'Pearce Pool'. The steep-sided rocky site presented great problems, but an excellent builder and two ranch workmen under Garfield's direction achieved this in time for an exceptionally hot and rainless summer. Grace told Judith in September: 'Only now ... does [Dad] realise – and I, too – how far from his normal self he has been all these months ... he is gay and teasing and happy. So don't WORRY ...'[1]

A major event towards the end of the year was the publication of Judith's book, *The Right to Say No*, dedicated: 'For my brave mother'. Grace told her she was 'greatly moved, delighted, proud, humbled'.[2] The book, the reviews of it and reactions to it, now became a major interest, and source of pride, to her parents.

1   JGT/JT, 7.9.72, J. Todd Papers.
2   JGT/JT, 12.12.72, ibid.

Garfield Todd: The End of the Liberal Dream in Rhodesia

In March 1973, Garfield began raising the weir below the house by four feet and, at the same time, building it up and broadening it to form a causeway which would allow cattle and people, and cars, to move across the Ngezi except when the river was in spate. 'Two water development people came to see the place the other day and came to lunch', Grace told Judith. 'They came with trepidation and no doubt reluctance and it is so interesting to see the thawing, the developing interest and eventually the friendliness which takes its place. What I would give to hear the conversations as they go on their way.'[3]

The months of great and unusual heat combined with little rain had brought the grass situation on the ranch to a critical point. In desperation, Garfield wrote to his Protecting Authority asking to be allowed to go to all the camps at certain hours over the next two weeks, and after that to be able to have each Monday and Tuesday morning from 6 until noon for camp visiting.[4] A month later came permission to do all he had asked for, until 31 October 1973.

'The permission for Gar to go about the Ranch on Monday and Tuesday mornings has made the most enormous difference to him. As you have guessed, just to be able to get into a car and drive off has destroyed so much of the mounting frustration. It has really been a terribly difficult year. The water in the Mtchingwe has now dried up and there is NO grass.' A most successful sale of 50 steers had cheered everyone up: 'Allan Ritson started them at sixty dollars and then had to give up as "he had neither the money nor the courage!"' [5]

***

By the end of 1972, ZANLA guerrilla activity had increased. They came across Rhodesia's rugged 760-mile-long border with Mozambique, with the help of FRELIMO – the Front for the Liberation of Mozambique – which was moving freely throughout that country. ZIPRA, the military wing of ZAPU, operated from Zambia against targets in western Matabeleland. On 21 December, guerrillas attacked Altena Farm, in the Centenary area 120 miles north of Salisbury.

A British counter-insurgency expert who made a private visit to Rhodesia at this time considered that the Rhodesian forces could contain the guerrilla war for, at most, another four years.[6] Grace's letters to Judith underline the growing seriousness of the situation: she writes of 'little hope for political relief ... the rising strains and hatreds because of woundings, killings, executions,

---

3   JGT/JT, 22.3.73, ibid.
4   GT/BSAP, 27.4.73, MS.1082/5/12, Todd Papers, NAZ.
5   GT/JT, 12.9.73, J. Todd Papers.
6   Private information.

unemployment'.⁷ She tells of a European counter hand in a Bulawayo store who was emigrating: 'This is my second spell in the valley this year and I'm not waiting.' And another: a friend of Paddy Fehrsen's (formerly Henderson) told Judith he was 'just back from his service in the valley and he told them that he could not stay as he could not take the treatment of the people in the valley by the troops'.⁸

Supremely cheering to the Todds was a visit from Robert Blake, whose book, *A History of Rhodesia*, was still in preparation. He brought the relevant chapter for Garfield to read and check. Grace wrote to Judith: 'From our point of view, excellent ... Blake's book is the first of real importance to deal with the "politics" of that period, and because of his standing and stature it is very important that the record should be clear. No historian of note following Blake could afford to ignore what he has written ... after years of calumny and misrepresentation and denigration, it gives us a wonderful feeling of relief and satisfaction to have this straight-forward account of what happened ... I am so happy for Dad ...'⁹

'Garfield says he could not have expected such a fair evaluation for fifty years, instead of 15 ... It is a matter of the most profound satisfaction to us as you may guess, and we are so happy, too, for the sake of all our loyal friends ... After the years of vilification this was a moment of great pride and satisfaction for us ...'¹⁰

Then came a letter from Bishop Donal Lamont, from Rome: 'Yesterday, I had a marvellous private audience with Pope Paul, during which I spoke of you. The Holy Father has asked me to assure you of his remembrance of you in prayer and has given me a lovely medallion of his pontificate as a sign of his admiration and respect. I hope to deliver it to you when I return to Rhodesia.'¹¹ Bishop Lamont never succeeded in getting a permit to visit the Todds, so he left the 'very beautiful bronze medallion ... "struck to commemorate the 11th year of Pope Paul's pontificate"' with Bishop Haene of Gwelo, who later brought it to Garfield. The accompanying message read: 'Given in private audience to the Right Reverend Donal R. Lamont O.Carm. with the request that it be delivered to the Honourable Garfield Todd. In making this gift and sending his good wishes the Holy Father desires to express his concern for prisoners of

---

7   JGT/JT, 19.8.73, J. Todd Papers.
8   JGT/JT, 22.8.73, ibid.
9   JGT/JT, 25.9.73, J. Todd Papers.
10 JGT/SP, 3.10.73, TPPC.
11 Bishop Donal Lamont/Todds, 16.11.73, MS.1082/4/12, Todd Papers, NAZ.

conscience everywhere in the world.'[12] Garfield subsequently gave the medal to Alycen's Roman Catholic family.

On 5 December 1973, Garfield was granted 'full range' of the ranch, and on New Year's Day 1974 Grace was in Rome to witness Judith's marriage to Richard Acton.

***

In February 1974, the British Prime Minister called a snap general election, in which the Conservative Party was narrowly defeated. Rhodesia would have to deal once again with its old enemy, Harold Wilson.

***

'The Africans no longer need ANY European to lead them or tell them what to do', Grace told Lady (Izo) Murray in South Africa. 'They are absolutely on the ball and there are so many excellently qualified, articulate and intelligent men now in the political leadership, they certainly do not need Gar. And they continue to be, in my estimation, so moderate in their demands. The tragedy remains and escalates and the whites in power still do not come to terms.'[13]

The Todds were concerned for the Murrays, for Izo had been diagnosed with TB, and Sir John was old and very frail. Garfield asked for, and received, permission to visit them, and on 15 November 1974 Grace told Judith: 'You are simply not going to believe this – I am beginning this letter to you in a comfortable cabin at Ranch Motel south of Pietersberg and Dad is stretched out on the other bed, reading the *Financial Mail*! There! We are on our way south to spend three days with John and Izo who don't have an inkling of our intentions, poor darlings … The local police were VERY nice, wishing us a happy trip and so on. … We reached Pietersberg about 3:30 and Dad found a barber and had his first professional haircut for three years.'[14] 'John put his hand on Dad's shoulder and said: "It is grand to see you again: 'the shadow of a rock in a weary land'".'[15]

Grace told the Murrays on her return home: 'I think perhaps one has to be deprived of freedom to realise fully what liberty means. We found that our requirements for happiness were remarkably modest. It was sufficient to be free and driving through beautiful South Africa with the prospect of seeing you both at the end of the journey …'[16]

---

12 JGT/A. W. Lee, NZ Church of Christ, 31.5.74, MS.1082/1/20, Todd Papers, NAZ.
13 JGT/Lady Izo Murray, 3.6.74, MS.1082/4/13, Todd Papers, NAZ.
14 JGT/JT, 15.11.74, J. Todd Papers.
15 JGT/JT, 17.11.74, ibid.
16 JGT/Murrays, 8.12.74, MS.1082/4/13, Todd Papers, NAZ.

Garfield wrote: 'I believe that Africans will probably make much better and much more devout Christians than most of us do but there will be as many evil men, as much lust for power among blacks as among whites ... If we had not been interrupted in 1958 we would have done it more gently but the end approaches and, while it may be delayed at increasing danger, it will not be evaded. As pressures increase and tensions grow I doubt if I will be released – nor will the 340 Africans who are also detained ... I am the one who has everything – except freedom ...'[17]

***

Garfield's 'belief that one should not be too cast down over a gloomy prospect, for one can never rule out the unexpected'[18] had been vindicated in mid-1974 as the log-jam in Rhodesia's affairs began to break up. The 1971 Home–Smith Settlement Proposals were, finally, 'taken off the table'. On 25 April, the Portuguese Army had mounted a successful, bloodless coup in Lisbon, largely on account of its antagonism to the colonial wars it was obliged to fight. The impact of the Lisbon coup was even greater on Rhodesia's southern neighbour, South Africa: while the centre of her *cordon sanitaire* – Rhodesia – still held, the right and left flanks – Portuguese East Africa and Angola – were about to crumble, leaving South Africa directly exposed to Black Africa. President Vorster's need for *détente* was now of paramount importance. Zambia, Rhodesia's northern neighbour, had arguably been more adversely affected by sanctions than the rebel colony, and Kaunda also saw in the new developments in Mozambique an opportunity to bring pressure for change to bear on Smith.

Secret negotiations between Vorster and Kaunda began, always bedevilled by nationalist in-fighting and the Rhodesian Government's obstinate refusal to consider majority rule; but optimism was generated by the release from detention of ZANU and ZAPU leaders to fly to Lusaka for talks. The Lusaka meeting on 6 December was unproductive, but two days later Kaunda announced that ZANU, ZAPU and a third, short-lived nationalist party, FROLIZI (Front for the Liberation of Zimbabwe), had agreed to unite and merge with the ANC. Smith was subjected to further pressure by Vorster, and on 11 December he announced a ceasefire, the release of African detainees – but not of Garfield – and the prospect of a constitutional conference without preconditions.

---

17 GT/Pauls, 24.11.74, TPPC.
18 JGT/JT, 28.4.74, J. Todd Papers.

78

'A Zimbabwe Man' – 1975–6

'Probably Vorster holds the key.'

Garfield Todd, 1966

'We are so happy to know that the men are being released now,' Garfield told Judith. 'The difference between them and me is that in my case release means permission to leave home, in their case it is permission to go home.'[1] Joshua Nkomo had asked for Garfield to be one of his advisers in his latest talks with Smith; but, as Grace told the Barhams, 'Smith had absolutely refused to release Gar, giving as his reason that he was a top security risk …'[2]

Hopes of a productive meeting faded early in the New Year, and the war resumed with a joint guerrilla force on 7 January 1975. In early March, Sithole was detained in Salisbury and charged with being a leader of ZANU. Muzorewa promptly broke off talks. On 18 March, before Sithole came to trial, Herbert Chitepo, ZANU's director of guerrilla operations, was killed by a car bomb in Lusaka. The assassination exposed the ZANU scene as a seething cauldron of personal ambition and rivalries, fear and petty betrayals – along with some genuine nationalistic fervour. Many Rhodesians in the Zambian capital were arrested, including Josiah Tongogara, but he was not brought to trial. No one has been convicted of Chitepo's murder, though most commentators consider Tongogara to be the likeliest suspect. Before the end of March, Robert Mugabe, another prominent nationalist, fled Rhodesia for Mozambique, where he established his leadership of the ZANU guerrillas with a headquarters in Maputo (formerly Lourenço Marques).

***

---

1 Todds/JT, 20.12.74, J. Todd Papers.
2 JGT/EB, 11.1.75, Mrs Collins' Papers.

'A Zimbabwe Man' – 1975–6

Garfield was now in his fourth year of restriction, never convicted, never charged, never even questioned. Businesses in Bulawayo were 'short-staffed, men called up and others left', Grace told Judith. 'And everybody just a bit on edge – And still Smith does not talk.'[3] By August, there were moves towards another conference thanks to the combined efforts of Vorster and Kaunda. Mugabe, Sithole, Nkomo and Smith were all there, at either end of a train on the Victoria Falls bridge over the Zambezi, the Rhodesian/Zambian border. The conference was full of rancour and bickering – and, again, almost totally unproductive.

***

'Armed conflict in Rhodesia has never seemed so likely as it does now', said the editorial in the *Guardian* on 21 October 1975. 'This is a tragic situation, brought on by white obduracy and black feuding ... The interested African Presidents have patched up truce after truce between them and none has lasted beyond nightfall ... [Vorster's] only course is to reach an agreement on the future of Rhodesia with Messrs Kaunda, Nyerere and Samora Machel and for all four to enforce it on their clients under threat of withdrawing all support ...'[4]

Garfield, aware of the strain on himself of the raising and dashing of hopes of his freedom, was very concerned for the effect on Judith, and this prompted him to write to the Secretary for Justice on 18 December for permission to make a short visit to London to see her. In the second week of January 1976, he walked into Grace's study 'looking positively white and stunned and whispered, "I'm allowed to go and see Judith!" Can you imagine the scene? I snatched the letter and nearly fainted myself. N.B. DO NOT TELL ANYONE ... Since that moment we have been able to think and talk of little else. We are still unbelieving.'[5] This was the last dealing Garfield had with his former lawyer, as on 1 February 1976 Hilary Squires took over the portfolio of Justice, Law and Order.

Rhodesia's sole white 'non-person' featured prominently in newspapers in Rhodesia as well as in Britain for the next three weeks. At Bulawayo airport, press photographers were allowed to take pictures of the Todds, but this was nothing compared with the reception at Heathrow. 'Strobe lights and flashguns lit the arrivals hall ... like a theatre when Mr Todd arrived yesterday ... He was clearly startled ... Mr Todd read out his restriction order before the cameras.' Asked if he was glad to see the talks between Smith and Nkomo, Garfield said:

---

3   JGT/JT, April 1975, TPPC.
4   *Guardian*, 21.10.75.
5   JGT/JT, 13.1.76, J. Todd Papers.

'"Oh, yes – what alternative is there … ?" Then he stopped himself: "It's very easy to break the terms of the order" …'[6]

'Mr Todd, tanned and in buoyant mood, said: "Anyone in the British tradition is a little upset to be restricted – as I have been." … The white-haired Mr Todd made little comment about the Rhodesian situation. However, he stressed: "I have hope of the Rhodesian situation and I believe in miracles." …'

Grace told friends 'tremendous interest had been aroused by the time, all unsuspecting, we flew into London … For the next few days the Press continued to come for interviews and to take photographs and we co-operated, because they were just so careful, so aware of the delicate nature of Garfield's position and that he would be going back into detention when he returned …'[7]

There was a meeting with the late Bernard Levin, who said he had met many who had come from detention and restriction 'but none so unmarked by his experience'.[8] On 19 April, Levin wrote an article for *The Times*: 'How rarely heroes live up to expectation and how satisfying when they surpass it! That is what, last week, I felt after meeting Alexander Solzhenitsyn for the first time – that, and the familiar and inexplicable feeling of exhilaration that comes from talking to those who know what it is to live in hell and who … nevertheless radiate a kind of vulnerable optimism that comes from within … I felt it intensely the night before I met Solzhenitsyn, when I met Garfield Todd. The gentle Rhodesian and the Russian titan could scarcely be more different, in the experiences they have undergone, the situation in which they find themselves, or the nature of their lifework; yet the same current of delight ran through me as I met them, and the same lightness of heart accompanied me as I left. Good, brave men, it seems, are the same the world over, and their goodness and bravery can no more be hidden than they can be counterfeited.'[9]

Grace did two interviews for the BBC. Garfield saw James Callaghan, British Foreign Secretary, and the New Zealand Foreign Minister. 'It was a wonderful and memorable visit for us', Grace wrote to friends. 'Garfield was accorded honour and affection wherever he went and after these years of restriction the stimulation of meeting and talking with so many people was a marvellous injection of vitality and interest … We have been most fortunate.'

Back in Rhodesia, Grace told Judith: 'I have always been sad that [Dad] has been a prophet without honour in this country. It is hard, year after year, in his circumstances here, to keep faith and hope high, though indeed he has done

---

6 *Sunday Mail*, 8.2.76.
7 JGT/'Friends', February 1976, TPPC.
8 JGT/EB, 2.3.76, destroyed file, c/TPPC.
9 *The Times*, 19.3.76.

so in a remarkable way. I have always hoped that the time would come when what he has done, what he has stood for, would be recognised and honoured. Well, it does not matter now if that never happens here, for it happened in such a delightful, and to us unexpected way, in London ... Dad has come back invigorated and revitalised, but of far greater importance is that he has recovered his old gaiety ...'[10]

***

The Smith/Nkomo talks broke down – and Jack and Ida Grant had been served with deportation orders. They were allowed to visit Hokonui before they left. Peter Niesewand, the *Guardian*'s correspondent, had also been deported – after a shattering experience of Lardner-Burke's brand of justice, law and order.

---

10 JGT/JT, 11.4.76, J. Todd Papers.

79

A Free Man – 1976

'My eyes were stained with tears of joy as they glanced at the headline of the 6th June Sunday Mail.*'*

F. Z. Mhlanga

On Saturday, 5 June, Senior Assistant Commissioner Wright arrived at Hokonui Ranch at lunchtime and handed Garfield a piece of paper:

REVOCATION OF AN ORDER MADE IN TERMS OF SECTION 19 OF THE EMERGENCY POWERS (MAINTENANCE OF LAW AND ORDER) REGULATIONS, 1976

To: REGINALD STEPHEN GARFIELD TODD

In terms of subsection (5) of section 19 of the Emergency Powers (Maintenance of Law and Order) Regulations, 1976, I hereby revoke the order at present in force against you with effect from the time that this revocation order is tendered to or served upon you.

Given under my hand at Salisbury this 5th day of June 1976

sgd. H. G. SQUIRES

Minister of Law and Order

Garfield told friends: 'Tea was served and Mr Wright explained that he had ruled that no Press car could enter the grounds of our home until he gave permission. So we enjoyed a quiet half hour while the Press waited, unquiet, at the gates ... And then they came with cameras and tape-recorders and old-fashioned ones with notebooks ... Then the phone joined in the celebrations and rang merrily until the last call at one a.m. Sunday: Radio New Zealand.'[1]

A Government statement on radio and TV on Saturday evening gave the news, adding: 'This follows a recommendation to the Ministry ... that adequate

---

1   GT/'Friends', June 1976, TPPC.

security grounds no longer existed for [Todd's] detention.'[2] But Advocate Anthony Eastwood may well have been right when he said in his Oral Archive that Garfield's detention was a 'personal' matter to Lardner-Burke – 'And it's true, the minute that Lardner-Burke was replaced by Hilary Squires, Todd was released.'[3]

'TODD FREED AFTER FOUR YEARS OF DETENTION', ran the *Sunday Mail*'s headline. 'Sitting on the veranda of his hilltop home on the banks of the Ngezi River, Mr Todd, dressed in a green safari suit, looked remarkably fit and relaxed as he gave his first interview in more than 4½ years', wrote reporter Frederick Cleary. '"I had no idea why I was arrested in the first place, and now I wonder why I was let out. But I am not going to argue about it. I'm just delighted ... I am as concerned today as I ever was regarding the situation in the country and my love for this country and for all its people ..."'[4]

'What of all the others who are being detained?', Garfield asked Bruce Loudon of the *Sunday Telegraph*, who wrote: 'Observers believe that in releasing Mr Todd, Mr Smith was influenced by intense international pressure ... Mr Todd is widely respected by African Nationalist leaders and has been considered a likely candidate to take part in renewed attempts to break the impasse over the country's future. He is admired by Mr Joshua Nkomo and President Kaunda of Zambia.'[5]

On Monday, *The Chronicle* called Garfield's release 'the end of a shameful episode in Rhodesian history ... Mr Todd is free now, but the shame lingers. So do the doubts, the questions ... How did he suddenly cease to be "dangerous"? ...'[6]

'I have never been a security risk', Garfield told the *Scotsman*. 'It was what I had to say that was not acceptable to the government.'[7] During a BBC interview at Hokonui, Garfield spoke of the country's need – '"the only way to get white political change in Rhodesia was by outside help" ... whites had "shown themselves unable to come to terms with the African people". If the whites, given 20 years' gradualism, had used this time correctly they would not now have been in trouble.'[8]

***

The first Saturday after freedom, Garfield arranged a feast for the ranch

---

2   *Sunday Mail*, 6.6.76.
3   A. N. H. Eastwood, Oral 260, NAZ.
4   *Sunday Mail*, 6.6.76.
5   *Sunday Telegraph*, 6.6.76.
6   *The Chronicle*, 7.6.76.
7   *Scotsman*, 7.6.76.
8   BBC interview, June 1976, MS.1087/1/20, Todd Papers, NAZ.

employees. Grace told friends of going to church at Dadaya again: 'When Garfield was first detained I made the decision that as far as I could I would sit it out here with him, going away only to do what needed to be done for him or for the Ranch. So I have not been to church ... We have been touched and very grateful to various ministers who have celebrated Communion with and for us here. But it is lovely to be back in the familiar church at Dadaya ... there are now no Europeans on the staff. We have been delighted to find the Church services beautifully conducted, the Church packed with 400+ students, all quiet, well-behaved and reverent ...'[9]

When Garfield made his first visit to Salisbury, he noted that 'My release is taken to mean that I never did anything in the first place and so only those who are less sure of themselves quickly glance around and slip by on the other side. Africans everywhere are welcoming ... my taxi-driver ... said "It is good to see you around again. You are part of the African's history and you will never be forgotten", which was rather a nice speech – off the cuff.'[10]

The last time Garfield had asked to see Ian Smith, he had been refused, but now the Prime Minister agreed to a meeting. Ten years later, Garfield divulged something of that interview: 'I said to him, "You are the one person who can save this country because whites will follow you." But of course he did not listen. He obviously never had any thoughts of coming to terms with the black population.'[11]

By mid-1976, no roads were really safe, certainly not after dark, as now it was not only the dirt roads that were mined. Garfield received advice from Africans that he should leave the country. They were afraid he was a marked man in the Government 'dirty tricks' department. Garfield took certain precautions, such as only travelling to Gwelo in the afternoon and in his recognisable Citroën. One day, 'coming from Bulawayo in the afternoon, I saw the guerrillas by the side of the road and they waved. It was very embarrassing for the guerrillas having Derrick and Cynthia (always with her gun) there. They were very vulnerable ...'[12]

In 2007, Graham Lord wrote in an article in the *Mail on Sunday*: 'During the civil war, Smith might well have had the liberal Todd hanged for treason, because Todd confessed to me that secretly he had helped Mugabe's guerrillas kill whites.'[13] Garfield's support for the guerrillas lay in food, cigarettes, toothpaste,

---

9   JGT/'Friends', July 1976, MS.1082/5/17, Todd Papers, NAZ.
10 GT/JT, 7.7.76, MS.1082/14/4, Todd Papers, NAZ.
11 *The Chronicle*, 7.7.86.
12 GT, interviews for this book, 1997.
13 *Mail on Sunday*, 25.11.2007.

aspirin, Coca Cola and, on one occasion, 180 pairs of boots. Garfield was once asked if he did not recognise that by not telling security forces of the presence of guerrillas, these men might then go on to kill white people. Yes, he admitted, there was guilt in that, but Garfield would never have helped anyone – guerrilla or soldier – to kill anyone. But, as Grace said, 'Wherever your sympathies were … you were supporting people who were using violence.'[14]

***

On 9 August 1976, Rhodesian armed forces raided Nyadzonya, a camp in Mozambique supported by the United Nations High Commission for Refugees, killing 1,000 Zimbabweans, mostly refugees. The reaction to the massacre among Rhodesia's whites was 'one of absurd, almost pathetic, elation', Sir Robert Tredgold told his nephew, Mr Sandford Stretton. 'This government has done much to expedite the coming of majority rule, but nothing more than this.'[15]

On 11 August, Bishop Donal Lamont issued an 'Open Letter to the Rhodesian Government: "Conscience compels me to state that your administration, by its clearly racist and oppressive policies and by its stubborn refusal to change, is largely responsible for the injustices which have provoked the present disorder and it must in that measure be considered guilty of whatever misery or bloodshed may follow. Far from your policies defending Christianity and western Civilisation, as you claim, they mock the law of Christ and make Communism attractive to the African people … You may rule with the consent of a small and selfish electorate, but you rule without the consent of the nation which is the test of all legitimacy."'[16]

The following month, the bishop was brought to trial, under the Law and Order (Maintenance) Act, on two counts of failing to report the presence of terrorists and two counts of inciting others to commit the same offence. Garfield told him: 'It is a tragic farce … Almost every act of this Government puts it on trial before the world and in charging you they put themselves on trial again … They just cannot win – for no matter what the verdict you have the respect and the love of 90 percent of our people who know that you stand, not for justice alone but that you will not shirk the cost of total love …'[17]

Garfield went to Umtali before the trial, though he knew it would be adjourned, telling Judith: 'I wanted to be present when Bishop Lamont appeared

---

14 JGT/SP, 1991.
15 RCT/Sandford Stretton, 12.8.76, MSS.Afr.s.1632 (Box VII), f. 62, Bodleian Library.
16 Bishop Lamont, quoted in his account of his subsequent trial: *Speech from the Dock* (1977).
17 GT/Bishop Lamont, 5.9.76, MS.1082/5/17, Todd Papers, NAZ.

first in court. The Press took a photo of us as I said goodbye to him and Grace is not sure that that was good for either Donal or me! ... I am sure he will just stand and in his usual fearless manner he will tell the whole truth. I am surprised that the Government is giving him the opportunity to tell the whole truth ...'[18]

On Sunday 19 September, Smith was in Pretoria negotiating with Vorster and Dr Henry Kissinger, Secretary of the American National Security Council Interdepartmental Group for Africa, who had brought proposals worked out with the British Government. 'We were told that K would not see Smith unless he had first received an assurance that majority rule was to come', Garfield told Judith. 'Now we hear that certain proposals have been put to Mr Smith and that Smith, Vorster and K are meeting now to finalise ??? [sic] What does it all mean? ... Well, the BBC at 10pm say that K has said that the Rhodesian delegation will give a satisfactory report to the cabinet on their return!!! If that is so he has ... led that group of Rhodesians through a detailed hell in full technicolour!'[19]

On the evening of 24 September, Smith said in a broadcast to the nation that he accepted 'majority rule'. But it was a 'majority rule' qualified by the word 'responsible'. The aim of the proposals Smith had been forced to accept was 'To sustain a united and civilian Rhodesia which guarantees a permanent home and equal opportunities for all its communities, which maintains responsible government and civilised standards'.[20] There were five main points, the first of which was 'Rhodesia agrees to majority rule within two years.' There would be a meeting in Geneva in October of Rhodesian Government representatives and Rhodesian African leaders to discuss the setting-up of an interim multiracial government to function until majority rule came in.

Mr Ivor Richard, Britain's Ambassador to the United Nations, was appointed chairman of the conference, which opened in Geneva on 28 October with delegations from Muzorewa's ANC, Sithole's ZANU and the new, uneasy Patriotic Front formed by Nkomo's ZAPU and Mugabe's ZANU, and the Rhodesian Government. Hopes were nowhere high. In addition to the difficulties already hinted at, the proposals carried the fatal flaw that had characterised earlier settlement attempts: Rhodesia's Africans had not been consulted. The Todds were surprised at the number of whites in Bulawayo who expressed relief that Garfield would be attending as one of Nkomo's advisers.

***

For Garfield, involvement in the conference was exciting; it was deeply

---

18   GT/JT, 15.9.76, MS.1082/4/14, Todd Papers, NAZ.
19   GT/JT, 19.9.76, TPPC.
20   Outline of Settlement Proposals, 8.10.76, MS.376/7/5, Todd Papers, NAZ.

satisfactory to be able at last to feel that he still could make some small contribution to solving Rhodesia's dire problems. And, from the start of his journey at Johannesburg, the following weeks were a series of happy, heart-warming reunions and meetings with old – and often long-detained – friends who maintained that the largest delegation at Geneva was of ex-Dadayans (twenty out of 150 black Rhodesians); 'and we have our father with us', added Clement Muchache.[21] Garfield told Grace that Cyril Ndhlovu had said: 'Smith was no doubt justified in detaining me ... "Dadaya has produced so many revolutionaries"'.[22] There were white friends, too: Dr Claire Palley and Leo Baron.

'Some of the scenes are really highly emotional as men who have not seen each other for ten years and more and have been through such suffering meet each other again,' Garfield wrote. 'An astonished press looks on at these scenes. The feeling of warmth and brotherhood is an experience I had never yet encountered in any gathering ...'[23] 'I am finding the time usefully spent, the most useful contribution being probably in talking to the men about the future.'[24]

Garfield told Grace: 'The problem is really the attitude of the UK to the conference and to the de-colonisation of Zimbabwe. The unwillingness of the UK to be fully involved, the purpose of the Council of State so designed as to leave us to the mercy of the Smith regime and the army in Rhodesia, etc., causes deep concern. Also there is plenty of news to show that Smith is not quietly and purposefully and honestly moving forward to majority rule. Under these conditions we seek to involve the UK more purposefully ...'[25]

Robert Blake sheds valuable light on the British Government's attitude to the conference in a letter to Sir Robert Tredgold: 'The government here is terrified of being involved in another Ulster situation, and this is why they are treating the crisis in such a gingerly fashion. Given the general situation in Rhodesia just now one could hardly be surprised at this, even if one deplores it ...'[26]

According to *The Times*, 'common sense is not the outstanding quality evident in the Palais des Nations ... Majority rule, yes. But there is no sense, whatever, among the Rhodesian leadership that power itself is to be passed to the Africans, that that is what the Africans want and whether anyone likes it or

---

21 GT/JGT, 19.11.76, TPPC.
22 GT/JGT, December 1976, TPPC.
23 Ibid.
24 GT/JGT, 21.11.76, TPPC.
25 GT/JGT, October 1976, TPPC.
26 Robert Blake/RCT, 29.10.76, MSS.Afr.s.(I), fos 234–5, Bodleian Library.

not that is what is going to happen.'[27] From first to last, the missing ingredient was trust. But one reason why the conference was doomed was that Vorster had removed the pressure on Smith to come to an agreement – and military supplies were once more on their way to Rhodesia.

Garfield wrote an interesting letter to Lord Alport at this time: 'You will be wondering what on earth we are doing but Ivor has had a very delicate task to perform ... Britain must take a greater part. I think it is a considerable compliment that the ex-colonies and the present African people of Rhodesia should seek such definite British participation. They want a governor – such as you – to come out, to take control of the army, to give a clear confidence in a very tricky and complex situation that things will go straight ...'[28]

On 1 December, Garfield addressed a meeting at Chatham House, headquarters of the Royal Commonwealth Society, in London. He believed 'The Geneva Conference [was] heading for disaster ... the time had come for a major British initiative and on this he is backed by the rival nationalist delegations at Geneva ... Britain should step in decisively.'[29]

***

The conference adjourned on 14 December. Garfield returned to Rhodesia to find dangerous roads, a tough call-up situation and the increasing exodus of whites. On his return to Rhodesia, Nkomo had been issued with a police warning not to hold political meetings or processions, or to address gatherings of more than ten in the Bulawayo area.[30] The *Rhodesia Herald* the following day reported more comments by Nkomo: the Patriotic Front's aim was the transfer of power '"to the people of Zimbabwe. And this includes those who are in power now" ... he did not want whites to leave. "Whites are part of a Zimbabwe that will be non-racial and non-tribal."'[31]

***

Garfield wrote two articles about the Geneva Conference, which were published in 1977. In the *Christian Advocate*, he said: 'I have not before been a small cog in an African political machine. This experience has proved to be a happy one for I find myself in a group of men and women who are dedicated to the setting up of a non-racial and democratic state ... My most forcible impression ... is the lack of bitterness. Many of my companions have been in prisons

---

27 *The Times*, October 1976.
28 GT/A, 18.11.76, MS.1082/5/19, Todd Papers, NAZ.
29 GT, Chatham House, November 1976, TPPC.
30 *Sunday Mail*, 19.12.76.
31 *Rhodesia Herald*, 20.12.76.

and detention camps for ten and more years; one for fifteen years! They have emerged mature, capable and determined, but not bitter ... It is understandable that the nationalists do not want to negotiate with Mr Smith ... Britain does have a continuing responsibility in providing a catalyst as things threaten to fall apart ...'[32]

In his long article for *Reality*,[33] Garfield quoted the British Foreign Secretary's statement in Parliament: 'Her Majesty's Government are ready to play a direct role in the transitional government if it is the general view that this would be helpful.'[34] Britain's acceptance of her responsibilities had been probably the only achievement of the conference.

***

Christopher Hitchins wrote in his Geneva Diary for *The Listener* in November 1976: 'Perhaps the two most impressive delegates here are as dissimilar a pair as could be imagined. Robert Mugabe and Garfield Todd both work for the Patriotic Front, but whereas one is a rich farmer and a former Prime Minister the other has just emerged from ten years of harsh confinement in Salisbury jail. Mugabe is ... quiet and very bright, with an army behind him in the bush which he doesn't boast or brag about. Todd, who also served several years in restriction, strikes one not just as a very nice guy so much as the nice guy who was saying all or most of this 15 years ago. By shutting him up, the stupid settlers lost all the years in which decent and peaceful plans might have been made for majority rule. Strangely, neither man feels any bitterness towards Ian Smith; Todd because he thinks Smith is a little guilty about him, Mugabe because "I couldn't dislike him any more than I did to start with".'[35]

---

32 *Christian Advocate*, vol. 57, no. 2, February 1977.
33 *Reality* magazine, May 1977, TPPC.
34 House of Commons, *Hansard*, vol. 921, 3.12.76, c. 219.
35 *The Listener*, November 1976.

80

The War comes to Hokonui Ranch – 1977

'The African majority is today convinced that no other choice remains open to them but violence.'

Bishop Adolph Schmitt, 1976

In January 1977, Smith called up all able-bodied white males aged between 38 and 50, which further harmed the economic life of the country and led to a net emigration of 6,000 in 1977. The scornful phrase 'taking the chicken run' began to be heard, describing those who drove away south over the border. To relieve the manpower shortage, mercenaries were recruited, from Europe and America as well as South Africa. The war continued: the guerrillas infiltrated into Rhodesia in growing numbers; the Rhodesian forces raided Mozambique – though not on the scale of the Nyadzonya raid until June, when hundreds of refugees, or unarmed guerrillas, were slaughtered at Mapai, many miles into Mozambique. Schoolchildren, singly, in groups, even a whole 'student body', started to slip over the border to join the guerrillas.

***

In spite of a poor start, the rainy season had been very good – and, as Garfield told John Stallworthy in Oxford, 'at Hokonui there is a false sense of beauty and peace', but 'life in Rhodesia is pretty dreadful. The "boys" (i.e. the guerrillas) [*sic*] with their AK automatic rifles are all through this area. Last week they opened two stores, including one of ours from which they just stole about 200 dollars' worth of clothing and blankets! The missionaries to the south of us, the Lutheran Church of Sweden, pulled out some months ago – and this week the Brethren in Christ from the States … have returned home.' All the neighbouring farmhouses were surrounded with security fences, and two had recently been burned down. 'We still go ahead feeding chickens and dipping the thousand

The War comes to Hokonui Ranch – 1977

cattle every week. David was happy to mention that "the cattle on a thousand hills are mine" – and I can find joy in the fact that the thousand cattle on our hills are ours – though some are mortgaged!'[1]

***

Bishop Donal Lamont's adjourned trial had taken place in September 1976, by which time a fifth charge had been added to the sheet: instructing his European nurses not to mention treating wounded guerrillas. Both Anglican bishops spent unavailing hours in the witness box on Bishop Lamont's behalf. He was sentenced to ten years in prison with labour. On appeal, this was reduced to four years with labour. However, Smith had no desire to make a martyr of him – so, instead, stripped him of his Rhodesian citizenship and deported him, on 23 March 1977.

On Good Friday, the Todds lost another dear and good friend: Sir Robert Tredgold died in hospital after a very brief illness. 'Robbie' had been one of the great influences on Garfield's life (the others he named were his grandfather and father, Grace, Dr A. L. Haddon, A. R. Mather and Sir John Kennedy). 'He was a wonderful man', Garfield said. 'After all, being the fifth generation since the Livingstones and his father having been Attorney-General in an earlier government, he was of the essence of the true Rhodesian – but they were the great exceptions, like Hardwicke Holderness, above the calibre of most Rhodesians.'[2] To Margaret Tredgold, Garfield wrote: 'He and I were at one on most issues and I depended on him, heavily, for advice.'[3]

In May, *Reality* printed Garfield's article: 'In the six months that have passed since Mr Smith's acceptance of the principle of "majority rule" on 24 September, the magnitude of the fraud which he tried to perpetrate has gradually been revealed ... It is now quite clear that at no time did Mr Smith intend to transfer power from white to black – Mr Smith has not changed ...'[4]

***

At the invitation of the African-American Institute, in May Garfield went to Washington to see the Vice-President and the Secretary of State. From Hokonui, Grace wrote to Garfield on the 23rd: 'It is all too terrible here. Daily people are losing their lives needlessly. Here we are now in a curfew area. There are soldiers everywhere, so presumably also "the boys". It was a great shock to learn last week that Dr Zhou had been murdered. The Press announced that he had been

---

1   GT/John Stallworthy, 20.2.77, MS.1082/5/17, Todd Papers, NAZ.
2   GT/SP, 1994, TPPC.
3   GT/Margaret Tredgold, 7.1.78, MS.1082/4/17, Todd Papers, NAZ.
4   *Reality* magazine, May 1977, TPPC.

killed by "terrorists" but none of the people around here will believe that.'[5] It was later established that a Government unit, the Selous Scouts, had committed the murder. Dr Zhou was long remembered for his 'selfless dedication and devotion to serve his people', John Mukokokwayira, one-time chief clerk at Hokonui, wrote in Garfield's 80th-birthday book in 1988. It also transpired that Garfield had been next on their list. John goes on to tell how he met a young man who 'freely confessed that he was one of the two assassins sent out by the regime to kill two men ... Dr Zhou at Mnene Hospital and Mr Todd at Dadaya. One dark night they gunned down Dr Zhou on his door steps, in cold blood. That was an easy task, he said ... The next was Todd. Easy target, he said. After a few trials they chose to give up – mission impossible ...'

***

On the 28th, Garfield wrote to Grace, asking: 'How is 77 going to finish? ... Thank you for your courage and steadfastness. If we both win through and through the settlement into peace in Zimbabwe our lives will really have been crowned.'[6] Garfield was enjoying his freedom: 'One is greeted by doormen and people everywhere so kindly. Had a splendid lunch with former Geneva comrades yesterday ... a happy meal and warm fellowship, but no belief that the UK initiative means much at all.'[7] He had visited his tailor, who commented on the suit he was wearing: '"This one has worn well, sir." "Yes, but I did not wear it during my years in prison or detention." Laughter. "A phrase not heard here before, sir."'

Garfield's programme in the USA was even more hectic than usual: meetings, press conferences, TV and radio interviews. On the first day, he met Andrew Young, permanent US representative at the UN. The *New York Times* on 6 June reported on the meeting, with Garfield 'quietly and dispassionately' describing 'neighbours and acquaintances he said had been shot or taken away by the secret police in his home district of Shabani ... He has met Secretary-General Kurt Waldheim and will testify before a congressional committee, all with one purpose in mind: "to get the Rhodesian war stopped". Mr Todd views the Rhodesians' incursions into neighbouring Mozambique this week ... as "an act of desperation". He says it was intended to boost the morale of the white minority. In his talks in this country Mr Todd said he was advocating measures to cut off oil shipments, which are continuing to flow to Rhodesia through South Africa. Since South Africa

---

5   JGT/SP, 23.5.77, TPPC.
6   GT/JGT, 28.5.77, TPPC.
7   GT/JGT, 31.5.77, TPPC.

The War comes to Hokonui Ranch – 1977

ignored trade sanctions, the only recourse was to cut off the oil at its source.'[8]

Garfield met Senator Hubert Humphrey, who was pleasant and helpful; and the Vice President, Walter Mondale, who assured him 'that the USA had only one desire – to help. They would go in fully, or go half in, or stay out – anything that was required ... [Mondale said] We have entered the Rhodesian sphere not because we must do so to counter Russian moves in that part of Africa, but because we want to see all the people share in government on a universal franchise.' Garfield's notes of the meeting end: 'Not one thing emerged upon which we disagreed.'[9]

***

Garfield met business and banking leaders in Salisbury who were completely disillusioned with Smith. Grace told Judith: 'Dad was very frank ... What was a bit surprising was that most of those present agreed with Dad about Smith. But the nicest thing was that afterwards Kipps Rosin[10] said to Dad that what impressed him was Dad's complete lack of bitterness. Dad replied that he had so many things for which to be thankful, among them a happy marriage and a good digestion. Kipps said he also had a happy marriage, but if he had had to endure the things "those bastards" had done to Dad he would be bitter as hell, and then said, "I think you must be a very fine Christian" which coming from a Jew of Rosin's standing is a remark I shall treasure.'[11]

***

Years later, after the independence of Zimbabwe, Garfield told the Toronto *Globe & Mail*: 'of course we were co-operating with the guerrillas. I'd have 20 of them sitting with their arms and their ammunition and their rocket-launchers on the front stoep in the middle of the night. Very dangerous.'[12] 'If ever the divide-and-rule strategy failed, it was at Hokonui Ranch,' writes Julie Frederikse. 'There on the border of the divide between Mashonaland and Matabeleland, the armies of both ZANLA and ZIPRA fought the regime's soldiers, while the people tilled the land, herded cattle and supported all the guerillas that passed through.'[13] Garfield told Frederikse: 'Confined here as I was, under house arrest for four and a half years, I saw a lot of action. I was never actually involved in any violent act, but we felt there was no option but

---

8   *New York Times*, 6.6.77.
9   TPPC.
10 Salisbury surgeon. His wife, Muriel, had been a URP MP 1953–8, then UFP Federal MP.
11 JGT/JT, 11.8.77, J. Todd Papers.
12 *Globe & Mail*, 19.2.88.
13 Frederikse, 1982, pp. 230–2.

to support the nationalist cause. And, you know, the violence came, first of all, from the government. People don't realise that violence generates violence, and that when you have your detention camps and your prison cells and your executions, naturally there is going to be a reaction on the part of the people. So that the Smith regime, they were the terrorists, in my estimation, who begat the guerilla war. Then of course when the people rose, naturally one's sympathy was with them, although one hated the violence …

'We could never see a day where, with policies of oppression, whites could ever be safe in this country. So that when people thought we were betraying the whites, we believed that we were taking the only way of safety for the whites … If the whites were going to stay here and be happy and safe here, they had to go along the way of change. We would rather it had been the peaceful change that we had worked for, but we had failed. After all, if anyone failed, it was I, being the Prime Minister. I had power and I had failed, and been thrown out. So there was violence and there was violence right here on this ranch. There were many mines placed on our property and much fighting right here. We had the ZIPRA boys on the one side of us and the ZANLA boys in control here …

'There were a few occasions when the boys came to the house to see us, but usually they were very good; they kept away, largely because it was known that it was putting us into great danger should people actually come to me personally. So they came to our people, using people who were known intermediaries. They just gave the list of what they wanted, and it was drawn from the stores, and the storekeepers kept a list of what had been given … They wanted mostly toothpaste, cigarettes, sugar, clothing … oh yes! aspirin. Of course there was always a need for drugs …'

***

In August 1977, the Todds' neighbour on Wedza Farm (formerly Bob Mattison's Tugela Ranch), 29-year-old Noel Webb, was killed. Two days earlier, Allan Ritson from Tsomo Ranch, Filabusi, had been murdered. This was probably the worst moment of the war for Grace and Garfield. He had been a good friend – 'the only white farmer to visit me during my years of detention', Garfield told Frank Ferrari.[14] Allan's teenage sons asked Garfield to see to all the details of the funeral. This was at Dadaya Church, where he had married Allan and Heidi, and where he had taken Heidi's funeral. She had been buried in the Mission cemetery, and Allan was buried beside her. Derrick, on the hills above, with his PN rifle, kept watch over the committal.

Grace told Judith: 'We have lost a friend, one who brought into our lives

---
14 GT/Frank Ferrari, August 1977, MS.1082/1/22, Todd Papers, NAZ.

a new dimension. He has of late, since the curfew, not come to dinner, but dropped in for coffee on his way home to Tsomo from Shabani. His stories were always fabulous, there was always laughter and fun. Already I miss him terribly. Whatever he was to others, "He was my friend, faithful and just to me". We are left now with a feeling of dread as to what could happen to Derrick. Both Dad and I have tried to persuade him to go, but he will not move ... But Noel Webb's death has shaken them both. Noel was in Derrick's "stick", and a good friend ...'[15]

Three years earlier, Grace had given the first hint of the Todds' anxiety for the Edge family. Now the two murders so close to home finally persuaded Derrick and Cynthia to leave. Their decision, Garfield told Judith, 'gives us relief and comfort and fills us with the greatest sadness. We have pled with them to do just that but now that it is happening we are desolate ... They will go to the UK just as soon as passports are ready ... we have just one concern – to get them out safely ...'[16]

There was a rocket attack on the white railway families' village at Bannockburn in September. This was right beside the ranch's commercial centre. Next morning, the soldiers came and interrogated everyone, and a group from the reserve coming in to the grinding-mill was challenged. Garfield told Judith: 'One little boy of seven, son of Kennias who used to work for us – ran – and was shot dead. You are supposed to stop when you are challenged.'[17] 'The times are terrible', Grace wrote to Judith. 'I find myself echoing Polycarp, who died in the year 155, calling on God to ask why he had been spared to see such times to see such things. Distress and horror are no new things. But there remains beauty everywhere, even in some people.'[18] Then came the wrench of the departure of Cynthia, Derrick and Kim, Garfield driving them to Johannesburg to catch their plane – and Grace, desolate, watching the car go down the drive and round the hill and out of sight.

***

In the last week of November, Rhodesian forces raided two ZANU bases at Chimoio and Tembue deep inside Mozambique, killing, at a conservative estimate, 1,200 guerrillas – and considerably raising white morale. Buoyed up by these successes, Smith announced that he was ready to start negotiations, with a view to majority rule, with three black internal leaders: Bishop Abel

---

15   JGT/JT, 11.8.77, J. Todd Papers.
16   GT/JT, 24.8.77, J. Todd Papers.
17   GT/JT, 14.9.77, MS.1082/4/14, Todd Papers, NAZ.
18   JGT/JT, 6.10.66, J. Todd Papers.

Muzorewa, the Rev. Ndabaningi Sithole and Senator Chief Chirau. But there was still no dialogue with the guerrillas, so it was difficult to take the move seriously. Talks between the four 'internal partners' began on 2 December and continued until March 1978. Meanwhile, the war went on and the casualties mounted on both sides. Garfield did not believe that Muzorewa and Sithole controlled the guerrillas.

Garfield went to Bonn for more talks with the Protestant Central Agency about funds for Dadaya School's projected expansion to include a sixth form; and to Lusaka to see President Kaunda and Joshua Nkomo. When Garfield returned to Hokonui, he took with him Robert Blake's book *A History of Rhodesia*, which he had read on his travels. It will be remembered that the Todds had earlier seen the chapter on Garfield's ministry. Garfield now told the author: 'Being unashamedly human I started at Chapter 19, "Southern Rhodesian Society 1946–1953", and read to the end before I began at the beginning ... my first reaction was to say "Thank you" with all my heart – for me – but even more especially for Grace who has endured much suffering, criticism and virtual ostracism from our own community for all these years ... What we are especially grateful for is that you, Robert Blake, conservative, historian, whose judgements may be questioned but not lightly dismissed by anyone who wishes to be taken seriously, have concluded that it was right to strike out in 1953 to establish a unity among the people on the basis of sharing power ...'[19]

Blake's book 'made' Grace's Christmas. She wrote: 'It is superb by any standards, but for us it is the appraisal for which we have waited and longed, from an impeccable and authoritative source.'[20] She told Robert Blake that 'What pleases and satisfies me most, however, is that without being moralistic you have made certain judgements ... Along with the pleasure of reading the unfolding story of Rhodesia I have the deep satisfaction of finding our own values endorsed ... Besides our own personal satisfaction I am glad of this for our friends (the nicest and most intelligent people left in Rhodesia!) for it vindicates their faith and loyalty, too, and their adherence to those former policies ...'[21]

---

19 GT/Robert Blake, December 1977, TPPC.
20 JGT/SP, 31.12.77, TPPC.
21 JGT/Robert Blake, 29.12.77, TPPC.

81

SMITH'S RHODESIAN SOLUTION – 1978

'The Salisbury Agreement is the culmination of our history of perfidy.'

Garfield Todd, 1978

Smith and the 'internal leaders' proceeded with their discussions, although the British Government warned Smith that any deal that excluded the Patriotic Front would not be acceptable. But, in all the confusion, the only really significant question was: who controlled the guerrillas? Muzorewa and Sithole claimed they did – Mugabe and Nkomo *knew* that *they* did.

At the end of January 1978, guerrilla and security force activity in the Bannockburn and Dadaya area was almost at its height. A big, permanent army camp not far from Hippo Lodge was attacked during the night; and, at 11 p.m. on the 30th, a group of guerrillas, armed with 'everything up to rocket-launchers', went to Dadaya Mission and ordered the principal to assemble all pupils and staff in the dining room. Garfield told Dr Augustini, of EZE: 'My information is of course second-hand ... The guerrillas wanted medical supplies and the Principal ordered the school nurse to supply whatever was asked for. The group also wanted cash ... they would not touch school funds but would the staff like to help? ... so twenty-nine dollars was donated.' While men with sub-machine guns lined the walls of the dining room, the leader addressed the pupils. He said that 'the guerrillas would not lay down their arms until there had been a transfer of power from white to black; that they were not interested in Mr Smith's internal settlement ... They told the pupils that they did not require more recruits and that their job was to stay at school and do their best to get the finest education possible so that they would be able to take their places in the new Zimbabwe.'[1]

---

1 GT/Dr Augustini, 31.1.78, TPPC.

***

On 15 February, Smith reached agreement with Muzorewa, Sithole and Chief Chirau. This provided for a constitution requiring a three-quarters majority for any alteration, and 28 white seats in a 100-seat assembly – thereby giving whites the power to veto any proposed alterations. The whites would, for ten years, control the army, the police and the civil service. Garfield told the magazine *Life and Times* that 'this is quite unacceptable to the people as a whole. I believe, with some justification, that the Patriotic Front has the support of the majority of the people in Rhodesia.'[2]

***

David Caute gives us a vivid picture of Hokonui Ranch in February 1978: 'A remarkable man lives here with his no less remarkable wife ... Now he's an old man and a legend; but his life hangs by a fine thread ... Hokonui ... bouncing slowly along a rutted track I come across a white lady, ankle-deep in mud and surrounded by cattle. An outbreak of ear tick, she explains: the normal dips don't cure it ... Here, west of Shabani ... ZANLA and ZIPRA forces confront one another in a tense, distrustful stand-off ... Shabani ... is the nerve-centre of a ruthlessly conducted counter-insurgency operation involving the Special Branch, the Selous Scouts, Fireforce units of the RLI [Rhodesian Light Infantry] and – by mid-1978 – black "auxiliaries" loyal to one or other of the "internal" nationalist parties. One thing they all have in common ... is an intense dislike of Garfield Todd.' In a memorable phrase, Caute writes of 'the blue-green silence of insurgent Africa', and goes on: 'The house at Hokonui has no security fence, no Agric-Alert system, no sign of a weapon. Its sole means of defence resides in the heads of the natives and in the Bible ...'[3]

***

On 3 March, Smith, Muzorewa, Sithole and Chirau signed their Settlement Agreement – 'little more than a device for keeping real power in the hands of Rhodesia's small white minority and already suspect in black African eyes', commented the *New York Times*.[4] Within two weeks of the signing of the agreement, it had been rejected by the UN Security Council, and a few weeks later Muzorewa was refused a hearing by the Council.

On 21 March, the nine ministers (three from each black party) were sworn in, not by the President or Chief Justice but by the Anglican assistant bishop in Mashonaland, Patrick Murindagomo, a quietly staunch nationalist. The

---

2 *Life and Times*, 1978, MS.1087/1/34, Todd Papers, NAZ.
3 Caute, 1983, pp. 193–202.
4 *New York Times*, 5.3.78.

four members of the Executive Council – Smith, Muzorewa, Sithole and Chief Chirau – were all sworn in as 'Prime Minister', equal partners. Their decisions were required to be unanimous – so Mr Smith had a veto. Just days before the Settlement Agreement was signed, control of all the security forces had been handed to a streamlined national war council under Lt General Peter Walls.

Reporters from *Illustrated Life Rhodesia* visited Hokonui in May. Chris Ashton's article was published in the magazine's issue of 25 May. Of Garfield, he wrote: 'To the western world and particularly the British media, he is seen as the lone voice of dissent against entrenched minority rule; white Rhodesia's liberal conscience. Missionary, rancher and politician, his personality is stamped above all by the mission experience ... For all his disappointments in the political arena, the hostility that mention of his name still excites in many white Rhodesians, he gives off a sense of being at peace with himself ... "I've been particularly fortunate in my life ..."

'With Todd and his wife Grace you sit on the terrace of their homestead high above the Ngezi river ... You admire the weir below, built by Todd during his detention ... You drive through the 19,500-acre ranch, noting how well his cattle look, how spruce his yards and outbuildings; all the signs of sound farm management. You ask yourself how rancher, builder, politician, visionary and idealist can combine in a single being. And then you recognise a survivor of a species you have only read about and imagined was long extinct, the gentleman farmer of nineteenth-century England; Christian, scholar and reforming liberal, man of many parts, passionately committed to the perfection of mankind.'[5]

***

Attempts to arrange a ceasefire began in early May, with amnesties offered to guerrillas who wanted to return, but few took up this offer. Muzorewa's and Sithole's proud boast of control over the guerrillas was shown to be as false as many had suspected.

The Chronicle reported on 18 May the deaths of 50 black Rhodesians in crossfire between security forces and terrorists. The massacre caused little stir among whites who, a month later, were horrified and furious at the murder of nine British missionaries and four of their children at the Elim Pentecostal Mission near the Mozambique border. Suspicion fell equally on the guerrillas and the Selous Scouts. After the war, it was generally agreed that the guerrillas had been responsible.

At the end of June, four helicopters and a plane launched an attack on a guerrilla camp on Wedza mountain. The following day, when Garfield was at

---

5   Chris Ashton, *Illustrated Life Rhodesia*, 25.5.78.

Bannockburn for stock-taking, news came through 'that when bombs were dropped, four guerrillas were killed, two girls were killed, three girls were wounded and one man'.[6] 'In the afternoon the four bodies of the guerrillas were displayed at Wedza School. I understand the parents of the two girls got their bodies – the girls had taken food up to the camp and the four wounded were hiding in the veld, for the soldiers had returned this morning to comb the villages. Two of the wounded are very serious and there are no medical facilities. It was almost more than I could bear to carry on stock-taking when all one's inclinations, experience and training demanded that I should go and try to help. However, my team was quite clear on this – you could not go and put yourself in the position of "assisting terrorists" …'

The four bodies were displayed at the school; one was unrecognisable but the others were found to be local men, including a ranch employee. 'Since then the worst wounded have been located and taken to hospital … Wedza is sad and families are shocked and horrified at what has happened.'[7]

An outbreak of foot-and-mouth disease in Lundi Tribal Trust Land had broken through the veterinary cordon. Animal-health inspectors paid three visits to Hokonui in the week following the Wedza raid. Garfield told Judith about these: 'It is interesting to see the reactions at the dip when the Inspectors come … The military concertina vehicle and a landrover arrive in quick succession. There is an immediate silence with people going on quietly with their work – no smiles – no chatter. The vehicles pull up and 3 or 4 black soldiers from each jump out, race to surround the dip, turn outwards with automatic rifles pointed into the bush around. The two whites get out … both have large automatics strapped to their waists. They are pleasant and get on and do their work. With counts and inspections completed they enter the vehicles – the soldiers run and clamber aboard – the doors are shut and the vehicles move off. Gracie sits down again at her little table/chair, work is under way, chatter and laughter are again the order of the day. And the old white woman and her twelve black assistants are back to normal.'[8]

Grace wondered what the young white officers thought as they drove off. 'We are the only people around here who do not carry guns and have no security fence to lock ourselves behind at night', she told Elsie. 'Perhaps we are foolishly trusting. But we know we are trusted in return by the people among whom we live. That is not to say that there are not others "who knew not Joseph" whom we should fear. But we must live a life, and we feel it is no way to do it

---

6   GT/JT, 25.6.78, J. Todd Papers.
7   GT/JT, 28.6.78, ibid.
8   Ibid.

if we have to tote guns around. Anyway, by doing so one immediately declares oneself ... The one certain thing, in this area anyway, is that "the boys" and the people are one, and the army, especially the black troops, are the feared and the hated ..."[9]

In his letter to friends, acknowledging all the good wishes he had received on his 70th birthday, Garfield wrote: 'Perhaps the most useful period was our time at Dadaya Mission ... In that period especially we have come to know the worth and ability of the people among whom we were living ... we know black men and black women who are better educated, more liberally endowed with natural gifts and who are finer Christians than we are. In this lies hope for Rhodesia – humility for ourselves ... While there is just as high a percentage of the selfish and the corruptible among blacks as there is among whites, we have faith in the eventual outcome of the good and the true. So we pray for the emergence of a free and peaceful Zimbabwe in the year ahead ...'[10]

**

In August, Smith had another abortive meeting with Nkomo in Lusaka, but on 3 September there occurred a horrible incident that effectively ruled out all contact with the ZAPU leader. The Rhodesian forces were known to use civil airliners to transport troops, as well as to carry civilian passengers. Now Nkomo earned the lasting hatred and contempt of the whites when a ZIPRA surface-to-air missile succeeded in bringing down an Air Rhodesia Viscount carrying mostly white families back to Salisbury from holidays at Kariba. Thirty people died in the crash, but – even worse – ten of the eighteen survivors were killed on the ground by ZAPU guerrillas. 'I do not believe they were killed by our people. I hope not', Nkomo writes.[11]

Nkomo was interviewed on radio and caused further anger and distress when he appeared to giggle about the disaster. He says in his book that he was laughing at his remark that the plane was brought down by 'throwing stones' (he did not want to admit having SAMs) – not at the deaths of the people, which included an Indian friend and his whole family. But no explanation for his laugh would have been acceptable. The following year, another Viscount was brought down – Nkomo asserting that it was targeted because it was believed that General Walls was on board. (He was in a plane which took off a few minutes later.[12])

The Government banned ZAPU and ZANU and declared martial law in

---
9   JGT/EB, 28.6.78, c/TPPC.
10 GT/'Friends', 17.7.78, TPPC.
11 Nkomo, 1984, p. 167.
12 Ibid.

certain areas, including Shabani. Rhodesian forces conducted massive raids on ZAPU camps in Zambia – it was estimated that 1,500 guerrillas had been killed or wounded and large quantities of equipment destroyed. Similar raids were carried out on ZANU camps in Mozambique.

Smith allowed Muzorewa and Sithole to build up their own private militias to police the rural areas, thus freeing up the regular forces. There would now be five competing 'armies' to harass the desperate people, who were trying to lead some semblance of normal life. Colin Legum wrote in the *Observer*: 'Rhodesia is at the point where the ultimate disaster of uncontrollable chaos and massacres can be prevented only if Britain takes over responsibility for the country's security ... On the white side now morale has begun to crack ... On the black side, there is an intensification of the power struggle among the four major leaders – Nkomo, Mugabe, Muzorewa and Sithole ... The only hope of preventing chaos has lain in arranging all-party talks; but any hopes of achieving this appear to have been finally lost through the abortive Smith–Nkomo talks and the emotional aftermath of the Rhodesian air crash ...'[13]

***

On 13 September, both Garfield and Grace set out for the USA, where they were to receive honorary degrees in recognition of their 'outstanding lifetimes of ministry in the Churches of Christ'[14] from Eureka College, Indiana, the alma mater of Emory and Myrta Ross (and Ronald Reagan). Grace told Judith in 1977: 'The whole thing horrifies me ... I have not earned or deserved this in any way, so it is a sham and I can hardly bear it. But having told you this I do now intend to be good about this. People have been most caring and kind and I know I must do them honour, as they are doing us ...'[15]

By August 1978, Grace had become so far reconciled to the idea as to welcome the chance to get away from Rhodesia: 'The strain of life in Rhodesia now is considerable. The people suffer so. We have so much to tell you that we may not write', she told me.[16] Garfield told Judith: 'Of course we leave with a good deal of concern for the people we are leaving behind. This last week, Victor, one of the herders, came to say soldiers had burned his house and all his possessions and that he did not know where his wife and four children had fled to. We will tackle the matter this morning ...'[17]

---

13 *Observer*, 17.9.78.
14 Dr Gilbert/GT, 18.10.77, MS.1087/1/33, Todd Papers, NAZ.
15 JGT/JT, 7.11.77, J. Todd Papers.
16 JGT/SP, August 1978, TPPC.
17 GT/JT, 20 and 21.8.78, J. Todd Papers.

Smith went to America at the invitation of 28 conservative Republican senators. That Garfield should be in the USA at the same time as Smith had not been intended, but it was useful. He saw US Secretary of State, Cyrus Vance; and, according to Frank Ferrari of the African-American Institute, the meeting 'certainly reinforced whatever doubts the Secretary of State had about Smith and the Internal Settlement'.[18]

Garfield received the degree of Doctor of Laws; Grace the degree of Doctor of Humane Letters. She told Alycen afterwards that the Convocation 'was a very grand affair – or so it seemed to me'. Held in the Reagan Gymnasium, the academic procession was headed by pipers playing 'Amazing Grace'! Dr Daniel D. Gilbert, the college president, said that Garfield and Grace 'personify the dedication and selfless leadership, to which Eureka has been devoted. First in their church and nation and today around the world, [they] offer a noble example of service to humanity.'[19]

Garfield gave an address to the Congressional Black Caucus Dinner in Washington, where Andrew Young was his host, having earlier given a lunch for them. Garfield had 'just over an hour with Mr Vance and Mr Morse', he told Harold Hochschild.[20] 'It was a delightful and warm meeting and when I returned to the hotel I said to Grace that it could well have been one of the most important hours of my life.'

The magical Fall colours formed the backdrop against which their whole visit took place, and, literally, coloured it all for Grace, who was overwhelmed by the beauty of the country and the kindness she received. Now she could understand why Garfield kept on returning to the USA.

On their way home, Garfield addressed the Reform Group of Britain's Conservative Party during its annual conference in Brighton. The *Guardian* reported on 13 October that Garfield 'urged Conservatives yesterday not to support the internal settlement of Mr Smith and Bishop Muzorewa. Mr Todd … was heckled and jeered when he told the meeting that the guerillas in Rhodesia were supported by the majority of the black population … Many of his audience were in angry mood.'[21] However, following that meeting, both Edward Heath and Lord Carrington asked to see Garfield.

A special occasion was a gathering at Judith's home of members of the wider

---

18 Frank Ferrari/Todds, 25.10.78, MS.1087/1/12, Todd Papers, NAZ.
19 Eureka Convocation, 23.9.78, MS.1087/1/33, Todd Papers, NAZ.
20 GT/Harold Hochschild, 14.11.78, MS.1087/1/33, Todd Papers, NAZ.
21 *Guardian*, 13.10.78.

Todd family: Grace and Garfield of Rhodesia; and three sisters, Garfield's cousins: Jessie Harrison, now living in England; Nell Wood of New Zealand; and Louie Todd of Moscow. Louie, a dedicated communist, had gone to live in the Soviet Union nearly 50 years before. She had survived the siege of Stalingrad and had been given the task of checking a Russian–English dictionary but, finding it inadequate, had revised it in its entirety in two of the three years allotted to her for the job.

Before the Todds returned to Rhodesia, they learned of the death in Cambridge of C. G. 'Jack' Grant. Garfield gave a tribute to him at the memorial service.[22] Grace told me he spoke of his 'long friendship with Jack and Ida and of their never to be forgotten kindness to me, for it was at their house I used to stay in Salisbury when I used to go to visit Judith at Marandellas and Gar at Gatooma …'

***

Grace wrote on her return: 'I went as you know reluctantly on this trip, and have been humbled and rebuked by the lovely experience of friendship which we have enjoyed.' She admitted she had 'certain apprehensions as the time for leaving came near'; but, on her return to Hokonui, Grace told Elsie: 'this is our place for as long as may be … We are delighted with the way our assistants have managed the affairs of business and ranch … our people have shown that they can cope.'[23] The full effects of martial law in the Dadaya/Bannockburn area were also becoming apparent. Stores were being closed, which meant that people had to go 15 or 20 miles into Shabani to buy meal, sugar, tea and so on – all with the object of making life more difficult for the guerrillas. So far, Hokonui's stores remained open, including Bannockburn, which had been threatened with closure. All grinding mills had been put out of action, and any load of more than 10 kg of meal was confiscated. 'The people are suffering terribly and it is becoming increasingly difficult for them to exist at all', Garfield told Judith.[24]

---

22 JGT/SP, 20.11.78, TPPC.
23 JGT/EB, 9.11.78.
24 GT/JT, 8.12.78, MS.1087/1/34, Todd Papers, NAZ.

82

FACING REALITIES AT LAST – 1979

'Will we wait until reason has been fed with blood?'

Garfield Todd, 1966

On 1 January 1979, Senator Chief Jobe Mafala Matshazi was ambushed by guerrillas near his home at Old Dadaya. He and his armed guard were killed and their bodies burned in the wrecked car. The little boy whose life Garfield had saved had in due time succeeded to his father's dignities – and been appointed a Senator. To the guerrillas, he was a 'sell-out'. The security forces, alerted by the shots, were quickly on the scene and set about burning the villages of his people. Learning what had happened from terrified women and children whom he met on the road to Bannockburn, Garfield went there immediately. He told Judith: 'Wide destruction was taking place. I went in to see Barbara, Chief Mafala's wife … I sat for half an hour among the wailing people but was not able to do much except say my own prayers. On the wall were the prized photographs of the opening ceremonies of Parliament in which Senator Chief Mafala Matshazi had taken his part … all the signs of his great success in life – and all down the valley the homes of his people were burning as soldiers moved from empty village to empty village …'[1]

Garfield drove to Shabani but, having failed to find Mr Shaw, the District Commissioner, went to see the Commanding Officer of the Joint Operations Command to ask him to limit the destruction of the homes. On his return to Old Dadaya, Garfield saw that for a mile or more the houses were on fire and 'right across the valley the flames were rising. At the gate of the Chief's security fence there were two lorries … and a number of soldiers including four whites.' Mr Shaw was there and told Garfield that on the CO's instructions he had stopped

---

1 GT/JT, 6.1.79, J. Todd Papers.

the burning. 'I must say that I have never in my life encountered such intense, but unspoken dislike if not hatred', he told Judith.[2]

'I went to Shabani to get extra supplies of bread for the refugees … we are surrounded by people in despair. And now it is Friday evening. Hlambelo buried the chief this morning among a group of soldiers, the Chief's immediate family and two white officials … his people were scattered far and wide and 53 huts stood roofless to avenge his death.'[3] Almost 100 refugees were at Dadaya School, fortunately on holiday, and had been given blankets and food.

'I asked my old friend, J. N. Hlambelo, to find out for me exactly how many huts had been burned, how many granaries also. He is almost 80 and that fact was his protection. He walked with a stick along the valley … and brought me a report so that I could make adequate application for relief. Only in two kraals were the granaries set on fire … I have discussed assistance with Christian Aid and have told them that we can manage the immediate problems of blankets, food, soap, etc. etc. – and thank God for relief money raised by our Churches and some already in the Bank in Shabani … maybe, when things cool down a bit, I can go again to the CO and see if I can get any assurance that women at least can return to their stricken homes … the cattle are just wandering around and they have broken into the fields of growing crops and this means that there may be no crops for these villagers and help may have to be found for them for a whole year …

'Perhaps it was just in keeping with the whole distress and horror of the New Year's Day that, when I arrived home in the evening, a very quiet Grace should say that she had taken a message on the phone for me … "There was a plot to assassinate Mr Todd. Perhaps he should leave the country." Well, there was more to the message than that, but the man was pleasant and seemingly friendly and that was the gist of what he had to say.' When the specific threats were repeated at a small meeting of Sithole's people in the Shabani area, the Todds fitted very strong doors to the house, burglar bars to windows in the bedroom wing, grenade screens to their bedroom and bathroom windows, and four external security lights.

***

On 31 January, Smith won his referendum on the proposed new Constitution, with 85 per cent of the vote. The Commonwealth Secretary-General issued a statement: 'Rhodesian whites have not voted for genuine majority rule but for Ian Smith's latest tactic to postpone it. The new UDI … and the "election"

---

2   Ibid.
3   Ibid.

promised for April will not produce a solution to the Rhodesian problem: they are a masquerade for perpetuating the denial of majority rule.'[4] Smith later described the Constitution as 'so good that we cannot get the rest of the world to recognise it. That is the only complaint: it gives the white man too much. If we turn it down does anyone in their senses believe we could get a better deal?'[5] At the end of February, rule through the largely white Rhodesian electorate ended after 56 years.

***

Once again, in a very hot, dry season, Hokonui Ranch was desperate for rain. Grace told Elsie: 'For the first time I am seriously beginning to wonder about our future here. It is unwise to write too freely … up till now, we have felt protected by our good relationships with the people. But now the thing is complicated by the private armies of Muzorewa and Sithole, yet who appear to operate with the protection of the army. These people would, I believe, consider Gar an enemy of the Internal Settlement and one begins to feel pretty insecure …'[6]

The Governing Board and the Education Department agreed to close Dadaya School at the time of the election. The Todds thought it prudent to go into Bulawayo, where they had taken a lease of a house Allan Ritson had owned in the Suburbs area. Here quiet, wide streets were bordered with double rows of jacaranda trees; and the houses, mostly bungalows, were set in large, well-tended gardens complete with swimming pools. So far, 47A Heyman Road conformed; but the inside of the house was different, and suspicions that it had once been a private gaming-house were supported by the built-in bar and the shuttered grille in the heavy wooden doors into the high-walled garden. Grace told Elsie that the house 'defies description. It is definitely not our life style! But Gar loves it. He finds he can relax there as he cannot do here … there are great easy chairs, a TV, a fantastically appointed kitchen, with Benjamin.'[7]

Enormous pressure to vote was brought to bear on Africans by employers, the Government, local officials, and the army. The general election was held in April – for the whites on the 10th, when Smith won all the 'A'-roll seats; for the Africans, over twelve days later in the month. Two British journalists, Richard Lindley and Robin Denzelow, had persuaded the Government to attach them to 'one of their particularly potent units, mercenary-led. We went out on a number of patrols with them', Lindley told me. 'We felt we should also try to get a sense of what the boys in the bush were also thinking … Leaving our camera crew, we

---

4   Commonwealth Information News Release no. 79/3, 31.1.79.
5   *The Chronicle*, 19.3.79.
6   JGT/EB, 11.2.79, destroyed file.
7   JGT/EB, 7.5.79, c/TPPC.

went down to Hokonui Ranch. Garfield took us and introduced us in the early light of dawn. We set up our camera, Robin operated it ... Soon "boys" came out. I talked to these people and it was clear to me that they were the authentic face of black nationalism in that part of Zimbabwe. They were human beings with views on what they were fighting for. We got back without difficulty, left the country and put the programme out.'[8] It had all been very secret – but, when they left, Grace found that they had carefully signed their names in the Hokonui Ranch visitors' book.

On 31 May, white rule ended in the country that had been Southern Rhodesia, then Rhodesia, and now would, briefly, be Zimbabwe-Rhodesia. Smith wrote: 'It was all coming to an end, this tremendous nation of Rhodesians with their epic history of fighting a lone battle for freedom and western civilisation.'[9] Bishop Abel Muzorewa became the country's first black Prime Minister. His first priority, he said, was the creation of peace. He offered an amnesty to the guerrillas, but they ignored it and there was no peace.

***

The Conservatives had won the British general election on 3 May 1979. There was a danger that Mrs Thatcher might recognise Muzorewa's government, but within two days 34 Commonwealth High Commissioners had warned her against doing so and against removing sanctions. While the Todds were less enthusiastic about the Conservative victory, they greeted with relief the appointment of Lord Carrington as Foreign and Commonwealth Secretary.

A summit in Colombo of the Non-Aligned group of countries in June expressed strong condemnation of the 'internal Settlement' and warned the British Government against recognition. In July in Liberia, the OAU summit took a similarly strong position. Garfield, on a short visit to London, added his mite of warning and advice when he saw the new Foreign Secretary, whom he considered 'the best man the Conservatives have got for Foreign Affairs'.[10]

***

Garfield drank the third and last glass of brandy in his life at a guerrilla camp at Manjarira, in the Mazvihwa area on the other side of Shabani, on a Sunday in June 1979 that Samuel Mutomba, Principal of Dadaya School, described as 'the longest day I ever lived through'.[11] The complete story that follows is

---

8   R. Lindley interview, TPPC.
9   Smith, 1997, p. 299.
10 GT/Mrs David Hood, Carnegie Corporation, 4.6.79, MS.1082/5/20, Todd Papers, NAZ.
11 GT/Judith Acton, 4.7.79, TPPC.

told, partly in Garfield's letter to Judith and partly in an address he gave to the Zimbabwe Staff College in 1981.[12]

The previous day, Mr Mutomba had telephoned Garfield in Bulawayo at 5 p.m.: 'Garfield, you must come to Dadaya now. We face a crisis.' It was winter and would be dark by six, when the curfew came into force, and the roads around Gwatemba were particularly dangerous; but the Todds set out. 'I went straight to the office where Mutomba sat grim-faced. He held a letter which he had opened at 5pm. It said that he was to close Dadaya School immediately. If by Tuesday morning anyone remained on the place he would be shot. It apologised to Todd for what was being done but stressed that it was a command. To close Dadaya in June, send 600 scholars home and maybe bring to an end the formal education of many of them was unthinkable. The letter did not ring true but we did not dare take the risk … it came from Bungowa to the east of Shabani and we knew that the leader there was Garikayi whose signature appeared on the letter, on behalf of Mambo Mlambo' (the ZANLA District Commander, who once visited Hokonui at night, with several of his men).

Mutomba asked a schoolboy, Alfred, who came from that area, to be Garfield's guide, and he agreed. They set out for Mazvihwa early the next morning. Beyond Shabani, they passed an army camp; but there was no road block and no challenge, and they took the side road to Bungowa. They stopped at the first village to check for mines but were assured it was safe to proceed to the next village. There, they were told by a man to go no further. Alfred didn't believe him and went off to consult his aunt, who lived there. He returned, saying: 'we can go safely as far as St Verena School'. On reaching the school, Mr Maposa, 'the headmaster appeared, smiling and surprised. "I haven't seen a white man here for five years, and when I saw Mrs Grace Todd's car come I did not know what was happening."' (Grace had visited the villages to judge school choir competitions.)

When Garfield told Mr Maposa what he wanted, he replied that he had been with Garikayi the previous day, so he couldn't be far away; 'but of course the boys move on all the time. You wait at my house and I will try to find him.' After an hour of searching questions from the guerrilla 'chef', he returned and reported that Garikayi would meet Garfield at a village a few miles away. At the end of a long walk, Garfield was greeted by a short, stocky man with a bushy beard, carrying a rocket-launcher and with a quiver on his back holding three rockets. He was accompanied by a younger man whom he introduced as Tshaka. 'Both men shook hands with me … and took me to a table set under a

---

12 Leadership Address, GT, Zimbabwe Staff College, 6.11.81, MS.1082/3/13/1, Todd Papers, NAZ.

tree. There were three chairs and we sat down. Each of us had a tumbler with an inch of brandy …'

First of all, Garikayi asked to see the letter. Garfield explained that he had not brought it in case he was searched, but 'you must believe that I would not come out here for fun. "No, but you may have been sent by Smith"', replied Garikayi. Then he disclosed that he had not written the letter. 'A ton weight dropped from my heart and all I wanted was to rise and go with the good news, but that was not to be.' Tea and cakes were brought and consumed, and then there was a tour of the bases. At the third, water to wash was brought, and then food. Garikayi showed Garfield his AK47 and suggested he fire it. Garfield declined; the soldiers were not all that far away …

The party returned to the first base, and then Garikayi let Garfield go. '"Remember we would not close Dadaya: we support Dadaya." So I walked back to St Verena's school where Alfred waited for me. We turned the car towards Shabani, came to the road junction and the military camp – no road block – no challenge – and by dark we arrived at Dadaya School, where a tense Mutomba waited. '"All is well," I reported. Who sent the letter I do not know, but Dadaya stayed open for the whole of the war.'

***

When the British Prime Minister, Mrs Thatcher, and the Foreign Secretary reached Lusaka for the Commonwealth Conference, they found a powerful alliance of President Nyerere of Tanzania, President Kaunda of Zambia, Michael Manley, Prime Minister of Jamaica, and Australia's Malcolm Fraser determined to prevent Britain's recognition of Muzorewa. In addition, Presidents Kaunda and Machel were so appalled at what was happening in their own countries and to their own economies that they were prepared to apply the strongest pressure on the guerrilla leaders.

The Commonwealth Conference discussions on Rhodesia resulted in the 'Lusaka Accord', with a commitment to genuine black majority rule and the holding of a constitutional conference, to which all parties would be invited. On 6 August, Grace told New Zealand friends her heart was 'singing hallelujahs' because of the news from Lusaka: it looked 'as if the miracle has at last been vouchsafed'. 'Garfield never gives up hope, never rules out the possibility of a miracle … I believe the suffering black people of this country, who long for peace, will rejoice. Pray with us for the success of this initiative.'[13]

The constitutional conference was held at Lancaster House in London in

---

13 JGT/Church Women's Fellowship, Onehunga, 6.8.79, MS.1082/4/18, Todd Papers, NAZ.

September. Mugabe was reluctant to attend, but Samora Machel applied a successful combination of pressure and threats. Nearly twenty long, weary, bloody years had passed since Garfield had pleaded for Britain to call a Constitutional Conference on Southern Rhodesia.

This time, Garfield would not be part of any delegation, which meant he would be an entirely free agent to play his part in the creation of Zimbabwe. He kept a manuscript diary of his activities between 6 September and 10 November (but he later returned to London for a few more days), with notes of conversations with pretty well all the participants in the conference, as well as Tanzanians, the Zambian President and High Commissioner, and the President of Malawi. His objectives were, first, as Judith described it, 'running around seeing people – doing anything to bring the war to an end'; second, larding the wheels of heated discussions and negotiation behind the scenes, smoothing misunderstandings and 'sweetening discord' by his knowledge of and long association with many of the participants, particularly the Africans; and third, to try to ensure that decisions were made which, with his 45-year knowledge of Rhodesia and his understanding of her present needs, he felt were correct. He was particularly anxious about (and would later be dissatisfied with) the vital land provisions. When Garfield died in October 2002, his obituary in the *Lincolnshire Echo* included this: 'We in London were able to appreciate this handsome old man for what he truly was, determined but now magnanimous'.[14]

Much has been written about the Lancaster House Conference – not least by the participants, notably Lord Carrington, the Commonwealth Secretary-General (Sir 'Sonny' Ramphal), Smith and Lord Renwick – but a few small pictures here will serve to illustrate the contrast with what was going on in Zimbabwe-Rhodesia. Smith, speaking 'for himself, his party and "the whites of Zimbabwe-Rhodesia"', 'lashed out' at Muzorewa's acceptance of the British Constitutional proposals, 'the worst' since UDI.[15]

One encounter Carrington had with Smith is referred to by both. Smith writes: 'At one stage Carrington went to Washington for more than a week ... On his return I reminded him that innocent people were being murdered in our country every day, and this would continue until we finished our work – I hoped he would dedicate more time to our mission.'[16] Carrington writes: 'I think I had kept my temper throughout some pretty provoking moments at that conference, but on this particular occasion it was touch and go. I said

---
14 TPPC.
15 *The Chronicle*, 15.10.79.
16 Smith, 1997, p. 315.

to Smith: "Perhaps you might recollect that but for you nobody in Rhodesia would be being killed." I think it was a fair reply.'[17]

In October, Garfield returned briefly to Hokonui, 'still marginally hopeful' about the talks, Grace told me,[18] though both were very concerned about racial clauses in the proposed constitution. 'There are some really bad things in that proposed Constitution ... I do not want to be shoved willy-nilly onto a whites-only roll, and only given right-wing RF types to vote for ...'

Garfield told Lord Carrington about 'the present hell of our situation. While I was in England an attack by security forces at Lundi less than 30 miles from our home killed no guerrillas but did kill 20 men and 4 women from the villages with another 8 people wounded. These tragedies are not reported and troops in our area seem to have mounted a campaign of terror. Both sides continue their atrocities, but, on their own daily reporting, the security forces kill ten times as many people as do the guerillas.'[19]

More shocking events occurred near Hokonui, Garfield told the OMB in New Zealand. 'We have just paid out a hundred dollars to a widow with twelve children from 15 years down. Her husband controlled the water at an irrigation project near Wedza and was shot out of hand by soldiers as he walked to work.' He listed 75 dependants left after the Lundi attack.[20] 'In this area people are being shot, not just beaten up. The CO is a new man and a police-trained man and there is always some hope when the head man is both approachable and a man with standards. The vast mass of soldiers and guards with whom we have to contend daily are quite a different matter.'[21]

Tormented by the knowledge that the horrors going on around Hokonui would be repeated all over the country, Garfield wrote an impassioned letter to Muzorewa in London: 'I plead with you to take no step which would just intensify the horror of our situation. I cannot believe that you know what your security forces are doing in the Tribal Trust Lands ... I now plead with you not to enter into any agreement which is not able to stop the war.'[22]

On his return to London, Garfield went to see General Walls and found it much easier to talk to him than he had expected: 'He said that we could surely forget the whites now as they had lost most of their significance ... the PF seemed ready to fraternise with the whites and even with Ndiweni but not with

---

17   Carrington, 1988, p. 300.
18   JGT/SP, 11.10.79, TPPC.
19   GT/Lord Carrington, 11.10.79, TPPC.
20   GT/OMB, 6.10.79, MS.1082/5/20, Todd Papers, NAZ.
21   GT/OMB, 16.10.79, ibid.
22   GT/Abel Muzorewa, 16.10.79, MS.1082/5/20, Todd Papers, NAZ.

Facing Realities at Last – 1979

Muzorewa.'[23] Garfield listened to a late-night debate in the House of Commons on the conference. 'A commonwealth force was being assembled to monitor the ceasefire! Wonderful. Another step along the way.' But 'the prospects of success in the conference were nearly destroyed by massive Rhodesian raids into Zambia'. Renwick writes: 'It proved possible just in time to prevent [the Rhodesians] blowing up the Tete suspension bridge in Mozambique.'[24]

Before leaving London on 10 December, Garfield sent a message to Nkomo and Mugabe: 'Even the most sympathetic person could not comprehend the devastation which has engulfed people and villages in Zimbabwe … the thousands of men, women and children who have been killed are only a fraction of the price which is being paid for freedom. Thousands more have been wounded and those who have been crippled will have to be supported through all the years ahead. Hundreds of thousands of our seven-million population, peace-loving people, have had their homes destroyed, their schools, hospitals and clinics closed. They have had to abandon fields and cattle and seek refuge in towns, some with relatives, some sheltering under plastic sheets, owning nothing and utterly dependent upon the Churches and the Red Cross for a bare existence … Hundreds of young men and girls, too, have been shot as they fled the country or killed in battle when they returned. They lie in unmarked graves in the bush; many were not given burial; and the fate of thousands will be forever unknown to their families … the people have demonstrated their courage and determination in war and they have the vision required to win the peace.'

Finally, and against all the odds, agreement on the last, trickiest item – the ceasefire – was reached. The guerrilla forces were to stand down, move to assembly points, and accept disarmament. The country would revert to the pre-UDI constitutional position. Elections would then be held on universal suffrage, all parties participating. When Carrington announced that the first step would be the return of a British Governor, he feared an adverse reaction. Nkomo broke a stunned silence, asking: '"Really? Will he have plumes and a horse?" The whole conference dissolved in laughter. The day was saved.'[25]

The ceasefire arrangements were tabled on 16 November and agreed to by Muzorewa ten days later, but the Patriotic Front took more persuading. Garfield's verdict on the constitution as finally agreed was cautious: 'imperfect but workable'. While negotiation on details took many days, there was, almost unbelievably, a ceasefire, an end to the killing. Carrington didn't wait for the PF to agree – 'the Daimler and the furniture' arrived in Rhodesia on 19 November.

---

23 GT's Diary, TPPC.
24 Renwick, 1997, p. 54.
25 Carrington, 1988, pp. 301–2.

On 12 December, the new Governor of Zimbabwe-Rhodesia, Lord Soames, and Lady Soames arrived in Salisbury 'to the strains of "God Save the Queen"':[26] 'When he drove into Government House there was a handful of people with a union jack to welcome him – the same old bunch of starry-eyed liberals who had always been petrified at the thought of standing alone in this world.' In that small crowd were Sir Humphrey and Dame Mollie Gibbs. Governor Soames broadcast to Zimbabwe-Rhodesia in the evening: his 'task was to hold the government and the country in trust until independence'. And, that day, British sanctions were lifted.

On 20 December, the Zimbabwe-Rhodesian Parliament passed the bill which at last wrote 'Finis' on Smith's UDI; and the first British troops of the monitoring force arrived. On 21 December, the agreement was signed by all parties; in Salisbury, the Governor revoked the orders banning ZAPU and ZANU. On 27 December, small teams of the monitoring force were sent into the most remote and dangerous parts of the country. By midnight on the 28th, 39 rendezvous points for the guerrillas were in place, and 24 hours later the remaining five had been established.

On 28 December, the ceasefire came into force.

***

Garfield Todd, Garfield Todd,
How will it end?
In black votes, or red gutters
– You choose, my friend ...[27]

---

26 Smith, 1997, p. 326.
27 *Central African Examiner*, 1959.

83

DEATH THROES OF AN ILLEGAL REGIME – 1979–80

'To be honoured so greatly in New Zealand and then to be sent to prison in Rhodesia was all too much of a contrast.'

Garfield Todd, 1980

In December 1979, the Todds went to New Zealand. Grace had warned her sister, Elsie, of the toll the years had taken, and went on: 'I am the most ordinary of women and many others would have reacted to my circumstances in a far nobler and better way for all concerned. I still hate the limelight, am reluctant to take on responsibilities or rise to challenges ... It is just that we are stuck here in these strange circumstances, different from what most people have to face, and of course Garfield is, I think, somewhat special. Me, I just tag along, reluctant and complaining.'[1]

Garfield had many engagements during their five weeks in New Zealand; Grace, too, had a few commitments. There were also family visits and meetings with the Overseas Mission Board. An occasion of particular significance for Grace was a gathering of her 'whole clan ... for a feast spread under the trees on the original family farm at Pukerau. My McKenzie grandfather settled there over 100 years ago.'[2]

Garfield's graduation at Otago University, with the degree of Doctor of Laws, *honoris causa*, took place in Dunedin town hall. The public orator, Assistant Prof. R. G. Mulgan, spoke of Garfield's early years and his career at the university: 'He has had to wait a long time, indeed, exactly half a century from the year of his matriculation, before being enrolled among the university's graduates. But what a half-century it has been!'[3]

---

1   JGT/EB, 14.1.79, c/TPPC.
2   JGT/'Friends', November 1980, TPPC.
3   University of Otago citation, 7.12.79, TPPC.

The public orator told of the Dadaya decades and then reviewed Garfield's political career, introducing it: 'There are some, Mr Chancellor, who consider politics to be a profession somewhat less than reputable and one unworthy of a man of principle let alone a man of God. A politician must bargain and compromise; if he need not actually lie, he must often present the truth in the most favourable light. Yet politics, as Aristotle remarked, is the master science, which orders the conditions under which all other aspects of human life may flourish. If men of ideals abandon it, they leave it to men who have none. One of Garfield Todd's great achievements has been to demonstrate that politics and principles are not incompatible, that men of integrity and faith can be effective political leaders though, or rather because, there is always a point beyond which they will not compromise for the sake of retaining power. New Zealanders may take pride that they have produced a statesman who has become an international champion of racial equality …

'Historians agree that [1958] was a turning point in Rhodesian history. With the fall of Garfield Todd, the country lost its one chance of a peaceful transition to majority rule and legal independence … But the Smith government succeeded merely in confirming and enhancing his stature as opponent of racial segregation and an advocate of a free, equal Zimbabwe … Whatever the future of Zimbabwe, the chances that white and black may live there together have been greatly increased by his actions and life-long example …'[4]

Garfield began his address in reply: 'Fifty years ago I could not have imagined that I would have a part to play in a graduation ceremony of the University of Otago. You have given me great honour, and I would like to offer something to you young men and women whom it is my privilege to address … The only subject in which I have kept reasonably up to date is life itself. My concern has been with people, and there are certainly plenty of them …

'People! Living and adventuring with people! … From the University of Otago five men and women of my own tribe, and in my own lifetime, have gone from New Zealand to make their homes in China, India, the United Kingdom, Africa and Russia.' He told the story of Louie … 'Whether working on English–Russian dictionaries or in manual labour for the state she had fulfilled her life …

'Sometimes, however, a country stagnates: the vision dies … The common good is spurned in the pursuit of power or personal gain. Tragedy strikes. In Colonial Africa the breech-loading rifle and the Maxim gun made it possible for western nations to suppress the masses of the people for many years … Then came 60 years of peace and from 1896 until 1959 no-one in Rhodesia

---

4   Ibid.

was killed by policeman or soldier. In that period a subjected people found themselves again. They accepted churches and schools, were responsive to new ideas and lived at peace. In this exciting adventure we have shared for 45 years ... Soon there came demands for equality of opportunity – for an equal say in government. So the killing began again ...'

Garfield spoke of the fourteen years since UDI and the horror of the war: 'The political changes which the people demand could have come by peaceful evolution if there had been sympathetic understanding between the races ... The situation in Zimbabwe is our special tragedy and a new day will not dawn until dividing walls are broken down and people meet with a desire to understand one another ...

'In our life, day by day, we can play our specialised parts but we should also cultivate an awareness of our wider responsibilities. If we accept this doctrine, then at the end of the day we may find that although we have not achieved world-fame in our profession or have blazed new trails through the stars all will not have been lost if we can say – "I have adventured with people, I have lived."'[5]

The applause which followed Garfield's graduation was such that the Chancellor stated 'he had never seen so moving a tribute when a person was presented for a degree'.[6]

To the *Nelson Evening Mail*, Garfield said he did not believe 'a victory by Robert Mugabe would transform the country into a Marxist state. "I don't fear it. For a start, the population is not atheistic. It's a spirit-believing population."' Of the guerrillas, Garfield said: 'They come from our schools and villages. They have decided on the highest motivation to go out of the country because after 30 years they would not achieve what they wanted by peaceful means ... We owe Nyerere, Machel and Kaunda a tremendous debt of gratitude. We could not have come to Lancaster House without them ... All it needs to get Rhodesia on its feet again are peace and stability ...'[7]

An important part of the visit was the contact with the Churches of Christ, including the annual conference. There, both were honoured. Grace addressed the conference of the National Churchwomen of the New Zealand Churches (formerly the Christian Women's Auxiliary): 'Another special significance attaches to this visit. We are the last of the band of missionaries sent to Africa by our churches. Each one made a contribution, important and unique, according to each one's special gifts. Yet I surely believe that each one of those missionaries

---

5 GT, University of Otago, 7.12.79, TPPC.
6 GT/Edith E. W. Todd, 12.12.79, MS.1082/1/25, Todd Papers, NAZ.
7 *Nelson Evening Mail*, 18.1.80.

would testify that much importance lay in the lives we touched and influenced. No small band of white missionaries could account for the tens of thousands of Christian converts. The work of evangelism, the teaching and witness and example of the Christian way was the work of African men and women ... The task of the missionaries in Africa was the establishment of an indigenous church. That church is now a living and growing reality. It can be nurtured and sustained and helped in whatever way possible by Churches and individuals here but the relationship has changed, I believe, from the paternalism of the past to the sharing of brotherly concern. For Garfield and me it has been a life of great privilege in which you have always and faithfully shared ... Our visit now ... is a journey into the past, to our roots, to the country where we were shaped and prepared ...'[8]

***

At the end of January 1980, the Todds returned to Zimbabwe-Rhodesia – and, when the Governor revoked all ministerial detention orders, were joined by Judith. By this time, electioneering was in full swing, and Garfield found himself approached for donations by more than one party. He gave ZANU-PF, in the person of a man called Amin, a donation of 300 dollars to pay off a car loan. Three of the party's candidates were in the Shabani area, and two of them – Simbarashe Mnangagwa and Mrs Julia Zvobgo – held a private meeting in a teacher's house at Dadaya on the evening of 7 February. Both were subsequently arrested by Shabani police, together with their colleague, Richard Hove – of the 1964 *Daily News* protest.

On 8 February, Mr Samuel Mutomba, Principal of Dadaya School, was also arrested and taken to Shabani police station. As the telephones were out of order, his deputy, Mr Zebediah Sibanda, went to Hokonui to tell Garfield – but he was in Bulawayo. However, he saw Judith, who telephoned the news to her father. He promptly instructed a lawyer to take all necessary steps for Mutomba's release.

No sooner had Mr Sibanda left than three policemen arrived, also seeking Garfield. On learning he was due the next day, they said they would return then. Judith rang Heyman Road again, and the Todds set out immediately for Dadaya. After seeing Mr Sibanda, Garfield telephoned the police to find out what it was all about. They said that if he went to Shabani at 8 a.m. the next day they would tell him. Garfield said it was such a serious matter he would go in that night; but, no, the police would see him the next day. He then telephoned this rather ominous news to one of the New Zealand election

---

8   *New Zealand Christian*, February 1980.

monitors, Mr Peter Wilkinson, in Salisbury, who said he would tell a member of the Governor's staff.

Garfield went into Shabani early on Saturday morning – and, as Grace told Elsie, 'the sky fell on us'.[9] He was arrested 'in the name of the Queen' under the Law and Order (Maintenance) Act. As an amnesty had been proclaimed, Garfield found his arrest quite unbelievable. He drove back to Hokonui with a police escort, Mr Gibbard. It was 1972 all over again, but this time under a British Governor. Once again, Grace rose to the challenge: once again she ordered tea and sandwiches for prisoner and escort. Once again, Garfield packed a bag for prison. When he asked to visit his sister, ill in her house 200 yards away, Gibbard went with him. Judith promptly telephoned the journalist Martin Meredith in Salisbury, who promised to ring the Governor.

Judith went with her father into Shabani. That the court was full of undisguised hostility came as no surprise to Garfield; but that the magistrate should remand him in custody until 22 February came as a profound shock. Only then did he learn that he was charged with two counts under the Law and Order (Maintenance) Act – 'aiding a person in commission of acts of terrorism' (the 300-dollar loan to Amin, as shown in Amin's 'diary' now in the possession of the police); and failure to report the presence of a terrorist (Amin).

Garfield was taken out of court, and Judith drove back to Hokonui, where she telephoned Lord Soames's office, which moved quickly – 'Get that man out of jail!' – and, by the time Garfield had at last been provided with a large enough prison uniform, he was told to change back into his own clothes to appear before a hastily reconvened Shabani Court, where he was remanded on 500 dollars' bail. Gibbard took Garfield back to Hokonui. Before Garfield was due back in court on 22 February, the Attorney-General decided 'to terminate the criminal proceedings'.[10] His 500 dollars were returned; and, after Independence, the charges against him and Mr Mutomba were struck from the books.

In true Rhodesian style, Mr Mutomba was not so fortunate – he didn't return home for a fortnight, during which he was badly treated by the police.[11] Garfield's postal agent, Ephraim Thebe, who had witnessed the meeting with Amin, was even more unfortunate. He was beaten up by the police and forced to sign an untrue statement of Garfield's criminality (which he subsequently repudiated).

***

---

9   JGT/EB, 8.3.80, destroyed file, TPPC.
10   Attorney-General, 115/80/GD, 21.2.80, MS.1082/2/13/1, Todd Papers, NAZ.
11   Caute, 1983, p. 409.

When Garfield was interviewed by the Rev. Colin Morris for a BBC programme many years later, he admitted helping the guerrillas. Morris asked: '"So, in actual fact, what you were doing was high treason?" "Oh, yes," replied Garfield, "One knew that you had no defence … But there was no defence, because, everybody knew … so it was just nice that Lord Soames was in charge and I was freed within the twenty-four hours."'[12]

---

[12] Transcript, TPPC.

84

'This Peculiar, Rogue Colony'[1] – 1980

'Some Africans clearly persisted in the hope that sometime, somehow, something better would turn up.'

Pearce Commission Report, 1972

The job of the new Governor of Southern Rhodesia was to see that conditions for an election campaign were in place by March 1980 – and to see that the election itself took place peacefully. Robin Renwick, adviser to the Governor in Salisbury, writes that Lord Soames made up 'in force of personality what he lacked in real power',[2] which was just as well. One of his first actions was to replace the local 6 p.m. news with the BBC World Service.

'It was asking a great deal of the guerrilla armies to emerge from the countryside in positions where they would be vulnerable to attack', observes Renwick[3] – but, by the time the ceasefire came into force, the British and Commonwealth troops of the monitoring force were deployed around the country at the rendezvous points and the assembly areas. Derek Ingram, media adviser to the Commonwealth Observers, recalls sitting at one point manned by unarmed Australian troops, and the sense of excited anticipation, apprehension, even scepticism, as they waited for the guerrillas, for on the success of this initial step depended the whole process. He remembers, too, the frisson, and the sense of relief, of triumph, as the armed figures quietly began to emerge from the bush, that 'blue-green silence',[4] to be greeted by the Australian officer in charge, with a handshake and a cup of tea! 'The Australians were marvellous,

---

1 Lapping, 1985.
2 Renwick, 1997, p. 57.
3 Ibid., p. 53.
4 Caute, 1983.

relaxed and friendly, jollying them along.'⁵ The bizarre and unprecedented plan was beginning to work.

By 1 January, 4,280 guerrillas had come into the assembly points; by the 8th, 15,000; 20,000 by the 9th (though Soames recognised that many guerrillas who had recently entered the country remained in the bush). On the 6th, Muzorewa held an extravagant rally, with a lavish feast, but only a few thousand turned up. On the 13th, Joshua Nkomo returned in triumph to Rhodesia, drawing 100,000 to his rally. Sithole's rally on the 20th drew only a few thousands.

On 27 January, 50 ambassadors saw Mugabe off in style from Maputo airport – but at Salisbury airport he and his party were not so civilly received. His rally was attended by 200,000 ecstatic followers. Did the Rhodesians take note of these figures? The *Herald* reported that Mugabe had said: 'No Rhodesian need fear for his future under a ZANU(PF) government ... "We are pledged to the creation of a true democracy based on equality where there won't be any discrimination on the basis of race or colour."'[6]

For Rhodesia's whites, the relief at the ceasefire was so great that life quite soon returned to normal; but at Government House there was anxiety that the whites might yet try to stage a coup – and not without reason, as plans were indeed being laid. Fortunately, in the end, wiser counsels prevailed – including those of General Walls and the CIO's Ken Flower. The whites-only election took place on 14 February. There was muted electioneering – and not only because in fourteen of the twenty white seats Smith's candidates were unopposed. He himself was out of the country at the time of the election, but his party won all twenty seats.

The non-white election was to be held towards the end of February. The split in the Patriotic Front, caused by Mugabe's unilateral decision, immediately after the Lancaster House Conference, to fight the election as ZANU-PF, had been a grave disappointment to Nkomo (and to Garfield). There were now four separate parties fighting the election, which brought probably the most difficult of Soames's problems: intimidation. All parties were guilty – some more than others. Smith asked the Governor to exercise his powers to disqualify Mugabe's ZANU from participating on this account. Soames refused: 'In this race all our horses are going to start. They may fall and I may disqualify them but they must all leave the starting gate', reported Jim Buckley, Soames's Private Secretary in Salisbury.[7]

Shortly before the election, the Governor invited Robert Mugabe alone to an

---

5 Derek Ingram/SP, interview, January 2008.
6 *Herald*, 28.1.80.
7 Interview, Jim Buckley/SP, 16.5.2000.

informal meeting at Government House. Lady Soames recalled what happened: 'That meeting was crucial. Christopher was very plainspoken. He made it clear to Mugabe that he must control his people, that stories of intimidation were rife. And that it would be very bad for the election if my husband was forced to proscribe constituencies because of intimidation ... It was no good predicating a perfect plan, you had to work with the people you had, in the conditions you had, and with the passions that had been aroused.'[8]

The *Guardian* commented on 22 February: 'It is hard to find a Rhodesia-watcher who does not have the jitters. Surprisingly, though ... there are slightly fewer jitters in Salisbury than in London. What is most evident in Salisbury is that the cease-fire has been largely successful ... This change has been accomplished by a combination of pressure from the front-line states, realisation by the Rhodesian parties, whites included, that war has only just stopped short of destroying the country, and some knife-edge political judgements by Lord Soames, Sir Anthony Duff, General Acland and their team ...'[9]

There was now – widely if rather thinly – deployed around the country a team of experienced British election supervisors, under the chairmanship of Sir Maurice Dorman, who had been a member of both the Monckton (1960) and Pearce (1972) Commissions, and possessed a special sort of knowledgeable wisdom. There were also 281 foreign election observers and 680 journalists.

Polling took place on 26, 27 and 28 February – and, contrary to everyone's fears and expectations, Soames had all his horses in the starting-gate – and the race began. But, even at this late hour, there was 'a threatened military coup by the white Rhodesian army should Mugabe beat his rival Joshua Nkomo in the election', according to Rebecca de Saintonge in her obituary of Ian Smith's son, Alec.[10] 'The armoured tanks were already positioned in the streets of the capital ... just waiting for the moment ... [but] advised by the Governor ... the army quietly slid away.'

Mugabe flew to Maputo on the 27th but would return after the end of polling. Soames, Renwick and others visited polling stations and 'detected the first signs of a ZANU landslide', writes Renwick.[11] The UN Representative, Señor Perez de Cuellar, was 'extremely impressed by the conduct of the election. Like the World Press, he seemed to find both picturesque and reassuring the presence in remote parts of the bush of British policemen in helmets and shirtsleeves,

---

8 *The Times*, 20.4.2000.
9 *Guardian*, 22.2.80.
10 *Independent*, 14.11.2006.
11 Renwick, 1997, p. 96.

supervising the polling!'[12] (Several later emigrated to Zimbabwe.) That day, nearly half the electorate – 1,375,000 people – voted.

By the time polling ended on 29 February, 2.7 million votes had been cast – a 93 per cent turnout. 'Soames called on all the observers present at the elections to make public their opinions before the results were known ... The conclusions of all the official groups were unanimously favourable, including that of the Commonwealth team', writes Renwick.[13] The British election supervisors reported that 'the elections in general were a fair reflection of the wishes of the people ... the degree of intimidation and pressure was not so great as to invalidate the overall results of the poll'.

By 2 March, preliminary results of vote-counting showed support for Mugabe. Sir Anthony Duff and Renwick met the Rhodesian commanders. Walls considered the possibility of military action if Mugabe won, 'only to reject it', Renwick writes. 'It might have lasted 48 hours or more. Many people would have been killed. It would have been a chaotic state of affairs.'[14] He later made a TV broadcast 'urging people to accept the election results calmly'.

On the eve of Mugabe's great victory, Lady Soames said: 'We heard that all over Salisbury there were hundreds of families ready to leave ... their cars with tanks full of petrol, belongings packed up.'[15] All Rhodesia listened as the election results were broadcast. The Rhodesian Registrar of Elections, Mr Eric Pope-Symonds, the model of the incorruptible, correct, helpful civil servant, announced that Muzorewa had won three seats, Nkomo twenty (all in Matabeleland) and Mugabe 57. (Sithole and his political ambitions were swept away.) Mugabe therefore had an overall majority in Parliament. Sir John Boynton, the British Election Commissioner, 'declared the outcome "a reflection of the wishes of the people" and later defended its validity against those who argued that Mugabe had stolen power'.[16] So overwhelming was Mugabe's victory that it was obvious that, even without any intimidation, he would have won.

'On the part of the white community the news was received in stunned silence', writes Renwick.[17] Mrs Thatcher and Lord Carrington in Britain; Smith and Vorster in Africa; all were appalled.

On the evening of 4 March, Mugabe made an 'eloquent broadcast ...

---

12 Ibid.
13 Ibid., p. 97.
14 Ibid., p. 99.
15 *The Times*, 20.4.2000.
16 *Daily Telegraph*, obituary, 14.2.2007.
17 Renwick, 1997, p. 100.

"Greeting in the name of freedom", it began', writes Renwick.[18] 'His efforts would be directed towards the achievement of peace and stability ... He would be inviting Nkomo to join his government and also the representatives of other communities. His government would respect the constitution. It would not interfere with pensions or individual property rights ... His government would bring change, but change could not occur overnight.' Canon Victor de Waal quotes further: 'Only a government that subjects itself to the rule of law has any moral right to demand of its citizens obedience to the rule of law', and goes on to describe 'an immense wave of relief' sweeping 'over the white community. The next day the whites were back at work and the children back at school.'[19]

Over 30 years later, some of this rings a little hollow. In April 2008, Lord Renwick was asked if he had had any 'inner fears' about Mugabe. He replied: 'Yes, I did because I had seen his methods for winning power in existence at villages at night ... but at that time they were fighting against white rule and they did have support. He did have majority support and this is why we installed him and his government as the first government of the democratic Zimbabwe.'[20]

'Mugabe's victory was won on the battlefield,' commented *Current Affairs in South Africa*. 'The elections only confirmed that victory. The African people voted for ZANU on the basis that it had already won independence from white control through force of arms.'[21]

***

Garfield was unsurprised at Mugabe's victory. Grace never forgot the 'tremendous excitement' over the election.[22] They prudently went into Bulawayo to stay at Heyman Road over the time of counting and the announcement of the results. 'None of our white friends imagined that Mugabe was going to win. They were quite sure there was going to be some sort of accommodation between Nkomo and Smith. I think Soames was expecting that. It was a landslide and there was absolute consternation on the part of the whites and then 24 hours later Mugabe made that reconciliation speech which absolutely changed the situation and people just listened to it with hope and relief and almost disbelief ...'

In the video, *Hokonui Todd*, first Garfield and then Grace reflected on the 'Soames election': 'From 1958 until 1980 was a long span, and all of that time we were waiting for independence, so we were fortunate that we were the ones

---

18 Ibid., p. 101.
19 de Waal, 1990, p. 47.
20 BBC Scotland radio interview, 17.4.2008.
21 *X-Ray: Current Affairs in South Africa*, March/April 1980.
22 GT and JGT/SP, interviews for this book, TPPC.

who lived through and saw our dreams come true ... And then the day came that Rhodesia became Zimbabwe and Mugabe had won an election, and a black government, a majority government was formed. I, too, felt liberated.'[23]

Mugabe invited Nkomo to become Zimbabwe's first president. He declined, but accepted the portfolio of Home Affairs in the new cabinet. There were four other ZAPU cabinet ministers and three junior ministers. To the great relief of the white community, David Smith, formerly of Ian Smith's cabinet, was made Minister of Commerce; and Denis Norman, President of the National Farmers' Union, became Minister of Agriculture.

To their friends, Garfield wrote on 6 March: 'Rejoice with us. On Tuesday, March 4th 1980, Zimbabwe emerged from persecution and war with a clarity of decision which has taken the world by surprise. This overwhelming expression of the people's will is our recipe for peace. Our happiness is so great that it has almost banished the fear and anxiety under which we have lived for so many years; yet the joy and thankfulness which we share with almost the whole of the black people of Zimbabwe cannot eradicate the memories of what has happened ...

'The great contribution which has been made by the Commonwealth, and especially by Britain, has been the Lancaster House Conference and the provision of an election in which the people ... gave the two parties whose guerilla fighters they had supported during the war, their almost exclusive support ...

'Mr Mugabe, as Prime Minister designate, addressed the nation last evening and his message was one of reconciliation and of hope. Not in many years have we listened to a speech by our Prime Minister so unambiguous, so articulate, so carefully conciliatory. At the same time people from both sections of the Patriotic Front were dancing and singing in the townships and in the villages, brothers in the struggle and in the victory.

'The war has cost over 20,000 lives [an estimate finally revised to 37,000], the detention and imprisonment of tens of thousands of people, the destruction of innumerable homes, but we are now emerging into the sunlight of hope ... I know that there will be problems and disappointments; there are wounds of the body and of the spirit which can hardly be healed but the people have massively spoken for peace.'[24]

Grace wrote to Elsie: 'We were certain that Robert Mugabe was going to poll the largest number of votes, but even we were not prepared for Muzorewa's defeat.' Grace goes on to speak of 'the amount of pressure and violence of the Security and other pro-Muzorewa elements. Only by knowing about this can

---

23 *Hokonui Todd*, 1992.
24 GT/'Friends', 6.3.80, TPPC.

one understand the significance of the massive pro-Mugabe vote. I think it is a vote for radical change. I see Mugabe's great challenge as gauging the speed of change necessary in relation to the need to allay the fears of the whites, and only hope he will not be tempted to be too soft and conciliatory in the latter direction ...

'It is extraordinary that our papers, completely biased until now, are already reporting various bodies, e.g. Railways, Commerce and Industry, Cattle Commission, etc., making hopeful prognostications ... It would be foolish to expect that all our troubles are over for good or that there will be no further unpleasant incidents. Yet we are so happy and hopeful. The election was another miracle. It is tragic and should have been unnecessary that a bloody war had to be the prologue. Yet we dare now to hope that it is now going to be peace with justice and a brighter future for us all ...'[25]

Among the relieved and happy letters from friends, Margaret Tredgold wrote: 'Robbie's prophecy came true – that we would have Mugabe, "a kind of black Napoleon", when he knew him, so long ago ... He also foresaw that when Mugabe's day also has run its course our country will be ruled by the Matabele ...'[26]

***

Garfield went to Salisbury for a meeting of the Christian Council of Zimbabwe with members of the World Council of Churches. He also saw the new Minister of Information and Tourism, Nathan Shamuyarira, whom he had known for a quarter of a century, and the new Minister of Education, with whom he discussed the future of private schools like Dadaya. Then he saw Mugabe. At the end of their interview, Garfield thanked the PM for seeing him, and said: '"There is a convention in Britain and it used to hold in Rhodesia that a past PM had easy access to the present PM ... I am really asking two things of you – reasonably easy access for a past PM and an assurance that I will not be arrested." Mugabe laughed – then he leaned over and put his hand on my arm and said, "but I want you for the Senate". I was quite taken aback ... "You have made a great contribution to the struggle and you deserve it. It is time those who in the past dishonoured you should now see you honoured." I still protested because I could not clearly see what all the implications might be – age, travel, business at the ranch, the Dadaya Project – and when the PM saw my hesitation, he said, "but you know it will not be a dull house ...". And so the Prime Minister of Zimbabwe has asked me to be one of the six Senators

---

25 JGT/EB, 8.3.80, MS.1082/4/7, Todd Papers, NAZ.
26 Margaret Tredgold/Todds, March 1980, MS.1082/4/19, Todd Papers, NAZ.

whom he is able to name personally – and I am honoured.'

After that meeting, Garfield joined Grace in the car, and they left for home. When Garfield broke the news to Grace, 'she also was quite dumbfounded. Anyway, as the miles slipped by we thought it was not only a great honour but that it would be a pleasant and interesting position in which I might well make some contribution.'[27]

Grace told the *Hokonui Todd* TV interviewer: 'I had lived all those years after Garfield's defeat in Parliament knowing that he was denigrated by the European community, not by the Africans, and always hoped that somehow or other the day may come – that he would live long enough actually, to find that his policies had been vindicated and the people would understand and appreciate what he had done, what he had suffered in this cause'.[28]

The day after Garfield's astonishing interview with Mugabe, Grace wrote to Ida Grant: 'Yes, there have been miracles, a succession of them, and perhaps the greatest is that the people set aside all blandishments and in spite of threats and intimidation made their will clearly and firmly known. Since then Mugabe has been splendid and we hope and pray he may continue to show the same tolerance and wisdom ... I think a great many whites will still leave, as and when they can, but many are surprised and relieved at Mugabe's moderation and will stay on and see what happens ...

'It is now 2 April and I am in Bulawayo ... Gar will be coming in here this afternoon, so we shall have a nice quiet evening here and then shall meet Judith tomorrow ... I feel so happy as I sit here writing to you. We consider ourselves fortunate people to have lived to see the beginning of a new era, the birth of Zimbabwe.'[29]

Later, in a letter to Elsie, Grace wrote: 'What has given us great delight and satisfaction is the joy [Gar's] appointment has given our African friends, and all those around here with whom we are associated'.[30] Samuel Mutomba, so recently released from his ordeal in that filthy cell, and his wife, Raviro, wrote the most touching letter of all: 'While Zimbabwe celebrates her finest hour, Dadaya celebrates its proudest hour. We salute you and we share with you in this well-deserved and well-earned honour. It is the least Zimbabwe could have done in recognition of your heroic stand during the last fifteen years. Dadaya has been honoured and recognised and this is our proudest moment.'[31]

---

27 GT/JT, 21.3.80, MS.1082/5/22, Todd Papers, NAZ.
28 *Hokonui Todd* transcript, TPPC.
29 JGT/Ida Grant, 29.3.80, TPPC.
30 JGT/EB, 12.5.80, destroyed file, c/TPPC.
31 R. and S. Mutomba/GT, n.d., MS.1082/3/5, Todd Papers, NAZ.

Mutomba also wrote to the Overseas Mission Board in New Zealand: 'Dr Garfield Todd's ... open and heroic stand during the war, often at great personal risk, endeared him to all of us here at Dadaya and all our people out in the Reserves. His personal courage and deeply rooted faith were an inspiration to all, especially to us here who have the pleasure of working closely with him ... I held a special assembly for the students to inform them of what had happened. I was literally stunned by their reaction: they broke into spontaneous applause, wildly cheering and whistling and clapping their hands in approval ... As a community we feel gratified that this really is the climax to all the sacrifices and the troubles we have shared with Dr Garfield Todd during the grim war years. We are proud that Zimbabwe has elevated the Father of our community in this way, and we share in his joy and personal triumph ...'[32]

***

On 16 April, the Prince of Wales, representing the Queen, arrived in Salisbury and was greeted by Lord Soames, General Walls and the ZANLA and ZIPRA commanders. The Prime Minister of India, Mrs Gandhi, arrived, as did the Prime Minister of Australia, Malcolm Fraser, and Dr Waldheim, Secretary-General of the United Nations. Lord Carrington arrived to represent the British Government.

On the evening of the 17th, there was a great reception at Government House. Dr Megahey writes: 'It was probably the last great colonial occasion in the country, as the Gibbses and Todds and Putterills mingled with the new black ministers designate.'[33] Garfield told Harold Hochschild: 'As I walked in Government House grounds with my sister, my daughter and my wife after a break of 20 years I could hardly believe what was happening.'[34] At sunset, the Union Flag was lowered. Sir Humphrey and Dame Mollie, of course, had seen it all before.

---

32 Samuel Mutomba/OMB, 21.4.80, MS.1082/4/19, Todd Papers, NAZ.
33 Megahey, 1998, p. 182.
34 GT/Harold Hochschild, 28.4.80, MS.1082/4/19, Todd Papers, NAZ.

PART VI – ZIMBABWE, 1980–92

◆•◆

85

'Free, Legal and at Peace' – 1980

'This is Africa and it is going to end up black and nothing anyone is going to do is going to stop it.'

Sir John Moffat, 1960

Garfield, Grace and Judith were among the excited crowd of 100,000 in the National Sports Stadium on 18 April 1980. Grace told Elsie: 'When we climbed up into our seats a hand came down to help and it was Bishop Lamont ... At midnight the new flag was hoisted and the formal ceremony of the inauguration of the republic of Zimbabwe was performed ... all very emotive and happy.'[1] Among those who had returned for the great day were Guy and Molly Clutton-Brock and Bishop Kenneth Skelton, who stayed a few days at Hokonui. 'What a wonderful and moving occasion Thursday night was!' he later wrote. 'Though it made me wonder what the last 15 years had been about

---

1   JGT/EB, 17.5.80, MS.1082/4/17, Todd Papers, NAZ.

'Free, Legal and at Peace' – 1980

– it could all have been done 15 years ago. What a waste of lives and time.'[2]

On Independence Day, Lord Alport wrote to Garfield: 'I am so glad that you are once again in a position of influence ... We will not dwell on the dangers ahead. I have admired your role over many years and thank goodness we were able to field Peter and Christopher at this moment.'[3] Garfield replied: 'We look foward with a great deal of hope for the future ... Peter Carrington especially deserves great honour. There were times when I disagreed with both him and Lord Soames, but now that the plans have been successful I ask myself whether my criticisms were valid or not ...'[4]

Grace told Isobel Knapp: 'We just hope that all dissidents will soon give up and accept what has happened. There are some big problems. It is to be expected that after seven years of a particularly horrible war and with young men trained to arms, and guns and grenades still all too freely accessible, and all aggravated by unemployment, there would be lawlessness. And so there is. Armed robbery is a serious threat.'[5] In Grace's mind will have been Ralph Palmer's wife, Margareta, gunned down by an armed robber on their farm.

To other friends, Grace wrote: 'Yet with all this seeming return to normality there can hardly be one home not tragically affected by the events of the war years. There are hundreds of thousands of displaced persons, war-wounded and refugees, children who have lost years of schooling; homes destroyed and cattle dead. The problems of reconstruction are enormous and the promised aid small in comparison with the need ... Yet for the first time in very many years we are full of hope.'[6] Grace thought the common experience of personal loss and grief had helped to draw black and white together.

***

Garfield used his Senate speeches to put across, very carefully, his anxieties occasioned by actions and speeches of the Government or individual ministers, but for a long time he was careful not to criticise the Prime Minister. He also put forward ideas which he felt were worthy of consideration to deal with some of the many problems that were arising, particularly unemployment. It is hard to resist the feeling that he would have liked to have had a more active part in tackling, perhaps more urgently and more imaginatively, some of the country's problems.

In 1959, Garfield had written to Grace of his dream that one day Hokonui

---

2   Bishop Kenneth Skelton/GT, 22.4.80, MS.1082/6/2, ibid.
3   Alport/GT, 18.4.80, ibid.
4   GT/Alport, 27.4.80, ibid.
5   JGT/Isobel Knapp, 23.5.80, ibid.
6   JGT/Mr and Mrs L. Yates, 28.4.80, ibid.

would be 'a place that people will count a privilege to visit'.[7] This dream had been in the process of realisation for the succeeding twenty years and now was lavishly fulfilled. Grace's garden had matured into breathtaking beauty and variety and fruitfulness – and, once more, no bombs, no aeroplanes or helicopters drowned the sounds of the birds and the animals in the veld around.

***

The Zimbabwe Government was not happy with the existing ownership of the main newspapers by Argus Press of South Africa. The Nigerian Government gave a substantial donation to enable the Government to buy out the shares of the Rhodesian Printing and Publishing Company, and the Government set up the Mass Media Trust to receive the shares. The Minister of Information, Nathan Shamuyarira, invited Grace to be one of the trustees. She 'was a little hedgy about it', she said. 'I understood their desire to get the shares into their hands, but I did not like in any way the idea of the government controlling the press. I made it clear that I would have to be given assurances that this would not happen.'[8] When reassured on this point, she accepted.

Grace found her involvement with the Mass Media Trust very interesting in itself; and through it came a great deal of contact with the new Government and the leadership, as well as her co-trustees. Grace was appointed to one of the Trust's three seats on the board of directors of the new Zimpapers. She 'enjoyed the work as Director of Zimpapers much more than the Trust ... I learned so much just from the talk across the table. Then I discovered that one of the requirements of a Director was that he must have shares in the company, which meant buying 100 shares (and Garfield bought another 100 for me).'[9] These 200 shares marked the beginning of the Todds' interest in the stock-market – which on the face of it seemed so uncharacteristic, but which was heightened when the proceeds, first of the sale of cattle, then of Hokonui Ranch, were channelled into Zimpapers, Wankie Colliery and other carefully selected commercial concerns.

Garfield was asked by the Witwatersrand University Academic Freedom Committee to give the annual Richard Feetham Memorial Lecture – as he had done in 1964. The necessary visa, however, was not forthcoming from the South African government, so Garfield sent his 4,000-word script to the university – who promptly gave it to the *Rand Daily Mail*.[10]

In his 'speech', Garfield recalled remarks of 1964: 'I was despondent. Our tragedy was that peaceful evolutionary changes were being deliberately

---
7 GT/JGT, 4.1.59, MS.1082/3/1, Todd Papers, NAZ.
8 JGT/SP, TPPC.
9 JGT/SP, TPPC.
10 *Rand Daily Mail*, 25.7.80.

frustrated by decree ... Sixteen years ago I said: "I cannot see the way but the ideal is clear. I wish with all my heart that I could show you how easily the impossible will happen. I cannot, but there are two things I will say, I say them continually to myself: 'The first is that the impossible continually happens, and the second is that your responsibility starts with yourself.'"

'From Rhodesia to Zimbabwe is not just a cold event in history, not just the mechanics of a guerrilla war but the emergence of a nation from racial darkness into the light of hope ... We can fulfil the Christian ideal of being one in Christ. We can set aside prohibitions, overcome inhibitions – both white and black – we have been liberated.

'Of course there are dangers. Men have not changed. There will be greed and corruption and a lust for power in the new society and there are tensions because in the Lancaster House constitution our new wine has been poured into old wineskins. We will face the new challenges and I believe we will overcome.'

***

President Samora Machel of Mozambique paid an official visit to Zimbabwe in August. Garfield attended a luncheon given for him in Bulawayo. 'When I was introduced, the President, through his interpreter, asked for my name to be repeated. To everyone's surprise, he said: "Garfield Todd! But I have had you in my heart for 15 years! Bring a photographer." Everything stopped while a photograph was taken. Then the President said, "You must come and visit me."' A Mozambican general in Maputo later saw the picture and exclaimed: 'I know that white man! I met him in the mountains outside Shabani!' He had been FRELIMO's liaison officer with Garikayi's group.[11]

In November, Grace told Elsie: 'Last weekend there was an outbreak of violence between the two army units, ZIPRA, loyal to Nkomo, and ZANLA, loyal to Mugabe. This was in Bulawayo and for two days the various African townships were affected and at the end there were 50 dead and 500 wounded. It is horrible, appalling ... Yet, while such violent incidents are terrible, nevertheless good and important and constructive things are being achieved ... Schools and churches are everywhere reopened. Those which were damaged during the war are being repaired ... the government is demonstrating that it cares about and is determined to help the poor and the rural population ...'[12]

---

11 GT, TPPC.
12 JGT/EB, 17.11.80, MS.1082/4/19, Todd Papers, NAZ.

86

THE NEW ERA – 1981–3

'I have never held that Southern Rhodesia under an African government would be better governed than under a white government – probably the contrary is true.'

Garfield Todd, 1964

Cynthia and Derrick Edge had settled happily in Australia and now decided to remain there, but Judith and her husband, Richard Acton, came to live and work in Zimbabwe. Garfield designed them a bungalow in Harare (formerly Salisbury), and built it together with Gijima Mpofu.

Garfield's final attempt to sub-divide Hokonui Ranch – now 18,000 acres in extent – failed when discussions with the Government on the creation of a dozen 1,000-acre units came to nothing. But now the Todds were able to make a different kind of land contribution, handing over 3,000 acres of good arable land near Bannockburn (and near to power, water, road and railway) to a co-operative of unemployed, disabled ex-combatants. In time it would be home to 480 men and women, 'twenty-year-olds who have lost arms or legs or eyes or who go in wheel-chairs', Grace wrote. 'This new area has been named, by the men who settled there, "Vukuzenzele" which means "Wake up and help yourselves". Bricks are being made but the advance party of men live in tents …'[1]

The New Zealand Government donated the first cattle for the co-operative. Grace told me: 'We do not ourselves want to be involved in anything other than the gift of the land';[2] but before long Garfield was helping with fencing and piping water for 100 plots of vegetables. Then he and Gijima Mpofu built 40

---

1   JGT/SP, 12.12.81, TPPC.
2   JGT/SP, 26.10.81, TPPC.

cottages at Vukuzenzele, with money from EZE again.

***

The Senate took up a considerable amount of Garfield's time, and he continued, with great tact, to express disquiet at Government policies or ministerial speeches, making use of Adjournment Debates to highlight particular and immediate problems. His association with both the Christian Council and the United College of Education concluded satisfactorily, as he handed over responsibility to other Church of Christ members.

***

'The happiest day for Dadaya was June 19th 1981, when the Prime Minister of Zimbabwe ... and Mrs Mugabe, accompanied by 5 Ministers of State, visited Dadaya Mission', runs an anonymous, typed account of the day.[3] But Garfield was taken ill at the conclusion of the formal part of the day. Only Grace knew what was happening – and she quickly took him home. Dr Fehrsen saw him next morning, and he was admitted to hospital, where heart tests and a brain scan revealed all to be well. But Garfield was told straight to 'try to limit his working day to eight instead of eighteen hours, like any sensible man of his age', Grace told Cynthia. 'It has been a warning to us both, so the doctor says and I am sure he will be wise and do this.'[4] As Grace wrote, Garfield was attending the Senate in Salisbury – and on 13 July he celebrated his 73rd birthday. Garfield did his best to take life a bit more quietly and was helped in this by the drawing to an end of the four-year development programme at Dadaya, of which he had been not only the person with day-to-day responsibility, but also his own accountant and Clerk of Works.

***

'It is not given to every man to live to see his dreams, rejected 25 years ago, become official Government Policy', Grace quoted Garfield in her Christmas 1981 letter. 'The dreams of 25 years ago could really be summed up as "we work for the day when it will not matter to a child whether he is born white or black or of mixed race: all will have equal opportunity in our land". That sounds like the spirit of Christmas.'[5] But there were clouds on the horizon. (Alas, not rainclouds: the worst drought since 1946 held the Dadaya area in its grip.) Grace told her niece, Vicky Barham: 'The government has achieved almost miracles in the educational field ... basic wages have been raised and

---

3   TPPC.
4   JGT/Cynthia Edge, 9.7.81, MS.1082/3/5, Todd Papers, NAZ.
5   JGT, Christmas 1981, TPPC.

raised again, which makes for problems in a period of recession. There are many unsolved problems but I would say that many more people in independent Zimbabwe have a chance of the good life than was the case pre-Independence ...'[6]

***

On 17 February, Mugabe announced the dismissal of Nkomo, Chinamano and others, and ZAPU was eliminated from the ruling coalition. Two caches of arms had been found on ZAPU properties. In March 1982, two key figures in ZIPRA, Dumiso Dabengwa and Lookout Masuku, were arrested on treason charges. They were kept in prison for a year while awaiting trial, much of the time in solitary confinement. In April 1983 they were tried, acquitted, promptly rearrested and sent to Chikurubi Maximum Security Prison.

To try to put this into context, Garfield wrote an article for *The Times*. He explained that Zimbabwe had 'enormous problems: inflation, unemployment and underemployment. There are only a million jobs in the cash economy and if 800,000 families have to live as peasant farmers on an acceptable economic level then vast tracts of land will have to be acquired by Government from white farmers and made available for black farmers ...

'The discovery of caches of arms sufficient to equip 5,000 men has caused uproar, confusion and political storm. But there have been no mass arrests, no riots. Trouble there is, but not disaster. The Government has really not felt at risk and this should be reassuring ... Change I welcome. A one-party state I can accept if it enshrines the liberty of the individual to speak openly and to vote in secret. A one-party state could well be our best form of government for it would bring together the mass of our people who have similar political aspirations but who might divide on the grounds of tribe and personalities.'[7]

It was only when the appalling atrocities perpetrated by that secret, North Korean-trained 5th Brigade came gradually to light over succeeding years (to be confirmed by the Catholic Commission for Justice and Peace in Zimbabwe[8]) that Garfield – and everyone else – knew that although there were 'no mass arrests, no riots', there had been terrible oppression of mostly innocent peasants.

In April 1982, Grace turned 71 and the Todds celebrated their golden wedding anniversary. Garfield told friends that Grace had asked him: '"What do you want for the seventh?" "To wake up with you for the 18,000th time", I replied – and so it was. We are well though age refuses to be entirely ignored.

---

6 JGT/Vicky Barham, 23.1.82, MS.1082/3/6, Todd Papers, NAZ.
7 *The Times*, 19.3.82.
8 CCJP, 1997.

The blue in Grace's eyes has dimmed a little over the past few years.'[9] However, the fault lay not in her eyes but in his. In London, he had new acrylic lenses implanted – 'and a whole new world of light and colour came streaming in ... And there was a second miracle for when I looked with my new eyes I found that the brilliant blue in Grace's eyes had been fully restored.'[10]

After the opening of Parliament in June 1982, Garfield treated the Senate to some straight talking. He noted that there had been no 'mention of the word "reconciliation". In its place we have a great deal on security, on the maintenance of emergency powers, of the establishment of a people's militia, of an on-going military training ... That some terrible and outrageous things have happened since Independence, we all know. Some criminally stupid things have taken place. On my own ranch, we have suffered five hold-ups by armed men ... The law must be upheld but it should not be replaced by ministerial decisions ... We are not at war – the Government is not threatened – the Prime Minister is firmly in the saddle ... Let the light of public scrutiny, of the courts shine in on our problems so that we can see and understand.'[11] In 1983, Garfield met the US ambassador, Mr Keeley, and gave him information on the atrocities and on the suffering of the Ndebele people.

---

9 GT/'Friends', May 1982, TPPC.
10 Ibid.
11 Senate, *Hansard*, vol. 5, 16.1.82, cc. 24–31.

87

'Life is a Mixture' – 1983-5

'Unscrupulous men must be restrained from defrauding or maltreating the Natives ...'

Sir Harry Johnston, 1890

Grace celebrated her 72nd birthday on 3 April 1983 and wrote shortly afterwards: 'The year has been so far traumatic for us. The drought is catastrophic. We have had under six inches for the season and face slaughtering and selling through the butchery our total pure-bred Brahman herd. We are lucky to have this means of disposing of them ...'[1]

In May 1983, Garfield was invited to Germany to address the Tübingen Festival on the subject of 'Human and political relations in Southern Africa'. Garfield could not fail to speak about Gukurahundi. 'This year some Press reports have been extremely critical of us. We ourselves have had reason for distress but not for dismay as we faced serious trouble and much suffering in Matabeleland. Matabeleland lies in the south and shares a common boundary with South Africa. Across that border, after Independence, fled some thousands of political malcontents both black and white: men ready to turn against the Mugabe government if opportunity and support became available. Within our country were others, similarly disaffected. These dissidents, many of them ex-army and without work, others people just unwilling to accept the people's choice of a Mugabe government, have robbed buses and stores, assaulted and killed innocent people. Limited areas of the country were destabilised and the government was faced with insurrection. The security of the government itself was not threatened for it has the support of the vast majority of the people ...

'Government did not evade the issue and the Prime Minister himself gave

---

1   JGT/SP, 11.4.83, TPPC.

'Life is a Mixture' – 1983–5

an assurance that allegations would be examined, the situation considered and that soldiers involved in criminal actions would be apprehended and brought to trial. These assurances have been honoured and the situation rapidly improved … When we speak of human rights in relation to Zimbabwe there is one thing which should always be remembered. Many of our leaders, including the Prime Minister himself, suffered long years of imprisonment in their quest for justice and liberty and their crusade was not a selfish one – the struggle was for the country and the people. I do not wish to make our situation seem better than it is. In Matabeleland innocent people suffered and there was great distress, not only of the people but of the government also …

'I am upheld in my hope for the future of my country for I know that there is a host of young women and young men in Zimbabwe today whose vision is of a country where liberty and peace walk hand in hand. As for me – I would a thousand times rather be a Senator in a free Zimbabwe than be Prime Minister of the Self-Governing Colony of Southern Rhodesia'.[2]

***

The Todds sold all their cattle except 300 breeding cows and eight bulls which they would feed through the months until there was grass again. 'Perhaps we are mad at our age to contemplate beginning again', Grace told Elizabeth Collins, Elsie's daughter, 'but as you know the cattle are a source of interest and pleasure to us both – and we shall continue to hope for a good season next year.'[3] A moment of pure joy and triumph came for Grace watching the sale of 50 pure-bred young beasts. As they trotted into the sale ring, tough weather-beaten ranchers stood on their seats to get a look and marvel at their quality.

***

In May, Edith fell ill again, and after a week in hospital in Zvishavane (formerly Shabani) she died quietly in the night while her maid, Georgina, and Grace's cook, Jellinah, kept watch beside her. Her funeral at Dadaya Church, decorated with red roses from Grace's garden, was attended by 350 people, with a further 150 at the graveside in Dadaya Cemetery. Her death affected Garfield deeply. He and Grace were very distressed at not being with Edith when she died. Edith had done the Dadaya Governing Board minutes, and kept the Mission books for years; and Garfield told Lew Hunter, former Chairman of the OMB in New Zealand, that her work with the church and school were her 'major contribution and God was kind in leaving her until after the crucial [Governing

---

2   GT, Tübingen Festival, 28.5.83, TPPC. Portions of the address were reproduced in the *Sunday Mail*.
3   JGT/Elizabeth Collins, 24.4.84, MS.1082/3/5, Todd Papers, NAZ.

Board] meeting of April 28th ... It was all wonderful for we had, after years of some misery, a splendid meeting. People were united and enthusiastic and I did not keep a firm hold so that Edith's work was made doubly difficult. The next morning she brought me the draft minutes with apologies. I went through them and said, "They are perfect. No changes."'[4]

***

In August 1984, the ZANU-PF Congress decided that Zimbabwe should be a one-party state. Grace wrote about the Congress decision: 'What the overseas media has not highlighted is the statement in Congress that the one-party state would be brought about "in the fullness of time and in accordance with the Law and the Constitution", which ... we find immensely reassuring. In fact, one of Judith's journalist friends from outside the country said the Congress had been "a triumph of healing and moderation". Since then Mugabe was on TV on his question-answering session in the House, and Garfield, who watched it, said he was very good indeed.'[5] Yes, television had come – with some technical difficulties – to Hokonui, and in time it would be in colour. The set was firmly in Garfield's study, to spare Grace *Dallas*.

The *Rand Daily Mail* journalist, the late Michael Hartnack, picked up on Garfield's one-party-state remarks in the Senate speech: 'With 80% of Zimbabwe's population supporting ZANU the ruling party is assured of power for at least twenty years, Sen. Todd feels. But he believes much of the country's future history hangs on the mechanisms for peaceful change which Mr Mugabe (now 61 himself) builds into the new constitution when he scraps or changes the one inherited from Britain at Independence. "I would hope ZANU could be thrown out by means other than the army", says Sen. Todd, with a candour that is typically tactless and good-humoured ...

'Sen. Todd says ... "The biggest sadness to me has been the fact that ministers have considered themselves above the law – not that they would say that, but their actions, their statements, their threats, would make one believe they believe they have some magical power." He felt one of Zimbabwe's main problems since independence had been the delusion of government ministers that political power gave them total control over events.'[6]

In September, violence broke out in the Midlands – 'a major ... demonstration against the dissidents that had been prevailing in the area', according to the

---

4   GT/Lew Hunter, 12.8.84, MS.1082/2/13/3, Todd Papers, NAZ.
5   JGT/SP, 19.8.84, TPPC.
6   *Rand Daily Mail*, 17.9.84.

Minister of Lands.[7] As always, indiscipline and violence incensed Garfield, and he spoke forcefully in the Senate: 'It has been said that the forces of law and order stood aside while violence took place ... The Prime Minister himself said ... "The Police must be left to control a situation as they see fit. It is undesirable for any member of the public to interfere." I would have liked the Prime Minister to have been more explicit. People would like the assurance that that statement covers ministers, members of the military, as well as ordinary members of the public ...

'People believe ... that a certain minister, his name is well-known, went down to Que Que and explained that there were going to be party meetings throughout Midlands and instructed members of the police force to let the people have their own way, "people" meaning the youths ... What happened in the Midlands was a humiliation to the police and a serious blow to the prestige of the government ... this was in a time of peace in a peaceful area where there were no dissidents operating, where without explanation the thing blew up, and you can explain as you like why television cameras were there and why masses of young people were there ...'[8]

***

Two African Senators were murdered in their homes in November 1984, and there were violent and deplorable incidents in Shabani, where Garfield was held up by a youth militia roadblock but, on being recognised, was allowed through. Two soldiers beat up one of the ex-combatants at Vukuzenzele and then held Garfield up at gunpoint on the Bannockburn Road. He spoke of these incidents in the Senate, making 'a plea not just to the government, but to everybody ... we are faced on every side by a break-down of discipline. The percentage of our people who are involved with corruption, embezzlement, theft and a contempt for the rights of others, leading to assaults on homes, assaults on people, rapes, maiming, killing; the percentage is not very high but everything we are trying to achieve is threatened by these killings ... one of the fundamental weaknesses in the security situation today I believe has to do with the trespass of party influence upon the work and duty of the police ... the police must be freed from all political pressures ...'[9]

In one of his last Senate speeches, Garfield spoke of the 'feeling of great unity of concern, that we shared the deepest concern for the welfare of our country and the safety of our people. Senators have taken their duties seriously; on no occasion

---

7   Senate, *Hansard*, vol. 9, no. 18, 25.9.83, c. 583.
8   Senate, *Hansard*, vol. 9, no. 18, 25.9.84, cc. 574–81.
9   Senate, *Hansard*, vol. 9, no. 27, 12.12.84, cc. 985–7.

have we lacked a quorum in the House and our debates have been concerned with reason, not with vituperation ... Senators have set a good example.'[10]

Lawrence Vambe, former editor-in-chief of African Newspapers and a former federal civil servant, considers that Garfield 'made a tremendous impact on the Senate, he did influence in every way possible to make the Senate a fairly independent body and give it a position of being impartial and being able to look at legislation and national affairs with a kind of detachment and due consideration ... Garfield was certainly among those people who introduced a note of caution and wisdom and deliberate consideration ...'[11]

Garfield enjoyed the Senate and being part of the political scene once more: 'I was afraid that things were not just going as they should, and looking back we can see that that was so. The people I worked with were very good when I was being critical. As at a certain point in my Parliamentary days, people did not really accept what I was saying and see that it had enormous importance; even though it might have been the truth, they did not believe it was the truth.'[12]

***

In 1985, Mugabe was impatient to change the constitution to enable him to introduce a one-party state and executive presidency. To do this, he would need at least 70 seats in the forthcoming election. Twice postponed, this eventually took place in June and July. Intimidation and violence made campaigning difficult, particularly in the rural areas; and the continuing state of emergency in Matabeleland and the Midlands further hampered ZAPU. White voters largely stayed away from the election, on the one hand not wanting to endorse a 'whites-only' roll, and on the other not wanting to endorse a one-party state. In the event, the Independent Zimbabwe Group (which urged whites to accept the reality of black rule) won five seats, Smith 15. In the common-roll election, ZAPU won 15 seats, and ZANU-PF 64. An angry and frustrated Mugabe 'called once more for the "weeding out of the dissidents"'[13] and 'railed' against '"these racists" and in Shona threatened to "kill those snakes amongst us"'.[14] The succeeding years would bear witness to Mugabe's retribution against ZAPU and the whites who remained.

---

10 Senate, *Hansard*, vol. 9, no. 18, 25.9.84, cc. 574–81.
11 Interview, L. Vambe/SP, 13.7.1993.
12 GT/SP, interviews for this book, TPPC.
13 Auret, 2009, p. 89.
14 Ibid.

88

'FIFTY MARVELLOUS YEARS' – 1983–6

'Dadaya Mission had been our first love and had continued in that place.'

Garfield Todd

When Garfield said his life was just the thread that linked so many interesting events and people, the Reverend Ndabambi Hlambelo was one person he had in mind. In June 1983, Hlambelo died. 'He was preacher and teacher and a wonderful man', Grace told a Teachers' Seminar at Zvishavane.[1] He was even more than that: without Hlambelo's help in their early years at Dadaya, Garfield could not have succeeded. One morning, the old man of 81 – 'always a wizard with machinery' – tried to start his tractor with the self-starter, but, when it did not work, he tried the handle. One enormous heave, and it roared to life – and Hlambelo fell to the ground. He was the only person at Dadaya who had known every missionary who came from New Zealand – from the Hadfield family in 1906 to Mrs Isobel Knapp, who in 1974 was the last serving missionary to leave Dadaya.

The Todds were very conscious of the fact that in July 1984 they would celebrate 50 years at Dadaya Mission, and they felt that it was time they finally withdrew from the work. They thought they had done this when Garfield went to Salisbury in 1953, but with Ray Knapp's sudden death in 1964 they had responded to the emergency with total commitment. Now, after twenty years, Garfield was preparing to step down as chairman of the Governing Board. He might be contemplating retirement, but he would never lose his interest in Dadaya and its students; so, when an invitation reached them to attend the inaugural meeting of the Association of Dadayans – the 'old boys and girls' of

---
1 JGT, 23.7.83, TPPC.

Dadaya School – at a Harare hotel, it was accepted with delight. He wrote about the gathering in his New Year 1984 letter: 'About 300 young men and women (they must have been young for Grace had taught them) including Cabinet Ministers, the Party Whip, business men, teachers, farmers attended and the chairman was Mr Sam Mpofu, Managing-Director of Longmans (Zimbabwe).

'The Chairman announced that the deliberations would be opened by prayer by Herbert Chikomo, head-boy in 1946 ... today Moderator of the Presbyterian Church of Zimbabwe and Chairman of the Heads of Denominations'. The last item on the agenda was a motion by Professor George Kahari that Grace and Garfield be elected patrons of the society. Garfield's 'keynote address' was entitled 'Dadaya: Yesterday, Today and Tomorrow'. Yesterday, for Dadaya, was 1906; and Garfield started there as he recalled the significant happenings of the past 80 years, of Hadfield and Hlambelo down the years to Mutomba and Garikayi. The inauguration of the Association of Dadayans was timely, 'because changes are taking place in the control of the school, and responsible help and guidance will be welcome ... Dadaya is an institution but it has become a tradition also and you are the essence of that tradition ... as we bow out it is cause for great satisfaction that to you we can hand on the Torch!'[2]

***

In April 1984, there was a meeting of the Governing Board to smooth the transition to a new board and to establish the process for electing its membership. The day had come which Garfield had foreseen 40 years earlier, when 'the European missionaries will have fulfilled their purpose and worked themselves out of a job'.[3] After twenty years' devoted service to the Governing Board (and more years than that to African education), Peter Nathan had retired to the USA, where his wife's family lived.

On 13 July 1984, Garfield celebrated his 76th birthday – and they all celebrated the 50th anniversary of the arrival in Southern Rhodesia of Garfield, Grace and Alycen. An extract from the Minutes of the Overseas Mission Board meeting in Nelson on the 17th was sent to them: 'This Department places on record its thanks to God for the outstanding and devoted service of Sen. R. S. Garfield and Mrs Grace Todd over the past 50 years in Zimbabwe ... we think especially of:

> (1) The compassion shown by Drs Garfield and Grace Todd, particularly in their concern for the oppressed, and for their willingness to help in any way, including medical help, when called upon to do so.

---

2   GT, Association of Dadayans, Harare, 10.12.83, TPPC.
3   GT's monthly Report to New Zealand, October 1943.

(2) The way the school at Dadaya was built up ... for the training which was given to pupils which has enabled them to be today's leaders in Zimbabwe: for the high esteem in which Mrs Todd is held because of the initiation [sic] she took in promoting African education:

(3) The courage shown by both of them during the years of restriction, the time in prison, and dangers of the civil war:

(4) The national and international influence of Dr Garfield Todd; his assistance to the British Government during the time leading up to Independence: his ability to secure financial assistance for Dadaya High School from the Protestant Churches in Germany which gave the school the requirements to take pupils to 6th Form Level.'[4]

Grace wrote in her letter of thanks to the Secretary of the Overseas Mission Department: 'The mutual trust which was evident through all the years was our source of strength. We look back the long view over fifty years and realise with deep gratitude how fortunate and happy we have been in the work and with the people we love ...'[5]

The formalities for the Todds' withdrawal were rather long-drawn-out, but, on 10 November, the new chairman was elected, to take over in March 1985. The result of 50 years' work on the Todds' part was there in the new Board of nine members: a former Dadaya head boy, Samson G. Mpofu, Chairman; David Mkwananzi, a schoolboy at Dadaya in 1934, re-employed retired Headmaster; M. M. Nyoni, former Principal of Dadaya and Deputy Regional Director of Education, Midlands; Mpande Nyoni, head at Msipani School and Church Conference Chairman; Shadrach Gumbo, retired teacher, active in Church and Rural Councils; T. L. Ncube, once a primary schoolboy at Sibozo, now Inspector of Secondary School English in part of Mashonaland; John Ngara, Law Adviser, PM's Office; S. Nyoni, deputy Headmaster of a Kwe Kwe school; Dr Sibanda, born at Mapansure, Secretary to the Department of Manpower, Planning and Development – and future Ambassador to the Soviet Union.

After Garfield's last Governing Board meeting on 2 March, Grace told Stella: 'we could hardly speak for relief and relaxation. We still can hardly believe it. It is a strong and capable Board ... We can happily and with great relief leave the future to them. Since that day – only five days ago – Gar has had a kind of reaction. Not of any sadness of farewell. Simply a kind of disbelief that his long period of responsibility and the burden of it all is over. It is difficult to realise. And also that after all our concern and anxiety these

---

4   Minutes, OMB Meeting, Nelson, 19.7.84, MS.1083/4, Todd Papers, NAZ.
5   JGT/OMB, 23.8.84, TPPC.

people are so capable and so committed. We ought not to be surprised that God has managed everything so exceedingly well!'⁶

***

Now the Todds sold all that remained of their 6,000 acres, comprising the house and gardens and the land across the river they overlooked. Their purchaser was Sam Mpofu, who as a fourteen-year-old schoolboy at Dadaya had visited the Hokonui homestead, looked out over the valley, the hills, the river and Wedza mountain, and known this was what he wanted. The agreement was that the Todds would continue to run the place for a few years while he built up his herds – an agreement that suited everyone.

'The nice part about it all,' Grace told Stella, 'is that the cattle remain here, I continue to organise them and the business continues. No interruption to our schedules or to our employees. The new owner will want us to stay on and continue to manage it all as long as we wish, or are able, which is ideal. In the meantime we are going ahead with a few alterations to Heyman Road ...'⁷

Grace was also relinquishing responsibilities to the Mass Media Trust and Zimpapers. When the Trust chairman received Grace's formal letter of resignation, he replied: 'The Trustees particularly asked me to convey to you how much they have enjoyed working with you over the past four years. Your contributions to the Trust's deliberations which have always been stimulating and penetrating will be sadly missed ...'⁸

***

The year 1985 had written (or so the Todds thought) a concluding chapter in their association with Dadaya Mission. It also provided an exhilarating postscript to Garfield's long-ago prime ministership, in the form of Hardwicke Holderness's long-awaited history of the Eighth Parliament of Southern Rhodesia, 1953–8. The account is so fresh and immediate that it is hard to believe it incubated for a generation.

Garfield wrote in his Foreword to the book: 'the story is sparkling, sensitive and authoritative. It covers much more than the five critical years at the close of which the opportunity to continue on the road to peaceful political evolution was supplanted by the growing danger of civil war. Hardwicke spent his early life in the old Salisbury among the white community. I spent my first twenty years in Southern Rhodesia in the Lundi "Native Reserve" with a black community. From such different backgrounds our views were eventually to merge ...

---

6   JGT/SS, 7.3.85, MS.1082/3/6, Todd Papers, NAZ.
7   JGT/SS, 10.9.86, MS.1082/4/22, Todd Papers, NAZ.
8   Dr Sadza/JGT, 17.6.85, ibid.

'Fifty Marvellous Years' – 1983–6

'This book is largely an account of the experience of a group of men and women who in the forties and fifties attempted to educate their fellow citizens and to inspire such changes in our political life as would bring us all together within a politically viable nation. 1953–8 was a period of hope for those whites who recognised that, in the long term, safety and progress for all depended upon a sharing of political power – theirs for the time being – with an ever-increasing number of blacks. This hope could not have been sustained had there not been black men and women who were prepared to reciprocate in both thought and action. Fortunately the liberal whites were matched by a group of outstanding black men and women, many of whom are today's national leaders and two, Leopold Takawira and Herbert Chitepo, have their honoured place among the heroes of the revolution …

'I am deeply indebted to Hardwicke Holderness for his vision, his tenacity of purpose, his warm friendship and now, for his book.'[9]

***

The Prime Minister of New Zealand, Mr David Lange, paid an official visit to Zimbabwe in April 1985. The Todds dined with them in Harare at the official Government guest house where they were staying – Northward – a return after 27 years. Mr Lange asked Garfield if he would accept an 'honour'. He replied that he would be honoured and delighted, but asked that anything of the kind should be cleared with the Zimbabwean Government. The early months of 1985 brought poor health to Garfield and Grace, but also brought a visit from Cynthia – 'the same lovely, gentle, affectionate person'.[10] Her month-long visit did much to help their recovery.

After Christmas, Grace wrote to Alycen and Cynthia: 'In the middle of December Judith … was phoned from Athens by the NZ Ambassador to Greece. (There is no Ambassador or High Commissioner in Africa.) He … asked her to tell Dad that the honour of Knight Bachelor was being conferred upon him by the Queen in the New Year's Honours list … We have been in a daze whenever we have thought about it since that moment, hardly believing it all. It never entered our minds that it would be that kind of honour, or anything like it.'[11] When Garfield told David Lange that they thought it would be 'some letters after his name', he uttered a laconic 'For a PM? Go on!'

On 27 December, telegrams came from New Zealand. One was from the Governor-General of New Zealand, informing them of the knighthood; and the

---

9   Holderness, 1985, Foreword, pp. 2–3.
10   JGT/SP, n.d. [?June 1985], MS.1082/4/22, Todd Papers, NAZ.
11   JGT/Alycen and Cynthia, 28.12.85, TPPC.

other was from David Lange, with congratulations. 'So it was true after all ... It was such good fortune that we had agreed to have dinner with Paddy and Paul [Fehrsen] that evening. We took the copies of the telegrams and shared with them the excitement and joy. We are so happy. Thrilled, honoured, delighted. Dad is seventy-seven. It is a recognition, a reward, an accolade, and from the Queen ... this is the final and most splendid recognition for Dad after the pain and struggle of the past. We could not have had this if first we had not suffered that.'

89

SIR GARFIELD AND LADY TODD – 1986-7

'... heard the Comrade had been knighted.'

David Mukonoweshuro, January 1986

The *Herald* placards on the streets of Harare on 31 December 1985 read: 'GARFIELD TODD KNIGHTED'. The Zimbabwe press greeted Garfield's honour warmly – as did the British and New Zealand press, and friends all over the world. Garfield told David Lange about some of the letters he had received in the five weeks following the announcement: 'Your decision to ask the Queen to bestow a Knighthood on me certainly came as a surprise – everywhere … A wonderful flood of phone-calls, cables and letters descended upon us … The Curia, Rome, a splendid Rabbi now retired in London, Bishops of both Catholic and Anglican churches here and overseas, a Muslim friend in Paris, Church leaders in Britain, Australia, Switzerland, USA, New Zealand, Sister Jayant of Raji Yoga, London; Ministers in New Zealand as well as local, Lord Brockway, Ted Heath, Lord Alport, who was High Commissioner here at one time; Humphrey Gibbs, our last legal Governor before Soames, wrote: 'What adds to its value is the fact that it is the only Honour given to this country for the past fifteen years and probably the last that will be given to anyone here …'

'There are many facets of delight and the co-operation is one of them. New Zealand proposed, Zimbabwe agreed, the Queen conferred. Messages have come from many of my white friends of the fifties and sixties who thought with us and fought with us. I sense that the Queen's honour somehow vindicates us all.'[1] Former British Prime Minister Ted Heath began his letter: 'Dear Prime Minister – for that is how so many of us will always think of you … this award so long overdue …'

---

1 GT/David Lange, 7.2.86, MS.1083/4, Todd Papers, NAZ.

Grace was revelling in the just appreciation of Garfield ringing through the letters, telling Isobel Knapp: 'The sentiment which comes through is one of joy and delight that a simple, good man should be selected for such an honour'.[2] Sir Ian MacLennan, who had been Britain's High Commissioner to Rhodesia in the years 1950–5 – and not always a whole-hearted admirer of Garfield – wrote: 'You have shed so much lustre on New Zealand by your many years of work in Zimbabwe, distinguished work in which Grace has shared to the full, and when we rejoice to think, and speak, of Sir Garfield, we think with equal satisfaction that we are in future to refer also to Lady Todd.'

K. D. Dube, Director of the UN Information Centre in Nairobi, wrote: 'My dear Mfundisi [teacher], Great vision, love for fellow-men and respect for the dignity of the human person led you in your courageous and exemplary contribution to the creation of Zimbabwe. Congratulations to Nkosikazi [the lady], too, who has facilitated your efforts and who has enabled many a Zimbabwean to gain education for life coupled with high leadership qualities.'

But the letter 'which moved and pleased [the Todds] most' came from a stranger, 'Peter' in Australia, who wrote: 'As a non-Christian (and non-believer) it is perhaps fitting for me to confess to the overwhelming feeling that Christians may today hold their heads very high indeed. The years of selfless sacrifice and of faith in the eventual outcome; the residue of trust across the divide of a race war; and the magnanimity of the victors – all these are suggestive of something more than simply human goodness and virtue. Some day let us hope the full story will be told. But in a sense there is really nothing to add to the record of Garfield Todd's contribution: yours has been a shining example throughout the darkest days, inspiring many of your countrymen not only with hope for a better future but also with the heart to forgive.'[3]

***

Garfield's private investiture took place at Buckingham Palace on 5 June 1986. There, to their surprise and delight, David Lange joined them. This was one of the occasions when Grace asked herself: 'What am I, little Grace Wilson from Winton, New Zealand, doing here?' Mr Lange spoke of the occasion twenty years later: 'With an equerry with spurs on his boots we clanked forward with Garfield looking sort of tall and strong and straight-backed ... Here was a guy who went to get knighted at Buckingham Palace with all that grandeur and when he went home that night he had to put a shilling in his meter to get his room warm. Such a contrast. His whole life had been that of course, moving in and

---

2   JGT/Isobel Knapp, 27.2.86, MS.1082/4/22, Todd Papers, NAZ.
3   Quoted in JGT/SS, 13.12.86, MS.1082/4/22, Todd Papers, NAZ.

out of contradictory worlds, really. The overall feeling one had about Garfield Todd was an extraordinary sense of fitness he exudes. It is not just physical fitness. It has got some other wholesomeness or fitness or strength ... It is an occasion to meet Garfield, quite apart from the build-up ... there is an aura ...'[4]

The New Zealand High Commissioner gave a reception for the Todds at NZ House. Here they saw many friends – but, as they entered the room, it was not friends they saw, but Alycen and John Watson, from New Zealand. Grace had put their names, and Cynthia and Derrick's, on the suggested guest list – and the seven Watson sons and daughters had seen to it that their parents went to London.

***

Immediately after the London visit, Garfield wrote to David Lange: 'Our holiday of a lifetime was thought up by David Lange and organised by the New Zealand High Commission who provided cars and drivers and staged a happy and delightful party in such a magnificent setting for our UK friends ... The Investiture, with my third meeting with the Queen, was a great occasion. Grace and I were greatly honoured by your presence and we are fully appreciative of your great kindness on this occasion also ... words are as inadequate in expressing our gratitude as they would be if we tried to describe the Trooping of the Colour ... Our presence there was also the work of the High Commission and as the tickets came from the Palace we sat in the best seats ... At my age, I had not thought to find myself so deeply indebted to a new friend. Thank You.'[5]

***

Grace had had nine months' freedom from pain, but on her return to Zimbabwe 'wasted three weeks' suffering in bed. Mugabe was given the freedom of the City of Bulawayo, and the fitful Unity talks between ZANU and ZAPU went on. Lookout Masuku had died, but Dumiso Dabengwa was released from detention, in time to see his father before the grand old man of Gwatemba died.

In New Zealand, Elsie Barham died. Grace wrote: 'I think you will understand that my first and overwhelming emotion was of relief that Elsie's cruel bondage was at an end and her bright spirit at last set free. But though I continued to feel relief there is an inescapable sense of sadness and loss that the ties of a lifetime have been broken ... I felt far away and sad ... Garfield was in Harare which, without reason, made it seem worse.'[6] Soon after Elsie's death, Stella, Garfield's

---

4 Interview, David Lange, Auckland Airport, 1994, TPPC.
5 GT/David Lange, 17.7.86, TPPC.
6 JGT/SP, 18.12.86, TPPC.

sister, was diagnosed with cancer. She had always been the person to whom he could write completely freely and frankly.

***

On 27 October 1987, Mugabe signed a Unity Accord with Nkomo, merging ZAPU and ZANU-PF into a single party. An amnesty was granted to security-force members as well as the remaining dissidents. Members of the Catholic Commission for Justice and Peace had taken part in the protracted negotiations, as had the Heads of Denominations. Remembering Garfield's long association with that body, it is good to read in *A History of the Church in Africa*: 'The contribution in 1987 of the Heads of Denominations to the question of national unity was a major achievement'.[7]

---

7   Sundkler and Steed, 2000, p. 283.

90

Tributes and Tribulations – 1988-90

'Inside or outside politics I have never been a great party man but on my 80th I really enjoyed myself.'

Garfield Todd, 1988

The Unity Accord had brought Garfield great satisfaction, but he was ever aware of the dangers of poverty and unemployment. Early in the year, he attended the funeral of Chief Wedza and was deeply saddened by evidence of great poverty after years of drought when the people harvested nothing at all for food. That there was even a poor feast was due to supplies from Bannockburn Store. Garfield visited a village where a couple with six children lived. They had had to take in sixteen impoverished relatives – and there was no food. Bannockburn Store again was able to provide enough to keep them going. And, in a typically imaginative gesture, Garfield had sent a cake of soap and a little bottle of scent to a girl on her eighteenth birthday.

***

Garfield was 80 on 13 July 1988. Judith, with Michael and Eileen Haddon, gathered reminiscences from scores of his friends and compiled an 80th-birthday book for him. On the evening of 12 July, the New Zealand High Commissioner, Chris Laidlaw and his wife, Helen, gave a party 'to surprise Sir Garfield on his 80th birthday'. Grace wrote of the guests, who included Alycen's youngest daughter, Judy: 'a delightful and interesting mixture – cabinet ministers, diplomatic representatives, old boys from Dadaya now in positions of national importance, friends from School, Church and State – including David Mkwananzi who was in Standard 3 at Dadaya School when we arrived in 1934 ... It was a lovely party. I did not want it to end.'[1] 'I wish I had a copy

---
1 JGT/SP, TPPC.

of the excellent speech which Chris made', Grace wrote, 'for he paid tribute to our marriage, and also to Garfield who, he said, during his years of striving for justice in this country had "tilted" events towards the final happy solution ...'

The next day, on the birthday, Grace and Judith gave a dinner for 30 at the Laidlaws' official residence, catered for by friends. So many of the familiar names were there: Dr Paul and Paddy Fehrsen, Hugh Prosser, Joshua Nkomo, Chief Justice Enoch Dumbutshena, Professor George Kahari, Sam Mpofu. The Chief Justice proposed the birthday toast 'and told in a happy speech how twenty-six years ago when he was in political exile in London Garfield had been instrumental in overcoming what seemed to be insuperable problems so that he had been accepted in Gray's Inn ... [he] is proving to be courageous and wise in his vitally important office.

'In his happy and humorous reply Garfield spoke of the "Book of Letters" which he had received the previous evening. He said he had time only to dip into the book, where he had already found "some truth" (even at eighty a man could not be expected to bear the burden of the whole truth), some romanticism based on a modicum of truth, some delightful falsehoods – an enthralling mixture which he would enjoy for the rest of his life ... When we finally arrived home from Harare, Garfield said he was still "tingling" with the enjoyment of it all, so for us it was all completely successful and happy ...'[2]

***

The Quinquennial World Conference of the Churches of Christ took place in Auckland in 1988. Garfield had not intended going – but, when he learned his sister Stella (though suffering from terminal cancer) hoped to be present, and learned that their work at Dadaya was to be the main topic, he changed his mind. (He and Stella shared a hotel suite and had quiet hours together.) Grace's osteoarthritis had decided her against travelling to New Zealand.

The first day of the meeting was the occasion of the 'Recognition of fifty-four years of service in Zimbabwe of the Todds'. There were 400 in the audience, including David and Naomi Lange. There were many 'panegyrics of praise' of the Todds, some pretty fulsome; but Hugh Scott, whose own service at Dadaya gave him a solid foundation of knowledge of the school, the place, the country and its history, made a 'perfect' speech, Garfield wrote. Hugh said: 'I personally too, want to thank you for the way in which your home has been an oasis of calm, peace and encouragement for many Zimbabweans and also for many New Zealand missionaries and visitors. Thank you for persevering ... We honour you today, we love you and we thank you both. We wish you both many happy

---

2   JGT, GT's birthday, TPPC.

years of relaxation and reflection together ...'

When Garfield rose to speak, he was given a standing ovation; 'and the PM behind me said, "This is done only at party meetings", a comment I immediately passed on – to much laughter ... It's a very wonderful day for me. I'm just tremendously sorry that Grace is not with me.' Garfield told some of the early Dadaya stories. 'Life has been good ... Grace and I have now come to the end of a chapter. It's been a period of great happiness, though of course, there have been periods of doubt and uncertainty when we had to hold hard to God and to each other ... In a world of change, our responsibilities as Christians remain clear and strong ...'

***

Once more back at Hokonui, Garfield was badly burned in a petrol fire – and he and Grace and Judith began 'the worst time they had ever endured ... a trek through hell'.[3] A letter from Judith tells some of it: 'The evening of the accident [my father] was about 27 kilometres away from ... Zvishavane, feeding petrol into the carburettor of a car when the petrol caught fire. As the upper part of his body was leaning over the engine, under the bonnet, you can imagine the extent of the burns – face, ears, hair, neck but most especially his hands.'

Christine Mukokokwayira was in the car and instinctively threw Garfield to the ground and extinguished the flames with earth. 'A teacher passing from Dadaya ... rushed him into Shabanie Mine Hospital ... where he fell under the excellent care of the medical superintendent who is both a doctor and a surgeon, Mr Mataka.' Judith, in Harare, on hearing the news, had rushed to the hospital. 'My father's hands were in huge bandages and his left upper chest and shoulder were burned. His head was a black, swollen football covered with a miracle white salve ... although he could recognise what was happening around him and could speak, his mouth was also burned ... His head was a little cap of white and brown burned hair which wasn't touched for some days ... almost immediately we knew for sure that his eyes were going to be fine ...

'That Sunday Mr Mataka told us that the first 36 hours were the most critical and, as my father had survived them, he was now over the hump. We were enormously relieved not really understanding that he was specifically speaking of actual survival and not really realising what yet lay in store. The following Thursday, my father, still on a drip, was transferred by ambulance to the Mater Dei Hospital in Bulawayo where he had skin grafts on his left hand', and later on his right hand. Blood transfusions helped considerably, but there followed

---

3   JGT/'Friends', 4.3.89, TPPC.

weeks of great pain for Garfield and great anxiety for them all. Mr Mataka said it was only Garfield's strength that saved him; and it was the skill of Miss Rosemary Hepworth, plastic surgeon, that restored his hands to 70 per cent of normal use.

Garfield would repeat the following story frequently over the years: 'One day they got me into the bath and the sister came running in, saying, "The President's here, the President's here!" So I said, "fine, there's a chair" but they got me back into bed as quickly as they could and in came Mugabe and behind him Nkomo! And others behind them. It was after the Unity Accord and they were there together. The hospital did not know he was coming and there was a roaring of sirens and so on and the cars drew up. We don't forget that. Nice that he did not warn them. The Ward Sister was a very fine woman who had had a lot of experience with burns and we depended on her a great deal. She had been hassled by the security people who said, "Hurry up, the President's waiting!" She replied, "You do your job and leave me to do mine. Mine is my patient and I will look after him."'

On 6 April 1989, Garfield wrote from Hokonui: 'Here I am at my desk and trying out the typewriter: actually trying out myself! ... My people have done so well here during my absence ... I am being given a very warm welcome home ... Grace is taking me into Zvishavane this morning to present me for inspection to Mr Mataka who sent me to the Mater Dei where my life was saved ... Well, this is my first typed letter so I have made a start and I am feeling well and very thankful and happy.'4 Grace added a note from a full heart at the foot of Garfield's letter: 'Garfield is both typing and writing better than ever. He is incredibly patient and persevering. He cut off the top of his egg at breakfast and spread his own toast! Praise God from whom all blessings flow.'

Grace told Elizabeth Collins: 'We have experienced the most amazing outpouring of love and concern – unrestrained on the part of Africans from taxi-drivers to clerks at the post office and of the assurance of their prayers from friends of many faiths and different denominations. The Rabbi had prayers with his congregation in the Synagogue in Harare, the RC Bishop Karlen came faithfully even when visitors were not allowed, Fr. Odilo came each night to the hospital to give him his blessing.'5 A week after Easter, Garfield wrote appreciatively to the President and Joshua Nkomo – signing 'Garfield. (Like the Apostle Paul: with mine own hand!)'

Grace's birthday was 'not so much a birthday celebration as a time of thanksgiving', she wrote. 'We had shared so much, the pain and fear and hope

---

4   GT/SP, 6.4.89, TPPC.
5   JGT/Elizabeth Collins, Easter 1989, Mrs Collins' Papers.

and recovery and it was simply blissful relief to be together knowing that Garfield was truly recovering …'[6]

***

In May, the Todds learned that Stella was not well enough to visit them in June as had been hoped. Then Grace went down with the worst attack of 'flu she had ever experienced. While she was still in bed, they had a phone call from Stella: a friend (Mrs Helen Cramer) had arrived from the USA and, when told of Stella's cancelled visit, offered to accompany her if she still wished to make the trip. Stella leapt at the offer. A difficult and week-delayed journey finally brought them to Hokonui. Over succeeding days Garfield, Grace and Helen took four-hour shifts at Stella's bedside while she gradually slipped into unconsciousness. Early on the morning of Sunday 28th, Stella died, very peacefully and – to his great comfort – during Garfield's watch. Stella was 'laid to rest in the little Mission cemetery beside our sister Edith', Garfield told a friend. 'It is quite remarkable that my mother's three children, born in Waikiwi, will rest together in Zimbabwe, with the girl from Winton who is my life.'[7]

***

On the last day of 1989, Grace wrote: 'Before the day ends – which also marks the end of the year and the decade – I want to think of you and write to you. I have been thinking of words and trying to make sentences to tell you, dearest and most constant of friends, of our love and thanks … We have had a quiet and happy Christmas … tomorrow it will be 1990. For us this old year has brought fear and suffering, but also relief and joy. And now at the end we are spectators at the incredible spectacle of the "breaking out" of democracy in Eastern Europe … What will 1990 hold for us?'[8]

***

The year 1990 began with some significant visitors to Hokonui Ranch: a TV team from New Zealand, led by Richard Driver, to make an hour-long film on the Todds; and Garfield's biographers. He wrote in his New Year 1991 letter: 'For many years friends have asked if I "was writing?" I thought that a biography should be written at the end of one's life. At 82 I have surrendered … Over a period of some months came long interviews with Ruth Weiss, a German writer from South Africa, and Jane Parpart, a history researcher from the Dalhousie University in Canada.'

Grace was horrified at the thought of the film but glad about the biography.

---

6   JGT/SP, 10.4.89, TPPC.
7   GT/Gavin Munro, n.d., MS.1082/6/5, Todd Papers, NAZ.
8   JGT/SP, 31.12.89, TPPC.

Ruth Weiss visited Hokonui to 'experience the atmosphere', Grace wrote to me. 'We were dismayed at how much we seemed to have forgotten as we answered her questions, or tried to ... I am of course apprehensive about anyone, other than you, writing this biography. But at the same time I am impressed with Ruth ... It is now Sunday 11 February, a date which surely will never be forgotten in the history of Africa. Garfield was, by good fortune, the preacher at this morning's service at Dadaya. The school had evidently not heard that Mandela is to be released today, and when he spoke of it a great murmur went through the Church. He gave a splendid address in which John the Baptist, Gorbachev, the Christian Church, Dadaya School and Mandela all figured! And his voice seemed young and strong! – It is difficult to believe that we are actually living through all these amazing events ... This time last year we did not know whether he would live. How much for which to be ever thankful ...'[9]

---

9   JGT/SP, 10.2.90, TPPC.

91

LAST YEARS AT HOKONUI RANCH – 1990-2

'Of course there are dangers. Men have not changed. There will be greed and corruption and a lust for power in the new society.'

Garfield Todd, 1980

In 1980, Garfield had pledged his support to the man who would win the election, and this turned out to be Mugabe. By 1990, Mugabe had forfeited his support, and Garfield began to speak out against him – about the manner in which he was establishing a one-party state, about the corruption among his ministers and appointees, about official disregard of poverty and unemployment, and the undermining of press freedom. He was particularly concerned about the possibility of the appointment to the board of Zimpapers of one or two civil servants. When this took place, Garfield set about the gradual disposal of all his shares.

Mugabe called a general election in April 1990 and focused his campaign on the issue of white-owned land. Already he had handed over 8 per cent of the former white land which the Government had acquired to his ministers, senior officers, civil servants and their cronies and rich businessmen – not to the landless peasants.

***

The NZTV unit was in Zimbabwe for five weeks, and by all accounts (including Richard Driver's) the five members revelled in the experience. They filmed Garfield addressing the National Chamber of Commerce in Harare; the interment of the journalist Willie Masururwa at Heroes' Acre; and Garfield preaching at the Sunday service at Dadaya. They filmed the loading at Bannockburn station of 50 steers on their way to sale.

'[T]hey have stayed at the Nilton Hotel and we have had them for morning tea, lunch and drinks before they went back to Zvishavane each evening. In a way it has been stressful but the people were very nice indeed and we enjoyed their company. They were with us for about ten days but for two days I was with them at the Hwange Park and the Falls Hotel ... Grace was very apprehensive about her interviews but in the end she was the best of the three of us.'[1]

Grace 'didn't know where to start!' when she wrote on the 22nd. 'The NZTV team left us here last Tuesday ... When they left here Garfield and I collapsed! They were five very pleasant people and worked like slaves all the time they were with us. When they flew in from NZ they stayed at the Sheraton but already in New Zealand had booked themselves into the Nilton in Zvishavane ...! We were terribly concerned about this as the Nilton is nowadays – and always has been – pretty basic. We need not have worried. They loved it! The Sheraton, they said, was like any great, modern hotel anywhere in the world. The Nilton was something different! They were apparently much welcomed and fussed over and left with regrets and protestations of friendship on all sides ... In between times they rushed off to take shots all over the place ... the Hokonui sign, the weir, the hippo who were shy at first but went through their paces later.' There were visits to classes at Dadaya School, to Vukuzenele, and to a village church where three congregations had gathered for an Easter service: 'they loved it all, especially the women dancing, and the concern of the people over Garfield's hands, which were fondled and kissed! ... they came with me to the Dip to see me record a breeding herd there, and were impressed with the Bulls ... Richard Driver is the producer ... But, dear Sue, you know how I have disliked (indeed hated and feared) the publicity which my family attracts and I did find it all exhausting, and also dislike the whole idea of making all this public, shown indiscriminately all over the place. And of course our version of events will not commend itself to many who have a different view ...'

Garfield went to Harare with the team when they left for New Zealand. While there, he received the first rough draft of Ruth Weiss's book and brought it home. 'And do you know,' Grace wrote, 'I have not dared to look at it and neither has Judith! Garfield thought it good, but that it portrayed him as aggressive and tough.'[2]

***

Towards the end of 1990, and early in 1991, there was a spate of strikes and rioting at the university and at secondary schools around the country. Dadaya was not spared. On Sunday 18 November, Garfield was at Dadaya Church

---

1 GT/SP, 19.4.90, TPPC.
2 JGT/SP, 22.4.90, TPPC.

with Grace, and he sensed there was 'trouble' somewhere and invited some of the Upper Sixth pupils to come over to Hokonui that afternoon. 'It was the bonus weekend, when everybody had got their bonuses and gone off to spend the money. There were only one or two [teachers] left at the school, but the one or two who were left were obviously worried because the Canadian family came across to our house and stayed ... Then a teacher who was getting worried brought his car and asked if he could leave it at our place ... I was not on the Dadaya Governing Board so although I was worried to hear these reports I had no responsibility to go over and take charge ... Then somebody rang up towards evening and said that the mission was on fire. At that point I really did act.'[3] He and the teachers and a couple of plain-clothes policemen who had come in response to a telephone call did what they could, removing furniture from the principal's house and so on, and finally got the fire under control.

Before the Governing Board could do anything to assess the damage or make enquiries of any kind, the Education Department acted unilaterally and prematurely by closing the school the following day. Garfield was furious and, as Chairman of the Dadaya Mission Trust, the owners of Dadaya School, issued a statement which *The Chronicle* printed on the Wednesday: 'The burning of three laboratories, a classroom and the Principal's house is a dastardly crime and I believe that the Police will find those who are responsible and bring them to Court, to conviction and punishment. That is justice. However, the official reaction seems to be that all 850 students were responsible for the crime and that they and their parents, who have spent a million dollars to send their children to Dadaya this year, must be given the maximum punishment, the immediate closure of the school and no opportunity given to the 250 'O' and 'A' level students to sit examinations. In practical terms there was no reason for the closure of the school ... the Dadaya Trust, unable to atone for the injustice done to parents and scholars in 1990, will turn to the daunting task of repairs, renovations and the opening of the School in January 1991.'[4]

The Governing Board wasted no time in coming to grips with the situation. Garfield's nephew, Allan Todd, and his wife, Marjorie, were providentially visiting Zimbabwe, and he was immediately co-opted onto the Board – and to the reconstruction committee (Sam Mpofu, the headmaster, Garfield) – as secretary. Over the next two years, Garfield sought and obtained money for the reconstruction of the three laboratories, classroom, storerooms and Principal's house – and then supervised the rebuilding.

3   GT, interviews for this book.
4   GT's statement, *The Chronicle*, 21.11.90.

Ten days after the fire, Grace wrote: 'It has been a terrible blow to Garfield, as well of course to innocent parents and scholars. I watched Gar age over those first few days and lose his gaiety and ebullience. I was deeply glad Allan and Marj were here. They have been splendid and the most excellent help. There was a governing Board meeting on the next Saturday and the following day Marj and Allan came in here to attend a church service, already arranged. Allan reported it had been a splendid Board meeting, with all concerned positive and determined Dadaya should reopen in January and ready with plans and ideas. They begged Allan to stay on for a three-month period to help in the reconstruction and they have agreed ... Allan is energetic and competent and experienced and also well-liked ... I imagine the burden will mostly fall on Garfield so once again I am deeply grateful that Marj and Allan are here to help and consult and advise. Gar is better again, but he tires easily. Still I think on the whole he is glad to be involved himself in this way, instead of having to watch others dragging their feet and making mistakes!'[5]

The school reopened on due date. The reconstruction of Dadaya took pretty well the whole of 1991, and along with Allan Todd's almost miraculous availability (in the end he stayed nearly two years) came Garfield's old friend, Samuel Mutomba, as Dadaya's new Principal, and with him 'the vital change in the spirit of Dadaya Church and School'.[6]

***

During the days when Rhodesia's whites thought Garfield 'so liberal he might almost be a communist', it was a secret amusement to him that his own first cousin, Louie Todd, was a genuine communist living in Soviet Russia. For decades there was never any news of her and her daughter; but, once communication had been restored, both had enjoyed their correspondence. And there had been the memorable Todd family gathering in Judith's London home. Now, in February 1991, Garfield decided it was time for him to visit Louie.

'Russia was grim', Garfield told the Bakers in Edinburgh; 'I am sad for my cousins who live there. Louie M.A., now 89, had as her last task the compilation, with many professors, of the latest English–Russian dictionary. Her daughter Anne is an engineer and has just retired at 60. Louie was always an agnostic, and Anne has just discovered Christ; and all her family, with the exception of the husbands, are now Christians.'[7] Grace wrote that from what Garfield had told her, 'Louie herself believes she has had a good and interesting

---

5   JGT/SP, 27.11.90, TPPC.
6   GT's New Year letter 1992, TPPC.
7   GT/Mr and Mrs Bill Baker of Edinburgh. I am grateful for sight of this and other letters.

life and that she has made a good contribution to contemporary society ... It is her daughter Anne who is the rebel and resents that Louie's decision in all these things deprived her of her Western birthright, as well as the fact, terrible to us all, that she was brought up without any religious faith. Anyway, Garfield has done what he has for long wanted to do and has gone to Moscow to see Louie and her family.'[8]

In London on his way back to Zimbabwe, he told me their plans for the future: they would leave Hokonui at the end of 1992 and go to live in Bulawayo. He spoke enthusiastically of what Grace was accomplishing at Heyman Road, with its few, spacious, comfortable rooms, its large 'troubled' swimming pool and easy-maintenance garden. Then he said, in his own inimitable way: 'Grace knows she has to die first so that I can look after her to the end.' And that was how it was.

'Gar has set 31st March, the end of our financial year, as the final date of handing over all responsibilities of the Ranch to Sam. And I shall hand over my books and records this coming weekend. I am sure this is right but will nevertheless miss my visits to the cattle and contacts with "the men". But bit by bit I shall now disengage myself from here ... I am determined to do this without regrets. It has been a lovely and satisfying place in which to live (and from which to wage our battles). But I let it go without too many backward glances, but with very precious memories.'[9]

***

In April, *Hokonui Todd* hit New Zealand's TV screens. Richard Driver described his film as 'simply the story of a remarkable human being'.[10] In his 'Week in Review' column in the *Otago Daily Times* of Saturday 27 April, John Kennedy wrote: 'In an article written fifteen years ago for *The Times* of London, Bernard Levin described how he experienced "an uplift of spirit" whenever he met men who had risen through misery, cruelty and oppression to true greatness of heart and mind. He singled out two men, Alexander Solzhenitsyn and Garfield Todd, of Rhodesia, and he exclaimed "how rarely heroes live up to expectations and how satisfying when they achieve it".

'That, I am sure, is how thousands upon thousands of New Zealanders felt last Tuesday night as they watched the documentary, *Hokonui Todd*. Deeply moved, I switched off the box and reflected for a while on what I had just seen. Then I resumed reading Levin's *Taking Sides*. A few pages later the quotations I have just cited fairly jumped out at me ... "Good brave men, it seems, are the

---

8   JGT/SP, 17.4.91, TPPC.
9   JGT/SP, 19.4.91, TPPC.
10   *Otago Daily News*, 27.4.91.

same the world over, and their goodness and bravery can no more be hidden than it can be counterfeited".

'Amen to that, except that after watching *Hokonui Todd* I amend that phrase "good, brave men" to read "good, brave men and women". One of the features of that splendid documentary was surely its portrayal of Sir Garfield's wife, Grace, as equally courageous in the face of constant danger and vindictive persecution. What an amazing story theirs is, and how well television told it! ... The whole thing was beautifully done. Indeed, the lives of this couple stand out like a beacon on a hilltop for their deep faith, the dedication they have shown to their work, their courage in facing challenges when others wilted, their humour in the face of oppression and their steadfast trust in their God.

'There was another aspect of importance. That was the way in which the radiant beauty of a lifelong, loving marriage came through. Their stand for principle, backed by that rich, vibrant family life made their persecutors seem futile and petty ... the idealism and faith to be found in lives such as these are precious and rare, and perhaps the greatest gift we can hand our youth in today's rather grubby society.'[11]

***

The Todds' Hokonui Ranch became Sam Mpofu's Zibombo Ranch in April 1991. Judith sold her Harare home and bought a house in Bulawayo, five minutes' walk from her parents'. In August, Grace wrote from Hokonui: 'Here I sit at my desk lifting my eyes to look up the river to the satisfying shape of Wedza. The view is still as lovely as ever, always in our sight as we pass from bedroom or office to living and dining rooms, always delighting us with its still beauty. Winter seems to be over here and the days are sunny and delightful, soon I fear to be hot and windy. Garfield is on his way from Harare and will be here for lunch ... I spent last week in Bulawayo planting my first twenty roses ...'[12]

The last year at Hokonui was heartbreaking for Garfield. Judith writes: 'He was devastated watching his beloved ranch, which he had built up so painfully, being wrecked not only by the drought, but also by the new owner. Fences weren't being mended. Pumps weren't repaired. Herders were not paid. Bulls were starving ...'[13]

Meantime, of course, Garfield was supervising the reconstruction at Dadaya by Gijima Mpofu and his fourteen-man team – and they went to see the Queen, again, twice, this time in Bulawayo and Harare, as the Commonwealth Heads of

---

11   *Otago Daily Times*, 'Week in Review', John Kennedy, 27.4.91.
12   JGT/SP, 9.8.91, TPPC.
13   J. Todd, 2007, pp. 370, 368.

Government meeting was being held there. Grace wrote one of her fascinating accounts of both occasions, finishing: 'I'm afraid I've rambled on. But it is very unlikely that there will be another such occasion to report to you.'[14] (The Queen did not forget the Todds: she sent Garfield a message when Grace died. When Garfield died, Her Majesty's High Commissioner attended his funeral, with a message from her. And, after the Service of Thanksgiving for their lives in London in February 2003, a message from the Queen was read out to their family and friends.)

In his New Year 1992 letter, Garfield wrote: 'Although, in health, Grace's problem is that she is almost as old as I, we have both successfully entered our eighties, have lived at Dadaya for 57 years and may this year complete 60 years together – but there will be no diamonds.'[15] Garfield was wrong: there was a little diamond in the centre of the Victorian gold-and-pearl brooch he presented to Grace on 7 April 1992.

***

At the Commonwealth meeting, the 'Harare Declaration' was signed, which 'made human rights a Commonwealth benchmark for the first time. Mugabe himself took little notice', Steve Crawshaw wrote in a profile of Mugabe in the *Sunday Independent* on 9 April 2000. In 1992 came the launching of the Zimbabwe Human Rights Association, with two patrons: former Chief Justice Enoch Dumbutshena, and Garfield. The *Sunday Mail* explained that 'Zimrights seeks to foster among individuals and groups respect for human dignity ... It will promote the practice of social, economic, political and legal justice ... The organisation will also encourage the Government to ratify all important International human rights instruments and to perform their duties under such instruments ...'[16]

Garfield began his speech by paying tribute to the Catholic Commission for Justice and Peace 'for its years of valiant service to Zimbabwe ... Zimrights hopes, with a wider constituency, to be its parallel for justice and peace ... Zimrights is of course deeply concerned with politics, but its greatest strength, so far, is that it is not involved in Party politics ...

'The Press, and through them the ... citizens of Zimbabwe can be informed of only what Government thinks it desirable for them to know ... We have a frightening responsibility for the hundreds of thousands of our people throughout the land who are hungry, thirsty, who sleep and then wake in terror.

---

14 JGT/SP, 19.10.91, TPPC.
15 GT, New Year 1992, TPPC.
16 *Sunday Mail*, 30.8.92.

Life is slipping away from them. They watch their cattle die. They cannot properly sustain their children, or themselves. We here have the physical strength to dedicate ourselves to relieve their plight. Let's hope we all have the unflagging moral stamina to be able to do so ...'

Garfield pleaded for the police to be free of all political influence, and went on: 'I have been privileged to see colonialism go. But, as I'm now 84, alas, what I have always longed for, democracy, I may not be able to see fully established in Zimbabwe. This is a good day. Zimbabwe is a marvellous country ... Here, together, we are dedicated only to the good of our country and to the safety and well-being of our people ...'

Garfield finished by quoting Article 40 of the Magna Carta of 1215 – 'and Zimrights might take this as a guide: "To none will we sell, to none will we refuse, to none will we delay – Right and Justice". Seven hundred years later, in Zimbabwe, let's strive even to better Magna Carta!'[17]

***

At the end of August, Garfield handed over the stores and butcheries to Sam Mpofu. He had always enjoyed his work with them and the opportunities it gave him to be with the people who lived around them. For 57 years, their whole lives had been tied up with the local people – and cutting these ties was very painful.

'We are doing our move the wrong way round,' Grace wrote. 'I had intended doing all sorting and disposing at Hokonui ... Now Garfield, who is commuting between Hokonui and Bulawayo, does not want me to go there and see it in its derelict state. Instead, he sends in a truck load every day or so and I am sorting, arranging, disposing, here.'[18] Garfield's decision was typical of his imaginative solicitude for Grace. The day he went to Hokonui to collect a last load, Sam Mpofu died.

'This is now Tuesday 29th. I have just been through to see Garfield triumphantly finish his third letter on his computer ... He is now excited and intrigued by the possibilities ahead. Very good news indeed – endless interest and fascinated occupation. No room for boredom ... Garfield speaks often of the beauty and the comfort, which give me in turn comfort and joy, since it has been my aim to make this place attractive enough to him to lessen the pain of leaving Hokonui.'[19]

---

17 GT, Zimrights, 29.8.92, TPPC.
18 JGT/SP, 9.12.92, TPPC.
19 JGT/SP, 28.12.92, TPPC.

PART VII – RETIREMENT, 1992–2002

'Grow old along with me!
The best is yet to be,
The last of life for which the first was made.'

Robert Browning

♦•♦

92

Bulawayo –1992–5

'Grace says these are the most joyful and privileged days of our life. She is right.'

Garfield Todd, 1995

One of the reasons the days were so 'joyful' for Grace was that she no longer had to 'share' Garfield with the Mission, or politics, or the ranch. In moving from Hokonui to Heyman Road, Grace, at the age of 81, accepted with relief the opportunity to let slip from her shoulders all responsibility save for her immediate family and her household – and those she shared with Garfield. As his outside interests gradually diminished, and her pain and illness increased, Grace and her comfort, her care, became his total and loving concern.

Garfield was obviously still suffering from the loss of Hokonui when he wrote at the end of 1993 that 'everything is on a vastly smaller scale than at Hokonui. The stand is one fifth of an acre instead of a wide ranch, a tiny garden instead of a panorama ... Over the years we have lived within a large African community where standards were low and people were dependent on one another, where people in need came to the door ... Now to be encapsulated in a beautiful house with every comfort is delightful but constricting ... Gladly I report that one doesn't ever really leave Dadaya for wherever we go there are Dadayans to greet us. Even the small "white" thread remains unbroken since 1906, for the third and fourth generations of the original Hadfield missionary family are leaders in the Churches. Miss Hazel Mansill conducts a Sunday School for hundreds of children ... We are really never lonely for we are still part of the Dadaya Family.'[1]

In April 1993, Grace had reported that Garfield was 'really very happy and contented. I am greatly relieved that the move to Bulawayo has not been as traumatic for him as we had feared. I am sure that still having the link with the business has been helpful. When Garfield is here at Heyman Road he spends most of his time on his computer, and that is giving him endless interest also.'[2] But the death in May of Dr Paul Fehrsen, who had been so dedicated a doctor and so faithful a friend, was a great sadness. Garfield gave the address at his funeral in St John's Cathedral.

***

The New Zealand board of the Church of Christ put up a two-storey administration block at Dadaya. In spite of strong protests from Garfield and Grace, it was called the Todd Building. Allan was once more at Dadaya – this time helping to set up computer training systems for the pupils. Garfield and Grace both spoke at the laying of the foundation stone on 18 September 1993. Grace took her audience back to 1934 and through the decades since; 'but it was our African colleagues who were the real agents of change. In the churches it was the African evangelists, in the schools it was the African teachers who daily extended knowledge to the community. Soon in hospitals and workplaces throughout the country it was the Africans who worked and taught and preached and produced. If and when the history of Dadaya is written, the names which will dominate the story will be Hlambelo, Sithole, Phiri, Ncube,

---

1   GT, New Year 1994, TPPC.
2   JGT/SP, 12.4.93, TPPC.

Mkwananzi, Dube, Mukonoweshuro, Mutomba, Nyoni, Mpofu, Msipa – and on and on. The list of names is long, and each one is deserving of high praise. These names live. Some have passed on, but their work and influence remain.'[3]

In November, Grace wrote: 'It is jacaranda time and the city is clothed in shimmering beauty ... It is next weekend that Garfield finally hands Maglas to the Mine. He goes out on Friday 15th when he expects that Christine and co. will have emptied the store. That night there is to be a little party there ... Mr Mutomba and Mr Sayakayi (of Shabanie Mine) are invited as well, since they have always been so helpful ... on Monday, by which time the whole of Maglas is to have been scrubbed out, he will hand the keys to the Mine management. And so will end a long association of thirty-three years. Of course he will have feelings of regret, but at the same time great relief and gratitude ...'[4]

***

In February 1994, Garfield was interviewed by John Edlin, a *Southland Times* (New Zealand) correspondent then in Harare. 'Today,' Edlin writes, 'fourteen years after the Union Jack was lowered over Harare for the last time, Todd is less than enthusiastic about the self-proclaimed Marxist ... "the radical rhetoric drove investors away and cost our young people untold thousands of jobs" ... Had the British heeded his advice in 1960, said Todd, independence could have dawned under a moderate black politician who could have handled the economy more skilfully. Instead, Mugabe tried to draw on failed economic policies from the Eastern Bloc and North Korea, plunging black Africa's potentially richest nation into ruin. "Zimbabweans, having suffered so much under white rule, have been denied the rewards that are rightfully theirs", said Todd. "Zimbabweans are law-abiding and want Zimbabwe to succeed but Mugabe has shown lately that he holds the electorate in total contempt."'[5]

***

Garfield liked to say that 'having given up ranching cattle, he was now ranching kids' – as he and Grace were supporting a number of children through school. First equipping them, then visiting them at their various schools, gave Garfield great pleasure and an opportunity to get behind the wheel of his favourite car and to drive through the countryside he loved. In April, he wrote that he was, 'after fifteen months, really emerging from the compelling interest and work associated with closing down the various businesses. Sometimes I wonder how we coped with ranch and cattle and grinding mill, stores and butchery,

---

3   JGT, laying of Todd Building foundation stone, 29.5.93, TPPC.
4   JGT/SP, 10.11.93, TPPC.
5   *Southland Times*, 23.2.94.

Zvishavane business, church, school, shadows of politics. I have continued to be so busy during the period that it has numbed the pain of breaking so many contacts with life and lives.'[6]

Sam Mpofu's death had also meant the Dadaya Governing Board had to elect a new Chairman: Cephas Msipa, Sam's brother-in-law. On 29 May 1994, Garfield attended his last Dadaya Governing Board meeting, as a member. 'He came home enthusiastic, saying he thought it the best he had ever attended', Grace wrote.[7]

***

In 1990, with the rest of the world, the Todds had watched Mandela walk to freedom; now in 1994 with the rest of the world, they watched South African citizens queue for hours to cast their votes for the first time in a free election. On 11 May, Grace wrote that they were 'still in a state of euphoria … yesterday's incredible – unbelievable – swearing-in ceremony in Pretoria of Nelson Mandela as the first President of a non-racial, democratic South Africa. Brave words! But it actually happened.'[8]

On 23 December, Garfield wrote his annual letter: 'Forty years ago in Rhodesia, I had hoped for, and worked to accomplish, what President de Klerk successfully brought to pass in the Union of South Africa today. It seemed like a miracle and all people of goodwill rejoice with South Africa and acclaim the magnificent performance of Nelson Mandela. We paid the price of civil war for freedom …'[9]

***

Garfield's discovery of the German theologian Hans Küng had been a milestone in his theological thinking. Küng seemed to articulate his own ideas on what constituted Christianity – certainly he seemed to validate what Garfield had sought to do during his life. 'All through one's life, one has been concerned with Christianity today', he said in interviews for this book.[10] 'The thought of Christianity as a way to heaven has not been one's first interest as much as Christianity opening up the "more abundant life" that Christ said he was to bring. I was fascinated with Küng because he was of the Catholic Church and of course his teaching for a start was not terribly popular with the Church itself. It did bring new ideas but a lot of it was not new to me. Here I was finding put

---

6   GT/SP, April 1994, TPPC.
7   JGT/SP, 30.5.94, TPPC.
8   JGT/SP, 11.5.94, TPPC.
9   GT, Christmas/New Year letter, 23.12.94, TPPC.
10   TPPC.

into words a lot of the things that I was thinking myself. I would think that that was the excitement because I was going along a path with Küng that I was already treading myself ...

'I was interested in life and coming to Rhodesia and setting up in a little mission station – and being cut off, in a way, from the world, you did your own thinking along those lines. Then you came to the wider world, to Johannesburg – to me life was always tremendously exciting. But it was tremendously exciting also because this was the life, this was what Christ, I hope, had come to offer the people ... The light came, the way people responded and I think a lot of this came into the writings of Küng ... I thought, here is something that I can go along with. He speaks of the things that should happen in the Church and a lot of these things were almost from my own background when, 150 years ago, the Churches of Christ were set up: "In essentials unity – in all things charity." Then he had another big letter on reforming the Church. A lot of that, too, were things that were part of my understanding. It was exciting and challenging – and in beautiful language ...

'Sending me a book like Hans Küng's *New Horizons* can be dangerously disturbing ... many hours of fascinating reading and [it] has sent me back to *On Being a Christian* ... but we are still looking and the search for final answers will no doubt have to continue until they arrive! I look around at the miracles which we have seen in the lives of the people among whom we have lived. Admittedly the observable miracles are the lives of children who came from villages where there was little of this world's wealth ... The Churches were welcomed and developed into calls for schools and from the schools came the added enlightenment which brought "Independence" in 1980.

'I don't regret the time, energy, prayer and cost of our part in it but there is such a long way still to go. I acknowledge that we owe a great debt to Mugabe for the fact that we have had relative peace since 1980 but he, personally, has had too great an influence on his ministers ... Kangai states today that if there are Civil Servants who are not loyal first to the Party, then he would want to weed them out. We have no understanding of democracy let alone a love for it.'[11] When Garfield was asked if democracy would ever come to Zimbabwe, he replied: 'I don't think it will come. Everything is at risk if they do that.'[12]

In 1957, Garfield had told the 25th Divisional Rotary Conference at the Victoria Falls Hotel on 10 April: 'democracy ... was much more than a system of government. It was a set of values and founded upon discussion and tolerance.

---

11 GT/SP, 14.1.95, TPPC.
12 GT/SP, interviews for this book.

"Of course democracy has always had its weaknesses ... Let us hold very dearly the principles of liberty and dignity for the individual, for upon such rests the whole fabric of our social life and from it comes another principle – that government is a trust given by the people of their own free will to those who govern; a trust that can be gained and can be withdrawn."[13]

***

In August 1995, David Mkwananzi died. His funeral took place at Dadaya. More than 1,000 people came from Harare, Bulawayo and Gweru. Garfield wrote: 'I had already rung Cephas Msipa suggesting that we offer a grave that we had prepared at Dadaya and that the burial should not take place till Sunday ... This was Judith's first experience of a funeral at Dadaya and I think it was important. David was the Chairman of our Churches, had taught for 40 years. It really turned into a great Thanksgiving Day ... The church was filled with a thousand people and at the cemetery people stayed and met and talked and the pain was eased, as so many old friends recalled the years.

'My sermon was interpreted by Kingsley Dube but later in the programme the service gave way to reminiscences. Eva Mkwananzi had had her head down all the time, but when I said that while everyone else was telling of David's life, I was the only one able to tell of his boyhood, and as I told some stories showing his determination to change things, I was delighted to see Eva raise her head as she listened to boyhood happenings and to see her join heartily in the laughter which accompanied my stories.'

Towards the end of his sermon, Garfield said: 'We give thanks to God for the life of our friend and brother, David. How glad we are that we can do this with joy, with love and appreciation for what David has meant to us over the years of his fruitful life ... I am old. David was old. We had both outlived the scriptural span of three score years and ten, but while it was no doubt more appropriate for me to think of David as a brother, I have more often thought of him as a son, a son whose achievements in life gave my wife and me the greatest pleasure – my son, my brother, my friend ...'[14]

***

Grace's attacks of osteoarthritis became more frequent during the early years in Bulawayo. 'I have been carefully and tenderly looked after', she wrote after one long spell of pain, 'and know myself to be a fortunate woman to have such comfort and such care.'[15] Painkillers of various kinds had very limited

---

13 *Rhodesia Herald*, 11.4.57.
14 GT/SP, 6.9.95, TPPC.
15 JGT/SP, 21.8.94, TPPC.

benefit, and both she and Garfield had nights of only broken sleep, during which Garfield would get up and make hot drinks. He gave a vivid picture of the pain Grace was in: 'Her hands squirmed on the sheet like little fishes. X-rays were taken which revealed that there were three vertebrae in the neck which had gone soft, having not only lost their protective strength but also closed in on the spinal cord.' Mr Themba Ncube, Bulawayo's leading orthopaedic surgeon, operated on Grace. Fifty years before, she had taught his father. 'You motivated my father,' Mr Ncube told Grace, 'and he motivated me.'

Garfield typed at Grace's dictation on 29 January 1996 to say 'the incisions were healed, including the critical one down the front of my throat. As Surgeon Ncube had chosen to follow the line of a deep wrinkle, provided by me, there is little to see. Thank you for that also, Mr Surgeon. I was given the most wonderful care at the Mater Dei Hospital, was waited on by a devoted husband (me) who was in attendance from 5:30am (excluding meals and other breaks) till 7:30pm and am now, seven days later, safely, happily and comfortably in my own bed at home. My leg was paralysed because the bone required to weld the vertebrae was taken from my hip. Feeling has now warmly risen from my toes to my outraged hip and I am learning to walk again. Then will come new spectacles on February 12th and I will once again be in reasonably good shape! ... I expected the surgeon to make an entry through the back of my neck where I had always understood my backbone was located.' Garfield signs off with 'God is good'.[16]

When Garfield wrote on 21 February, he said Grace had 'received her new spectacles yesterday so her nine weeks' starvation comes to an end. It has been a very trying time for her and she is also extremely weak. I am hoping that the spectacles will bring a lift to her spirits ... In general things are going well.'[17]

---

16 GT/SP, 31.1.96, TPPC.
17 GT/SP, 21.2.96, TPPC.

93

'This Haven of Peace and Security' – 1996–9

'He that would live completely happy must, before all things, belong to a country that is of good report.'

Simonides (c. 500 BC)

Alycen's youngest daughter, Judy, wished to be married in Zimbabwe so that Garfield could take part in the ceremony. Alycen and her husband, John Watson, and their three youngest children – Colleen, Paul and Judy – together with Judy's fiancé, also Paul, spent a fortnight in the country. Garfield arranged a tour to the Victoria Falls and Great Zimbabwe for their first week, and then they went to Bulawayo. Garfield had made all the arrangements for the wedding with Bishop Khalen, Roman Catholic Bishop of Bulawayo. The bishop's chaplain, Fr Pius Ncube (later Archbishop of Bulawayo), performed the ceremony in the bishop's private chapel, and Garfield blessed Judy and Paul.

There were many memorable moments during this visit – a meeting between Alycen and her childhood companion Rua (Rebekah), and a tour of Dadaya High School. They stood on the weir Garfield had built and looked up the steep side of the hill on which stood Hokonui homestead, and the trees around it, all sleeping silently in the sun. It looked remote, romantic, a fairytale castle.

***

Grace had her second cataract operation in November, and on 'Day 7 of 1997' wrote that she was better and stronger than at any time during 1996 'and look forward to a more useful 1997. We are having good rains with hopes of good harvest.'[1]

Grace received a letter from a stranger questioning the rightness of missionary endeavour in Africa. Garfield wrote that he and Grace 'felt that our life work

---

1   JGT/SP, 7.1.97, TPPC.

was in jeopardy, and Grace picked up a pen and put our point of view. I thought that her reply was compelling and vindicating.'[2] Grace's letter is their apologia, written near the end of their lives. She wrote:[3]

'Garfield and I came into this scene as young people to a Christian Mission. In those days the ... Christian belief and teaching was still basically and strongly missionary. We were taught, and accepted, Christ's command to go into all the world and proclaim His Gospel. That does not mean we came as superiors or conquering cohorts. It was not the "Onward Christian Soldiers" ethic. More like, "Oh brother man, fold to thy heart thy brother" ... We came into an already established 40-year-old colonial system, and found a people whom we liked and respected and grew to love. For various reasons and circumstances, we, Garfield and I and our small family, were the only "Whites" on the Mission and it continued thus for nearly 20 years. How did one react? We at once established accord on the religious level because of the strong belief of the people in a spirit world, beginning with their belief in the creator, "Umkulumkulu", the Great Great. For myself, I soon became aware that my own loved and comforting belief in those lovely allusions to the "choir invisible", the great "cloud of witnesses', the "souls of just men made perfect", etc., was not the spirit world of our African friends, or at least not the reality in their everyday life.

'We found a people ruled by fear. Anything that went wrong – sickness, crop failure, disaster small or great, was immediately attributed to the displeasure of "the spirits" – the newly dead or the relatives, as well as the ancestors. Then followed the search for the victim, the cause of the displeasure, and the punishment, and the cleansing. "Harmony and joy" were not everywhere visible. It was certainly present in the song and dance, a community activity enjoyed often. It was probably present in the activity of hunting. The population then was one million, instead of the eleven million today, and game was plentiful. But what seemed evident to us was the need, the cry for help, to learn to cope with the new environment. The twentieth century would not go away. They needed to learn to cope with it. And so we found ourselves meeting the need, as we saw it, of people desperate to learn and eager to "improve". They did not look to Government, as they do now. Government was far and alien. Near at hand was the missionary, the teacher, the school. And for the next 20 years these people, this way, was our life – totally absorbing, wholly fulfilling and rewarding, so it seemed to us. Of course, we learned to test our own received values, our "conventional wisdom" against that of the people we lived with. There was no wish or attempt to destroy an existing culture, rather to add to

---

2   GT/SP, 27.2.97, TPPC.
3   JGT/Mrs N..., 24.2.97, TPPC.

and enrich it. The young, especially, were so eager to learn. There were no books in their language, no text books for teachers. We felt so fortunate, so privileged, to be in there at that particular time, to become aware of, absorbed in, their longings, their hopes, their fears.

'The rest, the record, is there now in books. I just wanted, in answer to your own questionings, to tell you what it was like to meet these people at that particular time. What else could one do, but try to meet their need? I was a teacher. My work was in the school. For Garfield it was everywhere; in the community, the fields, in brickmaking and building, in helping the sick, pulling teeth, delivering babies. This was all before there were clinics. And so gradually to be one with them in their awakening national identity and their struggle against being second-class dwellers in their own land. Who could have then foreseen how greed would grow with power, how injustice and corruption would flourish; so that in this new era one would have to fight against even greater injustice than they had identified earlier?

'Yet we grew up with these people and everywhere we know and respect those who strive, even now, for a more caring society. Just as many do in Britain, Europe, and everywhere else in the society of "The Takers". One just has to go on striving for good – for how long? Until the end of Time.'

***

'Grace and I have been tardy in recognising our age and it is reluctantly, very reluctantly, being forced on us because of Grace's medical experiences of the past days, weeks, months and years,' Garfield wrote at the end of April 1997: Grace was 'strong and joyful for the whole morning. Visitors are welcome and she directs her gardener and enjoys greatly the preparation of the spring garden. Judith usually pops in ... Grace consistently beats both Judith and me at Canasta and Scrabble, so we have to take our appropriate place! On Monday mornings we attend the Communion Service at the Cathedral at 7 o'clock and then two other mornings are taken with a trip to the Library and one to the Hairdresser.'[4]

***

Garfield's constant concern was Grace. In August, he wrote: 'My ambition is to be here, strong and able to look after Grace, who is the be-all of my wish to continue living. That I most fervently pray for.'[5] Garfield 'really touched bottom' at that point, but when he wrote early in September was emerging 'from a sort of miasma'. 'A wider consultation with doctors has brought full clarification and now we are coping with the pain.' Valoron was the only thing that gave Grace

---

4   GT/SP, 27.4.97, TPPC.
5   GT/SP, 14.8.97, TPPC.

relief, but the doctors were concerned because it was 'addictive − (?at 86) − It seems we have the pain quite under control but Grace is very weak. However, in the past couple of days ... there is real improvement and I am recovered! ... I am happy today.'[6]

By October, Grace was writing freely again, and fluently, as twenty years earlier, but regretted that she could no longer drive herself on long journeys. 'I can't quite believe, or accept, that that ability is no longer mine. I think often, and happily, of the past, and the hard work required and enjoyed both at Dadaya and Hokonui. I would not be capable of any of that now. Instead, I find myself surrounded by comfort and with help, pleasantly even eagerly offered, to make my life easy. And all thanks to my beloved husband who out of storms and battles has brought us both to this haven of peace and security such as I have not until now known. I am daily and hourly grateful. Thankful, too, that at least in the matter of driving, once indispensable to him, he is willing and glad to have Thoko drive him everywhere. But each day we achieve less. When I am sad and guilty about this, he smiles his lovely smile and says we must accept that for us the days of achievement are past. But there is for me still the duty of acceptance in all this, and I believe I am daily learning. This all sounds a bit mournful and melancholy. But that is not an ingredient of our lives ...'[7]

***

The *Financial Gazette* published a letter from Garfield on 19 February 1998 in its 'Readers' Forum' column: 'Zimbabwe can be saved from financial disaster only by our President. Problems of mealie-meal, petrol, rocketing prices and falling standards of living, future pensions − even for ex-combatants − will not be solved and our financial situation made viable until the river of our economy flows again, and most of our "catchment area" is overseas where the World Bank, the International Monetary Fund and other donors live ... The river of our salvation is blocked by the unwillingness of President Robert Mugabe to give a public and personal assurance that the government will, in its negotiations and in its use of funds made available to it, honour the Constitution of Zimbabwe and the laws of our country. That personal and public declaration by our President must be made and honoured.'[8]

News in Garfield's letter to me of 23 February was uplifting: 'Judith and I attended a meeting last Friday in an overcrowded City Hall. After all these

---

6   GT/SP, 4.9.97, TPPC.
7   JGT/SP, 11.10.97, TPPC.
8   *Financial Gazette*, 19.11.98.

years both the Chairman and the Head of Zimrights drew attention to the fact that Judith and I were in the audience. In fact we had to stand up and, humbly but gratefully I can report that we received the biggest accolade of all. So unexpected but so heartening from many angles.'[9] In May, there was another packed meeting in the large City Hall, the audience virtually all black and young. There was a cross-aisle about halfway back where Garfield and Judith sat, and everyone who passed greeted them with delight. When the meeting began, he was invited onto the platform, amid a storm of applause and whistles, where he spoke briefly of the dire straits Zimbabwe was in.

But Garfield at 90 was frail, and his health was poor – he couldn't stand for long, and finally a urinary infection and malaria combined to send his temperature rocketing, and he became delirious. Grace immediately rose to the crisis and took on the nursing, but his 90th birthday was lost in a day of confusion and great distress of mind. However, within a day or two he was up and rather shakily opening presents and cards.

To brighten this sombre period came Cynthia: 'At the last moment we rang and said she should wait a month because I was rather low', Garfield wrote. 'But she came and it was the right decision because almost the day she arrived my problem had been solved and the correct medicine applied. I have been getting better ever since, though Grace was weak ... We were very thrilled with everything about the visit ... we had such tremendous enjoyment and Grace especially had lots of quiet times and long conversations.'[10]

'When I was so ill I was fortunate to be able to hand over all our affairs to a very capable Judith. Now that I am recovering I do miss the business but at 90 it is high time that I gave up, and how fortunate we were to have Judith ready to take over, which she has done. I especially miss dealing with our children in school, though I still do see them.'

Garfield's old friend and political colleague, Cyril Hatty, invited the Todds to his 90th-birthday lunch. In regretfully declining, Garfield wrote: 'I must say I hadn't planned to live this long, but I have no objections either. Together we can look back on fifty years of friendship and, in a shared political life, that is an accomplishment achieved by mutual respect and trust, based on Christian faith and affection. How fortunate we have been in the love, support and devotion of our wives, Doris and Grace, and how bountifully we have been fulfilled in our families. So at 90 we look back over the years with unbounded gratitude and joy ...'[11]

Garfield's Christmas letter for 1998 told their friends: 'we live under a cloud

---

9   GT/SP, 23.2.98, TPPC.
10 GT/SP, 25.9.98, TPPC.
11 GT/Cyril Hatty, November 1998, c/TPPC.

of fear which has been generated by a regime of "absolute power". This is a devastating disappointment but we believe that it will pass. There is a strong leaven of splendid, good people in Zimbabwe who know and believe that it is not power and privilege, but "righteousness which exalteth a Nation" ...'[12]

A few days later, Grace wrote: 'My writing is still unpredictable ... Judith is sensitively protective over anything affecting us. But for Judith I believe we could not continue here. She has been a tower of strength during this last rather difficult year ...'[13]

***

At the end of March 1999, Grace was once more in pain and discomfort. On 25 April, I had a letter with the superscription 'Thoughts Grace: fingers Garfield': 'Grace is easier and with no real pain, but no strength at all so she is spending a great deal of time in bed ... On April 3rd I realised that Grace had wakened pretty much as usual at 2:30am ... I asked if it was time to begin the birthday and she agreed. I went out and came back with a little silver tray on which was the most beautiful blue/white orchid I have ever seen; grown in Bulawayo. And beside the orchid were the cards and greetings and gifts. So at 3am on 3 April we were celebrating Grace's 88th and being thankful for our friends and loved ones who were joining with us ... The weather is beautiful and Judith came for tea and Grace came out and joined us for half an hour.'[14] Grace added a little message in slightly shaky writing but was well enough a day or two later to attend a little birthday lunch Paddy Fehrsen gave for her.

On 9 May, Grace wrote a note to me: 'My own writing, so bad, yet good! My heart lifts when I think we shall see you soon. And I can still play Scrabble and Canasta – and may even occasionally win!!' Grace and I had our games of Scrabble – and she frequently won – and Garfield joined us for Canasta – and the house was filled with music. On my last day, Grace waved me off from the house, her aureole of white hair framing her lovely old face against the dark green tickey-creeper – and it was the last time I saw her.

---

12 GT, Christmas 1998, TPPC.
13 JGT/SP, n.d. [January 1999], TPPC.
14 GT and JGT/SP, 25.4.99, TPPC.

94

SADNESS AND SERENITY – 1999–2000

'We stood with courage against white racism. Now we must stand against Mugabe and the spread of black terror.'

Garfield Todd

Joshua Nkomo died on 1 July 1999 and was buried a hero at Heroes' Acre as eulogies rang out among the tombstones. Three years later, Garfield wrote: 'I was just so sad for Nkomo who, now that he is dead, is portrayed politically as the ideal Zimbabwean, Father of Zimbabwe, dedicated to taking the land back, no friend of the whites: not able now to defend himself. Maybe this is fine and his name will continue to be revered, as it should be for he really had to give himself over to being Mugabe's shadow, when in fact his life and conduct, his attitude, were all quite the opposite from the Mugabe who has emerged.'[1]

Stephen Taylor, author of *Livingstone's Tribe*, visited the Todds as he journeyed from Zanzibar to Simonstown along the old missionary route. Garfield quoted from the book in his Christmas 1999 letter: 'The Todds were not the kind of people you felt pity for. They are dignified, gracious and self-contained. Sir Garfield, missionary, rancher and the only liberal white politician ever to hold power in Southern Africa, was now almost ninety. Judith, his daughter, ally, confidante and a campaigner in her own right, lives a few blocks away along a tree-lined avenue of suburbs. It was a tranquil spot for a venerable figure to be living out his days.'[2]

Professor Terence Ranger gives another little picture of Garfield: 'At 90, he is reading as never before and thinking quite new thoughts about the past and the present.'[3]

---

1 GT/SP, 29.7.2002, TPPC.
2 GT, Christmas 1999, TPPC.
3 Ranger, review of Weiss and Parpart, *Sir Garfield Todd and the Making of Zimbabwe* (1999), in *BSOAS*, vol. 63, no. 1 (2000), p. 155.

Sadness and Serenity – 1999–2000

***

'Here I am on January 4, at 6am, wanting to talk to you,' Garfield wrote to me, 'but you are not around so I decided to write and send some of the news because I miss you when I need to talk.'[4] Over the turn of the year, a combination of drugs prescribed for Grace had disturbed her mind to the extent that she did not know where she was, though she replied quite lucidly to questions Garfield had asked her about important times in their lives. They talked and prayed, and she went to sleep. Garfield lay beside her, wakeful, all night, and when she woke in the morning Grace was herself again.

Garfield wrote again on 22 January: 'we have everything that is available and that is of assistance, and everyone around is most sympathetic and helpful. We are fortunate people ... Things here are really dangerous. We are out of fuel and the farmers, with their planting and ploughing are in real trouble. Buses, cars stranded on the streets of Harare. South African banks cutting credit lines with Zimbabwe banks.'[5] During 1999, Mugabe's new draft constitution was published – 'a licence for eternal political life', according to the *Sunday Independent* of 9 April. Opposition from the Zimbabwe Congress of Trade Unions and the National Constitutional Assembly ('an umbrella of civic organisations and individuals') consolidated into the Movement for Democratic Change (MDC). The draft of Zimbabwe's new constitution provided for land expropriation without compensation, but at the referendum on 12 and 13 February Zimbabweans voted 'NO', by 55 to 45 per cent. The editor of the *Zimbabwe Independent*, Iden Wetherell, headed his comment 'Thank you Zimbabwe'. 'As in 1972, this week's verdict in the referendum is a vote of protest against a government that has misused power, manipulated the media, and denied us the elementary rights to which we are entitled. The *Zimbabwe Independent* ... saw the constitutional commission and the way it went about its business as symptomatic of everything that was flawed in the way we are governed as a nation. In particular we pointed out the hypocrisy and deceit the nation was being fed in the commission's and the government's public relations offensive ... Like Smith in 1972, this regime will never be the same again.'[6]

Garfield wrote the same day: 'There is reason for rejoicing but in some ways nothing has changed ... in a most important way, everything has changed, for there is now hope and great excitement. Mugabe has been

---

4 GT/SP, 4.1.2000, TPPC.
5 GT/SP, 22.1.2000, TPPC.
6 *Zimbabwe Independent*, 18.2.2000.

defeated: the impossible has happened …'[7]

When Garfield wrote on 7 March, he was concerned with the first manifestation of Mugabe's revenge for his referendum defeat: 'Within Zimbabwe things are disastrous. "War veterans", many of doubtful credibility, are invading white farms in their hundreds, being bussed in by Government lorries and have taken over more than 100 farms so far. Dumiso tells them to get off the farms but earlier it was the President who said Government would not stop the invasions, so they are paying no attention …

'Cyril Hatty, who keeps irregularly in touch with me, was on the phone last week: "our telephone lines have been cut and our neighbouring farmer has been invaded by 'war veterans'". They have been given eight hours to pack and get off the farm! There is nothing he can do but get off. There seems no law, and the Police say that they cannot act as this is all a political matter and beyond their authority … Zimbabwe is on the brink of Anarchy.'[8] A month later, Garfield wrote: 'Cyril Hatty rang yesterday to say that his family were packing him off to a son in Johannesburg …'[9]

On 20 March, Garfield wrote: 'The High Court has instructed the invaders to leave within 24 hours and have instructed the police to move the people out, but the police refuse to budge. There is no law and order now and it is frightening for everyone, not just for the white farmers. Mugabe rules supreme!'[10]

***

The Chronicle published a letter by 'Samu Zulu' in its 'Guest Column'. Reporting on whites queueing up to register as voters for the forthcoming election, Zulu wrote that none of the whites based in Zimbabwe 'can equal or surpass the respectability of 91-year-old Sir Garfield Reginald Todd, his wife Grace and daughter Judith … being the TRUEST [sic] white friend Zimbabwe has ever had, Garfield is still with us and he continues to speak without fear or favour. This "white brother" certainly deserves the medal and knighthood he received … because he really is an advocate of "peace and justice". But how many Africanised whites are like Sir Garfield Todd?'[11] Garfield's comment: 'Imagine our surprise and happiness to read this …'

'Samu Zulu' wrote again on Grace's birthday: 'As usual, Todd was with his wife, Jean Grace Isobel [sic] – better known as Lady Grace – who turns 89 today. Is this the couple everybody talks about? … Do the Todds, human as we

7   GT/SP, 18.2.2000, TPPC.
8   GT/SP, 7.3.2000, TPPC.
9   GT/SP, 16.4.2000, TPPC.
10 GT/SP, 20.3.2000, TPPC.
11 *The Chronicle*, 22.3.2000.

all are, really deserve the immense idolisation the world has showered on them or can an impartial black journalist unearth certain blemishes, which may have been hidden by the white paparazzi? ...

'These two former missionaries of the New Zealand Church of Christ ceased to be "private individuals" when they first arrived in Bulawayo on July 13 1934 to serve "a benighted people in darkest Africa". The Todds contributed more than any other white family.' Zulu goes on to write of Dadaya School and to list some of 'the luminaries from this prestigious school' and tells the story of the Todds' life during the liberation war.[12]

On 15 May, Garfield wrote: 'We are living with evil. This is not just incompetence or even greed but the intelligence and determination of the Government are a manifestation of evil and it is frightening ... This morning, 60,000 British passport-holders have been told that their Zimbabwean passports are cancelled so they are just British, and therefore foreigners, and therefore will have no vote in the coming election. I doubt there are 60,000 of these people who hold two passports but of course we know friends who are now disenfranchised ... This is evil we face ... Judith's very positive role adds to Grace's concern.'[13]

The Todds were threatened with a war vets' 'invasion'. Judith enlisted Dumiso Dabengwa's help, and the invasion did not materialise; but, as she writes in *Through the Darkness*: 'This event marked the beginning of my mother's spiritual and mental retreat from Zimbabwe ... she could feel that something was up and from about that moment she reached the most devastating conclusion possible for both of them. [She] took me aside at the first possible opportunity and informed me that her husband, my father, Garfield Todd, had been kidnapped by war veterans. The man now looking after her so tenderly and lovingly was an imposter. She couldn't understand his role in her life, but she valued him enormously. However, above all, she mourned the loss of my father and was desperately worried about him. Where was he, and how could we rescue him?'[14]

We know that Garfield was the 'sun, the moon and the stars' to Grace and that his absence was the worst thing that could happen. Her question to Judith, 'Where was he?', was the deepest anguish for her. From now on, Grace would inhabit two worlds, with 'Gar' in the real world, replicated by 'Garfield' 'looking after her so tenderly and lovingly' in her 'other' world. The redeeming feature for Garfield of this heartbreaking situation was that Grace was always

---

12 *The Chronicle*, 3.4.2000.
13 GT/SP, 15.5.2000, TPPC.
14 Todd, 2007, pp. 414–15.

Grace, the same person and personality he adored, and this remained so until the end, just the same Grace.

***

The Zimbabwe election was scheduled for 25 and 26 June 2000. Forty opposition supporters, including three white farmers, were murdered. But an MDC rally on 15 June at the large City Hall in Bulawayo passed off peacefully. The *Farmer* magazine of 20–27 June had a photograph of Garfield on the cover. Inside, the story ran: 'At a packed rally ... Sir Garfield Todd endorsed Zimbabwe's MDC.' If he were 40 years younger, 'he told about 3000 supporters who came to listen, "I'd be asking you to vote for me. Instead I'm asking you to vote for the MDC." Accompanied by whistles and cheers, Sir Garfield told the rally "to think of those who've died, of all those who've suffered in these hard times". Described by a MDC official as Zimbabwe's oldest living freedom fighter, Sir Garfield talked of the evil that was taking place, describing Mugabe's cabinet as a "cabinet of jellyfish".'[15]

David Coltart, one of the MDC's doughtiest fighters, said the meeting was 'absolutely packed, standing room only. Garfield was on the platform on a freezing night and spoke for 5–10 minutes. He spoke a bit about his past and said that he had fought his whole life for democracy in the country and that ZANU-PF had betrayed the ideals of the liberation struggle. He concluded by giving an unequivocal endorsement of the MDC. He had a wonderful reception from a 90% black audience, 60% under 25 years of age ... I remember feeling absolutely amazed by his clarity of thought, by his gentle nature, by his humour. It was a remarkable performance from a 91-year-old. He had people literally hanging on to every word. The young black voters were completely fascinated by the appearance of this old ex-PM of Southern Rhodesia whose ideas were as progressive as theirs. He was far more in touch with modern democratic thought than was the party led by people several decades younger than him.'[16]

On 22 June, Grace wrote: 'I've left all the horrid election news to Gar. Here we are happy and peaceful to date, but can we remain so, even if it is our side which wins – and that seems likely ... So, darling Susan, continue to pray for us, and all like us, living in a very precarious state, part peace, part hideous violence.'[17] The MDC won 57 of the 120 contested seats, thereby denying Mugabe the two-thirds majority he needed to amend the Constitution.

***

---

15 *The Farmer*, 20–27 June 2001.
16 Telephone conversation, David Coltart/SP, 19.1.2001, TPPC.
17 GT and JGT/SP, 22.6.2000, TPPC.

'Grace prays to get better but spends most of the time in bed, and the weeks pass and she is not gaining in strength. She is wonderful and lovelier than ever and my heart goes out to her. I give her 20 drops of Valoron, every three hours around the clock, but I think she is losing hope and I wanted you to know … We are in love but I can't find a cure. Your prayers will be with us', Garfield wrote on 26 July.[18]

'The special pills which we started to take 15 days ago have taken away the "burden" of fear and have brought even a new brightness', Garfield wrote on 28 August. 'Grace is lovely but once or twice recently she talks to me, so sweetly, about Gar. Once she asked me if I knew him, and when I said I did, she asked how he was, and was delighted with the news. Then I quietly led her back to where we were and that Judith would soon be in, and then that I was Gar. "Are you sure?" So we quietly retraced our steps. It is all so beautiful, every day that passes while we are together is so happy and precious …'[19]

Garfield wrote of Grace's '"burden" of fear'; in 1977 Grace had written to her sister, Elsie: 'I don't mind at all the implications of the passing of the years and the coming of old age. If only one could be sure that one could retain one's mind and strength. You say you dread loss of memory, remembering Mother. I do, too, of course, but the worst fear is fear itself.' Elsie's memory and mind disintegrated. Grace's memory was intact in 2000; as to her mind, she was still beating Garfield and Judith at Canasta; but, as she herself had written all those years earlier, 'the worst fear is fear itself'.

At the beginning of a letter Garfield wrote on 20 September 2000, he warned me that it was 'not going to be in the ordinary run of letters … you are my friend of many years and we have an understanding together, which is unique in my life. That means that I can quietly talk to you, not so much wanting help from you, but giving help to myself. I need to talk … For some weeks now I have noticed that Grace "wanders" a bit but recently it has become more noticeable. We love talking about earlier days and special occasions … However, sometimes it is Grace telling me in detail of shared memories but she turns the conversation into a story about "Gar". Then, after we have gone on a while, she stops, looks quizzically at me and says, "but you know this, don't you? You are Gar?" … Anyway, this situation, which is one of love but occasional uncertainty, is not worrying.

'This is not a regrettable phase of my life but rather emphasises the challenges which are still before me and of course, the most immediate and of the greatest concern is that I recognise and act on anything which can concern Grace … The

---

18 GT and JGT/SP, 26.7.2000, TPPC.
19 GT/SP, 28.8.2000, TPPC.

parting must come but I pray that hospital doesn't have to separate us before that occasion ...'[20]

By 1 October, Grace had 'fully accepted' Garfield as '"Gar" and is a bit embarrassed that there was any doubt. Grace is lovelier than ever and we spend day and night together ... We sit in the lounge a good bit, with lovely music. Just wanted you to know that the love story is all new again, with much joy.'[21]

***

In 1995, I had given Garfield and Grace a first draft of the 'long' version of the biography up to 1953. Now, in November 2000, Garfield wrote: 'I have been reading extracts to Grace from your early writings and we find them fascinating. Of course we are deeply involved but the stories, the experiences are so interesting ... I rang you of course – 44 years of communion and I needed some help. Thank you for being there.'[22]

Garfield's last Christmas letter reviewed their lives, and ended: 'So, in our nineties, we no longer look for challenges but find peace in St Paul's assurance "and now abideth faith, hope and love, and the greatest of these is love". Faith is never easy, hope springs eternal, and love, the greatest, we know – and in love we place our faith.'[23]

---

20 GT/SP, 20.9.2000, TPPC.
21 GT/SP, 1.10.2000, TPPC.
22 GT/SP, 12.11.2000, TPPC.
23 GT, Christmas 2000, TPPC.

95

'HER NAME IS GRACE' – 2001

'The girl from Winton who is my life.'

Garfield Todd

In February, Garfield reported: 'Grace is really so much improved in health, and so much like her old self (a new, old self) that days are happier for us all and full of hope. She is even arguing again and the kitchen is once more coming under her control …'[1]

'Grace and I, whose love overwhelms us both as the days pass, is [sic] really without much interest in life except for me to stay beside her. She loves to see Judith and also Paddy … She looked at me and said, "I wish this could go on forever, but we know it can't." … As we really cannot discuss the horrors of the day, Judith finds it difficult to stay but when Grace is strong enough we enjoy Canasta, and Grace does her best because she feels that the three of us can be fully relaxed together, while playing and not talking.'[2]

Garfield's letters recounted political news as he watched, horrified, what Mugabe was doing to his beloved Zimbabwe; but 'what I cannot forgive is how many people he has corrupted'.[3] 'Cephas Msipa (chairman of the Dadaya Governing Board) and now Sam Mumbengegwi, whose brother is our High Commissioner in London, destroy families we were so proud of', he wrote.[4] 'I am not suggesting that I am without hope. To know so many wonderful African people, to know their families, assures me that Christian love reigns in the hearts of many people and to believe that love will overcome, rules out despair.'

1 GT/SP, 13.2.2001, TPPC.
2 GT/SP, 3.3.2001, TPPC.
3 Todd, 2007, p. 422.
4 GT/SP, 25.3.2001, TPPC.

Grace was 90 on 3 April 2001. Mr Aeneas Chigwedere placed in her hands the manuscript of his just-completed book, *The White Heroes of Zimbabwe*, about 'the British Methodist the Rev. John White, who, from the end of the nineteenth century until 1930 was a great champion of the rights of the Native People in their conflicts with the Government. The second third is devoted to the life of a High Anglican Priest, the Rev. Arthur Shearly Cripps, who kept the battle going till the 1940s, and the final third is on the Todd Family (1940–1980).'[5]

Garfield wrote after the birthday and 'Our 70th wedding anniversary': 'both opened badly but by 10am on the third, Grace was dressed and on the stoep and in splendid form, so that she happily and delightfully took calls that came from her relatives in New Zealand and from our people in Australia; then came visits from Paddy and from Alison Rudd ... What can you give your wife on a 70th Anniversary? I decided on an Orchid but it was not the season for orchids.' However, with the help of the secretary of the Orchid Society he found a beautiful white orchid, which a florist arranged with other tiny orchids, for a table centrepiece. 'It was really the most beautiful and perfect gift from a 92-year-old husband. We were both delighted.'[6] It was actually their 69th anniversary. Probably Garfield was well aware of this but feared (rightly) that Grace would not see 7 April 2002, and wanted to make 7 April 2001 as special as he could.

Garfield was 93 on 13 July: 'We had decided not to leave the house on the 13th and Grace had a good day with Paddy and Judith joining us for wine and a fine birthday cake (Grace's Mother's recipe) which Benjamin had baked for us. It was, as usual, a beautiful day, and a very happy one, with Grace in fine form, which made my day ...'[7]

Between the declining state of the country and Grace's slow, gentle withdrawing from life, Garfield was obviously in some anguish on 29 July: 'I have just written to you, but I have been with Grace for the rest of the day and I just feel that my letter is nonsense so I will send news, later. At 93 why should I be unable to face facts? Of course if I were to meet Jesus of Nazareth I would be saying, I don't want pleasures beyond our imagination, just a continuation throughout eternity of the fellowship and love of the past 70 years. Forgive this. I will write or phone soon. Our love.

'... and now it is 3:30am on Monday the 30th. Grace is, I think, asleep and

---

5   GT/Karl du Fresne, Wellington, NZ, 2.2.2002, c/TPPC.
6   GT/SP, 8.4.2001, TPPC.
7   GT/SP, 12.7.2001, TPPC.

will stay so for a while ... Grace should now have all my time and I am going to stop letter-writing and, so as to keep in touch, ask you to phone me ... Judith and Grace and I are as safe as we can be, and are financially as safe as we can be. So I will conclude this letter and just have quiet phone calls, based on our common knowledge of each other's circumstances. Prayers for our little family, selfishly, and for our country and its beleaguered people.'[8]

The telephone calls continued, but Garfield resumed his letter-writing on 19 August: 'In the past two weeks we have had some difficult days but Grace comes round marvellously each time and we are quiet and enjoying life ... I have been thinking that although everything is limited, we are able to give happiness and security and hope to our ten "children" ...'[9]

Garfield wrote on 30 August: 'Sometimes I feel I am living in a strange unknown world. But quite all right. Grace had a difficult morning yesterday ... this morning Grace is fine but very confused ... But I suppose another concern is Dadaya. It has become a school for the rich! ... Dadaya was once known as the poor man's school and when a child was admitted he or she never left until the course was over. In 20 years no child was ever expelled for any reason, nor had to go because fees were not forthcoming ... I really can't leave the house for I am Grace's link with life and if I am not around she is lost ... Grace says she is happy sitting on the stoep and has sent me to get on with my letter ... She sends her love ... I didn't really intend to write as miserable a letter but there is little joy for the people today ...'[10]

***

'The Government has now begun a programme of Ethnic Cleansing. Thousands of farm workers are being driven off the farms which the Government is taking over for resettlement of "landless people". Tens of thousands of workers whose grandfathers or great-grandfathers came to Rhodesia from Malawi, Mozambique, etc. are to be sent HOME [sic]. Many of them won't know where Malawi is ... Thousands of the people are now camped along roads or are getting shelter from friends. But this applies to us! Judith can't get a passport unless she has a certificate to say that she has renounced, under New Zealand law, any right she may have through her father to settle in New Zealand. This is catastrophic for hundreds of thousands of people, black and white, and the countries which can be affected by mass immigration from Zimbabwe are appalled! ... I do not have a valid Passport but have applied to Harare for one ...'[11]

---

8   GT/SP, 29.7.2001, TPPC.
9   GT/SP, 19.8.2001, TPPC.
10 GT/SP, 30.8.2001, TPPC.
11 GT/SP, 6.9.2001, TPPC.

***

As I completed final drafts of the chapters about Garfield's PM years, I sent them to him. The reliving of happier past times became a great interest to him. 'I read the chapters immediately, with the greatest of joy. Of course we are loving recollecting so much of what we have enjoyed in past years, and lots of it I am deeply moved by … I like your use of "Garfield".'[12] 'Of course I am scared of Heaven, not only because there is no marriage there but because of the time it will take to make amends for earthly failings and misunderstandings. However, I will just wait and not go into details before I have to.'[13] That was the first glimmer of humour for many months.

'Dadaya stays as the centre of things. I can hardly believe that Grace and I had 20 years there, 20 years of unbelievable privilege, began our family, started political life … but anyway I am a happy man who has been too greatly privileged: then I look across and see Grace so soundly sleeping – and realise that we are both in our nineties! – lying in our so comfortable bed, which sleeps five, but only in emergencies! …

'At that point my door opened and framed in it, in her dressing gown, was a little old lady who, for the moment, could have been my adored grandmother! I left the letter … just stayed beside Grace for the whole of the day. She is so pathetically glad to have me "back" after a long absence and doesn't want me to leave the room … Grace is so sweet in her present state that I find it hard to want to change again …'[14]

The last months of Grace's life, when 'Garfield' disappeared for periods, however 'brief' or 'long' they seemed to her, resonate poignantly with her anguish when Garfield went on visits to Britain and the USA during the difficult years on Hokonui Ranch, and illustrate more vividly than anything else, even her letters to him, the depth of the anxieties she endured at those times. 'My love for you and need for you is all mixed up by my longing for you to be here to look after the pump. To such depths have I come.' 'I only know that even now I do not know how to face the remaining weeks until you come.' Grace told Elsie that her relationship with Garfield, 'while my life lasts, is more important to me than any other aspect of life itself'. Grace's amazing acceptance of the worry and difficulties of Garfield's five-and-a-half years' restriction was firmly founded on the relief that he was there, with her, and *could* not go away.

***

---

12 GT/SP, 13.9.2001, TPPC.
13 GT/SP, 16.9.2001, TPPC.
14 GT/SP, 26.9.2001, TPPC.

'Her Name is Grace' – 2001

On 2 October 2001, a delegation from the Rotary Club of Bulawayo visited Heyman Road to hand over to Grace the Services Rendered Award for dedicated and lifelong service to education at Dadaya Mission and Zimbabwe. 'As Grace could not come out,' Garfield wrote, 'I accepted a very beautiful framed certificate of achievement from the delegation, one African, one Indian and one White ... Grace was really pleased and fully appreciated what had taken place.'[15]

In November 2001, Garfield wrote: 'There is so much to be thankful for in that Grace is happy. I would dearly love to clear away the miasma but if it has to stay then it almost seems I am courting Grace a second time ...'[16]

In September the previous year, Garfield had written: 'I pray that hospital doesn't have to separate us'. Nor did it: Grace did not have to leave her own home, her own bedroom, her own bed, but by December Garfield had to bring in nurse-aides to help in looking after her. 'I have found that the strain is increasing, and I don't always get the sleep I need, so I have now totally surrendered ...

'Duduzile Sithole we have known for only three weeks but if you could see her with Grace you would think they were mother and daughter. If not doing anything else, Dudu will be sitting with a hand of Grace's in her own hands, and just chatting away ... It is wonderful to see Lindiwe and Duduzile in action. Patience and smiles all the way.' One night when Grace was in distress, Garfield heard Duduzile singing to her, very quietly, from the Psalms.

'Of course I am not suggesting that things are well with Grace. She has really been ill for three years and there is not much left in her life except that she is surrounded by the love of Judith and Gar, and we are in the fortunate position of being able to provide what comfort is available, and I have all the drugs that are needed, which is more than the majority of our people could afford or obtain ... Grace is now living in a world of make-believe but is calm and is now in no doubt about our life together, both our history and now. This, to me, is just so satisfying.'[17]

On 12 December, Garfield wrote: 'It is now five months since Grace was able to join us on the stoep to play Canasta. I checked and the final score, which we have kept for years, shows that Grace is 8 games ahead of Judith and me! It was always that way ... For pure kindness and courtesy [Grace] gets 100%. Never a criticism, always an amazement at the kindness she receives from all. She holds that "kindness" is the premier virtue ... I came to be fully recognised again and utterly depended upon, after all our 70 years of such a blessed time together.

---
15 GT/SP, 7.11.2001, TPPC.
16 GT/SP, 7.11.2001, TPPC.
17 GT/SP, 3.12.2001, TPPC.

So we wait quietly now and Grace is happy and still finds life interesting, and marriage unbelievably happy. I just thank God that all is going so quietly and so happily ...'[18]

The week before Christmas, Garfield's 'strength gave in in a frightening way', and among other things he could not work his computer. He wrote on Christmas Eve: 'This is how it is at the moment and I will have to give up. It is just a case of utter exhaustion. The Medical Aides have arrived in the nick of time. Already I have slept hours and hours but there will be a gap of some days –

'December 27th 2001 ... I spoke to you last night and I was registering some improvement. However, I will limit myself to this one note for today ... Of course, we have had a very quiet but, within present limits, a happy Christmas and have much to be thankful for, as we are. Benjamin had roasted a chicken big enough to meet the appetite of the Todds and their staff, which is now quite large! I am personally so much improved in health, after some rather grim days so that I will be starting the new year in good heart ...'[19]

'Grace and I had discussed what was to happen when she died.'[20] 'Can you really imagine that quietly, and out of a silence, Grace should say: "You will wear a white shirt and a black tie and you will make a good speech"? To remember it moves me to tears.'[21] She also asked him to give 'Aaron's Blessing'.

'Grace did not suffer much pain, and even the last days were still wonderful. We were together and in full communion and speech till just five minutes before she passed away and that was just the greatest privilege.'[22]

Grace died at 10 p.m. on Sunday, 30 December 2001.

***

'Of course I am devastated,' Garfield told friends. 'To have to part after 70 years together seems almost unbelievable, but it has happened. When I endeavour just to think rationally, I can tell myself of the many reasons why I am glad that Grace did not have to face another month or more of life in this sad country and I am happy that she was shielded from violence of any kind ... Grace died on a Sunday night and the funeral was scheduled for two Sundays ahead. Our graves had been prepared, in the Dadaya Cemetery, about 15 years ago, so we were granted more years than we had expected but 70 years together was not enough – I am 93, and I look forward, with Grace, to eternal life which has been promised.

---

18 GT/SP, 12.12.2001, TPPC.
19 GT/SP, 24–27.12.2001, TPPC.
20 GT/'Friends', 18.1.2002, TPPC.
21 GT/SP, 15.2.2002, TPPC.
22 GT/Rev. Dr W. A. Curwood, 6.2.2002, c/TPPC.

'Her Name is Grace' – 2001

'Grace and I knew that, with problems of no petrol and even today's threat of no maize meal, there would be a very small congregation at the funeral, but how wrong we were. Dadaya is a very isolated place and anyway at 90, so many of one's friends have preceded us, so there could not be many to attend. We were so wrong! The Church was filled to overflowing and the service was beautifully conducted, with the singing as delightful as one could expect from a congregation largely African men and women, but with so many white friends from all over Zimbabwe. From New Zealand came Allan Todd and from Edinburgh a special friend of ours ... A committee just seemed to appear. In Zvishavane there was no mealie meal, no cooking oil, no meat available and what could we do when we found that many friends from as far distant as Harare were intending to come to Dadaya? I personally was relieved of all responsibility.

'The Dadaya School was on vacation but, as the new term was to start on the Tuesday following Sunday's service, the Dadaya School staff was on duty and loyal friends worked miracles. The Dadaya staff planned to cater for 1,000 people and on Sunday the 13th of January a thousand people filled the Church and after the service they enjoyed a delicious meal with unlimited ice-cold orange drink, on a hot Sunday. To me, it all seemed unbelievable. Vukuzenzele donated an ox and the Mukokokwayira family who now own a small but beautiful farm, also once part of Hokonui Ranch, donated an ox. Generosity knew no bounds. Various friends contributed to the service but of special note was the contribution of the Hon. Aeneas Chigwedere, the Minister of Education. His speech was warmly accepted, especially by me. I have always recognised the national importance of Grace's work in education and it is now given official recognition ... This letter endeavours to bring just a few bits of information, but my grieving heart is my own. Grace---'[23]

***

On Sunday morning, the church was already full when Paddy Fehrsen went in to place her exquisite flowers on Grace's coffin, the congregation singing hymns, interspersed with tributes given by people who fondly remembered Grace. One of the churchwomen spoke about Grace's insistence on punctuality – to be followed by a happily smiling Pastor Albert Nyoni apologising for the fact that the programme was running half an hour late! Much laughter ...

The Dadaya Choir sang, and Minister Cephas Msipa, heads of churches and members of the Education Department arrived. Judith took her place beside them at the front of the congregation, and then the 1,000 people in the church

---
23 GT/'Friends', 18.1.2002, TPPC.

stilled as Garfield, in his black suit with 'white shirt and black tie', walked slowly through the door on to the platform and to his chair near the reading desk. Tall, thin, frail, but straight-backed, his presence was electrifying. Dr Michael Ndubiwa, former Town Clerk of Bulawayo, the MC, announced the first hymn: 'How Great Thou Art'. (It would be sung at Garfield's funeral a few months later, and at the thanksgiving service for the lives of Grace and Garfield at the Church of St Martin-in-the-Fields in London the following year.) David Mukonoweshuro – 'the best headmaster there had ever been at Dadaya (but not headmistress)' – led the prayers of the congregation, and he was followed by the Minister of Education with his remarkable tribute to Grace – 'On behalf of the Government of Zimbabwe I am here to join you in bidding farewell to a great daughter of Zimbabwe and a legend in Education circles … all the Africans here who did primary education before 1980 are children or grandchildren of the Grace Todd Education System.'[24]

After the singing of 'The Lord is My Shepherd', Garfield went to the reading desk to give his tribute to his beloved Grace – to make his 'good speech'. He spoke, at no great length, slowly but unfalteringly about their arrival in Southern Rhodesia, the early days at Dadaya, some of the people – and related events from his 'son' David Mkwananzi's life to illustrate how the changes came among them. He spoke of his gratitude for the minister's address and his contentment that Grace's work had been so richly acknowledged – and a little, a very little, of his own loss. And then he raised his hand and gave 'Aaron's Blessing': 'The Lord bless you, and keep you: the Lord make his face to shine upon you, and be gracious unto you: the Lord lift up the light of his countenance upon you and give you peace, now and for evermore. Amen.'

Kingsley Dinga Dube, David Hlambelo, Bafundi J. Mpofu, Cephas Msipa, Benjamin Ncube and Paul Themba Nyathi bore Grace's coffin out of the church. (A few months later, they would perform the same office for Garfield.)

***

It took a long time for the congregation and the procession of cars to make its way to the cemetery. There was a covered area of chairs near the graveside, and the people stood all around as prayers were said. Then Allan, as representative of the Associated Churches of Christ in New Zealand, gave his address, telling how Grace had 'inspired us and indeed the whole New Zealand Todd family over many years. Grace, we loved you and cherish the fondest memories of your love, consideration of others, and the marvellous times we have had together …

'We, the New Zealand Churches, have basked in the acclaim given for the

---

24 See Chapter 24, n. 7.

tremendous work, the deep involvement, the aroha, the "love-in-action" of Grace. Her work and her life have inspired us all ... Grace ... We especially remember your work, your energy, your love in making life more meaningful for young women. You took the New Zealand Churches down radical, reformist paths where sometimes they followed most reluctantly. But you never wavered – your love overcame every problem. You have given all of us encouragement and hope, to make a difference in this challenging world ...'[25]

There were more prayers, and then 'little Grace Wilson of Winton, New Zealand' was gently lowered into the dry, stony earth of Dadaya Mission, the scene of her great contribution to Zimbabwe. Scores of men stepped forward in line to spade the earth into the grave, while men and women came forward to shake hands with Garfield and Judith. The spell broke, and 'people stayed and met and talked, and the pain was eased, as so many old friends recalled the years', as Garfield had written of David Mkwananzi's funeral.

'I, Garfield, with Alycen, Judith and Cynthia, while we are understandably and enormously proud of the service which Grace gave our land and people, desperately miss her presence and her daily love of each of us. To us, she was a loving and delightful wife and Mother.'[26]

---

25 Allan Todd, TPPC.
26 GT/'Friends', 18.1.2002, TPPC.

96

'A MIGHTY TREE HAS FALLEN IN THE FOREST' – 2002

'For my beloved, with my devotion and thanks for a lifetime of love and care. Go well into the future, my darling.'

Grace Todd on Garfield's 70th birthday card

Garfield seemed to find increased strength after Grace's funeral. He wasted no time in writing to thank all those who had made the arrangements at Dadaya, and to Dr Chigwedere for his address. All the tributes to Grace that arrived gave him such joy that he wanted immediately to respond: 'a completely wonderful person', 'incredibly kind, incredibly courageous'; 'a most wonderful woman'; people's memories of Hokonui Ranch, of Grace's garden, her food and the warmth of her welcome; 'innovative educationalist' (from former Principal Ron Chapman); 'a life so positive, productive and inspiring'; 'a genuine hero'; 'she lived up to her name, Grace'.[1]

Grateful as Garfield was that, as he so desired, he had been able to care for Grace to the last and that his strength had held out for the funeral, and buoyed up as he was by these tributes, he was exhausted – and unspeakably lonely. On a visit to Grace's home in Winton in 1959, he had written to her at Hokonui: 'I am lonelier than I have felt for a long time for I am sitting in the front room … at Queen Street and you are not here but everything speaks of you. I felt tonight that this would be the feeling I would have if you had passed on and I were left behind.'[2]

***

'I still put out my hand when I waken … Gracie is being given the attention she deserves, but if her spirit is now at home with her dear departed she doesn't

---

[1] TPPC.
[2] GT/JGT, 27.1.1959, MS.1082/3/1, Todd Papers, NAZ.

require earthly recognition. Nevertheless I am grateful for it all, being VERY human.'[3] 'With my calling, with my age at 93, with the most wonderful 70 years with Grace, I suppose I should not only consider myself the most fortunate person in the world, but also be the happiest ... but I am broken-hearted', Garfield told the Rev. Dr W. A. Curwood.[4]

***

Mugabe chose this moment to take his revenge on 93-year-old Garfield. On 12 February, Garfield made a statement to the press: 'Today I received notice from the State that I have ceased to be a citizen of Zimbabwe and that I have lost my right to vote. I have also lost my right to travel ... I have been a citizen of this country for 67 years. Today I must shoulder the responsibility of totally rejecting the disenfranchisement of Zimbabweans by ZANU(PF). I totally reject the theft of our citizenship (approximately 2 million Zimbabweans are affected) by ZANU(PF). I am horrified by the destruction of our economy, the starving of our people, the undermining of our Constitution, the torture and humiliation of our nation by ZANU(PF).

'Just as we stood with courage against the racism of the past so, today, we must stand with courage against the terror of the present. Come what may, I will, next March, be going to the polling station to claim my right as a very senior citizen of Zimbabwe to cast my ballot for good against evil.'[5]

On 20 February, Garfield wrote: 'My life is not empty. My disenfranchisement has caused a real stir and letters are coming in from all over the world ... Grace's passing and the citizenship issue have resurrected so many unknown friends!'[6]

Garfield's mind was carried back to the Eighth Parliament by the draft chapters that he received. After reading my chapter on the Land Apportionment Act 'carefully for the third time', he commented: 'It is the heart of the matter and the subject of land will have no end. I found it fascinating although I knew it well. Every speaker makes his case so definitely, as I remember them: Jackie Keller, Wightwick, Stumbles, Ben, one had to put up with a lot from them, but Ben had the harder job. When I think of the speeches Ben had to make during those years I feel almost sorry for him ... How grateful I am for Hardwicke and his contributions ...'

***

March brought the Presidential election. Garfield went to the polling station,

3   GT/SP, 3.2.2002, TPPC.
4   GT/Rev. Dr W. A. Curwood, 6.2.2002, c/TPPC.
5   GT, Statement, 12.2.2002, TPPC.
6   GT/SP, 20.2.2002, TPPC.

at Hamilton High School, where a former headmaster of Dadaya School, Mr Noyce Dube (whose parents he had married), was polling officer. Tall and erect, as at Grace's funeral, Garfield walked past the queues, where waiting voters recognised him and murmured their approval; and, as he entered, Mr Dube approached him, so apologetically, and said he could not vote. Garfield smiled and walked up to the ballot box. He stretched out his hand, still shapely in spite of the burn scars, towards the box before turning and walking slowly away.

***

The first week of April was never going to be easy for Garfield. He wrote on the 3rd: 'This is a special day. It is Grace's 91st birthday, which is the first she has missed ... When Grace died, at 90, which I also hardly believed, I would have liked just to press a button and to go along too. Time is passing. Chapters are arriving.'[7] 'Oh, I am missing Grace,' Garfield wrote on the 5th, 'but people are thoughtful and kind.'[8] Their actual 70th wedding anniversary was on 7 April – also the first Grace had missed.

Contemplating the state of Zimbabwe brought him only pain and grief. The business, both sad and joyful, of replying to letters about Grace had got him through the first month or so, but his 'interest in the lives of others' was what really kept Garfield going during the months after she died. Garfield taped the televised funeral of the Queen Mother: 'It followed on from such a fresh memory of Grace's passing that I found comfort in the national demonstration of faith, and joy in the wonderful pageantry ...'[9]

'I simply cannot imagine what Zimbabwe would be like without its *Daily News*', Garfield wrote on 30 April. 'The Government harasses its editor and even its vendors, daily ... Well, there have been delays. First you posted chapter 13 on the 4th and it took 21 days to arrive. Then I had problems with my printer, so my enthusiasm to respond immediately to that wonderful chapter was delayed, but here I am ... Then came the visit to the United Kingdom (1954). Really Grace and I had a marvellous time and fifty years later I am deeply moved as I read your story of the wonderful occasions, the marvellous receptions given to us: our reactions. My great joy is of course that I shared with Grace all those wonderful meetings with people, and later, the unbelievable occasion with Her Majesty when I became Sir Garfield and Grace shared the honour with me ... It was such a joy to be reminded of what happened to us. Every event you mention was a joy and brought to my mind a myriad more. Chapter 13 is a personal

---

7   GT/SP, 3.4.2002, TPPC.
8   GT/SP, 5.4.2002, TPPC.
9   GT/SP, 18.4.2002, TPPC.

treasure house and thank you ... I rejoice in the knowledge that, with all her anxieties and political suffering, Grace and I were privileged to have such a long and joyful life together.'[10]

Garfield had resumed his reading with *The Gifts of the Jews* ('the book which precedes Genesis'), which Dr Gelman had lent him. Then, 'I have turned to the *Good News Bible*. I have read only the occasional excerpt from it over the years but, having read only Genesis in the new book to date, I think I am really going to like the experience, though some phrases do jar when one is used to the writings of King James ...'[11]

'The fascinating chapter on Kariba has brought much joy to me', Garfield wrote on 23 May. 'As always, I wish I could read it to Grace ... A chapter like Kariba makes me regret losing even a line in the final edition of the Book, but I know that really cannot be. The Kariba chapter though, the uncertainties, the human prejudices, Jimmy tracing a new road termed "impossible" by the surveyors, and having to turn to the wisdom and experience of the local elephants who marked out the way so many years ago, the political strains and stresses, Malvern's ultimate joy and the final triumph of Jimmy Savory. It's such a story in itself ...'[12]

'You so rightly underlined my statement that "Peasant farming was not the answer to the African problem" and now we have, 50 years later, gone back to peasant farming and 60% unemployment ... My statement that the European has a right to be here today, BUT the African's right should be underlined. Today, the European has no rights and no protection under the law. Maybe I have really lived too long ... And then the Georgetown University and my agreeing that the African will eventually assume political control!!!! well, well!!'[13]

In his letter of 7 July, Garfield was back with the *Good News Bible*: 'I am finding the exercise very satisfying. I am getting near the end of the O.T. now and am looking forward to the N.T. Actually, if I were a member of the appropriate Commission, I would remove quite large parts of the O.T. from the Canon! ... Grace. Oh how I miss her but life does go on. I stopped swimming a week ago as the temp dropped to 5 degrees. I will wait till it rises to 7 and I think that won't be so long. I have really enjoyed the daily dip and I know I benefit from it ...'[14]

When Garfield wrote on 24 July, he had received the chapter on African

---

10 GT/SP, 30.4.2002, TPPC.
11 GT/SP, n.d. but between 14 and 23.5.2002, TPPC.
12 GT/SP, 23.5.2002, TPPC.
13 GT/SP, 9.6.2002, TPPC.
14 GT/SP, 7.7.2002, TPPC.

education and 'was overjoyed with your account of this very important section ... The debates on Education were really very good ... I was delighted to be reminded of the cost of the five-year plan, of the financial impossibility of carrying it through and then the outrageous and dangerous suggestion that the tax should be doubled! Looking back on it I am almost frightened at the dangers as my ministers saw them, and of the faith we had in the African reaction ... It really was an exercise in faith which terrified Ben and Co., but how very wonderful that it worked out; that the people were so determined and so sure of what they wanted – and believed that we would really spend their money as we promised them ...'[15]

When Garfield wrote next, he was still concerned about African education: 'We came to preach the Gospel and that was just fine with the New Zealand brotherhood, but "education", I suppose everyone knows, that is a matter for the State not for our Churches! Anyway, I pray that the preaching of the Gospel was effective and I think that in so many lives it was, but there is no doubt that the Dadaya contribution in education covered the country and is now the basis of hope for the future. ...

'Remembering with pleasure A. R. Mather. I'm glad I got to visit him at home in the States and I am touched by the thought of his pointing out the chair that the PM had sat in. We really had some wonderful people: Stark, Finkle, Davies, Mather, not only capable servants but such pleasant people to work with. I speak of our Education Dept. but, except for dear old Ben and then Stumbles and the last and least minister, Jack Quinton, we were so fortunate in the team. The story of drafting the Five Year Plan and getting it into operation is probably the highlight of the period. The wonderful thing about it was that it carried on after the minister departed ... The loveliest event was, of course, Samkange's tribute to Grace. "If the minister had problems he should not consult with his cabinet but should ask Mrs Todd." It was such a wonderful tribute and Grace loved it – as, even more, did I ...'[16]

'Of course I do recognise some of the imperfections of the speeches I made from time to time but looking back there is only one speech of which I felt ashamed and that was the St Andrew's speech I gave in Bulawayo (1957). Things were getting tense (my excuse) and Ministers were quite open that my support of African development would lose them the coming election ... I have felt so close to Grace as I write you. She loved your writing ...'[17]

Garfield wrote again after receiving the chapter on his visit to the USA in

---
15 GT/SP, 24.7.2002, TPPC.
16 GT/SP, 28.7.2002, TPPC.
17 GT/SP, 29.7.2002, TPPC.

1955. 'When I rang yesterday I was feeling out of touch and so many lovely things had been coming in, particularly chapter 18 which seemed almost unbelievable as I remembered the people, the incidents, the hospitality, the meeting with so many interesting people. All very wonderful to look back upon and be thankful for ...

'The situation here is sad and terrifying for so many people. There is absolute confusion: people starving and Mugabe takes delivery of the latest state of the art armoured Mercedes Sedan ... All the farmers concerned should have left their farms yesterday. Word is that most have not moved! ... Judith is waiting for her passport to come back from the South African Embassy with her S.A. visa, and then she will be off for a month, I hope. My health is fine and Judith realises she can leave with confidence.'[18]

'This letter has no special reason behind it', Garfield began his letter of 24 August. 'It is a beautiful morning (as usual) and I have just been speaking with Judith, who is having a wonderful holiday ... I have just completed my reading of the *Good News Bible*. I doubt I have increased in virtue but it has been a good exercise and there has been clarification of some passages. However, I would not recommend the exercise to a friend. The Old Testament, with of course certain exceptions like the Psalms, Ecclesiastes, Song of Solomon and others can be boring ...

'Having completed the reading of the whole Bible I now turn to its history and commentaries in, I suppose, further confirmation of my reunion with Grace and so I pass the days. I am really the most fortunate of men. There is always sugar and milk for my porridge and we still have some bread in the deep freeze. I encourage Judith to stay away for a month but we shall see ... my privileged life of course depends on her.'[19]

'Yesterday was a big day for me', Garfield wrote on 30 August. 'Chapters 20 and 21 arrived together and I found it exhilarating to think that a man Todd, whom I once knew, could rise to the occasion when he had 'flu, and find it possible to give as good an address with the help of a few notes: I find it difficult to believe! ... Geoff and Cyril were wonderful in their planning and, of course, in their splendid prophetic outlook ... I am afraid that it is true that the Federal Government simply was not fully aware of its weaknesses, but over all, the liberal stance of the SR Govt, not supported in principle by the [Commonwealth Relations] Office, brought matters to a climax. Welensky was neither astute enough or liberal enough to give the leadership which just might

---

18 GT/SP, 8.8.2002, TPPC.
19 GT/SP, 24.8.2002, TPPC.

have saved the situation …'[20]

'Yesterday Washington Samsole, who claims to be in charge of us till Judith returns, brought four loaves of bread … The arrival of three new chapters in the one mail was truly exciting. I have greatly enjoyed the chapters …'[21]

On 23 September, Garfield wrote: 'I so enjoyed your phone call and when I went back to my office, your long and delightful letter of the 9th was put on my desk. With the call and the letter I really feel up to date … It will be good to have [Judith] back but servants and friends have been wonderful … I would dearly love to visit Dadaya and the Churches but I'm afraid that isn't going to happen … The arrival of *Tears of the Giraffe* [by Alexander McCall Smith] will give great joy to me and upwards through the family … after the 8 o'clock news I will retire and begin reading … Again, thank you Sue and John for the pleasure you bring us. My love, Garfield'[22] (in his own hand).

That was the last letter I received from Garfield. In the week following, we spoke twice. On 30 September, Judith returned to Bulawayo. That evening, Garfield went for his customary swim – and had a stroke. As usual, Benjamin was hovering nearby – and, seeing Garfield in difficulties, went into the pool and brought him out.

Garfield spent two weeks in the Mater Dei Hospital, with the best medical attention he could have from his doctor and specialists, and devotedly looked after by the nursing staff, while Judith kept vigil by his bedside. He died in the early morning of 13 October 2002.

***

Bishop Jim Thompson began his 'Thought for the Day' on BBC Radio 4 the next morning with the words: 'A prophet has died in Zimbabwe'.

***

On 27 October, Garfield was buried beside Grace in Dadaya Cemetery.

---

20 GT/SP, 30.8.2002, TPPC.
21 GT/SP, 12.9.2002, TPPC.
22 GT/SP, 23.9.2002, TPPC.

Epilogue

In 1991, the *Hokonui Todd* NZTV interviewer asked Grace what epitaph she would choose for Garfield.

'The verse from Browning's *Asolando*,' she replied.

'And for you?'

'Just to be beside him.'

> *One who never turned his back but marched breast forward,*
> *Never doubted clouds would break,*
> *Never dreamed, though right were worsted, wrong would triumph,*
> *Held we fall to rise, are baffled to fight better,*
> *Sleep to wake.*

♦•♦

Sources

United Nations
Proceedings of the United Nations General Assembly:
28 November and 19 December 1961

New Zealand
Hocken Archives, Dunedin
Early Settlers' Museum, Dunedin
Transcript of NZTV film *Hokonui Todd*

Zimbabwe

Archives:

National Archives of Zimbabwe, Harare
    Public Records Office, NAZ
    Oral Archives (at NAZ)
    Sir Garfield Todd Papers
Historic Reference Collection (of Bulawayo Public Library)
University of Zimbabwe History Department Library

Hansard:

Debates of the Legislative Assembly of Southern Rhodesia
Debates of the Federal Assembly (1953–63) of the Federation of Rhodesia and Nyasaland
Debates of the Zimbabwe Senate (1980–5; incomplete) at the Parliament of Zimbabwe

Newspapers and periodicals (Southern Rhodesia/Zimbabwe):

Rhodesia Herald, Salisbury
Sunday Mail, Salisbury
The Chronicle, Bulawayo
Sunday News, Bulawayo
Central African Examiner
Gwelo Times
Umtali Post

Bantu Mirror
African Daily News (later the *Daily News*)
African Weekly

South Africa

Newspapers and periodicals:

Drum
The Rand Daily Mail
South Africa

United Kingdom

Archives:

Public Records Office, Kew
Bodleian Library African and Commonwealth Collections, University of Oxford: papers of:
Sir Roy Welensky, KCMG
Major-General Sir John Kennedy, GCMG, KCVO, KBE, CB, MC
Vice-Admiral Sir Peveril William-Powlett, KCB, KCMG, CBE, DSO
Sir Robert Tredgold, KCMG
Sir Edgar Whitehead, KCMG, OBE
Sir Godfrey Huggins, CH, KCMG, FRCS (Viscount Malvern)
Hardwicke Holderness, DSO, DFC, AFC (including follow-up *Lost Chance* project)
Professor Kenneth Kirkwood
Hirsel Archives (Earl of Home)
National Library of Scotland
Edinburgh Central Library
Edinburgh University Library

Hansard:

Proceedings of the House of Commons

Journals:

Journal of Southern African Studies

Reports:

The Monckton Commission, 1960
The Pearce Commission, 1972

Sources

Newspapers and periodicals:

The Times
The Guardian (earlier: *Manchester Guardian*)
The Scotsman
The Listener
East Africa and Rhodesia

Todd Papers Paul Collection (private):

Monthly Reports of the Superintendent of Dadaya Mission to the Foreign Mission Union/Overseas Mission Board of the Associated Churches of Christ in Nelson, New Zealand

Garfield Todd's 'Notes on recent happenings in the political situation in Southern Rhodesia, 23.1.58'

Hardwicke Holderness's 'Notes giving gist of remarks by HHCH to the General Meeting of the Salisbury North Branch of the United Rhodesia Party, 3/2/58'

Private files of J. Grace Todd (subsequently destroyed by her)

Monthly letters from Mrs J. Grace Todd of Dadaya Mission to the Christian Women's Auxiliary of the ACCNZ

Monthly letters to the boys and girls of the Bible classes of the ACCNZ by Garfield Todd/Mrs J. Grace Todd/other missionaries

Letters from Garfield and Grace Todd to Susan Paul, 1970–2002

Garfield Todd's draft autobiography (c. 1974, unpublished)

Sundry papers, newspaper cuttings about and letters to/from Todds (to 2003).

Select Bibliography

Auret, Michael. 2009. *From Liberator to Dictator: An Insider's Account of Robert Mugabe's Descent into Tyranny* (Cape Town: David Philip Publishers).

Banana, Canaan. 1996. *The Church in the Struggle for Zimbabwe* (Uppsala: Swedish Institute of Missionary Research).

Barber, James. 1967. *Rhodesia: The Road to Rebellion* (London: Oxford University Press).

Berlyn, Phillippa. 1978. *The Quiet Man: A Biography of the Hon. Ian Douglas Smith, I.D., Prime Minister of Rhodesia* (Salisbury, SR: M. O. Collins).

Birkenhead, F. W. F. Smith, Lord. 1969. *Walter Monckton: The Life of Viscount Monckton of Brenchley* (London: Weidenfeld & Nicolson).

Birmingham, David and Terence Ranger. 1983. 'Settlers and liberators in the South', in David Birmingham and Phyllis Martin (eds), *History of Central Africa: The Contemporary Years since 1960* (London: Longman).

Blake, Robert. 1966. *Disraeli* (London: Eyre & Spottiswoode).

—— 1975. *The Office of Prime Minister* (London: Oxford University Press).

—— 1977. *A History of Rhodesia* (London: Eyre Methuen).

Bloomfield, G. W. 1960. *1960: Last Chance in the Federation* (Universities' Mission to Central Africa).

Blundell, Michael. 1994. *A Love Affair with the Sun: A Memoir of Seventy Years in Kenya* (Nairobi: Kenway Publications).

Boynton, Graham. 1997. *Last Days in Cloud Cuckooland: Dispatches from White Africa* (New York: Random House).

Brown, Robin. 1989. *Bye Bye Shangri-la* (London: Weidenfeld & Nicolson).

Bull, Theo (ed.). 1972. *Rhodesian Perspective* (London: Michael Joseph).

Burrough, Paul. 1988. *Angels Unawares* (Worthing: Churchman Publishing).

Butler, R. A. 1971. *The Art of the Possible: The Memoirs of Lord Butler* (London: Hamilton).

Carrington, Peter, Lord. 1988. *Reflect on Things Past: The Memoirs of Lord Carrington* (London: Collins).

Casey, Michael W. 2007. *The Rhetoric of Sir Garfield Todd: Christian*

Imagination and the Dream of an African Democracy (Waco, TX: Baylor University Press).

Catholic Commission for Justice and Peace/Legal Resources Foundation. 1997. *Breaking the Silence, Building True Peace: A Report on the Disturbances in Matabeleland and the Midlands, 1980–1988* (Harare: CCJP/LRF).

Caute, David. 1983. *Under the Skin: The Death of White Rhodesia* (London: Allen Lane).

Cecil, David. 2017. *The Young Melbourne & Lord M* (London: Pan Macmillan).

Cleary, Frederick and Ann Field. 1998. *Kamoto: The Life of Winston Joseph Field, 1904–1969* (St Arnaud, Victoria: Ann Field).

Clements, Frank. 1959. *Kariba: The Struggle with the River God* (London: Methuen).

—— 1969. *Rhodesia: The Course to Collision* (London: Pall Mall Press).

Clutton-Brock, Guy and Molly Clutton-Brock. 1972. *Cold Comfort Confronted* (London and Oxford: Mowbrays).

Creighton, T. R. M. 1960. *The Anatomy of Partnership: Southern Rhodesia and the Central African Federation* (London: Faber & Faber).

de Waal, Victor. 1990. *The Politics of Reconciliation: Zimbabwe's First Decade* (Cape Town: David Philip).

Doig, A. B. 1997. *It's the People That Count* (Edinburgh: The Pentland Press).

Dunn, Cyril. 1959. *Central African Witness* (London: Victor Gollancz).

Fisher, Nigel. 1973. *Iain Macleod* (London: André Deutsch).

Flower, K. 1987. *Serving Secretly. An Intelligence Chief on Record: Rhodesia into Zimbabwe, 1964–1981* (London: John Murray).

Foot, Sir Hugh. 1964. *A Start in Freedom* (London: Hodder & Stoughton).

Frederikse, Julie. 1982. *None but Ourselves: Masses vs Media in the Making of Zimbabwe* (Harare: Zimbabwe Publishing House).

Gann, L. H. and M. Gelfand. 1964. *Huggins of Rhodesia: The Man and His Country* (London: Allen & Unwin).

Godwin, Peter. 1996. *Mukiwa: A White Boy in Africa* (London: Picador).

—— and Ian Hancock. 1993. *Rhodesians Never Die: The Impact of War and Political Change on White Rhodesia, c. 1970–1980* (Oxford: Oxford University Press).

Goodman, Arnold, Baron. 1993. *Tell Them I'm On My Way* (London: Chapman).

Grant, Jack. 1980. *Jack Grant's Story* (Cambridge: Lutterworth).

Gray, J. A. (ed.). 1969. *South Africa Today* (London: St Bride Foundation Institute).

Gray, Richard. 1960. *The Two Nations: Aspects of the Development of Race Relations in the Rhodesias and Nyasaland* (London: Oxford University Press).

Greenfield, Julian M. 1978. *Testimony of a Rhodesian Federal* (Bulawayo: Books of Rhodesia).

Hadfield, F. L. 1954. *Christ and the Colour Bar in Southern Africa* (South Africa: Central News Agency).

Hailsham, Quintin Hogg, Lord. 1990. *A Sparrow's Flight: The Memoirs of Lord Hailsham of St Marylebone* (London: Collins).

Hancock, Ian. 1984. *White Liberals, Moderates and Radicals in Rhodesia, 1953–1980* (London: Croom Helm).

Hanna, A. J. 1960. *The Story of the Rhodesias and Nyasaland* (London: Faber & Faber).

Harris, Norman. 1971. *The Fly-Away People: A Portrait Gallery of Outstanding Expatriate New Zealanders* (London: Baynard-Hillier).

Hastings, Adrian. 1979. *A History of African Christianity, 1950–1975* (Cambridge: Cambridge University Press).

Holderness, Hardwicke H. D. 1985. *Lost Chance: Southern Rhodesia, 1945–58* (Harare: Zimbabwe Publishing House).

Home, Alec Douglas-Home, Lord. 1976. *The Way the Wind Blows: An Autobiography* (London: Collins).

Hope, Christopher. 2003. *Brothers under the Skin: Travels in Tyranny* (London: Macmillan).

Houser, George M. 1989. *No One Can Stop the Rain: Glimpses of Africa's Liberation Struggle* (New York: Pilgrim Press).

Hudson, Miles. 1981. *Triumph or Tragedy? Rhodesia to Zimbabwe* (London: Hamish Hamilton).

Hughes, Richard. 2003. *Capricorn: David Stirling's Second African Campaign* (New York and London: Radcliffe Press).

Ingram, Derek. 1962. *The Commonwealth Challenge* (London: Allen & Unwin).

Keatley, Patrick. 1963. *The Politics of Partnership: The Federation of Rhodesia and Nyasaland* (Harmondsworth: Penguin).

Kirkman, W. P. 1966. *Unscrambling an Empire: A Critique of British*

Colonial Policy 1956–1966 (London: Chatto & Windus).

Lamont, Donal. 1977. *Speech from the Dock* (London: Catholic Institute for International Relations).

Lapping, Brian. 1985. *End of Empire* (London: Grenada Publishing).

Lawley, Jonathan. 2010. *Beyond the Malachite Hills: A Life of Colonial Service and Business in the New Africa* (London and New York: I.B. Tauris).

Lessing, Doris. 1993. *African Laughter: Four Visits to Zimbabwe* (London: Flamingo).

Leys, Colin. 1959. *European Politics in Southern Rhodesia* (Oxford: Clarendon Press).

Lockhart, J. G. and C. M. Woodhouse. 1963. *Rhodes* (London: Hodder & Stoughton).

Lord, Graham. 1991. *Ghosts of King Solomon's Mines: Mozambique and Zimbabwe: A Quest* (London: Sinclair-Stevenson).

Lusby, J. Lowell. 1990. *Historical Survey of the Central Africa Mission, Zimbabwe* (Grayson, KY: Kentucky Christian College Press).

Macmillan, Harold. 1972. *Pointing the Way, 1959–1961* (London: Macmillan).

—— 1973. *At the End of the Day, 1961–1963* (London: Macmillan).

Martin, David and Phyllis Johnson. 1981. *The Struggle for Zimbabwe: The Chimurenga War* (London: Faber).

Mason, Philip. 1958. *The Birth of a Dilemma: The Conquest and Settlement of Rhodesia* (London: Oxford University Press).

—— 1960. *Year of Decision: Rhodesia and Nyasaland in 1960* (London: Oxford University Press).

Megahey, Alan J. 1998. *Humphrey Gibbs, Beleaguered Governor: Southern Rhodesia, 1929–69* (Basingstoke: Macmillan).

Meredith, Martin. 1979. *The Past is Another Country: Rhodesia 1890–1979* (London: André Deutsch).

—— 2005. *The State of Africa: A History of Fifty Years of Independence* (London: Free Press).

Moorcraft, Paul. 1979. *A Short Thousand Years: The End of Rhodesia's Rebellion* (Salisbury: Galaxie Press).

Mugabe, Robert G. 1983. *Our War of Liberation: Speeches, Articles, Interviews, 1976–1979* (Gweru: Mambo Press).

Mungazi, Dickson A. 1999. *The Last British Liberals in Africa: Michael*

Select Bibliography

Blundell and Garfield Todd (Westport, CT: Praeger).

Niesewand, Peter. 1973. *In Camera: Secret Justice in Rhodesia* (London: Weidenfeld & Nicolson).

Nkomo, Joshua. 1984. *The Story of My Life* (London: Methuen).

Nkrumah, Kwame. 1976. *Rhodesia File* (London: Panaf Books).

Nyarota, Geoffrey. 2006. *Against the Grain: Memoirs of a Zimbabwean Newsman* (Cape Town: Zebra Press).

Olssen, Erik. 1984. *A History of Otago* (Dunedin: John McIndoe).

Palley, Claire. 1966. *The Constitutional History and Law of Southern Rhodesia, 1888–1965, with Special Reference to Imperial Control* (Oxford: Clarendon Press).

Parker, John. 1972. *Rhodesia: Little White Island* (London: Pitman).

Partridge, W. G. McDonald. 1985. *United College of Education, Bulawayo 1967–1985* (Bulawayo: Louis Bolze).

Phimister, Ian. 1994. *Wangi Kolia: Coal, Capital and Labour in Colonial Zimbabwe, 1894–1954* (Harare: Baobab Books).

Ranger, Terence. 1995. *Are We Not Also Men? The Samkange Family and African Politics in Zimbabwe, 1920–64* (London: James Currey).

—— 2000. Review of Ruth Weiss and Jane Parpart, *Sir Garfield Todd and the Making of Zimbabwe* (London: British Academic Press, 1999), in *Bulletin of the School of Oriental and African Studies*, University of London, vol. 63, no. 1, 154–155.

—— 2008. 'A Todd succession? A political family and modern Zimbabwe', *Journal of Southern African Studies*, vol. 34, no. 1, 225–227.

—— 2013. *Writing Revolt: An Engagement with African Nationalism, 1957–67* (Harare: Weaver Press).

Renwick, Robin. 1997. *Unconventional Diplomacy in Southern Africa* (Basingstoke: Macmillan).

Royle, Trevor. 1996. *Winds of Change: The End of Empire in Africa* (London: John Murray).

Sanger, Clyde. 1960. *Central African Emergency* (London: Heinemann).

Savage, Murray J. 1949. *Achievement: 50 Years of Missionary Witness in Southern Rhodesia* (Wellington: A. H. & A. W. Reed).

—— 1970. *Haddon of Glen Leith: An Ecumenical Pilgrimage* (Dunedin: ACCNZ).

—— 1980. *Forward into Freedom: Associated Churches of Christ in New Zealand Missionary Outreach 1949–1979* (Dunedin: ACCNZ).

Savory, James. 1984. *Never a Dull Life* (Albuquerque, NM: Stocks Publishing).

Shamuyarira, Nathan M. 1965. *Crisis in Rhodesia* (London: André Deutsch).

Shepherd, Robert. 1994. *Iain Macleod: A Biography* (London: Hutchinson).

Skeen, Andrew. 1966. *Prelude to Independence: Skeen's 115 Days* (Cape Town: Nasionale Boekhandel).

Skelton, Kenneth. 1985. *Bishop in Smith's Rhodesia: Notes from a Turbulent Octave, 1962–1970* (Gweru: Mambo Press).

Smith, Ian D. 1997. *The Great Betrayal: The Memoirs of Ian Douglas Smith* (London: Blake Publishing).

Sundkler, Bengt and Christopher Steed. 2000. *A History of the Church in Africa* (Cambridge: Cambridge University Press).

Taylor, D. 1955. *The Rhodesian: The Life of Sir Roy Welensky* (London: Museum Press).

Thorpe, D. R. 1996. *Alec Douglas-Home* (London: Sinclair-Stevenson).

Todd, A. B. 1906. *The Poetical Works of Adam Brown Todd. With Autobiography and Portrait* (Edinburgh: Oliphant, Anderson & Ferrier).

Todd, Judith. 1966. *Rhodesia* (London: MacGibbon & Kee).

—— 1972. *The Right to Say No* (London: Sidgwick & Jackson).

—— 2007. *Through the Darkness: A Life in Zimbabwe* (Cape Town: Zebra Press).

Tredgold, Sir Robert C. 1968. *The Rhodesia that was My Life* (London: Allen & Unwin).

Vambe, Lawrence. 1972. *An Ill-Fated People: Zimbabwe Before and After Rhodes* (Pittsburgh, PA: University of Pittsburgh Press).

—— 1976. *From Rhodesia to Zimbabwe* (London: Heinemann).

Vincent, J. J. 1970. *The Race Race* (London: SCM Press).

Weiss, Ruth and Jane Parpart. 1999. *Sir Garfield Todd and the Making of Zimbabwe* (London: British Academic Press).

Welensky, Sir Roy. 1964. *Welensky's 4000 Days: The Life and Death of the Federation of Rhodesia and Nyasaland* (London: Collins).

West, Michael O. 1992. 'Ndabaningi Sithole, Garfield Todd and the Dadaya school strike of 1947', *Journal of Southern African Studies*, vol. 18, no. 2, 297–316.

Wilson, Harold. 1971. *The Labour Government, 1964–1970: A Personal Record* (London: Weidenfeld & Nicolson).

Wood, J. R. T. 1983. *The Welensky Papers: A History of the Federation of*

Rhodesia and Nyasaland (Durban: Graham Publishing).

—— 2005. *So Far and No Further! Rhodesia's Bid for Independence during the Retreat from Empire, 1959–1965* (South Africa: 30 Degrees South).

—— 2008. *A Matter of Weeks rather than Months: The Impasse between Harold Wilson and Ian Smith; Sanctions, Aborted Settlements and War, 1965–1969* (Bloomington, IN: Trafford Publishing).

Wrong, Michela. 2000. *In the Footsteps of Mr Kurtz: Living on the Brink of Disaster in Mobuto's Congo* (London: Fourth Estate).

INDEX

Abrahamson, A. E. ('Abe') xxiv, 191, 221, 223, 224, 230, 237, 263, 264, 321
ACCNZ (Associated Churches of Christ in New Zealand) *see* Church of Christ
Acland, General 447
Acton, Judith Garfield *see* Todd, Judith Garfield
Acton, Lord (John) 378
Acton, Lord (Richard) 400, 458
Adams, Alf 239, 243, 259
Addecott, George 134, 278
Addison, William 108
African Affairs Board (Federal Assembly) 204, 205, 315
African Affairs Department 207
 see also Department of Native Affairs
African nationalism 77, 147, 156, 166, 211, 276, 289, 322–3, 337, 341
African Newspapers xix, 138, 252, 466
African Voters' League 69
Aid Rhodesia Movement 362
Aitken-Cade, Stewart 178, 261
Aldington-Hunt, Archdeacon 90
Allen, John 268–9
Alport, Lord (Cuthbert) 306, 307, 309, 379, 380, 412, 455, 473
Alvord, Henry 35
ANC (African National Congress) (Northern Rhodesia) 161, 206–7, 332
ANC (African National Congress) (Nyasaland) 161, 206–7, 285
ANC (African National Congress) (Southern Rhodesia)
 conference (1958) 263
 creation of new ANC 118, 137, 207–8, 209–13
 franchise issue 193, 199
 on GT and corporal punishment at Dadaya 76
 GT's concerns re new ANC 211–13
 Native Land Bill 85
 state of emergency (1956) 171
 state of emergency and arrests (1959) 286, 290
 Whitehead's Bill to ban SR ANC 289
ANC (African National Council) 381, 401, 410
Anderson, Major-General John 340, 346
Anglo-American Corporation 109, 208
Appleby, John 348
Apprenticeship Bill (1957) 182
Arden-Clarke, Sir Charles 145
Armitage, Sir Robert 299
Armstrong, Jack 115, 224, 225, 261
army
 see also warfare
 role in Gukurahundi massacre xxxiii
 role in Wankie Colliery strike xxxii, 111, 112, 113
 Selous Scouts 416, 422, 423
ARNI (Association of Rhodesian and Nyasaland Industries) 220–1, 221, 224
Ashton, Chris 423
Ashton, Dr Hugh 78, 149, 286
Asian Adult Education Institute 105, 143
Augustini, Dr 421

Bamford, Reverend Thomas 15
Banda, Dr Hastings Kamuzu 281, 286, 298, 299, 326, 344, 386
Bango, Grey 253
Bannockburn 282, 317, 343, 383, 419, 421, 424, 428, 429, 458, 465, 477
Barham, Clarence 104
Barham, Elsie (née Wilson) (Grace's sister) 12, 463, 475
Barham, Vicky 459
Baron, Ben 151, 191, 251, 264
Baron, Leo 343, 348, 353, 354, 358, 411
Barrow, Sir Malcolm 90, 175
Bassoppo-Moyo, James 154
Batonka people 130
Beadle, Hugh 84
Beadle, Shirley 91, 282
Belgian Congo 154, 285, 299, 300
Bell, Mr and Mrs A. W. 68, 82
Benoy, Barney 346

541

Benson, Sir Arthur 150, 196, 203, 205, 252–3, 299, 313
Berkeley, Humphrey 296
Berlyn, Phillippa 355
Biddulph, Jim 350, 357
Blake, Dr Eugene Carson 367–8
Blake, Lord (Robert) 134–5, 256, 275, 277, 340, 374, 399, 411, 420
Blampied, Ray xxv, 52, 94
Blundell, Sir Michael 175
Boddington, Mr 16, 52
Bohé, Father 52
Bolton, Mr 16, 52
Bottomley, Arthur 347, 352, 354
Bowen, C. A. 15, 16, 20, 21, 22, 23
Boynton, Graham 295
Boynton, Sir John 448
Britain
  see also Federation of Rhodesia and Nyasaland; Northern Rhodesia; Rhodesia; Southern Rhodesia
  CDC token loan 139–40
  Commonwealth Parliamentary Association 119, 131, 148, 180–1
  Conservative Party 148, 281, 292, 378, 400, 427, 432
  federation discussions 83–4, 88–90
  general election (1959) 292
  general election (1964) 345
  general election (1971) 378
  general election (1979) 432
  issue of Federation's status 201–2
  Labour Party 292, 345
  Smith's UDI (1965) 346, 347–55
  UN and issue of SR's independence 329–31
British Council of Churches 372, 381
British South Africa Company 18, 151
Brockway, Lord 473
BSAP (British South Africa Police) 18, 19, 106, 110, 190, 382, 392
Buchan, Max 190, 191, 192, 232, 264, 297
Buckley, Jim 446
Bulawayo
  arrival of Todds 21
  divided society 131
  possible capital city 124
  railway strike (1956) 169, 170

riots (1960) 304, 312, 317
Todds at Heyman Road 431, 449, 470, 487, 491–2
Bull, Mr 206
Bunche, Dr Ralph 156
Burman, Reverend Reg 48, 94
Burton, Lilian 299–300
bus boycott 166–9
Butler, R. A. 135, 333, 336

Caley, F. S. 261
Callaghan, James 180, 404
Campbell, Dr Colin 291
Campbell, Evan 340, 346
Campbell, Marshall 58
CAP (Central Africa Party)
  CAP statement and reactions 303, 304–12
  collapse 291–2, 294, 333
  Federal Review Conference (1960) 320–1
  GT on Federation 337
  GT and unrest (1960) 302–12
  successor to URP 283, 286–7, 291–2, 296–7
capital city issue 22, 122, 124–5, 178, 315
Capricorn Africa Society 132, 274, 277
Carden, Hugh 91, 92–3, 97
Carden, Mrs 91, 93
Carrington, Lord 427, 432, 435–6, 437, 448, 453, 455
Casey, Professor M. 312
Cathedral Club 132
Catholic Commission for Justice and Peace in Zimbabwe 460, 476, 489
Caute, David 422
CDC (Colonial Development Corporation) 139–40
ceasefire 437–8, 445–6
Cecil, Lord David 64
censorship 353, 354, 358, 489
Centre Party 373
Chamber of Mines 182, 183
Chapman, Ron 362, 520
Chataway, Chris 296
Chesterton, A. K. 193
Chichester, Archbishop Aston 206
Chidzero, Dr Bernard 297

Index

Chigwedere, Dr Aeneas 98, 512, 517, 520
Chikerema, James xxxii, 118, 166, 198, 207, 209, 263, 344
Chikomo, Dr Herbert 367, 468
Chikurubi High Security Prison 389, 460
Chinamano, Josiah 341, 352, 381, 386, 391, 393
Chinamano, Ruth 341, 386, 391, 393
Chipunza, Chad 214
Chirau, Chief 420, 422
Chirwa, M. I. Wellington 107, 147–8, 202, 314
Chitepo, Herbert 118, 132, 402, 471
Christian Council of Rhodesia/Zimbabwe 360–1, 367, 370, 371–2, 377, 381, 397, 451, 459
Christie, Lansdell K. 173, 228, 242, 247, 249, 282–3, 326, 328, 341, 361
Church of Christ
   see also Dadaya Mission
   Allan Todd at Grace's funeral 518–19
   Bible College 8, 9, 13, 16
   Commission of Enquiry into Carden controversy 94
   Foreign Mission Council (FMC) 20, 92, 93
   member of Christian Council of Rhodesia 360–1
   missions 15–16, 19–20, 51–2
   origins and principles 5
   Quinquennial World Conference (1988) 478–9
   Todds' New Zealand visit 441–2
   in USA 5, 145, 426
Churchill, Sir Winston 347
City Youth League 166–7
Clarke, C. F. S. 159–60
Clarke, Gerald 203, 224
Cleary, Frederick 47
Clements, Frank 242, 255
Cleveland, R. M. 192
Clutton-Brock, Guy 86, 210, 212, 213, 233, 286, 290, 376, 454
Clutton-Brock, Molly 376, 454
CMED (Central Mechanical Equipment Department) 121, 157
Cochrane, T. P. 240, 243
Cold Comfort Farm Society 376
Cole, David M. 124
Collins, Elizabeth xxv, 463, 480

Coltart, David 508
Commonwealth Conference (1959) 283
Commonwealth Conference (1979) 434
Commonwealth Heads of Government 488–9
Commonwealth Parliamentary Association 119, 131, 148, 180–1
Commonwealth Prime Ministers' Conference (1957) 202, 343–4
Commonwealth Relations Office 84, 134, 203
Confederate Party 105, 107, 109
conferences
   ANC (Southern Rhodesia) conference (1958) 263
   Church of Christ conference (1988) 478–9
   Constitutional Conference (1961) 319, 326
   Federal Dissolution Conference (1963) 336
   Federal Review Conference (1960) 320–1
   on federation (1951) 83–4
   on federation (1953) 89
   Geneva (1976) 410–13
   Kenya Constitutional Conference and agreement 296, 298–9
   Lancaster House constitutional conference (1979) 434–6, 436–8
   Missionary Conference (1936) 44, 57, 64, 65
   Victoria Falls (1949) 83
   Victoria Falls (1975) 403
Congo *see* Belgian Congo
Conservative Party (UK) 148, 281, 292, 378, 400, 427, 432
constitution
   Constitution Amendment Bill (1957) 204–5
   constitution proposals referendum (1979) 430–1
   Constitutional Conference (1961) 319–20, 326
   constitutional proposals (1969) 368–9, 370
   Lancaster House constitutional conference (1979) 434–6, 436–8
Courtauld, Sir Stephen 269
Coyne, André 128, 129

Cramer, Helen 481
Crathorne, Lord 314
Crawford, Alyce 9
Crawford, Ann *see* McKenzie, Ann
Crawshaw, Steve 489
Crichton-Stuart, Lord James 175
Cripps, Reverend Arthur Shearly 36, 138, 512
Cumings, Sir Charles 151
Curwood, Reverend Dr W. A. 521

Dabengwa, Dumiso 460, 475, 506, 507
Dadaya Mission
  Association of Dadayans 467–8
  Church of Christ conference (1988) 478–9
  daily life 24–7, 42–3, 45
  David Mkwananzi's funeral 496
  development of Africans 49, 50
  during warfare 421, 425, 428, 430
  establishment 9, 20
  false order to close school (1979) 432–4
  funding 420
  Golden Jubilee 98, 174
  Grace's Dadaya Schemes 47–8, 97, 98, 365–6
  Grace's funeral 517–19
  GT's appointment 15–17, 21–3
  GT's concern re deteriorating situation (1963) 337–9
  GT's reports 23, 30, 33, 40, 43, 50, 52, 56, 57, 59, 62, 76
  GT's resignation as principal (1953) 92, 94–5, 97
  GT's retirement (1984) 467, 468–70
  GT's return as chairman (1966–7) 357, 360–1, 377
  history 18–20, 98
  language issues 28, 46–7
  medical matters 37–41, 52–3, 57–8
  Missionary Conference (1936) 44, 57, 64, 65
  new missionaries 91–4, 97
  new site on Hokonui Ranch 81–2, 174
  principal Samuel Mutomba 432, 433, 434, 442, 443, 452–3
  reconstruction and building 488, 492–3
  school closure at election (1979) 431
  schooling 25–6, 28, 30, 43, 46–9, 51, 58, 64
  status and education of girls and women 27, 32–3, 44–5, 47
  strike and issue of corporal punishment xxxi, 73–7
  teacher training 64
  village schools 34–6
  violence and fire at school (1990) 484–6
  visit from Mugabe (1981) 459
Daily News banning 344–5
Danziger, Max 49
Davenport, Sir George 101, 109, 191, 229–30, 234, 259, 261, 262, 274
Davies, C. S. ('Steve') 48–9, 141, 249, 524
Davies, Jessie *see* Todd, Jessie
Davies, R. M. 137
De Haas, J. 183
De Waal, Victor 449
Denzelow, Robin 431–2
Department of African Education 141, 142
Department of Native Affairs 19, 42, 103, 109, 110, 114–15, 141, 153, 154, 166, 207, 245, 277
Department of Native Development (Department of Native Education) 15, 21, 25
detentions and imprisonment
  detentions and restrictions (1964) 341
  detentions (1970) 373
  imprisonment of GT and Judith (1972) 382–91
  Nkomo at Gonakudzingwa Camp 341, 347, 381, 395
  restriction of GT and Judith to Hokonui Ranch (1972) 391, 392, 393–4, 396
  restriction of GT to Hokonui Ranch (1965) 350–2, 356–9, 362
  restriction of GT to Hokonui Ranch (1972) 397–8, 400, 402, 403
  revoking of detention orders 442
Devlin Commission 285, 290
Dewa, Richard 72
Dhlamini, Bishop 206
Dillon, I. B. 269, 270, 292
Doig, Dr Andrew 147, 205
Dominion Status 180–1, 201–2, 207, 280–1
Dorman, Sir Maurice 447

Index

Douglas-Home, Sir Alec
  Banda's release from prison 299
  on Britain's role in SR 331, 342
  CAP statement 304–6, 310, 311
  comment on GT 276
  on Constitutional Conference 319
  on Federation 321
  Foreign Secretary 309
  franchise views 194
  memo from African deputation 297
  Pearce Report 393
  Secretary of State for Commonwealth Relations 145, 148, 281
  settlement proposals (1971) 378–9, 382, 401
  Smith's reasons for GT and Judith's arrests 389
  visit from GT (1960) 296
DP (Dominion Party)
  by-election (Mrewa 1957) 192
  by-elections (Sebakwe and Gwelo 1956) 159–60
  criticisms 268
  franchise issue 193
  general election (1958) 269, 270, 275
  growth 207, 211, 214
  SR Constitutional talks 326
Driver, Richard xxvi, 481, 483, 484, 487
Dube, Kingsley Dinga xxiv, 103, 252, 474, 493, 496, 518
Dube, Noyce 522
Duff, Sir Anthony 447, 448
Duffaut, Tisne and Misson 128
Dumbutshena, Enoch
  at Government House 352
  Chief Justice's recommendation 296
  on effect of Devlin Commission 290
  fears at intended party fusion 214
  GT's 80th birthday 478
  mediation with African nationalists 337
  member of Capricorn Africa Society 132
  patron of Zimbabwe Human Rights Association 489
  talks with British Government (1960) 297
  talks with GT (1960) 296, 304
  on Welensky and Greenfield 256
Dunn, Cyril 102, 172, 185, 192, 204–5, 225, 227, 239, 242, 243, 279

Dupont, Clifford 334, 353, 371

Eastwood, Anthony xxiv, 407
Edgar, Professor 9
Edge, Cynthia Gay Garfield (née Todd) (daughter of GT)
  birth 80–1
  GT's knighthood 475
  living at Dadaya Mission 97
  living at Hokonui 317, 325, 353, 408
  living in London 357, 361
  marriage 373
  move to Salisbury 103–4
  move to UK/Australia 419, 458
  visits to GT and Grace (1985, 1998) 471, 502
Edge, Derrick
  GT's knighthood 475
  living at Hokonui 376, 385, 396, 408, 418
  marriage to Cynthia Todd 373
  move to UK/Australia 419, 458
Edlin, John 493
education
  at Dadaya Mission 25–6, 28, 30, 32–3, 43, 46–9, 51, 58, 64
  debate and Kerr Commission 80, 87–8
  Grace's Dadaya Schemes 47–8, 97, 98, 365–6
  GT's article on Native Education 321–2
  GT's five-year plan 186–8, 524
  launch of Department of African Education 141–3, 174
  village schools 34–6
Edwards, Superintendent 384, 385, 388, 390
elections
  by-election (Bulawayo North 1950) 84
  by-election (Hillside, Bulawayo 1958) 263
  by-election (Mrewa 1957) 192
  by-elections (Sebakwe and Gwelo 1956) 159–60, 174
  general election (1946 Southern Rhodesia) 65
  general election (1948 South Africa) 78
  general election (1953 Federal) 105, 107
  general election (1954 Southern Rhodesia) 105, 107–9, 276
  general election (1957 Federal) 256

general election (1958 Southern Rhodesia) 199, 211, 215–16, 263, 267, 268, 269–70, 272–5
general election (1959 Britain) 292
general election (1959 Northern Rhodesia) 287
general election (1961 Nyasaland) 326
general election (1962 Northern Rhodesia) 332
general election (1962 Southern Rhodesia) 333
general election (1964 Britain) 345
general election (1965 Southern Rhodesia) 348
general election (1970 Republic of Rhodesia) 373
general election (1971 Britain) 378
general election (1979 Britain) 432
general election (1979 Republic of Rhodesia) 431
general election (1980 Zimbabwe-Rhodesia) 445–50
general election (1985 Zimbabwe) 466
general election (1990 Zimbabwe) 483
general election (2000 Zimbabwe) 508
Presidential election (2002) 521–2
Electoral Amendment Act (1957) 198, 199–200
Elim Pentecostal Mission murders 423
Ellman-Brown, Geoffrey
  bus boycott 168
  cabinet crisis 216, 225, 226, 232, 233, 234, 374
  franchise issue 196
  GT's defeat 251
  immorality issue 191
  member of URP 105
  Minister of Roads and Road Traffic 109
  Monckton Commission 314
  support for GT's withdrawal 264
  UFP Congress (1958) 244–5
  URP Congress (1957) 180
  Whitehead's new cabinet 259
  working with GT on economy 120, 121, 123
Evans, Sir Athol 229
exchange-control measures 371

Federal Party
  see also UFP
  by-election (Mrewa 1957) 192
  by-election (Sebakwe 1956) 159
  formation 105
  general election (1953) 107
  GT's speech on need for change 123–4
  issue of party fusion 160–5, 214–15
Federated Chambers of Commerce 220
Federation of African Trade Unions 154
Federation of Rhodesia and Nyasaland
  see also Northern Rhodesia; Nyasaland; Southern Rhodesia
  African attitudes 147–9
  effects of formation 105, 105–6
  Federal Dissolution Conference (1963) 336
  Federal Electoral Bill (1957) 203–5
  Federal government's relationship with SR government 115, 116, 120–5, 158
  Federal Referendum (1953) 89
  Federal Review Conference (1960) 320–1
  federation discussions and formation (1953) 83–4, 88–90
  general election (1953) 105, 107
  general election (1957) 256
  GT's criticisms and fusion proposals 160–5
  importance of SR Prime Minister 101
  issue of Dominion Status (1957) 180–1, 201–2
  Monckton Commission (1960) 313–16
  need for funding 122, 123, 144
  secession of Nyasaland and Northern Rhodesia (1962) 332–3
Fehrsen, Paddy xxiii, 399, 472, 478, 503, 511, 512, 517
  see also Henderson, Paddy
Fehrsen, Dr Paul 282, 357, 459, 472, 478, 492
Ferrari, Frank 418, 427
Field, Winston 268, 333, 336, 340
Fingland, Stanley 357
Finkle, H. C. 141, 524
Flag of Rhodesia Bill (1968) 365
Fletcher, Lady Dollie 260
Fletcher, Sir Patrick ('Ben')
  on apparent unity of cabinet 180

backbencher 261
capital city issue 125
concerns re 1958 general election 211
criticism of 'partnership' concept 156
father-in-law of Dr Mavros 343
GT's cabinet crisis 216, 217, 218, 224, 225, 228, 232, 234, 237, 238, 239
GT's defeat 251, 258–9
on immorality issue 189–90, 190, 191
knighthood 224
land issue 521
Minister of Native Affairs 109, 524
reaction to Ghana's independence 176
support for GT's resignation 264
UFP Congress (1958) 244, 247, 247–8, 252, 255
United Party congress (1953) 101
wage regulations 221
Wankie Colliery strike 111
Flower, Ken 106, 288, 446
Foot, Dingle 298
Foot, Sir Hugh 303, 309, 329–30, 331
forced removals 63–4, 377
franchise
  disenfranchisement of Zimbabweans 521
  Federal Electoral Bill 203–5, 315
  growing dissatisfaction of Africans 79
  qualifications issue 69, 84–5, 149–52
  SR Constitutional talks (1961) 326
  Tredgold Commission (1957) 151, 193–200
  withdrawal of GT's citizenship and right to vote xxxiii, 521–2
Frankel, Professor S. Herbert 253–4, 274
Fraser, Malcolm 434, 453
Frederikse, Julie 417
FRELIMO (Front for the Liberation of Mozambique) 398, 457
FROLIZI (Front for the Liberation of Zimbabwe) 401

Gandhi, Indira 453
Gardiner, Lord 347
Garikayi 433–4, 457
Gatooma Prison 383–91
Geneva conference (1976) 410–13
Ghana xxxii, 84, 145, 148, 175–6
Ghoko Block 64

Gibb, Mary *see* Todd, Mary
Gibbard, Mr 443
Gibbs, Sir Humphrey 101, 336, 353, 369, 438, 453, 473
Gibbs, Dame Mollie 369, 438, 453
Gibbs, Peter 182, 296
Gilbert, Dr Daniel D. 427
Goddard, V. J. ('Tom') 269, 270
Goddard, V. W. ('Vic') 65
Gold Coast *see* Ghana
Goldberg, B. 341
Gonakudzingwa Camp 341, 346, 347, 348, 381
Gott, Richard 378
Grant, C. G. 'Jack' 387, 393, 405, 428
Grant, Ida 387, 393, 405, 428, 452
Grant-Dalton, Erskine 273–4
Gray, J. A. 197, 234, 255
Gray, Professor Richard xxvi, 86, 87, 278
Greenberg, Benjamin 361, 362, 363
Greenfield, Julian M.
  criticism of GT 276
  franchise issue 150, 151, 203, 205
  GT's advocate 75
  GT's cabinet crisis 229, 237
  member of Legislative Assembly 79
  Minister of Internal Affairs and Justice 84, 85, 101
  mistrust of British Government 148
  party fusion 163–4, 165, 215, 240
  refusal for Moffat to visit Banda 298
  role in GT's removal 255, 256, 258
  smear campaign against GT 178
  UFP Congress (1958) 240, 242, 243, 247, 250
Griffiths, James 175
Grundy, Trevor xxvii, xxix, 312
guerrilla warfare
  air crashes 425–6
  attack on Bannockburn village 419
  ceasefire 437–8, 445–6
  control of guerrillas 421, 423
  devastation of warfare on people 437
  GT's support for guerrillas 408–9, 436
  increased activity 398–9, 421, 422, 423
  infiltration across borders 414–15, 417–20
  legislation on terrorism 371, 372
  murder of Chief Matshazi 429–30

murder of ZANU's Chitepo 402
Nyadzonya camp raid 409, 414
rejection of amnesty 432
Gukurahundi xxxiii, 460, 461, 462–3
Gumbo, Shadrach 469
Gwelo 124, 159, 160, 174, 283, 296, 389

Habanyama, H. C. 314
Haddon, Dr Arthur Langan 8, 13, 16, 94, 415
Haddon, Michael and Eileen xxiv, 350, 477
Hadfield, F. L. 20, 23, 40, 44, 65, 95, 98, 197, 357, 467, 468
Hadfield, Philip 21
Hadfield, Vonna (née Phillips) 21
Haene, Bishop 399
Haldane, A. G. 254
Hall, Percy 283
Halliday, Dr 62
Hamadziripi, Henry 166, 168
Hancock, Ian 227, 248, 269
Harare Declaration 489
Harari 166–9, 209, 236–7
Harari African Cultural Association 141
Harper, William 292, 363
Harris, Norman 256, 281, 325, 374
Harrison, Jessie 428
Hartnack, Michael 464
Hatty, Sir Cyril
  90th birthday 502
  by-election Bulawayo North (1950) 84
  cabinet crisis 216, 216–17, 217, 228, 232, 233
  capital city issue 125
  GT's defeat 251
  immorality issue 191, 192
  land invasions 506
  Minister of the Treasury xxiv, 109
  role in SR economy 120, 121, 123, 141, 157
  UFP Congress (1958) 245
  Whitehead's new cabinet 259
Heads of Denominations 372, 468, 476
Heath, Edward 378, 427, 473
Henderson, Alan 174, 247, 249
Henderson, Paddy 174, 179, 247, 249
  see also Fehrsen, Paddy
Hepworth, Rosemary 480

Herbert, John 2
Heroes' Acre 210, 483, 504
Hickman, Colonel A. S. 110
Hillary, Sir Edmund 133
Hirsch, Dr I. M. 159
Hitchens, Christopher 413
Hlambelo, Bethuel xxiv, 75, 286
Hlambelo, David 518
Hlambelo, Reverend Ndabambi 22, 68, 75, 99, 286, 430, 467, 468, 492
Hochschild, Harold 269, 427, 453
Hokonui Ranch
  after independence 455–6
  Bannockburn 282, 317, 343, 383, 419, 421, 424, 428, 429, 458, 465, 477
  Christie's partnership 173–4, 228, 234, 242, 247, 249
  Christie's repayment demand 282–3, 365
  drought 295, 459, 462, 463
  film and biography of GT 481–2, 483–4
  Grace's involvement 32, 284, 295, 324–5, 327, 328
  GT as rancher (1961) 324–7
  GT and Judith's restriction (1972) 391, 392, 393–4, 396
  GT's management 282–3
  GT's restriction (1965) 350–2, 356–9, 362
  GT's restriction (1972) 391, 392, 393–4, 396, 397–8, 400, 402, 403
  home 259–60, 268, 342, 373–5
  new site for Dadaya Mission 81–2, 91, 331
  purchase 70–2
  sale of land and cattle 363, 369, 456, 463, 470
  Shirley Beadle as manager 91, 282
  Todds' handover 487, 488, 490
  Vukuzenzele 458–9
  warfare infiltration 356–7, 415–16, 417–20, 422, 423, 428, 430, 431, 432, 436
Holderness, Hardwicke
  on African desire for equal participation 157
  attack by Fletcher 156
  cabinet crisis (1957) 215, 226, 230, 231, 232
  CAP member 309, 312

Index

exceptional Rhodesian 415
on Federal Government 121, 122, 147
franchise issue 149, 151, 195, 197, 198
general election (1958) 268, 269
history of Eighth Parliament of SR 470–1
on Ian Smith 340
immorality issue 189, 190, 191
on Industrial Conciliation Bill 184
land issue 87, 118, 521
member of Select Committee for labour bill 154
on National Congress 207
on Parliament (1954) 114
on railway strike 171
refusal of cabinet minister post 109
relationship with new SR ANC 210
support for GT 102, 104, 108, 264
at UFP Congress (1958) 242, 246
URP candidate 107
visit to London with GT (1964) 341, 342
Whitehead's new cabinet 258, 259
Holland, Alf 35–6
Home, Lord see Douglas-Home, Sir Alec
Hone, Sir Evelyn 299, 300
Hope Fountain Mission 21, 22, 372
housing 88, 134, 138–40
Hove, Byron 345
Hove, Michael M. xxiii, 138, 278
Hove, Richard 442
Huggins, Sir Godfrey (Lord Malvern)
 backbencher 104
 creation of Federal Party 105, 107
 criticism of Smith's UDI 355
 death 376–7
 desire for independence of Federation 148
 franchise issue 203
 on Ian Smith 340–1
 Kafue vs Kariba 126–7, 128, 129
 need for establishment of university 118
 opposition to fusion proposals 165
 Prime Minister of Central African Federation xxxi, 90, 102, 123, 124, 160, 201
 Prime Minister of Southern Rhodesia xxx, 63, 65, 66, 67, 78, 79, 83, 89, 100, 101
 retirement 148–9
 support for Whitehead 269–70
human rights 318–19, 463, 489
Humphrey, Senator Hubert 417
Hunter, Guy 309
Hunter, Lew 52, 338, 349, 463

immigration 63, 64, 68, 121–2, 122
Immorality and Indecency Suppression Act (1916) 189–91
imprisonment see detentions and imprisonment
Indemnity Bill 365
independence issue 298, 329–31, 340, 341–2, 343, 345–6, 347–55
Independent Zimbabwe Group 466
Industrial Conciliation Act (1934, 1945) 153, 155, 184
Industrial Conciliation Bill (1957) 182–5
Ingram, Derek xxvi, 445
Inter-Territorial Movement of Persons Bill 106
Interracial Association 171, 196–7, 198, 232
Ireland, Dr Alfred J. ('Sonnie') 37, 42, 58, 74, 92

Jenkins, Peter 378
Joelson, F. S. 287
Johnson, James 202
Jones, Arthur Creech 83
Jones, Sir Glyn 385, 386
Jowitt, Mr 15, 23, 25

Kafue Dam vs Kariba Dam 106, 122, 126–30
Kahari, Professor George 468, 478
Kamba, Walter 321
Kariba Dam 103, 106, 122, 126–30, 161
Karlen, Bishop 480
Kaunda, Kenneth 300, 301, 332, 343, 401, 403, 407, 420, 434
Keatley, Patrick 255, 298
Keeley, Mr 461
Keith, Robert C. 294
Keller, Jack 113, 146, 184, 198, 199, 261–3, 521
Kennedy, John 487
Kennedy, Sir John 100, 101, 102, 415
Kenworthy, Major Peter 261

Kenya
  GT's visit (1954) 322
  Kenya Constitutional Conference and agreement 296, 298–9
  Mau Mau movement 106, 119, 187
Kermode, Jean 91, 93
Kerr Commission (1952) 80, 87–8, 139, 154, 206
Ketteringham, R. N. 110
Khalen, Bishop 498
Khami Prison 286
Kilmuir, Lord 132
Kirby, John 174, 259, 282, 325
Kirkwood, Professor Kenneth 269
Kissinger, Dr Henry 410
Knapp, Isobel xxv, 81, 93, 97, 339, 455, 467, 474
Knapp, Ray 4, 81, 92, 97, 338, 338–9
Knight, Reginald 151, 192, 259
Küng, Hans 494–5
Kutama Mission 44, 60, 166

labour affairs
  general workers' strike (1948) 78, 106
  Harari bus boycott 166–9
  Industrial Conciliation Act (1934, 1945) 153, 155, 184
  Industrial Conciliation Bill (1957) 182–5
  need for better labour legislation 153–6
  railway strike (1956) 169–72
  review of African wages (1957) 220–5
  Rhodesia Railways firemen's strike (1954) 115–16
  RISCOM (1954) 121
  Wankie Colliery strike (1954) 109–13, 153
Labour Party (SR) 65, 84, 105, 314
Labour Party (UK) 292, 345
Ladbrook, Albert and Queenie 81, 97
Laidlaw, Chris and Helen 477, 478
Lamont, Bishop Donal 370, 372, 399, 409–10, 415, 454
Lancaster House constitutional conference (1979) 434–6, 436–8, 446
Land Husbandry Act see Native Land Husbandry Act
land issue
  farm workers evicted from farms 513

Land Apportionment Act (1930) 63, 86, 117–19, 151, 189, 232, 277, 521
land expropriation without compensation 505–6
land invasions 506
Land Tenure Act (1969) 370, 371, 377
Mugabe's land policy 483
Native Land Bill (1951) 85–7
Native Land Husbandry Act (1951) 136–8, 328
'reserved land' legislation 328
urban housing 138–40
Lange, David xxv, 471, 472, 473, 474–5, 478
Lange, Naomi 478
Lardner-Burke, Desmond
  appeal for independence 349
  attitude towards GT 331, 407
  banning of Daily News 344
  deportation of Grants and Niesewand 405
  on detainees 373
  GT's imprisonment 382, 388, 391
  GT's restriction 362, 407
  permission for Judith Todd to travel 396
  on terrorists 371
Laundy, Philip 274
Law and Order (Maintenance) Act (1960) 332, 409, 443
Law and Order (Maintenance) Bill (1960) 318–19
Law and Order (Maintenance) (Amendment) Bill (1960) 335
Law and Order (Maintenance) (Amendment) Bill (1970) 371
League of Empire Loyalists 193
Leary, L. 108
Legge, Ronald 358
Legum, Colin 149, 275, 321, 426
Levin, Bernard 404, 487
Liberal Party (NR) 272, 332
Liberal Party (SR) 79, 84
Lilford, D. C. 334
Lindley, Richard xxvi, 431–2
Livingstone, Dr David 7, 22
Llewellin, Lord 89, 175
Lloyd, Paddy
  advice to GT after imprisonment 390–1

approval of GT and Nkomo meeting 212
cabinet minister 230
CAP congress 296
on chiefs' *indaba* 346
immorality motion 191, 192
liberal critic of GT 171
loss of seat 275
resignation from UFP 265
support for GT 264
unavailable as cabinet minister 109, 151, 259
Logan, John 2, 3
Lord, Graham 408
Loudon, Bruce 407
Lovegrove, John 296, 308, 309
Lovemore, Jessie 274
Lowe, George 133
Lundi Reserve 20, 25, 33, 47, 81, 136, 282, 342–3, 436
Lundi Tribal Trust Land 424
Lusaka Accord 434

McAdam, Mr 'Bossman' 42
Macauley, Lord 46
McCulloch, Rua (Rebekah) 26, 48, 58, 81, 498
Macdonald, John ('Matabele Mac') 177, 178, 191
McGovern, Senator George 367
McHarg, Dr James 187
Machel, Samora 403, 434, 457
McKenzie, Alexander 11
McKenzie, Ann (née Crawford) 11, 14
McKenzie, Annie *see* Wilson, Annie
McKenzie, James 11
MacLennan, Sir Ian 474
Macleod, Iain 281, 296, 298, 298–9, 300, 307, 341–2
Macmillan, Harold
  Banda's release from prison 299
  Prime Minister of Britain 281, 309
  resignation 340
  visit to Ghana and Central Africa 295
Maglas Township 326, 358, 382, 493
majority rule
  constitutional proposals (1969) 368–9
  referendum (1969) 369
  referendum (1979) 430–1

Smith's 'acceptance' of proposals (1976) 410, 415
Smith's rejection 341–2, 364, 378, 394
Malaba, Hay I. 366
Malawi Congress Party 326
Malherbe, Professor E. C. 274
Malianga, Moton 297, 303
Malunga, Lida 40
Malvern, Lord *see* Huggins, Sir Godfrey
Mandela, Nelson 482, 494
Mangena, Todd 39
Manley, Michael 434
Mansfield, Philip 389
Mansill, Hazel 20, 25, 28–9, 492
Mansill, Madge 20, 25, 28–9
Mansill, William 20
Mantjojo, Jonah 40, 286
Mapai slaughter 414
Maposa, Mr 433
Marandellas Prison 383, 384, 387
Maripe, Knight 170, 253
Marlborough resolution 160–1, 162–3
Marquand, H. A. 307
Marsh, Rua *see* McCulloch, Rua (Rebekah)
martial law 425–6, 428
Mashona people 19
Mason, Philip 151–2, 309, 310
Mass Media Trust 456, 470
Masters and Servants Act 110
Masuku, Jellinah 325, 463
Masuku, Lookout 460, 475
Masururwa, Willie 483
Matabele people 18–19, 22
Matabeleland atrocities 460, 461, 462–3
Mataka, Mr 479, 480
Mather, A. R. 21, 23, 25, 30, 34–5, 36, 43, 47, 48, 95, 141, 415, 524
Matimba, Patrick 189, 190
Matopo Mission 51
Matshazi, Senator Chief Jobe Mafala 40–1, 429–30
Matshazi, Chief Mafala 40–1
Mattison, Bob 363, 418
Mau Mau movement 106, 119, 187
Maudling, Reginald 300
Mavros, Dr 343
Mawema, Michael 297, 302
Mbirimi, S. M. 296, 309, 312

MDC (Movement for Democratic Change) 505, 508
media
  censorship 353, 354, 358, 489
  Daily News banning 344–5
  government control 348
Mass Media Trust 456, 470
Megahey, Dr Alexander 453
Meikles Hotel 67, 206, 247, 258
Meredith, Martin 443
Merrington, Mr 42
Metcalf, Rupert 218–19
Mhambi, D. G. 274
Millerick, Dr 74
mining
  Chamber of Mines 182, 183
  Mineworkers' Congress (1957) 183
  Wankie Colliery strike (1954) 109–13, 153
miscegenation debate (1957) 189–91, 232
Mkwananzi, David xxiv, 51, 56, 68, 73, 74, 76, 469, 477, 493, 496, 518, 519
Mkwananzi, Eva 496
Mkwananzi, Leah 68
Mlambo, Mambo 433
Mnangagwa, Simbarashe 442
Mnene Mission Hospital 41, 44
Moffat, John (missionary) 22, 31
Moffat, Sir John
  attempt to visit Banda 298
  defeat in general election (1962) 332
  on Federal Electoral Bill 204–5
  letter from GT 272
  meeting with GT re NR election 283
  Northern Rhodesia talks 300
  parliamentarian 147
  on 'partnership' 90
  role in CAP 287, 291, 297, 307–8, 312
Monckton, Lord 314
Monckton Commission (1960) 307, 313–16, 321, 395
Mondale, Walter 417
Moorcroft, George 363
Morris, Stan E. 346
Moyo, J. Z. 171
Mozambique
  see also Machel, Samora
  Chimoio and Tembue raids 419

guerrilla warfare 334, 377, 398, 402
Mapai slaughter 414, 416
raid of Nyadzonya camp 409
raids on ZANU camps 426
Mpofu, Bafundi J. xxiv, 518
Mpofu, Gijima 458, 488
Mpofu, Samson G. 30, 468, 469, 470, 478, 485, 490, 493, 494
Msipa, Cephas xxiv, 493, 494, 496, 511, 517, 518
Muchache, Clement 411
Mugabe, Robert
  cause of Zimbabwe's ruin 493, 505–6
  control of guerrillas 421
  desire for one-party state and executive presidency 466
  dismissal of Nkomo et al (1982) 460
  educated at Kutama Mission 166
  freedom of City of Bulawayo 475
  general election (1980) 446–7, 448, 448–9, 450–1
  general election (1985) 466
  Geneva Conference (1976) 410, 413
  GT on possible Mugabe victory 441
  GT's criticisms 483, 501, 502–3, 511
  GT's message (1979) 437
  Lancaster House conference (1979) 435
  land expropriation without compensation 505–6
  leader of ZANU in Mozambique 402
  Mugabe's Senator offer to GT 451
  power struggle 426
  Prime Minister 464, 465, 495
  return from Maputo (1980) 446
  teacher at Dadaya Mission 60
  Unity Accord with Nkomo 476
  Victoria Falls conference (1975) 403
  visit to Dadaya Mission (1981) 459
  visit to GT after burn injury 480
  withdrawal of GT's citizenship and right to vote xxxiii, 521–2
Mukokokwayira, Christine 326, 479, 517
Mukokokwayira, John 416, 517
Mukonoweshuro, David 392, 493, 518
Mulgan, Assistant Professor R. G. 439–40
Mumbengegwi, Sam 511
Mungazi, Professor Dickson 279
Murindagomo, Bishop Patrick 422

Index

Murphy, Sir William 109, 253, 269
Murray, Lady (Izo) 400
Murray, Sir John 151, 400
Mushonga, Paul 166, 297, 304
Mutambirwa, J. A. C. 274
Mutomba, Raviro 452
Mutomba, Samuel xxiv, 432, 433, 434, 442, 443, 452, 486, 493
Muzorewa, Bishop Abel
  at Lancaster House conference (1979) 436, 437
  breaking off talks 402
  criticism by Smith 435
  first black Prime Minister 432
  general election (1980) 448, 450
  Geneva conference (1976) 410
  head of African National Council 381
  Lusaka Accord 434
  negotiations with Smith (1977) 419–20, 421
  power struggle 426
  private militia 426, 431
  rally (1980) 446
  Settlement Agreement (1978) 422–3
Mvubu, Jackson 99
Mzingeli, Charles 154, 253

Nasser, Colonel 147
Nathan, Mrs 91
Nathan, Peter xxiv, 91, 338, 356, 468
National Constitutional Assembly 505
National Council of Women 192
National Party (SA) 78, 84
National Union of South African Students (NUSAS) 344
Native Affairs Department *see* African Affairs Department; Department of Native Affairs
Native Education Bill (1957) 186
Native Industrial Workers' Unions Bill (1954) 154, 184
Native Labour Boards Act (1947) 153
Native Land Bill (1951) 85–7
Native Land Husbandry Act (1951) 136–8, 328
Native Reserves 15, 19, 25, 117, 137
Native Tax 142, 158, 277, 524
Native Trade and Production Commission 85–6

Ncube, Benjamin 431, 512, 516, 518, 526
Ncube, Fr Pius 498
Ncube, T. L. 469, 492
Ncube, Mr Themba 497
Ndebele people *see* Matabele people
Ndebele, P. J. Mkoka 51, 56, 68, 73
Ndhlovu, A. L. 75
Ndhlovu, Cyril 411
Ndoda, David 76
NDP (National Democratic Party)
  1961 proposals 326–7
  arrests and riots 302–4
  banning 328
  Federal Review Conference (1960) 320–1
  formation 294
  GT's CAP statement and consequences 304–12
  talks with British Government 297
Ndubiwa, Dr Michael 518
Nelson, Reverend Thomas 2
Ngara, John 469
Ngedhleni (headman) 41
Ngole, Tom 99
Ngome mission 20
Nicolle, Hostes 346
Niesewand, Peter 383, 389, 390, 405
Nkomo, Joshua
  see also Patriotic Front; ZAPU
  acceptance of 1961 proposals 326
  African National Council 381
  African nationalist xxxii, xxxiii, 166
  on arrests in Salisbury (1960) 302
  at conference on federation (1953) 89
  at Gonakudzingwa Camp 341, 347, 381, 395
  at Government House 352
  at Lancaster House conference (1979) 437
  cabinet minister 450
  CAP statement 304–6
  commission on transport 168
  consulted re trade unions (1955) 154
  control of guerrillas 421
  death 504
  desire for peaceful evolution 278
  dismissal by Mugabe (1982) 460
  evidence to Pearce Commission 395
  Federal Review Conference (1960) 321

formation of People's Caretaker Council 337
general election (1980) 447, 448, 449
Geneva Conference (1976) 410, 412
GT's 80th birthday 478
GT's concerns re new SR ANC 211–13
on GT's UN appearance 330
message from GT (1979) 437
power struggle 426
President of new SRANC 209, 233, 253, 263
rally (1980) 446
release from detention 402
response to air crashes 425
support for GT 407
talks with Smith 402, 403, 405
Victoria Falls conference (1975) 403
visits with GT 296, 420, 480
Nkrumah, Kwame xxxii, 84, 175
Norman, Denis 450
Northern Rhodesia
see also CAP; Federation of Rhodesia and Nyasaland; Zambia
Constitutional Conference (1960) 320, 326
Federal general election (1953) 107
federation discussions 83–4, 88–90
general election (1959) 283, 287
general election (1962) 332, 333
growth of nationalism 156, 161, 206, 207
Kafue Dam issue 126–30
miners at Wankie Colliery strike (1954) 110, 112
Rhodesia Railways strike (1954) 116
road to independence 202, 299–301, 346
violence 105
visit by Macleod 299
Northward 103, 104, 133, 179, 259, 471
Nyadzonya camp 409, 414
Nyandoro, George xxxii, 85, 118, 137, 166, 207, 209, 212
Nyasaland
see also Federation of Rhodesia and Nyasaland
Banda's imprisonment and release 298–9
federation discussions 83–4, 88–90

general election (1961) 326
independence issue 202, 299, 344
return of Hastings Banda (1959) 281
riots and State of Emergency (1959) 285–6, 290, 299
secession from Federation (1962) 332
Nyathi, Paul Themba 518
Nyemba, J. 76
Nyerere, President Julius 403, 434, 441
Nyoni, Pastor Albert 517
Nyoni, Manikidza M. 53, 356, 469
Nyoni, Mpande 469, 493
Nyoni, S. 469

OAU (Organisation of African Unity) xix, 432
Odilo, Fr 480
Official Secrets Bill (1970) 371
O'Hea, Father 44
Overseas Mission Board 277, 356, 357, 360, 361, 362, 439, 453, 468–9

Paget, Bishop Edward 44
Palley, Dr Ahrn 289, 303, 319, 333, 346, 348, 373
Palley, Dr Claire 215, 256, 411
Palmer, Eric 110, 191, 230, 233, 264, 296
Palmer, Margareta 455
Palmer, Ralph 110, 177–8, 188, 191, 230, 264, 296, 308, 309, 310, 320, 321, 455
Parker, John 131
Parpart, Jane 481
Paton, Reverend John G. 7
Patriotic Front
Geneva conference (1976) 410, 412, 413
inclusion in talks 421, 422
Lancaster House Conference (1979) 436–7, 437, 446
Peace Preservation Act (1953) 105–6, 111
Pearce Commission 382, 385, 389, 392, 393–5
Pearce, Lord 382, 386, 389, 391, 392, 393
Pearce, Mike 177
Pedder, Tony xxiv, 309, 321
Pennant-Rea, Rupert 346
People's Caretaker Council 337, 341
Perez de Cuellar, Señor Javier 447–8
Perrott, Roy 357
Phillips, F. John 20, 53

Index

Phillips, Mary 53
Phillips, Vonna *see* Hadfield, Vonna
Plewman, R. P. 178
Plewman Commission 178, 253
Pope-Symonds, Eric 448
Portugal 401
Powell-Duffryn Ltd 109
Prain, Sir Ronald 269
Preservation of Constitutional Government Bill (1963) 335
Preventive Detention (Temporary Provisions) Act (1959) 341
Programme to Combat Racism 367–8, 373
Prosser, Hugh 478
Protected Places and Areas Act (1959) 289
Pswarayi, Dr 294
Purnell, George 332

Quinton, Jack 192, 233, 237–8, 245

race relations
 see also white community
 attempts to break down barriers 131–3
 GT's attitudes 35–6, 54, 59, 61–2, 66, 118–19, 133, 208–9
 racism consultation 367–8
 regarding land 117–19
 separate development policy 360–1, 371–2
Railway African Workers' Union 154, 169
Ramphal, Sir 'Sonny' 435
Ranger, Shelagh 334
Ranger, Professor Terence xxiii, xxx, 108, 210–11, 292, 303, 304, 309, 311, 312, 334, 504
Reay, Peter 246
Reith, Lord 139, 140, 174
Rendell, W. F. 248, 252
Renwick, Lord 435, 437, 445, 447, 448, 449
Rhodes, Cecil John 18, 19, 166, 197
Rhodesia
 see also Rhodesian Front; Smith, Ian Douglas; Southern Rhodesia; Zimbabwe
 constitution proposals referendum (1979) 430–1
 constitutional proposals (1969) 368–9, 370
 end of white rule 432
 general election (1970) 373
 general election (1979) 431
 Geneva conference (1976) 410
 independence issue and UDI 347–55
 Lancaster House constitutional conference (1979) 434–6, 436–8
 Lusaka Accord (1979) 434
 Republic declaration 371
 Settlement Agreement (1978) 422–3
 settlement proposals (1971) 378–80, 381–2, 393–5
 Smith's ongoing talks 359, 364, 402, 405, 408
 UDI declaration (1965) 346, 347–55
 Victoria Falls conference (1975) 403
Rhodesia Corporation 70
Rhodesia Iron and Steel Commission *see* RISCOM
Rhodesia National Affairs Association 87, 108, 151, 210, 331
Rhodesia Party 105
Rhodesia Railways
 attitude towards Hokonui Ranch 282
 firemen's strike (1954) 115–16
 importance 106, 110
 review of wages 220
 workers' strike (1956) 169–72
Rhodesian African Teachers' Association 365–6
Rhodesian Front (RF)
 see also Rhodesia; Smith, Ian Douglas
 closure of technical college 187
 general election (1962) 333
 general election (1965) 348
 general election (1970) 373
 group of anti-establishment forces 334
 Ian Smith as leader 340–1, 348, 349
 Independence referendum 345–6
 participation of William Harper 292
 'reserved land' legislation 328
Rhodesian Light Infantry 422
Rhodesian Republican Army 317
Rhodesian Women's League 189
Richard, Ivor 410, 412
RISCOM (Rhodesia Iron and Steelworks Commission) 121, 157

555

Ritson, Allan 398, 418–19, 431
Ritson, Heidi 418
Roberts, Farewell 74
Roberts, John 260, 300
Robins, Lord Eric 191–2
Rosin, Kipps 417
Rosin, Muriel xxiv, 107, 264–5
Ross, Dr Emory 173, 282–3, 328, 426
Ross, Myrta 173, 426
Rotary Club 97, 495, 515
Royal Institute of International Affairs 283
Rudd, Alison xxiii, 512

St Faith's Anglican Mission 86, 210
Salisbury
  as capital city 122, 124–5, 315
  Harari 166–9, 209, 236–7
Salisbury, Lord 336
Samkange, Sketchley 302, 303
Samkange, Stanlake
  comments on GT and Congress 242, 246, 253, 258
  on Dominion Status 202
  member of CAP 287, 312
  on new ANC 208
  support for GT 197
  unrest (1960) 302, 303
  vice-president of CAP 291, 296, 309
Samkange, Reverend Thompson 76, 142
Samsole, Washington 526
sanctions 355, 356–7, 416–17, 438
Sandys, Duncan 309, 321, 340
Sanger, Clyde 225, 240, 242, 263, 271, 286, 289, 318
Savanhu, Jasper Z. 89, 334
Savory, Jimmy 40, 126, 127–8, 128–9, 129–30
Sawyer, Sydney 255, 258, 259
Sayakayi, Mr 493
Scott, Edith *see* Todd, Edith
Scott, Hugh 478–9
Scott, Jean 91
Second World War 52, 53, 55, 63
Segregation Society 193
Selous Scouts 416, 422, 423
separate development policy 360–1, 371–2
Settlement Agreement (1978) 422
Seward, Mr 384

Shabani
  see also Dadaya Mission
  GT's constituency 79, 108, 268, 269–70, 292
  mining community 20, 42–3, 48
  violence 422, 425–6, 429–30, 465
  visit by Sir Godfrey Huggins 65
Shabanie Mine 48, 326, 358, 382, 493
Shamuyarira, Nathan
  on bus boycott 168–9
  on GT's acceleration of African education 186
  on GT's contribution 276, 278–9
  on independence 303
  on Land Husbandry Act 137–8
  member of Capricorn Africa Society 132
  Minister of Information and Tourism 451, 456
  observer at UFP Congress 242, 243, 244, 249
  on role of Africans in URP 157
Sharfe, Mr and Mrs Paul 91, 93
Shaw, Mr 429–30
Shawcross, Lord 314
Sheriff, John 19–20
Shona people 19
Sibanda, Dr 469
Sibanda, J. M. T. 351
Sibanda, Joram M. 30, 81
Sibanda, Wesley 99
Sibanda, Zebediah 442
Sinclair, Jim 349
Sithole, Canaan 74, 75, 76
Sithole, Duduzile 515
Sithole, Edson 166
Sithole, Ndabaningi
  acceptance of 1961 proposals 326
  at Dadaya Mission xxxi, 40, 41, 58, 60, 64, 65, 73, 74, 75, 76
  detention (1975) 402
  formation of ZANU (1963) 337
  general election (1980) 448
  Geneva conference (1976) 410
  leading nationalist 257
  move from CAP to NDP 297
  negotiations with Smith (1977) 419–20, 421
  power struggle 426

Index

private militia 426, 431
rally (1980) 446
Settlement Agreement (1978) 422, 423
Victoria Falls conference (1975) 403
Siziba, Philemon 343
Skeen, Brigadier Andrew 346, 348
Skelton, Bishop Kenneth 335, 349, 353–4, 356, 357, 360, 371–2, 372–3, 377, 454–5
Smedley, H. 385, 386
Smith, Alec 447
Smith, C. D. 197
Smith, David 450
Smith, Ian Douglas
  constitution proposals (1969) 368–9, 370
  constitution proposals referendum (1979) 430–1
  criticised by Ahrn Palley 289
  criticism of Grace 351
  franchise 194
  general election (1962) 333, 334
  general election (1980) 446, 448
  Geneva conference (1976) and majority rule 410–12, 415
  GT's concerns 341
  Independence referendum 345–6
  influence on white population 343
  Lancaster House Conference (1979) 434–6
  leader of Rhodesian Front 340, 348–9, 356
  negotiations with black internal leaders 419–20, 421
  new member of Legislative Assembly 79
  pressure by Vorster 401
  Prime Minister xxiv, 340
  reasons for GT and Judith's arrests 389
  Settlement Agreement (1978) 422–3
  settlement proposals (1971) 378–80, 382, 394, 401
  talks with GT 408
  talks on HMS *Fearless* (1968) 364
  talks with Nkomo 402, 403, 405
  talks with Vorster and Kissinger 1976) 410
  talks with Wilson on HMS *Tiger* (1966) 359
  UFP Congress (1958) 242
  in USA (1978) 427
  Victoria Falls conference (1975) 403
Smith, Leslie 65
Soames, Lady Mary xxvi, 438, 447, 448
Soames, Lord (Christopher) 438, 443, 444, 445–50, 453, 455
Solzhenitsyn, Alexander 404, 487
South Africa
  address by Macmillan 295
  general election (1948) 78, 84
  influence on trade unions 154, 183–4, 277
  Mandela as president (1994) 494
  negotiations between Vorster and Kaunda (1974) 401
Southern Rhodesia
  see also Federation of Rhodesia and Nyasaland; Rhodesia; Zimbabwe
  antagonism of whites towards GT 317
  arrests and riots (1960) 302–12, 317–18
  Britain's attitude and responsibility 334–5
  cabinet crisis (1957) 216–19, 221–5, 226–9, 236–9
  congress and GT's resignation (1958) 190, 231, 232, 239–41, 242–50, 251, 252–3
  effect on whites of atrocities in Congo 300
  Federal government's relationship with SR government 115, 116, 120–5, 158
  federation discussions 83–4, 88–90
  formation of Whitehead's cabinet (1958) 258–9, 260, 260–1
  franchise issue 193–200, 203
  general election (1946) 65
  general election (1954) 105, 107–9
  general election (1958) 199, 263, 268, 269–70, 272–5
  general election (1962) 333
  general election (1965) 348
  GT's criticisms of Federal Government and fusion proposals 160–5
  GT's debate on majority rule 341–2
  GT's new cabinet and Caucus meeting 230–5
  history 18–19
  immigration 63, 64, 68, 121–2, 122
  independence issue 329–31, 340, 341–2, 343, 345–6

Independence referendum (1964) 345–6
SR Constitutional talks (1960–1) 319, 320, 321, 326–7
State of Emergency (1956) 169, 170, 171
State of Emergency (1959) 284, 286, 287, 287–90
State of Emergency (1965) 348, 353
white immigrants 63, 64, 68
Southern Rhodesia African National Youth League 193
Southern Rhodesia Immorality Suppression Ordinance (1903) 189
Special Branch 210, 393, 422
Squires, Hilary 403, 406, 407
Stallworthy, John 353, 414
Stallworthy, Peggy 342, 353
Stallworthy, Sally 342
Stark, George 62, 95, 98, 524
Steere, Loyd V. 144
Stewart, Dr Garfield (cousin of GT) 6
Stewart, Jimmy 48, 51, 56, 92, 95, 274
Stockil, R. O. 187, 198, 262
Straw, Norman 180, 198, 199, 259, 264
Stretton, Sandford 409
strikes
  bus boycott (1956) 166–9
  Dadaya strike (1947) 73–7
  general workers' strike (1948) 78, 106
  Rhodesia Railways firemen's strike (1954) 115–16
  Rhodesia Railways workers' strike (1956) 169–72
  RISCOM strike (1954) 121
  Shabanie Mine strike (1972) 382
  Wankie Colliery strike (1954) xxxii, 109–13, 153
Stumbles, A. R. W. ('Rube')
  franchise issue 151, 198, 199, 232
  GT's cabinet crisis 216, 232, 237
  GT's defeat 251, 259
  immorality issue 191, 192, 232
  land issue 151, 521
  member of United Party 105
  portfolio of African Education 187–8, 524
  support for GT's withdrawal 264
  UFP Congress (1958) 242, 245
Swadel, Sydney 254, 260

Swinton, Lord 100–1, 109, 135, 140
Symons, Moira 372

Takawira, Leopold 132, 294, 302, 326, 373, 471
Tangwena people 377
Tapsell, Sir Peter xxvi, 296, 307
Taylor, Don 149, 238, 256
Taylor, Stephen 504
terrorism *see* guerrilla warfare
Thatcher, Margaret 432, 434, 448
Thebe, Ephraim 443
Thomas, Sir Miles 83
Thompson, Bishop Jim xxiv, 342
Thomson, Mavis *see* Walsh, Mavis
Todd, Adam 1–2, 2
Todd, Allan (nephew of GT) xxv, 485, 486, 492, 517, 518–19
Todd, Alycen *see* Watson, Alycen
Todd, Anne (daughter of Louie) 486, 487
Todd, Cynthia Gay Garfield *see* Edge, Cynthia Gay Garfield
Todd, Edith (née Scott) (mother of GT) 6, 49, 102
Todd, Edith (sister of GT) 6, 49, 325, 353, 463–4, 481
Todd, Eliza (aunt of GT) 2 4, 6
Todd, Elizabeth (née Wright) (grandmother of GT) 2, 3–4, 6–7, 9
Todd, Helen (aunt of GT) 11–12
Todd, Ivy (sister-in-law of GT) 8
Todd, Jane (aunt of GT) 6
Todd, Lady (Jean Grace Isabel) (née Wilson) (wife of GT)
  see also Dadaya Mission; Hokonui Ranch
  90th birthday 512
  adoption of Alycen 14, 16, 23
  apologia for rightness of missionary endeavour 498–500
  on arrests (1960) 303
  awards 97
  birth, childhood and education 12–13
  birth of Cynthia 80–1
  birth of Judith 57, 58
  death 97–8, 489, 516–19, 520–1, 522
  early relationship with GT 9–10
  effects of GT and Judith's imprisonment 383–4, 386–7, 387–8, 388–91

Index

furlough (1941–2) 52, 53–6
furlough (1949) 81
health 13, 49–50, 92, 94, 178–9, 282, 358, 471, 475, 481, 492, 496–7, 498, 500–1, 503, 505, 507, 509–10, 511, 512–13, 514, 515–16
marriage 13–14
move to Bulawayo 487, 488, 490, 491–2
move to Hokonui Ranch 259–60, 268
supportive role as Prime Minister's wife 103, 104, 174, 242–3, 247, 249
wedding anniversaries 177, 179, 460–1, 489

Todd, Jessie (née Davies) 6
Todd, John (uncle of GT) 5
Todd, Judith Garfield (daughter of GT)
birth 57, 58
books 312, 397, 507
David Mkwananzi's funeral 496
education 103–4
Grace's Dadaya Schemes 48
Grace's death 517
GT on marriage 14
GT's 80th birthday 477, 478
GT's arrest (1980) 442–3
GT's burn injury 479–80
GT's letter on 30th birthday 50
imprisonment and hunger strike (1972) 382, 383, 384, 385, 387, 388, 389–90, 391
living at Dadaya Mission 97
living at Hokonui Ranch 376
living in London 357, 361, 396, 403–5, 427–8
marriage 400
move (1981) from UK to Harare 458
move (1991) from Harare to Bulawayo 488
protest against banning of *Daily News* (1964) 344–5
restriction to Hokonui Ranch 391, 392, 393–4, 396
settlement proposals (1971) 379, 380, 393–4
substitution for GT at Edinburgh University 351, 352
support for ageing parents 500, 501–2, 502, 503, 504, 507, 511, 512, 513, 515

visit to New Zealand (1949) 81
visit to SA (2002) 525, 526
Todd, Louie (cousin of GT) 428, 440, 486–7
Todd, Marjorie (wife of Allan Todd) 485, 486
Todd, Mary (aunt of GT) 6
Todd, Mary (née Gibb) (great-grandmother of GT) 1
Todd, Matthew (great-grandfather of GT) 1
Todd, Matthew (uncle of GT) 2, 3
Todd, Nathaniel (uncle of GT) 5
Todd, Sir Reginald Stephen Garfield
see also CAP; Dadaya Mission; Hokonui Ranch; URP
80th birthday 477–8
90th birthday 502
achievements and contributions 276–9
adoption of Alycen 14, 16, 23
arrest (1980) 442–3, 444
biography and film 481–2, 483–4, 487–8
birth of Cynthia 80–1
birth and early childhood 6–7
birth of Judith 57, 58
burn injury 479–81
car enthusiast 7
charismatic speaker 104, 108
Christian beliefs and values xxxiii, xxxiv, 7, 34, 44, 523, 525
death 489, 526, 527
disenfranchised by Mugabe xxxiii, 521–2
early ministry 14–15
education and theological training 7–9, 10
family relationships 6–7
furlough (1941–2) 52, 53–6
furlough (1949) 81
Grace's death and funeral 516–19, 520–1, 522
health 357, 363, 388–9, 391, 393, 459, 461, 471, 479–81, 502, 516
importance of Grace's support 104, 295–6
imprisonment (1972) 382–91
knighthood 471–2, 473–5
marriage 13–14
Minister of African Education 141, 142
Minister of Justice and Internal Affairs 109

559

Minister of Labour 220, 222
Minister of Labour and Social Welfare 259, 260–1
move to Bulawayo 487, 488, 490, 491–2, 493–4
move to Hokonui Ranch 259–60, 268
political beliefs 65–6, 67–8, 68–9, 78–80, 84–5, 236–7
Prime Minister appointment (1953) 90, 91, 98, 100–6
Prime Minister crisis and resignation (1958) 188, 215, 218, 242–50, 258–9
on racial issues 35–6, 54, 59, 61–2, 66, 118–19, 132, 133, 134, 287
resignation from Whitehead's cabinet (1958) 264–6, 267, 281
restriction to Hokonui Ranch (1965) 350–2, 356–9, 362
restriction to Hokonui Ranch (1972) 391, 392, 393–4, 396, 397–8, 400, 402, 403
revocation of restriction order 406–8
Senator 9, 451–2, 455, 461, 464–6
support of children through school 493
tractor rescue 90
value of missionary career 96, 105, 145
wedding anniversaries 177, 179, 460–1, 489
Wits University studies 60–2
Todd, Robert (uncle of GT) 5
Todd, Stella (sister of GT) 6, 9, 14, 37, 40, 49, 393, 469, 470, 475–6, 478, 481
Todd, Thomas I (grandfather of GT) 1, 2–5, 5–6, 6, 415
Todd, Thomas II (father of GT) 3, 4, 5, 6, 9, 17, 50, 415
Todd, Thomas Frederick Davis (half-brother of GT) 6, 8
Tomlinson, Superintendent 382, 383
Tongogara, Josiah 402
Tracey, Leonard 248
Trade Union Congress 154
trade unions 153, 154, 155–6, 182, 183–4, 193, 277
traditional chiefs 25, 85, 86, 327, 345, 346, 394
travel
  1941–2 leave in New Zealand 52, 53–6
  1949 leave in New Zealand 81
  1954 UK 134–5
  1955 USA and Canada 141–2, 144–5, 525–6
  1956, 1967 holidays at Noetsie, SA 174, 361
  1959 UK and France 292–3
  1960 USA and London 295–6
  1961 UK and USA 327–8
  1967 USA, UK and New Zealand 361–2
  1971 UK, Paris and Greece 376–7
  1976 UK 403–4
  1977 UK and USA 415, 416–17
  1978 USA and UK 426–8
  1979/80 New Zealand 439–42
  1986 knighthood in London 474–5
Tredgold, Lady (Margaret) xxvi, 415, 451
Tredgold, Sir Robert
  autobiography 364
  belief in Mugabe 451
  on British attitude at Geneva Conference (1976) 411
  Commissioner 151, 194, 203
  consultation with GT 227
  criticism of tightening of Acts 332
  death 415
  denunciation of Bills 289
  on Federal Constitution 89
  on Federation 313
  on GT's abilities 131
  on GT's downfall 255, 257
  on raid of Nyadzonya camp 409
  resignation as Chief Justice of Federation 318–19
  on Rhodesia as police state 335
Tredgold Commission (1957) 151, 193–200
Tübingen Festival speech 462–3

UDI (unilateral declaration of independence) (1965) 346, 347–55
UFP (United Federal Party)
  black-on-black intimidation 327
  Congress (1958) 239–41, 242–50
  general election (1958) 268, 269–70
  general election (1962) 333
  GT on UFP 228
  John Roberts as leader in Northern Rhodesia 300
  meeting (1958) 238–9

opinions on Congress vote 251–7
party fusion issue 215
Wightwick's criticism of GT 222
UN (United Nations)
address by GT 341
Bunche on no need for violence 156
rejection of Settlement Agreement (1978) 422
SR and independence 329–31
support for 1980 election conduct 447
United Club 132
United College of Education 397, 459
United National Independence Party 332
United Party xxx, xxxi, 65, 66, 84, 101, 102, 105
United People's Party 348
Unity Accord 476, 477
Unlawful Organisations Act (1959) 331–2, 341
Urban African Affairs Commission 178
Urban Industries Native Labour Board 220
URP (United Rhodesia Party)
see also Southern Rhodesia
Annual Congress (1956) 160–3
Annual Congress (1957) 179–80, 211
by-election (Gwelo 1956) 159–60
cabinet crisis (1957) 216–19, 221–5, 226–9, 236–9
congress and GT's resignation (1958) 239–41, 242–50, 251, 252–3
defeat in general election and Gwelo conference (1958) 283, 291
formation (1953) 105
franchise issue 195–6, 198, 199
general election (1954) 107–9, 276
issue of party fusion 160–5, 214–15, 239–41
no-confidence motion by Opposition (1958) 261–3
opinions on Congress vote 251–7
revival of party and general election (1958) 267–71, 272–5
Whitehead's by-election (1958) 263
Whitehead's desire for Todd's withdrawal from politics 263–6
Vambe, Lawrence
on ANC 210
at GT's 85th birthday xxix
on bus boycott 167–8, 169

on City Youth League 166
on colour barrier 131
on general election (1958) 275–6
on GT and Central Africa Party 292
on GT as senator 466
historian xix–xx, xxiv
on land issue 138, 143
member of Capricorn Africa Society 132
on NDP 294
on Palmer brothers 230
on respect for Huggins 78
Vance, Cyrus 427
Vickery, Ray 8
Victoria Falls Conference (1949) 83
Victoria Falls Conference (1975) 403
violence
see also warfare
Gukurahundi xxxiii, 460, 461, 462–3
post-independence 464–5, 484–6
Vorster, President John
dismay at Mugabe's victory 448
negotiations with Kaunda (1974) 401
removal of pressure on Smith 412
talks with Smith and Kissinger 410
Victoria Falls conference (1975) 403
Vukuzenzele 458–9, 465, 484, 517

Wakatama, Matthew 337
Waldheim, Kurt 416, 453
Walls, Lt General Peter 423, 425, 436, 446, 448, 453
Walsh, Mavis (née Thomson) 14, 22, 23
Wankie Colliery strike (1954) xxxii, 109–13, 153
Wankie Native Labour Board 112
war veterans 506, 507
warfare
ceasefire 437–8, 445–6
conscription of white males (1977) 414
counter-insurgency operation 422
guerrilla warfare 398–9, 402, 408–9, 417–20, 421, 422, 432
increased attacks 423–4, 425–6, 436
murder of Matshazi by guerrillas 429–30
raid on Nyadzonya camp 409, 414
raid on ZANU bases Chimoio and Tembue 419

Rhodesian raids into Zambia 437
Watson, Alycen (née Todd) (daughter of GT)
  adoption 14, 16, 23
  correspondence from Grace 427, 471
  GT's knighthood 475
  living at Dadaya Mission 22, 26, 45, 48, 57, 58, 468
  marriage of Judy 498
  move back to New Zealand 103, 400
  visits to New Zealand (1941, 1949) 55, 56, 81
Watson, John 475, 498
Watson, Judy 477, 498
Webb, Noel 418, 419
Wedza, Chief 477
Wedza Mountain 22, 423–4
Weiss, Ruth 481, 482, 484
Welensky, Sir Roy
  attempt to avoid NR's independence 299, 300
  Banda's imprisonment 298, 299
  claim of African support 263
  criticism of GT 341
  demand for Dominion Status 280, 285
  failure of Federation 336, 337
  Federal Review Conference (1960) 321
  franchise policy 203
  GT's cabinet crisis 237–8, 238–9, 239
  on GT's Inyanga house 177
  introduction to Macmillan's Salisbury speech 295
  issue of party fusion 164, 215
  leader of the Unofficial Members of the Legislative Council 83
  London agreement on Federation status 201–2
  member of Federal cabinet 90, 107, 124, 147, 148, 162, 336
  Monckton Commission 314, 321
  President of Federal Party 165, 214, 217
  Prime Minister of Federation 149, 175
  role in GT's removal as SR Prime Minister 255, 255–6
  support for Kafue project 127, 129
  support for Whitehead 264
  UFP Congress (1958) 240, 241, 242, 243, 244, 248, 249, 252
  union official 115–16

Went, Maurice 274
West, Michael 76, 77
Weston, A. 110
Wetherall, Iden 505
White, Reverend John 512
white community
  attitude towards GT xxxii, 159, 237, 317, 486
  comparison with Todds 506
  concept of white supremacy 316, 369, 377, 394
  effect of Federation 114
  emigration 336, 412, 414
  fears 106, 118, 300
  general election (1980) 446, 448, 449, 450, 452
  general election (1985) 466
  GT on need for change 322, 331, 418
  opposition to equality xxxi, 84, 306, 365, 407
  support for Smith 343, 422, 430
Whitehead, Sir Edgar
  achievements 277
  banning of NDP 328
  by-election disaster (1958) 263
  desire for Todd's withdrawal from politics (1958) 263–6
  Federal Review Conference (1960) 319–21
  formation of cabinet 258–9, 260, 260–1
  franchise 194
  general election (1958) 269–70
  general election (1962) 333
  proposal for party fusion 165
  SR Prime Minister 178, 185, 239, 242, 244, 247–8, 249, 251, 252, 296
  SR talks and violence (1960–1) 320, 321, 326–7
  state of emergency (1959) 286, 288, 289
  tightening of Unlawful Organisations Act and Law and Order Act 331–2
  unrest (1960) 302, 303, 317, 318
Wightwick, H. D. 180, 196, 199, 221–3, 225, 261, 262, 521
Wigley, F. L. ('Freddie') 70, 71–2, 296
Wilkinson, Peter 443
William-Powlett, Admiral Sir Peveril 131, 287–8, 289, 292, 314, 336, 346

Index

William-Powlett, Lady 131
Williamson, Robbie 113, 159
Wilson, Annie (née McKenzie) (Grace's mother) 11–12, 12, 17, 81
Wilson, Elsie (Grace's sister) *see* Barham, Elsie
Wilson, Grace *see* Todd, Jean Grace Isabel
Wilson, Harold
  general election (1974) 400
  meeting with GT 352–3
  refusal of SR independence 349
  sanctions 355
  talks on HMS *Fearless* (1968) 364
  talks on HMS *Tiger* (1966) 359
Wilson, James 12
Wilson, Madge (Grace's sister) 12
Wilson, Winifred (Grace's sister) 12, 81, 357–8
Wingfield, N. S. 199, 264
Wood, Professor J. R. T. xxiv, 352
Wood, Jim 92, 93
Wood, Nell 97, 428
Wood, Hon. Richard 180
Woodhouse, Susan xix–xx, xxi, xxix
World Council of Churches 367, 368, 372, 373, 451
Worrall, John 356, 357, 367
Wright, D. W. 392, 406
Wright, Elizabeth *see* Todd, Elizabeth
Wright, Robert 2
Wright, William 2
Wrong, Michela 300

Yamba, Dauti 107
Young, Andrew 416, 427
Young, J. R. Dendy 107

Zambia
  see also Northern Rhodesia
  independence (1964) 301, 332, 346
  negotiations between Vorster and Kaunda (1974) 401
  raids on ZAPU camps 426
ZANLA (Zimbabwe African National Liberation Army) 398, 417, 418, 422, 453, 457
ZANU (Zimbabwe African National Union)
  see also guerrilla warfare; ZANLA
  banning (1978) 425
  detention of Sithole and murder of Chitepo 402
  detentions and banning 341
  Geneva conference (1976) 410
  GT on betrayal of ideals 508
  Lusaka talks (1974) 401
  raid on Chimoio and Tembue (1977) 419
  revoking of banning (1979) 438
  WCC grant 373
ZANU-PF (Zimbabwe African National Union (Patriotic Front))
  general election (1980) 446, 447
  general election (1985) 466
  GT on disenfranchisement 521
  GT's donation 442
  one-party state decision (1984) 464
  talks with ZAPU (1986) 475
  Unity Accord 476
  use of force against own people 169
ZAPU (Zimbabwe African People's Union)
  see also Nkomo, Joshua; Patriotic Front; ZIPRA
  air crashes 425–6
  banning (1962) 332, 337
  banning (1964) 341
  banning (1978) 425
  dismissals and arrests by Mugabe (1982) 460
  general election (1985) 466
  Geneva conference (1976) 410
  launch 328
  Lusaka talks (1974) 401
  raids by Rhodesian forces 426
  revoking of banning (1979) 438
  talks with ZANU-PF (1986) 475
  Unity Accord 476
  WCC grant 373
Zhou, Dr 415–16
Zibombo Ranch 488
Zimbabwe
  see also Rhodesia
  disenfranchisement of Zimbabweans 521
  farm workers evicted from farms 513
  general election (1980) 445–50
  general election (1985) 466
  general election (1990) 483

general election (2000) 508
Independence Day 454–5
one-party state decision (1984) 464
Presidential election (2002) 521–2
referendum on land expropriation without compensation (1999) 505–6
ruin by Mugabe 493, 505–6, 507, 525
Unity Accord 476
Zimbabwe Congress of Trade Unions 505
Zimbabwe Human Rights Association (Zimrights) 489–90, 502
Zimbabwe-Rhodesia 432, 435, 438, 445–50
Zimpapers 456, 470, 483
ZIPRA (Zimbabwe People's Revolutionary Army) 398, 417, 418, 422, 425–6, 453, 457, 460
Zvishavane 463
see also Shabani
Zvobgo, Dr Eddison 97
Zvobgo, Julia 442

Lightning Source UK Ltd.
Milton Keynes UK
UKHW011058211221
396027UK00012B/843